823   Kaplan, Fred, 1937-
DIC
         Dickens

$24.45

DATE		

DICKENS

ALSO BY FRED KAPLAN

BIOGRAPHY:
Thomas Carlyle, A Biography, 1983

CRITICISM:
Miracles of Rare Device: The Poet's Sense of Self in Nineteenth-Century Poetry, 1972

Dickens and Mesmerism: The Hidden Springs of Fiction, 1975

Sacred Tears: Sentimentality in Victorian Literature, 1987

AS EDITOR:
Charles Dickens' Book of Memoranda, 1981

DICKENS

❧ A BIOGRAPHY ❧

Fred Kaplan

William Morrow & Company, Inc.
New York

Library of Congress Cataloging-in-Publication Data

Kaplan, Fred, 1937-
Dickens.
Includes bibliographical references and index.
1. Dickens, Charles, 1812-1870—Biography. 2. Novel-
ists, English—19th Century—Biography. I. Title.
PR4581.K28   1988   823'.8 [8]   88-12859
ISBN 0-688-04341-0

Printed in the United States of America

3   4   5   6   7   8   9   10

BOOK DESIGN BY CATHRYN S. AISON

TO JULIA, NOAH, AND BEN

AND

TO THE MEMORY OF MY FATHER

Contents

8

Illustrations

Dickens' . . . steady practicality withal; the singularly solid business talent he continually had; and, deeper than all, if one has the eye to see deep enough, dark, fateful silent elements, tragical to look upon; and hiding amid dazzling radiances as of the sun, the elements of death itself. . . .

—THOMAS CARLYLE TO JOHN FORSTER

Constituted to do the work that is in me, I am a man full of passion and energy, and my own wild way that I must go is often—at the best—wild enough.

—CHARLES DICKENS TO MARY BOYLE, 12/9/1858

Freud . . . in accepting the Goethe Prize in 1930, said . . . the goal of biography [is] to bring a grand figure nearer to us. "It is unavoidable . . . that if we learn more about a great man's life, we shall also hear of occasions on which he has done no better than we, has in fact come nearer to us as a human being."

—DANIEL GOLDMAN, "New Insights into Freud, from 'Letters to a Friend,'" *The New York Times Magazine*, 3/17/1986, p. 92

DICKENS

CHAPTER ONE

Scenes of His Boyhood
(1812-1822)

❧ I ❧

On an exquisite September day in 1860, Charles Dickens burned "the accumulated letters and papers of twenty years." The flames rose into the sunlight in the field behind the house at Gad's Hill. Every letter he owned not absolutely on a business matter went up into fire and ashes, letters from friends and family, from the obscure and the famous, from Thomas Carlyle, William Makepeace Thackeray, Alfred Tennyson, William Harrison Ainsworth, John Forster, Wilkie Collins, Leigh Hunt, letters from his mother, father, brothers, and sisters, letters from his wife, letters from Ellen Ternan. He was mercilessly indiscriminate, absolutely insistent. Henry and Plorn, his two youngest sons, gleefully carried one basketful after another from his study to the bonfire. They soon "roasted onions on the ashes of the great." His daughter Mamie begged her father to save some of the letters. She held them in her hands momentarily, recognizing the handwritings and the signatures. Letters were ephemeral, he responded, "written in the heat of the moment." As the fire destroyed decades of correspondence, he remarked, " 'Would to God every letter I had ever written was on that pile.' " The articulate smoke rose into the sky "like the Genie when he got out of the casket on the sea-shore." With the disintegration of the last letters, the sky darkened and it began to rain "very heavily. . . . I suspect my correspondence of having overcast the face of the Heavens."[1]

Fearing that they would be published to an audience that had no business with them, he could, and now did, destroy every private letter he received.[2] Aware that fame generated its own detractors, that the exposure of secrets had as much excitement within public discourse as within fiction, he feared the Victorian equivalent of his phone being tapped. He had no belief in or commitment to the idea of a public record about private matters. His books would speak for him. All other voices should be silenced. His art, not his life, was public property. But no amount of discretion could gainsay that he earned his living as a public man, a writer and an entertainer reading from his own works. The incessant traveling during the readings made his presence in his novels a real voice heard and an actual face seen in innumerable high streets, hotels, and railway stations. Only between 1862 and 1865, when he withdrew temporarily from the reading stage, were his public appearances interludes in an essentially private life. His face, though, was always prominently displayed in bookshop windows across the country. The success of his journal *All the Year Round,* "Conducted by Charles Dickens" emblazoned in bold print on the cover, kept his name before the public with weekly persistence. One could hardly turn one's head toward a newsstand or a bookstore or a reading table without seeing it. The more famous he became, the more certain it was that his letters would eventually be published. The Heavens would send back some of the smoke.

Born in Portsmouth on Friday, February 7, 1812, Charles Dickens was the second child of a slim, dark-haired, pretty woman. On the night of his birth, Elizabeth Dickens, who apparently declined to act the part of an invalid, and, like her son, loved to dance, had attended a ball. She was a woman of energetic, aggressive self-definition. His father, who made his living as a clerk in the payroll office of the navy, performed as if he had been placed below the rewards that his talents and his love of life merited. John Dickens proudly took the unusual step of trumpeting in the local newspaper that unto him had been born "on Friday, at Mile-end Terrace, the Lady of John Dickens, Esq., a son."

In his adolescence, Dickens constructed the compensatory myth of Friday's special child, just as he would do later for David Copperfield. As an adult, he considered Friday his lucky day, needing to believe that he had been born with great expectations and the talent and will to realize them. Named Charles John Huffam Dickens (he never used the two middle names and "never" forgave his mother and father for them), he was baptized on March 4 in St. Mary's near the modest, narrow house on Mile End Terrace that his family rented.3

His earliest memory, from a time when he could have been no more than two, was of a "small front garden." He remembered being watched by a nurse and trotting about "with something to eat, and his little elder sister," Fanny, with him, three motifs that were to become important in his life and fiction, the woman who is the nurturer-protector but who also has the potential to be the vehicle of deprivation; the food that nourishes one, and of which, like Oliver Twist, one often wants "more"; and the lovely sister-wife who represents the ideal woman and the completion of the self. Afterward, he recognized the very spot on which he had as an infant watched a military parade. He had been brought out from the garden to see the soldiers exercise, and he had carried away a vividly remembered "little picture of it, wonderful, accurate." A few years later, "my poor mother . . . put me up on the ledge of a . . . low wall with an iron railing on the top . . . so that I might raise my hat and cheer George 4th—then Prince Regent—who was driving by."4

His references to his parents in his letters and in his fiction suggest that the infant had both a heightened sense of dependency and a strong fear of their untrustworthiness, particularly his mother's. One of his favorite stories was of the little boy lost and the little boy found, of the child separated from his family, like the chimney sweep who had "been stolen from his parents in his infancy [who] . . . was sent in the course of his professional career to sweep the chimney of his mother's bedroom; and

. . . being hot and tired . . . he got into the bed he had so often slept in as an infant, and was discovered and recognized therein by his mother."5 Such recognition scenes happen often to young adolescents in his fiction, in time to revive some earlier ideal model when child and mother lived together in blissful harmony. The scenes generally occur without benefit of father, who is usually absent, sometimes dead. Whether or not such a time ever existed for him is doubtful. His need to be recognized by his mother seems always to have been unfulfilled.

Born in 1785, his father, John Dickens, was the second son of a steward, William Dickens, and a servant, Elizabeth Ball. Both were trusted employees of John Crewe, a member of Parliament who became Lord Crewe in the early nineteenth century. They had married in 1781 at St. George's Church, Hanover Square, London, the same church in which funeral services were held for William Dickens fourteen years later. The younger of two sons, John was ten years old at his father's death. Other than the claim that he competently managed the household at Crewe Hall in Chester and perhaps on Grosvenor Street, London, William Dickens has no personal history. His background is the recordless blank of the eighteenth-century servant class, illiterate, anonymous functionaries in a world in which their social importance was local and generic. His wife survived him by thirty-nine years, rising to the position of housekeeper to the Crewe family. Her background is as obscure as her husband's. She was remembered years later not by her grandson, to whom she bequeathed her husband's silver watch, but by members of the Crewe family, particularly for her powers as an impromptu storyteller. Though she never learned to read or write, apparently she created romances and fairy tales, the "invention of her clever and original brain," for she possessed "strong story-telling powers."6 The claim has its symbolic resonance, the movement from the oral expression of folk tales and romances by an illiterate woman to the great written literature of her descendant two generations later. When she died, Charles was twelve years old. She makes no recognizable appearance in his comments about his family or in his fiction. But through her influence with her employer, nineteen-year-old John Dickens was appointed in April 1805 an "extra clerk" in the navy pay office in Somerset House, London, at five shillings a day. Two years later, he rose to fifteenth assistant clerk on the permanent staff at a total salary of about one hundred pounds a year. He was thought careless with money, irresponsible about work, and too eager to enjoy the pleasures of conviviality.

Born in 1789, the year of the French Revolution, which was to be the setting for one of her son's most successful novels, Elizabeth Dickens was the second of the ten children of Charles Barrow and Mary Culliford, who had married in 1788. A lieutenant in the navy as a young man, Barrow became a partner in his father-in-law's musical-instrument firm in London. Then, in the first year of the new century, he was appointed a clerk in the navy pay office in Somerset House. The Barrows were modestly affluent, successful in the wool business, then in journalism and the civil service. Soon Barrow became "Chief Conductor of Monies in Town," his salary rising to £330 a year. In June 1809, Charles Barrow's twenty-year-old daughter married his twenty-four-year-old colleague. The groom had been working in Portsmouth, probably since November 1807, with frequent trips to London to court Elizabeth, who had bright hazel eyes and a slim waist. He kept his servant-class origins out of sight as much as possible. The newlyweds soon settled in Portsmouth, where John Dickens now earned a salary of £110 a year. Like his father-in-law, he handled payroll accounts. Within the year, his annual salary increased to a little over £200. By November 1809, Elizabeth was pregnant. In January 1810, an extraordinary scandal exploded. Her father, Charles Barrow, who had found his income insufficient to cover the costs of a comfortable life for himself and his family, was caught secretly pocketing large amounts of government money. The system made it easy for him to do so—temporarily. The discovery stunned family and friends. Shame, remorse, guilt: Where had all the money gone? He pleaded "the very heavy expenses of a family of ten children, increased by constant illness."[7] When criminal prosecution became almost a certainty, he fled to the Continent and then to the Isle of Man, beyond the reach of British law.

The financial difficulties that plagued the Dickens family during Charles's youth had their beginnings in the first years of his childhood. The pleasures of conviviality were essential for John Dickens, but the family soon found that laughter was costly. The paterfamilias had little sense of the importance of adjusting his needs to his income. His wife either had not been taught economy or was a poor learner. The young couple enjoyed dinners, parties, family gatherings, and assumed that their income would be sufficient sooner or later to redeem their current expenses. Still, the family seems to have been solvent during these Portsmouth years. In late June 1812, perhaps as an attempt to economize, they moved from Mile End Terrace to 16 Hawke Street. At Christmas 1813, they made another local move, to 39 Wish Street, where a second son, Alfred, was born. Charles may perhaps have been responsive enough to feel the gloom in the household when, in September, the infant died "of water on the brain."[8]

None of them were likely to have been pleased when John Dickens was transferred back to London in late 1814. At this time Elizabeth's eldest sister, Mary Allen, whose husband had died the previous year, lived with them. They were a family of five, with another child visibly on the way. The move increased the financial burden. John Dickens' salary, which had included a special "outport" supplement, now fell to two hundred pounds per year. They moved to 10 Norfolk Street, between the crowded Tottenham Court Road area and Great Portland Street, in the heart of the city in which Dickens was to live much of his adult life. This stay in London lasted about two years. A second daughter, Letitia Mary, was born in April 1816. At the baptism her father listed his station in life as "gentleman." Time passed, and the crucial years between two and four never seem to surface except in the interstices of fiction, where autobiography merges into the wish to transform and the wish to forget. At the beginning of January 1817, John Dickens was transferred to Sheerness, in Kent, probably glad to have his "outpay" restored. In March, with retrenchment at Sheerness, he was transferred again, about twenty miles distant, to the pay office of the naval yard in Chatham, adjacent to Rochester.

❧ 2 ❧

THE "MASSIVE GREY SQUARE TOWER" OF ROCHESTER CATHEDRAL dominates the fertile landscape into which the young boy first came to youthful consciousness. The rooks, as they ascend, circling that stable tower in every season, survey the narrow streets of the old cathedral town, the magnificent ruin of a once mighty fortress, the naval dockyard at Chatham, then the glittering river Medway, which gradually widens and disappears into its estuary and the cold waters of the Channel. The hills across the river and the landscape of Kent glitter peacefully, quietly. London is too distant to the west and north to be seen.

That landscape was the primal home of Dickens' imagination. All his "early readings" dated from this place. In his memory, he bathed that vista in a glow of calm summers, of celebratory winters. That radiant landscape became forever associated with the time in which he felt young and loved. The garden of his creative fruitfulness, a place initially almost without dark shadows, it was the home to which he regularly returned, in his novels and in his life, his place of refreshment until refreshment was no longer possible. And his final but incomplete novel, whose last words he wrote on a bright June day in a summer house from which he could see the traffic on the Medway, unites the nurturing Kent of his boyhood with the death that resides in all natural things.

Like all paradises, Kent was retrospective. As an adult, he remembered its sights, scenes, and experiences vividly. Often they were associated with his father, the articulated presence that set his values and sense of self. An event that stuck in his memory, that he wrote about years afterward as a defining myth, brought father and son past an imposing late-eighteenth-century house on the Gravesend Road called Gad's Hill Place, the hill associated with Falstaff's adventures in Shakespeare's *Henry IV*. To the small boy, used to his lower-middle-class world and the cramped houses of his earlier childhood, it seemed a palatial wonder. If he "were to be very persevering and were to work hard," his father told him, he "might some day come to live in it."[9] The association of Shakespeare, his favorite author, with success; his father's encouragement to think nothing impossible for the assiduous and the talented; and the association of writing with money and status, all must have produced feelings and connections that had a strong influence on him.

Since Chatham and Rochester were adjacent, the towns formed a continuous playground. In one direction lay the dignity and history of Rochester, in the other the excitement of the bustling modern dockyard. Chatham provided the drama of action, the streets overflowing with soldiers and sailors, the marketplace busy with buying and selling, often by those with either too much or too little in their pockets, and the clamorous noises of the large dockyard, where convict labor did most of the hauling and pulling. He was fascinated by the ships, by mechanical devices such as a crane to lift and sort logs, which he called the "Chinese Enchanter's Cart," and by the men, "these busy figures . . . bending at their work in smoke and fire."[10]

Rochester provided the dignity of an ancient city, stimulation for his historical imagination: the cathedral, Fort Pitt, the Tudor buildings, the moon-faced clock suspended over the narrow high street, the coaching inns, the Theatre Royal, where he first saw Shakespeare performed, the *gravitas* of the town and the townspeople. The stolid bridge across the Medway carried the London road northward and left Rochester the other way toward Dover and the mysterious world called "abroad." Some distance downriver huge gray ships were used as jails, the hulks from which Pip, in *Great Expectations*, hears the gunfire that signals the escape of a prisoner. Charles may have heard from others or from the voice of his imagination that "people are put in the Hulks because they murder, and because they rob, and forge, and do all sorts of bad; and they always begin by asking questions."

Like most precocious boys, he himself had the reputation of being an incessant questioner. And "it would be difficult to overstate . . . the intensity and accuracy of an intelligent child's observation." The running water of the river encouraged his daydreams. Spending hours by its bank, he remembered himself as "a young boy, with an intelligent face burnt to a dust colour by the summer sun, and with crisp hair of the same hue," listening to the tide, watching the boats on the river, wandering in the marshes. In his moments of most idyllic memory, "peace and abundance were on the country-side in beautiful forms and beautiful colours, and the harvest seemed even to be sailing out to grace the never-reaped sea in the yellow-laden barges that mellowed the distance."

During the little over five years that he spent in Chatham, the family was at its most stable. In his memory, it was never winter by the Medway. In April 1817, they happily moved into

2 Ordnance Terrace, a new Georgian-style house opposite a large field. Despite his lithe figure and quickness of movement, he was unusually small and not very athletic. When he did participate, he competed vigorously. But his enthusiasm was undercut by a touch of sickliness, occasional attacks of renal colic.[11] Eager to be accepted, he expressed himself warmly and cheerfully with his parents, his sisters Fanny, Letitia, and Harriet, the latter born in 1819, his brother Frederick, born the next year, two servants, and Mary Allen, called Aunt Fanny. Their nearest neighbors were the Stroughill family: George, a little older than Charles, Lucy, with blond curls, a kind of playmate sweetheart whom he later invoked when writing about an early birthday celebration. He remembered her as a "peach-faced creature in a blue sash . . . whose life I supposed to consist entirely of birthdays." Living on the same street, Richard Newnham and his wife became friends of the family. Mrs. Newnham became the model for the old lady in *Sketches by Boz*.

During his wanderings, Mary Weller, his thirteen-year-old nurse, was his closest female companion, replacing an earlier nurse, Mercy, who had told him vicious horror stories. His mother, of whom his memories were perhaps purposely hazy, taught him to read. He faintly remembered "her teaching me the alphabet." He soon attended a school on nearby Rome Street. In 1821, he transferred to a more substantial local academy, run by a young Oxford student and Baptist minister, William Giles. At first he walked the distance from Ordnance Terrace to the schoolhouse next to Providence Chapel. Soon he became an after-school friend of his teacher's younger brother Samuel, with whom he "rambled together in the same Kentish fields, and mingled in the same sports." When the family moved in late spring 1821 to a modest house called The Brook, he walked the short distance to Giles's school, proudly sporting the white top hat the schoolboys were required to wear. A voracious reader, he could not keep away from the books available to him. For Dickens, the experience of imaginative engagement expressed itself physically, as if the mind alone could not contain the mind's activity. He would "sit with his book in his left hand, holding his wrist with his right hand, and constantly moving it up and down, and at the same time sucking his tongue . . . reading as if for life."[12] Later, when he became a writer, he sometimes acted out with his face and his body the appearances and the actions of his characters while creating them. When he became a public reader of his own works, he combined the inner world of his imagination with a visible physical performance.

From the world of his early reading he took his lifelong models of human nature. He read Tobias Smollett, Henry Fielding, Oliver Goldsmith, Samuel Richardson, Daniel Defoe, Cervantes. From "that blessed little" attic room in The Brook (his father's book and magazine collection probably was available to him at Ordnance Terrace also) "a glorious host" came out to keep him company.[13] The structure of fiction, of narrative mythmaking, became more closely identified with essential truth than the constructs of philosophy. Much of what he has to say in his novels about human nature and the world that human beings have made derives from widespread eighteenth-century views whose most accessible and powerful expression is in the novels, poems, essays, and plays that he read as a child and continued to read throughout his life. Fiction was, he felt from the beginning, morally didactic, a powerful force for teaching goodness in the general sense of providing models of moral and immoral character and action. The young boy probably now had his first glimpse of the possibility that he too could be a writer and achieve the fame and fortune his father had held up to him as a vague ideal on the day that he had seen Gad's Hill Place for the first time.

THE OUTWARD WORLD OF PEACEFUL KENT HAD ITS PARALLEL IN THE shining face of a boy eager to learn and eager to please. Standing on chairs or tables, he gladly performed for his family and his father's friends. He had a good way with a tune and with lyrics, a voice, a lilt, and a look for vocal comedy. He was short for his age, and thin; he was also clever, responsive, and sensitive. He had an expressive, mobile face, with pale skin, thin nose, and eyes indeterminately shading between gray and light blue, "a sort of green hazel grey." Later, his myopic eyes frequently were remarked on as mysterious, ever-changing, and powerfully intense. His nasal voice was not especially attractive, with a characteristic family slurring of speech, a tendency to talk very quickly, and the high alto of childhood when singing.

The family was musical. His mother loved dancing. His sister Fanny had talent, soon translated into piano and voice lessons and then specialized training for a musical career. Charles's "comic singing gave the sociable John Dickens such delight that he often hoisted [him] up on a table to entertain the guests . . . or strolled down into the lower part of the town with the youngster to show him off there." No doubt these songs, Dickens recalled, "were warmly applauded by all, and justly so, for they were admirably sung." But he later remarked that he "must have been a horrible little nuisance to many unoffending grown-up people who were called upon to admire" him. His father pulled the strings. He "never recalled [these performances] that his own shrill little voice of childhood did not again tingle in his ears."14 From early on, he developed a performance personality, encouraged to believe that applause was approval.

The theatre was his model. In a culture unable to transmit voice or image except through print and illustrations, the living stage flourished. In the city and in the country, from serious drama and opera to comedy, spectacle, and musical, in established theatres and in temporary outdoor sites frequented by traveling companies, the theatre was a magical presence, a precious alternate world. The excitement of the stage and of the histrionic, of an exaggerated bright spectacle that heightened life, caught his imagination from an early age. The first theatre performance he saw seems to have been a pantomime, of the sort he described when he edited for publication the memoirs of Joseph Grimaldi, the best-known clown of his childhood. "The delights—the ten thousand million delights of a pantomime . . . [to] which a long row of small boys, with frills as white as they could be washed, and hands as clean as they would come, were taken to behold the glories. . . . What mattered it that the stage was three yards wide, and four deep? *We* never saw it. We had no eyes, ears or corporeal sense, but for the pantomime." His dazzled eyes were wide open when he saw Grimaldi perform in London during the 1819–20 holiday season. In response to "the humour of Joe," he clapped his "hands with great precocity."15

There was also theatre at home, both in the household and

in the Theatre Royal in Rochester. Charles brought his friends
into the living room for impromptu performances of charades,
pantomimes, comedies, melodramas, magic-lantern shows.
Actor, director, producer, even script writer, he could conceive
of and control the entire world of performance, the clever child
glowing with the satisfaction of being center stage. In the autumn of 1821, he wrote a tragedy called *Misnar, the Sultan of India,*
a brief adaptation of one of James Ridley's pseudo-oriental *Tales
of the Genii* (1794), and enjoyed the notoriety his authorship produced in his childish circle. A new friend, James Lamert, the son
of Aunt Fanny's suitor, Dr. Matthew Lamert, stimulated his
imagination by organizing and directing sophisticated amateur
theatricals. He also took him to the Theatre Royal, on whose
stage the tragedian Edmund Kean and the comedian Charles
Mathews performed. He saw his first professional performances
of serious drama. Shakespeare's *Richard III* and the witches in
Macbeth made his heart "leap with terror." Goldsmith's depiction of "the funny countryman . . . of noble principles," who
would "crunch up his little hat and throw it on the ground, and
pull off his coat, saying 'Dom thee, squire, coom on with thy
fistes then,' " brought tears of laughter to his eyes.[16] Shakespeare
and Goldsmith became the charged poles of his imagination.
They were to be the two favorite authors of his maturity.

❧ 4 ❧

BUT NEITHER THE GLITTER OF THE THEATRE NOR THE BENEFICENCE
of Kent could disguise the fact that he was also nightmare's
child. Some of his fears were those widely shared by all children.
He felt the unavoidable youthful anxieties, particularly about
his separation from his mother. He felt the burden created by
his father's expectations. As an adult, remembering his childhood, he recognized that, whatever the widespread pattern, he
had been the victim of what he humorously but seriously called
frequent acts of "boyslaughter." Some of them were benign.
They came from the hateful changes that time works on everyone, including the demolishment of his boyhood landmarks.
When he returned to Rochester in middle age, he remarked that
the owner of the new coach business had done him an injury by

tearing down the familiar building and substituting new buildings and a different name. Like many others, he had "committed
an act of boyslaughter, in running over my childhood in this
rough manner."[17]

The fragility of life struck him with a particularity that
expressed itself in singular images. He was taken by Mary
Weller through the streets of Rochester to lyings-in, so many
that he wondered afterward if he hadn't escaped his true profession of midwife. As often as not, the infants died. He accompanied Mary to the receptions for the mothers of the dead
children. In one instance, a multiple birth had produced four or
five dead infants, who were laid out "side by side, on a clean
cloth on a chest of drawers," which reminded him "of pigs' feet
as they are usually displayed at a neat tripe-shop."[18] As the
increasingly reluctant father of ten children, he did not escape,
as he later joked painfully, many lying-in scenes of his own,
separate from his novels. He heard the voices and moans of
women in labor, the wails of newborn children. His novels
memorialize the dying of children, the deaths of brothers, like
the first Alfred, and sisters, and the rows of small tombstones
that dominate Pip's early childhood, and the imaginative trans-
mutation of those dead infants into food laid out in the butcher's
window. Many of his most potent descriptions of death and
dying associate the bodies of the dead with food for the living.
As an adult, he frequently expressed his feeling that he had
become the sole source of food for an impossibly large family.
From childhood on, he became obsessed with cannibalism, with
images and scenes of human beings ingesting other human beings, of people being transformed into food, and also with the
act of eating, both as festival and as Thyestes' feast. When he
projected the pattern onto the world at large, it became a key to
his understanding of relationships between people and an image
of society's exploitativeness.

His need as a child to protect himself against diminishment, even annihilation, had its special points of location and
expression. Reading was a way to augment the self with a private protective treasure. Writing became a way to increase the
self. Probably he heard family discussions, if not arguments,
about money. Early acquainted with its value, he had little or
none in his pocket. What he had, he protected. When a subscrip-

tion was being raised for the mother of the dead infants, he was frightened that the little bit of pocket money he had might be pressured out of him. When he "was earnestly exhorted to contribute," he "resolutely declined: therein disgusting the company, who gave me to understand that I must dismiss all expectations of going to Heaven."[19] At an early age he began to learn to say no, to exert his will to protect himself. The likelihood, though, of not going to a literal heaven had little terror for him. His family was not religious. Neither ritual nor theology had a place in its daily activities, except insofar as the public calendar mandated for people of such easygoing Anglicanism occasional attendance at church and the celebration of holidays. From an early age, hell was a place of the mind, an inner world of tensions, anxieties, and nightmares, the more terrifying because it could not be controlled.

For the demons of the mind to emerge aggressively, all one had to do was put one's head down on the pillow. "Are not the sane and the insane equal at night as the sane lie a dreaming? Are not all of us outside" the madhouse "who dream more or less in the condition of those inside it, every night of our lives?" Fascinated by dreams, he later located the primal force of life in unconscious and semiconscious states, for dreams are "the insanity of each day's sanity," significant and frightening in what they reveal about our true selves. He made the voyage into dreams, folk tales, horror stories, unwillingly but inescapably. They did much to determine the phantasmagoric and nightmarish tone of his own stories and novels. Like the tale of Captain Murderer, which Mercy apparently told him frequently, many of the stories of his childhood and his own later fiction were stories of cannibalism, of the self being dissected, devoured, served for someone else's sustenance, of the nightmare destiny of both the devoured and the devouring. They were Faustian stories, such as the one, which he later wrote out in detail, in which a shipbuilder named Chips makes a compact with the devil in the form of a rat. No matter how hard he tries to escape, the rat sticks to him "like pitch." The devil-rat multiplies into many rats on shipboard, gleefully exclaiming, though only the privileged Chips, who has special powers of understanding and language, can understand them, "we'll drown the crew, and we'll eat them too! . . . And what the rats—being water-rats—left of Chips, at last floated to shore, and sitting on him was an immense over-grown rat, laughing. . . ." Boyslaughter and laughter were part of the same voyage.[20]

❦ 5 ❦

SOME OF THE LAUGHTER IN THE HOUSEHOLD BEGAN TO BE MUTED BY family misfortunes They were of the most hauntingly pernicious kind for people aspiring to retain their lower-middle-class gentility. John Dickens could not maintain his style of living without small loans, most of them from tradespeople in the currency of goods and services, to be paid for in part or in full at the next payday. That he was paid quarterly made the pattern of small borrowings seem sensible. He began to find himself with more debts and anticipated expenses than cash. He borrowed money from his mother, to be deducted from what would be his share of her small estate. It was painful to him to confirm her opinion that he was irresponsible, "that lazy fellow John . . . against whose idleness and general incapacity she was never tired of inveighing." In the summer of 1819, he borrowed two hundred pounds in a business arrangement to be repaid at 26 pounds a year for the rest of his life. He did not keep up the payments. His brother-in-law Thomas Barrow, who had countersigned the loan, was forced to retire it in full in 1821. Dickens never repaid him. His friend on Ordnance Terrace, Richard Newnham, also lent him money, which some years later he generously forgave.[21] Tradespeople, though, could not afford to be forgiving. Their knocking at the door trying to collect small debts frayed the family's nerves and threatened their sense of self-worth.

The happy occasion of Mary Allen's marriage to Matthew Lamert in December 1821 had the inconvenient consequence of depriving them of her regular contribution to the family budget. The Lamerts moved to Ireland, though young James Lamert, Matthew's son by a previous marriage, stayed behind, living with the Dickens family temporarily. In March 1822, Alfred Lamert Dickens was born, the sixth child of the household.

Meanwhile, Charles's attendance at Giles's school fed his aspirations toward gentility. The curriculum emphasized penmanship, elocution, vocabulary, arithmetic, history, geography, and Latin. He won a prize for a recitation. His white beaver hat became a symbol of his sense of his own worth. It represented his need for praise, his hope for distinction, his sense that Gad's Hill Place and what it represented could be his one day. Fortunately, the family's financial discomfort did not impinge upon his school attendance.

In June 1822, unexpectedly, John Dickens was transferred back to London. The ten-year-old Charles must have heard the laughter of the devil-rat. The family was on the move again, with the loss of "outport" pay, with the difficulty of finding housing, and under the strain of unpaid bills and almost no cash. Chatham and Rochester had been a comfortable home, the place he most identified with, the center of his personal security in a world that had become constructively stabilized. The cathedral had been like a pillar anchoring his world. What was happening was threateningly destabilizing. Where would they live? What school would he go to? Would he have friends, people to care for him, to nurture his sensibility and his aspirations? Despite his terror, he had to imagine that he would. He could not have anticipated that the reality would be even more damaging than he feared.

CHAPTER TWO

The Hero of My Own Life (1822-1834)

❧ I ❧

PREPARATIONS TO LEAVE WERE SOON UNDER WAY, THE FAMILY'S possessions packed and shipped to London by boat. Unexpectedly, at the last moment, a special arrangement was made for Charles. He would not go to London with the family. Staying with William Giles, he would attend school in Chatham for another quarter. Given a temporary reprieve, he had one last summer in Kent. Three months later, his teacher gave him a book of essays by Goldsmith as a going-away present. On a dismal day in September 1822 he was packed "like game," amid the odorous damp straw, into the Rochester-to-London coach, and forwarded to Cheapside. "There was no other inside passenger, and I consumed my sandwiches in solitude and dreariness, and it rained hard all the way, and I thought life sloppier than I had expected to find it."[1]

Delivered to his parents' new home at 16 Bayham Street, Camden Town, he found casual disorder, the chaos of domestic and financial confusion. His salary insufficient to pay current expenses and previous obligations, John Dickens struggled to

33

pay an outstanding "bond" with the only recourses available to him, the pursuit of new loans and the curtailment of current expenses. Both created the tensions of humiliation and deprivation. Probably the parents were less vulnerable than Fanny and Charles, who were old enough to feel the anxiety and observe the daily insults but not old enough to have any sense of control over their own lives. John Dickens may have been sure that "something would turn up."[2] But the effort to deal with retrenchment, avoid creditors, and find new sources of money drained the family's emotional resources.

That fall and winter of 1822–23 contrasted bleakly with his previous years in Kent. "Solitude and dreariness" were the initial qualities of the London life to which the coach from Chatham had brought him. He had hoped that at least his new life would be no worse than what had been before, but he quickly discovered that his comforting assumptions were unwarranted. He was caught in the trap of his parents' preoccupation with survival. Benign neglect soon became pernicious irresponsibility. He had expected to be enrolled in school, even if the particulars of his future were somewhat vague. Whatever the details, he had already imagined himself a man with a profession, enjoying success. He would be a gentleman by talent and achievement. Such was the implied promise of his father's expectations, and of the praise that he had received from family, friends, and teachers. As the months passed, though, he was not enrolled in school. Left mainly to drift, he did minor chores in and outside the house, polishing his father's boots, going on odd errands, looking after his younger sisters and brothers.

Fortunately, there was relief from boredom and failure, especially since his parents desired to maintain as normal a family life as possible and their stubborn emotional resilience helped them to survive their continuing embarrassments. Both had a reckless kind of mercuriality, an ability to turn quickly from tears to laughter. Unlike their son, they could compartmentalize misfortune. One of Charles's pleasanter memories of this time was a toy theatre that James Lamert, still living with them, made for him. But that preferable alternative world could be sustained only in the imagination. Another helpful diversion was visits to Christopher Huffam, his godfather, at Church Row, Limehouse, on the Thames, and to Thomas Barrow, his

uncle, who lived on Gerrard Street, Soho. Just as the toy theatre
provided continuity with his childhood theatrical obsession, the
visits to Huffam affirmed his powers as a performer and his
visits to Barrow his view of himself as a serious reader and
potential author. The Huffam family had been in the ship-rig-
ging business for two generations. Huffam and John Dickens
had become friends, probably through the navy and marine
connection. Encouraging Charles's song-and-dance performances, Huffam pronounced the boy a prodigy. Thomas Barrow, Elizabeth's brother and John Dickens' colleague, indirectly
provided him with books. Having recently had a leg amputated,
the result of a serious break years before, he lived over a bookshop whose widowed owner, Mrs. Manson, took a maternal
fancy to Charles. She regularly lent him books, Jane Porter's
Scottish Chiefs, Hans Holbein's *Dance of Death*, George Coleman's
comic descriptions of London scenes, *Broad Grins*.3

The visits became excursions into the wider world of London experience. Though excluded from the advantages of formal education, he discovered that the streets had their texts and
lessons. A comic description of Covent Garden in *Broad Grins*
intrigued him sufficiently to tempt him to "steal down to the
market by himself to compare it with the book." The smell of
rotting cabbage leaves became fixed in his memory. The stateli-
ness of St. Paul's, the squalor of Seven Dials, these first restless
days in London began his observation and absorption of the
multiplicity of the city, the mediation that language provides
between the individual and the fullness of the world. Even at
this early age, he began to develop his sense of himself as the eye
that observes, records, and evaluates. Some years and many
walks later, he found the words that his eyes anticipated in
Covent Garden and Seven Dials. He saw "dirty men, filthy
women, squalid children, fluttering shuttlecocks, noisy bat-
tledores, reeking pipes, bad fruit, more than doubtful oysters,
attenuated cats, depressed dogs, and anatomical fowls." St.
Paul's, as for other literary Londoners, took on a special emotional significance. It seemed to tower above and dwarf the child
and the man. But his interest, from the beginning, was more in
the rotting cabbage leaves than in the monumental structures.
Some of what he observed, he had an impulse to describe. Influenced by his teething on eighteenth-century essays and fic-

tion, he thought in terms of the character sketch, the memorability of distinctive people. He wrote one sketch describing his uncle's barber in Soho, another describing a deaf old woman servant at Bayham Street.4 Though he thought them clever and admired them himself, he showed them to no one.

✿ 2 ✿

WHATEVER TALENT HE HAD, IT WAS OF NO PRACTICAL USE TO HIS distracted parents. They were of little use to him. At his age, and in these circumstances, to be intelligent, sensitive, articulate, and attracted to literature was as much a burden as a blessing. What could he do, as eight months went by and no provision was made for him other than to continue, by default, his desultory life? What he most wanted was direction, involvement, and attention. Restless, he was filled with undirected energy. Convivial and friendly by strategy as well as by nature, he needed companionship of the sort that his siblings and his parents did not provide. Even when the temper of the household was amiable, it did not speak directly to his needs. The digressions of the toy theatre, of visits to his uncle and his godfather, of reading and of street scenes, were unsatisfying without a focus from which they could be diversions.

Suddenly his sister Fanny, who had shown talent as a pianist and vocalist, was given an unusual educational opportunity. That she was two years older and her musical ability had professional potential, whereas his did not, may have influenced their parents to make use of the good offices of Thomas Barrow's neighbor, "the eminment pianoforte maker, Thomas Tomkison," to nominate her to be a student at the newly founded Royal Academy of Music in Hanover Square. The total fee, including living costs, amounted to thirty-eight guineas. In light of the £350 a year John Dickens earned, it was a modest expense—if there had been no debts. In April 1823, she passed her entrance examination and began her professional training, studying under a fine faculty, including Ignaz Moscheles, who had been a friend and student of Beethoven's.5 Whatever Charles's feelings then, whatever his love for his sister, his situation soon took a grim, pervasively damaging turn that keenly

BOOKMOBILE

28 days

attacked his sense of his own worth and stirred feelings of sibling resentment.

The cultural situation was one in which his parents were victims also. Neither of them had the resources or discipline to plan for prosperity. Each had developed a psychology of entitlement. John had acquired the manners and habits of minor affluence, of a gentleman with an income. Elizabeth snobbishly assumed her social superiority, accepting her comfortable view of herself as a young woman of beauty and high culture. Neither was especially intelligent or hardworking. Without religious or vocational vision, neither had an anchor for their values outside the limitations of their personalities. Insufficiently afraid of ill fortune, they were sufficiently easygoing to be able to live with debt and muddle. They needed capital to invest in themselves and their children. They needed the profits of capital to purchase the pleasures of life. Without self-denial or enterprise, John Dickens' employment as a pay clerk could not supply any excess capital at all. In March 1820, he had attempted to supplement his income by publishing a report of a major local fire in the *Times,* probably through Elizabeth's brother, John Henry Barrow, a reporter on the newspaper.6 But whatever he was paid, his extravagant donation of two guineas to the survivors of the fire was more than he could afford. Unable to increase his income or decrease his expenditures, he borrowed regularly in a society in which capital was scarce.

When the costs of Fanny's education were added, what had been serious financial difficulty reached the threshold of crisis. Tradespeople began to decline any further credit. So John Dickens delayed paying his first quarter's householder tax. The authorities issued a summons. He did the same for the next quarter's, and did not pay local maintenance rates.7 Soon the family's penchant for the wastefully unrealistic expenditure asserted itself. Elizabeth Dickens determined that she would open a school to be called "MRS DICKENS'S ESTABLISHMENT." Christopher Huffam, she imagined, had East Indian connections that would provide her with pupils. Advertisements would bring others. John Dickens, having failed to provide alternatives, and perhaps taken with the idea, was in no position to oppose the plan. Elizabeth either did not seek or did not take advice. A large, expensive, newly built house on Gower Street

North was rented for the family, the students, and the school. Charles was sent around the neighborhood to distribute advertisements. On the day after Christmas 1823, they moved into the new house. Elizabeth Dickens did not get the opportunity to demonstrate that she was unsuited to fulfill her professional aspirations. Not one student enrolled.

Without capital, the family had only its labor to offer. John Dickens was fully engaged at the pay office. Elizabeth had tried and failed. Alfred, at two, Frederick, at four, and Letitia, at eight, were too young to help. At almost twelve, Charles was employable in a society in which child labor provided an opportunity for additional income for hard-pressed families and capital advantage for eager employers. Children were cheaper to use than the few machines available in industries in which repetitive tasks needed to be performed. The same James Lamert who had made him the toy theatre now became the agent of his imprisonment. Thinking to help the family, he offered employment for the boy in a shoe-polish factory and warehouse that he managed and his cousin George Lamert owned. Certainly, given the family situation, some other employment would have been found for Charles if Lamert had not made the offer. The salary was six shillings a week. His parents accepted on their son's behalf. Soon after his twelfth birthday, probably by mid-February, 1824, he began the daily grind at Warren's Blacking, 30 Hungerford Stairs, the Strand.[8]

What was a future scholar and gentleman doing in a dingy factory repetitively pasting labels onto pots of black shoe polish? He should have been at school, he believed, like his sister, neatly and appropriately dressed, with the opportunity for suitable companionship instead of in this "crazy, tumble-down old house . . . on the river . . . literally overrun with rats." Sitting at a table, in a recess on the first floor overlooking the coal-barges, he spent his days covering "pots of paste-blacking, first with a piece of oil-paper, and then with a piece of blue paper," then tying them with a string, clipping the paper edges, and pasting on a label. At first, James Lamert spent the hour from noon to one teaching him "something," and at first he was kept apart from the other boys doing similar work downstairs, one of whom, Bob Fagin, showed him the trick of using the string and tying the knot. Soon the noontime lessons stopped. Then he was moved downstairs. His companions were lower class and ignorant. Though they provided fellowship, he felt keenly the humiliation, the humbling of middle-class self-identity and self-worth. He was also personally wounded. His snobbish facade became a cover for "the secret agony of [his] soul" as he felt his "early hopes of growing up to be a learned and distinguished man, crushed in [his] breast."[9]

Suddenly his father's fragile house of debt collapsed. Arrested on February 20, 1824, for failure to pay 40 pounds to his neighborhood baker, a large amount to owe unless the sum involved cash loans, three days later he was moved from a temporary jail to the Marshalsea prison on the south side of the Thames.[10] Fortunately, the navy continued to pay his salary, probably a local decision prompted by sympathetic awareness of the family's situation. Most likely his colleagues at Somerset House knew about his imprisonment, even if his absence from work was justified officially as sick or personal leave. His salary went to keep creditors at bay and to pay the necessary expenses for the family at Gower Street and his own in prison. Appeals to friends and relations to discharge the forty-pound debt were not successful. If he appealed to his mother, she also declined. His legacy would have to await her death. Many of the family possessions, including the small library, were pawned or sold. Only one solution was available. John Dickens decided to declare himself an "insolvent debtor," even at the cost of submitting his family to the humiliation of the Insolvent Debtor's Act's provision that the possessions of the family not be valued at more than twenty pounds. Initiated in early March, the slow legal proceeding followed its deliberate calendar. The family's possessions, even the clothes Charles wore to work, were assessed. John Dickens was released from prison "per Insolvency Act" on May 28, 1824.

A month before his release his mother died. Her youngest son could not attend the funeral. None of the £450 left to him would be available until the will had gone through probate, a lengthy procedure. As welcome as the money would be, it could not help in his present situation. Stressing that she had already lent him money years before, his mother made painfully clear in the will how low had been her opinion of him. She had so little confidence in him that she had stipulated that in the event of the death of her eldest son, her sole executor, his wife rather than her youngest son was to succeed him. On the same day that John was released from prison, his brother William was sworn as his mother's executor. The will was proved on June 4, 1824. Part of the legacy, available in the autumn, was used to pay outstanding debts and current expenses, particularly desirable since, under the terms of the Insolvency Act, his salary could be and was partly attached by his creditors. The legacy was not used, though, to pay Fanny's outstanding bills from the Royal Academy, which threatened to expel her for nonpayment. Her father sent them an IOU with his promise to redeem it, "for a circumstance of great moment to me will be decided in the ensuing term which I confidently hope will place me in comparative affluence, and by which I shall be enabled to redeem the order before the period of Christmas day."[11]

Whether or not he could continue in his position at the navy pay office had become a pressing concern as soon as he was imprisoned. If he stayed in jail, he was sure to be discharged. If he gained his release by claiming insolvency, his employer might consider him compromised beyond forgiveness and deny him his pension. A minor urinary problem that had made desk work and regular hours uncomfortable suddenly appeared to him in a new light. What if his kidney difficulties could serve as a means to resolve his dilemma? Disguising the fact of his imprisonment, he wrote to the Treasurer of the Navy, two weeks after being jailed, requesting early retirement. He enclosed a medical certificate, signed by a surgeon, stating that his "infirmity of body, arising from a chronic infection of the Urinary Organs, incapacitated [him] from attending to any possible duty." His request was forwarded to a higher administrative level with a recommendation for approval that stated he had discharged his duty satisfactorily for over nineteen years and the navy would stand to gain financially. His pension would be half his salary, £145 per year. His replacement would cost only £90. The procedure was a slow one. The application lapsed and was renewed. In the meantime, he returned to work at Somerset House. The admiralty, though, raised questions about whether the retirement was requested because of medical reasons or because of his taking the Insolvent Debtor's Act. Would granting the request set a precedent? William Huskisson, who had approved the petition, humanely responded in December that "I am equally unwilling that he should remain in office, or be entirely dismissed without provision, for he can plead a service of nearly 20 Years, and a Wife & Family of 6 children totally dependent on his Income for life. . . . I shall immediately make a regulation . . . that hereafter Clerks attempting to take the benefit of the Insolvent Act shall be discharged from their situation." On March 9, 1825, his retirement became official. At the age of forty, John Dickens was unemployed.[12]

While his father was in prison, Charles had been earning his own living, trudging each day through much of February and March the five miles from Gower Street to the Strand and back. Unready to be an adult, he was forced into trying to think and perform like one. Bewildered at being deprived of his father, he did errands and carried messages. In the Marshalsea, father and son cried together in a frightening reversal of roles. Since John Dickens could not leave the prison, his family, as was not unusual, came to stay with him at a considerable savings after selling the possessions at the Gower Street house. His mother, Letitia, Frederick, and Alfred moved into the Marshalsea, keeping one servant, who was lodged nearby. Fanny remained at the Royal Academy. Charles was sent to lodge on Little College Street in Camden Town with an old friend of the family, Mrs. Elizabeth Roylance, with whom his maternal grandfather had lodged temporarily years ago before fleeing to the Continent. Perhaps his father paid Mrs. Roylance for Charles's share of the room he occupied with two other children. He never knew. He knew only that he had to make his six shillings cover all other expenses for the week. On Sundays, he and Fanny visited the family. From "Monday morning until Saturday night" the twelve-year-old boy had "no advice, no counsel, no encouragement, no support, from any one. . . ." Deeply lonely, he eventually persuaded his father to allow him to move to lodgings close to the prison, on Lant Street, in a run-down neighborhood.[13] He then spent many evenings in the Marshalsea. Intensely curious about the prisoners and prison life, keenly observant of its social structure, he encouraged his garrulous father to tell stories about it. As soon as he had been imprisoned, John Dickens had begun to impose his fantasies on his surroundings, to distinguish himself from his fellow prisoners by assumptions of superiority.

Constantly underfed, Charles sniffed hungrily at the food in the London stores and streets. He played mental games about whether to buy one type of pudding or another or to buy attractive food now and have no money later or to buy attractive food later and have no food now, or to act like a grown-up and plan sensibly. Occasionally he regaled himself with a culinary treat, like coffee and bread and butter in a coffee room, where the letters read backward impressed themselves on his memory as a searing reminder of his loneliness and degradation. He could not buy parental attention and the security of a home. His schoolboy's few clothes became increasingly shabby and he detested the difficult-to-remove and defiling polish that grimed his hands and fingernails. As an adult, he would be obsessive about cleanliness. He would also be fetishistic about his clothes, from the dandy splendor of his twenties and thirties to the elegant seriousness of his later dress. At twelve he was still short and noticeably slight in build and he sometimes experienced attacks of severe pain in his left side. During one severe spasm, his fellow workers compassionately attended to him. Still, he had the sense of being frighteningly alone. Through much of his life, at times of emotional stress, the attacks would return.

Unexpectedly, his father's liberation from the Marshalsea in late May 1824 made matters worse. First, they all temporarily lodged with the sympathetic Elizabeth Roylance. Then, in June, they moved to 29 Johnson Street, a shabby neighborhood between Somers Town and Camden Town. There was a touch of euphoria in the air. Not only was prison behind. There was also the expectation of the legacy as soon as John's mother's will was probated. Charles could not help but be confused by the gap between his daily drudgery at Warren's and the new financial optimism, and there was no mention of his being freed from servitude. Whereas everyone else had been liberated, he was still imprisoned. John Dickens resumed his London life, with its companionability and bonhomie. Charles kept pasting labels on pots. When the factory moved from Hungerford Stairs to Chandos Street, in Covent Garden, he was placed, with the other boys, in a window alcove through which passersby could observe their dexterity. One day, his father came to Warren's with a friend, Charles Wentworth Dilke, on business or amusement that had nothing to do with his son. Dilke saw the boy at work and gave him "a gift of a half-crown," for which he received "a very low bow." At the end of June, they all went to applaud Fanny receiving a silver medal for good conduct and a second for piano from the hands of the Princess Augusta before a fashionable audience at the Royal Academy. It was the stuff of which family dreams were made. The tears ran down Charles's face. He may not have wished that his sister was in the blacking factory, but he certainly wished that he was on that stage receiving prizes. He could not bear to think of himself "beyond the reach of all such honourable emulation and success . . . I felt as if my heart were rent. I prayed, when I went to bed that night, to be lifted out of the humiliation and neglect in which I was. I never had suffered so much before."14

Charles's deliverance from the blacking factory was unpredictable and bewildering. For reasons he never learned, his father quarreled with James Lamert. Perhaps his pride had been offended by his son working in the window to full public gaze. John Dickens seemed more concerned about himself than his son, and his anger, the substance of which was communicated in a letter that Charles was forced to deliver, conveniently expressed itself only after his release from prison and his awareness of the coming legacy. With characteristic self-indulgence, he could not have been thinking of his son's situation when he made him the bearer of his letter to Lamert, since it was predictable that Charles would feel the force of Lamert's anger even if it was not directed at him. Lamert told him that "he was very much insulted about me; and that it was impossible to keep me after that. I cried very much, partly because in his anger he was violent about my father, though gentle to me." He felt the anger directed against his father as if it were directed against himself. Depressed, "with a relief so strange that it was like oppression," he went home. But the atmosphere there was hardly one in which he could recover or find the security and love he had been craving. "My mother set herself to accommodate the quarrel, and did so next day. She brought home a request for me to return next morning. . . . My father said I should go back no more, and should go to school."15 Achieved at great cost, it was a redemption that his mother opposed. But it must have been additionally painful to him that his liberation resulted from his father triumphing over his mother in a conflict in which he could feel that he was both only a pawn and at the same time the cause of such a bitter quarrel.

For a long time he had taken his father as his model, having identified closely with him from early childhood. But he had been in the process of separating from his mother since infancy. Regardless of its cause, Charles began to develop the sense at an early age that he hardly had a mother. Now that separation took a dramatic and overdetermined leap forward into anger at himself for being so badly treated and into increased feelings of worthlessness because his mother could treat him that way. Fortunately, he was able, in time, to turn his anger away from himself and toward her. "I do not write resentfully or angrily," he claimed over twenty years later, "for I know how all these things have worked together to make me what I am: but I never afterwards forgot, I never shall forget, I never can forget, that my mother was warm for my being sent back."16 His anger was the necessary, liberating culmination of that stage of the relationship. But it was a stage that his feelings and his imagination remained in close touch with throughout his life. He created many variations on this experience in his fiction, dividing his pain into the two women of his fantasy life, the oppressive, witchlike, or carelessly self-indulgent mother he felt he had, and the idealized, loving antimother of wish fulfillment.

THE NEXT TWO AND A HALF YEARS WERE THE CALM AFTER THE emotional firestorm. Typically, John Dickens sent his son to inquire about the cost of becoming a day student at a local school, Wellington House Academy. Apparently no effort was made to determine what might be the best school for him. This one was there; it had turned up, so to speak. The pretentious name may have appealed to his father. Sometime in the summer or fall of 1824, he was introduced to the tyrannical headmaster, William Jones, to the flute-playing lame head usher, who was responsible for most of the teaching, and to the Latin master.17 Each day he walked from Johnson Street to Hampstead Road, just below Mornington Crescent, delighted to be at school again, delighted to be a boy again. In emotional intensity, the years at crowded Wellington House Academy were like days; the months he had spent at Warren's Blacking were like years.

The school provided the usual assortment of subjects and personalities. The headmaster specialized in corporal punishment, a minor sadist of the rod and cane. The Latin master seemed burned out by years of drilling declensions into the minds of indifferent students. The dancing master was fat, the French master brisk. Aspects of these teachers appear in various dismembered and composite ways in his fiction, in the vicious Squeers of *Nicholas Nickleby,* the fuming Creakle, the gentle Mell, and the absent-minded Dr. Strong of *David Copperfield,* the murderous M'Choakumchild of *Hard Times,* and the explosively repressed Bradley Headstone of *Our Mutual Friend.* Teaching was not a profession that he especially admired. Frequently he depicts teachers as self-serving instruments of false values and a repressive society. After railroad construction had destroyed Wellington House Academy, he remarked that the world had "little reason to be proud of Our School." His years there, though, seem to have left few scars. Despite Jones's sadism, perhaps an early contribution to the boast of Pip's sister in *Great Expectations* that she had brought him up "by hand," the experience was a benign one, partly because he was there by choice, partly because some of his needs were being well served. Studying Virgil, he added to the Latin he had learned in Chatham, winning a prize for Latin proficiency and the good humor of his classmates for his punning.[18] He had practice in composition, penmanship, history, arithmetic, geography, French. The most important subject, though, was money. "A profound respect for money pervaded Our School, which was, of course, derived from its Chief." The school was a business, its values materialistic.

The controlled rough-and-tumble of street and schoolroom provided his most sustained pleasures. He seized the opportunity to have the ordinary experiences of his age and situation. The boredom of bad teaching, the low level of intellectual challenge, the threat of physical punishment, were infinitely preferable to the blacking factory. And they were easily outweighed by the opportunity to observe and learn, by the high spirits of

games and hobbies, by the delight of having sympathetic classmates. For the first time in years he had friends of his own age.
They lent one another books, traded valuables and favors,
played street games. They created a scrap-paper *Our Newspaper*,
lending it to read on payment of marbles and pieces of slate
pencil. Some of the boys were exotic and romantic, mysterious
pupils from foreign countries, or older boys who were rumored
to be wealthy or vicious or both. Many of them had pets, particularly white mice and canaries, kept in their desks and pockets.
Elaborate houses were built for the mice, early lessons in Victorian engineering. "One white mouse, living in the cover of a
Latin dictionary," was trained to run up ladders, draw Roman
chariots, shoulder muskets, turn wheels, and even make "a very
creditable appearance on the stage as the Dog of Montargis."
Later, he "fell into a deep inkstand, and was dyed black and
drowned." At least once he entertained his friends at home,
singing "The Cat's Meat Man," a comic song that for years had
been a staple part of his repertoire. He wrote a small tragedy in
blank verse based on the association of one of the mysterious
students with "the sea, and with storms, and sharks, and Coral
Reefs," and he participated in school theatricals, performances
of lifelong favorites such as the melodramatic *Miller and His
Men*. [19]

Though the theatre provided a stage for his dreams and
hopes, he still had to return each day to the muddle of his
father's world. The time at Wellington House Academy provided rest and renewal, the replenishment of his diminished
emotional resources, the possibility that he could once again feel
in control of his life. Against this as counterpoint was his family's continuing financial instability. As an insolvent debtor, his
father was subject to the law's provisions, administered by the
court. Though he could no longer be held in lieu of payment,
his pension and other possessions could. His friend Richard
Newnham, who had been appointed trustee to deal with creditors, refused to act. In October 1825, a new trustee was appointed. Some of the creditors gradually received satisfaction.
Pursued by debts, evicted for nonpayment of rent, the family
moved between 1825 and 1831 to the Polygon, to Norfolk Street,
to George Street, to North End, Hampstead, and then to Belle
Vue, Hampstead.[20] The views may have changed but the situa-

tion did not. In December 1831, the court intervened again. John
Dickens' pension was attached to satisfy a creditor. The "circumstance of great moment" that would place him "in comparative affluence" was an expression of unchanging personality
rather than of realistic expectation. And it was a personality
with which his son had to come to terms. Charles did so by
responding to the second termination of his schooling in a noticeably different way.

His mother was the agent of his expulsion. In early 1827, at
a time when the family was feeling the pinch of unpaid bills,
including Fanny's at the Royal Academy, she met a young solicitor, Edward Blackmore. The junior partner in the firm of Ellis
and Blackmore, at Holborn Court, Gray's Inn, lodged nearby at
the home of her aunt, Elizabeth Charlton. Blackmore thought
the fifteen-year-old boy "exceedingly good looking and clever."
She prevailed upon him to take Charles on as a law clerk.
Dressed in "a Russian jacket and a soldierly young cap," he took
his seat in Blackmore's office probably in May 1827, perhaps as
early as March.[21] He left Wellington House without regret. He
probably also left with unpaid bills. He seems not to have resented his mother's initiative, aware that, among other things,
whatever future he had would not be served by remaining at
school. Visions of Oxbridge, if he had had them, had evaporated
into airy fantasy. Boys from Wellington House Academy did
not go there. In fact, his father could not support him anyplace.
So he began the process of showing himself and the world that
he could do things in a different and better way than John
Dickens. That his clerkship was in a solicitor's office was hap-
penstance. But it contributed to an ambition, sustained for some
years, to become a barrister, though not for the purpose of
practicing law.

The world of the law extended the world of Wellington
House Academy. It was a more fluid, varied world, though, in
which he could move from his clerk's stool into the streets, into
legal chambers, into the law courts, into administrative offices.
It provided colorfully dramatic variations, with their rules and
players, on the serious games that society plays and that ultimately are society itself. It was a grown-up world in a way that
Wellington House was not. He took his turn with the office
tasks, such as keeping the petty-cash book. He ushered people

in and out. He impressed the partners with his eagerness, his amiability, his malleability, his intelligence. He spent much of his time prowling the halls of various "circumlocution" offices, delivering documents and messages, running errands for the firm, which specialized in representing provincial solicitors. "His knowledge of London was wonderful, for he could describe the position of every shop in any of the West End streets." An excellent mimic, he entertained his fellow clerks with imitations of "the low population of the streets of London in all their varieties" and "the popular singers . . . whether comic or patriotic. . . . He could give us Shakespeare by the ten minutes, and imitate all the leading actors of that time."[22]

During his year and a half with Ellis and Blackmore the question of vocation became a problem. In November 1828, he moved to the firm of Charles Molloy, at 8 New Square, Lincoln's Inn. His motive may have been an increase in salary. It may have been some disagreement or dissatisfaction or restlessness. Perhaps he was attracted by the idea of working in the same office in which his friend Thomas Mitton was serving his apprenticeship as a solicitor. Mitton and Dickens had met through their families, who had been neighbors. Born in the same year, they each had their ways to make in the world. Eager conversationalists, they were youthful allies in a world in which companionship helped to alleviate some of the anxieties of work, family, and future. An overweight, lumbering man, unselfconscious about his appearance, Mitton was a warmly loyal companion. His possessive affection was transformed into the desire to be a helpful friend. Intelligent, successful, and ultimately noticeably eccentric, he later acted as Dickens' solicitor. It was the first of many sustained friendships that helped him establish a community of support and security.[23]

He stayed with Molloy, though, only a few months. The legal tedium seemed insufferable, "a very little world, and a very dull one." It was frustratingly slow, if not creaky, in its rewards. Starting at ten shillings a week, he ended at fifteen or a little more. Though his salary did meet his small expenses, the law by itself would not bring him, or bring him quickly enough, to the possession of Gad's Hill, at least the law as embodied in a clerkship. He considered alternatives: finding some business opportunity abroad, perhaps in the West Indies, finding some business opportunity at home, some substantial firm for whom his skills, his intelligence, and his suitability for the position of manager or heir would be irresistible, studying for the bar, becoming a reporter, going on the stage. Unfortunately, there was no sound business opportunity for him anyplace. He decided, though, not to go back to a law office.

Since he had some small savings, and he still lived with his parents on Norfolk Street, Charles did not feel pressured to find new employment right away. In February 1830, immediately after his eighteenth birthday, he obtained an admission ticket to the British Museum, where he became a regular for the next year. He was still as avid a reader as he had been when Mary Weller observed him concentrating on his books as a child in Chatham. He now devoted himself for some time "to the acquirement of such general literature as I could pick up in the Library of the British Museum," reading widely from Shakespeare to Goldsmith to Holbein to *Lights and Shadows of Scottish Life*. [24]

The important aim was not to be like his father. The obvious way of doing that was to avoid debt, to transform his labor into capital, to earn adequate money through initiative, assiduousness, and achievement. In 1829, the bar seemed a possibility. After he left Molloy, he kept open that alternative until the early 1850s, in the event that being a barrister would make it more likely that he would be appointed to a civil-service position. Another attractive profession, with less status but with fewer qualifying hurdles, was journalism. It had become his father's. As with everything John Dickens did, he practiced it in a desultory way. Beginning in late 1825, with only his half-salary pension, he had looked to put to profit his writing skills, his sociability, and his contacts. In 1828, his brother-in-law, a shorthand writer and successful reporter who had helped him before and who was the founder and editor of the *Mirror of Parliament*, employed him. In the autumn of 1826, John Dickens had written a series of articles on a controversy about marine insurance, which was published, probably with the help of Barrow, in the *British Press*. Charles may have done some legwork for his father and perhaps contributed small newsworthy items. When the newspaper failed, John Dickens wrote to Lloyd's, the company whose interests his articles had supported, stating "that the failure of the Newspaper had caused him serious pecuniary inconvenience and he trusted [Lloyd's] would not permit any effort on behalf of the subscribers to go uncompensated." Whether or not there had been a previous arrangement, Lloyd's sent him a check for £10.10.[25]

Tutored by his uncle, Charles had no difficulty adding to his reading at the British Museum the challenge of learning the well-established Gurney system of shorthand writing, "with a view to trying what I could do as a reporter—not for the Newspapers, but legal authorities—in our Ecclesiastical Courts." Having "tamed the savage stenographic mystery," he soon had regular work as a free-lance court stenographer. By early 1831, in time to help with the task of recording the first of the Reform Bill debates, his cooperative uncle elevated his nephew to the staff of the *Mirror of Parliament*. Charles began to take his turn in the galleries, often working through the night. Fortunately, not only did one not need a degree to practice journalism but, as a profession, it had the flexibility, fluidity, and openness to reward talent and hard work. Grub Street teemed with talented reporters and editors attracted to the glamour of opinion-making, the hope of political and literary influence, the attraction of making a living by becoming an articulate part of London and national life. Being a parliamentary reporter meant stenography more than creativity, but Charles did not mind. Suddenly, he had more than a job. He had a vocation.[26]

JOURNALISM WAS NOT A PROFESSION THAT WOULD SERVE HIM WELL in the love affair that began when he met Maria Beadnell in May 1830. His preoccupation with her over the next four years "excluded every other idea."[27] With an obsessiveness unprepared for by any other experience, he fell in love. His notion of an appropriate object reflected his lower-middle-class Anglican upbringing, his image of feminine sexuality the blond, curly-haired ideal, embodying both the pure sister and the innocent wife, on the golden wings of whose spirit, education, and social position he would ascend to bliss. His need was for a woman who, unlike his mother, would nurture and support him, who would be the good, beautiful, and morally elevated genius of his aspirations. In the case of Maria, his judgment was significantly off-target. She was too much like his mother, self-involved and emotionally frivolous. That he fell in love at the age of eighteen, with a seriousness so deep that he desired to marry, dramatizes the extent of his unfulfilled need and the emotional poverty of his experiences as a son.

There was also a social difference. She belonged to a class to which he aspired. Two years older than he, she was the daughter of a moderately prosperous clerk in a banking firm that her uncle managed.[28] A class-conscious, determined woman, Maria's mother devoted herself to managing her household and the lives of her daughters. With three marriageable girls, the Beadnells entertained frequently, creating as favorable a setting as possible for the celebration of their attractions. Well educated for marriage in the ornamental fashion of the day, Maria, the youngest daughter, like her sisters, enjoyed the security of being admired and pursued within the rules and values of her parents' world. Having just returned from finishing school in Paris, she was introduced to Dickens by Henry Kolle, a bank clerk of twenty-two who was about to become engaged to her sister Anne. Maria was blond, petite, and conventionally pretty. His first sight of her "in a sort of raspberry colored dress . . . with a little black trimming at the top . . . captured . . . his boyish heart" and brought him eagerly back to the Beadnell home on Lombard Street as often as he was permitted to visit.

Quickly drawn into their circle, he played the role of entertaining suitor, charming both the daughters and the parents. At parties he sparkled with all the wit and performance he could muster, much of it in the style of elaborate compliment, gentle irony, and deep sentiment. He wrote strained acrostics, parodies, and poems in Maria's album, eager to flatter her.[29] He was more desirable, though, as a friend and a guest than as a member of the family. Despite her claim to the contrary twenty-five years later, there is no reason to believe that she ever took him seriously. He was an underaged suitor, with modest employment on the fringes of journalism, one among numbers with whom she delighted to flirt and from whom she accepted flattery. Her parents did not need to disapprove. Young women who thought of themselves as witty, well educated, and beautiful, with the security of a substantial middle-class home, rarely married economically insecure younger men who were less experienced, less well educated, and socially inferior. Maria apparently had no sense of her painfully persistent suitor as special as a human being or as a lover. She was "a blessing too great for us children of clay," he wrote in a parody of one of his favorite Goldsmith poems, which he called "The Bill of Fare" and presented to the Beadnells sometime in the autumn or winter of 1831. He still hoped that his love would be returned.

While she and her friends, with a firm grasp of the social reality, enjoyed the teasing badinage of flirtation, he was able to imitate the style infrequently. Too serious, too much in love, he created in his mind fantasies of marriage. Almost immediately confessing himself in love, he wore his heart on his sleeve. With the humiliation of the blacking warehouse fresh in his emotional memory, he was at pains to dress as handsomely as possible. His attractiveness, though, did not prevent his poses and confessions, widely made to friends, family, and intended, from becoming the subject of mild ridicule. "When I, turned of eighteen," he later parodied himself, "went with my Angelica to a City Church on account of a shower . . . and when I said . . . 'Let the blessed event, Angelica, occur at no alter but this!' . . . My Angelica consented that it should occur at no other—which it certainly never did, for it never occurred anywhere." The Beadnells were hospitable to the boyish entertainer, not to the serious suitor. Though he got some help from his sister Fanny, who had become a member of the Beadnell circle, Maria's parents soon encouraged both their daughter and her young suitor to limit or stop their communication. His family criticized his obsessiveness. With the collaboration of Mary Anne Leigh, a gossipy friend, he sent secret messages. Playing the role of confidante and intermediary, Mary Anne sometimes pleased herself in the game of hearts, flirting with him to tease Maria and to flatter her own vanity. He attempted to give Maria presents, to involve her in literary ideas, to make himself useful. She mostly discouraged him.[30]

As the months went by, his friendship with Kolle flared. His friendship with Mitton strengthened. Probably through his father, he met Thomas Beard, a young reporter, five years older than himself. Beginning in 1832, John Dickens and Beard were

colleagues on the staff of the *Morning Herald*. A generous, enthusiastic young man, Beard, a talented reporter from a family of
brewers in Sussex, provided amiable companionship on long
walks and in evening entertainments at taverns and in theatres.
They were soon to be colleagues, and to begin a lifelong personal and family intimacy. Still living with his own family,
Charles moved with them from one residence to another, ending
finally at 18 Bentinck Street, near Cavendish Square. When his
parents were inconveniently located, he rented furnished lodgings for himself, including rooms on Cecil Street and, in 1831,
rooms that he shared briefly on Buckingham Street.[31] He began
to work long hours, transcribing debates. Having impressed his
uncle with his intelligence and competence, he was awarded
with some managerial and secretarial responsibilities at the *Mirror of Parliament*. In November 1831, for the second time, John
Dickens declared himself an insolvent debtor, a kind of painful
bad joke played out in the background of his son's attempt to rise
in the world and win a bride.

Charles's effort to triumph with Maria persisted for about
two years. With the details of his family history obscured by
silence, he behaved as if they had never been poor, let alone
debtors. He believed that he could persuade Maria and her parents, the former with "the simple truth and energy" of his love,
the latter with the claim that he would "raise himself by his own
exertions and unceasing assiduity." He had little real sense of
what a poor match she would be for him. By the spring of 1832,
the end of the painful game was becoming clear to him. His
struggle to accept defeat lasted for another year. At the beginning of February 1833, at a coming-of-age party, which he seems
to have originated and paid for, but for which his mother sent
out the invitations, Maria apparently insulted him, though without being aware how deeply, by telling him that he was a boy.
The word "scorched [his] brain."[32]

In the months ahead he elaborately justified himself. He
accused Maria of "heartless indifference" and he dramatized his
wounded feelings. He also ferociously attacked Mary Anne
Leigh for meddling mischieviously, and he denounced his sister
Fanny, whom "no consideration on earth shall induce me ever
to forget or forgive," because she had not told him of Mary
Anne's interference and misrepresentation. There was more

temporary rhetorical bluster in his criticism of Fanny than long-lasting anger. He was unable, though, to distinguish between them. In May, he told Maria that "I have no hopes to express nor wishes to communicate. I am past the one and must not think of the other." He was true to his feelings when he too readily exclaimed that "I have been so long used to inward wretchedness, and real, real misery." He also claimed that toward Maria he had "never had and never can have an angry feeling." Later in May, aware of the futility of his proposals, "sans pride, sans reserve sans anything but an evident wish to be reconciled," he made one final effort to convince her of his worthiness. "I never have loved and I never can love any human creature living but yourself . . . and the love I now tender you is as pure, and as lasting as at any period of our former correspondence."33 His rhetoric was self-defining. His intensity was at its highest at the moment when the loss was irrecoverable. Fortunately, the relationship was at an end. Two years later he had no trouble pledging his love to someone else.

SITTING IN HIS RENTED OFFICE IN THE DULL WORLD OF THE ECCLESIAS-tical courts, he wrote in March 1832 to George Bartley, the manager of Covent Garden Theatre, requesting an audition. He told him how young he was "and exactly what I thought I could do; and that I believed I had a strong perception of character and oddity, and a natural power of reproducing in my own person what I observed in others."34

Vocation had become a problem much on his mind. His uncertain earnings as a free-lance stenographer at Doctors' Commons, the ecclesiastical court, and his lowly status in the hierarchy of journalism neither helped him with Maria nor fulfilled his own ambition. Since childhood he had been fascinated by theatrical performance, the brilliance of Grimaldi, the terror of Shakespeare, the histrionics of Charles Kean. He could not stay away from the theatre. Eager to please in a childhood world in which he needed to demonstrate that he was worthy of being loved, he had developed a performance personality, wearing the various masks that would earn him applause.

He had been an entertainer, a song-and-dance child, singing for his emotional supper. He had become a self-conscious actor and playwright, performing in his own and other people's stage dramas. Perhaps he could solve his vocational problem by becoming an actor.

For some time, he had been attending the theatre constantly. Fortunately, it was cheap, with half-price admission after the first act. He later claimed to have gone to some performance—pantomime, comedy, farce, extravaganza, spectacle, ballet, opera, melodrama, tragedy—every night for about three years. In late 1832 he saw the famous William Charles Macready perform at Drury Lane. For "three or four successive years" he regularly attended the *At Homes* of the comedian Charles Mathews, whom he idolized, "travelling entertainments" that emphasized imitation and mimicry. Apprenticing himself to the best acting available, he practiced diligently all the movements and gestures, "often four, five, six hours a day." From a well-known manual he learned a widely practiced system for memorizing parts that he used successfully throughout his life both in amateur theatricals and for public speeches.

To Charles's delight, Bartley responded to his request for an audition "almost immediately," setting an appointment for April. Fanny agreed to be his accompanist. Though unpaid bills had forced her to leave the Royal Academy at the end of June 1827, she had become an instructor there, and had been earning a living as a teacher and professional accolades as a performer. With high hopes, Charles practiced his repertoire of comic songs and skits. When the day came he "was laid up . . . with a terrible bad cold and an inflammation of the face." Though he commented years later about how near he "may have been to another sort of life,' his heavy cold may have been as much ambivalence and stage fright as organic illness. Whatever his fascination with the theatre, he might have found the life of an actor ultimately as tediously repetitious as the duties of a court stenographer. His need to control the conditions of his professional life would have been much more difficult to achieve in the world of the Victorian stage than in a writer's study. He wrote to Bartley, explaining his indisposition, and "added that [he] would resume [his] application next season."[35]

By then, though, his restless imagination was being increasingly absorbed by the new interest he felt in journalism. At the same time, with a flurry of confused, self-lacerating correspondence, he was liberating himself from Maria. His hopes were over. But the theatre was still a preoccupation. By April 1833, he had given up the idea of becoming a professional actor. Yet, as if to affirm the theatre's enduring importance to him, he plunged into organizing, producing, directing, and acting in an evening of private theatricals at the Dickens home on Bentinck Street. Rooms were emptied and furniture rearranged. "The whole family was infected with the mania for Private Theatricals." During the month in which he made his last proclamations of undying love for Maria, he not only worked long hours in the gallery but carried on the preparation for the performances of an opera in two acts, *Clari, or, The Maid of Milan;* an interlude, *The Married Bachelor;* and a farce, *Amateurs and Actors.* He wrote a prologue, organized rehearsals, assigned parts, supervised costumes, lighting, staging, and scenery, with an enthusiasm for total control that energized himself and his colleagues.

Enlisting his friends and family, he became the absolute manager. Henry Kolle and Henry Austin, an architect and engineer who soon was to marry Dickens' sister Letitia, were in charge of the lighting. Austin acted as his secretary. Austin's sister Amelia read the prologue. There was a band and scenery. A playbill was printed. He sent the actors, in Austin's handwriting, a peremptory list of regulations: "1. Mr. Dickens is desirous that it should be distinctly understood by his friends that it is his wish to have a series of Weekly Rehearsals for some time, experience having already shown that the Rehearsals are perhaps the most amusing part of private Theatricals. . . . 2. It is earnestly hoped that Ladies and Gentlemen who may have somewhat inferior parts assigned them in any piece, will recollect the impossibility of giving every performer a principal character, and that they will be consequently induced rather to consult the general convenience and amusement than individual feeling upon the subject. . . . 3 [Costume]. 4. . . . a punctual attendance at Rehearsals, and an early knowledge of the several parts, are most especially necessary. 5. It is proposed that a Rehearsal shall take place every Wednesday at 7 o'clock precisely—Charles Dickens, Stage Manager."[36]

In honor of Shakespeare's birthday, the plays were per-

formed on April 23, 1833. Dickens played the starring roles in a
cast that contained most of his friends and family. Only his
mother was excluded. Thomas Mitton, Henry Austin, Letitia
Dickens, Fanny Dickens, his younger brothers Frederick and
Alfred, and even John Dickens, as the farcical Mr. Elderberry,
had parts. Like his son, the portly journalist delighted in foot-
lights and performance, though he was always limited in his
son's casting to one role. The next year he played it explicitly,
performing as the "Great Unpaid" in another private theatrical,
a musical parody of *Othello* written and arranged by his son, in
which he sang,

> Oh! take me home to my "missus" dear;
> Tell her I've taken a little more wine
> Than I could carry, or very well bear:
> Bid her not scold me on the morrow
> For staying out drinking all the night;
> But several bottles of soda borrow,
> To cool my coppers and set me right.[37]

The final break with Maria, amid a flurry of angry communications, came the next month. It left him posturing that he
had a broken heart, that he would never cease to love her. The
break, though, was a timely one. That he had the courage to
accept it marked a stage in his maturity. In his fiction he would
transform Maria into a youthful version of his mother, the prototype of the flighty, self-indulgent coquette whose feelings
never run deep enough to know and express real love. In his life,
he remained both attracted to and critical of such an embodiment of female ego, whose physical beauty and domineering
manner attracted him erotically. Pain and pleasure, rejection
and acceptance, were closely allied in his emotional and sexual
life. Against that attraction, against women like Maria and his
mother, he needed an antidote, a pure sister, an ideal wife. He
also needed to find a counterbalancing satisfaction in his work,
in the praise, admiration, and love of his friends and admirers.
By 1832 he had begun to create a circle, an extended family.
Though some of his family members belonged, he reached out
to Mitton, Austin, Kolle, and soon Thomas Beard, in his first
successful effort at building a supportive, protective community
whose love for him would be unqualified.

His journalistic work began to take on a new energy and

excitement. In March 1832 he had become a parliamentary reporter for a new paper, the *True Sun*, while continuing to work for the *Mirror of Parliament*, where his uncle expanded his responsibilities. In his effort to gain recognition as the official parliamentary record, Barrow drew on his nephew's organizing skills to create "masses of papers, plans, and prospectusses." Much of the work was done at his uncle's home in Norwood, where he was well enough over Maria by late 1833 to be attracted by "a very nice pair of black eyes." Recognized as extraordinarily competent at shorthand and a disciplined, vigorous worker, "the most rapid, the most accurate, and the most trustworthy reporter then engaged on the London press," he began to be asked to do special assignments, many of which were to take him in the next few years across and around England to report on important elections and to transcribe lengthy speeches.[38]

Still living with his family on Bentinck Street, he saw his father not only at home but at work. On the surface, he dealt considerately with him and with his mother, and warmly with his two sisters. Two of his brothers, Alfred and Frederick, toward whom he felt affectionate and protective, were becoming teenagers. When he had begun working at Ellis and Blackmore in 1827, his mother had been nursing an infant. With their usual disregard for the relationship between income and expenses and with the same inability to prevent conception that their son later displayed, the Dickenses had had another child, named Augustus, at a time when children were neither emotionally nor financially desirable.

Soon disaster struck again. In November 1834, John Dickens was arrested for an outstanding bill owed to his wine merchant. Pressed for rent arrears at Bentinck Street, John confessed that "we have been living in apartments . . . much beyond our means . . . our establishment is about being broken up . . . Charles . . . into chambers and your humble servant 'to the winds.' " Charles had previously resolved "to leave home."[39] He could now afford it, and the independence essential to his maturity had become a necessity that he needed to embrace.

CHAPTER THREE

The First Coming
(1834-1837)

❧ I ❧

He had not been cast by his family for the role of eminent writer, let alone genius, of his age. "None of us guessed at it," his father said, "and when we heard that he had become a reporter . . . my brother-in-law Barrow . . . and other relations anticipated a failure."[1] No one had seen harbingers of distinction. At school, he was no more than bright and responsive, with a retentive memory. His preoccupation with theatre and literature enriched his inner life, adding to his social presence more than expressing special talents or unusual promise. As a child, his frailty undercut his natural energy. Severely depressed by his six months in the blacking factory, recovering gradually from the diminishment of expectations inflicted on him by his parents' limitations, he began to reveal energy and compensatory self-confidence. But initially he had no vocational focus. Much of his childhood energy had gone into keeping himself as healthy as possible in a repressive environment. Much of the energy of his next decade had been absorbed by the slow process of emotional healing. He neither steadily glowed nor fitfully sparkled before an impressionable world. When he left his legal clerkship to attempt to be a reporter, his family thought he had aimed too high. When, in the next two years, he went from legal to parliamentary reporting, they expected a failure. Understandably, they were unprepared for the explosive release of energy and talent that transformed him in a three-year period into an internationally celebrated writer. Even he was startled. His ability to reimagine himself could not keep pace with his achievements.

In August 1834, he applied to become a reporter for the *Morning Chronicle*. Since at twenty-two he hardly looked his age and had little formal education, almost no one thought he could be competent.² On the recommendation of his uncle, who had unsuccessfully attempted to get him employed by *The Times*, and with the help of Thomas Beard, already on the staff, he unexpectedly got the job. By December he had been working for the *Chronicle* for five months. When the family dispersed in December, Dickens was ready. Since publishing his first "article" in the *Monthly Magazine* in December 1833, he had published seven more by the time of his appointment to the *Chronicle*, and another seven by the end of 1834. The *Monthly Magazine* paid nothing for them. It seemed possible, though, that he might persuade the editor of the *Chronicle*, who had given thought to the possibility that it would be a good thing to publish some of his employee's sketches, to pay him for them. Here, then, was a potential additional source of income. When he and fourteen-year-old Frederick moved into 13 Furnival's Inn in Holborn, even having to borrow small sums to cover his moving expenses did not dampen his triumphant sense of having come into his own. One of his first impulses was to make a housewarming party.

The *Chronicle* paid him five guineas a week. Unlike his income from court stenography and the *Mirror of Parliament*, it was a secure annual salary. When Parliament was not in session, he was assigned to do theatre reviews and general reporting. His duties were demanding, and meant long hours, usually nights, taking his turn with other *Chronicle* reporters in the hot crowded gallery of the House, and rapid coach, carriage, and horseback trips to provincial political events in order to record important speeches and to get the transcriptions into print as soon as possible. The need to beat out the competition put an added premium on quickness and accuracy and on making rapid-express arrangements to get the copy back to the office. Just a few weeks after joining the *Chronicle*, he was sent to Edinburgh to report on a political banquet given for Earl Grey. It was his first travel outside southeastern England. Journeying by steamer up the coast, Dickens and Beard were a professional team on the first of a series of ventures that bound them together as friends and colleagues. In November, he reported a meeting of the Birmingham Liberals. At the beginning of January 1835, they spent almost a week reporting on the general-election nominations in Colchester, Braintree, Chelmsford, Sudbury. and Bury Saint Edmunds. In May, they reported on the Exeter speech of Lord John Russell, the leading Whig politician of the day, in November his speech to the British Reformers in Bristol, then an election meeting in Birmingham, a "town of dirt, ironworks; radicals, and hardware." In December, they covered the by-elections at Northampton. At the end of January 1836, they attended two political dinners given for the Irish nationalist Daniel O'Connell in Liverpool and Birmingham. On one occasion, after two good-natured colleagues held "a pocket handkerchief" over his notebook during a rainstorm to keep it dry, he returned to London with "a slight touch of rheumatism" and "*perfectly* deaf." In every kind of weather, from sunshine to pelting rain, dry or soaked, clean or muddy, indoors or outdoors, he observed the British political process at work.[3]

The reporting genre demanded transcription rather than narration or interpretation, objective dryness rather than local color. Developing his eye for the humorous, he included in his account of the dinner in Edinburgh a description of one of the guests, who, having grown tired of waiting for Lord Grey, began the dinner by himself, "one of the few instances on record of a dinner having been virtually concluded before it began." The scenes were colorful, the hotels and inns bustling, the roads filled with interesting human detail. Some of the elections were rowdy, most of them corrupt, some both. At the Northamptonshire by-election a virulent confrontation stopped just "short of murder and riot." His growing detestation of the Tories, "a ruthless set of bloody-minded villains," spilled over into his report of the Tory horsemen purposely "bearing down all before them with . . . ruffianly barbarity, and brutal violence," for which no Tory expressed the least regret.4 Developing a critical pen, he reported the rhetoric of deceit and false claims, of promise and prevarication, increasingly convinced that political life was essentially corrupt. What he experienced and observed, much of which could not go into his newspaper reporting, became part of his memory and imagination.

Eager to earn more money, he was dissatisfied with being only a parliamentary reporter. The articles that he had began to write in December 1833, soon to be called "sketches," focused his imagination in ways that newspaper reporting could not. He had a commitment to reporting. He felt "the genuine fascination of that old pursuit," and he enjoyed his comradeship with his professional brothers. Still, he had begun his first efforts at authorship with an expectant heart.5 Fearing rejection, he had dropped his first sketch into "a dark letter box, in a dark office, up a dark court in Fleet Street . . . with fear and trembling." When "A Dinner at Poplar Walk" appeared in "all the glory of print," his eyes had overflowed with joy and pride. The pleasures of authorship clearly exceeded those of newspaper work. The distinction was discreet and personal. Authorship resonated with the expectations of childhood, of his walks with his father, of Gad's Hill Place. It made him feel in control in a way that he had never felt before. His success as a reporter brought him to a threshold that he eagerly crossed. Satisfying work, travel, new friendships, finding a better, more compatible Maria—all of these things were possible.

Immediately responsive to his first sketches, the *Monthly Magazine* had soon received more amusing stories, for which they paid nothing. Dickens liked doing them. They attracted attention and praise. It was in his interest to be printed and reprinted, to become a visible author, whose terms in the future might be different from those in the present. In January 1834, he had published "Mrs. Joseph Porter," in February "Horatio Sparkins," in April "The Bloomsbury Christening," reprinted the next month in another small magazine, *The Albion*. These and the two sketches that followed, "The Boarding-House—No. I" (May 1834), and "Original Papers," in *Bell's Weekly Magazine* in June, were unsigned. He needed a signature, something to identify the articles as his. He decided on a pseudonym, a nasal

corruption of the nickname Moses, with which he had chris-
tened one of his younger brothers, taken from one of his favorite
characters in Goldsmith's *Vicar of Wakefield*. Boses became Boz.
By August 1834, when his first signed article, "The Boarding-
House—No. II," appeared in the *Monthly Magazine*, the previous
stories had been sufficiently successful to make anonymity as
self-protection unnecessary. Many of his friends and colleagues
already knew that he was Boz. Now John Black, the editor of
the *Morning Chronicle*, his "first out-and-out appreciator," admiring what seemed to him Dickens' "original genius," encouraged
him to do less general reporting and more original writing.
Black thought that this "fresh, handsome, genial young man,
with a profusion of brown hair, a bright eye, and a hearty
manner," had unusual literary talent, even the possibility of
brilliance.[6] Beginning in September, the *Chronicle* published his
series of "Street Sketches," five in all appearing in the autumn
and winter of 1834.

Black's admiration and Dickens' own initiative were about
to make him a professional author. Dickens was also assisted by
a new friend, a colleague who asked him in January 1835 to write
a sketch for the first issue of a new paper of which he had been
put in charge, the *Evening Chronicle*, published by the owners of
the *Morning Chronicle*. A fifty-one-year-old reporter and editor,
George Hogarth was a Scotsman by birth and inclination. Having given up law for journalism, he had bounced from London
to Exeter to Halifax and then back to London again, where he
joined the staff of the *Morning Chronicle* in the summer of 1834.
Dickens readily agreed to write the sketch, assuring his colleague that he would do so even without being paid for it. But
would his employers be willing to add "*some* additional remuneration" to his salary if he were to agree to do a series of
sketches for the *Evening Chronicle*? That would be only "fair and
reasonable . . . I should receive something for the papers beyond
my ordinary Salary as a Reporter."[7] Surely this must have been
on his mind since September, when his first *Chronicle* sketch had
appeared. With Hogarth's support and with Black's prediction
of "future greatness," the owners agreed to raise his salary from
five to seven guineas a week. It was the first money he ever
earned as an author. He never again wrote without being paid.
In the sixty sketches that he published between December 1833

and December 1836, he created, with the most tentative and belated of overall planning, a comic city with dark corners and threatening relationships that introduced some of the major colors, styles, and tensions of the fiction that he was to write for the next thirty-five years.

The sketches were a testing ground for an apprentice author whose talent enabled him to progress precociously. With a keen eye for social observation, he began to portray satirically, though affectionately, the variety and comic oddity of human nature in the social guises of early Victorian life. Many of the characters are stock representations of conventional eighteenth- and early nineteenth-century literature. The plots are often minimal or nonexistent, a visit to an uncle or a friend, the staging of amateur theatricals, an attempt to tangle or untangle oneself from an amorous relationship. When they are more fully developed, they are stereotypical exercises in the machinery of plot development, as in "The Great Winglebury Duel" and "A Passage in the Life of Mr. Watkins Tottle." Often the tone ranges between humor and irony in a slightly stiff style that echoes the distancing effects of the eighteenth-century essay and contemporary humorists. Some of the sketches, such as "The Streets—Night," reveal elements of his mature style. The tone, the diction, the surreal elements, the rhetorical devices, and the sentence rhythms combine to create a sketch that could have been written two or more years later, stylistic preludes to *Oliver Twist*. In "Gin-Shops," a sympathetic but outraged social consciousness dominates, his first identification of poverty, filth, and pollution as social crimes. "The Misplaced Attachment of Mr. John Dounce" and "Sentiment" transform his painful romantic misadventure with Maria Beadnell into comedy while at the same time lightly touching the exposed nerve of courtship, sex, and sexuality. They are sketches of repression and frustration in search of appropriate language. In "The Pawnbroker's Shop," his fascination with prostitutes makes its first dramatic appearance. The ameliorative, optimistic Christmas totem that would reach its culmination in the Christmas tales of the 1840s makes its thematic debut in "A Christmas Dinner."

Aspects of his personal experience flow through the porous filter of the partly fictional, partly observational genre. "The First of May" invokes sanitized images of a golden childhood in

Kent. "Astley's" invokes his recollection of learning the alphabet from his mother. "Seven Dials" reflects his fascination as a
child with the slums of London. "The Broker's Man" and "The
Pawnbroker's Shop" contain memories of early family life, and
the main character of "A Passage in the Life of Mr. Watkins
Tottle," like John Dickens, is jailed for debt in a prison like the
Marshalsea. "Mrs Joseph Porter" satirically describes an example of the mania for private theatricals similar to the performances that he directed and in which he performed. "The
Steam Excursion" is based on a trip taken by Dickens and his
friends, and "Early Coaches" draws on his traveling experiences
as a reporter. But the more dramatic, less obvious currents of his
life flow with surprising power through those sketches whose
subject matter forced him into contact with his own deepest
concerns and began his lifelong pattern of being attracted to
fictions of displaced autobiographical exploration. In "Our
Next-Door Neighbour," he presents the fantasy of the dead boy
and the grieving mother, an echo of the childhood fantasy in
which his self-worth and worthiness to be loved become clear
to his mother only after his death. In "The Pawnbroker's Shop,"
his family's insecurity, the origin of his obsessiveness about
money, is dramatized in the description of the visitors to the
shop: A small boy is beaten, a man and a woman fight bitterly,
a prostitute, "the lowest of the low; dirty, unbonneted, flaunting and slovenly," has a moment of human sympathy in response to another woman who may have to travel the same road
she is on, which has "but two more stages, the hospital and the
grave." In "The Hospital Patient," a brutally abused dying wife
is idealized as the ever-forgiving female whose father had said
five years before that "he wished [she] had died a child."

"A Visit to Newgate" starkly synthesizes the social and
psychological themes that ran through these sketches. In November 1835, he visited the prison, beginning his lifelong practice of visiting social institutions to help him with impressions
for his writing. He also went to the Coldbath Fields prison the
same month but did not write about it because the "gallows" is
more dramatic than the "Tread-Mill." The prose of "A Visit to
Newgate" is incisive, evocatory. Some of the characters anticipate *Oliver Twist*. The emphasis on dream states as both escape
from reality and imprisonment, on guilt, betrayal, murderous-

ness, and altered states of consciousness, takes him back to his childhood and forward to his future novels. The powerful sketch "The Black Veil" combines Gothic horror, imprisonment, madness, and death with a self-preserving reversal of his sense of himself as the good son with the bad mother. In the story, the boy's mother is perfectly good, "a widow . . . who had denied herself necessaries to bestow them on her orphan boy." She expressively loves her son, no matter what his faults. With a dead father, a selfless mother, the boy has no one but himself to blame for his "career of dissipation and crime." That was one way out of the blacking factory, one way to go back even further into childhood and into the myth of the blameless mother, whom he would have much preferred to the mother he had.

❧ 2 ❧

IN LATE 1834 OR EARLY 1835, GEORGE HOGARTH INVITED HIM TO HIS home in York Place, Chelsea, "standing opposite orchards and gardens extending as far as the eye could reach." There he found a moderately prosperous middle-class family, with interesting and cultured Scottish connections, who welcomed him warmly and whose warmth he returned.[8] Hogarth played the role of paterfamilias with a combination of amiability and competence. He had had professional though not financial success as a lawyer in Edinburgh, a writer to the Signet, and as the trusted adviser of Sir Walter Scott. But he had moved more in literary and musical than legal circles. Having recently begun his career as a journalist, he soon became a distinguished music critic, feature writer, and author. In 1814 he had married Georgina Thomson, whose grandfather one year later organized the first Edinburgh music festival. Among his many distinctions, he had engaged Scott, Robert Burns, and Beethoven to write words and music for a collection of Scottish songs. Georgina Hogarth bore the burden of her family of ten children and tight budget with a strong sense of maternal propriety. Forty years old when Dickens met her, she had recently given birth to another daughter to add to a moderately pretty, mildly cultivated, and charmingly domestic threesome. Catherine had just had her nineteenth birthday. Mary was a pretty fifteen-year-old, Georgina a gamineish seven. The dominant Hogarth complexion was creamy pale, with touches of natural pink, the eyes bright blue, the chin recessive, the hair blond, the spirit light, the accent Scottish.

The young writer became a regular visitor, whose promise the Hogarths appreciated and to whom their eldest daughter responded. With heavy-lidded eyes and turned-up nose, Catherine had a becoming tendency to carry her shortness into full-figured plumpness. Though not quick of wit or foot, she was warm, engaging, eager to please and to be pleased, and clearly on the marriageable side of adolescence. Unlike Maria, she was not flirtatious or fickle.[9] Shaped by his mother's aloofness, conditioned by Maria's rejection, Charles wanted a woman whose world he would be the center of, whose feelings and actions would revolve around his needs. He also wanted a family he could identify with, who would provide the intimacy and stability that his own lacked. He courted her deliberately, self-confidently, having chosen someone not likely to refuse him. Since May 1833 he had elevated himself to a respectable position with a rising annual income. He had also become a promising writer for whom some people, like his prospective father-in-law, were predicting great things. Unlike the prosaic Beadnell household, the Hogarth home, whose patriarch was a talented musician and a competent writer, valued culture and appreciated the arts. Dickens radiated the intensity of his work ethic and his ambition. His talent and its demands were clear, at least to George Hogarth. Early in May, Charles proposed marriage. There seem to have been no rivals. Catherine quickly accepted.

That she had little sense of the life of the imagination did not matter to her suitor. At twenty-three, he needed to come into his patrimony. There was to be no financial inheritance. His emotional legacy was mainly an unhappy one. He needed to create his own good fortune, both material and emotional, to become father to himself. He wanted to match his emancipation with the full symbols of adult responsibility. With a strong sense of having been deprived of a familial hearth, he used the Hogarths' as the threshold of his own. Marriage to an amiable, conventional, sweet-tempered, and domestic woman, who would cooperate with his desire to be master of his own home, to be in control of his life and work, to have compliant, contained, and unthreatening sexual relations, to have children with whom to express his own familial needs, was strongly attractive. To be closer to her, he took lodgings in June 1835 on Selwood Place, Chelsea, around the corner and a few hundred yards from the Hogarth home. Eager for domestic blandishments, he encouraged her to make it a practice to visit him, sometimes, for propriety's sake, with her sister Mary, to prepare his breakfast after he had spent late nights at the House. Once he sent her a note at five in the morning, before going to sleep, to tell her that he would awaken at one. "You will lunch with me at that hour, of course—I shall not rise until you *call* me." On another morning, having returned home just before dawn, he proclaimed with amiable bossiness, "I shall *fully expect* you and Mary to breakfast with me this morning . . . I take *no denial on any pretence.*"[10] Catherine had no desire to deny him. She defined her engagement in conventional terms. Eager to be attended to and flattered as much as possible, she felt pleasure in her fiancé demonstrating his love through his demands on her.

He had a surer sense of her nature than she of his. Those things about her that he did not like he did not hesitate to criticize. He did not like her narrowness of vision when it prevented her understanding him; he did not like her temperament when it rubbed against the grain of his emotional needs. Sometimes she seemed to him childishly self-involved and foolish. She frequently teased him in small ways. Though the battles were minor skirmishes that she quickly lost, she attempted initially to resist his total dominance, to reserve aspects of herself from his control. Aware that her power was limited and temporary, she tried stubbornly to assert some of her needs. She was better, though, at capitulation than at self-transformation, at suppression than at change. He gave absolute emotional sincerity. When he was there, he was involved totally, among other reasons because he had an immense desire to get the relationship right. So much depended on it. When, from his perspective, it was going wrong, he could be aggressively, even callously frank. If she could not be the way he wanted her to be, he did not want her at all. When she expressed herself angrily, he labeled it "*hasty* temper." When she withdrew her warmth, unaware of what deep resonances that would have for him, he responded to this "uncalled-for coldness" with the threat that she frankly confess that she had tired of him. He would not be used as a toy that "suits your humcur for the moment . . . I shall not forget you lightly, but you will need no second warning."[11]

What he wanted was that she be infinitely responsive to his feelings, mainly through compliance, cheerful toleration, and nurturing supportiveness. When she was ill—both Catherine and her mother had scarlet fever in October 1835—he could be tenderly reckless. He visited them constantly, aware of the danger to himself and willing to suffer the illness for the sake of being there for her then. When, in a teasing mood, he played the game of pet names, he sometimes crossed the boundary between generosity and possessiveness, between respect and defamation. He needed her cooperation in feeling fully justified in loving her. He smugly reported to her Mitton's supportive but possibly evasive comment, "whatever I do must be right; and that whoever I love, must be faultless."[12]

If there is any ironic self-awareness in the remark, there is also both wishful thinking and coercive pressure. He desired absolute loyalty from friend and lover. He was prepared to give it in return, filtered through his energy, his restlessness, and his ambition. As a reporter, he spent long hours traveling and at the House. He had a certain amount of business at the office. As an apprentice writer, he could practice his craft only in odd hours. When he made a commitment, he unswervingly kept it. The specter of his father's irresponsibility hovered always in the background. What was for him a necessity of his personality and his life became for Catherine a marker of his priorities. He tried indirectly and unsuccessfully to tell her about his childhood, to help explain what drove him to work so hard, often to the point of exhaustion.[13]

From the beginning, she struggled to resist the likelihood that he cared more for his work than for her. He would not admit that that had any validity. From the beginning, he presented himself as an unchanging and unchangeable given. He had no desire to be any other way. His protestations expressed the stiff formalism of self-deceit. When his back was up, he was a master of sincere excuses, of the heightened rhetoric of justification. On one occasion, having moved back to Furnival's Inn, he sent his brother Frederick to tell her that he would not keep their appointment that evening. "If you knew how eagerly I long for your society this evening, or how much delight it would afford me to be able to turn round to you at our own fireside when my work is done . . . you would believe me sincere in saying that necessity and necessity alone, induces me to forego the pleasure of your companionship for one evening in the week even. You will never do me the justice of believing . . . that my pursuits and labours such as they are are not more selfish than my pleasures, and that your future advancement and happiness is the main-spring of them all."[14]

When she satisfied him, she was "My dear Kate" or "My dearest Katie" or "My Dearest Girl." When she did not, she was "My Dear Catherine," frozen in both acid and ice. When she complained that his letters were stiff and formal, he was surprised. "I don't know how it is, but I am quite certain I had no notion of its being so, and if it really were (which I can hardly believe) it was quite unintentional." There was never either retreat or awareness in his words and tone. His most frequent complaint was that she was "ill-tempered," a code phrase for insensitivity to his needs and feelings. He regularly applied the carrot as well as the stick, sometimes in the same letter. "Your note my love . . . displays all that amiable and excellent feeling which I know you possess. . . . If you would only determine to *shew* the same affection and kindness to me . . . I should have no one solitary fault to find with you. Your asking me to love you 'once more' is quite unnecessary—I have never ceased to love you for one moment, since I knew you; nor shall I."[15] The courtship had its loving moments, its times of endearment and optimism. In her effort to weather the complexities of his personality, hoping that the storms would be short, she had a fund of little-girl mispronunciations, pet names, and cute phrases to deflect his anger and relieve her anxiety. She may have compared his assertiveness and persistence with her lack of emotional strength. He had been educated in a hard environment. She had been educated in the easygoing amiability of the Hogarth household. She needed to marry almost as much as he did, but less for personal than for social and cultural reasons.

The courtship went on, with breakfasts, lunches, short excursions, brief visits to York Place, and with visits to the theatres, particularly to see plays he had been assigned to review. In late November 1835, keeping his eye open for a place to live, he looked at houses in Pentonville that were "extremely dear." His own small apartment did not even have a kitchen. They needed space for Fred, who would continue to live with his brother, for Mary Hogarth, who had become Catherine's closest companion, and for a servant. Just as he had helped his parents by taking Fred off their hands, the married couple would help relieve the crowded Hogarth household by taking Mary. The solution was next door, at 15 Furnival's Inn. He took the lease, from Christmas 1835, of the "three-pair front south," with a kitchen in the basement, at fifty pounds a year for three years. In mid-February 1836, he and Fred moved in. In March, he purchased most of the household furnishings, and suggested to Catherine, with a peremptory force that could not be denied, that they honeymoon in Rochester. The golden days he had spent in Kent in his childhood drew him back. At the end of the month, maneuvering around his heavy work schedule, *he* fixed the date as "Saturday next." They were married in St. Luke's Church, Chelsea, near the Hogarth home. Catherine was dressed modestly, becomingly, "a bright, pleasant bride." In addition to the Hogarth and the Dickens families, a few friends were present, including Beard, who acted as his best man. "It was altogether a very quiet piece of business." The wedding breakfast was held at York Place. As a present, the groom gave his bride an ivory-fitted workbox inscribed FROM CHAS. DICKENS TO KATE, APRIL 2ND, 1836, an appropriate symbol of her domestic mission.[16] Sometime during their week-long honeymoon in Chalk, near Chatham, or in the next few weeks, Catherine became pregnant.

THE PREVIOUS AUTUMN HE HAD HOPED THAT THEY MIGHT MARRY AT Christmas 1835. But he did not feel secure enough. With a developing entrepreneurial self-confidence, he had no need for an absolutely fail-safe net of security, and was willing to take limited risks. He had had, though, painful experience with overextension. The misery of trying to survive on less than a reasonable minimum was all too familiar. His only income still came from his salary, sufficient to maintain a single person but not a family. He needed additional money. Unexpectedly, the sketches he had been writing for almost two years, the only income from which had been two guineas a week added to his salary by the *Morning Chronicle*, became a property with a potential buyer, an ambitious twenty-six-year-old publisher who had just come to London. The inexperienced but shrewed John Macrone offered Dickens one hundred pounds for the copyright of the sketches that were already in print.[17] He would bring them out, augmented by additional sketches, in two volumes, under the title *Sketches by Boz*, with a preface by the author and with art by a well-known illustrator. Undercapitalized, reflecting the severe depression in the publishing industry in the early 1830s, Macrone had just borrowed five hundred pounds on the security of good looks, charm, and a promise. It seemed a clever proposal.

In making the offer, Macrone had taken the advice of his unofficial literary adviser, William Harrison Ainsworth. *Rookwood*, Ainsworth's melodramatic novel, to which Macrone had bought the rights, had been a smashing success in 1834. Ainsworth had come to London in 1824 at nineteen years of age to train as a solicitor in the expectation of taking over his father's Manchester practice. After completing his training, he had given up law for the more exciting practice of literature. The elderly essayist Charles Lamb introduced him to various literary figures. Early in 1830, the industrious Ainsworth, soon "a dandy and a literary lion," notorious for quickly written, widely popular, sensationalistic fiction, became a founding member of a group of writers and artists associated with *Fraser's Magazine* and called the Fraserians. By the autumn of 1835, when he brought Dickens and Macrone together, he had been for some time a well-established, even distinguished member of a disparate circle that included William Makepeace Thackeray, Bryan Procter, William Maginn, William Jerdan, and Daniel Maclise, some of whom were to become Dickens' intimate friends.[18] Ainsworth, who also knew Leigh Hunt, John Forster, and George Cruikshank, became his first channel into this world.

Having purchased the copyright, Macrone would take all the risk as well as all the profit. To protect his investment, he engaged the usually difficult and always arrogant Cruikshank to do the illustrations. Mercurial, vulgar, moody, with a flare for the personally dramatic, Cruikshank had a "hawk nose, broad forehead . . . black hair and whiskers." His "steely blue eyes had

no merriment—only keenness and a certain fierceness in them."
Usually dressed in a "blue swallow-tail, a buff waistcoat, grey
pantaloons, and Hessian boots with tassels," at the age of forty-
two he already had had a distinctive career. Trained with his
brother in the studio of his artist-father, "cradled in caricature,"
he had brilliantly illustrated in a series of cartoons the political
fortunes, misfortunes, and corruptions of Britain and France in
the late Napoleonic age. Afterward, collaborating with various
writers and creating miscellaneous independent plates for separate sale, he took as his subject the pretension and corruption of
urban life. The result was his successful *Life in London.* Like
Dickens, he knew the city "better than the majority of Sunday-
school children know their Catechism." At the height of his
powers, with a distinguished reputation as an artist, he had
already agreed to do twelve etchings for Macrone's fourth edition of *Rookwood,* to be published in May 1836.[19] To Ainsworth
and Macrone, Cruikshank and the young writer seemed made
for one another, the experienced, successful artist, the talented,
youthful author, both sharp satirists and London visionaries.

When he and Dickens met in November 1835 they quickly
transformed a working relationship into a social extravaganza.
Joined by Ainsworth, they created a dining and theatre trio,
Dickens' first artistic circle supportive companions in business
and pleasure. Cruikshank's domestic life centered around a wife
half his age, a house on semirural Myddleton Terrace in Islington, and frequent visits, in "clouds of tobacco smoke, and over
foaming tankards," to "all kinds of strange and queer places."
Ainsworth, whose marriage had collapsed in 1835, lived harmoni-
ously with two female relatives at Kensal Lodge, in easy distance
of Cruikshank and Dickens. From the beginning, his relationship with Cruikshank had its tensions. The few years of collaboration, though, were productive, and the friendship retained
some warmth even when it lost its intimacy. Ironically, a relationship that began with buoyant consanguinity became
strained by Cruikshank's departure from the banquet table and
the wine bottle when he later became a crusading teetotaler.

Excited by Macrone's projection of a Christmas 1835 publication date, Dickens, despite his heavy schedule, had no doubt
that he would be ready. But, to his irritation, Cruikshank did not
have the plates for Christmas. The coordination of the project

among author, illustrator, and publisher was taking more time than had been anticipated. Having rushed to get additional sketches done to fill out the volume, he pressured Macrone and Cruikshank. The illustrator, used to being the dominant partner in such ventures and assuming that he had absolute authority to choose what scenes to illustrate, declined to finish the plates until he had the entire manuscript in hand. Probably he was also busy with other projects. Dickens steered his resentment into conciliatory rationalizations. He also had incorrectly assumed that each plate would have two rather than four illustrations, consequently misreading Cruikshank's progress. Under pressure from Macrone, he wrote a puff for the book to appear in the *Morning Chronicle* and elsewhere. He sent out notes and directed review copies to likely places and people. He sent a sycophantic letter, with a copy of the book, to Lord Stanley, whose long speech on the condition of Ireland he had taken in shorthand in a private session in February 1833 after Stanley had been dissatisfied with the published newspaper transcription. Closer to home, his father-in-law-to-be, who "knows all the sketches by heart, and takes an interest in the book in no way secondary to my own," wrote a "beautiful notice" for the *Morning Chronicle,* which appeared three days after publication, February 8, 1836.[20] Hogarth's partisan claim that it was "the work of a person of various and extraordinary intellectual gifts . . . a close and acute observer of character and manner, with a strong sense of the ridiculous," who can produce "tears as well as laughter," was confirmed by the reviews and the sales of the next few months.

An unexpected success, *Sketches* repaid Macrone's gamble on a relatively unknown author. Dickens soon received another £100 for a second edition; then he received £150 for a new volume of previously uncollected sketches, published in December 1836, designated the second series; and finally he was paid £100 for the copyright of both volumes. The initial £100 for the first series was a welcome minor supplement to his income. As Macrone's profits mounted, eventually to more than £2,000, the author had reason to regret that he "was never a partner in the work, and never shared in the profits from it."[21] As his expenses increased, he needed more income. "Head over ears in work," he juggled commitments, intent on exploring whatever might be artisti-

cally and financially profitable. The success of the book suggested that a further try at articles combining fiction, reportage,
and realistic observation might provide a vehicle for fulfilling
his ambition to be a successful professional author. There were
other possibilities, though, one of which was the theatre. He had
no special preference at this time for any particular genre. Eager
to try his hand at anything that had potential, he had the energy,
ambition, and financial need to take on as many projects as
possible, even simultaneously. He preferred exhaustion to de-
pletion, and the harder he worked the more energy he seemed
to have, its level rising to meet the exhilaration he felt in his
achievements.

When, in late December 1835, while waiting for Cruikshank, he was queried about doing the libretto for a comic opera,
he responded enthusiastically. Among other things, it spoke to
his lifelong fascination with the stage. Fanny introduced him to
John Hullah, who wanted to create a comic opera, to be called
"The Gondoliers," based on a stereotypical Venetian subject.
Emphasizing that he was at home in England but abroad in
Venice, Dickens convinced the composer that they should collaborate on a comedy of English country manners. Set in the
eighteenth century, with the musical-dramatic structure of John
Gay's *The Beggar's Opera*, it would have the tone of eighteenth-
century pastoral satire and the moral values of a relaxed Victorianism. With a mixture of dialogue and song in the English
ballad opera tradition, it would gently parody popular Italian
opera. He would do the libretto, based on one of his unpublished
stories, Hullah the music. An untalented versifier who had written some squibs, comic verse, and sentimental ballads, he would
write the rhymed verse for the songs as well as the dialogue.
"The characters would act and talk like people we see and hear
of every day." Though they do nothing of the sort, the final text
and score of *The Village Coquettes*, his share of which he wrote
and revised throughout the first half of 1836, persuaded John
Braham, a popular tenor and the owner-manager of the new St.
James's Theatre (built as an expensive speculation that soon
failed), to produce it and to perform in it. George Hogarth,
influential as a music critic, helped convince Braham that the
opera, ready by the end of July, would run easily for fifty or
sixty performances, especially since the popular John Harley

was engaged to play the leading role. But revisions, rehearsals, and managerial complications delayed the production from the anticipated October opening until early December 1836.

Always fascinated by the theatre, Dickens now had access to the professional stage. He eagerly attended rehearsals, even when he had to travel distances and suffer inconveniences. Able to afford new clothes, he began to dress theatrically, in the dandy tradition, partly to recompense himself for the rags of his adolescence. On one occasion, he did not appear at a dinner party partly because his clothes had gotten muddy and he did not have fresh things into which to change. Impatiently waiting for the appearance of *The Village Coquettes,* he adapted for performance, with Braham's encouragement, "The Great Winglebury Duel," which had appeared in the first series of *Sketches by Boz.* Retitled *The Strange Gentleman,* it opened on September 29, 1836, at the St. James's Theatre, with songs and music that allowed Braham to call it a burletta. Harley's talent helped the farce run for over fifty performances, one part of a series of entertainments that made an evening at the St. James's. For this minor critical and financial success Dickens received only the thirty pounds for which he had sold the copyright. He made great personal capital, though, buoyed by the excitement and rewards of a premiere, of evenings at the theatre, of being a successful dramatist. When *The Village Coquettes* finally opened on December 6, with the fiftieth performance of *The Strange Gentleman* completing the evening's bill, Dickens, his family, and his friends were in the theatre. His contribution had been advertised in the playbill. At the end of the performance, the audience "screamed for Boz." It seemed surprised when it got only the ordinary-looking Dickens rather than one of his fictional characters. The reviews also were tepid, and one of them, by John Forster, the music critic of *The Examiner,* was ponderously unfriendly. Despite Hogarth's partisan effort in the *Chronicle,* the opera closed after nineteen performances.[22]

THOUGH HE FELT DISAPPOINTED, HE WAS ALREADY PREOCCUPIED with another, this time extraordinary, literary venture. In February 1836, the publisher William Hall unexpectedly came to see him at his lodgings at 13 Furnival's Inn. Chapman and Hall, at 136 Strand, had been in business for six years, surviving the steep depression in the book industry with the help of prudent commitments, including *Scenes and Recollections of Fly-fishing*, a sixpenny weekly, *Chat of the Week*, and a *Topographical Dictionary* in twenty-four monthly parts. For the Christmas trade of 1835, they published *The Squib Annual*, a coffee-table volume with illustrations by the humorist Robert Seymour. Brisk and businesslike, with an accountant's fluency with figures, Hall handled the firm's money matters. Retiring and contemplative, with wide knowledge and a keen sensibility, Edward Chapman represented the firm's literary sensibility. Once decisions had been reached, Hall handled the negotiations. Chapman and Hall admired *Sketches by Boz* and were about to publish one of the stories, "The Tuggses at Ramsgate," in their *Library of Fiction*. The success of *Sketches* had brought Dickens to their attention as someone to whom it might be appropriate to make a proposal that had already been turned down by a number of writers. When he responded to Hall's knock at the door, Dickens, to his surprise, recognized the man from whom in December 1833 he had bought the copy of the *Monthly Magazine* in which he had seen his work in print for the first time. Though he had not realized it then, it had been in Chapman and Hall's bookshop that he had made the purchase.[23]

Having had considerable success with *The Squib Annual*, the publishers had agreed to Seymour's proposal that they put out a volume of his humorous illustrations on the subject of Cockney sporting scenes. Seymour suggested that the focus be the adventures of a club of sporting gentlemen. A hardworking, practical artist who had been immensely productive, perhaps to the point of overwork, and who had had a nervous breakdown in 1830, Seymour agreed to the suggestion that it be a monthly serial accompanied by brief textual descriptions. Chapman and Hall had good reason to believe that there were financial advantages to publishing what would eventually be a book volume in monthly parts. In need of a journeyman writer, they proposed to Dickens that he provide each month a sheet and a half, or twenty-four printed pages, of text to accompany four comic illustrations. The pay would be £14 3s. 6d. "for each number [monthly serial part] to be made always on the day of publication, which is understood to be the last day of every month." For the first number, he was "to provide copy . . . by the first of March [1836] and sufficient for the second by the 15th," future numbers always to be ready "*two months* before the date of publication." The contract called for "a book illustrative of manners and life in the Country." Chapman, Hall, and Seymour had in mind a volume whose primary selling point would be the illustrations. On the evening of the day that Hall made the offer, Dickens wrote to Catherine that he had been asked "to write and edit a new publication . . . entirely by myself; to be published monthly and each number to contain four wood cuts."[24] Seymour was not mentioned in the letter. Within a week, the young author gave his "entire concurrence" to the proposed terms, with the one proviso that he be allowed to provide copy five rather than eight weeks in advance. Chapman and Hall probably had no knowledge of his other commitments and little sense that they were involving themselves with someone who was about to make additional ones.

Despite a delay of a few days because of moving from 13 to 15 Furnival's Inn, he assured his new publisher on February 18, 1836, that "Pickwick," a name taken from a stagecoach owner he remembered from his travels, "is at length begun in all his might and glory. The first chapter will be ready tomorrow." When Seymour did a sketch of a thin Pickwick, Chapman protested that he "must be a fat man; good humour and flesh had always gone together since the days of Falstaff." When, on the twenty-first, both Chapman and Hall came to see what their new man had done, the first number was ready. They apparently liked it. Dickens had more trouble with the second, though he had it ready by the middle of March. They had scheduled the first number to come out on March 31, dated April 1. That second number, ready by mid-March, was insurance that there would be an April 30 appearance of the May 1 number. Thereafter he would provide his text about the end of the third week of the month for publication about five weeks later. In mid-April, Dickens glowingly proclaimed, on the basis of scanty evidence, "PICKWICK TRIUMPHANT." Actually, the sale of the press-run of a thousand copies of the first number had been modest. Chapman and Hall reduced the run of the second to five hundred copies.

While they were at work on the third, a shocking event brought progress to an abrupt halt. Overtired, irritated, sensitive about his lack of education and his working-class background, Seymour shot himself to death on April 20 in the garden of his home in Islington. The coroner's verdict was "temporary derangement." Having returned from his honeymoon ten days before, Dickens had praised the artist for "how much the result of your labours, has surpassed my expectations." He had urged him, though, perhaps uneasy at having inserted into the second number an interpolated "Stroller's Tale" that he had written some time before, to redo the etching to accompany it, since "it is not quite my idea; and as I feel so very solicitous to have it as complete as possible, I shall feel personally obliged, if you will make another drawing." On the seventeenth, Seymour had spent a short time with him at Furnival's Inn, their only meeting, probably trying to get clear what his young colleague wanted and assessing with whom he was dealing.[25]

The artist's legacy to his associates was a business problem. He had provided four illustrations for the first number but had completed only three for the second. What, then, should they do with *Pickwick Papers*? So far, it had been neither a success nor a failure. Ready with a bold proposal, Dickens recommended that they continue it, with some changes that would improve the chances for increased sales. Why not have two instead of four illustrations each monthly number, and thirty-two pages of text instead of twenty-four? With sixteen pages between illustrations, he "could expand his scenes and amplify his characterizations in ways he could not when he had to invent a new comic climax every six pages." The diminution of the role of the illustrator would give him more control over the book. His words would now unarguably be more important than the illustrations. And the publisher would have to pay more attention to the author than to the artist, for the success of the work would depend on the text. For every two sheets, or thirty-two pages, he had proposed that he should receive twenty pounds, a raise of one pound per sheet over the rate of payment for the first two numbers. "If the Work should be very *successful* . . . I apprehend you would have no objection to go a little further."[26]

The economics were clear to Chapman and Hall. Abandoning the project meant a substantial loss in stock and in cash outlay as well as the inevitable need to find another investment that might or might not be less risky. They had reason to be pleased with what Dickens had done in the first two numbers, though they had not yet and might never gain from it financially. The continuing success of *Sketches* confirmed that he was still a good author in whom to invest. His youth and ambition were much in his favor. Seymour could be replaced easily, especially since, with the changes that Dickens proposed, there would be less need to employ a well-known, highly paid illustrator. They soon decided that the proposal was worth accepting. Business associates recommended Robert Buss. A young artist, inexperienced with the etching process in book illustration, Buss had worked on Chapman and Hall's *Library of Fiction* and was available at short notice. Buss, despite his own reservations, was induced by Hall to give it a try, with the understanding that his initial stumblings in the learning stage would be tolerated until he had a chance to prove himself. He did the two illustrations for the third number to everyone's dissatisfaction, including his own, and was promptly fired.[27] He and Dickens had never met.

With word out that an illustrator was needed, two young artists separately approached him. A tall, pudgy-faced, well-educated young man, William Makepeace Thackeray, came to see him at Furnival's Inn. Eager to be selected, among other reasons because he wanted to marry, he brought "two or three drawings . . . which, strange to say," Dickens "did not find suitable."[28] A self-trained artist, who, like Thackeray, had been educated at Charterhouse and had studied medicine, John Leech sent him some designs, on Cruikshank's recommendation. Dickens thought them "extremely well-conceived, and executed." But when Leech threatened to call on him in late August, he fobbed him off to Chapman and Hall. Dickens and the publisher had already selected the right person. Hablot Knight Browne is "a gentleman of very great ability, with whose designs I am exceedingly well satisfied, and from whom I feel it neither my wish, nor my interest, to part." Probably he had been chosen for the assignment in the process of the firing of Buss. Three years younger than Dickens, he had trained from an early age as an apprentice illustrator. In 1832 he had won a medal for the best illustration of an historical subject. Now Chapman and Hall's main illustrator for the *Library of Fiction*, he had effectively illustrated Dickens' recent pamphlet broadside *Sunday Under Three Heads*, directed against a legislative attempt to prohibit all work and recreation on Sunday, which Chapman and Hall had published in June. He had proven himself a rapid, reliable, and observant worker who most likely could work readily under Dickens' direction.[29] A modest and broodingly private man, Browne was a talented illustrator without any painterly or fine-arts ambitions.

For the third number, in June 1836, the first to reflect the new arrangement, the print run was restored to one thousand copies. Even if they had all been sold, the return to the publisher would have been too small to cover expenses. Short of capital, Chapman and Hall needed to use all the proceeds beyond their fixed costs to pay for the production of the next number. They innovatively created a nation-wide distribution network by enlisting provincial booksellers to take each month at no risk a stack of the thirty-six pages of text and two illustrations, bound like a pamphlet in a green paper cover with a design and inserted advertisements, the unsold copies to be returned at the publisher's expense.[30] With the introduction in the fourth number of the lively, vividly depicted Sam Weller, with his humorous Cockney wisdom, helped by the increasing efficiency of the provincial network, the sales began to increase rapidly. In August the delighted Chapman and Hall voluntarily increased his remuneration as of November to twenty-five pounds per number. Soon *Pickwick Papers* was indeed triumphant. Monthly sales rocketed toward forty thousand copies. Profits were immense. By August 1837, when the sixteenth of the twenty numbers appeared, the publisher made an additional settlement with their now prize author of two thousand pounds for the twenty numbers eighty pounds per number more than the agreement with which they had started. With the copyright entirely theirs, Chapman and Hall made at least ten thousand pounds' profit on the book.

What was most on Dickens' mind, though, was not money, marriage, publishers, a new series of *Sketches*, newspaper reporting, the theatre, or the pressure of his schedule and commitments, important as these things were. His energies were fast becoming immersed in the all-absorbing challenge of creation. Writing had become a daily confrontation with the sacred, with his craft, his art, and his life. He needed to remind his publisher and himself that *Pickwick* had a claim on permanence, that it was literature and that he was an artist. Schedules had to have the flexibility that art demands. "The spirits are not," he told Chapman and Hall, "to be forced up to Pickwick point, every day." Sometimes his imaginative energy outpaced the speed of his pen. Sometimes his nervous energy brought him out of his chair. Sometimes he sat "down to begin a number, and feeling unequal to the task," he would "do what is far better under such circumstances—get up, and wait. . . ." With a strong sense of high stakes, of the call to fame and fortune, he began to build on partial truth a myth of total self-sufficiency. *Pickwick Papers* marked the first conclusive moment of his triumph over early deprivation. "If I were to live a hundred years, and write three novels in each, I should never be so proud of any of them, as I am of Pickwick, feeling as I do, that it has made its own way"— that *he* had made his own way—"and hoping . . . that long after my hand is withered . . . Pickwick will be found on many a dusty shelf with many a better work."³¹ At twenty-four years, he was aware that he was creating great literature. He felt *Pickwick Papers* flowing out of himself and his life.

In these comic idealizations, he created the purest myth, touched by a manageable darkness, of his own and his culture's recovery from economic and emotional deprivation. In the *Pickwick* world the recovery occupies the present of an optimistic consciousness without ever denying the past or promising that the future will be undeviatingly bright and inclusive. It is a novel of personal myth, not history, of the brightness of his own first triumphant self-assertion, of his young adulthood and his temporary liberation. The historical world stands still in *Pickwick Papers* at the moment in which the bright sun of Mr. Pickwick and his circle flares out with the energy of stagecoaches, rural travels, unshakable comradeship, happy times. After the trauma of the Reform Bill, in the brief pause before the Victorian spurt into social consciousness, the British reading public found its message of optimism, class harmony, benevolence, and comic reconciliation irresistible. The social problems created by poverty, industrialization, undercapitalization, and a restrictive class structure that he knew so well from his own experience are mostly excluded from the novel. At its core is a definition of human nature as essentially benevolent, as desirably Pickwickian. The scenery of Kent, the dignity of Rochester, the comedy of farce and remediation, the glow of Christmas, dominate the Pickwickian self-definition.

In his childhood, he had experienced isolation and fragmentation. The universe of Mr. Pickwick, though, is fraternal and cohesive, with a penumbra of comicality that transforms a fallen world into a pleasurable place of harmless eccentricity. Matthew Lamert becomes Dr. Slammer. Dodson and Fogg are balanced by the morally responsible Perker. The reprobate Jingle and Job Trotter are redeemed by their response to Pickwick's benevolence. The corruptions of the political world of Eatanswill, based on what he had seen as a political reporter, cannot touch the essential triumph of right feeling. The world of darkness, nightmare, and insecurity, the laughter of the devil-rat, Chips, is narrowed, imprisoned, so to speak, in the very place in which his father had been incarcerated. Refusing to pay Mrs. Bardell's legal costs, Pickwick accepts the consequences as an affirmation of who and what he has decided he wants to be. His imprisonment in the Fleet parallels but transcends John Dickens'. Since he consciously chooses to assert his moral integrity, his loss of liberty is an ascension into greater freedom. Through material incompetence, through flaws of personality, through insufficient self and family protectiveness, his father had descended into an imprisonment that he could not avoid. In the depiction of Pickwick's imprisonment, Dickens plays sensitively with one of the most painful experiences of his childhood. Among other things, he creates in his fictional character an idealized version of his father, an antifather who voluntarily chooses prison as an exemplification of his moral stature and as an expression of his control over his own life, the kind of control that Charles had been so eager to achieve for himself. That John Dickens had not achieved such liberation was painfully clear to his son. While he worked on *Pickwick Papers,* his father found his success a valuable resource. Reminding the publishers "how your interests are bound up with those of my son," he attempted to borrow money from Chapman and Hall without his son's knowledge.[32]

Pickwick's final stasis and happiness, though, demand his separation from adventure and the world, his retreat into the upper-middle-class seclusion of his protected enclosure of self-sufficiency in his pleasant house in Dulwich. Unlike John Dickens, he has managed to liberate himself entirely from financial pressures. There is nothing he cannot afford, nothing that the material world can deny him. The novel never calls into question the applicability of that solution. *Pickwick Papers* is a novel of exclusion. The Pickwick world is satirized with loving, comic acceptance. No doubt, the novel implies, Pickwick could, if he desired, go out into the world again, a little wiser, adventuring into resolvable farce, ultimately returning to his happy home. But he does not and will not. It is a containment that embodies the new structures of personal relationship, of marriage and of professional life, that Dickens had created for himself, though it is more rarefied, static, and narrow. The novel ends, Pickwick stops. Dickens, though, hardly paused.

CHAPTER FOUR

Charley Is My Darling
(1837-1841)

❧ I ❧

WHILE HE WORKED "LIKE A HOUSE O' FIRE" ON A MORNING IN LATE
June 1837, writing the fifteenth number of *Pickwick Papers,* the
bells of St. Paul's began to toll for the death of King William IV.
"If you know anybody," he wrote to John Forster, "I wish you'd
send round and ask them not to ring . . . I can hardly hear my
own ideas."[1] He had neither the power nor the inclination to
hold back the new. On the contrary, he and his friends greeted
the death of the old king with a combination of personal indifference and communal relief. By the middle of 1837, the twenty-
five-year-old author had become important to an expanding
circle of writers and artists, most of whom delighted in the
prospect of ringing out the old, inaugurating a new era of high
seriousness, fervent companionship, and artistic achievement.

In late 1836 he had been introduced to a successful young
artist, Daniel Maclise. Irresistible, "very mad & Irish, but very
affectionate," Maclise was the son of a poor tradesman. From
childhood he had shown outstanding ability at drawing. The
star student at the newly opened Academy of Art in Cork, he

created a stir and received high praise from his subject when he drew Sir Walter Scott. A highly skilled portraitist who excelled in catching likenesses in rapid sketches, he began to make his living as a professional artist in 1825. Arriving in London in the summer of 1827, the twenty-one-year-old, tall, well-built, handsome Irishman, with long "dark hair . . . in heavy waves," looked Byronic and ambitious.[2] Often moody, sometimes depressed, he had an energy for adventures, passions, and jokes that outpaced his capacity for withdrawal and darkness. He quickly became a member of the Fraserians. Novelists like Ainsworth, Edward Bulwer, and soon Thackeray, artists like Cruikshank, journalists like William Jerdan, Douglas Jerrold, Francis Mahony, and William Maginn, poets like the attractive and ambitious Letitia Landon, and an assortment of Bohemian figures ranging from the romantically dissolute to the dandyesque met regularly in the *Fraser's* back room. Maclise introduced Dickens to many of them. Fun-loving, handsome, and talented, with an attraction for and to women, he was a well-known social and amorous man-about-town who appealed immensely to Dickens and soon was to become one of his two most intimate companions. He was to sit for Maclise's pen and brush many times. But Thackeray's 1836 drawing of himself, Maclise, Mahony, and a rakishly smoking Dickens at St. James's Square bring writer and artist vividly together for the first time.

When he met the young critic and biographer John Forster in the winter of 1836, introduced by Ainsworth, Dickens began the most sustained friendship of his life. Despite stormy moments and some brief estrangements, the fraternal bond resonated warmly for almost thirty-five years. Forster's passion for him had its fullest expression in his biography of his friend, shaping posterity's view of the novelist for close to a century. They first shook hands in the year in which Queen Victoria came to the throne. They were buried over three decades later in the same cultural grave. Forster became a force to be resisted as well as embraced, grist for Dickens' satiric mill, parodied early in their friendship in Dowler in *Pickwick Papers* and later in Podsnap in *Our Mutual Friend*. But when Forster's eldest brother died in 1845, Dickens reminded him that "you have a Brother left. One bound to you by ties as strong as ever Nature forged. By ties never to be broken, weakened, changed in any way. . . ."

Born in the same year as Dickens, Forster began his literary mission as a young man in Newcastle upon Tyne, his mother the daughter of a farm laborer, his father a butcher and cattle dealer. Their enlightened Unitarianism brought him firmly into the secular world. His uncle's prosperity paid for his fees at the secular Royal Grammar School, where he became head boy, eager to justify the confidence of his uncle, his "best friend all through life . . . a true good man." Like Dickens, he needed to imagine and create an environment different from his family's. As a boy of sixteen, he went to Cambridge to study classics, with his uncle's support. Within months, he left for London University to study law. Despite a diligent effort, aware that he was disappointing many, aware of the potential loss of income, Forster soon gave up studying law. He could not resist envisioning himself a man of letters and of the theatre. Like Dickens, he had an avid imagination fired from childhood by literature. The law had certainty, security. His writing and argumentative skills, his avid support of the Reform Bill, his tenaciousness, his energy, and his imposing physical presence could carry him far. His teacher Thomas Chitty believed that had he remained at the bar eventually he would have become lord chancellor.3 But he readily exchanged the fantasy of being lord chancellor for that of being what Dickens later good-humoredly called the "Great Mogul" of literature.

Forster's passion for the theatre had also begun in childhood. At fifteen, he wrote an argumentative "Vindication of the Stage" in response to a puritanical pamphlet that the mother of one of his friends thought he would benefit from reading. The next year his quasi-Byronic but moralistic *"Charles at Tunbridge or The Cavalier of Wildinghurst . . .* by a gentleman of Newcastle" was performed and favorably noticed, with the prediction that he would "one day become an ornament of his country," by the editor of the Newcastle newspaper for which he had begun to do reviews. His creative talents, though, were more managerial than histrionic. He could play only one role—the evaluator, the arbitrator, the enthusiast sure of his middle-class values and his aspirations for himself and his culture. With an expressive reading voice, "rich and melodious, and full of varied intonations," he performed only the stentorian part.4 Brought up in a narrow world of provincial Unitarianism, he had confidence in a combination of reason and force of personality that made him at times

a self-deceptively imperceptive man. With only a little poetry
and less imagination, his preference for the straight and narrow
was deeply embedded in his simplistic rationality. Unlike Dickens, he had no ability to fall, only to remain steadily conventional. Like Dickens, he defined literature and theatre as moral
exemplars. But he had no visible alternative forces operating.
Though he acted it brilliantly, he could act only one role.

When he reviewed *The Village Coquettes* in December 1836,
the tall, dark-haired, handsome, twenty-four-year-old Forster
had been active in London journalism and literature for almost
seven years. With prodigious enthusiasm, he had pursued
every available opportunity, reviewing for the *Newcastle Mercury* and the *New Monthly Magazine*, promising to write a series
of biographies of civil war figures, making a start at a biography of Oliver Cromwell, publishing a volume of execrable
verse, *Rhyme and Reason*, becoming drama critic of the radical
newspaper the *True Sun*, and then, in late 1833, of the Liberal
newspaper *The Examiner*, originally founded by Leigh Hunt.
Mostly with a young man's hero worship, always with a sense
of mutual mission, he pursued Charles Lamb, one of Dickens'
favorites, "the original, kind-hearted, veritable Elia," and then
Hunt, "the first man of letters of any note worthiness I ever
knew," who "influenced all my modes of literary thought at
the outset of my life" and "confirmed me in Literature as a
profession."⁵ Hunt's influence helped turn him away from the
law. Poised between Romantic and Victorian generations, he
sought the continuity of holding with one hand the remnants
of Romanticism, Wordsworth, Southey, Lamb, Hunt, and
Walter Savage Landor, and, with the other, the young soon-to-
be Victorians, Edward Bulwer, Robert Browning, Daniel Maclise, and Charles Dickens, and the two transitional figures
who touched both cultural modes, William Charles Macready
and Thomas Carlyle.

His appearance at the premiere of *The Village Coquettes* was
in response to a note that Dickens had sent to Albany Fonblanque. The editor of *The Examiner* assigned his young reviewer to see what the talented author of *Sketches* had done.
Dickens took with good grace Forster's criticism that the libretto was "totally unworthy of Boz" and his humorous condemnation of the unprofessional appearance of the author and

the composer on the stage after the performance, in response to the cheering crowd. Dickens could not, though, help laughing, "for the life and soul of me," at the comment that the audience was "left in perfect consternation that he neither resembled the portraits of Pickwick, Snodgrass, Winkle, nor Tupman. Some critics in the gallery were said to have expected Sam Weller."[6] Friendly feelings were expressed in March 1837 and the two men began to see one another socially. By late May, the formality of "My Dear Sir" had been replaced by the intimacy of "My Dear Forster." Forster's ecstatic response, "the highest of all praise," to Dickens' new novel in progress in *Bentley's Miscellany* and his strong sympathy for Dickens' pain in the midst of a personal tragedy in May encouraged Dickens to take Forster more into his confidence. Forster's good business sense and skill soon came to seem wonderful assets to an ambitious author increasingly damaging himself by compulsively signing disadvantageous contracts. Through Forster, he met Macready, the prickly, sometimes morose, most brilliant actor of the early Victorian stage, and Thomas Noon Talfourd, the facile, good-natured, rather bland poet-dramatist and member of Parliament who earned his living as a barrister. Shortly, mainly through Forster and Maclise, he knew almost everyone worth knowing.

Macready and Talfourd were almost contemporaries, Talfourd forty-two years of age and Macready forty-four in late spring 1837 when Forster introduced them to Dickens. Talfourd combined the security of law and the civil service with the glamour of literature. Dickens already knew him by reputation as a dazzling speaker and conversationalist. He also knew him by sight, having reported for the *Morning Chronicle* Talfourd's parliamentary activities and his role in the scandalous Norton-Melbourne trial for adultery on which Dickens had loosely based the Bardell-versus-Pickwick trial.[7] Talfourd was gifted with a great deal more ego and vanity than talent. Macready, who had preferred not to become an actor, who abhorred his profession, and who looked forward to saving enough money to retire from a world that his society did not consider respectable, had an equal amount of both. He had introduced to the theatre naturalistic techniques, stylized poetic devices, and the value or at least illusion of absolute performance sincerity. He also emphasized the desirability of authenticity in costuming and setting, particularly the importance of creating individualized sets rather than all-purpose scenery. With the help of literary allies, he attempted to reestablish the dignity of the theatrical profession. Collaborating on scripts with his friends, taking on the management of Covent Garden Theatre, reviving Shakespeare's plays, stripping away the bowdlerizing encrustations of the eighteenth century, he had become, by the late 1830s, a theatrical tyro whose energy was transforming the English stage.

An unsuccessful actor and theatrical manager, his father had been, like Dickens', an imprisoned bankrupt. But he had sent his son to Rugby to become a gentleman. Unlike his father, Macready embraced the theatre as a distasteful duty at a time of economic necessity. With his spinster sister, the stern guardian of his mind, he trained a young actress with whom he had fallen in love to become the dutiful wife of a gentleman and the mother of his family. Before marriage, she was "Katie." Afterward, she was invariably "Catherine." With a growing family, eager for respectability, he bought a country home in Elstree, seventeen miles from central London. Combining Victorian earnestness with Romantic resentment, inflamed sometimes by an almost uncontrollable temper, he became a moral tyrant both on and off the stage. Deeply compassionate, he elevated duty to a religious law and moral rigor to kindness. Though he breathed happily outside the world of the theatre, the stage was the center around which his friendships revolved.

Dickens, who later claimed that he went to the theatre every night for two or three years in the early 1830s, first saw the "eminent tragedian" perform in December 1832. Forster had contrived to meet Macready in May 1833 at the funeral of his rival the actor Edmund Kean, where he also met the successful marine painter Clarkson Stanfield, who had done stage sets for Kean, Macready, and Sheridan Knowles. Knowles was the improvident, overworked Irish dramatist who had written *Virginius*, one of Macready's most successful vehicles. Forster appeared to Macready "quite an enthusiast; I like him." They soon took pleasure in long conversations in which the younger man's admiration for and support of him became paramount. With access to the theater, with his position as drama critic of *The Examiner*, with his energy and ambition, Forster became intimate with Macready's friends, particularly Stanfield, Talfourd, and Bryan Procter, a lawyer and civil servant who wrote poetry and plays under the pseudonymn Barry Cornwall. In mid-June 1837, he came into Macready's dressing room at Covent Garden, where he was a familiar visitor, "with a gentleman, whom he introduced as Dickens, alias Boz." Macready was "glad to see him."[8] With theatrical stars in his own eyes, Dickens was strongly attracted to the actor's courage, warmth, and dignity He seemed a figure of steel-gray assiduousness, so different from his father and so like the model of his own aspirations. Before he had been a visitor to the theatre. Now he became Macready's guest. Before he had been on the lower level of the widespread free-ticket arrangement. Now he became part of the preferential world of those who were acknowledged to belong.

When *Pickwick* was published in book form in late 1837, he dedicated it to Talfourd, partly because the latter had introduced into Parliament a copyright bill that Dickens avidly supported. The pirated versions and imitations of *Pickwick* that its success immediately spawned had made him realize how much he was losing because of the national and international disregard of an author's rights to his property. When *Nicholas Nickleby* was published in book form in October 1839, he appropriately dedicated that most theatrical of novels to Macready. When *The Old Curiosity Shop* was published in 1841, he dedicated it to another, even more patriarchal representative of the older generation, the lame banker-poet Samuel Rogers, known for his cruelly sharp tongue, his humanitarian principles, and his celebrity breakfasts. In 1840, Forster introduced him to Walter Savage Landor, the irascible Romantic poet and essayist, who soon became partly an uncle, partly a father figure, whose admiration and love he quickly responded to. In the same year, he met Thomas Carlyle, to whom, over ten years later, he dedicated *Hard Times*. Such dedications had one eye on professional advantage another on warm personal gratitude, inseparable elements in his personality and in the increasing professionalization of literature in early Victorian society.

❧ 2 ❧

THOUGH THE BELLS TOLLING THE DEATH OF THE OLD KING WERE loud, they were emotionally muted. But the unexpected death, in May 1837, of his seventeen-year-old sister-in-law, Mary Ho-

garth, rang a devastating emotional change. It touched him to
the depths, providing a personal and a cultural touchstone for
his definition of himself and his fictional world. She died in his
arms, the first time he had literally embraced both life and death.
While he courted Catherine, the lively Mary became another
sister to him. The "sweet interesting creature" had seemed to
sparkle with sensitivity and intelligence. A cooperative chaperone, especially at those bleary-eyed breakfasts at Selwood Place,
she and her brother-in-law-to-be exchanged small tokens of affection. In April 1836, she spent "a most delightfully happy
month with dearest Catherine in her own house . . . she makes
a most capital housekeeper and is as happy as the day is long—I
think they are more devoted than ever since their Marriage—if
that be possible." Her successful brother-in-law was "such a
nice creature and so clever he is courted and made up to by all
the Literary gentlemen." Delighting in her liberated role, her
eldest sister's frequent guest and companion, she participated
energetically in the blessings of her second family, attending
parties and the theatre, shopping with her brother-in-law, and
helping Catherine in her confinement. With the birth of the
Dickenses' first child on January 6, 1837, she was "so taken up
with [Catherine] and her Baby that I have not been able to think
of anything else."9 Throughout January, she kept house for her
sister, who was incapacitated and depressed after giving birth.
At the end of March, when they moved from Furnival's Inn to
48 Doughty Street, Mary was a quietly cherished participant in
the household. Without apparent strain or threat to either of
them, she had become Charles's intimate friend, a privileged
sister and domestic companion.

On Saturday evening, May 7, 1837, she accompanied her
sister, her brother-in-law, and her parents to the St. James's
Theatre. She had stayed that previous week at Doughty Street,
and probably had been among the "numbers of elegant females"
in the gallery at the Literary Fund dinner five days before.
Looking exceptionally lovely, she leaned "her sweet face" over
the box toward the stage on which Dickens's comic burletta *Is
She His Wife?* was being performed, followed by two musical
dramas in which the lead parts were sung by Henry Burnett,
Fanny's fiancée. Braham and Dickens were attempting to capi-
talize on the success of *The Strange Gentleman* and the popularity

of *Pickwick*. The contretemps in the play between the two contentious, confusing marriages, with lines such as "How little did I think when I married you six months since that I should be exposed to so much wretchedness" and "If you are perpetually yawning and complaining of ennui a few months after marriage, what am I to suppose you'll become in a few years," may have suggested to Mary some of the recent tensions between her sister and brother-in-law. The local bickerings, the conflicting personalities, and his occasional emotional substitution of Mary for Catherine and Catherine for his mother probably created sufficient tension for even the innocent and the denying to be aware that there were problems, though not yet quite of the kind that could justify Dickens' claim years later that "Mary . . . understood . . . in the first months of our marriage" that the marriage was "as miserable a one as ever was."[10]

After the performance, they returned home. Having retired to her bedroom to undress for sleep, soon after midnight Mary suddenly became severely ill. Medical assistance was requested immediately. The doctors suspected heart disease of long standing, a stroke resulting from gradual arterial weakening. "Every remedy that skill and anxiety could suggest" was tried. The Hogarths came, Mary's mother increasingly hysterical to the point of insensibility. Charles, Catherine, and Mrs. Hogarth stayed up with her all night. The daybreak brought no relief. Having seen her perfectly healthy just hours before, the family at first could not imagine that she was dying. By early Sunday afternoon the likelihood was apparent. After she took a little brandy from him, he held her in his arms. "The very last words she whispered were of me." Sinking, as he held her, into a "calm and gentle sleep," she died at three in the afternoon. "The light and life of our happy circle . . . passed quietly away to an immortality of happiness and joy." Catherine could be more powerfully succinct: "I never saw her look so lovely and the next morning she was dead!"[11]

Charles responded to her death with controlled hysteria, the immense pain destroying his usual equilibrium. The next monthly number of *Pickwick Papers* and the installment of the new novel that he had begun publishing in *Bentley's Miscellany* were aborted, the only time in his life in which he did not keep a writing commitment. As an ultimate act of homage and as an expression of his own paralysis, he wrote nothing for the rest of the month. With the baby, in the middle of May he and Catherine went to a small farm in Hampstead "to try a fortnight's rest and quiet." Three months pregnant, Catherine miscarried. She became pregnant again by the middle of June with a Mary who was to be. To Charles Mary's death seemed a desertion so devastating that he kept her memory alive with conscious memorials and in recurrent dreams. His mother had distanced herself from him in his infancy, reinforcing his feeling of abandonment when she had argued for his remaining in the blacking factory. Maria Beadnell had provided the pain of romantic rejection. He had recently allowed himself, though, to believe that such painful experiences were behind him. Idealized as the female who genuinely loved him and whom he could trust, Mary had been elevated into the perfect sister. Unlike Fanny, she would not be his rival but his supporter. She had sympathized "with all my thoughts and feelings more than anyone I knew ever did or will. . . . If she were with us now . . . I think I should have nothing to wish for, but a continuance of such happiness." Her presence among them had been a special dispensation, a golden age of perfection in which "we were too happy together to be long without a change."[12] The faultless Mary had been a better mother, a better sister, and a better Catherine, an alternate Catherine, a completion of Catherine, adding insight, sympathy, and intelligent understanding.

Having held her mortality in his arms, he had also held his own. He strained to translate her into the permanence that he wanted to have available for himself. He could control both the pain of desertion and the fear of mortality by insisting, in an ever-rising rhetoric of transcendental affirmation, that "she is sentient and conscious of my emotions *somewhere.*" The faultless Mary, who, like Richardson's Clarissa, was "far above the foibles and vanity of her sex and age . . . is now in Heaven." There is, he insisted, "the certainty of a bright and happy world beyond the Grave, which such young and untried creatures (half Angels here) *must* be called away by God to people." With typical emotional recklessness, he gave himself up to his grief, finding in an exaggerated language of bereavement a strategy for dealing with his strong feelings. Though he attended Sunday services regularly, he had no real commitment to the Anglican faith. But he found it impossible not to seek the emotional satisfaction of a general Christian belief in a personal afterlife. For years he had the same dream of Mary visiting him, whose "perpetual repetition is extraordinary."[13] In the fiction he wrote during this period, he anticipated the emotional ramifications of her death in his depiction of the death of Oliver's mother and he dramatized these feelings in the death and ascension of Little Nell. Thereafter, though the force of what she had been to him remained strong, the rhetoric of heaven weakened and almost disappeared from his fiction.

His response to her death had an additional focal point in the novel that he had begun to write in January 1837, the month of the birth of his first child, "a son and heir," Charles Culliford Boz Dickens. In a sense his first novel, *Oliver Twist*, unlike *Sketches* and *Pickwick*, was conceived as a fiction unified by a plot, which he had the idea for as early as December 1833.[14] Years later, Cruikshank, who did the illustrations, claimed that the notion of presenting the story of an orphan among London thieves had been his. *Oliver Twist* is so powerfully autobiographical that the "illustrious" George's claim seems irrelevant. Written almost entirely in the year and a half after Mary's death, the novel dramatizes some of Dickens' deepest emotional patterns. It is a successful inward voyage of reconciliation of a sort that he was to make much more readily and regularly in his fiction than in his life. His own experience had made the child figure central to his imagination, the sensitive youth whose sense of his worth is assaulted by a hostile world from infancy onward. The assault precedes adolescence, and adolescent experience is a late stage of the reenactment of early-childhood loss. The most powerful expression in his fiction of such loss and deprivation is to be born an orphan or near orphan, as are Oliver, Pip, Little Nell, David Copperfield, and Esther Summerson, or to have lost one parent, like Nicholas Nickleby, Florence Dombey, and Amy Dorrit. In the first of his fictional child heroes, he contrasts the emotional impact of his own mother's distance and rejection with the absence of Oliver's, as if to say that a dead mother is preferable to a deadening one. Unlike his own, Oliver's mother dies while giving birth to her son. It is a tragic sacrifice that Dickens provides as an expression of the unqualified love of the perfect mother for her only son. Like Mary, she dies "Young Beautiful And Good," and her angelic presence at crucial moments in the novel provides Oliver with both an assurance of his self-worth and, since it is she he resembles, a visible connection with the world of love, benevolence, and innate moral values.[15]

Neither an obstacle nor an enemy, his father has been removed considerably before Oliver's birth. That convenience allows Dickens to focus on his relationship with his idealized mother and on the conflict between potential substitute fathers, the benevolent Mr. Brownlow and the devilish Fagin. In providing Oliver with a vicious brother, his father gives him the opportunity to demonstrate that he is innately good and Monks innately bad. Dickens may have found it emotionally attractive to identify with the father's good son, to create a drama of alternate children, or of the one child divided into two children, in which the child whom he believes himself to have been shows himself worthy of love and respect. In Mr. Brownlow, Oliver eventually finds a loving father, who fills "the mind of his adopted child . . . his own son . . . with stores of knowledge" of the sort that Dickens fantasied about when he believed that he would grow up to be a learned man. Father and son "were truly happy."[16]

In the beautiful seventeen-year-old Rose Maylie, conceived a little more than a year after Mary's death, he created an elegiac representation of his lost but ever-present sister. Like Mary, Rose seems made for heaven. "Cast in so slight and exquisite a mould; so mild and gentle; so pure and beautiful; that earth seemed not her element. . . . The very intelligence that shone in her deep blue eye, and was stamped upon her noble head, seemed scarcely of her age or of the world." Unlike Oliver's mother or Mary Hogarth, Rose is destined for fulfillment and happiness here on earth. She "was in the lovely bloom and spring-time of womanhood . . . the smile; the cheerful, happy smile, were made for Home; for fireside peace and happiness." In the reconciling magic of fictional representation, he both elegizes Mary and affirms that she is alive. "In all the bloom and grace of early womanhood," Rose Maylie marries and becomes "the life and joy of the fire-side circle and the lively summer group."[17]

❧ 3 ❧

HAVING BEEN DEEPLY PAINED BY THE POVERTY OF HIS CHILDHOOD, conditioned by his father's impecuniousness, Dickens needed more financial security than the *Morning Chronicle* and his payments from Macrone and Chapman and Hall provided. He wanted to devote himself full-time to writing fiction. Though his confidence as a writer and his sense of what it was possible for him to achieve had grown considerably, his remembrance of what it had been like to have had very little made it impossible for him to assess his position realistically. His awareness of his own market value for a short time, particularly before the success of *Pickwick*, lagged behind the reality. Between May and November 1836, he did himself considerable damage, abetted in his self-laceration by the widespread practice of publishers' purchasing full copyright rather than sharing profits through a royalty system and also by his own intemperateness. Afraid that the sun might go into eclipse, he wanted to make as much hay as possible while it still shone. He had little experience, though, with market predictions. Excitable, always eager to seize the day. insistent on resolutions even before the full problem had been revealed, he made a number of burdensome commitments.

In May 1836 he agreed to write for John Macrone, with whom his relations were cordial, a three-volume novel, to be called *Gabriel Vardon, the Locksmith of London*. In the same month, he easily persuaded the publisher to employ his brother Fred, a "sharp young fellow," now sixteen years old, as a clerk. In the early stage of writing *Pickwick*, without consulting anyone, let alone Chapman and Hall, he had committed himself to deliver this long novel "on or before the 30th. day of November next, or as soon afterwards, as I can possibly complete it," for which he would receive the "sum of *Two Hundred Pounds*" for the first one thousand copies and half of the profits thereafter. The writer Macrone had signed to do *Sketches* had been a relative unknown learning his craft. By May 1836, the first series had been a decided success; "Boz" had appeared beneath the title of two *Pickwick* numbers; and he had other projects in hand. But the success of *Pickwick*, even its continuance, could not be guaranteed in May as it could be two months later. The terms of the contract were reasonable. He had the satisfaction of signing an agreement that would provide him with a share of the profits rather than only a lump-sum payment. But he would have been wise to sign no contract at all at this crucial time, especially one that provided no payment until the delivery of the manuscript. What advantage was there except that he had a contract for a book before its quality could be evaluated? It was a form of being in debt without having received any money. Both inexperienced in such matters, the author ambitious but hasty and insecure, the publisher pressed for funds and eager to sign promising manuscripts, Dickens and Macrone did themselves a mutual disservice. By August, Dickens knew that he had made a mistake. *Pickwick* sales were skyrocketing, imitations were being created, a loosely adapted dramatic version was being staged. Readers, in the grip of the novel's power, were sending him suggestions for new episodes based on their own experiences. Chapman and Hall, anticipating an equally successful sequel, made a handsome proposal in the fall of 1836, which he verbally accepted.

Unable to resist turning almost any prospect into an agreement, he had responded positively in August 1836, this time to an offer from Richard Bentley. An experienced publisher with more prestige than Chapman and Hall, the forty-year-old Bentley, who had begun as a printer, had been in partnership for some years with Henry Colburn. After a bitter quarrel, he had bought Colburn out and gone into business for himself at 8 New Burlington Street. His loss of Ainsworth to Macrone in 1834 did not seriously disturb his profitable list of reprints and successful authors. Assertive and quarrelsome, he had a strong sense of his importance, a quick temper, and a buoyant, aggressive personality. After consulting with "some confidential friends," whose advice was no better than his own confused judgment, Dickens, perhaps flattered to be solicited by Bentley, proposed that the publisher raise his offer to five hundred pounds "for the *copyright* of a Novel in Three Volumes," reminding him that he was "dealing with an Author not quite unknown, but who, so far as he has gone, has been most successful." He seems temporarily to have forgotten the unhappy consequences of selling the full copyright of *Sketches* to Macrone. His misjudged aggressive-defensive comment that he "should be very sorry to appear anxious to drive a hard bargain, as nothing is more opposed to my habits and feelings," expressed his self-defeating vulnerability. Shrewder than Macrone, Bentley easily persuaded Dickens to sign a contract that committed the author to two three-volume novels for which he would be paid five hundred pounds each with two crucial provisos: He was not to receive any of the money until the first manuscript had been delivered and he was to undertake "no other literary production . . . until the completion of the above mentioned novel."[18]

As if this were not sufficiently damaging, a little more than two months later Dickens signed another contract with Bentley. He apparently found the second offer irresistible, partly because it provided him with the opportunity to play a leading role in London literary life. It called for him to edit for one year, with a three-year renewal option, a monthly publication, *The Wits' Miscellany* (soon changed, to everyone's relief, to *Bentley's Miscellany*). For twenty pounds per month, he would solicit articles, handle the correspondence, evaluate and select articles, and supervise revisions. He would also "furnish an original article of his own writing, every monthly Number, to consist of about a sheet of 16 pages," for which he would be paid another twenty pounds. Cleverly, Bentley wrote into the contract that the publisher would have veto power over the inclusion of any article, which in effect made him co-editor. During the life of the agreement, Dickens could not edit any other periodical publication, by which Bentley meant not only a magazine but a novel published in monthly parts, with the exception of the ongoing *Pickwick*, but not excluding a sequel. Aware that he could postpone the sequel indefinitely, Dickens probably deluded himself into believing that Macrone had already or would soon release him from *their* three-volume-novel contract, whose terms now seemed ludicrous. Macrone had no such intention, and may have resented that Dickens had not given him the opportunity to respond to Bentley's offers. Dickens may have assuaged his discomfort in regard to Macrone by remembering that his contract contained the phrase "or as soon afterwards, as I can possibly complete it," which allowed him indefinite postponement. So too did his verbal agreement with Chapman and Hall. The sequel to *Pickwick* had no deadline or conditions. An agreement that he had recently made to write a children's book for one hundred pounds was child's play in both senses, an agreement he terminated when he signed his August contracts with Bentley.[19]

Assuring Bentley that he felt completely satisfied that his new responsibilities "will not interfere with Pickwick," though it was to Chapman and Hall that he owed that assurance, he also had other creditors and promises to deal with. He resigned from the *Morning Chronicle* immediately. The proprietor, and probably John Black also, expressed unhappiness at his abrupt departure, reminding him that he had promised additional contributions for which they felt they had already paid. He emphatically rejected the claim. The most outraged creditor was Macrone, who had already begun to feel nervous when Dickens agreed to do, at a high payment, some stories for the *Carlton Chronicle,* and then fell behind schedule with copy for the second series of *Sketches,* announced for October 1836. When Macrone learned of his two agreements with Bentley, he felt misused and betrayed. Their personal friendship and their business relationship began to collapse. Eager to salvage whatever he could, Macrone asked Ainsworth to act as intermediary. Ainsworth criticized Macrone's short-sightedness and his hypocrisy in criticizing Bentley for stealing Dickens.[20] Though he believed Dickens legally bound, Ainsworth also knew that the resolution had to be a negotiated settlement in which Macrone would get less than he had originally estimated. As leverage, Macrone threatened to put out a new edition of the *Sketches* in monthly parts, as he had the legal right to do, in imitation of and in competition with *Pickwick.* Dickens became furious. The negotiation was a complicated one. In June 1837, with the help of John Forster and the business wisdom of Chapman and Hall, Macrone was induced to cancel his contract for *Gabriel Vardon* and to sell to Chapman and Hall his copyright interest in the *Sketches* and all his stock, including Cruikshank's plates, for £2,250. When the settlement was reached, Dickens and Macrone were no longer on speaking terms.

Gradually over the next two years, Dickens' labors for Bentley became as poisoned as his relationship with Macrone, and for some of the same reasons. Having entered into financially disadvantageous contracts with him, Dickens soon transformed Bentley into the "Burlington Street Brigand." He

treated both Macrone and Bentley as if only *he* were the mistreated party. Only his grievance was justified. The problems,
though, were just as much moral and emotional as they were
legal. He characteristically transformed a situation in which he
was morally culpable into an emotive thunderstorm whose main
point was that he had been abused and that his abusers were
immoral. The result of such treatment was intense anger and
resentment, the anger that allowed him to misuse legally and to
assault emotionally both of his publishers.

Dickens' combination of insecurity, arrogance, and intemperateness had legally bound him to provide two novels for
Bentley and to edit *Bentley's Miscellany*, as well as to contribute
a substantial article to each number, while at the same time he
had *Pickwick* to complete and a commitment to write a sequel of
about the same length. also to be published in monthly numbers.
Fortunately, Chapman and Hall were essentially benign. Bentley, though, was self-protectively clever and pettily vindictive.
Dickens wanted the disadvantages of the law to be subordinated
to expressions of the spirit. The publisher wanted what he
strongly believed he was entitled to. He saw no reasons other
than business ones for altering contracts that he had not coerced
Dickens into signing. Ultimately, he cooperated with Dickens
only because a dissatisfied writer, ready to go to extremes, could
so damage the product as to undermine, if not destroy, the
publisher's investment. Dickens' sense of humor was reveal-
ingly, if unconsciously, on target when he commented to Bentley that "I like to assume a virtue, though I have it not."[21]

The August 1836 agreement to write two novels for Bentley
was still operative, though Macrone continued to claim that he
had the rights to *Barnaby Rudge,* the second of the two. In January 1837, Dickens protested to Bentley about liberties that he felt
the publisher had taken with one of the contributions. Working
regularly on *Pickwick,* writing for the *Miscellany,* selecting, revising, and proofreading articles and corresponding with authors,
he became "extremely unwell" toward the end of January, "half
dead with fatigue." In spite of an infant and a depressed wife at
home he began work on his weekly contribution to the magazine. "I have thrown my whole heart and soul into Oliver Twist,
and most confidently believe he will make a feature in the work,
and be very popular."[22] With the exception of June and October

1837 and September 1838, an installment appeared every month from February 1837 to April 1839.

Soon it became crucial, as a matter of self-esteem, that Bentley accept *Oliver* in lieu of one of the two novels Dickens had pledged himself to write in the agreement of the previous August. By midsummer 1837, Dickens began to pressure Bentley to have *Barnaby* count as the first contracted novel and the ongoing *Oliver* as the second. The publisher resisted. In August, Dickens responded by finding an excuse not to write an installment for the September *Miscellany*, perhaps on Forster's advice. Having negotiated the agreement between Dickens, Macrone, and Chapman and Hall, Forster had became his adviser on all such matters, much to the annoyance of Bentley, who exaggerated both his role and his influence.[23] Using his objection to Bentley's contractually permissible editorial interference as his justification, Dickens raised the stakes in September. Claiming that he had been "superseded" in his position as editor, he resigned abruptly.

Bentley immediately retreated. Dickens resumed his editorship and the novel. Late in September, the publisher reluctantly agreed that *Oliver* would count as the second novel, with the new, later delivery date of October 1838 for *Barnaby*. Dickens then proposed that *Barnaby* appear in the *Miscellany* rather than that he be obligated both for it and for a substantial contribution to the magazine. In January 1838, he edited for Bentley, for the flat fee of one hundred pounds, the *Memoirs of Grimaldi*, with the help of John Dickens, who mostly took dictation. It was partly a sentimental nod in the direction of the theatrical fantasies of his childhood. By the spring, Dickens was furious with the publisher, though Bentley had made all the concessions, for deducting small sums from his fees for the installments of *Oliver* because they were shorter than had been agreed upon. Having been ground down by Dickens, Bentley expressed his resentment in this and in other petty ways, such as not keeping appointments. In September, author and publisher signed a new agreement, basically repeating the provisions of the earlier contracts, though slightly more financially favorable to Dickens and with the stipulation that *Barnaby* appear in the *Miscellany* after *Oliver*. In January 1839, Dickens peremptorily insisted that there be a further delay in *Barnaby*, that the financial provisions be renegotiated, "for I do most solemnly declare that morally, before God and man, I hold myself released from such hard bargains as these." Forster advised prudence and reconsideration. But Dickens had had enough of Bentley, of the frustration that must have been all the more difficult to bear because of his need to suppress the obvious fact that he was fully responsible for the contracts he had signed. With an aggressiveness characteristic of him when he was even partly, let alone fully, in the wrong, he castigated the publisher as a prelude to halting all communication with him. "I do *not* . . . I will *not* consent to extend my engagements with you. . . . If you presume to address me again in the style of offensive impertinence . . . I will from that moment abandon at once and for ever all conditions and agreements that may exist between us, and leave the whole question to be settled by a jury as soon as you think proper to bring it before one."[24]

At the end of the month, he again resigned as editor of the *Miscellany*. For a full day Dickens, Forster, and Ainsworth sent notes to one another and to Bentley, attempting to persuade the publisher to appoint Ainsworth the new editor under favorable terms. Reluctantly, he agreed, though both Dickens and especially Forster felt that Ainsworth had bungled his negotiations, settling for less money and editorial control than he could have gotten. Dickens turned over to his lawyer his negotiations with Bentley, who accepted his resignation and agreed to pay him two thousand pounds on the delivery of the manuscript of *Barnaby Rudge*, which was to be published only in book form, and another two thousand pounds if the sales should be strong.[25] In fact, after the completion of *Oliver* in April 1839, Bentley was never to publish anything of his again. Represented by Mitton, and with Forster as his literary spokesman, Dickens had burst the self-imposed "Bentleian bonds."

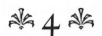

UNLIKE HIS CONTRACTS WITH BENTLEY, HIS BOND WITH HIS PARENTS was unbreakable. He tried to adjust it to make the relationship more satisfactory. Elizabeth Dickens had only her youngest son, ten-year-old Augustus to look after by the time of the completion of *Pickwick*. By the early 1840s, she balanced matriarchal stoutness with some affectations of youthfulness, particularly "the juvenility of her dress" and her semicomic confusions of speech. Her son described her wardrobe as "the attempt 'of middle-aged mutton to dress itself lamb fashion.' " The incongruity between her increasingly "worn, deeply-lined face" and her love of "youthful amusements," particularly dancing and party games, amused casual onlookers. Though it apparently made her son uncomfortable, she was a frequent guest at dinner, at family Sundays, on vacation holidays. He did sometimes recognize that she had practical abilities, and he expressed no outward disrespect. But he kept his emotional distance, aware that his anger at her early neglect of him prevented any effort on his part to find nurturing there.

Though he could be sentimental about them, and perfunctorily generous, his hostility to his parents was sufficiently close to the surface to explode, sometimes into wrath, even into bitterness. On one occasion, provoked by his father's using his name to guarantee a loan, Charles thanked "God for one thing especially—that His [own] Gracious Providence had saved him from dying in the gutter or in the penitentiary, so infamously had his father neglected him in his young days." With a preference both for staying out of prison and for not antagonizing his son, John Dickens in 1837 tried again to borrow from Chapman and Hall, requesting that they prevent "a breech of a most distressing nature" by not telling Charles. Disgusted and frustrated, his son repaid Edward Barrow the money he had loaned his father in a crisis in December 1834. Whether or not there were "most discreditable and dishonest dealings on the part of the father towards his son," as Charles's sister-in-law Georgina later maintained, by March 1839 he had had enough of his father's efforts to borrow against his credit and reputation. As unconfessed additional debts came to light, he was furious. "And so it always is;—directly I build up a hundred pounds, one of my dear relations comes and knocks it down again."[26]

Bitterly, he paid the most recent debts, probably with scenes in which his father played the role of the prodigal son. Dickens accurately described his father as "an optimist—he was like a cork—if he was pushed under water in one place, he always 'bobbed up to time' cheerfully in another, and felt none the worse for the dip." The portly, good-humored John Dickens seemed constitutionally incapable of not borrowing against his son's credit. Charles decided to have the satisfaction and the advantage of having the "Governor" out of sight. With peremptory incontrovertibility, he decided to exile his parents, with Augustus, to a cottage in a rural village. He went himself by coach to Devonshire, found a house in Alphington, near Exeter, made the basic arrangements for their comfort, and provided them with a carefully calculated but realistic allowance. It was true, but also convenient for his conscience, that it was "a jewel of a place . . . in the most beautiful, cheerful delicious rural neighborhood I was ever in." He expected them to like it, "if they will."[27] For his parents, it was a painful rejection, an exile to the distant provinces, where low cost was bought at the price of dullness. For him, it was self-protection with a touch of revenge.

By spring 1839, the basic contours of his family life had been drawn for the next decade. None of his siblings had more than minor to nonexistent artistic talent. Acting the part of father to his brother Frederick, he soon used his influence to secure him a position as a junior clerk in the treasury department, where he gradually ascended over the next twenty years to the post of second-class clerk. Alfred, who was studying civil engineering, soon became a surveyor and assistant engineer working for the railroads. Letitia and Fanny had married in the summer of 1837, Letitia to Henry Austin, the architect and engineer, Dickens' friend and companion in amateur theatricals since 1833. Fanny had married a fellow music student, the singer Henry Burnett, who began with a burst of theatrical promise that took him as high as Macready's Covent Garden company in 1838. Dickens felt affection and respect for both his brothers-in-law, which did not diminish when in 1841 Burnett's childhood religious training surfaced so strongly that he retired from the stage because of "scruples" and moved to Manchester, settling, with Fanny, into a pietistic life of dissenting observance. Burnett's voluntary retirement from the stage seemed to Dickens partly unintelligible, partly ironic. Dickens' every energy had been exerted to place himself stage center. Even Macready, though, had impulses similar to Burnett's, reflecting a culture in which early religious training often focused opposition to worldly ways in the image of the theatre as vanity.

Dickens' own household became an expanding domestic

theatre dominated and controlled by the author-manager. Not having had a dependable family to look after him as a child, he began to create a family so dependent on him that in the long run their neediness would become a burden. But for now he reveled in the role of household manager and paterfamilias. By 1841, when his friends looked at Dickens they saw a youthful-looking, brown-haired, fancifully dressed, immensely successful author. Slim, of medium height, with a clear complexion and a mobile, expressive face highlighted by attractive gray-blue eyes, he seemed to have been destined by timing, talent, and personality to be center stage at his personal hearth and the star actor on the stage of the family of Victorian culture. As the family grew, it needed more elbow room, especially since his social and professional elbows expanded widely as the boy-wonder of *Sketches* and *Pickwick* revealed a mature staying power. In April 1837, he took a three-year lease on 48 Doughty Street, at a rent of eighty pounds a year, the twelve-room house just large enough for Charles, Catherine, Frederick, visits from Mary Hogarth, and the son born the previous January. In retrospect, the two and a half years at Furnival's Inn and the brief time at Doughty Street before Mary's death seemed golden, the happiest of his life. With a heavy writing schedule, he sometimes worked nights as well as mornings. But his energetic confidence and casual conviviality made the workload a source of pride and strength. He sometimes wrote even when there were guests quietly conversing around the fireside in the same room.[28] In March 1838, his first daughter, Mary, named after Mary Hogarth, was born, then, in October 1839, Catherine (Kate) Macready Dickens.

Now, with a family of three children, with the need for live-in servants, with occasional guests, and with an increased sense of social expansiveness, he began to look in the autumn of 1839 for a new house. By mid-November, he was "in the agonies of house-letting, house-taking, title proving and disproving, premium paying, fixture valuing, and other ills too numerous to mention." Disposing of the remaining time on the Doughty Street lease, he bought, at a cost of £800 and an annual rent of £160, the eleven years remaining on the lease of 1 Devonshire Terrace, York Gate, a handsome, sizable house near Regent's Park.[29] On the basis of his talent alone, in a few short years he had established himself as decisively upper middle class. And the "agonies" were irresistible pleasures for the expansive, managerial Dickens, who orchestrated carpenters, painters, and masons like a master producer who could not get enough of being in charge. A few weeks before Christmas 1839, the family moved into their new home, where the next decade of childbearing and Christmases were suffered and celebrated.

Catherine did much of the suffering. She bore her children at the price of the usual pain and exhaustion. Ironically, like her husband, she was in this line a steady, hard, though semivoluntary worker. After the birth of her first child, Charles Dickens, Jr., she had a difficult two months. To help her recovery, during February 1837 they took a cottage at Chalk, in Kent, not far from his boyhood haunts and where they had spent their honeymoon. Dickens had been sick as well, and overworked, and the notion of an escape into the country appealed to both of them. Her sister's death in early May 1837 shocked her into a miscarriage, and then numbed her into a depression from which she rallied slowly. Becoming pregnant again during their subsequent stay in Hampstead helped her through her grief. After the birth of Mary, in March 1838, she became "alarmingly ill," in "great pain."

Her husband was not insensitive to the dangers of childbearing both to the mother and to the baby. Finding the latter part of confinement and delivery a great strain, he probably had in back of his mind the image from his childhood of dead infants laid out like pigs' feet or skinned rabbits. With a sigh of relief, he commented, after the birth of his second daughter, "Thank God it is just now all safely over, and Kate and the child . . . as well as possible." In 1841, Catherine came through the delivery of the first of the children born at Devonshire Terrace, Walter Savage Landor Dickens, "not merely as well as can be expected, but a great deal better."[30] The wear and tear, though, of four children in four years took its toll on her nerves and appearance. While his world expanded, hers narrowed.

From the birth of his first son onward, Dickens could afford the advantage of summer holidays and impromptu stays by the seaside or in the country. Since he needed to work closely with his illustrator and publisher, his inclination was to go far enough away so that it would be a real change but close enough so that he could commute to London some days each week. In September 1837, they spent two weeks in Broadstairs, falling in love with the glittering ocean and the convivial days and weather, and then a week in Brighton. The next summer, they vacationed for two months in Twickenham, and they were in Broadstairs again for most of September 1839. Dickens did not conceive of such holidays as private times with Catherine. They were family vacations, and his extended family was included. He needed the support and companionship of his friends. Calls went out from Twickenham and Broadstairs to his widening circle to join him for comradeship, excursions, and play. Marital intimacy had its pleasures and its consequences, but even at his most intimate he kept his distance. Though he rarely even whispers of marital sex in his letters, he seems to have had little difficulty in allowing his general good feeling to overflow into expressions of endearment. He apparently took Catherine into his confidence, partly because she was his wife, partly because she was there, partly because he tended to be expressive. She could be a convivial, amiable, tolerant companion, adequately competent in managing herself and the obvious things of the household. Her emotional focus alternated between her efforts to survive when pregnant and ill and her desire that her all-encompassing domestic world be pleasant and relaxed.

For a brief while there was another woman in his life, whom he shared with his friends and with the nation, and who provided a nonthreatening alternative to middle-class domesticity. Playfully alert, imaginatively restless, and incapable of being fully satisfied in his relationship with Catherine, he began the first of a series of tightly controlled amorous flirtations. This one was totally in his imagination. It was partly an elaborate joke, partly a serious expression of romantic passion. In June 1838, he and his friends watched Queen Victoria's coronation procession from a third-floor room he had rented. The next February he distantly rubbed shoulders with the young glamorous queen at Covent Garden. In full court dress, she watched Macready's performance in Bulwer's *The Lady of Lyons,* a play on which Bulwer, Forster, and Macready had spent long hours collaborating. She had read and liked *Oliver Twist,* which she probably had learned about from Maclise, whose paintings she adored. While there is no reason to believe that she adored

Maclise, the handsome Irishman had many female admirers, including Lady Henrietta Sykes, whose affair with him, after her affair with Disraeli, had become a public scandal. The news appeared on the front page of the *Morning Chronicle* when she "was caught in the arms of Maclise . . . in her own Bed, in her Husband's House in Park Lane."[31]

Alert to gossip, prone to tease his friends, Dickens had learned that Forster, before they had met, had been in love with Letitia Landon, the sentimental poetess of bland language and modest talents who had been the darling of the poetry annuals and keepsake books for a few years in the early 1830s. Forster had used the rumor that she had been the lover of the editor and writer William Maginn to withdraw his proposal. Rumor maintained that she had been among Maclise's conquests as well. By the time of her death in 1838, Dickens had a good sense of the past and present amorous aspirations and involvements of Maclise and Forster. He delighted to tease both of them. One revealing tease was a love letter to Forster from Dickens, loosely disguising himself as "Louisa," a name close enough to Letitia to have serious resonances. The spurned Louisa, who "wished with all a woman's ardour that you were mine," confesses her love—"think me capricious—strange—romantic"—and hopes that "you may be happy, as happy, Mr. Forster, as you deserve."[32]

In the world of London artistic society, pietistic prohibitions and middle-class idealizations had less force than in the community as a whole. London street life, particularly around the theatres, was openly bawdy, Drury Lane Theatre an active marketplace for prostitution. On the higher levels of social life, sexual arrangements, some romantic, many mercenary, flourished with a freedom that evangelical reform and middle-class values hardly touched. Maclise, whose artistic success and good looks had opened many drawing-room and bedroom doors, was an aggressive womanizer. Forster was inhibited and conservative. Unlike Dickens, they were bachelors. On one occasion, Forster urged Ainsworth to come with him "to see a *wonderful actress* and most fascinating woman (with whom your unhappy friend is over head and ears in love)." Passionately in love with Talfourd's niece, Maclise joked seriously about the "ruthless devastator of feminine blossoms." The married Dickens found an extraordinary excitement and a special bonding with his

bachelor friends in the fiction that they were all in love, though
he and Maclise more so than the phlegmatic Forster, with the
beautiful young queen.33

With the titillation of multiple participants, this imaginary
affair reached its climax in February 1840 in the self-consciously
humorous and arousingly voyeuristic focus on the queen's honeymoon at Windsor. For Dickens, it was an opportunity for the
safest kind of alternative to the domestication of his emotional
and sexual life at Devonshire Terrace. Aware of his good looks,
a "Fancy Man" himself, dressing elaborately in the colorful
dandy fashion, he particularly enjoyed the line in a song popular
in the London streets immediately before the royal wedding,
"Prince Hallbert he vill alvays be/My own dear Fancy Man."
The erotic joke was irresistible. It could not be suppressed,
especially since it was perfectly safe to express it humorously.
"I have fallen hopelessly in love with the Queen, and wander up
and down with vague and dismal thoughts of running away to
some uninhabited island with a maid of honor." He had in mind
the beautiful Lady Frances Cowper, whom he soon "dreamt of
. . . all night." When he and Maclise "sallied down to Windsor,"
they "prowled about the Castle, saw the Corridor and their
private rooms—nay, the very bedchamber (which we know
from having been there twice) . . . bespeaking so much bliss and
happiness—that I . . . lay down in the mud . . . and refused all
comfort. . . . I am very wretched, and think of leaving my home.
My wife makes me miserable, and when I hear the voices of my
Infant Children I burst into tears." He would rescue the beautiful lady from her groom by "heading some bloody assault upon
the palace and saving Her by my single hand."34 It was a satisfying fantasy whose characteristic humor did not disguise the
need it served.

MUCH OF HIS ENERGY, THOUGH, WENT INTO HIS WORK AND INTO HIS
friendships, the most alert of which by 1839 were with Forster
and Maclise. After some tension with Ainsworth, he had been
dropped from the "Trio Club," and the new trio relaxed under
the banner of the "Cerberus Club." Dickens had a growing

sense of personal and professional power, of being a man whose presence and ideas counted, and a sense that relationships were best developed within the structures of a formal community. A founding member in 1838 of the short-lived Shakespeare Club, he soon became a member of the Parthenon Club, where he frequently dined, then of the Garrick and the Athenaeum. Though they were sometimes forums for contention (he resigned from the Garrick in support of Macready, who had argued with the management, and rejoined some years later), the clubs were mainly places of elite male conviviality into which neither women nor domesticity could intrude. In personal relationships and in club life, he developed a network of supportive friendships essential to him and central to the Victorian literary community. He needed friends to encourage him in his work and to assist him as he assisted them in creating an artistic and practical environment in which their works would be appreciated and rewarded.

Forster was the closest of these friends. His irascibility sometimes produced violent scenes, tests of pride and friendship. During one argument, Catherine fled the room in tears. But as the most reliable, devoted of his friends, the disciplined, hardworking, domineering, deeply loyal Forster became his literary negotiator and private editor. The novelist absorbed his eager friend into the gray area between his creativity and his business. Forster was ever given responsibility for final cuts in monthly numbers when the length exceeded the required amount of pages. He was empowered to make these according to his own judgment, for "I knew so well you would do it in the right places." Equally austere in his tastes, Macready also played seriously. He was dissatisfied with the state of the theatre, and he suffered from his sense of belonging to a profession and a society that valued pantomime more than Shakespeare. With the support of Dickens, Forster, Talfourd, Bulwer, Knowles, John Payne Collier, the eminent Shakespeare editor, and Charles Knight, whose pictorial biography of Shakespeare had become the standard life, he attempted to restore high artistic seriousness to the English theatre. Dickens, who delighted in any theatrical performance, from the ludicrously amateurish to the professionally brilliant, readily enlisted in the Macready corps. He was constantly involved with the theatre anyway. While

Pickwick was still in progress, the first stage adaptation appeared. *Oliver Twist* was produced in numbers of versions. So theatrical was *Nicholas Nickleby* that it became, in a version with which Dickens cooperated, a financial success.35 He usually attended at least one performance of the stage adaptations of his novels, though he at least once seems to have writhed on the theatre floor with laughter or embarrassment.

On the level of principle, Dickens subscribed to the value of serious drama as part of the dignity of the literary profession. Macready's Shakespearean performances were among the most moving artistic experiences of his life. The effort to reform the theatre soon rallied around Shakespeare's fame. Through the Shakespeare Club, the Stratford restoration, and a Shakespeare museum, literary values could be affirmed. Led by Forster and Macready, he and his friends raised money, created publicity, and supported a curatorship for a Shakespeare museum. They also made themselves into a formidable clique, supporting Macready's innovative management of Covent Garden and then Drury Lane Theatre. Both management efforts failed. In a profession notorious for arrogance, Macready had made enemies in the theatre just as quickly as he made literary friends outside. Since only two theatres were licensed to produce legitimate drama, his scope for performance and principle was limited. As the star at Covent Garden, unhappy with his treatment and with the profession as a whole, one evening in late April 1836, blinded with anger, he had physically assaulted Alfred Bunn, the theatre manager. Talfourd had defended his friend in a trial for assault in which a jury levied damages against him that were small enough to allow both sides to claim victory. When, in 1837, the management of Covent Garden and then, in 1841, of Drury Lane, had become available, though at considerable financial risk, Macready had decided to gamble for his own artistic freedom and for the renewal of the English theatre. Dickens attended almost every performance, thrilled by Macready's Lear and Richard II especially. He cheered a series of brilliant Shakespearean productions that created the Shakespeare that the modern theatre knows.

The Cerberus trio frequently entertained themselves with excursions by river to Greenwich and Richmond. Sharing dinners and drinks in city and country inns, rapid overnight trips to Kent, late-night walks through London streets, cigars, brandy, and conversation, they amused themselves with elaborate badinage, jokes about women, about eccentricities, about escapades. Maclise shared with Dickens his appreciation of "the wild attractions" of a beautiful actress, "the small waist, the neatly turned leg . . . you will like her, love her, doat upon her." In 1841, Dickens tried to lure Maclise to join him on a holiday, telling him that "there are conveniences of *all kinds* at Margate (do you take me?) and I know where they live."[36] Never more truthful than when expressing himself humorously, in the security of such friendships Dickens could express his feelings in displaced and playfully creative ways.

With friends and business associates, he began the practice of celebrating the completion of each of his novels with a grand dinner. Amid glittering confectionery, elaborate dishes, and grandiloquent speeches, *Pickwick*'s success was toasted, in November 1837, by Ainsworth, Macready, Forster, Talfourd, Browne, Jerdan, Chapman, Hall, and even John Dickens, at a costly restaurant banquet for which the proud author paid. It was his way both of showing appreciation and of showing off. His father may have wistfully or even proudly noted that the cost was slightly more than what in 1824 he had gone to prison for being unable to pay. "Talfourd proposed Dickens' health in a very good speech, and Dickens replied—under strong emotions—most admirably." The "too splendid" *Nickleby* dinner in October 1839 took place at an even more expensive restaurant. Macready, who took the chair and felt uneasy about the ostentatious expense, thought Dickens not up to his usual toast-giving form. At similar future dinners, the vinous self-congratulations overflowed into both the exuberance and the tedium of "then Everybody proposes everything."[37] Dickens, though, soon became adept at toasts and public speeches. The techniques of memorization that he had learned while studying acting and while working as a shorthand reporter helped him overcome the disadvantage of his nasal voice and his tendency to talk too quickly. A prominent advocate of liberal causes, he soon began receiving speaking invitations, mostly to fund-raising dinners.

One engagement that he happily accepted was to a banquet in his honor in Edinburgh in late June 1841. He and Catherine traveled to her native city with unrestrained pride. Staying at the Royal Hotel, with a handsome view of the castle, they were besieged by admirers and the curious, their calendar filled with invitations to social events from literary, legal, and political notabilities. Formally elected a burgess, he was granted the keys to the city. Catherine was taken to visit the house in which she had been born. The public banquet had been arranged by a new friend, Francis Jeffrey, the Whig lawyer and politician who was still at the heart of Edinburgh literary society, though he had resigned as editor of the *Edinburgh Review* ten years before. Gregarious, enthusiastic, with a strong sense of propriety and a moderate Romantic disposition, the elderly Jeffrey found Dickens irresistible. Having supported and patronized Thomas Carlyle, though more at ease with his wife, Jane, than with the writer himself, Jeffrey found his relationship with Dickens less complicated.[38] It was unequivocally warm, and his enthusiasm for the novelist's female characters, particularly Little Nell, was unrestrained.

In a cool northern June, Edinburgh's warmth of heart provided a gala welcome for the young author. John Wilson, the Tory journalist and essayist, looking "as though he had just come down from the Highlands, and had never in his life taken pen in hand," described Dickens as "perhaps the most popular author now alive" to the over 250 distinguished men who had eagerly paid their subscription fee to attend the banquet. After dinner, 200 ladies, led by Catherine, entered the gallery to hear the toasts and speeches. "The room was crammed to the throat." People were turned away. As Dickens came through the door and entered the hall, the orchestra struck up, to "tumultuous" applause and "shouts of delight," the popular music-hall song "Charley is my Darling." He was escorted to the high platform for full viewing. Their darling, "a little, slender, pale-faced, boyish-looking individual, the very last man in the room" whom someone who did not know him "could have picked on as being the author of Pickwick," was thrilled. It "was very remarkable to see such a number of grey-headed men gathered about my brown flowing locks; and it struck most of those who were present very forcibly."

When he rose to speak, the silence was anticipatory. Immediately surprising and delighting the audience with his fluency, he responded to two toasts, one to Scottish literature, the other to Lord Jeffrey and to the recently deceased painter David Wilkie, whom he had met and become friendly with in London. Implicit in his toast to Scottish literature was the memory and ghost of Sir Walter Scott, whom many in the room had known, and the general awareness that Scott was an influence on his novel-in-progress, *Barnaby Rudge.* The young author exuberantly accepted his hosts' flattery and in return flattered them and "this capital of Scotland . . . which I shall love while I have life." By midnight, the "most brilliant affair you can possibly imagine" was over.39

His Scottish travels continued with a Highland holiday, guided by Angus Fletcher, a sculptor with whom Dickens had become friendly in London. With enthusiastic inefficiency, Fletcher took them through the rugged, rain-and-wind-swept terrain of his native Highlands from Edinburgh into the Trossacks, from Loch Katrine through the Glencoe pass to Ballachulish (they were prevented by the hostile weather from going to Oban), back through Glencoe to Inveraray, Loch Lomond, and finally Glasgow. Constantly wet, cold, exhilarated, and sometimes frightened, Dickens could not get the chill out of his bones even with large amounts of Scotch whisky. The passage through Glencoe was terrifying, "an awful place . . . shut in on each side by enormous rocks," like "the burial place of a race of giants," with "great torrents . . . rushing down in all directions . . . such haunts as you might imagine yourself wandering in, in the very height and madness of a fever." Then not only to have to go through the "terrible" pass again but to have to cross a dangerously swollen river. "It had rained all night, and was raining" still. Since the carriage had been damaged, they came down hills without sufficient drag, and had to hang out the back to keep it from flying downhill. At the crossing, they all got out. Catherine agreed to do so only at the last minute. They crossed precariously, dangerously, on a wooden platform, the carriage almost overturning, the horses almost drowning.40

He was glad to have his pen in hand each evening by a warm fireside, to write long accounts of his adventures to Forster, who possessively revealed their existence but declined to show them to Maclise, though Dickens meant the letters for him also. He was overjoyed to get letters from home, from the friends he desperately missed, including Macready and John

Elliotson, a professor of medicine whose experiments with mesmerism fascinated him. He missed the faces of his friends in the audience at the Edinburgh banquet. He missed the children also. With home-turning enthusiasm, having arranged to have Forster and Maclise at Devonshire Terrace to meet them, he hurried back from Glasgow to London for a reunion with friends and family on July 18, 1841. He had looked forward to this reunion "with a delight past all expression."[41]

❧ 6 ❧

DICKENS WAS, THOUGH, AT HEART A TRAVELING MAN, ALTERNATING between love of hearth and restlessness. Home was a willful construct, an abstraction made flesh. The road was a preexistent reality, a pattern of movement first created by his family's moving from Portsmouth, to London, to Kent, and back to London. During his youth, London seemed universe enough, a place in which one could travel almost endlessly and not walk the same street twice. Increasingly aware of his own restlessness, he worked the harder at creating domestic stability and a circle of friends whose center would be stable, unmoving, secure. He found an anchor for his personal instability in London and Kent. Though he helped elevate domesticity into a national totem, he nevertheless needed, even during the first decade of his married life, to find safe ways in which to express his need for change, travel, and adventure.

Writing itself generated an impatience that he embodied in his nervous prose, frequently exorcised in city walks and country hikes. As a child, his moves were involuntary. He accompanied his parents from one residence to another. But he had been intensely curious about the world, with a gift for observation of a sort that prompted him to look and explore. As an adult, his intellect was observational and satirical rather than abstract and meditative. He thought with his senses and his feelings. Gifted with a fluency of feeling and a fluency of descriptive and expressive language, he recognized that the road was his natural environment. As a reporter, he had his first opportunity to see England. With the success of *Pickwick*, he took his first trip abroad, in July 1837, a whirlwind week-long holiday, with Catherine and Hablot Knight Browne, to Calais,

Ghent, Brussels, and Antwerp. In February 1838, he visited Yorkshire with Browne, mainly because he wanted his illustrator to observe the setting for the early part of *Nicholas Nickleby*. In November 1838, with Browne and Forster, he toured North Wales and the Midlands, continuing his lifelong pattern of finding landscapes and communities in which to set his fictions.

The demands of his career, though, forced Dickens to spend most of his time in or near London. Long trips seemed out of the question. In March 1838, he had begun his "sequel" to *Pickwick Papers*, another long novel in twenty monthly parts for Chapman and Hall. Then, having liberated himself from daily editorial tasks by resigning from *Bentley's Miscellany*, he finished the last weekly installment of *Oliver* in April 1839. The extraordinary demands of *Nicholas Nickleby* kept him to the remunerative grindstone until late September 1839. During the brief period between the *Nickleby* dinner in early October and the start of a new, demanding project, he wrote for Chapman and Hall the brief *Sketches of Young Couples*, a follow-up to the anonymously published *Sketches of Young Gentlemen* of early 1838, pleasantly perfunctory humor for which he was paid a flat fee. (This was about the time he brought his relationship with Bentley to a close, except for the still unwritten *Barnaby Rudge*, and moved to Devonshire Terrace.) The new project, for which he signed an agreement in March 1840, was a weekly magazine called *Master Humphrey's Clock*, twelve of whose sixteen pages were to be his own original material, initially envisaged as a series of stories linked together by the pretense that they were manuscripts, and placed in the case of a large clock.

When the sales of the second and following issues of the weekly plummeted, apparently because readers realized that they were not being provided with an ongoing story, he tentatively began in June 1840, as the twelfth number of *Master Humphrey*, a new novel, *The Old Curiosity Shop*. Soon, feeling "the story extremely myself" and "warmly interested in it," he had set out on a journey with his characters that brought him and his readers to a pitch so intense that it became the Victorian touchstone for the empathetic novel, in which author and reader create a community of shared feeling. It quickly became an extraordinary success, culminating in widespread public mourning for the death of the main character.[42]

With the completion of *The Old Curiosity Shop* in February

1841, he began, finally, to write *Barnaby Rudge*, which had been conceived in 1836. He had started to write it in November 1839 only to give up in disgust. In July 1840, with a substantial loan from Chapman and Hall, he bought back from Bentley for £2,250 his contract for *Barnaby*, settled his rights in the *Miscellany* and other copyright agreements, and transferred the novel to Chapman and Hall, who seemed more like friends and private bankers than publishers. Though his relationship with Chapman and Hall was to have its difficulties, he had good reason to insist to Edward Chapman that he and his partner were an exception, "the best of booksellers past, present, or to come; and my trusty friends."43 With the success of *The Old Curiosity Shop* in the weekly format of *Master Humphrey's Clock*, it made sense to publish *Barnaby* in the same way, though he was less keen on weekly publication than on a novel in monthly numbers. In the weekly format he felt his artistry more cramped, his schedule more intensely hectic.

His first venture into historical fiction, *Barnaby* was written with Sir Walter Scott's example in mind, both Scott's ability to vividly re-create a historical past that spoke meaningfully to the needs and values of the present and his immense commercial success. Having read some of the obvious sources for the George Gordon antipopery riots of 1780, he solicited oral accounts from those who had memories of the events. With a novelist's sure sense of artistic efficiency, he distorted and simplified the historical facts in order "to select the striking points and beat them into the page with a sledge-hammer." In the climactic riot scenes, conveying his own and Victorian England's attraction to and abhorrence of revolution and mass movements, he brilliantly fulfilled his desire "to convey an idea of multitudes, violence, and fury" seen "dimly, through the fire and smoke."44 It is a novel whose historical placement anticipates the French Revolution and the revolution that the English Victorians hoped to avoid. It also dramatizes Dickens' personal aspirations toward domestic security and his sense of the complicated relationships between fathers and sons alternatively with the problems of private and public madness in a moment of cultural anarchy. *Barnaby* began its appearance in February 1841, and mercifully ended, as far as the tired author was concerned, that November. Even while dashing through the wind and rain of the Scottish Highlands in July, he had hardly been able to afford not to keep at it. In that sense, he had been traveling very hard.

For his fictional characters, from Pickwick onward, he created self-defining and culturally expressive journeys. In the three major novels he wrote in the late 1830s and early 1840s, the lives of the main characters are projected outward into the world as a pilgrim's progress, limited voyages toward personal fulfillment. In *The Life and Adventures of Nicholas Nickleby*, Nicholas travels a series of roads that cover the map of the traditional English *Bildungsroman*, the novel of the education of an instinctively good young man whose progress toward maturity bridges the landscape of country and city, north and south. It is a voyage of noble ambition in search of a home, toward whose domesticity Nicholas aspires as the highest affirmation of his self-worth. As with Dickens, the road is one of hard work guided by talent and a good heart. No evil, no obstacle, can defeat his energy, and his travels affirm the inevitable and decisive victory of goodness. Like Dickens, Nicholas feels omnipotent. No career is closed to him, not even a career in the theatre. In *Nicholas*, Dickens celebrates, through parody as well as praise, the magic of the theatre, drawing on his fascination with the stage and his friendship with Macready, absorbing his theatrical experiences into the plot, delighting in depictions of actors, actresses, and performances, from the absurdly banal to the humorously serious.

A performance personality, Nicholas can act out on the theatrical stage or in life the emotional soundness and the moral strength of his self-definition. He can be defined and valued in terms of his presence. He is in his sense of his own value a member of the upper middle class. His status as a Victorian-bourgeois gentleman cannot be undermined. Appropriately, Nicholas' father, an improvident man who, like John Dickens, leaves his family in want, is disposed of before the novel begins, freeing his son of paternal impositions. In Ralph Nickleby, the good father dead becomes the bad father alive whom Nicholas defeats in honorable battle. An aspect of Elizabeth Dickens becomes the totality of Nicholas' mother, the vain, ineffectual, verbally comic Mrs. Nickleby, another fictional neutralization of the pain in his relationship with his own mother. Unlike Elizabeth Dickens, Mrs. Nickleby, whatever she is "keen" on, has no power over her son. Allied with other good hearts, bound together with fraternal passion, finding both the perfect sister in Kate Nickleby and the perfect sister-wife in Madeline Bray, Nicholas, like Dickens in 1839, ends his triumphant journey as "a rich and prosperous merchant" whose first act is "to buy his father's old house" and surround himself with a "group of lovely children." He is elevated by honor, truthfulness, and talent to the center stage of British Victorian culture.

A more somber but beatific version of the pilgrim's journey, of ceaseless travel toward transformation, is dramatized in the voyage of Little Nell and her grandfather in *The Old Curiosity Shop*. Addicted to gambling, her improvident grandfather, who loves but cannot provide for his surrogate child, takes his place in Dickens' vivid gallery of failed fathers. Without discipline, work values, or social responsibility, even the good heart of a well-intentioned father cannot provide security for his child. Little Nell becomes father to her grandfather, parent to an elderly child. The orphaned Little Nell must become both father and mother to herself. Like Mary Hogarth, echoing the inscription he composed for her tomb—"Young Beautiful And Good"—Little Nell is an "angel," whose celestial destiny both affirms and alleviates the pain parents feel when children die.[45] Aware of the strength of wickedness in the world, embodied in the character of the dwarf, Quilp, Dickens attempts to show the triumph of goodness over evil and assert the innate goodness of the human heart to solace those who have lost beautiful and young souls to death. *The Old Curiosity Shop* is a novel haunted by the inseparability of the pain and blessedness of death, which transforms living angels into ever-living or heavenly angels and provides the catharsis of tears for those who remain behind.

Little Nell possessed his dreams, as Mary did, and the act of writing her demise had inherent within it the anguish of "slowly murdering" her. "When I think of this sad story . . . dear Mary died yesterday. . . . Nobody will miss" Little Nell "like I shall. It is such a very painful thing to me, that I really cannot express my sorrow. Old wounds bleed afresh. . . ."[46] His initial intention had not been to kill his main character. That her death was inherent in her beginning and in her situation gradually became clear to him. When Forster suggested that her death would be the appropriate resolution to the novel, he realized that, instinctively, unconsciously, he had from the beginning made that resolution inevitable. He consciously faced that necessity, though, only when the plot and the themes demanded it be made explicit. Forster advised him to do only what he already knew had to be done. The "Pilgrim's Progress" that is strongly on Nell's mind, when she and her grandfather look back at the "Babel" of London, with "Saint Paul's looming through the smoke, its cross peeping above the cloud . . . and glittering in the sun," as they begin their travels, is a progress whose final moment must be a heavenly ascension.

Half a year after completing *The Old Curiosity Shop*, he was again painfully reminded of the loss of Mary. Recently having had minor surgery, the removal, without anesthesia, of a fistula from his rectum, he was still in the postoperative recovery period and also struggling with the closing chapters of *Barnaby* when another Hogarth child died. Mary's younger brother was twenty-one. Under pressure, his own good sense asserting itself against the force of his feelings, he agreed to relinquish the opportunity for himself and his "dear children" to be buried next to Mary's grave "if it will be any comfort" to her mother. His rights to the gravesite were proprietary as well as emotional, since he had arranged and paid for it. He consoled Mrs. Hogarth with echoes of Little Nell, signifying that such pure angels wait for us to join them in heaven. Still, he had become obsessed with the inappropriate idea of being buried in the same grave with her. "It is a great trial to me," he privately wrote to Forster, "to give up Mary's grave; greater than I can possibly express. I thought of moving her to the catacombs, and saying nothing about it. . . . I cannot bear the thought of being excluded from her dust . . . I ought to get the better of it, but it is very hard. I never contemplated this—and coming so suddenly, and after being ill it disturbs me more than it ought. It seems like losing her a second time." But he did get the better of it. Within days, he was absorbed in *Barnaby*. "In the midst of this trouble and pain, I sit down to my book, some beneficent power shows it all to me, and tempts me to be interested, and I don't invent it—*really do not*—*but see it*, and write it down."[47] Through the same autumn, he was making plans for further travel. He had decided to cross the Atlantic.

CHAPTER FIVE

The Emperor of Cheerfulness (1842-1844)

I

TOSSED BY HEAVY ATLANTIC SEAS, EVEN THE BUOYANT DICKENS feared drowning. Sparks, exploding from the funnel of the coal-burning steamship *Britannia*, "full of fire and people" and without lifeboats, fell onto the wooden deck. He could not help imagining that the ship would catch fire. It rolled "from side to side . . . now on the top of a mountain; now in the body of a deep valley . . . with her masts in the water at every plunge; and the lightning streamed through the skylight, awfully." Optimism and cheerfulness, his surface response to challenges, were insufficient to calm his nerves on one of the stormiest midwinter crossings in recent memory. Like the other eighty-five passengers, including Catherine, he felt frequently nauseous and dizzy. During much of the voyage, high waves at right angles to the ship seemed to wall in the deck, eliminating the horizon. Their cabin seemed as small as a postage stamp. "I don't know what to compare it with. A small box at a coffee room is much too big. So is a hackney coach." The crossing took fifteen days. Finally, near Halifax, the pride of the Cunard fleet went aground in a shallow channel. Two days later, approaching Boston, Dickens strained his eyes for his first sight of "American soil. . . . A sharp keen wind blew dead against us; a hard frost prevailed on shore; and the cold was most severe."[1] Angry and frightened, partly because he believed the new technology unsafe partly because he had underestimated the perils of a winter crossing, he vowed not to take a steamship back. For the next half year he did not tire of repeating how unsafe the voyage had been. He returned to England six months later, through balmy June weather, on an old-fashioned American sailing packet, the *George Washington*.

When the *Britannia* had left Liverpool on January 3, 1842, Alfred and Fanny, representing the family, had waved him off. Forster had concluded his emotional embrace with a gift of a pocket Shakespeare, which he carried "constantly . . . an unspeakable source of delight," like a green patch of England in an English-speaking but foreign world. The thirty-year-old Dickens was not a seasoned traveler except in his imagination. Other than brief visits to Wales, the Midlands, Yorkshire, Scotland, and Belgium, his experience had been limited to London and southern England. European languages and cultures had no special attraction for him. His fictional travelers, Pickwick, Nickleby, and Little Nell, find England sufficient for their wanderings. He does not seem to have daydreamed about following in the carriage tracks of the eighteenth-century Grand Tour or to have thought of Paris and Rome as a young Englishman's finishing school. Unlike his older friends Landor and Rogers, he had had neither the learning nor the leisure to become a cultured European. Though the Channel was not as formidable a barrier as the Atlantic, his strong English commitment directed his imagination toward his own culture and its extensions.

Even if a continental adventure had appealed to him, he needed to transform adventure into commerce. Little to no British market existed for European travel books. There was, though, a substantial reading audience for books about America. His restlessness, his need for refreshment, his desire to find stimulation among fresh scenes there, could be reconciled with his need to maintain his income. In July 1839, he had speculated about crossing the Atlantic in the profitable footsteps of Frances

Trollope and Captain Frederick Marrayat, "to write from thence a series of papers descriptive of the places and people I see...." The British book-buying public continued to be curious about its cousins in America. The American impressions of the most popular English novelist would most likely sell widely. The trip would be financed by an advance against royalties from Chapman and Hall. In Dickens' mind, and in the general European consciousness, America was a newfound land of potential riches whose origin as a resource for the entrepreneur, as well as for the underemployed masses, could not be forgotten no matter how sophisticated the scheme. To the extent that it was marketable, English culture was a commodity. In response to Macready's financial worries, Dickens had suggested a mineral that "isn't to be found in England"—American gold.[2]

Before departure, he had signed a contract with his publisher, who put into his account at Coutts and Company an advance of £800 against the security of three life insurance policies he had recently obtained. In total, his "honourable, manly, and generous" publisher had agreed to provide £1,800 against the earnings of the book that he would write about his American adventures and a new full-length novel on an English subject to be published in monthly numbers. *American Notes* would extend the breadth of his social observation, comparing American institutions to British. He did not intend "pressing the Americans" into his service in the novel. Throughout he denied that he planned to write any book at all about America, though he had had one in mind from the beginning and had signed a contract to write it. There was some rough justice in his deceit. Unlike Macready, who had been paid cash for his American performances in 1826–27, the hardworking Dickens had received and could expect to receive nothing from the immense sale of his novels in the United States. Beginning in 1834, pirated editions had sold widely to American buyers who had little incentive to become party to an international copyright agreement. The American readers who waited in anxious anticipation on the docks of Boston and New York to receive the installment of *The Old Curiosity Shop* that might break their hearts with the news of Little Nell's death paid Dickens nothing for their tears. He bewailed, ironically, "the exquisite justice of never deriving sixpence from an enormous American sale of all my books."[3]

Having already spoken up for increased copyright protection in Britain and for a British-American agreement, he had it in mind to advance a just cause from which he and others would benefit. Ignorant of the complications of copyright politics and of the recent severe depression he crossed the Atlantic with the naïve expectation that in this republic of his imagination elemental notions of fairness would triumph over politics and power relationships, as if America were some elegant utopia exempt from the rough-and-tumble vicissitudes of human nature and ordinary society.

His American aspirations, though, were far from only commercial. From *Sketches* on, he had increasingly turned his literary eye toward social conditions. What he would see in America would qualify his belief that much of European misery had its roots in social, political, and economic exploitation embedded in the class structure and reflected in the attitudes of a corrupt ruling hierarchy that had not incorporated basic Christian principles into economics and government. With a sure sense of his feelings, the unsophisticated Dickens declared himself a "republican" who expected to find the realization of his humanistic dream in the United States. In April 1841, he had resumed a correspondence with Washington Irving, the warmth of whose fraternal hand he grasped "over the broad Atlantic." He anticipated an American community of friends. By September 1841, "still haunted by visions of America," he had decided to go, looking forward to walking on "the soil I have trodden in my day-dreams many times." He relished all "the wonders that await us . . . in your mighty land." He expected to find a model against which British failures could be measured and criticized, an experiment in democracy whose successes would strengthen his commitment to reform and his self-definition as a radical. His American hosts expected to give to a grateful recipient, an ambassador of goodwill, the homage of lionizing admiration, though British-American relations were severely strained by recent events. America had defaulted on foreign-owned state bonds, had aided Canadian rebels, and had become embroiled in an American-Canadian boundary dispute, which would be resolved by the Webster-Ashburton treaty that summer. Relations had been further exacerbated by British insistence on searching American ships suspected of engaging in the slave trade.4

Imitating his hero from pantomime, the buoyant Dickens bounced onto the American stage with one of Grimaldi's favorite tag lines, "Here we are!" He seemed to the young Boston publisher James T. Fields "the Emperor of Cheerfulness on a cruise of pleasure." Though he came to America as a private traveler, he could not resist stepping onto the public platform that his American hosts assumed was his natural place. As the *Britannia* pulled into Boston Harbor, a dozen newspaper editors "came leaping on board at the peril of their lives" to interview the international celebrity.[5] Every town in America wanted the honor of entertaining him publicly, as if to authenticate its cultural status. Every newspaper wanted interviews, quotations, anecdotes, exclusives, publicity. Wined, dined, toasted, interviewed, and celebrated in Boston, where he stayed for a month, and then Worcester, Hartford, New Haven, and New York, he could neither gauge nor appreciate the public nature of American life in which the "Inimitable Boz," as if hoisted on the petard of his own celebrity, was defined as a personality who belonged to his audience, the captured British lion on display. Used to English reticence, to tight boundaries between public reputation and personal privacy, he immediately learned that such distinctions meant little to Americans.

At the Boz Ball in New York, on February 14, repeated two nights later (he was prevented from attending the reprise because of a sore throat) and sensationalized in *The Extra Boz Herald*, three thousand people in full dress danced quadrilles around Dickens, who danced quadrilles until he was "no longer able even to stand." The ballroom was decorated with Dickens medallions. At one end were *tableaux vivants* of scenes from his novels. Torn between vanity and disgust, he thought it was "the most splendid, gorgeous, brilliant affair."

When not on public display, he was denied privacy by the curious who came to enforce their right as Americans not only to be equal to anyone else but to have sight of and talk to their famous visitor. He soon began to feel overexposed, even abused. Uninhibited by libel laws, in an early stage of developing the techniques of sensationalistic journalism, the newspapers raucously, aggressively, treated him the way they would any glamorous public figure. Soon he felt "so beset, waylaid, hustled, set upon, beaten about, trampled down, mashed, bruised, and pounded, by crowds, that I never knew less of myself in all my life, or had less time for those confidential Interviews with myself whereby I earn my bread. . . ." A sober young man in Worcester expressed some of the cross-cultural puzzlement from the American perspective. "His external appearance did not answer to our puritanical notions of a literary man: his dress was that of a *genteel rowdy* in this country and no one, who did not know, could have supposed him to be 'the immortal Boz.' A stout Prince Albert frock coat, a flashy red vest with a lark figured scarf about his neck, fastened with a pin to which was attached any quantity of gold chain and his long flowing hair gave him the air of a fashionable young man. . . ." But "when introduced to him he gave you a cordial shake of the hand which instantly made you feel at ease. From his dress his character is not to be judged: in his countenance there is a field for deep study, it is capable of a greater variety of expression than I recollect to have seen. In conversation his eye sparkles and lights up his whole face."[6]

Only a literary lion. Dickens walked into the political and economic den of public pressure groups like an ignorant Daniel. At a dinner in his honor in Boston, at the beginning of February 1842, he urged the merits of an international copyright agreement. A week later, in Hartford, he enforced his argument with the announcement that he had "made a kind of compact with myself that I never will, while I remain in America, omit an opportunity of referring to a topic in which I and all others of my class on both sides of the water are equally interested. . . . I would beg leave to whisper in your ear two words, International Copyright."[7] He argued that literature was property to be protected by rules of equity and that a native American literature could flourish best in circumstances that encouraged American publishers to pay American authors rather than have foreign authors free. The opposition maintained that literature, like all imaginative creations, should not be regulated by law and commerce, that undercapitalized nations, without public libraries, needed inexpensive access to ideas and entertainment that they could not generate themselves or afford to purchase at high rates, and that the free availability to publishers of an author's works did more to advance his reputation and long-term earnings than the restricted circulation created by the higher price of books on which a copyright royalty was paid. American opinion, across every interest group, including authors, was divided, though most book, magazine, and newspaper publishers were opposed. But the notion of entering into an agreement that would send capital abroad at a time when national growth was struggling against economic depression had little appeal even to those not in the book trade.

With no sense of the economic reality or of American irritability on such matters, Dickens had one overriding feeling: A great injustice was being done. While he could argue, even elegantly, potential advantages to both parties, he was constitutionally incapable of subordinating his definition of justice to a temperate and larger perspective. Already sensitive to the slander that "every rotten-hearted pander who . . . struts it in the Editorial We" might inflict on public figures, still he was unprepared for the absolute freedom of American editorial comment on his personal and public life. Having had their national pride insulted, American journalists rarely hesitated to accuse him of cupidity, an "unmanly and ungenerous" accusation from which he recoiled painfully, partly because of his vulnerability. Of all living writers he stood to gain most by a copyright agreement. Though most of his English fellow-authors supported his lobbying, some, like Bulwer, as well as numbers of his new American friends, thought his speeches unseemly and his position awkward. With Forster's assistance, he had rallied some of the best-known British writers to sign a procopyright collective letter, which he circulated in America as if it had been spontaneously generated rather than conceived and managed by himself. He quickly realized, though, that his initial hope that legislation would be passed soon was hopelessly naïve. Increasingly stubborn, he defined himself as a gadfly of righteousness whose efforts would bear fruit in the distant future, if not in time for himself, then for the writers of the next generation.

Dickens also realized that his strength was being exhausted by his intense public schedule. The winter weather wore him down with flu, toothaches, overheating, overexposure, vexation, exhaustion, weariness of spirit, a steady grind of public occasions. He was "sick to death of the life I have been leading here—worn out in mind and body—and quite weary and distressed." He could not, however, forgo expressing his position on an issue of principle. He was "iron upon this theme; and iron I will be, here and at home, by word of mouth and in writing, as long as I can articulate a syllable, or hold a pen." But by the middle of February 1842 he had decided on no "more public entertainments or public recognitions of any kind."⁸

❦ 2 ❦

PRIVATE ENTERTAINMENTS WERE ANOTHER MATTER. WITH A GIFT for friendship, Dickens found American friends after his own heart. In spite of these new relationships, his thoughts turned often to England, particularly to his friends and family. Macready, with his wife, was looking after the four children. For both parents, but especially for Catherine, it had been wrenchingly painful to leave them behind. After some hesitation, Dickens had concluded that it would be both dangerous and inconvenient to bring them. Gradually, through mutual tears, he had persuaded a reluctant Catherine, torn between competing loyalties, that her companionship was essential to him. His restlessness made it easier for him than for her to leave children and friends, though he warmly participated in the ritual of setting out in great state on each stop in their American travels Maclise's pencil drawing of three of the children. He deeply missed them, more pointedly as the weeks passed. He also particularly missed Forster, to whom he wrote long letters that they had agreed would form the basis of his travel book. "How I miss you . . . how seriously I have thought many, many times . . . of the terrible folly of ever quarreling with a true friend. . . ."⁹

Catherine's companionship did not compensate for such losses. Even more than he, she was susceptible to colds, sore throats, and fatigue. She had begun the voyage with a painful toothache. The crowds, the drafts, the dislocation, despite the help of her stoic Scottish-born servant, Anne Brown, kept her physically off-balance. She needed more rest than her frenetic husband, who tramped with his hosts from one end to another of each city they visited. Exerting herself to be a good sport and eminently presentable, she attended balls and dinners in Boston and New York, impressing their hosts with her quiet amiability and easygoing friendliness. She seemed a compliant, slightly overweight, "mild, rosy young woman—not beautiful, but amiable," a "small woman" embarrassed by being the "lion's mate." Some snobbish Boston patricians emphasized that she was her husband's social superior. Catherine, though, had for some time revealed a "propensity" for minor accidents. "She falls into, or out of, every coach or boat we enter," her husband remarked. She "scrapes the skin off her legs; brings great sores and swellings on her feet; chips large fragments out of her ankle-bones; and makes herself blue with bruises." In spite of this, on their difficult trip westward in March and April, she proved herself, to her husband's surprise, "a *most admirable* traveller" and "perfectly game."[10]

But Dickens' new friends, not Catherine, served as a partial recompense for the temporary loss of Forster and Maclise. On the *Britannia,* he had become companionable with Lord Mulgrave, George Constantine Phipps, later the second Marquis of Normanby, a good-looking young aristocrat returning to his regiment in Canada. In Boston, he met a group of talented patrician writers and intellectuals, particularly Cornelius Felton, Charles Sumner, Richard Henry Dana, Jr., and Henry Wadsworth Longfellow. Clever, portly, fair-haired, and genial, Felton was both a successful professor of Greek at Harvard and a *bon vivant.* If he had not previously, Felton soon "entertained a profound conviction that Dickens was the most original and inventive genius since Shakespeare" and that his judgment was at least half right. Traveling in February 1842 on the same boat to New York from New Haven, where Dickens had been serenaded at night beneath his hotel window by Yale students, they "drank all the porter on board, ate all the cold pork and cheese, and were very merry indeed." He paid his "unaffected, hearty, genial, jolly" American friend the highest compliment: He is "quite an Englishman of the best sort." In New York, they shared their mutual passion for oysters, whose reputation as an aphrodisiac Dickens had written about humorously in "The Misplaced Attachment of Mr. John Dounce," originally called "Love and Oysters." They strolled up Broadway together like urban sophisticates, unconcerned about being seen exploring the high and low life of a great city, "the grave Eliot Professor and the *Swelling,* theatrical Boz—the little man with the red waistcoat."[11]

With Sumner, a strong spokesman against slavery, trained as a lawyer but now committed to a literary career, Dickens developed an immediate rapport. Sumner became his most adventuresome and tireless Boston host, who showed him the back alleys and tourist sights as well as Beacon Hill drawing rooms. The twenty-seven-year-old Dana cast a keen, initially cold eye on the dandyesque celebrity. The son of a distinguished, strongly Anglophile Boston family, at the beginning of a brilliant career as a lawyer and writer, he had recently published *Two Years Before the Mast* (1840). Forster had praised the book to Dickens, who, years later, pronounced it "about the best sea book in the English tongue." "We have heard him called 'the handsomest man in London'&c," Dana wrote. "He is of the middle height (under if anything) with a large expressive eye, regular nose, matted, curling, wet-looking black hair, a dissipated looking mouth with a vulgar draw to it, a muddy olive complexion, *stubby* fingers & a hand by no means patrician, a hearty, off-hand manner, far from well bred, & a rapid, dashing way of talking. He looks 'wide awake', 'up to anything', full of cleverness, with quick feelings & great ardour. You admire him, & there is a fascination about him which keeps your eyes on him, yet you cannot get over the impression that he is a low bred man. . . . Take the genius out of his face & there are a thousand young London shop-keepers . . . who look exactly like him." Like many New Englanders, Dana thought Dickens vulgar, intellectually superficial, and morally suspect, even if only because of his flaming waistcoat in a society of men dressed in sober black. But, like many of his skeptical hosts, Dana marveled at his naturalness, geniality, and humor, as if he were a phenomenon of beneficent energy. "He is the *cleverest* man I ever met. . . . He impresses you . . . with the alertness of his various powers." He soon came close to sharing his father's view that Dickens' "whole countenance speaks *life* and *action*—the face seems to flicker with the *heart's* and mind's activity." Like another sun, "You cannot tell how dead the faces near him seemed. . . . He is full of life."[12]

Longfellow was among those who were happy to discover that there was more of the dandy in his manner and dress than of the New England puritan or patrician. To some Americans, he seemed vulgar, frivolous, and inappropriately young. Colorful and playful, even slightly risqué in his conversational remarks, he combined a lower-middle-class mentality with Cockney bad taste. But Longfellow, the first professor of modern languages at Harvard, a talented poet in quiet rebellion against the limitations of his Cambridge life, found attractive the very qualities his compatriots found distasteful, his "gay, free and easy character," with a slight dash of irresponsibility and social charm. Visiting Dickens at his hotel with Sumner late in January, Longfellow accompanied his old and his new friend on one of their long walks. Dickens, who thought him a "noble" fellow, admiringly read *Ballads and Other Poems,* which had just come out. Early in February 1842, Longfellow played host to a large breakfast party at which Dickens was the guest of honor. Dickens responded to some gossip about the notorious Mrs. Caroline Norton, the playwright Richard Brinsley Sheridan's beautiful granddaughter, having further damaged her reputation by assisting a young friend to elope, "I'm sure I should be very happy to help anybody run away." Longfellow was soon to run away from some of the pressures of Boston to the comparative freedom of Europe, first to the water cure in Germany, then to a visit with Dickens in London, where he became briefly a minor member of the Dickens circle.

In New York, Dickens met David Colden and William Cullen Bryant, with the exception of Irving the man he "most wanted to see in America." A wealthy, strongly Anglophile lawyer and philanthropist, whose father had been mayor of New York, Colden had become intimate with Macready in 1826 during the actor's first American tour. Known for his generosity, he was eagerly responsive to Dickens. The older man took an active role in entertaining the novelist and in the practical arrangements for the Boz Ball and Dickens dinner. When he left New York, Colden graciously handled business arrangements and forwarded his mail. With a lovely wife, Frances, with whom Dickens, half humorously, fell "deeply in love," Colden was "as good a fellow as ever lived." The meeting with Bryant proved slightly dissatisfying, at least to Bryant. Of all American poets, Dickens had the highest opinion of Bryant, who had made an international reputation in 1817 with the publication of "Thanatopsis." His support of Dickens' position on international copyright, though mostly privately expressed, was in his favor also. But, when they breakfasted together in late February, Dickens thought him "sad . . . and very reserved." Slightly put off, Bryant remarked that though he "liked [him] hugely . . . the number of dispatches that came and went made me almost think I was breakfasting with a minister of state." In a sense, he was breakfasting with an unofficial ambassador so engulfed by letters and invitations that he had already hired a full-time secretary, George Washington Putnam. Putnam served him efficiently, and Dickens immensely enjoyed his singing, painting, Hamlet-like silences, general sentimentality, and comic absurdity. Twenty-eight years later, Putnam praised "the full beauty and purity of [Dickens'] nature" and Catherine's attractiveness, her "high, full forehead, the brown hair gracefully arranged, the look of English healthfulness in the warm glow of color in her cheeks, the blue eyes with a tinge of violet, well-arched brows, a well-shaped nose, and a mouth small and of uncommon beauty," with a sweetness and "calm quietness" of temperament.[13]

The long-anticipated embrace of Irving took place immediately after Dickens' arrival in New York, in the middle of February. Irving greeted him with wide-open arms. The best-known American prose writer, he chaired the New York dinner in his honor, attended by 250 men and a small number of women, including Catherine, who were admitted to the balcony for the speeches. One of the few Americans who stood to gain by a copyright agreement, Irving, though more sophisticated than Dickens about the politics of the issue, toasted "International Copyright." Another speaker praised "the gifted minds of England—Hers by birth; ours by adoption." Copyright had some American champions. It was later extolled as "the only honest turnpike between the readers of two great nations." Only a small portion of Dickens' speech touched on that issue, much of it an extended paen to Irving, the "Knickerbocker" who had written the humorous *A History of New York; The Sketch Book of Geoffrey Crayon, Gent.; Tales of a Traveller;* and *The Legends of the Alhambra.* "Why, gentlemen, I don't go upstairs to bed two nights out of seven, as I have a credible witness near at hand to testify [laughter],—I say, gentlemen, I do not go to bed two nights out of seven without taking Washington Irving under my arm upstairs to bed with me [uproarious laughter]." He found Irving, known for taking small naps at other people's tables, "*a great* fellow," and developed a strong affection for him, a delightful companion in the New York social whirl that went on until the beginning of March. Urged by Dickens, Irving later joined him briefly in Washington—though he was there primarily to receive his instructions before leaving as ambassador to Spain—and then in Baltimore. Irving "*wept heartily* at parting."14 An international celebrity himself, Irving looked forward to their meeting again in England.

Determined to observe American manners and scenery, Dickens set out on a hectic voyage to see the wonders of the New World, first its main cities in addition to Boston and New York, then the South and the West. Early in March, he descended by train to Philadelphia, Baltimore, and then Washington. American manners seemed to him warmly courteous. "When an American gentleman is polished, he *is* a perfect gentleman," and "the whole people," who are especially courteous to women, "have most affectionate and generous impulses." But warmth sometimes became presumption and imposition. American hygiene struck him as primitive, particularly the widespread habit of spitting a combination of saliva and tobacco juice, sometimes into spitoons, usually onto the closest available surface. On one train ride, "the flashes of saliva flew so perpetually and incessantly out of the windows all the way, that it looked as though they were ripping open featherbeds inside, and letting the wind dispose of the feathers." Another time, he disgustedly wiped the "half dried flakes of spittle" from the large, caricaturishly American raccoon coat he wore against the winter chill. Fastidious, from a middle-class culture that stressed public decorum, and never able to forget the dirt of his blacking-factory days, he was repulsed: "I can bear anything but filth." Used to fresh air and milder winters, he gasped and sweated in overheated interiors. The practice was rarely to open windows in the winter. The ubiquitous Franklin stove made the air chokingly uncomfortable in hotels. He could not get over the "bilious and trying" weather of the northeastern United States. "One day it is hot summer, without a breath of air; the next, twenty degrees below freezing, with a wind blowing that cuts your skin like steel."15 The unexpected non-Englishness of the country gradually made him an increasingly cranky traveler.

In Philadelphia, he was manipulated into a public reception of the sort in which he had sworn not to participate. He stood, shaking hands and bowing, for hours. In Baltimore, he met Edgar Allan Poe, on Poe's initiative, and had a long talk about literature. He glanced at Poe's *Tales of the Grotesque and Arabesque*, a gift from the proud author, who admired Dickens and had been influenced by "A Madman's Manuscript" in *Pickwick Papers*. Poe had reviewed favorably his two most recent novels. The relationship was aborted, though, by Poe's fury two years later at being slighted in an article on American poetry published by Forster but which he believed written or at least contributed to by Dickens, since the article paraphrased what he and Dickens had said about American writers during their two conversations in Baltimore.

In Washington, much of which British invaders had burned thirty years before, the celebrity-ambassador met the ruling elite, including Henry Clay, "one of the most agreeable and fascinating men I ever saw. He is tall and slim, with long, limp, grey hair—a good head—refined features—a bright eye—a good voice—and a manner more frank and captivating than I ever saw in any man." John Quincy Adams, "a fine old fellow . . . with most surprising vigour, memory, readiness, and pluck," now a formidable member of the House of Representatives, though not an admirer of his novels, also entertained the novelist. Like an imperious statesman himself, Dickens shocked the company by leaving the former president's luncheon so early as to seem either impolite or arrogant. The beetle-browed Daniel Webster called. Dickens had met him in 1839, when Webster had impressed British society, including Carlyle, with his "Parliamentary intellect and silent-rage."[16]

A private interview with the rather dull but "mild and gentlemanly" John Tyler, who had assumed office on the death of President William Henry Harrison, was pleasantly perfunctory. Struggling with British-American tensions and his stalemated relationship with an antagonistic Congress, the mild-mannered president must have been able to make little of Dickens' visit and Dickens himself, though a few days later the novelist recognized that the president was embattled and unhappy. "He expressed great surprise at my being so young. I would have returned the compliment; but he looked so jaded, that it stuck in my throat like Macbeth's amen." Ignorant of

Washington protocol, he declined a dinner invitation from Tyler, but successfully suggested lunch instead. After visits to Congress, where he lobbyied on behalf of international copyright and presented a petition from American authors at the head of which was Irving's name, he concluded that most American politicians were very much "like our own members— some of them very bilious-looking, some very rough, some heartily good natured, and some very coarse."[17]

❧ 3 ❧

HE HAD INTENDED TO GO AS FAR AS CHARLESTON. HAVING ALREADY begun to take into account his limitations of time and energy, among other reasons because he very much wanted to go to the Far West, he soon heeded warnings that the roads, the weather, and the accommodations in the South would be uncomfortable. Keenly interested in American social institutions, particularly hospitals and prisons, some of which he had visited in Massachusetts, New York, and Pennsylvania, he had no doubt about his antagonism to slavery. He had not anticipated, though, that the South itself would seem to him a prison in which the very existence of slavery denied him his own freedom. So repulsed was he by what he saw of slavery in Virginia that the practical grounds on which he had canceled Charleston came to seem a blessing only afterward revealed. Its sights, stench, and distortions sent him reeling with disgust. The "accursed institution," a blight on the land, seemed to bring, or at least to be accompanied by, gloom and decay, economic and spiritual distress. The distortion of logic, reason, ethics, and the Bible by defenders of slavery seemed not only self-serving but also self-destructive, as if "cruelty, and the abuse of irresponsible power . . . were one of the greatest blessings of mankind." The "mere fact of living in a town" where slavery existed was "positive misery." After a few days he left the South for Washington and Baltimore, where he and Irving sipped a huge mint julep "far into the night." He felt his "heart . . . lightened."[18]

From Baltimore, he journeyed into an America whose boundary of comfort was the eastern seaboard and whose boundary of civilization was just slightly beyond the Mississippi, "the renowned father of waters." The railroad extended twelve miles west of Baltimore. After that, it was stagecoach and river travel only. On the seaboard, he had experienced the American experiment with democracy leavened by the high culture of the British inheritance. Traveling westward, he expected to see not so much the frontier but the wilderness, the exciting but comfortable European myth of the scenically sublime and exotic, a vast region of natural beauty suffused with transcendental power. With a taste for the picturesque as well as the sublime, he found the Susquehanna valley beautiful. At Harrisburg they boarded a canal boat to Pittsburgh, whose industrial smoke reminded him of Birmingham. From Pittsburgh, they took a steamboat, on which there was "no conversation, no laughter, no cheerfulness, no sociality, except in spitting." They traveled down "this beautiful Ohio, its wooded heights all radiant in the sunlight," to Cincinnati, "a very beautiful city . . . the prettiest place I have seen here, except Boston," whose "suburbs . . . turf-plots and well kept gardens" probably reminded him of England.[19]

But his journey to St. Louis up the Mississippi, "the beastliest river in the world," was distressing. The constant jarring efforts, especially at night, to avoid the steamboat's colliding with floating logs, frightened him. Pressured into attending receptions at various cities en route, he felt that "the Queen and Prince Albert could not be more tired." The farther he moved into unsettled, fragmentary communities, the more frightened he became. He had the sense of a society without supportive circles and communities of friends. In Cairo, Illinois, at the junction of the Ohio and Mississippi, later made famous by Mark Twain as the free city that Jim and Huck Finn never reached, he had found an epitome of ugliness that he afterward anathematized, "a dismal swamp, on which the half-built houses rot away . . . on ground so flat and low . . . a breeding place of fever, ague, and death . . . the hateful Mississippi circling and eddying before it . . . an ugly sepulchre, a grave uncheered by any gleam of promise: a place without one single quality, in earth or air or water, to commend it." The edge, the frontier, the open spaces, seemed to him empty or, even worse, savage. Deserted and decaying settlements along the riverbanks quickly slipped back into the wildness of nature. The settlers soon reverted to instinctive barbarism. Civilization was more fragile, more superficial, than he had imagined. What stuck most in his mind about St. Louis was Bloody Island, the dueling ground. When he visited the Looking-Glass Prairie, slightly beyond the city and the western boundary of his travels, he was disappointed—"It would be difficult to say why, or how. . . . Looking towards the setting sun, there lay . . . a vast expanse of level ground; unbroken, save by one thin line of trees, which scarcely amounted to a scratch upon the great blank. . . ."[20]

Despite all the adulation he had received on his journey, he felt even his professional self-definition challenged by this near-wilderness. Without community and hierarchy, the artist could have neither subject nor position. American individualism, in the marketplace, in politics, and now on the frontier, seemed to him anticommunal, intolerably lonely, brazenly selfish, inherently materialistic, and threateningly brutal. Ultimately, it emptied life of its highest joys. Such open spaces were a "great blank," a world of chaos, decay, and death, nature unredeemed by man and community. There could be no morality or God in such an unhierarchical society and in an empty continent. The frontiersmen, so different from the Yankees, seemed "heavy, dull, and ignorant," their manners increasingly offensive as he moved westward into a world that was paradoxically larger in its empty spaces but narrower, more confined, in barges, boats, and stagecoaches. It was difficult to be either a gentleman or an artist in such a world. The frontier was community at its most inchoate, landscape unredeemed by either man or God, a world of "swamps, bogs, and morasses" whose limitations were embodied in the country's commercialism, corrupt politics, and obsession with the inescapable issue of slavery. Despite all the similarities to English culture and corruption, he increasingly saw America as distinctive in its vices. Back in Ohio, on his way northward to British Canada by stagecoach, from Cincinnati to Columbus to Sandusky, he had a moment of relief as he passed through "a beautiful country, richly cultivated and luxuriant" that made him feel he "might be travelling just now in Kent."[21] As soon as he crossed the border, he felt, with immense relief, as if he were breathing native air.

"Weary of travelling," he visited Toronto, Kingston, Quebec, Montreal, and Queenston. His pace was slower, more restful than in his hectic dash across thousands of miles of the United States. Graciously entertained by Lord Mulgrave in late May in Montreal, he transformed Canadian raw material into an English stage performance. Before an elite British-Canadian audience of almost six hundred people, he put on for charity a comedy, *A Roland for an Oliver;* a farce, John Poole's *Deaf as a Post;* and an interlude, with a band, gas lighting, and borrowed stage props. Officers from the Montreal military garrison played various roles. Catherine acted in the farce. The major part in all three plays was performed by "Mr. Charles Dickens." He was also the stage manager, and not "for nothing," he told Forster, for "didn't I come Macready over them . . . ? Only think of Kate playing! and playing devilish well, I assure you!" The private was followed by a public performance, with professional actresses substituting for the amateurs in the interest of propriety. Unlike his sustained three-month appearance on the American public stage, he now had the satisfaction of being in control of the performance. Filled with self-congratulations—"I really do believe that I was very funny"—the great pains and perspiration that he expended through ten days of organizing and rehearsing were part of the pleasure of self-assertion, which was followed by the reward of applause.[22] Canada allowed him to be himself again.

At the end of April 1842 he saw Niagara Falls, "this Great Place . . . the most wonderful and beautiful in the world." At last he felt in the presence of the sublime. He viewed it initially from the American and then, more pleasurably, from "the *English* side," where he rested for over a week. For the first time he saw in America what he had expected to see, felt what he had wanted to feel. It was the only natural scene whose beauty fulfilled his idealized vision of God and eternity in nature, providing a visual equivalent of the Romantic myth of transcendence. He felt he was in the presence of "Peaceful Eternity" and his "Creator. . . . What voices spoke from out the thundering water; what faces, faded from the earth, looked out upon me from its gleaming depths; what Heavenly promise glistened in those angels' tears, the drops of many hues, that showered around, and twined themselves about the gorgeous arches which the changing rainbows made!" The voice that spoke most clearly and sweetly to him from the thunderingly peaceful waters was

Mary Hogarth's, as if she were in his presence again, as if she, who was out of time, visited regularly, at this sublime place, the time that he was still within. Here the visible and the invisible were made manifest to one another.[23]

Even Niagara Falls, though, had its fallen element. Some tourists had written facetiously vulgar remarks into the guest book. With vigorous priggishness, he described these remarks as so disgusting that "my wrath is kindled, past all human powers of extinction." It was "a disgrace and degradation to our nature," "the vilest and the filthiest ribaldry that ever human hogs delighted in." He would "force these Hogs to live for the rest of their lives on all Fours. . . . Their drink should be the stagnant ditch, and their food the rankest garbage; and every morning they should each receive as many stripes as there are letters in their detestable obscenities." Six months later, his outraged feelings still exacerbated by what seemed to him a significant attack on his idealizations, he continued his tirade. "It is humiliating enough to know that there are among men brutes so obscene and worthless, that they can delight in laying their miserable profanations upon the very steps of Nature's greatest altar." They "disgrace . . . the English language in which they are written (though I hope few of these entries have been made by Englishmen)."[24] His response was intensely self-protective, resonating with his own memories of defilement, aggressively raising his growing concern that human nature had more of the base in it than he had previously been willing to recognize.

He himself was delicately balanced between graffiti and the sublime. The American experience threatened that balance. It made the oppositions starker, the threat of imbalance clearer. On the one side, there was idealism, optimism, community, and friendship. On the other, there was pragmatism, pessimism, fragmentation, and isolation. The republic of his imagination turned out to be worse than England, partly because it had disappointed him, partly because his naïveté had been exposed. His unwillingness to formulate the gap between the idealizations that fiction could convey and the messy, mixed realities of the American scene heightened his anger. On one level, it was a class matter. Eager to be a democrat and an egalitarian, he had discovered that he preferred a hierarchy based on birth and talent rather than on money and equality. He preferred to help the lower classes rather than to live in a society in which purported classlessness was a disguise for a class system based on wealth, in which bad manners and the tyranny of the majority made daily life ugly and suppressed free speech. Having struggled out of the blacking factory to be a gentleman of the sort that America did not encourage, he identified with the upper middle class's assumption of aristocratic personal values and liberal middle-class politics. The class system, many of whose faults he vigorously criticized, still seemed to him the solid structure on which a civilization higher than the American had been constructed. Though he would not claim that his family was old and distinguished, he did not hesitate to use as his bookplate a coat of arms, a lion with a Maltese cross in its hands, which his father claimed was the family escutcheon originating in the sixteenth century. Ironically, he had a poor but ambitious carpenter with literary talent, John Overs, whom he assisted but also firmly patronized, carve the mold from which the bookplate was made.

As his date of departure approached, he could hardly restrain his eagerness. "Of course there is no place like England. There never was, and never will be." He had previously allowed himself to express that sentiment mainly in formal terms, a "yearning after our English Customs and english manners, such as you cannot conceive." The emphasis, though, had become increasingly personal, his desire to see his children and his friends again, his need to be liberated from the oppression of an alien world. At the end of May 1842, they left Montreal, traveling by steamboat, railroad, and stagecoach to New York via the St. Lawrence River, Lake Champlain, Albany, and the Hudson. To avoid the social entanglements of New York, he immediately took "a short excursion up the Hudson," visiting a Shaker community, West Point, and Albany, returning the day before sailing. "As the time draws nearer, we get FEVERED with anxiety for home. . . . Oh home—home—home—home—home—HOME!!!!!!!!!!!!" "We shall soon meet," he wrote to Forster, "and be happier and merrier than ever we were, in all our lives."[25] He hoped to surprise his friend, if he could, in his chambers at Lincoln's Inn Fields, and to burst in upon Macready and the children unexpectedly, to stand among his "household deities again" like a redeemed prodigal son and brother whose casual good-byes had not anticipated how much he would miss his beloved friends and home. Ironically, having come miserably on a British steamship, he returned happily and comfortably on an American sailing vessel that left New York on June 2, 1842. On shipboard, he played perpetually on an accordian that he had bought in March and on which every night he had played "Home Sweet Home" as they had traveled through America.

❧ 4 ❧

AMERICA HAD BROUGHT HIM SHARPLY TO THE CONCLUSION THAT there were no easy solutions to long-standing social problems. Radical changes in systems of government hardly guaranteed anything more than the perpetuation of old vices in new forms. British liberal monarchism had as much or as little promise in that regard as any other system. Mankind needed a reformation of heart before it could substantially reform the political and economic structures it had created. Justice and charity in the public world could only come from such virtues in the private individual. Much depended on how powerful were the voices calling for reformation, how responsive the ears and hearts that heard. As a novelist, he could move other hearts toward higher levels of compassion and idealism and "strike a blow" against identifiable evils. As a public voice, he could speak out strongly against social injustices and communal failures in forums other than his fiction. Persistent efforts to call attention to injustice and exploitation might in the long run do more to elevate the level of life in Britain than any revolution or experiment in radical democracy. Having gone to America thinking himself a radical, he returned recognizing that he was a left-of-center Whig.

In America, he had continued a practice of visiting prisons, workhouses, hospitals, and lunatic asylums begun when he had visited Newgate in late 1835. Dickens' morbid enthusiasm for variations of misery and its institutional treatment spoke deeply of his fascination with alternative lives that he could imagine vividly and present dramatically in his fiction. The poor, the imprisoned, the physically and emotionally deprived, were the familiar other, what he had had the potential to be but had not become. They were alternative versions of himself. Despite his depiction of Oliver as an alter ego immune from conversion to sin, his attraction both to figures like Oliver and Bill Sikes, and to a large gallery of overt and covert criminals in his later novels suggests the depth of his identification with and his sense of having escaped from degradation. He combined a personal interest in the lives and personalities of social and physical deviants with the reformer's enthusiasm for analyzing and improving social institutions.

One of the public issues, the silent system versus the solitary or separate system, that preoccupied his assessment of American prisons had decidedly personal resonances.[26] The silent system demanded that prisoners work next to one another but not speak. The solitary system deprived them of the sight as well as the sound of one another. He found the solitary system thoroughly, frighteningly repugnant. At the Eastern Penitentiary near Philadelphia, its facade modeled on a medieval castle, he saw the solitary system in operation. On the one hand, it separated criminals from one another's contaminating contact. On the other it tortured long-term prisoners into mental anguish so severe that he felt he "never in [his] life was more affected by anything which was not strictly [his] own grief" than by the "indescribable something" which he saw in such prisoners, "distantly resembling the attentive and sorrowful expression you see in the blind—which is never to be forgotten. . . This slow and daily tampering with the mysteries of the brain" seemed to him "immeasureably worse than any torture of the body." A prisoner in solitary confinement "is a man buried alive," like Dr. Manette in *A Tale of Two Cities*, "to be dug out in the slow round of years; and in the mean time dead to everything but torturing anxieties and horrible despair."[27] Later in the year, writing *American Notes*, he expanded this description into a sustained quasifictional representation of what he imagined it felt like to be imprisoned alone, with a "phantom in the corner," when "the world without, has come to be the vision, and this solitary life, the sad reality."

One bright winter morning, visiting the Perkins Institution and Massachusetts Asylum for the Blind in Boston, he was fascinated by the faces of the blind. As the guest of the director, Samuel Howe, a doctor, social reformer, and abolitionist who the next year married the remarkable Julia Ward he was intro-

duced to his most interesting case, the blind and deaf-mute
Laura Bridgman. He admired Howe's administration of the
institute, particularly fascinated by his success, supposedly the
first of its kind, in teaching the intelligent Bridgman to use her
limited resources, such as her sense of touch, as language with
which to communicate. It seemed a heartening example of what
intelligent, compassionate attention to and administration of
social misery could achieve. But it also fascinated him, to the
extent that he quoted at length in *American Notes* from Howe's
descriptive pamphlet. Bridgman's condition represented his
own fear of enclosure, of being cut off not only from other
people but from all communication, of the great blank that he
had seen in the distance from the Looking-Glass Prairie, of the
society that was deaf, mute, and blind, turned in upon itself,
without art, without community, without language.

Soon after returning to England, he entered the public
debate on another variation on human misery, the working
conditions for women and children in the coal-mining industry.
Interested in the issue for some time, in 1841 he had promised to
write an article on it for the *Edinburgh Review*. In America, he
had visited the model factories in Lowell, Massachusetts, impressed by the enlightened paternalism that provided housing,
education, libraries, attractive working conditions, and cheerful
dignity to the workers, all of whom were women. They worked
willingly, combining a due sense of their position in the class
structure with a sincere appreciation of what advantages this
system provided. In writing about them, he anticipated the anxieties of those who feared that the Lowell experiment would
undermine the distinction between classes. He simply denied
that it would, hinting at his own ambivalence about class,
though not so strongly that his identification with proper class
distinctions was not absolutely clear.

There was no need for any ambivalence in his public statement, a long letter published in the *Morning Chronicle* on July 25,
1842, under the signature "B," about the brutal mistreatment of
children and women in the largely Tory-owned collieries. Min-
ing and factory conditions in Britain seemed to him worse than
any working conditions he had seen in America other than those
imposed on slaves. An ardent evangelical, Lord Ashley, who
became the seventh Earl of Shaftesbury, later described Dickens

as one who did the work of the Lord, being of the evangelical party without knowing it. Ashley had introduced into the House of Lords a bill, which had already passed the House of Commons, on mines and collieries. It would banish women and children under thirteen from the mines, institute safety regulations, and improve working conditions. Dickens did his best to influence favorable consideration. With Swiftean reversals, parodic exaggerations, and sardonic irony, he dissected and dismissed the arguments against the bill.[28] An altered but still effective version of it passed.

His satisfaction at the passage of even the watered-down bill may have been greater than Ashley's, who resented the Duke of Wellington's congratulating him on what he felt to be a disappointment. The experience probably encouraged Dickens to think that he could advance reform through direct engagement with political and social issues. The possibility that he might run for office or be offered an appointment to administer some aspect of social reform had occurred to him. But the dominance of Tory administrations discouraged him from responding, in 1841, to the Liberal electors of Reading, Talfourd's constituency, and then to the Glasgow electors in the spring of 1842. Initially flattered, he realized that the cost of a contested election and the loss of income from writing would be too great. "Why wasn't I born with a golden ladle in my mouth as well as a pen . . . ?" Without an independent income, he could not afford political office. With a growing family, he needed more, rather than less, money. He had little to no savings, partly the result, the thrifty Lord Jeffrey chidingly insisted, of living beyond his means and his needs, even to the extent of having to arrange through Thomas Mitton in July 1843 a private loan to get him through some shortfall of income and unexpectedly heavy expenses.[29]

A government appointment, though, might speak to both his desire to engage himself actively in social reform and his need for additional income. The prospect of being appointed a police magistrate appealed to him. He wanted to put to practical use the combination of mercy and wisdom in the service of fairness for which his novels had been praised. He would be the good magistrate, like Henry Fielding, sternly but charitably fair, the opposite side of the coin of the vicious Mr. Fang in

Oliver Twist. He still maintained his nonactive enrollment as a law student at Gray's Inn with the notion that it might afford him some extra consideration for such a position. Although "the Jails and byplaces of London" were old sights to him, he was "more than ever amazed at the Ignorance and Misery that prevail." He "would never rest from practically shewing all classes how important it has become to educate, on bold and comprehensive principles, the Dangerous Members of Society." It was more realistic, though, to hope that in a Whig government his friends might provide him with administrative responsibility for educational reform, a subject that he had revealed strong opinions on in the depiction of Dotheboys Hall in *Nicholas Nickleby.*

It became an explicit concern in September 1843, when, for the first time, he visited, with Clarkson Stanfield, one of the newly established church-run slum schools, on Field Lane, almost adjacent to Fagin's house in *Oliver Twist.* They were called "ragged" schools, because they were "exclusively for children raggedly clothed. . . . My heart so sinks within me when I go into these scenes, that I almost lose the hope of ever seeing them changed." Supported primarily by the teachers themselves, whose "moral courage . . . is worthy of the apostles," the school was "held in three most wretched rooms on the first floor of a rotten house." The children were ignorant, diseased, and streetwise, the teachers badly trained if not incompetent, the school building a foul slum.[30] Remembering his own childhood vulnerability and neglect, he saw a chance to exert his energy on behalf of reform in an area in which he felt especially qualified.

Convinced that the first and most important line of protection against the criminality of adults was the education of children of both sexes, he warmly supported the ragged-school movement. And he suddenly found himself with the unusual opportunity of helping in a well-financed private effort. In 1838, Dickens had been introduced, on her initiative, to Angela Burdett Coutts, sole heir to her maternal grandfather's immense banking fortune, probably through Edward Marjoribanks, a partner in Coutts and Company, where Dickens had opened a small checking account. Dickens was sufficiently famous as a writer for Majoribanks to take notice of his patronage and to extend him special courtesies, including social overtures. Curious to meet the young novelist, the shy, tall, angular, badly complexioned Miss Coutts, two years younger than Dickens and reputedly the richest woman in England, invited him to her mansion in Piccadilly numbers of times. He finally had dinner with her in July 1839. By the end of the year, he described himself, with self-serving exaggeration, as "on terms of intimacy with Miss Coutts, and the other partners."[31] From America, he brought back presents for the heiress and her closest friend, the opinionated, domineering Hannah Meredith, who had been her governess and who remained her lifelong live-in companion. Miss Coutts combined evangelical ardor for strict Church of England sectarian good works with shyness, insecurity, loneliness, immense fear of being exploited, and a coolness of temperament that kept her always on the distant side of warmth. She was the insecure child of a hysterically invalided mother and an arrogant, wealthy father, Francis Burdett, the radical political leader of the 1820s, who turned sharply conservative and whom she worshiped even the more when he had allowed her to become his private secretary.

Whom Miss Coutts would marry was a topic of ceaseless gossip and ambition during the decades of her spinsterhood. Her idealization of her father directed her toward older men, particularly the Duke of Wellington, her neighbor in Piccadilly, whose advanced age of seventy-seven did not prevent her falling in love with him in 1846. Her interest in Dickens and his in her seem never to have been amorous. Though he was an inveterate flirt, she was not to be flirted with. He was to develop "a most perfect affection and respect for her." Years later he described his feeling for her "as always the love of a brother," though the relationship seems to have had little of the playful warmth of his idealized fictional brother-sister relationships, with their unselfconscious edge of incestuousness. She was to rely on his energy, idealism, and enthusiasm for assistance in channeling some of her money into charitable projects, both individual and institutional. With an eye toward his children's future, he was to accept her godmotherly patronage of his eldest son, edging his remarks to her with the hint of the possibility of her doing even more for him and his family. It was always a delicate balancing act between independence and dependency, between service for others and self-service. By the summer of 1843, she was relying on him for advice on petitions, and he had become "a faithful steward of [her] bounty."[32] His balked aspiration to be an active instrument of social reform could be fulfilled through making Miss Coutts dependent on his assistance. As long as he dealt with her tactfully, with respect for her limitations, without presuming on their relationship, and with due deference to Miss Meredith (who became Mrs. William Brown in 1844), he would have the chance to see some of his favorite projects supported.

When he saw the conditions at the Field Lane school, he immediately advised her that "I deem it an experiment most worthy of your charitable hand." He was at her service, and he had little difficulty persuading her to respond favorably to the advertisement for subscriptions placed by the Field Lane committee in *The Times*. He had no success, though, in getting government support. Increasingly identified with educational and social reformers like Dr. James Kay-Shuttleworth and Dr. Southwood Smith, Dickens found himself subordinating personal preferences for political advantages, uneasily submitting to boring personalities and lengthy tedium in the service of reform. The whirl of ideas and principles among competing groups sometimes frustrated progress. Sectarian religious positions were more important to most institutional reformers than substantive progress. The Ragged School Union, formed to advance the schools in the growing movement, was essentially evangelical in spirit, drawing support from dissenters and from the low church. Pious Anglicans like Miss Coutts were suspicious and doctrinally disapproving. But Dickens was convinced that the imposition into the ragged-school classroom of religious doctrine, let alone religious sectarianism, had a damaging effect on the children. The teaching already seemed weak, narrow, and unimaginative, like the heavy respectability of Bradley Headstone's lugubrious school of the "ghastliest absurdities" in *Our Mutual Friend,* which Charley Hexam attends after going to a ragged school in "a miserable loft in an unsavoury yard." It should not be further weighed down by religious dogma, Dickens felt, especially "any system of Education, based exclusively upon the principles of the Established Church."[33]

During the next few years, he advocated support for the ragged schools, among other things writing a strong letter to the *Daily News* in early February 1846. Educated children were likely to become socially productive citizens. His exposure to hardened adult criminals had convinced him that criminality was progressively self-determinative. The best antidote to criminal irreversibility was to catch the criminal in formation, in childhood, before poverty, disease, and ignorance had transformed the malleable child into the hardened malefactor. Universal education was essential, for all classes, from an early age, and the ragged schools seemed to him a start. The movement gradually provided industrial training (including, ironically, the Ragged School Shoeblack Society) and encouraged emigration to the colonies, both of which he approved of. Aware, though, of the inadequacies of the Field Lane and other ragged schools, eager to show what he himself could do and what could be done, he proposed to Kay-Shuttleworth "an experimental Normal Ragged School," based on a system of his own devising in which "the boys would not be wearied to death, and driven away, by long Pulpit discourses. . . . They might be amused, instructed, and in some sort reformed," and "we should have some data to go upon."34 Unfortunately, he could not find adequate support for the plan.

In the spring of 1846 Miss Coutts suggested a project that struck a responsive chord with Dickens. There existed little interest in suppressing, let alone eliminating, the numerous London brothels, frequented mainly by the upper middle class, the leisure class, and foreigners, that specialized in male and female prostitution across a wide range of sexual interests. But the eyesore of widespread street solicitation at all hours, with pimps operating as openly as their employees, weighed heavily on the religious and middle-class conscience and on the nervous susceptibility of a culture that needed to define itself as moral. From the window of her mansion in Piccadilly, Miss Coutts could see prostitutes at work. From his childhood on, Dickens had noticed what he had a predilection for not avoiding, the exploited victims of a repressive culture in which chance often determined opportunity and social destiny. Prostitutes were a type of criminal. If they were intercepted at a young enough age they too could have their evil destiny averted. That they were women, often quite young, made the prospect of reformation even better. For he believed, and dramatized in his sketches and through Nancy in *Oliver Twist*, that "there is much more Good in Women than in Men, however Ragged they are," though "people are apt to think otherwise, because the outward degradation of a woman strikes them more forcibly than any amount of hideousness in a man."[35] Miss Coutts's idea was to create an "asylum" for "fallen women" whose purpose would be to help them renounce prostitution. For the plan to work, though, two questions had to be answered. What were they to become in a positive sense and how could the change be effected? During the next ten years, Dickens devoted considerable time and effort searching for the answers.

❦ 5 ❦

ON HIS RETURN FROM AMERICA IN JUNE 1842, THE SUNBURNED AUthor flew into the long-sought and warmly open arms of friends and family. England never seemed more familial. From Liverpool, he and Catherine had the delight of a surprise arrival one day earlier than expected. They stunned Macready and Forster. He scooped the excited, even bewildered, children into his arms, kissing them through the bars of the house gate, so eager was he to reestablish intimacy. The five-year-old Charley went into brief nervous convulsions from being "too glad." Attended by Dr. Elliotson, he recovered quickly. On the last day of the month, they moved back into Devonshire Terrace, where Dickens made it a practice to sit on a new rocking chair that he had brought from America, a symbol of his domesticity, and to sing comic songs "to a wondering and delighted audience" of admiring children. He warmly thanked Mrs. Macready, whom they never could thank "enough in all our lives," for looking after the children. Within days, the old intimacies and routines were resumed with all his friends. George Cruikshank came home from the elaborate dinner in Greenwich that Forster had organized to celebrate Dickens' return in Dickens' carriage, standing on his head, so drunk that "he was last seen, taking Gin with a Waterman." To a large group of celebratory diners Dickens good-humoredly hinted that the "great pleasure of going to America" was "the pleasure of coming back."[36]

Coming back was soon accompanied by the challenge of having to be at work again. He had been away from his desk for

over six months, and he had committed himself to write two
books, against which he had received a substantial advance to
pay the cost of his travels and the maintenance of his family.
Fortunately, he had the assistance of the lengthy letters he had
written to Forster for the purpose of helping with his travel
book. Having lied consistently to his hosts about his intentions,
he now had the unenviable task of revealing his disingenuous-
ness. The more sustained challenge, the novel on "English Life
and Manners" in twenty monthly parts, would have to wait
until *American Notes* had been written. Before starting, he wrote
and had printed a circular addressed to "British Authors and
Journals" stating that he would no longer negotiate with American publishers to provide them with early proofs of any of his
writings. Since he was paid a small sum for the advance proofs,
he intended this to be a statement that he would renounce any
profit at all rather than cooperate with a system that denied him
a reasonable return. The "American Sketches" that were "shaping themselves" in his head and the introductory chapter that
he had written by the middle of July were preceded by this
statement of principle and intention, reflecting his preoccupation with the local issue of most importance to him. He urged
his colleagues to do the same. His feelings about American materialism and immorality were additionally exacerbated by the
appearance on August 11, 1842, in the *New York Evening Tatler*,
edited by Walt Whitman, of a forged letter that Dickens had
purportedly written on July 15, which harshly denounced
American manners. Though he raged bitterly against the forgery, its main points, ironically, were sufficiently close to his to
be both an effective caricature and an anticipation of *American
Notes* and the American section of *Martin Chuzzlewit*, as if it
prefigured and even helped to shape what was to come.

   To his surprise, Forster and Macready found the first chapter of *American Notes* tactless and counterproductive, "preparing
the reader for a much greater amount of slaughter than he will
meet with." Dickens' anger at the forged letter had become the
subtext of an explicit attack. Reluctantly, he agreed to omit it.
By the end of July, before going to Broadstairs, despite taking
time to write his lengthy letter on the minds and collieries bill,
he had finished the first four chapters. In the glittering sunshine,
writing chapters six and seven, he found his ironic title, *Ameri-*

can Notes for General Circulation. While writing the account of Laura Bridgman, he took on "a new protege . . . a wretched deaf and dumb boy whom I found upon the sands the other day, half dead. . . ." Pleased by Forster's delight with the first volume, "working, tooth and nail," he had done the description of Niagara by the middle of September, the penultimate chapter on slavery by the end of the first week of October, and finished in ample time for an October 19 publication. By the beginning of November, pirated editions were being sold in New York, Boston, and Philadelphia.

In both England and America the book had a mixed, lukewarm reception. Neutral readers found it persistently dull. To American nationalists, it seemed another stage in the war between English superciliousness and American naturalness. To some British critics, it was inferior to previous accounts of American culture, an overpersonalized view with a touch of sanctimoniousness that said too much about the author and too little about the United States. Some of his English friends, like Macready, who thought the book mean-spirited, wished that he had not written it. To his New England friends, the Dickensian combination of humor, severity, and idealism were admirably and effectively used to denounce slavery and materialism. To radical abolitionists, the main targets were well chosen, the tone appropriately condemnatory though insufficiently serious.37 Some critics, though, were distressed by Dickens the novelist pretending to be Dickens the social analyst, grafting his fictional talents onto alien soil. With a strong belief in his own moral stance and intellectual powers, but with a weak historical perspective, Dickens presented personal responses as if they were general truths, as if his evocative powers as a novelist allowed him to read and dissect a culture in intellectual terms.

Ralph Waldo Emerson, writing in his journal in November, was at least partly correct. "Truth is not his object for a single instant. . . . As an account of America it is not [to] be considered for a moment. . . . We can hear throughout every page the dialogue between the author and his publisher, 'Mr Dickens the book must be entertaining,—that is the essential point. Truth! damn truth.'" Distorting Dickens as much as *American Notes* distorted America, Emerson had no sense of how incapable Dickens was of not believing that his version *was* the absolute truth. Longfellow, who read his copy in Dickens' study in October and who had recently gotten over an "attack of *anti-English* spleen," was able, fortunately, to respond almost as happily to *American Notes* as he did to the pleasure of being a guest at Devonshire Terrace. But Dickens' commitment to his version of the truth lost him other American friends An essay in the *Foreign Quarterly* on the inferiority of American poetry, written by Forster but closely identified with Dickens, seemed another gratuitous insult. The American sections of *Martin Chuzzlewit* bitingly tore at what had been only surface wounds. Some, like Poe, became hostile. Some, like Irving, distanced themselves quietly by forgoing opportunities to visit and ceasing to correspond. Others, like Felton and Colden, whatever their opinion of his depiction of America, remained firm friends. They may have been as tacitly forgiving as Longfellow must have been when Dickens disingenuously told him in late September 1842, anticipating his visit, that "I have decided (perhaps you know this?) to publish my American Visit."[38]

With eager hospitality, Dickens brought Longfellow together with his circle of London friends. At Drury Lane, they saw Macready perform and shook hands with the actor in his dressing room. Dickens introduced Longfellow to Maclise, Stanfield, and Cruikshank at dinner, to Rogers at breakfast, and, a few days later, when they dined at Macready's, to Carlyle, with whose social views Dickens increasingly identified, then to the ailing Thomas Hood, to whose home he brought both Longfellow and a copy of *American Notes.* Longfellow met Landor on a rapid visit to Bath the day before the American's departure, and of course Forster, the member of the Dickens circle with whom he became most intimate and with whom he sustained a long correspondence. He reminded Forster a few years later that the two of them had been "the jolliest of all the youths at Dickens's table in the autumn of '42."[39] Dickens rounded the circle of his hospitality by taking him, under police protection, on a night excursion through the most sordid London slums and on a day tour of Rochester and environs. When he saw Longfellow off at Bristol the day after the publication of *American Notes,* neither of them could have anticipated that their next meeting would be twenty-five years later.

Fortunately, there were also new English friendships,

more sustaining because of their proximity. The old circle tightened in some parts, loosened in others. The bond with Macready was strengthened by the test of Macready's own departure for America in September 1843. Fearing to contaminate his friend by their being seen together soon after the appearance of the American sections of *Chuzzlewit,* Dickens painfully forwent seeing him off at Liverpool. But the late-August farewell party that he hosted in Greenwich was a smashing success, with Dickens at his sociable and oratorical best and Macready responding "more feelingly than eloquently."

With Forster, differences of temperament remained complementary. If anything, their intimacy increased, with walks, rides, and night excursions, with dinners at Devonshire Terrace and at their clubs matched by impromptu dinners that Forster hosted at his crowded chambers in Lincoln's Inn Fields. Dickens often "mixed the salad." Forster's increasing bouts with illness, which had begun as early as 1837, particularly violent rheumatic fever, and the likelihood of a weak heart, made him feel even more keenly the value of this friend.[40]

Though the bond between Dickens and Maclise remained as strong as ever, the painter was becoming less reliable. With the death of his mother in 1842, he had grown increasingly moody and obsessive. Solipsistic, even reclusive, he disappeared for long periods either to work or to brood. At his best, he was a jovial, carousing companion. Often, though, he rejected activities and people. "I am very wretched in going away," Maclise complained, "for I hate strange houses and strange people. And I suppose I shall be expected to make myself agreeable." Dickens also saw less of the busy Talfourd, though they remained warmly cordial, despite Talfourd's vanity and his amusing deference to his pretentious, tyrannical wife. The companionship of the genial, undemanding Stanfield, whose health had weakened and whose commitment as a Catholic convert had strengthened, became even more valued. Having especially enjoyed Carlyle's company at Macready's dinner party, Dickens hoped they would come "to know each other *well.* "

The circle expanded significantly, though, with the addition of two new friends. One of them, the artist John Leech, he had had a brief correspondence with when, writing the early numbers of *Pickwick,* he had needed to replace Robert Seymour.

Leech had had great success providing illustrations to the new
comic weekly *Punch*. Appreciative of both Leech's and *Punch*'s
genius, Dickens soon found the shy, thin, sincere, and good-
natured artist, who also had an improvident father, a delightful
companion. Dickens met in 1843 Leech's employer at *Punch*, the
editor Mark Lemon, and the two quickly became warm friends.
Burly, fat, full-bearded, both humorous and passionate at the
same time, Lemon was a shrewd, thoughtful editor keen on
liberal social positions. Uncle Porpoise, as he came to be called,
was a dedicated paterfamilias. Like his new friend, he loved
good food and entertaining company. He found Dickens as fascinating as Dickens found him companionable.[41]
    With Forster, Stanfield, and Maclise, Dickens took a week-
long excursion into Cornwall in late October and early November 1842, partly as another ritual celebration of his return from
America by this community of friends, partly because he had it
in mind to begin his new novel in a stormy Cornish setting.
They went into Devonshire by railroad, then traveled by horse
and carriage, Dickens in charge of the schedule and the money,
Stanfield the navigating, Forster the luggage. "Having nothing
particular to do," Maclise sang songs. They ate, and drank, and
played. Descending into the depths of mines, Dickens pursued
his social interest in working conditions. They explored "earthy
old churches" and climbed "to the tops of giddy heights" below
which "the unspeakably green water was roaring." Maclise and
Stanfield sketched, so that "you would have sworn we had the
spirit of Beauty with us, as well as the Spirit of Fun.' The Spirit
of Fun was later expressed in Stanfield's watercolor of the four
friends climbing the formidable Logan Rock and Thackeray's
caricature of them in their traveling carriage, drawn after he
had heard embellished stories about their wild adventures.
    In the same spirit Dickens began his custom of celebrating
Christmas, community, and his eldest son's birthday at elaborate Twelfth Night parties at Devonshire Terrace. For the parties, he organized and participated in charades, magic shows,
pantomimes, and elaborate amateur theatricals put on with an
expertise that raised them to a professional level. Stanfield became the resident technical genius, first creating an elaborate
toy theatre for Charley, which his fascinated father spent hours
helping construct and playing with. At one party, at the Mac-

readys', Jane Carlyle was whirled across the crowded dance
floor by Forster, who had "seized her round the waist" and
"made" her dance after she had refused an importunate Dickens,
who had almost gone down on his knees to persuade her to waltz
with him. She rubbed dancing shoulders with Maclise, "the
gigantic Thackeray &c. &c. all capering like Maenades!!" When
she "cried out 'oh for the love of Heaven let me go! you are going
to dash my brains out,'" Forster replied, "'your *brains*!! who
cares about their brains *here*? *let them go!*'" A wildly enthusiastic
dancer, Dickens found dancing exercise and exorcism. The
Twelfth Night and other parties had many rhythms, including
speeches, champagne, fancy dress, and late-night revelry. At a
grand ball at the Procters', Catherine looked "splendid . . . in
pink and satin and Mr. Dickens in geranium and ringlets."[42] No
Twelfth Night party was complete without the slim novelist, an
enthusiastic amateur magician, putting on a highly professional
sleight-of-hand performance, with props and costumes, and the
tall, burly Forster playing straight man to the man of magic.
Like the manager of a play, he staged and directed parties with
imagination and creativity.

Back from Cornwall, he had begun "the agonies of plotting
and contriving . . . A New Tale of English Life and Manners,"
pacing up and down the house and irritably "smiting [his] forehead dejectedly." He quickly gave up the Cornwall setting.
After a tortured beginning, which produced a discursive first
chapter, he got himself and the novel on track, creating Pecksniff and Tom Pinch and the Chuzzlewit brood, proudly reading
the opening to Forster toward the end of the year and "blazing
away" at his "new book." The first number was published on
January 1, 1843. After an adequate start, the sales of the next few
numbers unexpectedly declined, making author and publisher
uncomfortable, the first time that a novel of his had lost readers
while in progress. Late in March, he resolved to send Martin to
America, which he probably had been pondering for months.
His fury and frustration with American criticism of him had
not been put into perspective by distance. Constant reminders,
after the publication of *American Notes*, of the viciousness of
American journalism kept him in the mood to strike back. He
often dreamed that he was "in America again . . . endeavouring
to get home in disguise," with "a dreary sense of the distance."

In a novel whose theme was the destructiveness of greed and selfishness, the depiction of his idealized English main character visiting the country of greed and hypocrisy writ large must have seemed to him not only appropriate but brilliant. There would be personal satisfaction in striking this blow, in stirring up the hornet's nest. The American reaction came swiftly and almost unanimously. "Martin has made them all stark staring raving mad across the water." Its strength shocked even Dickens, who wondered why the intelligent among the Americans could not see the truth in his portrait of American culture as essentially materialistic, immoral, greedy, hypocritical, and debased.43

Just as he tested American equanimity, so too his publisher tested his. In June 1843, disappointed at the sales of *Martin Chuzzlewit* and exercising his accountant's pervasive anxiety about business, Hall mumbled in a casual conversation that the firm might have to invoke the clause that allowed it to reduce his payments by fifty pounds per number if the sales fell beneath a given figure. With a "fire . . . burning" in his head, "so rubbed in the tenderest part of my eyeballs with bay-salt," Dickens had made up his mind by the next day that the publishers whom he had warmly praised for years as honest and honorable were actually rascals. "I am bent," he told Forster, "upon paying Chapman and Hall *down*." That Hall had no real desire to invoke the clause and apologized made no difference. As soon as he could manage it, Dickens would repay the advances and settle any outstanding accounts. "And when I have done that, Mr. Hall shall have a piece of my mind."44 Except for the Christmas book that he was to write in the autumn, while continuing with *Chuzzlewit,* he was not to publish with Chapman and Hall again until 1859. And when his financial expectations for *A Christmas Carol* were disappointed, in his general fury he unwarrantedly blamed them.

Some of his anger resulted from the still raw wound of financial vulnerability, the memories of his childhood poverty inseparable from the pressures of maintaining an expensive family and entourage on his earnings as a writer. He gave brief consideration to editing a new liberal newspaper, which would satisfy both his desire to speak more directly and influentially on social issues and his need to find additional sources of income. A reliable salary would be helpful. When the potential sponsors proved unreliable or nonexistent, he gave up the idea for the time being. His never completely quiescent father became an economic embarrassment again. Using his son's name, he sent begging letters to Chapman and Hall and to Coutts and Company. Charles had nightmares about him, his bitterness rising to the rhetoric of calling him a leech from whom he desperately desired to be relieved. "I am amazed and confounded by the audacity of his ingratitude. He, and all of them, look upon me as a something to be plucked and torn to pieces for their advantage. They have no idea of, and no care for, my existence in any other light. My soul sickens at the thought of them. . . . Nothing makes me so wretched, or so unfit for what I have to do, as these things. They are . . . such a drag-chain on my life, that for the time they utterly dispirit me, and weigh me down." He hated being manipulated into paying extra bills after the fact. He writhed in anguish at the knowledge that his father was using his name with people whose good opinion he feared losing. In addition to his parents, he was also heavily subsidizing his three brothers, his "blood-petitioners."[45] There would be another petitioner soon, this one of his own making. Catherine was pregnant again.

Conceived in March 1843 and born in January 1844, Francis Jeffrey Dickens was a blessing of the sort of which he wanted no more. "I am constantly reversing the Kings in the Fairy Tales, and importuning the Gods not to trouble themselves: being quite satisfied with what I have. But they are *so* generous when they *do* take a fancy to one!" Years and more children later, he used the same verbal turn with an additional bitter twist, giving "a patriarchal piece of advice" to a young female friend not to "have any more children. If the childless Kings and Queens in the stories had only known what they were about, they would never have bothered the Fairies to give them families." Competent in his business and social affairs, he was noticeably incompetent in managing his sexual life, perhaps because of some conflict, perhaps because of a failure of imagination. He jokingly expressed his unhappiness as if it were Catherine's fault, for "I hope *my* missis won't do so never no more: but that's nothing to the purpose."[46] More likely than not, she played no determinative role, by nature and culture trained to respond to her husband. Though they usually used the phrases playfully, jokingly, he was "Bully" and she was "Meek." Apparently he thought he preferred it that way.

With his sister Fanny he got on, as he did with Letitia, better than with most other members of his family. Unlike Letitia, adequately supported by Henry Austin, Fanny needed occasional financial help. Henry Burnett's and her own income from singing and music lessons had decreased since their move to Manchester. She soon had two sons, one of whom, Henry, was crippled. Charles's resentment of Fanny's being sent to school while he was left idle and then condemned to the blacking factory had long since disappeared or at least been submerged. When, in October 1843, he went "to be victimised on the altars of the Manchester Athenaeum," where he gave a speech celebrating the importance of educating the lower classes, similar to speeches he gave early the next year in Birmingham and Liverpool, he stayed with Fanny and her family."[47]

The lost sister of blessed memory, whom he had dreamed of every night, was still sacred in his feelings and memory. By late 1842, she "has been my better Angel six long years." Eager for another sister, he adopted a new one, encouraging the fifteen-year-old Georgina Hogarth, slightly younger than Mary had been when she joined his household, to live with them. He found a striking resemblance between Mary's "mental features" and Georgina's, for "so much of her spirit shines out in this sister, that the old time comes back again . . . and I can hardly separate it from the present." Her mother and Catherine apparently found the arrangement satisfactory. The dependable, lively, moderately pretty Georgina would find ways to make herself useful while freeing the Hogarth budget from one of a large number of debits. Dickens clearly had no inclination to complain in this case about the cost. Probably by autumn 1842, certainly by Christmas, she had become a regular member of the household, one of his two "Venuses." "When we were first married," he told Longfellow, "there *was* another." Unlike his mother, Georgina would never undervalue or reject him. Unlike Mary, she would never desert him, but would be a dependable companion for the rest of his life. Unlike Catherine, she was feminine without being sexual or maternal. She was also competent, physically graceful, and attractively thin. The new sister and the old were united in the faithful Ruth, the idealized sister of Tom Pinch in *Martin Chuzzlewit.* "As light of foot and heart as in old days," she sits down beside her "tranquil, calm, and happy" brother, who plays at the organ a "noble music" that rolls "round her in a cloud of melody, shuts out the grosser prospect of an earthly parting, and uplifts her" brother "to Heaven!"[48] In his own grosser world, though, he had become so obsessively restless that he had decided to travel abroad again, this time with the entire family. At the beginning of July 1844, the Dickens entourage left for Italy.

CHAPTER SIX

An Angelic Nature
(1844-1846)

❧ I ❧

DESPITE HIS FLAIR FOR FLAMING WAISTCOATS, LONG HAIR, AND gold chains, Dickens embraced authorship as a profession and marriage as an institution with the discipline of an upper-middle-class entrepreneur. He wore the gray regularity of Victorian sobriety much before he and his contemporaries turned in their bright clothes for dark evangelical seriousness. In the red waistcoats that his American hosts found "rowdy," he expressed that aspect of himself that Victorian discipline could not contain. Forcing himself to write regularly every morning from nine or ten to three in the afternoon, to harness the muse economically, to take care of a large correspondence, to make his organizing presence felt daily in the life of his household, to find ways to be useful to the larger community, he felt the strain of mediating between his energy and his narrow outlets, between the spontaneity and freedom of his imaginative life as an artist and the restraints of his domestic patterns and values.

By midafternoons, he was eager for long walks or rides, the

physical exertion that would exorcise his restlessness. In the evenings he would be pleasant though sometimes moody company at home, at his clubs, frequently at the theatre with Forster, Maclise, and Stanfield. Quick to anger, particularly when he thought himself attacked, he had "a strong spice of the Devil" in him. To protect against the pain of criticism, he made "a solemn compact" with himself not to read reviews. He boasted in 1843 that he had never deviated from "this Rule . . . for five years." His reaction to America in 1842 and his preoccupation during the next two years with its response to him revealed how much he underestimated his own intemperateness and obsessiveness. His restlessness expressed aspects of himself that he was unable to comprehend or control. He often felt "at a great loss for a means of blowing my superfluous steam off." He needed to exert himself to use his compulsions creatively. Particularly restless when in the early stages of a book, he could not absorb his energy fully into his imaginative activity. Writing sessions were often followed by self-dramatized hikes. His long walks became, at periods of special tension, marathons, whose point was exhaustion. "I performed an insane match against time of eighteen miles by the milestones in four hours and a half, under a burning sun the whole way. I could get no sleep at night, and really began to be afraid I was going to have a fever."[1]

He turned some of his restless energy toward falling in love in ways that did not threaten his domestic security. In his idealization of Mary Hogarth as the perfect sister of his soul, he found a way to spiritualize romantic love. His relationship with Catherine had had from the beginning little romance and less spirit. It was simply one of the necessary foundations of his adult self-definition as a successful member of the middle-class community, entitled to its respect and rewards. He was young, handsome, and famous. He was also, by 1840, the father of three children, the support of a substantial establishment, and the husband of a frequently pregnant wife who settled quickly into the slack life of guaranteed fidelity. He felt the power of his attractiveness to people in general, to women in particular. With an eye for beauty, with a need to be appreciated, with a strong impulse to get from others the admiration that he felt his mother had denied him, he could be as romantic in flirtations as he could be businesslike in his work. He rarely resisted pretty women.

Between the ages of thirteen and twenty-three he had broken his "heart into the smallest pieces, many times." What he referred to as his "very small Cupid" became active again in the 1840s Before going to Broadstairs in 1840, he met twenty-year-old Eleanor Picken, "known as Emma," at the home of his friend Charles Smithson, Thomas Mitton's partner. An aspiring artist and the daughter of a minor Scottish writer, the blond-haired, attractive, lively Emma accepted the invitation of her relative, Mrs. Smithson, to spend the summer with the family in Broadstairs. Eager to surround himself with friends, Dickens found a house for the Smithsons next door to his own. With self-parodic intensity, conflating life and the theatre, he flirted with Emma and pretended to be in love with her red-haired friend Millie. This "sentimental flirtation" combined exaggerated rhetoric with uncontrolled energy in which the multileveled performance spoke of self-consciousness and deep disquiet.

One evening at dusk, on the pier, after they had been dancing, "he was in high spirits." Filled with "a demon of mischief," as if possessed—so Emma described it years later—he suddenly "flung his arm around me and whirled with me down the inclined plane of the jetty towards a . . . pole . . . at the extreme end," where "he intended to hold me . . . till the wild waves overwhelmed us." Gripping her tightly, despite her screams, as if acting one of his favorite roles, he urged her to " 'let your mind dwell on the column in the *Times* wherein will be vividly described the pathetic fate of the lovely Emma P——, drowned by Dickens in a fit of dementia! Don't struggle. Poor little bird! you are powerless in the claws of such a kite. . . . Think of the sensation we shall create!' " Cold and frightened, her "*best* dress," her "*only* silk dress," about to be ruined by the water that surged over their feet, she shrieked, " 'Mrs. Dickens! help me!— make Mr. Dickens let me go. The waves are up to my knees!' " " 'Charles! . . . How can you be so silly? You will both be carried off by the waves . . . and you'll spoil the poor girl's silk dress.' " He responded parodically with the rhetoric of romantic melodrama—" 'Dress! . . . Talk not to me of *dress*! When the pall of night is . . .' " Struggling "out of his grasp," she fled to her friends, "almost crying with vexation." They greeted her with quiet disapproval, as if she were responsible for the incident. After marrying the next summer, she saw less of Dickens, though she became warmly friendly with his brother Frederick. In Broadstairs, when not flirting or working, Dickens amused himself in the evenings with elaborate charades and vigorous dancing, in which Fred competed with him. "I feel that I could act a pompous ass to perfection! Let us get up some charades, and test our histrionic powers!"[2]

The bright beauty of Frances Colden, whom he "would go five hundred miles to see . . . for five minutes," remained in his mind's eye long after he had last seen her in New York. There was an advantage to falling in love with married women whose husbands might be sufficiently honored by his playful amorousness to accept it as both the price and the confirmation of friendship. His passions were often public performances, at dinners, in letters, both ostensible artifice and emotionally real, because, to him, performance was everything. Mrs. Colden had joined Catherine and the other select ladies who were permitted to hear the speeches at the New York dinner for Dickens. Though often irritated by such requests, he had taken the opportunity of responding to her plea, conveyed by Catherine, for a lock of his hair, not only sending it but having it set in a small brooch accompanied by a flirtatious letter. To Maclise, experienced in falling in love with beautiful women, he could put his passion into perspective, for "David Colden is as good a fellow as ever lived; and I am deeply in love with his wife." In a letter to her husband, he could refer to Frances as "the beloved Mrs. Colden, if I may make so bold as to trust that expression to your keeping." To Mrs. Colden, "My better Angel," he could write deeply expressive comic letters, signed "CupiD," urging her to "take no heed" of her husband. The passion of his romantic feeling often was socialized by its humorous rhetoric. He concluded a three-stanza comic "Love Song" with

> But vain reflection! who could rear,
> On scaffold, pier, or starling,
> A creetur half so bright or dear,
> As my unmentioned Darling!
> No artist in the World's broad ways

Could ever carve or mould 'un,
That might aspire to lace the stays
Of charming Mrs.......3

By wish and proxy, such erotic lacings came easily to the novelist. As words, they made dangerous realities into acceptable fictions. As passions, they were never acted on physically. As feelings, they expressed his desire to love and be loved in an active, spontaneous way, the romance that his marriage did not provide.

When he entered the large assembly hall of the Mechanics' Institute in Liverpool to take the chair in late February 1844, the organist played "See the Conquering Hero Come." It was Dickens, though, who was soon conquered by the piano soloist, Christiana Weller. Preoccupied the previous November and December with *A Christmas Carol* and *Martin Chuzzlewit*, he had persuaded the Liverpool committee to postpone their annual Christmas soiree so they could have a speech from him on the importance of education for the working class. "Rustling like the leaves of a wood," in an absolutely packed hall, the "ladies . . . in full dress and immense numbers," 1,300 people rose to receive him. The enormous place was decorated with flowers and "Welcome Boz . . . in letters about six feet high." Resplendent in a "white and black or magpie waistcoat," he created an immense sensation. His message, from his favorite contemporary poet, was that "Kind hearts are more than coronets," a fitting theme for a working-class educational movement that his life and fiction embodied. Meeting the nineteen-year-old piano prodigy for the first time, his kind heart responded strongly. In introducing Christiana to the audience, he remarked that he felt "some difficulty and tenderness in announcing her name." Within twenty-four hours he went from keeping "his eyes firmly fixed on her every movement" to telling his friend Thomas James Thompson, "Good God what a madman I should seem if the incredible feeling I have conceived for that girl could be made plain to anyone!"4

The previous February, her father, eager to elicit his support, had brought the name of his talented daughter to Dickens' attention. Christiana had been appearing with her elder sister as a child prodigy since 1834, with immediate success for her "brilliancy of execution." Strikingly attractive, her "highly prepossessing appearance" added an irresistible dimension to her musical skills. That night, at the town hall, Dickens also met her father, Thomas Weller, and the next day he *"invited himself"* and his friends to lunch at the Weller home.5 The friends included Thompson, whom he had met in 1838. A widower with two children who had been left a fortune by his Liverpudlian grandfather on the condition that he never work, Thompson enjoyed the best of London life and continental travel, a comfortable, cultured man who collected books and art. Though he and Dickens were of the same age and shared a passion for liberal reform, Thompson was free not only to fall in love but to act on his desire.

As soon as he left Liverpool, Dickens confided to Thompson that he could not even joke about Christiana. "For she is too good; and interest in her . . . has become a sentiment with me." He had no doubt, though, that his obsession would make him appear a madman to "sober people." From London, "perfectly exhausted, dead, worn-out, and Spiritless," he confided to his sister that his happy recollection of Christiana "has its tortures too." His depression resulted partly from separating himself from her. But the huge audiences that had "been driving [him] mad at Liverpool and Birmingham, with their loving cheers" had also allowed him to feel how pleasurable it is "to walk out of the room where one is shut up for so many hours of such a short life, into a sea of agitated faces, and think that they are always looking on." One face from that necessary audience looked at him with loving distinctness. He added to the amorous verses he had written in her scrapbook a volume of Tennyson's poems, "given to me by Tennyson himself," with an assurance that he would do anything in his power to help "the spiritual creature" who "started out alone from the whole crowd the instant I saw her, and will remain there always in my sight." A week later, Thompson, who had stayed on in Liverpool, confided to Dickens that *he* had fallen in love with Christiana. As Dickens read the letter, he "felt the blood go from my face to I don't know where, and my very lips turn white. I never in my life was so surprised, or had the whole current of my life so stopped, for the instant."6

Shocked partly because he had not imagined that Thompson could be as passionate as himself, he had mistaken either Thompson's nature or the power of love. He also felt both a proprietary right to Christiana and the superior enduring power of his attachment to her, as if his special ability to possess her permanently in his imagination counterbalanced his inability to have her physically. "I know that in many points I am an excitable and headstrong man, and ride O God what prancing hobbies!—and although I knew that the impression she had made on me was a true, deep, honest, pure-spirited thing, I thought my nature might have been prepared to receive it, and to exaggerate it unconsciously, and to keep it green long after such a fancy as I deemed it probable you might have conceived had withered." Suddenly shifting emotional gears, he responded to Thompson's request for advice and encouragement in the face of a hesitant Christiana and a resistant father with his own unreserved expression of what he would do if he were in Thompson's position. He would attempt to "win her if I could, by God," immediately! "I would answer it to myself, if my world's breath whispered me that I had known her but a few days, that hours of hers are years in the lives of common women."7 Though he had taken much of a year to court his earthy wife, he would condense a year into days for Christiana.

With resonances of the fate of Mary Hogarth, he saw in her the likelihood of an early death. He had seen "an angel's message in her face that day that smote me to the heart." There is no evidence, though, that she had any illness other than in his imagination. That fear should be used, he advised his friend, to persuade her possessive father that her best chance was for Thompson to take her to Italy, where "repose, change, a mind at rest, a foreign climate would be, in a springtime like hers, the dawning of a new existence." Having himself decided to go to Italy, he urged Thompson, for Christiana's sake, to take her there for "the quiet happiness we might enjoy abroad, all of us together, in some delicious nook. . . . Such Italian Castles, bright in sunny days, and pale in moonlight nights, as I am building in the air!" Thompson married Christiana Weller in October 1845. The novelist attended the wedding, wearing a bright waistcoat in which, he joked, he would *"Eclipse* the Bridegroom."8 Despite Dickens' disapproval, Frederick was to marry Christiana's younger sister in 1848. Though Christiana and her husband eventually came to Italy, it was after he had already left. That she lived to the age of eighty-five is not likely to have had anything to do with his "Italian castles" and his rescue fantasy.

❧ 2 ❧

WHEN IN AMERICA IN 1842, HE HAD LONGED TO BE AT HOME AGAIN. Within a year of his return, he mentioned to a French visitor plans for a visit to France he was to make shortly. While the visitor had no sense of the relationship between Dickens' inner life and his public performances, he intuitively saw in his appearance the possibility for role playing and alternative lives. For "the most popular novelist of the day" could easily have been taken for "the head clerk of a big banking house, a smart reporter of an assize court, the secret agent of a diplomatic intrigue, an astute and wily barrister, a lucky gambler, or simply the manager of a troupe of strolling players."9 At one time or another, he played some version of all these roles, except, perhaps, the lucky gambler. The one that he most self-consciously cast himself as was "the manager of a troupe of strolling players."

He was always, though, the head clerk of a private banking house. William Hall's careless reference to the penalty clause in the contract for *Martin Chuzzlewit* began the chain of events that led to his decision in November 1843 to go abroad for a year. But the inclination preceded the economic considerations. If he had made sufficient money from that novel, he would have unquestionably faded "away from the public eye for a year" to enlarge his "stock of description and observation" by seeing new countries before his family got any larger. "Already for some time I have had this hope and intention before me." With some French but no Italian, he and Catherine began to take Italian lessons from Luigi Mariotti, an Italian writer in exile whom he had met on the *Brittania* and who described him as "a bright-eyed, ready-witted, somewhat gushing, happy man, cheered by the world's applause, equally idolised by his wife . . . children . . . every member of his family." At first, the happy man thought he would leave his publication arrangements intact, rent his house, settle with a small entourage in someplace

"CHEAP and in a delightful climate, in Normandy or Brittany," and then travel throughout France and Italy. He would write a travel book, based on letters he would send to Forster, just as he had done when he had visited America, or perhaps send letters from abroad for publication in the *Morning Chronicle* or another newspaper. Anticipating Forster's objections, he granted that "leaving England, home, friends, everything I am fond of," would be painful, "but it seems to me, at a critical time, *the* step to set me right."[10]

Having been insulted by Hall, Dickens himself had stubbornly insisted on invoking the penalty clause. By the spring of 1844, he had decided to find another publisher, though Chapman and Hall would have been happy to provide him with anything that a new publisher would. Bradbury and Evans, Chapman and Hall's printer, hesitantly offered to take him on, with the hope that he would also edit a journal for them. Having run a flourishing printing business since 1830, they had no experience publishing books. Known as "the keenest man of business that ever trod the flags of Fleet Street," Frederick Evans was the junior partner. The senior partner, William Bradbury, a tall bright-spectacled, good-humored, Pickwickian figure, fit in well with the staff of *Punch*, one of a number of periodicals that the firm owned. Admiring Dickens' work and its popularity, they had become part of his outer circle of professional friends, attending the *Nickleby* dinner in 1839 and since then presenting the Dickens family annually with a Christmas turkey.

Soon they extended this seasonal association. *A Christmas Carol* had been a popular success in 1843. The unexpectedly small profits, though, disappointed him, and he had to borrow money. Furious, he blamed Chapman and Hall for inflating the cost of production, though he himself had dictated the format, and bungling the advertising, which Bradbury self-servingly referred to as "fatal negligence." Having told Chapman and Hall to "keep away from me—and be damned," he negotiated a contract with Bradbury and Evans ironically similar to the arrangement that he had made with Chapman and Hall four years earlier when he had wanted help in freeing himself from Bentley. On June 1, 1844, his new publisher agreed to advance him £2,800 against the security of a £2,000 life insurance policy and for "a fourth share in whatever he might write during the next

. . . eight years."[11] His share in copyrights held jointly with his former publisher or by himself were turned over partly or in whole to Bradbury and Evans. With the ongoing income from some properties remaining with Chapman and Hall, from the money advanced to him by Bradbury and Evans, from the anticipated income from the book based on his Italian visit, the new Christmas book, and a cheap edition of his works, he had the money both to pay Chapman and Hall the £1,500 he owed them and to live abroad for a year.

The necessary preliminaries were disposed of: finishing *Chuzzlewit*, the last double installment done by the middle of June 1844; rapidly renting Devonshire Terrace and moving into a rented house for three weeks; attending Christiana's concert at the Royal Academy, where, years before, while still a drudge in the blacking warehouse, he had heard Fanny perform. He also took a few days recreational yachting on Albany Fonblanque's yacht, despite his tendency to seasickness, and said hasty good-byes to friends and acquaintances. He said farewell en masse in Greenwich to over forty people on June 11 at a dinner that Forster had arranged. His intimate circle attended, except Macready, who was in America, as well as his extended community, most of whom two years before he had been so eager to return to. For reasons of health, Tennyson and Bulwer declined. Thackeray, who was in Ireland, could not attend. Carlyle also stayed away "from the inconvenience of a noisy, crowded dinner in Greenwich in the dog-days," though "I truly love Dickens; and discern in the inner man of him a tone of real Music." Unexpectedly, brought by Stanfield, "the great painter Turner" came. He "had enveloped his throat, that sultry summer day, in a huge red . . . handkerchief which nothing would induce him to remove. He was not otherwise demonstrative, but enjoyed himself in a quiet silent way, less perhaps at the speeches than at the quiet lights on the river."[12]

Having made up his mind to "see the world," Dickens bustled off to Dover in the "Magnificent Carriage" that he had purchased to carry his party of twelve. With them was a highly recommended courier, Louis Roche, a vigorous Frenchman whose skills and companionship he profited from and enjoyed throughout the year and on his next European trip. On June 2, 1844, they crossed the Channel. At Boulogne, proud of his French, which was more literary than conversational, he asked a bank clerk at length for currency and was answered in perfect English, " 'How would you like to take it, sir?' " The party spent two delightful but hectic days in Paris, which made "an immense impression" on him. He thought it "the most extraordinary place in the World" and promised himself that he would return for a substantial visit. The entourage descended by road to Chalon sur-Saône and then by steamboat to Lyons, "a great Nightmare . . . a fit of indigestion . . . an awful place." Finally, via a dusty road, they made their way to "dirty and disagreeable" Marseilles. There they had their first sight "of the beautiful Mediterranean." Dickens was already beginning to feel the benefits of change, the widening of vision, the heightening of perception. "Surrounded by strange and perfectly novel circumstances, I feel as if I had a new head on side by side with my old one." By late the next afternoon they "were steaming out in the open sea. The vessel was beautifully clean; the meals were served under an awning on deck; the night was calm and clear; the quiet beauty of the sea and sky, unspeakable."¹³

Coasting close to the shore, they passed Nice the next morning. In the afternoon, their destination came into view in the distance, Genoa, bright and beautifully cupped in the curve of its sparkling bay. It had been chosen by a confused, ill-informed process of recommendation and elimination. Angus Fletcher, the sculptor who had joined them in the Highlands, was waiting at the dock, and temporarily settled with them in a "perfectly lonely, rusty, stagnant, old . . . pink jail." the Villa Bagnerello in the suburb of Albaro, two miles from Genoa. The impractical sculptor, who was living in Italy, had rented it for an absurdly high sum. Its main advantage was a magnificent view of the Gulf of Genoa, the Alps on one far horizon, hills with forts on another, and the ocean right beneath them. "You go through the courtyard, and out at the gate, and down a narrow lane to the sea." Dickens' senses reeled with the perfume of the orange trees, the profusion of grapevines, the panorama of rose leaves, the intense blue of the sky, the "impatient and fierce" sun. The disorientation was delightful. The unfamiliar, despite the heat, was bracing. He felt "something of the lofty spirit of an exile. . . . I don't exactly know what I have done for my country in coming away from it, but I feel it is something, something great—something virtuous and heroic."¹⁴

Genoa, and Italy itself, seemed neither noble nor heroic. At first, it was not even comfortable. The city that had seemed so resplendent in the distance, on closer view was "mouldy, dreary, sleepy, dirty, lagging, halting, God-forgotten. . . ." Italy was still in the malaise of centuries, an unprofitable colony caught between Austrian occupation and French influence, divided into principalities, with most of its patriots, like Giuseppe Mazzini, in exile. To the Whiggishly liberal Dickens it was "a country gone to sleep, and without the prospect of waking again! . . . It seemed as if one had reached the end of all things— as if there were no more progress, motion, advancement, or improvement of any kind beyond; but here the whole scheme had stopped centuries ago, never to move on any more, but just lying down in the sun to bask there, 'till the Day of Judgment." He had no desire, though, to be political. He had no issues or ideals to exercise. Whereas he had had great expectations about republican America, he had no illusions about Austrian-occupied Catholic Italy. What reputation had promised—natural beauty, warm climate, ancient ruins, compliant people, cheap prices—Italy fulfilled. It also provided immense flies and mosquitoes, rudimentary sanitation, and intense heat during the summer months, which he either had not been warned against or had not taken warnings of seriously enough. Despite the heat and the inevitable tiredness after settling in, he managed enough energy to remember that he had a new Christmas book to write, which it would be best to do in August, September, and October, and to make general plans to travel through northern Italy in November, to go to Rome and Naples in February, to return to Rome for Easter, and then to spend a month in Paris before returning to England. Meanwhile, for the first time in his life, he enjoyed being lazy, going about "in a dreamy sort of way," reclining "on the rocks in the evening, staring the blue water out of countenance," strolling up the narrow lanes, and watching "the lizards running up and down the walls."[15]

Setting himself up to write each morning in the most attractive bedroom in the house, he was only a little nervous when it became clear that the writing was hardly coming at all. "The sun is off the corner window . . . by a very little after twelve; and I can then throw the blinds open, and look up from my paper, at the sea, the mountains, the washed-out villas, the vineyards. . . . It is a very peaceful view, and yet a very cheerful one.

Quiet as quiet can be." Soon it seemed too quiet, oppressively quiet. There was entertainment in Genoa: the commercial streets, the Teatro Carlo Felici, the puppet theatre, the English church, dancing parties at the French consel general's, entrée to the diplomatic and the British community. In Albaro, there was recreation, particularly swimming, whose pleasures he discovered for the first time, enlivened by outlandish costumes and Fletcher's amusingly absurd performances. "He always gives a horrible yell, when he first puts his foot in the sea . . . with his very bald head & his very fat body; limping over the sharp rocks in a small, short, tight pair of striped drawers."

In the midst of all these amusements, Dickens' five-year-old daughter, Katie, suddenly became seriously ill. Cuddling against the ministering hand of her father, she allowed no one else to give her medicine. With his usual seriocomic self-definition, he had for a few years already been referring to himself as "the physician." After a very difficult time of it, Katie gradually recovered. Dickens attempted to heal himself as well when, late in August, for no ostensible reason, he had "a short but sharp attack of illness," severe pain associated with the renal colic of his childhood. "It came on with the old unspeakable and agonizing pain in the side and yielded quickly to powerful remedies."[16]

His calls to friends now went out regularly, urgent invitations to Mitton, Maclise, Stanfield, Forster, even Edward Tagart, his minister at the Little Portland Street Unitarian Church, who had mentioned the possibility of traveling to Italy. The one certain visitor for a stay of a few weeks was his brother Fred, whose dandyish instinct he tempted by telling him that " 'Boots' are cheap here; and you can't do better than come and buy 'em." In the second week of September 1844, he was happy to have the excuse to travel by steamer to Marseilles to meet and escort Fred back, introducing him en route to "fleas of elephantine dimensions . . . gambolling boldly in the dirty beds" of the inns they stopped at. Having grown a moustache, he was annoyed to see that Fred had grown one also. "Either he or I must fall. Earth will not hold us both." Though they returned to Albaro, where Fred almost drowned on his first swim in the bay, Dickens had already arranged to move on the first of October into the Palazzo Peschiere in the heart of Genoa, an immense villa with painted walls and ceilings, with "a great vaulted roof higher than that of the Waterloo Gallery in Windsor Castle" and surrounded by the most delightful gardens, which he claimed would be easier to heat than the "pink jail" and which he had gotten cheaply. He needed more noise, more life, the semblance if not the fact of streets. "I seem as if I had plucked myself out of my proper soil when I left Devonshire-terrace; and could take root no more until I returned to it."17 He still found it difficult, even after having moved into town, to get started on his new Christmas book.

Before moving, he had been briefly ill again, with rheumatism in his back "and knotted round my waist like a girdle of pain." After being awake most of the night, he had a frightening dream in which "poor Mary's spirit" appeared, "full of compassion and sorrow" for him, the first time he had dreamed of her since February 1838. That she had the greatest compassion for him cut him "to the heart," as if he were unworthy of her love. He asked her, " 'What is the True religion?' " a question he afterward speculated had been prompted partly by there being an altar in his bedroom, partly by his having listened to the bells from a local convent before falling asleep, partly by his having had the subject of Catholicism on his mind in general. Perhaps, he prompted her, afraid that she might go away, " 'the Roman Catholic is the best'? . . . 'For *you,*' said the Spirit, full of such heavenly tenderness for me, that I felt as if my heart would break; 'for *you,* it is the best!' " Awakening with the tears running down his face, he "called up Kate, and repeated it three or four times over, that I might not unconsciously make it plainer or stronger afterwards. . . . I wonder whether I should regard it as a dream, or an actual Vision."18 Having invested in Mary an idealization of womanhood that invoked the Roman Catholic idealization of another Mary and of the mother church, in his dream, Mary, the eternal woman, is his guide, his adviser, his protector. Her compassion pained him because it implied his unworthiness, the distance between himself and such a heavenly creature, the tension between the flirtatious man of earthly passions and the man who defined himself as a noble soul in pursuit of the highest ideals.

Ruminating on the Christmas book that he still could not write, he had the supernatural on his mind. The previous fall he had found a topic that embodied his desire to create both a powerful social statement, "a Sledge hammer" that would respond to the abysmal treatment of the poor, and something appropriate for the Christmas season. With the encouragement of Chapman and Hall, he had created a new minor genre, the Christmas book, soon almost exclusively associated with his name. Published in mid-December 1843, *A Christmas Carol* was "a prodigious success." While writing, he was "very much affected by [it] and had an interest in the idea, which made me reluctant to lay it aside for a moment." Moralizing and Christianizing traditions of the supernatural drawn from Gothic fiction, he had created a social fable in which the supernatural structure of spirits and demons was taut enough not to offend Christians and loose enough to be acceptable to secularists.

Having been brought up in a nominally Anglican household, he associated organized religion with stale custom at best, with repressive fanaticism at worst. He aspired to a religion of the heart that transcended sectarian dogma. To the extent that he was habituated to Anglicanism, he sometimes found it benign enough to provide him an institutional way of expressing his admiration for the moral and religious example set by the life of Jesus. His novels resonate with phrases from the Bible and the Book of Common Prayer, whose ritual affirmations of eternal life moved him deeply. At the same time, he was aggressively anticlerical, antidogmatic, and antisectarian. While not a rationalist, he wanted a reasonable religion that would not try common sense with excessive emphasis, let alone reliance, on miracles like the Trinity, the Virgin Birth, and transubstantiation. In the context of liberal protestantism, he desired Jesus to be understood as an extraordinary human being rather than as the son of God. Searching for a community in which to express such views, in the winter of 1842–43 he had become a member of Tagart's Unitarian congregation. "Disgusted with our Established Church, and its Puseyisms, and daily outrages on common sense and humanity, I have carried into effect an old idea of mine, and joined the Unitarians, who *would* do something for human improvement, if they could; and who practise Charity and Toleration."[19]

Whether or not Mary's appearance was a dream or "an actual vision" made no difference. He believed in dreams as embodiments of truth, of the imagination as the force that made invisible realities visible, attesting to the external reality of what the imagination perceived. Since 1838, he had been a believer in mesmerism or animal magnetism, whose major tenet was that there existed a physical though invisible force, like electricity, that accounted for experiences and phenomena reason and science could not explain.[20] It brought him into closer contact with and encouraged a greater awareness of his unconscious life, providing a useful series of assumptions and metaphors about relationships between people and about cosmic givens that he gradually absorbed into his fiction. If magnetic force was ultimately amenable to rational investigation, the force itself and other such powers were the threshold to a sufficient credibility for the heavenly, the immortal, and the supernatural to allow at least occasional belief in a transcendent world. *A Christmas Carol*, though, did not *demand* more than the willing suspension of disbelief. The central emphasis was on human psychology and the felt realities of this world, the poverty, misery, miserliness, and misshapings as well as the generosity, lovingness, and redemptive capacities of the human heart.

Summoning up all his willful stubbornness, he stared at his blank sheet of paper on a morning in early October 1844. Unpredictably, "in one fell sound," the loud discordant noise of every church bell in Genoa suddenly seemed clanging, clashing, rushing through his ears and spinning his head and his unsettled ideas "in a whirl of vexation and giddiness." Suddenly he had his title and his story. "We have heard THE CHIMES at midnight, Master Shallow," he wrote to Forster. But he felt a restraint, a resistance. "Put me down on Waterloo-bridge at eight o'clock in the evening with leave to roam about as long as I like, and I would come home . . . panting to go on. I am sadly strange as it is, and can't settle." Soon, though, he had his "steam very much up," partly because his story possessed him, partly because he had decided that the distance between Genoa and London was not so great. "My whole heart is with you *at home,*" he wrote to Macready, who had just returned from America. By mid-October, when he sent Forster the first of what were to be four sections and a detailed overview, he had decided that he would add to his planned November touring schedule an additional journey that would bring him to London and the arms of his friends in early December.

The new Christmas book would be "a great blow for the poor Something powerful . . . but . . . tender too, and cheerful; as like the *Carol* in that respect as may be, and as unlike it as such a thing can be." Now, "in regular, ferocious excitement with the *Chimes*," he was up each morning at seven. After his cold shower, which he took each morning the moment he got out of bed, and then breakfast, he was at his desk, blazing away, "wrathful and red-hot, until three o'clock or so." All his "affections and passions got twined and knotted up in it." Given to self-dramatization outside as well as within his stories, he described himself as looking as "haggard as a Murderer." By the third of November, with full work days and many long walks in constant heavy rain, he had finished, "thank God," and had had a "good cry. . . . I believe I have written a tremendous Book; and knocked the Carol out of the field," though at the cost of almost having worn himself "to Death" by work and sleeplessness.

He was "still in the same mind about coming to London." Among other things, he wanted to have the emotional reward of seeing the faces of his dearest friends respond to his reading *The Chimes*. Placing great importance on the affective quality of his writing, he felt a compelling desire to see his audience's reaction to what he had written. Immersed in a solitary activity, he populated his fictional world with communities whose vividness and companionability paralleled the community for which he wrote, beginning with his family, his intimate friends, his extended circle, and then the audience of the English reading world as a whole. Like an actor, he wanted the pleasure of spontaneous applause, the immediate confirmation of his command of other people's feelings. In Genoa, now with only Catherine and Georgina on whom to try it out, he felt keenly the absence of immediate responses. Even with the addition of a few friends from the foreign community, the circle was too small. He confessed to Forster that he wanted "to inflict the little story . . . on dear old gallant Macready with my own lips, and to have Stanny and the other Mac sitting by." He particularly wanted Jane Carlyle present, whose "judgment would be invaluable," and Carlyle himself, whose recent book, *Past and Present*, he had read closely and whose criticism of British materialism had influenced the writing of *The Chimes*. He anticipated that to the extent that Carlyle would like the "radical" tendencies of his story, to that extent English Toryism would be outraged and hostile. Lonely, homesick, filled with an "unspeakable restless something," he urged Forster to "get up a little circle for me, one wet evening, when I come to town."[22]

Arriving in London on November 30, 1844, after three weeks traveling through northern Italy and France with Roche, he "rushed into the arms of Mac and Forster." The journey had been exorcism for his restlessness, the exhaustion that would give him energy. He had never "seen so much, and travelled so hard," from Genoa to Parma, Florence, Venice, Bologna, Cremona, Milan, Fribourg, Strasbourg, and then Paris. Venice had overwhelmed him, a reality so surreal that not even the imagination could fully comprehend it. Only the metaphor of the dream experience could give language to what was inexpressible. Venice, though, "is beyond the fancy of the wildest dreamer." He entered "*the* wonder of the world" by night, the "dreamy, beautiful, inconsistent, impossible, wicked, shadowy, damnable old place." When he stood in the piazza on the morning of November 12, "in the bright, cold, bracing day . . . by Heaven the glory of the place was insupportable!" On the road, dust, dirt, and rain, uncomfortable carriages and long, unbroken stages. In the towns, mediocre to bad accommodations, swearing innkeepers, urban decay, peeling frescoes, decaying monuments, medieval ugliness, boring tourists.

There had been occasional pleasures: chapels, works of art, quiet villages, courteous warmth. In Verona, he read *Romeo and Juliet*. In Milan, he admired the Corso, the cathedral, and, after the opera, a ballet called *Prometheus* at the "splendid theatre of La Scala." Soon "the Alps, stupendously confused in lofty peaks and ridges, clouds and snow, were towering in [his] path," in the immediate distance the lovely islands of Lake Maggiore. His eyes tingling with the cold, he was dazzled by the snow in the daytime and at night by "the brightest moon I ever saw." Crossing the Simplon Pass, he exalted in "daybreak on the summit . . . the Glory of which, making great wastes of snow, a rosy red: exceeds all telling."[23] Hardly sleeping except in carriages, he was ahead of the schedule that he had told Forster he would not fall behind, whatever the obstacles. On the twenty-eighth he was in Paris, which seemed "better than ever," but disappointed not to find Macready there. Eager to cross the Channel, within twenty-four hours he was in London.

The first reading of the *The Chimes* had already taken place. Having authorized them to adapt it for the stage, he had had Forster read it to Gilbert à Beckett, a journalist and dramatist, and probably Mark Lemon, both of whom had been shown advance sheets. Known for his self-control, Beckett "cried so much, and so painfully, that Forster didn't know whether to go on or stop." On Sunday, the first of December, Dickens read it to Macready, who could not be present at the long-planned reading at Forster's chambers. The most stringently professional public performer in his circle was "undisguisedly sobbing and crying on the sofa, as I read— . . . what a thing it is to have Power." On Tuesday, he read it at Lincoln's Inn Fields to a roomful of friends, including Carlyle, Stanfield, Douglas Jerrold, Laman Blanchard (a veteran journalist and literary figure), his brother Frederick, and Maclise, who made a sketch of the scene. "There was not a dry eye in the house. . . I do not think," the painter wrote to Catherine, "that there ever was such a triumphant hour for Charles . . . for every face was either extended into the broadest possible of grins, or else altogether hidden behind [a] handkerchief."

On Thursday, after dinner at Forster's, he read it again, to a smaller group, including Fonblanque, who, as editor of *The Examiner*, was among those he hoped would be stirred into action by his humanitarian plea for social justice. It was as if he could not read it enough, like the Ancient Mariner, with a tale to tell and a compulsive need to have an audience. He boasted to Fanny that this "staggerer of a book" that he had written "for Christmas . . . has made a decided effect upon a very difficult audience to whom I have read it here." Even "the printers have laughed and cried over it strangely. . . . When you come towards the end of the 3rd part you had better send upstairs for a clean pocket handkerchief."[24] When he left London a few days later, with the illustrations by Stanfield, Maclise, and Leech at the printers, publication set for December 14 and the stage adaptation to open on December 18, he could have reminded himself that the very different Tory audience, from the London *Times* on down, were likely neither to laugh nor to cry.

To his and his publisher's delight, it was an outstanding

commercial success. Still optimistic about such things, he maintained the illusion that, like *A Christmas Carol, The Chimes* also had made its mark in the public arena of humanitarian reform. If it did, it was only as a modest contribution to the century-long modification of the sensibility of the English ruling class that eventually allowed sympathy for suffering and deprivation to balance economic self-interest and class distinctions. The private readings, though, were an immense personal success. They strengthened his sense of the gratification available in direct contact with an audience. Whereas before he had acted only other people's words, now he had seen that his own could be transformed into dramatic performances that would combine the pleasure he had felt when raised onto the table to perform comic songs for his father and his father's friends and that derived from the most direct dissemination of himself as a serious author. Before leaving London, in this glow of acting enthusiasm, he had decided, with Forster and Stanfield, that they were going to put on a play as soon as he returned, and he told Forster for the first time about his youthful acting aspirations. "I have often thought, that I should certainly have been as successful on the boards as I have been between them."[25] After returning to Genoa, spending five days en route in Paris visiting Macready, and then sailing from Marseilles, he talked of it as a settled thing.

He was far from finished, though, with Christmas books. In December 1845, he published *The Cricket on the Hearth, A Fairy Tale of Home,* whose structuring idea had initially been proposed as the title of a weekly periodical. It sold more than double the number of its predecessors. He was to write two more Christmas books, *The Battle of Life* in 1846 and *The Haunted Man* in 1848, neither of which was to give him as much pleasure or to be as commercially successful as the first three. After *The Chimes,* the emphasis, partly derived from Carlyle, was on the reformation of the individual heart more than of the social system. Pressured by the demands of a new novel in monthly parts, he found that he had insufficient time and energy to do both the novel and *The Battle of Life.* He also chafed under the burden of a dangerously expansive story structure, given the limitations that a Christmas book demanded. *The Haunted Man* moved away from sentiment into psychology. Fascinated by the idea of the double, he awkwardly worked a new psychological pattern—which was to become increasingly a part of his long fictions—into a Christmas context that had begun with Gothic supernatural machinery.

The Christmas genre that had originated with such social force for him increasingly became an inappropriate expression of the themes of displacement and tension that had been central to his fiction from the beginning. The Christmas spirit was grafted onto situations and expressed in ways that no longer unambivalently celebrated Christ on earth, goodwill to men. For Dickens, the Christmas book increasingly embodied the misplaced benevolence or the antibenevolence of his own father, an unreliable deity who unfairly, exploitatively, took money from him. He wanted to be given to, not taken from. The true cry of the heart of the Christmas books is "My Father, my Father, why hast thou deserted me?" Compensating for emotional impoverishment, he transformed Christmas spirit into financial profit, at first through the Christmas books and then through the shorter Christmas stories he was to publish in the journals he owned and edited in the next decades. Christmas had its important commercial element. That the poor, in his idealizations, were thrifty, sensible, caring, and capable of appreciating the meaning of Christmas and of Christ did not help provide them with sustenance. Attracted by the notion of himself as physician, he was attracted in his Christmas performances to that aspect of himself in which he could feel that he was a Christ-like healer and provider. The necessary healing, though, was his own, the necessary profit for himself. Despite the threats of an exploitative father and an absent mother, of a demanding family and of self-serving publishers, his ambivalent triumph in such a circumstance was to become the supreme self-provider, the self-healer and self-sustainer. Through these Christmas books, he got sustenance of various kinds. It was a type of personal miracle.

WHEN THE PHYSICIAN RETURNED TO GENOA AT THE END OF DECEMBER 1844, he found immediate cause to exert his special skills. His newest patient was ill again with a "severe . . . attack of her sad disorder." Soon after moving into the Peschiere in October, he had met some neighbors, the Swiss-born banker Emile de la Rue, and his English wife, Augusta. Director of the Genoese branch of the banking firm founded by his grandfather, de la Rue was a well-educated, cultured businessman. He was a close friend of Camillo Cavour, later one of the founders of a united Italy, and he had married by 1830 the petite, attractive, but semi-invalided daughter of the religious leader of the British colony in Genoa. Socially prominent in local society, the childless couple entertained widely in their charming, comfortable apartment on the top floor of the Palazzo Brignole Rosso. Early in November, the day before Dickens left for northern Italy and England, he and Catherine had entertained a party of fourteen, including the de la Rues, almost certainly in return for hospitality extended to them. Deeply distressed by a mysterious neurological illness suffered by Augusta de la Rue, spasmodic muscular contractions of the face and extremities and convulsive seizures, Dickens had no desire to resist trying to help her.[26]

In early 1838 the newly famous author had attended one of John Elliotson's demonstrations at London University of the power of mesmerism. Dickens soon discovered that he, too, had the ability to mermerize people. He combined friendship with the foremost English exponent of this new therapeutic science, originally conceived by Anton Mesmer, with a strong belief that here was both a true overview of the nature of power in the universe and a therapeutic tool to help people improve themselves. "I should be untrue . . . to . . . myself if I should shrink for a moment from saying that I am a believer, and that I became so against all my preconceived opinions."[27] Professor of the Principles and Practices of Medicine at the university, Elliotson had introduced the stethoscope to England, had experimented brilliantly with the use of drugs in disorders of the liver and kidneys, had campaigned against corrupt medical practices, and, distressed by the limitations of the therapies available to him, had insisted on permitting mesmeric experiments at the hospital. Controversy soon became scandal. The short, dark-haired, resourcefully energetic doctor was forced to resign his teaching position in 1839.

The scientific mesmerists believed that there existed an invisible fluid, like electricity, that suffused the universe, the harnessing of which would provide valuable psychological and physiological benefits. Through special techniques of concentration, receptive individuals could be mesmerized (the word *hypnotism* did not become available until 1845) so that their normal state of consciousness was replaced by mesmeric trance in which they were able to have extraordinary knowledge about themselves and others through contact with the mesmeric fluid. In such states of heightened consciousness, subjects were not limited by the normal restrictions of reason and physical perception. They could dismiss the sensation of pain, which would be helpful in surgery, since anesthesia had not been discovered yet. Various illnesses, particularly those of the nervous system, could be ameliorated if not cured by the power of the mesmeric force when therapeutically administered. Mesmeric operators, putting their subjects into trance, had the opportunity to be physicians of the mind, special benefactors of mankind. They also had the opportunity to misuse their skills. The fluid in and of itself was neutral. It could be drawn on for any conceivable purpose, scientific or superstitious, noble or self-serving, sober or sensationalistic. Obsessed with possibilities of erotic subjection and domination, the Victorians especially feared that sacred taboos about sexual relationships might be transgressed by male operators with their mesmerized female subjects.

Dickens had no such fear. In 1842, while traveling in America, he had demonstrated for the first time his own mesmeric skills. Having been "holding forth upon the subject rather luminously" to some travel companions, he magnetized Catherine "into hysterics" within six minutes of making hand passes about her head, and then, to his alarm, into mesmeric trance. He successfully repeated the experience the next night. Increasingly fascinated by his own powers, after his return to England he began regularly to mesmerize friends and members of his family, sometimes for their social amusement, sometimes to alleviate illness.[28] The scientific mesmerists believed that during magnetic sleep mysterious healing and regenerative processes occurred. Since these powers had a healing effect, especially on nervous and mental disorders of the sort that had a hysterical origin, it seemed sensible to Dickens to offer his services to Augusta de la Rue. Apparently he had no difficulty persuading her to give it a try, and, at first, there was little resistance from Catherine. Emile warmly sup-

ported Dickens' efforts to help his wife, and tried unsuccessfully to learn to mesmerize her himself.

"Happy and ready to come to you" on a moment's notice,
at any hour, in late December 1844 and throughout January 1845
he mesmerized Augusta de la Rue frequently, even at four in the
morning, sometimes with her husband present, often not, going
back and forth between the Peschiere and the Palazzo Brignole
Rosso like an "anxious Physician." When she was put into mesmeric sleep, her convulsions stopped. Her body returned from
its rigid misformations into relaxation and natural form. After
a month, she "began to sleep at night—which she had not done
for years, and to change . . . in appearance." The etiology of her
disease fascinated him. While in trance, she spoke at length,
often freely associating, describing her dreams, hallucinations,
anxieties, usually in the symbolic language of displacement,
connecting her illness with a "Phantom" who often pursued
her. It was absolutely essential, he believed, *"that this Phantom,"*
which her incapacitating "thoughts are directed to, and clus-
tered round," should *"not regain its power."*[29] While she was in
trance, he engaged in extensive dialogue with her, asking questions, eliciting descriptions of her nightmares, searching for
clues to her illness in her trance visions, in her dreams, and in
her anticipations, some of them suggestively clairvoyant. Her
brother "Charles" became an obsessive part of her trance anxieties, soon replaced by her physician "Charles," whose brotherly
commitment had levels of intensity that neither doctor nor patient could readily unravel. Certain of his friend's noble intentions and eager to help his wife, Emile de la Rue constantly
consulted with Dickens. When the Dickenses left Genoa in late
January for Rome and Naples, Emile mailed him detailed, ongoing accounts, sheets from his diary, of his patient's condition.
The de la Rues had agreed to join him in Rome in late February.
Dickens urged them to come as soon as possible.

Catherine, though, was not at all eager for the de la Rues'
company. She had become uncomfortable both with the amount
of time her husband spent with such an attractive woman and
with the intensity of the relationship. Because of the proximity
of their residences in Genoa, she soon felt that her domestic and
marital primacy had been diffused if not assaulted, as if her
husband had two homes, in each of which he spent part of the

night. She may have been only slightly less distressed when, on the road from Rome to Siena, he often had "a strange and uncommon anxiety upon" him about Augusta de la Rue. He had arranged with his patient that he would think about her, mesmerizing her in his imagination every day for one full hour, starting at 11 A.M. At first Catherine knew nothing about the arrangement. They were traveling by carriage, Dickens within, Catherine up above for air. Concentrating on his patient, he was surprised to hear Catherine's muff fall. She had gone accidentally into mesmeric trance, her eyelids quivering in a convulsive manner. Her jealousy both infuriated and disgusted him. Having imagined that she had lost her husband's love, Catherine may have also thought that he and Madame de la Rue were having an affair, perhaps with Emile's approval. Fascinated with his own powers, insistent upon seeing himself as a thoroughly noble human being, Dickens refused to understand her jealousy, resentment, and sense of neglect. Characteristically he took refuge in feeling insulted by her suspicions. The experience was on one level "part of such a strange and mysterious whole," an explanation of cosmic energy, on another an absorbing flirtation with analysis.

During his separation from Madame de la Rue, he continued to be obsessed with her. In Rome, on the last day before Carnival, he awoke at two in the morning in a state of "horror and emotion," an anxiety connected with Madame de la Rue and her condition so intense that he thought about her "while awake and asleep" for the next three days and nights. He had "a sense of her being somehow a part of me, as I have when I am awake." She and her phantom were now his own creations. Needing desperately to mesmerize her directly, he urged the de la Rues to come to Rome immediately. When they were finally on their way, he insisted on coming out some distance to meet them. "Look out for a Gallant Figure, apparently possessing an Angelic Nature. All others are counterfeits."[30]

Catherine's unhappiness prevented her neither from becoming pregnant in late January nor from participating with her husband in an ascent of Mount Vesuvius on the night of January 21, 1845. With "six saddle-horses, an armed soldier for a guard," and, because of the harsh weather, twenty-two guides, they began the nearly perpendicular ascent at four in the afternoon. Georgina and Catherine "were put into two litters, just chairs with poles." Dickens was on foot, with a tough stick in hand. Deep snow covered a "sheet of ice from the top of the cone to the bottom." They formed a human chain to cross the ice. At the moment of sunset they reached the halfway point. Then, in the clear night, the moon brilliantly illumined the sea, the Bay of Naples, and the whole country visible below and behind them. From the cone, fire flared, "red-hot stones and cinders" exploding above it and then falling into the snow. Beyond the snow line, they climbed through what seemed like "a dry water-fall, with every mass of stone burnt and charred into enormous cinders, and smoke and sulpher bursting out of every chink and crevice." The night was red with flames, and they could hardly breathe. Everyone on foot now, "my ladies were dragged higher, without making the least complaint."

Only Dickens and the head guide went to the edge of the crater, Roche screaming that they would be killed. "Feeling at every step as if the crust of ground between one's feet and the gulf of fire would crumble in and swallow one up," Dickens insisted on climbing to the brink on the windy side and looking "down into the crater itself . . . into the flaming bowels of the mountain. . . . It was the finest sight conceivable," even "more terrible than Niagara," though equal "as fire and water are." In the presence of the flaming mountain, he felt the same elevated transcendence that he had felt in the presence of the great falls, the two locations of his experience in which the living and the dead, the natural and the supernatural, came together. He and the guide returned from the peak, "alight in half a dozen places, and burnt from head to foot." Catherine and Georgina, who had had their clothes almost torn off their backs by the heat and wind, covered themselves. Descending, the head guide staggered, slipped, and plunged head first "down the smooth ice into the black night, five hundred feet below!" A man behind them on the descent stumbled and rolled down past them, shrieking in pain and terror. Months later, Vesuvius still was burning in Dickens' thoughts, "beside the roaring waters of Niagara; and not a splash of the water extinguishes a spark of the fire; but there they go on, tumbling and flaming, night and day, each in its fullest glory."[31]

Italy, though, was less bold scenery than impressive cities

and a broad cultural experience. Unlike Vesuvius, Naples repelled him, its misery, degradation, and dirt, the "condition of
the common people . . . abject and shocking . . . so sunk and
steeped in utter hopelessness of better things, that they would
make Heaven uncomfortable, if they could ever get there." The
presence of such seemingly irremediable misery made *him* uncomfortable. The condition of the city seemed best typified by
the widespread practice of bearing the dead, "uncovered, on an
open pier," through the streets. The uncoffined bodies of paupers were flung into lime pits of which there was one opened and
sealed for every night of the year.

His initial impression of Rome disappointed him. Its commonplace suburbs and banal modern streets seemed as nonde-
script as those of London and Paris, "degraded and fallen and
lying asleep in the sun among a heap of ruins . . . no more my
Rome' of the imagination "than Lincoln's-inn-fields is." From
the distance, "it looked like—I am half afraid to write the
word—like London!!!" Having arrived at Carnival time, he
found the celebration "a very remarkable and beautiful sight
. . . a remnant of the ancient Saturnalia"—music, masks, horse
racing, street crowds, attractive women, and the rhythmic in-
determinacy of a spectacular urban theatre performance.

Soon the other Rome, the ancient city on which the modern had been imposed, asserted itself with a grandness that the
Coliseum and the southern side of the Campagna embodied.
St. Peters did not impress him. The unavoidable presence of
the Catholic Church stimulated his barely latent hostility,
creating a constant minor tension between his enthusiasm for
appreciating the vividness of his Italian experience and his
manageable but still strong English prejudices. The Italians he
gladly tolerated, with amiable condescension, as if they were a
special kind of children, who have "a natural enjoyment of
dirt, garlic, and oil." The ancient sections of Rome, though,
thrilled him. When he returned for much of March, the Colosseum, which "by daylight, moonlight, torchlight, and every
sort of light" is "most stupendous and awful," had become for
him an image of the ancient and the modern, of man's work
and time's destruction. He "went there continually, and never
could see enough of it."[32]

With a strong interest in art but with no pretension to high culture, he looked at a great many paintings, particularly in Rome, finding satisfaction mostly in those that had narrative drama and in portraits that emphasized individual personality. He delighted in those whose "tenderness and grace . . . noble elevation, purity, and beauty . . . relieve my tortured memory from legions of whining friars and waxy holy families." Untrained and unsophisticated in the painterly tradition or in art as formal composition, he needed always to make intellectual sense of the representational element in the depiction. He preferred art that was heroic and elevating, his paragon Maclise, who had begun work on his frescoes for the new Houses of Parliament. He also admired realistic paintings, especially if the subject was social, his models Hogarth and Cruikshank. Amused by the artists' bourse in the Piazza di Spagna, he had a keen eye for the ludicrous relationship between artists and models, "the falsest Rascals in the World," who, like actors, exhibited their poses to show their prospective employers how they were the very stuff of high art. Despite his superficial knowledge of the subject, Dickens was confident of his ability to recognize and respond to art. His distrust of the humbug of what others considered great art both liberated him to see for himself and imprisoned him in his unwillingness to see beyond his limitations. The problem persisted that much of the Renaissance painting he saw dealt with religious subjects in such a way as to reduce "every mystery of our religion to some literal development in paint and canvas, equally repugnant to the reason and the sentiment of any thinking man."[33]

When the de la Rues finally arrived, Rome took on a new emotional immediacy. Appropriately, Augusta became sick for three days. Her husband "called me up to her. . . . She was rolled into an apparently impossible ball, by tic in the brain, and I only knew where her head was by following her long hair to its source. . . . It was so alarming to see that I had hardly any belief in myself with reference to it. But in half an hour she was peacefully and naturally asleep, and next morning was quite well." The illness, though, could only be alleviated, not cured, despite his hope that his medicine would succeed eventually in discharging, even destroying, the phantom whose origin he believed to be his patient's disturbed nervous system. What relief he could give her, however, could be achieved only through constant concentration, frequent therapeutic sessions both to counteract the powerful dark figure and to increase her strength and confidence. Once, when she reported to him that she had seen the dark figure skulking in the shadows with his face covered he triumphantly took it as a sign that the phantom was withdrawing. Its defeat seemed imminent. Early in April, the two couples left Rome for Genoa. Every day he "magnetized her; sometimes under olive trees, sometimes in vineyards, sometimes in the travelling carriage, sometimes at wayside inns during the midday.'³⁴

Under the constant strain of her husband's neglect, Catherine began to express her fear and frustration. So frequently in her company, the de la Rues, of course, had become aware of her tension. Dickens assured Fletcher, though, that the four of them "are exceedingly happy, and don't fight much." Finally, the three-month-pregnant Catherine made a stand. She insisted that her husband tell the de la Rues that she was distressed by what seemed to her the impropriety of his relationship with Augusta. Embarrassed and angry, Dickens complied. He spoke to the de la Rues, but insisted on apologizing for Catherine's state of mind, calling her both oversensitive and insensitive to others. In his eyes, it was demeaning, irrational jealousy Years later, he castigated her with the unforgettable memory of her insult to him and to them. "Whatever made you unhappy in that Genoa time had no other root, beginning, middle, or end, than whatever has made you proud and honored in your married life, and given you station better than rank, and surrounded you with many enviable things."³⁵ He was simply being himself, and she had not been willing to take him "for better and for worse." The worse was as central and as necessary as the better, and if she chose to see his relationship with Madame de la Rue as something suspect, she ought to have known that it could also be seen—it *should* be seen—as an inherent expression of his creativity and nobility. It was part of the ground on which he held his greatest gift.

In the "charming spring days" in Genoa, after a visit to Florence, Dickens began to anticipate the end of his year in Italy. He had seen "so many wonders," including Herculaneum and Pompeii, each with "a voice of its own." But he would "leave here, please God," on the ninth of June, in order to be in

London again by the end of that month. In retrospect, he was happy with the experience. Part of April and much of May 1845 he spent lying on his "back on sofas, and leaning out of windows and over balconies, in a sort of mild intoxication." He even discovered that he had grown stouter, his "waistcoat-buttons flying off occasionally, with great violence."[36] The tension with the de la Rues decreased as the spring advanced. Catherine felt calmer after her confession and in anticipation of their departure. He continued to mesmerize his "sad invalid," and made efforts to teach Emile to administer the cure. Though he had initially intended to spend a month or two in Paris on his return trip, he had remained in Italy so long that he felt now he did not have time enough to make a long stay in Paris profitable, partly because he had decisions to make about transforming his Italian experiences into a book, mainly because he desired the familiarity of London and his own desk again after the longest time he had ever been away.

Dissatisfied with his letters to Forster, which would be the basis of his Italian travel book, he had been "half savage" with himself in the writing "for not doing better." He had written nothing but letters since December. The thought of his writing obligations created an undercurrent of expectation and anxiety. He had a great deal of income to earn and borrowed money to repay. In early June, reading *A Christmas Carol* to a group of his Genoese intimates, he seemed, uncharacteristically, "extremely nervous and insisted that no one should sit behind him." And the separation from the de la Rues must have been difficult, smoothed over by his insistence that not only would he never forget them but that he would visit them again and that they would visit him. "You must come to England. That's clear. And I must come back to Genoa too." They left on June 9, traveling to Milan and Lake Como, and then over the St. Gotthard pass, "the blue water tearing through the white snow with an awful beauty that is most sublime." Switzerland, which seemed much more like England than like Italy, delighted him even more in this summer weather. From Zurich and Frankfurt, they traveled down the Rhine to Cologne, and finally to Brussels, where Forster, Maclise, and Jerrold, having come out to meet him, welcomed the self-described "Inimitable B" into their eager arms.[37]

❧ 4 ❧

SOON AFTER REPOSSESSING DEVONSHIRE TERRACE IN JULY 1845, "once more in my own house!" and out of "the hideous confusion, and chaos of boxes," Dickens was again vigorously combining work and play. Brief excursions to Rochester and Brighton, September in Broadstairs, and hearty dinners at one another's homes brought the Dickens circle together again. Maclise and Forster visited like members of the family. He felt increasingly warm toward Stanfield and Jerrold, whose recent play he thought "incomparably the best" of his dramatic writings. Forster, whose serious illness the previous winter had worried him, had mended, though "he looks thinner, and roars out sometimes, without any notice, in consequence of rheumatic twinges in one of his knees." Maclise's inability to get the best out of himself, to "give his magnificent Genius fair play," distressed Dickens. In August, he published an extravagantly laudatory essay, "The Spirit of Chivalry in Westminster Hall," to give his friend's fortunes a boost. Maclise was often "very discontented and oh! how low in spirits." The writer Laman Blanchard's suicide, in February 1845, may have heightened his concern about Maclise's moodiness. "Dear Dick how good and kind he is," Maclise wrote to Forster—"he sets me in a glow while I read his warm praise." Ainsworth remained a friend in the distance, though he lived close by, despite Forster's efforts to bring him in. "You are," he chided him, "what Enobarbus broke his head for being, a promise-breaker and a fugitive. . . . We shall never be, in military parlance, 'as we were,' at this rate." Cruikshank was still "one of the best creatures in the World, in his own odd way . . . a live Caricature [of] himself."[38] David Colden visited from New York, without his beautiful wife. Though Mitton and Forster vied for who could be more indispensable to Dickens, Forster easily won.

For the author, no spontaneous fun could be as relaxing as that produced by the combination of exhaustion and exhilaration that he felt when organizing, arranging, directing, and acting in a play. With his usual Grimaldi reflex, he leaped onto the stage. After reading *The Chimes* in London in December 1844, he had rallied his friends to the commitment that they would put on a play when he returned. By mid-July, Ben Jonson's *Every Man in His Humour* had been decided on, to be accompanied by a farce, eventually *Past Two o'Clock in the Morning*, which he had done in Montreal. Anticipating "great amusement," he set to work, casting, organizing rehearsals, deciding on costumes, renting the small theatre on Dean Street owned by the flighty, officious, middle-aged actress Fanny Kelly, setting the ground rules for the amateur company, dreaming great things for this new adventure. Jonson's comedy had fine roles, the braggart Captain Bobadil for Dickens, the swaggering, rapacious Kitely for Forster, and parts for Jerrold, Leech, Lemon, Dudley Costello (a journalist whom Dickens had known since the late 1830s), Frank Stone, and Frederick Dickens. The participants shared the costs equally, about ten pounds each. Stanfield and Maclise were consulted about the scenery. The "perfectly good-natured and most agreeable . . . company" soon seemed to their perfectionist manager "*damned* bad." Forster, taking Macready as his model, to the extent that he even imitated "the great tragedian's" stage mannerisms, immersed himself in his role so passionately that he seemed to have defined acting as an act of aggression against his colleagues, whose nerves he severely strained. Acting opposite Dickens in one of the two roles in the farce, Lemon turned out to be an excellent actor, and Leech, in Robert Browning's judgment, superb.[39] Dickens, though, astonished his friends with the professionalism of his performance, as if he had been acting all his life. In fact, he had.

The performance was scheduled for September 20. Early in the month, "supernatural exertions . . . being made for the Great Play," he was still disappointed with some of the actors. "But they will improve perhaps, and come out better than I expect." Exhausting himself with management details, he had everyone working away at it "as if it were the whole business of our lives." Some of the company began to feel, as the night approached, "like used-up cab horses—going perceptibly at the knees." But he humorously boasted to Macready that "I think of changing my present mode of life, and am open to an engagement. . . . I will undertake not to play Tragedy, though Passion is my strength. . . . I consider myself a chained lion." The lion unchained performed brilliantly before an audience of five hundred invited guests, including Tennyson, Browning, Jane

Carlyle, Lady Holland and the Countess of Blessington, both of whom he had become friendly with, and the Duke of Devonshire, an "audience so distinguished for one thing or another—every one so elegantly dressed—all in such a state of excitement and expectation." The press, which had infiltrated the private event, widely praised the acting. Suddenly the company was inundated with requests to do additional performances, perhaps for charity. The idea of appearing as an actor before a general audience did not appeal to Dickens, nor, he thought, would it to the company. He had performed for a paying audience "in Canada, once—But that is far away, and quite another thing."[40] Though he could not stop thinking and talking about the experience, the company did not perform again in 1845, and in 1846 did only a benefit performance for Miss Kelly, for which Dickens wrote a prologue that Forster recited. Through much of the fall of 1845 he was busy writing *The Cricket on the Hearth,* and there were other serious drains on his time.

In addition to the theatricals, for the previous six months Dickens had been intensively planning the disposition of his letters from Italy, the agreement to edit a magazine for Bradbury and Evans, and the commitment to write a new novel in twenty monthly numbers. Whether to write a travel book or to publish the letters in a journal or newspaper had suddenly seemed in early July 1845 secondary to his enthusiasm for an idea for a cheap weekly periodical. It would be "partly original partly select; notices of books, notices of theatres, notices of all good things, notices of all bad ones; *Carol* philosophy, cheerful views, sharp anatomization of humbug, jolly good temper; papers always in season, pat to the time of year; and a vein of glowing, hearty, generous, mirthful, beaming reference in everything to Home, and Fireside." Above all, it would be a regular source of substantial income. The memory of his bitter experience with *Bentley's Miscellany* and the indifferent failure of *Master Humphrey's Clock* had faded sufficiently for him to think that this time he could pull it off. It would be necessary for the journal to be closely identified with him both in spirit and in ownership. He would need complete editorial control. He would need compliant publishers who would take the financial risk and forgo all interference. Optimistic that he had such a publisher in Bradbury and Evans, whose handling of *The Chimes* seemed to him infinitely superior to Chapman and Hall's of *A Christmas Carol,* though in fact the only difference had been that the former had been more popular with the public, he decided that *The Cricket* would be his title and that he would "chirp, chirp, chirp away in every number until I chirped it up to— well, you shall say how many hundred thousand!"[41]

By the end of the month, the idea had been abandoned, mainly because it had been replaced by another exciting notion, so bold that it absolutely amazed him. Bradbury and Evans proposed that he edit a daily newspaper, which would be known as the *Daily News.* Its politics would be liberal and financing would come from the railway directors, who, profiting from "the railway mania," wanted a public voice to counterbalance anti-industrial Tory interests. Its profits would be substantially augmented by advertisements for the financing and organization of new railroads. "Capital, *down and ready,* fifty Thousand Pounds!" Dickens claimed. The idea had probably been broached to Bradbury as early as 1840 by his country neighbor and financial adviser, the self-made Joseph Paxton, a talented gardener who had risen from garden boy to superintendent of grounds at Chatsworth, editor of gardening newspapers, and intimate friend of the Duke of Devonshire. His architectural genius was to produce the Crystal Palace for the Great Exhibition of 1851. His financial brilliance had made him wealthy from railroad-stock investments. By the autumn of 1845, he had "command of every railway and railway influence in England and abroad except the Great Western." His conservative business practices but liberal politics contrasted sharply with the speculative business practices and the self-serving Toryism of the flamboyant "railway king," George Hudson, who had also risen from obscurity to immense power and whose empire of over one thousand miles of railways rivaled Paxton's. By October 1845, as the plan matured, Dickens learned that Hudson "is with us in influence though not as a proprietor." Paxton, the moving force, "is in it, heart and purse."[42]

Tempted by the opportunity to have some direct say in the affairs of the country, he could not resist the blandishments of Bradbury and Paxton, the call of his own heart to do something striking for reform, and his expectation of the handsome salary he would receive. After spending October 18 at Chatsworth with

Paxton, he committed himself. "The venture is quite decided on; and I have made the Plunge." Forster, who "was to have some share in it," gave the news to Macready, who heard it with "a sort of dismay. . . . I fear the means and chances have not been well enough considered. I hope and pray all may go well with and for them." Dining together the next night, Dickens and his friends undoubtedly had a strong sense of the excitement as well as the danger of the venture. Two weeks later, reading his prospectus for the newspaper, Macready's apprehensions increased. He perceived his friend to be "rushing headlong into an enterprise that demands the utmost foresight, skillfull and secret preparation and qualities of a conductor which Dickens has not.' Forster agreed with his objections, "but he did not seem to entertain much hope of moving Dickens."43

Dickens himself, though, may already have had doubts. Catherine was about to give birth, he was having difficulty getting his next Christmas book, to which he had transferred the prospective title of his journal, started, he had at times been "half dead with [the] Managerial work" of the new acting company and now he was busily "trying to engage the best people, right and left," for the newspaper. He was planning to go abroad to set up the overseas offices, which would permit a visit to the de la Rues. At the beginning of November, his body began warning him that something was wrong with what he was doing. Still, on the third of December 1845 he formally accepted the editorship of the *Daily News*, asking and receiving double the thousand pounds a year that had initially been mentioned. He agreed to publish there his Italian letters and to write frequent short papers "from day to day . . . constantly exercising an active and vigilant superintendence over the whole Machine." He would not be a daily drudge, though. "When I am not there, or after I have left the office, I shall . . . have a Sub Editor to whom I can . . . hand over the practical management for the time being."44

An annual salary, though, was insufficient. He also wanted a portion of the ownership, his share of which "would then be a fine property." Partial ownership would be the reward that would make palatable a position that probably he, and certainly his friends, suspected was antithetical to his work as a novelist. Even with a reliable subeditor, it would be possible only at damaging cost to function as the editor of a daily newspaper and to write a novel in twenty monthly parts, which he was committed to do and needed to do to maintain his primacy as a novelist. It was unrealistic to think that he could subordinate editing a newspaper to his writing fiction so that "the new calling shall not long supercede the old one."[45] A glutton for detail and control, he did not balk at the likelihood that the amount of administration he would be compelled to do each day would far exceed anything he had ever taken on before. Whatever his managerial talents, they did not include delegating responsibility effectively.

Fortunately, the day after he had committed himself he was presented with the opportunity to back out. The arrangement that Paxton had made for financing the paper collapsed because of the "failure of a Great Broker in the City . . . which so affects two of my principal people that the Paper *cannot* be, on any proper footing." Having already hired a substantial staff at salaries that bested those of rivals like *The Times* and the *Morning Chronicle,* he felt that it would be embarrassing, even painful, to withdraw the contracts, especially in those cases in which the reporters, some of them personal friends, had given notice to their employers. "But never say die is the Inimitable's motto; and I have already pumped up as much courage as will set me going on my old track, please God, in four and twenty hours."[46]

As if saved from himself, he announced that he now had "no intention of connecting himself with any Newspaper." He advised Bradbury and Evans to cut their losses. There was no saving the *Daily News,* since the confidence of the publishing and business world had been shattered as had his own. If they insisted on going on with it, he would give them "every advice and assistance" in his power. "But I cannot connect myself with it, as I originally designed. Nor can I conceal from you that I believe in my Soul it would end in your Ruin." The publisher thought nothing of the sort. Additional money was raised. Despite efforts to persuade him, he at first held firm. After further discussions with Forster, Mitton, and Beard, the general opinion among his friends was that "to go on was desperate." He complained that he had "been involved for the last fortnight in one maze of distractions. . . . Everything I have had to do, has been interfered with, and cast aside. I have never in my life had so many insuperable obstacles crowded into the way of my pursuits."[47] Despite all this, and advice to the contrary, or perhaps because of it, by the fourteenth of November he had withdrawn his resignation, and on the seventeenth the proprietors signed a formal agreement. Since there was no mention of his share in the profits, probably that was to be worked out at a later date. He had not been able to resist triumphing over "insuperable obstacles." By the first of December 1845, he was able to date a letter from the "Office of the Daily News' at 90 Fleet Street.

Though the newspaper was to have a long life, his association with it was brief. He spent much of November and December organizing it and January and February realizing that it was a "Daily Noose." He found little to take pleasure in after the satisfaction of redeeming the staff appointments he had made initially, which now included Lemon, Forster, Fonblanque, and Jerrold as editorial writers. Costello as foreign editor, John Scott Russell as railway editor, George Hogarth as music and drama critic, Richard Henry Horne as Irish correspondent, William Henry Wills, a contributor to *Punch* and the former assistant editor of *Chambers's Edinburgh Journal*, as his personal secretary, the Countess of Blessington, at an impractical salary though only half the eight hundred pounds that she had originally proposed, for society tidbits, John Henry Barrow, his maternal uncle, as India correspondent, and the irrepressible John Dickens, popping up again "like a cork," in charge of the reportorial staff. The elderly gentleman took great pleasure in once more having a desk on which to put his feet. Bustling with enthusiasm, the portly father of the general editor took on his responsibilities with the bonhomie of a man who was back in familiar territory and the pride of a father being paid his due after long neglect by his son and the world. Rather than a stipend, he now had a salary.[48]

In addition to his position as general editor, Dickens took on, at no increase in salary, the chore of publicist for his "decidedly liberal" and, he anticipated, "extremely well written" newspaper. He quickly realized, though, that he had taken on tedious detail, infinite vexation, and the unanticipated frustration of problems with incompetent printers and nervous investors whose commitment to give him complete control over personnel was not fully honored. Bradbury angered him by what seemed unwarranted interference with his prerogatives, including treating his father in an insulting way. By the time of the trial edition on January 19, 1846, having corrected some of the initial problems, Dickens felt that "everything looks well for our Start." But the effort took its toll. "I can't sleep; and if I fall into a doze I dream of first numbers till my head swims."49 The editors and owners of established newspapers, like the *Times* and the *Morning Chronicle*, were relieved by the thin appearance of the first copies, redeemed only by installments of *Pictures from Italy* under the title "Travelling Letters" on January 21, 24, and 31, February 9, 16, and 26, and March 2 and 11, a little less than half the full book, which was published in mid-May 1846.

Dickens also took the opportunity to express strong opinions on a number of social issues, particularly on the relationship between criminality and lack of education, focusing on the potential of the ragged-school movement and on what seemed the ridiculousness of the advocacy of "total abstinence" because some people could not drink moderately. The widespread assertion that drunkenness was the cause of many evils rather than a result of already existing ones angered him, as if eradicating a symptom in any way dealt with the disease. Beginning with his earliest sketches, he had unequivocally claimed that societies with high levels of poverty and ignorance created the conditions that encouraged high levels of crime and alcoholism. The issue that most preoccupied him, though, was capital punishment. He dealt with it at length in five long letters published on February 23 and 28, and March 9, 13, and 16. It had been on his mind for many years, beginning with its indirect depiction in the accidental death by hanging of Bill Sikes, watched by a taunting, angry crowd, in *Oliver Twist*, the suicide by hanging of Ralph Nickleby, and the dramatic, extended presentation of the hangman and his work in *Barnaby Rudge*. With a strong touch of the obsessive voyeur, he found the highest drama in assaults on the body, in the depiction of the vulnerability of the human creature, who could be brought from wholeness to dismemberment, from life to death, in a moment of individual violence or state-sanctioned murder.

In early July 1840, on an impulse, he had gone to see the hanging of the Swiss-born François Benjamin Courvoisier. After a sensational trial, he had been convicted of robbing and

cutting the throat of his employer, Lord William Russell. Five
weeks earlier Dickens had expressed his support of the abolition
of capital punishment. He found himself drawn to the public
execution, as if he needed to see with his own eyes, like a burning remembrance, the primal scene. At first, he persuaded himself and his friends only to go "to see what is being done in the
way of preparation" for the hanging. Once at Newgate, the
magnetism of the crowd of forty thousand gathering to see
the spectacle and the single focus of the gallows became emotionally irresistible. "Just once I should like to watch a scene like
this, and see the end of the Drama." Despite their objections, he
took his friends and himself out of the obfuscating press of
thousands of people to an upper-floor room with an unob-
structed view. For a small rental fee, they had an excellent
vantage point. From that height, waiting from midnight until
dawn, they watched what his brother-in-law described as "the
sink of human filth" beneath them, the pickpockets, prostitutes,
drunkards, the idle curious, the morbid, the obsessive voyeurs.
He felt that he was both part of the crowd and an objective
observer of that live performance no other theatre could provide. Suddenly he caught sight of Thackeray, towering over the
people he stood among. The noise, though, prevented them
from getting his attention, the crowd so pressingly taut that he
could not have moved anyway. To get a better view people
shouted, "Hats off in front!" Suddenly, at eight in the morning,
as the body swung, the neck breaking, there was a moment of
complete silence at that "sight of helplessness and agony."[50]

Of this execution Thackeray wrote that "the poor wretch's
face will keep itself before my eyes, and the scene mixes itself
up with all my occupations." Dickens could not get the "horrible sight" out of his mind, a preoccupation that soon had a
fictional representation in *Barnaby*. The onlookers disgusted
him as much as the execution itself. "I did not see one token in
all the immense crowd . . . of any one emotion suitable to the
occasion. No sorrow, no salutary terror, no abhorrence, no seriousness; nothing but ribaldry, debauchery, levity, drunkenness,
and flaunting vice in fifty other shapes. I should have deemed it
impossible that I could have ever felt any large assemblage of my
fellow-creatures to be so odious." He immediately wrote to the
Morning Chronicle two letters, whose preoccupation with the

procedures of the trial did not disguise his radical statement that what the murderer had suffered by state barbarity made him conclude that he would never cooperate in bringing a murderer to justice.

When pressed by Macvey Napier for a contribution to the *Edinburgh Review,* an upper-middle-class Whig journal with a strong commitment to rational reform, he sketched out an argument in which he stressed that capital punishment was sufficiently harmful to society to warrant its being abolished. The spectacle of Courvoisier's death "was so loathsome, pitiful, and vile . . . that the law appeared to be as bad as he, or worse." Though he never wrote the article for Napier, his letters in 1846 to the *Daily News* (having by then left the paper's editorship) developed the main points: 1) Death has a great fascination for all people because of "the Dread and Mystery surrounding" it; 2) Those who are "criminally disposed" are influenced by such a psychologically fascinating sight, which, among other things, "engenders a diseased sympathy"; 3) The ignorant mass of people in general, seeing the state murder but not the crime for which it is a punishment, "will almost of necessity sympathize with the man who dies before them"; 4) Since "all exhibitions of agony and Death have a tendency to brutalize and harden the feelings of men," such public spectacles tend to make death less rather than more corrective. For him, death was a reminder of how precious life was, how moral its essence. Capital punishment denied both truths. And though the force of his argument was directed against the elimination of such public executions, he advocated the long-range goal of total abolishment, substituting "mean and shameful" punishments that would "degrade the deed, and the doer of the deed."[51]

Later, in 1849, having declined to attend a double public execution, with the added titillation of one of the condemned being a woman, he wrote two widely read letters to the *Times,* advocating elimination of public execution. Though he favored total abolishment, he had almost as much contempt for those who insisted on all or *nothing* as for the crowd that enjoyed the special excitement of seeing a woman hang. The law that created and condoned such an obscenity seemed to him barbaric. He felt almost as if he were "living in a city of Devils." Just as he had not for years been able to go near Warren's

Blacking on the Strand, he could not think of Horsemonger Lane Gaol, where the Mannings were hanged, without seeing in his imagination "the two figures still hanging in the morning air," figures whose execution he had not observed except in a vivid fantasy in which he saw "those two forms dangling on the top of the entrance gateway—the man's, a limp, loose suit of clothes as if the man had gone out of them; the woman's, a fine shape, so elaborately corsetted and artfully dressed, that it was quite unchanged in its trim appearance as it slowly swung from side to side."[52]

In February 1846, he liberated himself from the "Daily Noose." There had been some successes. With the help of his father and other experienced reporters, he had succeeded in setting up a network and a schedule that scooped other papers in getting into print an important speech by Robert Peel, evoking memories of his own reportorial achievements in the early 1830s on the hustings and in the House. Not even his friends, though, could pretend that the *Daily News* was a success. There is "nothing in it," Macready complained early in February. "How can this interest its readers? The persons employed do not understand their business." Elizabeth Barrett, who had earlier remarked that Dickens "has not . . . the *breadth* of mind enough for such work, with all his gifts," thought the editorial texture intellectually vapid. Forster may not have shared with his intimate friend his "very low spirits about *the paper*" and his view "that no one could be a worse editor than Dickens." But if not for the newspaper, then certainly for Dickens the road ahead looked to be a bleak, tedious one. He focused his perturbation on a new incident with Bradbury about personnel and his unhappiness with the newspaper's "one-sided" prorailroad policy. With cold anger, he told his publishers at the end of January 1846 that they would either do things his way or he would leave, and that he would probably leave anyway.[53]

Among other things, though, he had to assure Bradbury and Evans that his dissatisfaction with them as publishers of the *Daily News* did not extend to them as publishers of his novels. With Catherine, Georgina, Jerrold, and Forster, he went to Rochester at the beginning of the second week of February 1846, grounding himself in the old sites of his childhood, mulling over his situation, consulting with his friends, evaluating his sense of having gotten onto a wrong road. It was clear that he could not be both a novelist and the editor of a daily newspaper. On Monday the ninth, he announced his resignation. The owners agreed to Forster becoming the editor, a position he undertook with enthusiasm but from which, as Macready had anticipated, he unhappily resigned eight months later. "God knows," Dickens was to console Forster, "there has been small comfort for either of us in the *D.N.*'s nine months." With his letters on social issues, Dickens was to keep his hand in for some months and to receive some income from the newspaper thereafter. But by the end of February, "having subsided . . . into my old, and much-better-loved pursuits," the novelist was "contemplating a new story," which, by the middle of April, he had decided that he could "write . . . more comfortably and easily, abroad, than at home" and "I shall be saving money while I write." Though it was not an easy decision to uproot himself and his family so soon again, after "discussing the pros and cons of all these questions, with Forster . . . in a condition of incessant restlessness, uneasiness, and uncertainty," he soon made up his mind. "Abroad again. . . . I will write my book in Lausanne and in Genoa, and forget everything else if I can."[54]

CHAPTER SEVEN

As My Father Would Observe
(1846-1849)

❧ I ❧

AT THE END OF MAY 1846 THE DICKENS FAMILY DEPARTED FOR THE
Continent again, this time to Switzerland. Their sixth child,
Alfred D'Orsay Tennyson Dickens, had been born in October
1845. He had been named after the French-born count, arch-
dandy, and amateur artist, the intimate friend of the Countess
of Blessington, and after Dickens' favorite contemporary poet.
Both namesakes had attended the christening. Robert Browning
remarked that " 'Alfred' is common to both the godfather and
the—cevil-father, as I take the Count to be." He noted acerbi-
cally that his biological father's Unitarianism did not prevent
him from participating in a ritual of sponsorship that involved
allegiance to the Church of England. Unlike Browning, Dickens
hardly noticed such personal inconsistencies and did not take
formal religious matters seriously. He did take special pleasure
in his son having such distinguished godparents. And he was
forced to take seriously Catherine's objection to his desire that
they go to Italy again. She did not want her husband to be near
Augusta de la Rue. He explained to his disappointed friends that

Catherine's bad health in Genoa—she "was never very well there"—made it necessary that they go someplace else. For the present, he would "take a middle course . . . and, coming as near you as I could, pitch my tent somewhere on the Lake of Geneva—say at Lausanne, whence I should run over to Genoa immediately."[1]

During his remaining weeks in England, he was engaged for his "sins . . . to dinner every day." His sins were those of popularity and companionability. His obligations included attending his brother Alfred's wedding in the middle of the month, the pleasure of which was undermined by his fear that his sister Fanny was seriously ill. After examining her, Elliotson relieved the family anxiety with his opinion that her lungs were not affected. Though Dickens complained that he got "up every morning with an odious shadowing-forth of the evening that is to follow," he had ahead of him a clear calendar for the year.[2] There was a new novel to begin, "vague thoughts" of which had been making him restless since March and which had been on his mind since the previous November; there was another Christmas story to write; and with his propensity for social pleasures it was certain that he would find new companions to accompany him on afternoon walks and to fill his evenings.

He genuinely regretted having to turn down a farewell dinner invitation from Lady Blessington. In her late fifties, the portly widow had high literary aspirations, entertained lavishly, and ran an engaging salon at Gore House. She lived beyond her resources in a mysterious ménage with Count D'Orsay. Dickens found them both attractive, their attention flattering. They were also an entrée to Whig aristocracy, and his dining out was both an expression of his sociability and his compensation for a lower-middle-class childhood. Though he gradually learned to protect his time, he found invitations difficult to resist. By going abroad again, he would be out of the way of having to decline any invitations at all. By renting Devonshire Terrace, he would save money and take advantage of the power of the English pound on the Continent. He would gain time to write. He would have the stimulation of new places and new people, of the vast expanse of Alpine brilliance, of Europe again. And he had it in mind to go to Paris for the winter and spring, to experience

fully the city whose wonders had dazzled him when he had
made two brief visits on either end of his Italian year.

The trip was done efficiently, a combination of travel and
sleep that got them to the Hotel Gibbon in Lausanne on June
11, 1846. The final days were spent in three horse-drawn coaches
from which they had splendid views of the mountains. After a
brief temptation to look for a place in Neuchâtel, he decided on
Lausanne, which had more "booksellers' shops crammed within
the same space" on its "steep up-and-down streets" than any
other place he had seen, and was closer to Geneva, "in case I
should find, when I begin to write, that I want streets sometimes." He rented for ten pounds a month a small, scantily
furnished "perfect doll's house" called Rosemont, "which could
be put, bodily, into the Hall of our Italian Palazzo. . . . In the
most lovely and delicious situation imaginable," nestled into
"the hill that rises from the lake," it had just enough bedrooms
for the family with one to spare for guests. After rearranging the
furniture, as he did wherever he stayed, even if for only one
night, he relaxed into the beauty of the view of the lake and the
"eternally changing range of prodigious mountains—sometimes
red, sometimes grey, sometimes purple, sometimes black; sometimes white with snow; sometimes close at hand; and sometimes
very ghosts in the clouds and mist." The profusion of flowers
overwhelmed the garden "in a cluster of roses." He had the
pleasant sense of being in a new country in which he felt remarkably comfortable. It was so "leafy, green, and shady," with
even more singing birds than "in the richest parts of Devonshire," with excellent country roads, and with "green woods
and green shades" that reminded him of the warm shadows of
his childhood in Kent.⁵

Unlike Italy, this was an ordered, rational environment, a
landscape and culture that matched his need for harmonious
arrangement, without the confusions and superstitions of Catholicism. Like England, this was Protestant good sense at its
best, with the advantage of splendid scenery. Even the initial hot
weather soon cleared. Cool breezes from the mountains brought
him to his writing table refreshed. By late June, he was "contemplating terrific and tremendous industry—am mightily resolved
to begin the book in Numbers without delay—and have already
begun to look the little Christmas Volume in its small red face."

He cleared his desk of various correspondence and quickly wrote for his children half of a brief child's version of the New Testament. Suddenly, in the first weeks in July, he "BEGAN DOMBEY!"4

By the end of the month, when he sent the opening four chapters of *Dealings With The Firm Of Dombey And Son, Wholesale, Retail, And For Exportation* to Forster, he had outlined the novel's basic development, creating for the first time in his career an overall plan, revealing a coherence and a cohesiveness from the beginning of writing the book. When completing *The Old Curiosity Shop*, with resonances of Mary Hogarth in the death of Little Nell, he had been "very melancholy to think that all these people are lost to me for ever, and I feel as if I never could become attached to any new set of characters." The new novel also dramatically demonstrates his fascination with imaginary lives so real to him that his own self-definition demanded incessant renewal, new life for him through the creation of life for others. As he wrote, his spirits were brazenly high. Touching with unselfconscious frankness on both the imaginative source and the financial importance of such "dealings," he joked to his friend Henry Porter Smith, an ex-soldier turned executive of the Eagle Life Assurance Company, "you wouldn't entertain a proposal for ensuring imaginary lives, would you? If so, I would submit the name of ——." Additionally, during this period of what he described as "extraordinary nervousness" in getting the book started, Catherine became pregnant again.5

The excitement of plunging "head over heels into the story" did not eliminate a "besetting anxiety . . . of quite an intense kind." Were Bradbury and Evans competent to handle a novel in twenty monthly parts, the mechanics and the economics of which were crucial to a novelist keenly aware that his financial solvency depended upon wide sales? As publishers of the *Daily News,* they were tarred with his distaste for anything that had to do with that newspaper and with his distrust of their inexperience as book publishers. He feared that their preoccupation with the newspaper would deflect their attention from him. So great was his concern that he raised with Forster the thought of having them enlist the more capable Chapman and Hall, for whom the machinery of monthly numbers was "as familiar . . . as the ticking of their own watches."6 Some of the anger of his break with his former publisher had cooled. He had also determined, though, to give highest priority to practical considerations. These all were real issues, of course. But whenever he began a new novel it was necessary for him to have something to be anxious about, something onto which to deflect some of his restless nervousness about the primary task at hand.

Dickens had not anticipated how hard he would find it to get both *Dombey* and a new Christmas book started at the same time—so difficult that as the weeks went by he began to confront the possibility that he would have to abandon his commitment to do a Christmas book that year. But he would not give up easily. The idea for *The Battle of Life* was clear to him by mid-July, his imagination focusing on the use of a description of a battlefield to represent the transitory nature of life and memory and on an elaborate deceit that would enable two sisters eventually to marry satisfactorily. Unlike his previous Christmas books, it would be a domestic, nonsupernatural tale, though he also had in mind "a very ghostly and wild idea" that he would "reserve for the *next* Christmas book." At one moment, he felt "the suddenest and wildest enthusiasm" for the idea, at another "solitary and anxious consideration," partly because it seemed to demand greater length than a small Christmas book would allow, partly because his preoccupation with his new novel made him feel that he had too little time and energy for it. "It would be an immense relief to have it done, and nothing standing in the way of *Dombey.*" He wanted to finish it as soon as possible. Under such pressure, he could wishfully joke about not being able "satisfactorily [to] account for . . . not having been born to a fine property."7

By the end of August, he was hoping to get the writing started. In late September, after a very busy month, he painfully confronted the possibility that "there may be NO CHRISTMAS BOOK! . . . I have been brooding and brooding over the idea that it was a wild thing to dream of, ever: and that I ought to be at rest for the *Dombey.*" For the first time he approached the consideration of his own limitations. The novelist who had worked on *Oliver* while still writing *Pickwick*, *Nickleby* while still doing *Oliver*, and who had within a seven-year period completed five lengthy novels and various other literary tasks, who had thrived on the simultaneity of multiple literary challenges so that no amount of imaginative work seemed to daunt him, suddenly found his energy and emotional willfulness insufficient to his obligations. "If I don't do it," though, he told Forster, as if exhorting himself, "it will be the first time I ever abandoned anything I had once taken in hand; and I shall not have abandoned it until after a most desperate fight." The hot weather had returned. He felt a constant slight pain in his side. Suddenly he felt so debilitated by depression that he worried he was in serious danger of not getting anything done at all.[8] But to allow the book not to be written now was to permit indefinitely the possibility that some task was too great for him, that his energy was limited.

So he pushed on, aware of the resistance that made "getting on FAST" so difficult. As long as he still had the Christmas book to do, his progress on *Dombey* would be excruciatingly slower than his nervous system demanded. Never having attempted to write a full-length novel in parts while away from London, he suspected, and then concluded unequivocally, that his slow pace was due to "the absence of streets" and crowds. He felt no diminution of his creative powers, and his self-appreciative responses to the Dombey world he was creating reveal his awareness of being at the top of his form. But getting on quickly seemed impossible. "I can't express how much I want" city streets. "It seems as if they supplied something to my brain, which it cannot bear, when busy, to lose. For a week or a fortnight I can write prodigiously in a retired place . . . and a day in London sets me up again and starts me. But the toil and labour of writing, day after day, without that magic lantern, is IMMENSE!! . . . *My* figures seem disposed to stagnate without crowds about them."[9] The absence of the usual stimulant to his imagination left him restless in a self-consuming way.

After a brief visit in early September to the St. Bernard Convent, in "a great hollow on the top of a range of dreadful mountains," where he awoke early in the morning to the tune of "the solemn organ and the chaunting" with the thought that he "had died in the night and passed into the unknown world," he began writing the Christmas book. The experience on the mountain had been revivifying. Perhaps the sight of "the bodies . . . found in the snow" and kept "standing up . . . during the short days and the long nights, the only human company out of doors, withering away by grains, and holding ghastly possession of the mountain where they died," reminded him of the corpses of his childhood and brought him back into the possession of his own imaginative domain. Some of what he had seen in that "awful and tremendous place" remained in his memory for future use. He moved ahead satisfactorily with *Dombey*, but slowly with the Christmas book, and at the cost of some occasional giddiness and severe headaches, which were very unusual for him and which he again confidently attributed to the absence of streets. He was suddenly buoyed by the "BRILLIANT . . . success" of the first number of *Dombey*. By a little past the middle of the month, having felt "used up, and sick," he was done with his severe double work, feeling "floored: wanting sleep. . . ." Even after he had sent the Christmas book off to Forster, he felt deeply the limitations of what he had done and the prison that he had placed himself in. He dreamed for a whole week that "*Battle of Life* was a series of chambers impossible to be got to rights or got out of, through which I wandered drearily all night."[10]

He did only a little other wandering during these late-summer and early-autumn months of 1846. The neatness and regularity of the Swiss countryside delighted him. The scenery also astounded and moved him. In late July, he took a four-day trip to Chamonix, where he found the valley, Mont Blanc, and the Mer de Glace beyond his wildest expectations, "Gothic pinnacles; deserts of ice and snow; forests of firs on mountain sides . . . villages down in the hollow, that you can shut out with a finger; waterfalls, avalanches, pyramids and towers of ice, torrents, bridges; mountain upon mountain until the very sky is blocked away." He was amused and impressed with the Swiss fascination with rifle shooting, as if they were a nation of William Tells shooting targets for entertainment while at the same time keeping ready to resist tyranny. A visit early in August to the Castle of Chillon, with its torture chambers, "so terrifically sad, that death itself is not more sorrowful," reminded him of feudal retrogression. "The greatest mystery in all the earth . . . is how or why the world was tolerated by its Creator through the good old times, and wasn't dashed to fragments." In late September, with Catherine and Georgina, he spent a few days in Geneva, and then again for over a week in late October, having finished *The Battle of Life* and "running away from a bad head ache." Astonished by the civility of the bloodless anti-Royalist revolution that he had stumbled into observing, he admired the Swiss educational system, their "comfortable homes—great intelligence—and noble independence of character," and he sympathized with the revolution. "There is no country on earth . . . in which a violent change could have been effected in the Christian spirit shewn in this place, or in the same proud, independent, gallant style."[11]

One trip that he made alone was to Vevey in late August to meet the de la Rues, a quick journey from which he returned on the same day. Catherine's likely disapproval did not decrease the warmth of the reunion. Though he told his friends that it was important, "with a view to my next day's work, to return home that night," no matter how late, probably his wife's jealousy was at least an equally important spur for returning from that happy day on that day itself. He came back "rather drearily," in low spirits, hoping that they would have many more such days, "please Heaven, somewhere or other." By mid-August, he was comforting himself with the wishful belief that Catherine's pregnancy was a false alarm. It soon became clear that it was "the real original Fire Bell." He joked painfully to Macready, his soul mate in reproduction, that when he was asked by a lady if the mesmeric "influence might be exerted . . . for lessening the pain which ladies suffer, who love their Lords," that he had implored his questioner "never to hint at the possibility of that operation being made easy, or I didn't know what I myself, but mainly some of my friends (I meant you and Mrs. Macready) might come to!"[12]

To his delight, he found some new friends with whom daily socializing was comfortable for the entire family. Within a few weeks of arriving, they became intimate with a wealthy bachelor and two wealthy couples residing in Lausanne, "very agreeable people indeed." The hospitable, friendly English philanthropist William Haldimand, who owned a large estate just below Rosemont, with a beautiful house upon the lake, and the Swiss-born William de Cerjat, married to an Irish heiress, were permanent residents.[13] The good-natured, enlightened, fifty-eight-year-old Haldimand, having served as a director of the Bank of England and as a member of Parliament, had settled near Lausanne in 1828. Well known for his generosity, he contributed handsomely to charitable projects, and, like the visiting author, was avidly interested in improving care for the mentally and physically ill. Richard Watson and his wife, Lavinia, with an immense family estate at Rockingham in Northamptonshire, were, like the Dickenses, spending only the summer and a little more in Switzerland. An elegant, generous, quietly courtly man, Watson had served both in the army and in Parliament, where he had supported the Reform Bill. Mrs. Watson, four years younger than Dickens, with three small children, was a charming, urbane, pretty woman, interested in ideas and art. He immediately felt a warm brotherly affection for her. On June 29, 1846, while a tremendous storm raged, the Haldimands introduced their new neighbors to their old friends, beginning an interchange of dinner parties and group excursions through the next months that created an extended family of sympathy.

Dickens fame usually made him immediately welcome, a guest of distinction. Curiosity, in this case, was soon replaced by affection and delight with how unaffected he was with friends who took pleasure in sharing in his "extraordinary spirits," his amusing conversation, and the parlor games that he insisted on. He entertained them with whist, the tricks of the conjuror, the charades of the amateur actor, and the serious magic of the mesmerist, who, when Elliotson visited in mid-October, "magnetized a man . . . among unbelievers, and stretched him on the dining room floor." Among nonactors, he was a one-man performance. His respectable entertainments were usually irresistible. While delighting in being the object of attention, he warmly responded to the nonperformance personalities of Haldimand and Watson, whose honest silences and good hearts he admired and felt comfortable with. In mid-August, Haldimand took him to see "a remarkable case of a young man, deaf, dumb, and blind, who has been taught to *speak*, write and read," at the local home for the blind that he had founded and to which he eventually left his fortune. In early September, on the evening before they were to depart for the St. Bernard Convent, Dickens, "in a state of great animation," dined with his friends. The large party, led by Roche, went up to the convent together.[14]

Some old friends visited, though not as many as he had hoped. In July, the historian Henry Hallam, who was said "to have got up in the night to contradict the watchman about the hour and the weather," visited briefly with his niece Jane Brookfield, with whom Thackeray was in love. In August, the Thompsons became neighbors. Christiana was considerably pregnant, "a mere spoiled child . . . with a whimpering, pouting temper" who had not turned out "half as well as I expected." The Talfourds arrived in October for a three-day visit. Also that month, Elliotson. "The pleasure of a generous friendship," Dickens wrote to Jerrold, "is the steadiest joy in the world." Actually, the most surprising visit was Tennyson's in late August. At his namesake's christening, the poet had declined Dickens' invitation to accompany him to Switzerland, an inappropriate suggestion prompted both by his admiration for Tennyson as a poet and for the warmth he felt on his participation in the christening. Though Tennyson seems to have liked Dickens, he did not especially admire his novels and, ironically, feared that he would quarrel with him about his sentimentality. Probably he had Little Nell in mind. Having heard, perhaps from Hallam, that Tennyson was coming, Dickens anticipated "with fear and trembling" that he would not only be taken from his work "but required to smoke pipes by the Score." Late in the evening of a hot day, cogitating about *Dombey* and *The Battle of Life,* he saw "two travel-stained-looking men . . . of whom one, in a very limp and melancholy straw hat, ducked perpetually to me as he came up the walk. I couldn't make them out at all; and it wasn't till I got close up to them that I recognised Tennyson." He gave the poet and his companion, the publisher Edward Moxon, "some fine Rhine wine, and cigars innumerable." The visit went well.[15]

What went on best of all, though, once the Christmas book had been disposed of, was the writing of *Dombey and Son,* four numbers of which he had it in mind to complete before leaving Lausanne. The news from London was superlative. The sales had leveled off at over thirty thousand a number. This provided a provisional income, before accounts were settled, of one hundred pounds a month. The success seemed to him commensurate with the brilliance of what he was doing. He felt no false modesty on the matter, though his self-congratulations were mainly private. He did, however, begin reading sections of the novel to his friends in Lausanne. The first reading occurred on September 12, and was accompanied on Dickens' part by no feelings of dangerously premature exposure. The sober Watson noted that "he read remarkably well and we are all of opinion that the beginning of this work is more interesting than the commencement of any of his other works. He has great expectations of it himself." After reading the second number in October to his friends' "most prodigious and uproarious delight," he half seriously proposed to Forster that he give public readings of his works in London, since a "great deal of money might possibly be made . . . in these days of lecturings and readings." It would not be a gentlemanly thing to do. But "what do you say?" Should he take Miss Kelly's theatre "or shall I take the St. James's?" A few weeks later he carried on the serious joke by mockingly berating Forster for not exercising his usual good judgment and taking Covent Garden, which "is too large for my purpose," a joke that had its ironic fulfillment years later in his reading in equally large theatres. But the small theatre of his friends was sufficient for the moment. He anticipated that he would leave Lausanne, "if all goes well, in a brilliant shower of sparks struck out of them by the promised reading of the Christmas book," which he soon performed "with wonderful charm and spirit."[16]

By late October, the snow had already begun "closing in on all the panorama," and he was anticipating what awaited him in Paris, including the bustle of city streets to stimulate his imagination and to relieve his restlessness. At Lausanne, the winds blew unimaginably hard. Paris warmly glittered in the distance, "as bright, and as wicked, and as wanton, as ever." He also expected visits there from at least Forster and Jerrold. Though he regretted leaving his friends in Switzerland, he was not ambivalent about departure, partly because he felt that it was time to leave, partly because he felt certain that he would see them again, as visitors to Paris and London, and when he returned to Switzerland, as he imagined he would the next summer. He felt that he had "never left so many friendly and cheerful recollections in any place." In the middle of November, on the last night before departure, he felt quite miserable saying good-bye. Seeing the world through the eyes of his own gifts and gift giving, he felt that there were very few "dots on the map of the world where we shall have left such affectionate remembrances behind."[17]

❦ 2 ❦

BY LATE NOVEMBER 1846, DICKENS WAS SITTING AT HIS DESK BEFORE
a window in the small house that he had rented, after "the
agonies of house-hunting," at 48 Rue de Courcelles, watching
the heavy snow fall in an unusually cold, blustery Paris winter.
The wind entered the miniature "Paris mansion" as if it too
were a tenant. "There's not a door or window in all Paris—that
shuts; not a chink in all the billions of trillions of chinks in the
city that can be stopped to keep the wind out." It felt to him as
if he were experiencing real cold for the first time. "Everything
that is capable of being frozen, freezes, in every room in the
house, as hard as Marble." The bleak weather that went on for
months did not prevent him from tramping the wintry streets
after his morning writing sessions. "A wicked and detestable
place," Paris seemed wonderfully attractive. Dinners, small parties, the Paris theatres, other entertainments, occupied his evenings. He dined with Lord Normanby, now British ambassador
to France. Watson visited at the beginning of the new year.
"Ages seem to have elapsed since we left Rosemont." He wrote
to Haldimand that "I hear you trying to speak through what
now appear to me to be the fogs and hoarsenesses of my infancy."[18] While writing *Dombey*, he had constant reminders of his
childhood, of his family, and in the heavy snows that muffled the
sounds of the present and of the immediate past he heard more
clearly the voices of memory.

The sights of Paris occasionally provided striking external
representations of his emotional obsessions. The morgue particularly attracted him. It brought together his preoccupation with
death and an outward representation so stark and dramatic that
it encapsulated his deepest feelings. Even in Paris, the wages of
sin were death, death inexplicable, nontheological, a fact that
from childhood on he had had as an obsessive part of his imagination and consciousness. To look at a corpse was to look at the
ultimate, most threatening mystery, the body without spirit, the
flesh without animating life, turned into meat for carrion, into
the infant corpses in Rochester that had seemed to him as a child
like pigs' feet set out in a butcher shop, into the dead river-eaten
bodies of suicides fished out of the Thames, into the victims of

the devil-rat, Chips, into the corpses preserved by the cold at the great St. Bernard Convent, into the row of dead sibling infants represented for Pip by the small tombstones in the graveyard in Kent Unlike London, Paris had a central morgue where a large number of bodies could be viewed. It had become a morbidly fascinating tourist sight. "Whenever I am at Paris, I am dragged by invisible force into the Morgue. I never want to go there, but am always pulled there . . . with its ghastly beds, and the swollen saturated clothes hanging up, and the water dripping, dripping all day long, upon that other swollen saturated something in the corner, like a heap of crushed over-ripe figs." He went to the morgue many times during the winter "until shocked by something so repulsive that he did not have the courage for a long time to go back."[19]

Among the voices of memory, the voice of his sister Fanny spoke with particular plangency. Whether or not Elliotson's diagnosis in May had been correct, there was now "no doubt whatever that Fanny is in a consumption," an advanced case of tuberculosis. "Deeply, deeply grieved," he had to face the probability that his favorite sister would die within a few years, even with the best available medical care. Two weeks after he had settled into his Paris apartment, thinking of his own depressed state in the fall and associating it and his sister's illness with Mary Hogarth's death, he decided to leave Paris "for family reasons" three months sooner than he had intended; he would return to London at the end of March 1847 rather than in June. He could respond to Fanny's illness more helpfully at home than abroad, though he would be helpless to effect any real change. Given her condition and the medical treatment available, there was no basis on which to hope for recovery. Her singing and her music-lesson days were over. To add to Dickens' sorrow, Fanny's crippled eldest son, who had always had a fragile hold on life, seemed unlikely to outlive his mother by much, if at all.

Death and childhood had been prominently on Dickens' mind when he began *Dombey*. All his previous novels had had strong autobiographical elements, but *Dombey* and his next novel, *David Copperfield*, were to take the impulse into deeper, more effective, more discreet, and more revealing expressions. As his fame had increased, just setting the biographical record straight had become an occasional concern. In response to an American writer's brief, "wildly imaginative" account of him that had appeared in 1842, he had whimsically threatened that he might "one of these days be induced to lay violent hands upon myself—in other words attempt my own life." In 1838 and in 1845, he had provided two friendly biographers with brief corrective and controlling accounts, hinting that at some time he would himself provide fuller details. While in Lausanne in November 1846, Dickens discussed with Forster the possibility of writing a sustained autobiography. The desire was partly catalyzed by his preoccupation with episodes and feelings from his childhood that he was drawing on in the early episodes of *Dombey*, particularly the creation of Mrs. Pipchin's establishment in Bath, where young Paul Dombey lives for a short time. The memories were not all good ones. The episode resonates with the pain that he had suffered during what he felt was his period of neglect and exploitation. "We should be devilish sharp in what we do to children. . . . Shall I leave you my life in MS. when I die? There are some things in it that would touch you very much, and that might go on the same shelf with the first volume of Holcroft's."[20]

Whether he actually began to jot down brief accounts of crucial episodes from his early life while in Switzerland or in Paris, he clearly had it in mind to do so. In the next two years, perhaps while writing *Dombey*, certainly before beginning *David Copperfield*, he created a fragment of an autobiography that Forster eventually saw, perhaps some part of it soon after March or April 1847, when he brought up the subject again in a more sustained and detailed way, and the entire thing in January 1849. In the spring of 1849, he drew upon some of it almost verbatim for the fourth number of *David Copperfield*. Thomas Holcroft, in his widely read *Memoirs* (1816), had revealed that Holcroft's father's impoverishment had turned his childhood into a difficult apprenticeship to poverty and misfortune. By the beginning of the writing of *Dombey*, Dickens clearly no longer had in mind an autobiography that would decorously set the public record straight, but an intimate, subjective, revelatory account of his life in the Romantic tradition, in which nothing important would be omitted and no one would be spared. Such an autobiography would be difficult to publish while his parents were alive. Apparently he had no intention of doing more than leaving it as an unpublished manuscript for his children and posterity, which " 'he always *intended* to do.' " Indeed, "in the final months of his life." he talked " 'of taking it up again some day.' "[21]

With his childhood and Fanny's much on his mind, he absorbed into the heart of his novel-in-progress, sometimes directly, sometimes indirectly, many of the central relationships and situations of his early life. Soon after Paul Dombey's birth his mother dies. Paul and his sister, surrogates for Dickens, thus are deprived of nurturing and are left the victims of an unloving father whose pride elevates the son into a mirror image of himself and degrades his daughter, Florence, into exile and neglect in her own parental home. In Dombey senior, he created a version of John Dickens transformed into a self-contained monster of personal pride and love of self, that very aspect that had resulted in Charles's being sent to the blacking factory. Like John Dickens, Dombey becomes a bankrupt. The first step in his bankruptcy, ironically, is the death of his son, a projection of himself so intense that the son almost prefers to abdicate his life since so little of it is his own. As for many readers, the most moving episode in the story, the death of Paul from consumption, anticipating Fanny's, was a moment of solemn resonance for Dickens, who thought of Paul as a living part of himself. "Paul is dead," he wrote to Miss Coutts. "He died on Friday night about 10 o'Clock and as I had no hope of getting to sleep afterwards, I went out, and walked about Paris until breakfast-time next morning."[22]

Florence alone deeply, unselfishly loves Paul. It is with her that his soul is in touch. Unlike Dickens' sister, Florence Dombey lives, despite neglect, lovelessness, and victimization. A traumatized child whose feelings carry much of the resonance of his own accounts of his childhood, her essential goodness of heart, warmth of feeling, capacity for love, and nobility of nature allow her, in the idealizing resolutions of the novel, to triumph over adversity, to heal wounds, even to regenerate her father into a feeling, loving, repentant human being. Early on, he is a version of the nightmare father who devours his children. At the end, he is transformed into the benevolent father who loves his child more than himself, more than his own life. Believing in the superior "moral sentiments" of women, Dickens found it natural to create a female character whose moral sentiments are so deep and full that they embody his sense of himself at his best. Florence has none of his own bitterness, frustration, and vengefulness. His inability to forgive his mother and his unresolved anger at his father, which played themselves out ceaselessly in the crucial episodes of his life, have their fictional antimodel in the creation of a perfect sister to Paul and to himself, one of the many such sisters in his life and in his fiction.

The intense fictional world of each morning's writing did not obliterate the reality of Paris. Always eager to give the external world its due while the inner world sustained him, he made the best of the remainder of his winter abroad. Georgina rather than the pregnant Catherine accompanied him on daytime excursions, particularly to the glittering, infamous Palais-Royal. He was struck by the unmistakable contrast between English and French depravity. The Gallic alliance of cynicism and honesty compared strikingly with British hypocrisy. At first, he thought the French vapid, like the Americans at their worst, indifferent, careless, procrastinating, dishonest, with American "semi-sentimental independence" but without the characteristic "American vigour or purpose." As workmen, they were completely inferior to the English, "fit for nothing but soldiering." French charm, though, gradually lightened his criticism, creating an elegant environment for enjoyment and a general pleasure in life that contrasted favorably with English sobriety, with the dark Sabbath of British earnestness, some of whose values he shared but whose atmosphere frequently oppressed him. There was pleasure for him in his sense that, by late January 1847, he had become "an accomplished Frenchman," boasting that he had learned to speak like an educated native. Before he left in March he readily confessed to having "a much greater respect for the people than I had before." In fact, he had sufficient Francophile enthusiasm to exclaim that, despite their "odd mixture of refinement and coarseness," they were in many ways "the first people in the universe," and French culture noticeably superior to British in its "general appreciation of, and respect for, Art."[23]

Though he had only minor contact with the luminaries of

French artistic life, he admired Victor Hugo's genius and liked him "best." With Forster he visited Hugo on an evening in which the latter reminisced about his childhood and graciously flattered him. Hugo's wife impressed him, "a handsome woman with flashing black eyes, who looks as if she might poison his breakfast any morning when the humour seized her." With Forster again, he had dinner with the novelists Alexandre Dumas and Eugène Sue. A friend of Count D'Orsay, Sue oddly covered socialist ideas with dandyesque dress. They visited Théophile Gautier, Alphonse Lamartine, and "the sick and ailing Chateaubriand." He met and became friendly with the playwright Eugène Scribe, whose *Irène ou Le Magnetisme* he particularly admired. By himself and with friends, he went regularly to the theatres, delighting in the richness of the Parisian stage.

During the last weeks of January, when Forster came, they went sightseeing, "with a dreadful insatiability," mainly to places he had already seen, to the morgue, the prisons, the palaces, theatres, and hospitals, to the Louvre, Versailles, the Bibliothèque Royale, and Saint-Cloud, "whirled out of one into another with breathless speed." Those sites associated with the Revolution that he visited and revisited became fixed in his memory with a force and historical accuracy that he drew on years later for *A Tale of Two Cities.* Though he regretted Forster's demands on his time and the interruption in his writing schedule, as if he never "had anything to do with a book called Dombey," the friendship was not strained by the imposition. Dickens was at his best as a host. Forster delighted in having his friend and Paris at the same time.

Maclise, whom he had invited to join them, had regretfully declined the invitation, hard at work on an important project. Exercising his minimal talents as a comic poet, he begged Forster (and Dickens) not to forget him:

> When by the Seine thou rovest
> With the friend thou lovest
>   Still remember me.
>
> If Sue—or Victor Hugo,
> Geo. Sand—or Kock, to you go
>   Still, still remember me.

In Pere la Chaise while walking
O'er Montmartre while stalking
     Be sure remember me.

When with Dickens thou art dining
Think of him at 14 pining
     In fast—then think of me.

When with him you Lafitte drinking
Let not—your spirits sinking—
Of Lincoln's Inn then thinking
     a tear bedim your eye,
     and then remember me.[24]

During the week before Christmas 1846 Dickens had visited London, accompanied only by Roche, partly to consult about Fanny, mainly to participate in rehearsals of an authorized stage adaptation of *The Battle of Life*, initiated by his reading it to the cast and management. He also wanted to be in London on the day of its publication. Despite a severe cold, he enjoyed the company, at the reading and at dinners, of Forster, Macready, Lemon, Leech, Maclise, and Elliotson, though he felt too ill to attend the premiere. "There was immense enthusiasm at its close, and great uproar and shouting for me." On a second brief visit soon after the middle of February 1847, the Channel crossing was so rough that he felt more ill "than on our American voyage." Though the visit had been necessitated by his having underwritten the sixth number of *Dombey*, the first time he had ever done such a thing, he took advantage of the necessity both for business and pleasure. In addition to the one hundred pounds per month *Dombey* provided, the new accounts revealed, "thank God," an additional "£2000 clear" from the first four numbers alone. The financial projections for the future installments were joyously staggering. Arrangements for a cheap edition in numbers of all his completed novels also promised substantial profits. Finally enjoying a long-postponed dinner with Lady Blessington and other friends at Gore House, he had the pleasure of seeing his eldest son begin King's College School, with Miss Coutts paying the bill. No sooner had he returned to Paris late in February than an urgent message from Forster, to whom he had just said good-bye, told him that Charley had come

down with scarlet fever. "Forster and Ellictson removed him
... from School, wrapped up in blankets," crimson with fever,
and brought him to his maternal grandparents' home near Regent's Park.[25] Deeply concerned, he and Catherine returned to
London immediately.

THE SPRING AND SUMMER OF 1847 WERE A MODEST BUT NOTICEABLE
turning point. The hard work for over ten years of establishing
himself as a professional writer culminated in the success of
Dombey and Son. He never again had serious financial worries.
He had become independent, at least in the sense that his earning power was enormous. Whatever the pressures on him from
a large family, his actual resources readily sustained all expenses though his sense of being exploited, even harried, by
greed or incompetence or both, pained him. There was always
room for a hint of exasperation, an edge of bitterness, a rehearsal
of insecurities that no amount of success could ever discharge
fully. The size of his family, though, and their assumption of a
costly upper-middle-class style of life dependent on his achievements were compulsions and choices of his own.

He had also turned, with his new novel, *David Copperfield*,
more explicitly to fictional autobiography, to an exploration of
himself through his art more direct, more honest, more resolute
than in his earlier fiction. In the novels that were to follow, even
when they were not directly autobiographical, he was to use
autobiographical tonalities for more subjective portraiture and
psychological dramatization than in his earlier work. Additionally, with *Dombey*, he became a more careful, self-conscious
craftsman, with a controlling overview inherent in the inception and the initial plans. His sense of himself as a professional
author also expanded into bolder, more energetic efforts to define writers as socially valuable and communally cohesive
professionals caring about one another and about their position
in the culture. And in this effort and affirmation, he stepped
more fully onto the public stage as an actor and as a reader of
his own works in a series of performances whose underlying
energy hinted at failures within his marriage and discontent

with his life in general that quietly, slowly, perhaps inevitably, intensified the feelings and initiated the events that ten years later changed his life radically.

The idealized images of himself and of wives and sisters in his fiction had set a disquieting counterpoint to the reality of his relationship with Catherine. His awareness of her increasing emotional distance and his growing identification of her with women like his mother and Mrs. Nickleby expressed itself in his fiction long before he was able to confront it consciously. It was, though, all along unwittingly expressed in their relationship. The birth of Sydney Smith Haldimand Dickens, their seventh child, in April 1847, during which "my dear Kate suffered terribly," was one of those moments in which his relief was stronger than his anger at the sheer number of children they seemed not to be able to avoid having and the consequences to him. His bitterness was self-lacerating, and he felt increasingly ambivalent not only about the deaths but also about the births of children. Later, he freely gave the advice, "don't have any more children."[26] Over the next ten years, the youthful, handsome Dickens became, to his own shock, prematurely old. He grew painfully aware that one of the prices of hard work, success, and fatherhood was the unwanted assumption of middle age while inwardly feeling young, romantic, and unfulfilled.

Soon after his return to London in February 1847, he had attended William Hall's funeral "to pay that last mark of respect" to a man from whom he had been alienated. It was a moment of sadness and reminiscence. Hall had been only eleven years his senior. At the age of thirty-five, Dickens now had a sufficiently long personal history on which to focus his inherent tendency toward nostalgia. He detested the so-called good old times. But his increasing autobiographical orientation interwove the threads of nostalgia, sentiment, and personal history with an elegiac overtone for the lost self of his childhood and now sometimes also for the young man who had started his search for fame and fortune in the 1830s. He remembered vividly the day on which he had bought in a bookstore in the Strand, from William Hall's hands, "the Magazine in which the first thing I ever wrote was published," and another day, in 1837, when they had gathered in Chapman and Hall's office to drink claret and watch the young queen pass in a state procession on her way to the Guildhall.

Fortunately, though Charley's bout of scarlet fever had him in danger for a short while, there was soon no need to fear for *his* life. But the danger of disfiguring infection, even death, to Catherine and the child she was carrying forced both father and mother to stay away from their son until the danger was past. By late March, "Charley, thank God," was "quite well again."[27] Since they could not repossess Devonshire Terrace until the autumn, he took a short lease on 1 Chester Place, Regent's Park. "The children, servants, and Virgin" returned from Paris at the end of March 1847. With Charley's illness, Catherine about to give birth, and the dislocation of a strange house he had difficulty in getting the eighth number of *Dombey* under way, feeling "the "deepest of despondency (as usual in commencing Nos.)." Fortunately, he was soon back on schedule.

His family relations were cordial, even though he was not enthusiastic about Fred's being "transported to madness" for love of Anna Weller, "the most volatile little minx in existence." Taking his duties seriously, John Dickens continued working for the *Daily News*. Apparently his newspaper salary and pension were sufficient to keep him from pestering his son for loans or directing unpaid bills to him. In writing *Dombey*, and soon *David Copperfield*, Charles had his father frequently in mind, sometimes humorously, often painfully. He resonantly mimicked him to Forster, particularly his self-inflating, pretentious rhetoric, often with the tag line "as my father would observe—indeed did on some memorable ancient occasions. . . ."[28] Fanny's illness brought the family into a sense of shared sorrow, and John Dickens showed himself as anxious a father as did Charles a brother. With the Hogarths, he had a companionable relationship, little different from what it had been for years. Mrs. Hogarth remained a somewhat officiously hysterical mother and grandmother. George Hogarth, proud of Dickens' success, had gratefully seen three of his daughters absorbed into his son-in-law's household.

As soon as he returned from France, the Dickens circle reassembled. The rivalry between Maclise and Forster for Dickens had long been resolved in Forster's favor. It had been both a serious and a playful triangle. Among the observers who had noticed its intensity was Count D'Orsay, who, with French self-awareness and openness about such things, teased Maclise:

"Haave you concluded your little dam ridicule conquetterie avec that good Forster and Dickens. Bah! and we laughed joyously, and I told him he had exactly hit the very expression in coquetterie." Working on "a great picture of the Sacrifice by Noah," Maclise was increasingly preoccupied with his own professional frustrations. Dickens joked that "because he *couldn't* put in more than eight people" he fulfilled "his tendency always . . . to cram in, hundreds" by making "it up in Beasts." Feeling himself closer to Forster, Maclise sometimes resented the bond between Forster and Dickens. He felt with some anger that Dickens did not "care one damn" about his contributions to the Christmas books and sometimes treated him "harshly, not to say unjustly." When ill, he felt hurt at Dickens' neither calling nor writing. With moody confusion, he claimed, without the benefit of a pause between the clauses, "that I am really and truly unwell it may be hypochondria." After falling down "at the door of [his] painting room," he "had the most unquiet nights from palpitating fears." Increasingly reclusive, he passed his life "within the walls of my painting room. . . . I hate going anywhere and so I do *not* go." His immense Byronic vanity found middle age devastating. "My hair you will be delighted to hear is now quite grey. . . . This is the secret of keeping myself to myself. I quite understand Geo[rge] IV when his good looks departed, stopping at home." At times, though, he was still a good companion, and he and Forster visited frequently at Devonshire Terrace. In early 1848, Dickens and Maclise considered "going to Ireland for six weeks in the spring, and seeing whether anything is to be done there, in the way of a book."[29] They did not go.

Forster seemed "more silent than in the old days and his nose is higher," the elevation reflecting the combination of his tendency toward arrogance—Eliza Lynn, who met him at Landor's seventy-fourth birthday party in early 1849, thought him "pompous, heavy . . . ungenial . . . saturnine and cynical"—and the seriousness with which he took his role as a man of letters, a profession that he insisted was as dignified as the bar or the clergy. Still at work on his *Life of Goldsmith*, revising it again and again, "buried in Goldsmith and Examiner," he also took on the duties and the income of general editor of *The Examiner* at Fonblanque's retirement in early 1848. Yet he could twinkle with generosity and charm. Elizabeth Gaskell, who also met him in 1849, found him "little, and *very* fat and affected, yet *so* clever and shrewd and good-hearted and right-minded." Dickens and Forster were mutually possessive, and Forster, who handled all the proofreading when he was abroad and continued to proof-read *Dombey* as it went from printer to author to Browne to Forster and then to the printer again, probably still spent more time with Dickens than any of his other friends. But serious tension between them in the fall of 1847 threatened to end the friendship mainly because of Dickens' frustration at Forster's interfering arrogance. Forster spoke to Macready "as if the long and intimate friendship between himself and Dickens was likely to terminate or very much relax. They have both faults with their good qualities, but they have been *too* familiar." Macready hoped that Dickens was "not capricious—not spoiled; he has, however, great excuse."[30] The tensions were suppressed; the interdependence continued.

On one occasion Dickens volunteered to act as intermediary in a dispute between Forster and Thackeray. After years of barely successful journalism and fiction, Thackeray had begun to move emphatically through the gates of success with the beginning of the publication of *Vanity Fair* in monthly numbers in January 1847. Forster admired his talent but did not like the book, partly because it was "wicked." Thackeray strongly admired *Dombey* and generously praised it, particularly "that chapter describing young Paul's death: it is unsurpassed—it is stupendous!"[31] With a humorously wicked drawing pencil, Thackeray had for years been doing caricatures of his friends. Some were genial. Others touched raw nerves. Over the decade most of the Dickens circle and other well-known literary and artistic figures had had their peculiarities exaggerated, their weaknesses satirized, in his private doodles and drawings, some of which he shared with friends. Certainly the sensitive, irritable Forster had been one of his subjects. When a mutual friend, the sensible, good-natured journalist and dramatist Tom Taylor, made the error of telling Thackeray that in a moment of characteristic temper Forster had said that Thackeray was "false as hell," he responded, feeling that his honor had been attacked, by snubbing Forster at a party at Procter's house early in June 1847.

In a flurry of hostile and then conciliatory letters guided by Dickens and other intermediaries, the apparent insults became real misunderstandings. Taylor took the blame for being indiscreet. He had misjudged sensitivities. Forster took the blame for having expressed himself badly. Thackeray took the blame for having been ignorant of the context in which Forster made the remark, explained as a local, intemperate reference to a particular instance, most likely a response to one of his caricatures. Dickens' role was beneficent and constructive, though, unlike Macready, he did not think that the quarrel was only "words, words, words." Thackeray's series of caricatures of novelists in *Punch* had offended him, though he was not one of the subjects, as a demeaning of the profession of letters that "did no honor to literature or to literary men."

Having identified himself so fully with the effort to increase the status of the profession, Dickens felt personally affronted by Thackeray's dangerous indifference to sacred subjects. Though he did not find it easy to laugh at himself and his profession, he felt no personal hostility to Thackeray. At most, he felt some distance. That did not prevent him, though, from hosting a successful reconciliation dinner later in the month. Thackeray had a different sense of what was happening. "Jerrold hates me, Ainsworth hates me, Dickens mistrusts me, Forster says I am false as hell, and Bulwer curses me. . . . I was the most popular man in the craft until within abt. 12 months—and behold I've begun to succeed. It makes me sad at heart though, this envy and meanness. . . . Am I envious and mean too I wonder? These fellows think so I know. Amen. God only knows. I scarcely understand any motive for any action of my own or anybody else's." The next March, in response to Dickens' good-natured claim that "it couldn't be done without you," he happily attended, with Forster, Ainsworth, and others, a dinner at Devonshire Terrace in celebration of the completion of *Dombey*. [32]

With Hablot Knight Browne, the man with whom Dickens had the closest working relationship other than Forster, he communicated mainly by letter. Never a daily companion, "Phiz" had moved to the country. This businesslike relationship allowed Dickens the professional distance to control the content of the illustrations and to speak his mind unhesitatingly whenever he was dissatisfied. As long as Browne's work was satisfactory—it had in fact become an important asset—it was better that his artist friends like Leech, Maclise, and Stanfield, who had converted to Catholicism in 1846, be friends who were artists rather than collaborators, except for special occasions such as the Christmas books.

With two artists, the curve of intimacy was obverse. George Cruikshank still delighted him occasionally. His explosive vanity, though, and his increasing preoccupation with the dangers of alcohol set them apart. Cruikshank vigorously took up the temperance cause with the same extremism that had made him intemperate previously. In the summer of 1847, he published *The Bottle*, and one year later *The Drunkard's Children: A Sequel to the Bottle*, both of which Dickens reviewed in *The Examiner*. While he recognized the power of Cruikshank's art, he made clear in private conversation and in print that he thought "total abstinence" nonsense, an attempt by the weak-willed to make the temperate suffer for their inability to drink moderately.

With Frank Stone, a successful minor artist whom he had met at the Shakespeare Club in 1837 and who contributed illustrations to *The Haunted Man* eleven years later, he became warmly friendly in 1847. In the company of Stone, Leech, and Lemon, he now found himself setting off for long walks each week, the comradeship dubbed, with his passion for naming things, though without his usual flair, the "Walking Club." Occasionally a new friend accompanied them, the painter Augustus Egg, two years younger than Dickens, short, thin, sweet-tempered, and in poor health. An intimate of John Everett Millais, he also aspired to create an art that would embody the icons of Victorian modernity. At the end of March 1848, with Forster, Lemon, and Leech, Dickens went riding, "the greater part of it at full gallop," on the Salisbury Plain during a two-day holiday, visiting the "Druidical remains, and then coming home by the Great Western Railway."[33]

Soon after his return from France in 1847, Dickens declined to act in a performance of Sheridan Knowles's immensely popular melodrama *The Hunchback*, whose profits would go for famine relief in Scotland and Ireland. He gave "the Fashionables" who were putting it on the cold shoulder, partly because he did not think much of their ability, partly because he would not be able to control the proceedings, and also because he was busy with *Dombey,* with managing the transition from Paris to London, and with getting himself comfortable again. In addition, he had his own charitable projects to attend to, one of which, Urania Cottage, had been in the planning stage for some years and was now about to become a reality. Actively searching for a building to function as a home for former prostitutes, in early June 1847 he successfully negotiated for a house in Shepherd's Bush. In November, Urania Cottage opened. Deeply compassionate, Dickens' nature expressed itself more naturally in particularized and personally meaningful activities and objects of charity than in broad, abstract philanthropies. He was no more than ordinarily generous in giving to charity, partly because he received so many requests, partly because of his own pervasive financial insecurity. Once he had decided on a cause, though, no amount of trouble was too great. One of his young friends, George Henry Lewes, later remarked that he "would not give you a farthing of money, but he would take no end of trouble for you. He would spend a whole day, for instance, in looking for the most suitable lodgings for you, and would spare himself neither time nor fatigue."[34]

Seemingly indefatigable, he worked for the next ten years on behalf of Urania Cottage as if the redemption of a small number of fallen women symbolized the potential for wider salvation, for the triumph of humanistic liberalism, for the confirmation of his ability as a man of action to accomplish something in the real world of social problems, for the reaffirmation of his own idealized image of the higher moral sentiments inherent in the female. He wrote endless letters, both to Miss Coutts and to everyone who had to be corresponded with. He supervised the staff. He met almost every Tuesday with the governing board, on which his friends George Chesterton and Augustus Tracey also sat, both enlightened governors of well-known London prisons and his two most reliable conduits for likely residents of the home, which at any one time had no more than eighteen young women. He was familiar with the histories and personalities of every one of them, as if he had been given another chance to save Nancy from Bill Sikes. With an eye toward balancing the carrot and the stick, he instituted the marks system, a form of reward and punishment as inducement to improved behavior, and created a detailed "Explanation of the Mark Table" for internal Urania Cottage consumption. He wrote for public distribution an elaborate "Appeal to Fallen Women," combining compassion, common sense, deeply believed stereotypes, and some minor priggishness. Convinced that a new start offered the best hope for permanent reformation, he supervised arrangements to send promising residents to Cape Town or to Australia. Only the prospect of marriage in a context free of past associations could be sufficient incentive for former prostitutes to give up their long-learned and endured vices. He exerted himself to teach Miss Coutts that generally the carrot was better than the stick, though the stick had its necessary uses. Like readers of his novels, "these unfortunate creatures are to be *tempted* to virtue. They cannot be dragged, driven, or frightened."35

The notion of organizing his own amateur theatricals for charitable causes had been in his mind since 1845, when before privately invited audiences, his amateur company had successfully performed *Every Man in His Humour*. They had also done a benefit performance for Fanny Kelly and for a private hospital. Pressed to do more acting for various charities, he had declined. The notion seemed tainted by the change from private guests personally invited to public audiences buying tickets, even if the proceeds were for charity. The experience, though, had helped bind together Dickens and his friends. It had been pleasurable to most of them. And it had afforded him direct personal contact with an audience so much a part of his self-definition from childhood on. Restless, especially when writing, he needed additional outlets. Having organized his schedule when working on a novel so that he wrote during the first two weeks of each month, he usually had the next ten days or so free from the obligation to be at his desk. Even during the first two weeks of the month his schedule allowed late afternoons and evenings for recreation. In June 1847, while writing the tenth installment of *Dombey*, he brought together a number of inclinations and preoccupations: his fascination with the theatre, his constant search for ways to bind his community of friends together, his charitable inclinations with their personalized focus, and his increasing sense of himself as a member of a literary fraternity whose members should take communal responsibility for one another.

He and Forster began to explore the "half-formed idea of reviving [their] old amateur theatrical company for a special purpose," a series of benefit performances for Leigh Hunt. Hunt's always precarious financial affairs had taken a turn for the worse during the past year. The eminent Romantic journalist, editor, reviewer, and poet had preceded and then hovered in the background of the Dickens circle, like both the beneficent spirit and the harlequin from a Christmas pantomime, the deep favorite of Forster, a friend of Talfourd's, a legend whom the early Victorians inherited and embraced. Witty, bohemian, charming, politically liberal, even radical in his youth, he was a pleasant senior companion and a rallying cause for those, like Dickens and Forster, eager to assert the dignity of literature, the responsibility of the literary community to provide for its own, and the obligation of the government to reward merit in the arts by financial support. Hunt admired Dickens' novels and flattered him with how well he knew them. He warmly liked Hunt, with an affectionate respect that was a bow to the past and a recognition of his good company in the present. "Once when he and Dickens were coming away from a party on a very rainy night, a cab not being readily procurable to convey Leigh Hunt home . . . Dickens had made him get inside the fly he had in waiting for himself and the ladies who were with him, taking his own seat outside; upon which . . . Hunt put his head out to protest," quoting Mr. Mantalini in *Nicholas Nickleby*, " 'If you don't mind, Dickens, you'll *become a demd, damp, moist, unpleasant body!'* which was responded to by a blithe, clear laugh that rang right pleasantly in the dark wet night."[36]

By the end of the first week of June 1847, the party of amateurs had agreed to play again at one of the large London theatres for the benefit of Leigh Hunt, who "has done more to instruct the young men of England, and to lend a helping hand to those who educate themselves, than any writer in England," and also to perform once in Liverpool and once in Manchester. Dickens and Forster, who corrected Hunt's proofs, acted as his literary agent, and reviewed his work "regularly and influentially," had determined to pressure the government to provide a pension by putting on benefit performances that would dramatize Hunt's need and the government's irresponsibility. In June, in a review of his new book, Forster directly called for a state pension for Hunt. The strategy worked. Within a few weeks the government leaked the news that two hundred pounds a year had been granted. On the urging of Hunt, who had a long felt uncomfortable with benefit performances rather than a direct subscription, they canceled the performance at Covent Garden, but not those in Manchester and Liverpool, which would celebrate Hunt's pension, with a prologue written for the occasion by Bulwer and spoken by Forster, and also financially assist the impoverished, alcoholic former playwright John Poole, one of whose farces Dickens had put on in Canada. Forster and Talfourd had known Poole for years. The playwright had been living in squalor in Paris since that summer. Dickens, who had known him casually, probably had been influenced in some of the stories in *Sketches by Boz* by Poole's 1835 *Sketches and Recollections*.[37] Though a small portion of the anticipated profits would still go to Hunt, the lions would feed the lion's share to the destitute playwright, a combination of peer assistance and government help that Dickens thought salutary.

"Between Dombey and Management," he groaned, "I am one half mad and the other half addled." The Sparkler, as he often jokingly called himself, sparkled. "Gas," as he now jokingly called himself, flamed. The complaints came from a man who, reveling in overexertion, wrote "100 letters a day. about these plays."[38] By the end of June, with frequent trips to London from Broadstairs, where he was staying for the summer, he had made arrangements for the July 26 performance at Manchester and the July 28 at Liverpool. He had also, like a one-man staff, arranged for advertising. assembled the cast, and directed the initial rehearsals at Miss Kelly's theatre. They were to do Jonson's familiar *Every Man in His Humour* with, appropriately, a short interlude by Poole, *Turning the Tables*, and a farce, *Comfortable Lodgings*. As in 1846, he played Bobadil and Forster Kitely. All the members of the Dickens circle, with varying degrees of talent and cooperativeness, took their parts, including Jerrold, Leech, Costello, Stone, Lemon, and Augustus and Frederick Dickens from the original company. The vain, cantankerous Cruikshank, boasting that he had once considered an acting career, insisted on one of the substantial roles as the price of joining the cast. Dickens, who thought his name would be helpful, was also happy to have his two new young friends Augustus Egg and George Henry Lewes. Among other things, Lewes was a talented, semiprofessional actor and a writer of steamy romantic novels.

With companionable good humor, the company traveled to Manchester, lodging at the same hotel, dining together, celebrating together. There were some spouses and other relations, like Georgina, along for the adventure, including three pregnant wives, Catherine, Helen Lemon, who was to give birth in October, and Annie Leech, who shocked everyone into "great confusion and distress" by unexpectedly going into labor at the railway station in London. "Wheeled to the Victoria Hotel in a Bath chair," she was "there confined triumphantly. She was in my carriage; so I was a witness to the seizure and the wheeling. She is a capital little woman, and I'm glad it's over." The incident gave him the amusing but gauche idea for a story in which Mrs. Gamp, the comic, alcoholic midwife in *Martin Chuzzlewit*, "being informed that several of the ladies attached" to the theatrical company's trip northward "were in various stages of an interesting state, accompanied it, unbeknown, in a second cladge carriage, on the chance of being called in."

He had mixed feelings when the performances were over. "The success was brilliant, and you can imagine nothing like the reception they gave me at both places—standing up as one person, and shouting incessantly for a good ten minutes. . . . I never heard or saw such laughing in a theatre. The people were drooping over the fronts of the boxes like fruit." Christiana Thompson thought his performances wonderful. At the *"tremendous* supper afterwards,"* the company and their guests drank forty-six bottles of champagne into the small hours of the morning.[39]

Neither the pregnancies, though, nor the performances were over. When Annie Leech safely gave birth to a daughter, he prayed that "from any future personal participation in such achievements, may the humble individual who now addresses you (father of seven young children) be himself delivered!" The next year there were theatricals again, of a more sustained kind, directed toward what had now become a campaign to shame the British government into more generously funding the pension civil list for impoverished authors, artists, and scientists. In the fall of 1847, he attempted to regularize the amateur players into a system, with a secretary at fifty pounds a year. Frederick gladly undertook the position. In the late summer, he thought about and in the fall wrote a prospectus for "The Provident Union of Literature, Science, & Art . . . the Committee to consist of the Members of the Amateur Company." The plan was to invest each year the profits from two London and two provincial performances to create annuities for elderly indigent artists and their families. Having decided not to write a Christmas book for 1847, though "very loathe to lose the money," he found the time to take the new Society of Amateur Players through trial readings of several plays before they finally decided to add Shakespeare's *Merry Wives of Windsor* to their repertoire.

By early January 1848, the Society had made a commitment to raise funds to support a needy author as the permanent curator of the Shakespeare museum in Stratford. What better way to memorialize both the greatest English literary genius, whose reputation he had long been championing, and the profession itself? The Dickens circle soon decided that the most appropriate candidate for the first curatorship was Sheridan Knowles, who, despite the popularity of *The Hunchback* and *Virginius*, lived at the edge of poverty. Having become religious, Knowles, who had decided that "the Bible is the only book," was eager to be saved by the curatorship and to take time away from the Bible for Shakespeare.[40] Shakespeare's birthplace, in which the museum was to be housed, had been purchased the previous summer after years of fund-raising by a totally separate Shakespeare House Committee, a subcommittee of the London Shakespeare Committee, which had initiated the idea of the curator being "some Person honourably connected with Dramatic Literature," and had agreed to appoint Knowles if the novelist and his friends could raise the money. Early in December, Dickens attended a Shakespeare panorama at Covent Garden, organized to raise money to help repay funds borrowed to buy Shakespeare's birthplace, in which many leading actors performed. Dickens' amateur players agreed to raise the funds for the appointment of Knowles.

After speaking to the Leeds Mechanics' Institute at the beginning of December 1847, suffering from a heavy cold, he stayed for the first time with the Watsons at nearby Rockingham Castle. Surrounded by servants, he heard muffled distant footsteps echoing in the cavernous halls. Back in London, which was in "a very hideous state of mud and darkness . . . everybody . . . laid up with the Influenza," he worked at resolving how to present the erotic relationship between Edith Dombey and James Carker for the sixteenth number of *Dombey*. He provided sufficient ambivalence in the text to allow some readers to conclude that they had not had a sexual affair, others to think that they had. One of the former, Francis Jeffrey, eagerly awaited the author's late December 1847 visit to Edinburgh. Having been ill, the elderly Jeffrey constantly anticipated dying. On the journey from Edinburgh to Glasgow, where Dickens was to preside at the first annual soiree of the Glasgow Athenaeum, Catherine, about six months pregnant, "was taken very ill . . . a miscarriage . . . coming on, suddenly, in the railway carriage." Though she seemed better within a few days, "she was again taken violently ill." The second "famous Doctor" countermanded the orders of the first "famous Doctor." She was put to bed again immediately. While she was attended by servants and doctors, the bagpipes greeted him at the Glasgow Athenaeum dinner with "Welcome Royal Charlie." The crowd cheered wildly. Outside it was "snowing, sleeting, thawing, and freezing." Inside, "unbounded hospitality and enthoozymoozy the order of the day, and I have never been more heartily received anywhere, or enjoyed myself more completely."[41]

He spoke again in May 1848, this time at the annual dinner of the Royal General Theatrical Fund, of which he was a trustee. At his request, Edward Bulwer-Lytton presided. Associated with drama and the novel, the long-haired, full-bearded writer, his name recently hyphenated by a condition of his mother's will, had for some time been a friend and close working associate of Forster's, who helped make his closet dramas, *The Duchess de la Vallière, The Lady of Lyons,* and most recently *Money,* more practical for production by Macready. Bulwer-Lytton warmly supported Dickens' effort to provide financial help to impoverished writers. Having met as early as 1838, the two men had established a formal relationship that soon became an admiring, even intimate friendship. At the fund's dinner the next year, Dickens steered his way successfully between his

close association with Macready and Forster and the presence
of the actor Charles Kean, Macready's chief rival, who detested
Forster. With formal good humor, Dickens spoke in terms that
were resonantly personal and economically astute. "It is not
sufficiently recollected that if you are born to the possession of
a silver spoon, it may not be very difficult to apply yourself to
the task of keeping it well polished . . . but . . . if you are born
to the possession of a wooden ladle instead, the process of trans-
muting it into that article of plate is often a very difficult and
discouraging process. And most of all we should remember that
it is so at a time of general trouble and distress . . . for then the
peaceful, graceful arts of life go down, and the slighter orna-
ments of social existence are the first things crushed."[42] Famine
in Ireland, revolution on the Continent, cholera in London,
economic depression, government under financial as well as
ideological pressure—in such times support for the arts was
most vulnerable. The best resource was self-help.

In the same month in 1848, Dickens boasted that his amateur company "are all nearly worked to death" in preparation
for the upcoming performances. He drove them relentlessly.
"Stone is affected with congestion of the kidneys, which he
attributes to being forced to do the same thing twenty times
over, when he forgets it once. Beads break out all over Forster's
head, and *boil* there, visibly and audibly. Fred says upon his soul
he never saw anything like it in all his life. And Leech is limp
with being bullied." Rehearsing at the Haymarket Theatre "all
day and at Miss Kelly's half the night," he admitted that he
began "to wonder why one does such things for nothing." He
knew why, of course. He had "set [his] heart on seeing Sheridan
Knowles installed at Stratford on Avon, as the Curator of
Shakespeare's House."[43] Those who had played in *Every Man in
His Humour* expanded their talents and anxieties to *Merry Wives
of Windsor*, and the two plays were performed on consecutive
nights in London. In addition they performed in three farces,
Animal Magnetism; Love, Law, and Physic; and *A Good Night's Rest*,
the first in London and Birmingham and the other two in Man-
chester with *Every Man*. They also performed in Liverpool in
June and then in Edinburgh and Glasgow in July. Two years
later, in November 1850, the same company did Jonson's play at
Bulwer-Lytton's ancestral home, Knebworth, north of London,

for a new plan, a variant of the pension-and-insurance proposal for impoverished writers that Bulwer-Lytton enthusiastically supported.

A few professional actresses were added to the cast for the 1848 barnstorming. Dickens gratefully accepted the participation of an attractive, talented amateur, Mary Cowden Clarke, the wife of Charles Cowden Clarke, who had been a friend of Keats's and was a lecturer and writer on Shakespeare and other authors. Three years Dickens' senior and the author of *The Complete Concordance to Shakespeare*, Mary Clarke became the informal historian of the Dickens-Shakespeare revels. On opening night, while standing "at the side scene of the Haymarket Theatre . . . with Augustus Egg, waiting to make our first entrance together upon the stage, and face that sea of faces, he asked me whether I felt nervous. 'Not in the least,' I replied; 'my heart beats fast; but it is with joyful excitement, not with alarm.' " The London performances were an outstanding success, partly due to his driving the company, "ever present . . . superintending, directing, suggesting, with sleepless activity and vigilance," being torn to pieces, in his own view, "by the whole body of amateurs and Shakespeare House people." The supreme amateur, Dickens demanded perfection, of others and of himself. Influenced by Macready, he went to great lengths to attain historical accuracy and stage effectiveness in costumes and scenery. As Justice Shallow, "his own identity was almost unrecognizable . . . his impersonation was perfect," though Maclise thought that he did not have enough to do. To the star-struck Mrs. Clarke, Mark Lemon's Sir John Falstaff, a role to which his natural girth and good humor contributed, "was a fine embodiment of rich, unctuous, enjoying raciness. . . . John Forster's Master Ford was a carefully finished performance." In Maclise's view, it was "the best piece of acting" Forster had ever done. "John Leech's Master Slender was picturesquely true to the gawky, flabby, booby squire. . . . Mr. G. H. Lewes's acting, and especially his dancing . . . were very dainty, with a peculiar drollery and quaintness. . . . George Cruikshank's . . . Pistol was supremely artistic . . . fantastic, spasmodic, ranting, bullying."[44]

Driven by enthusiasm and restlessness, Dickens considered additional performances in Plymouth, Bristol, and other cities. At the same time as he arranged the details for Manchester,

Liverpool, and Birmingham, then for Edinburgh and Glasgow, he adjudicated the competition and rivalry among his cast; he also helped with the arrangements for a gala retirement benefit for Macready, who had been unprecedentedly honored by the queen's decision to attend. In Manchester, Liverpool, and Birmingham, the audiences were rapturous. In the middle of July 1848, they traveled to Edinburgh. There, he organized a visit to Holyrood and then to Loch Lomond, with Catherine and Georgina also in tow. After the last night in Glasgow, "he was in wildest spirits at the brilliant reception and uproarious enthusiasm of the audience . . . and said in his mad-cap mood, 'Blow Domestic Hearth! I should like to be going on all over the kingdom, with Mark Lemon' and 'Mrs. Cowden Clarke . . . and acting everywhere. There's nothing in the world equal to seeing the house rise at you, one sea of delighted faces, one hurrah of applause!' "45

⚜ 4 ⚜

AT HOME AGAIN IN JULY 1848, THE INEVITABLE REACTION SET IN. Exhaustion and dissatisfaction took their toll. Dickens' comic tone came to his rescue. He missed Mary Clarke, he missed the travels, the acting, the audiences. "I have no energy whatever—I am very miserable. I loathe domestic hearths. I yearn to be a Vagabond. . . . Why have I seven children . . . taken on for an indefinite time at a vast expence . . . ? A real house like this, is insupportable after that canvas farm wherein I was so happy." *Dombey* had been finished in March. He had gone "about perpetually persuading" himself that he was choking, though he knew that there was "nothing the matter" with him. Feeling "rather nervous after [his] hard work," he had turned to the theatricals for relief.46 The first thoughts of a new book were now dimly stirring, soon to be conceived in the undeveloped interstices between *Dombey* and the fragments of autobiography that he had written. And Catherine, whom he had described in March as "tremendously fat," added another pregnancy to her figure. Henry Fielding Dickens, conceived in mid-April and to be born in January 1849.

Fanny was painfully, unmistakably dying. Since his return

from France, her condition had deteriorated. He kept closely in touch, writing more than he had done before, describing his daily activities, chatting about his work, his health, and the family. As the spring had advanced, Fanny had declined, exhausted by seizures, racked with coughing, unable to keep food down. She worried incessantly about the fate of her children and husband. "*Rest* is the one great thing you want," her brother urged, as if some act of the will could provide the context and the ability to do what her illness did not allow. "So look that fact steadily in the face and rest at all risks." He combined tenderness with willful exhortation, as if there were nothing that could not be overcome. "Do not get worse when you may under God so easily get better." His pleas partly expressed his unwillingness to accept helplessness, partly his attempt to encourage her to efforts that would make her dying less unrelievedly bleak. He responded to the example of a suicide that Fanny found attractive with a warning about how powerful ideas could be. "There are times with me after mental excitement and toil when such a circumstance as the suicide of your neighbor would become a dreadful idea that I could not shake off. I have had sufferings of that sort sometimes the oppression of which has been horrible." Yet he knew she was dying, and thought it best that she know no more than she insisted on knowing. When she did learn how ill she was, he "promised her that [he] would faithfully assist and advise" her husband "at all times and endeavour to be your true friend and that of the dear children." It was a "sacred . . . promise . . . lying always close to my heart not for today and tomorrow but for my whole life."47

He wanted her out of Manchester, an unhealthy place. "If you decide to take a holiday . . . I will send you a hundred pounds whenever you say the word." For that or any other need he offered as much money as would be required. When performing in Birmingham and Manchester, he had visited the Burnetts, and soon after made arrangements that brought Fanny and her family by the beginning of July 1848 to a rented home in Hornsey, near London. The air was better than Manchester's. Good medical care and family attention were available. Expert opinion, though, made it clear that the most that could be done was to relieve the coughing and the pain. Though he had been able to forget much during the revels in mid-July, he had not forgotten his sister except for brief moments. During July and August he visited her almost daily. One day he brought Mamie and Katie to see their aunt, who "still lingers on, to the amazement of the doctors and all who see how worn and wasted she is." Exhausted himself, and in response to Catherine's "*un*interesting condition," he went with his family to Broadstairs at the beginning of August. Thinking about his next Christmas book, playing with the children, receiving friends, exercising he kept at his usual activities, aware of Fanny's pain, in touch with her, with Burnett, with his father and mother, who visited Hornsey regularly.

Aware that her life was an agony to her he both hoped and dreaded throughout August to receive news of her death. On September 1, he "found poor Fanny in one of those paroxysms described by my father . . . and could have conceived nothing more terrific. No words can express the terrible aspect of suffering and suffocation—the appalling noise in her throat—and the agonized look. . . . From that, she sunk into a kind of lethargy. Sleep seems quite gone, until the time arrives for waking no more." The next morning she died. Dickens made the funeral arrangements, spending the tremulous day with Forster, remembering what his sister had been like when they had been children together, when, as he wrote later in an autobiographical story, "he had a sister, who was a child too, and his constant companion." After the funeral, his hand shook. He could not hold his pen steady. He had the steadiness, though, to assure Burnett that he could "never forget the patience, gentleness and endurance of your affection for her." Early the next year, her eldest son, "the little deformed boy," the prototype of Paul Dombey, "whom my sister has left half unconscious of his bereavement," was also to die. Dickens felt "that the mercy of God [had] removed" him.[48]

With Forster and Stone, he returned to London in late September from Broadstairs via a walking tour that he had designed to bring them through the country of his childhood. In Rochester, they stayed at the Bull Inn, with resonances of Pickwickian glory, and walked through Chatham, where he remembered the years as golden. He retouched the places of primal memory, as if for Fanny's sake as well as his own. "Dim visions of divers things are floating around me; and I must go to work, head foremost, when I get home." The Christmas book had to be written. The dim visions may have included fragments of self and personal history, some glimmer of the possibility of creating an autobiographical novel or more fragments of an actual autobiography that would extend the fragments he had already written and put into writing what he had been saying about his past in conversations with Forster. With only the Christmas book to do, he spent a comparatively relaxed autumn, though once under way he fell into a "frowning . . . state of inaccessibility and irascibility which utterly confounds and scares the House. . . . Kate and Georgina quail (almost) when I stalk by them." The idea that he had conceived in Lausanne in 1846 and then postponed, after writing a few pages in September 1847, developed into a psychological tale of the supernatural, *The Haunted Man*, which he finished at the beginning of December 1848, "crying my eyes out over it—not painfully but pleasantly as I hope the readers will."[49]

One night that month he read it after dinner to an appreciative audience of friends, including the Watsons, Hannah Meredith and her husband, Dr. Brown, Miss Coutts, Forster, and Stanfield. "People will take anything for granted, in the Arabian Nights or the Persian Tales," he told a friendly critic of the story's mixture of supernaturalism and realism. "But they won't walk out of Oxford Street, or the Market place of a county town, directly into the presence of a Phantom, albeit an allegorical one. And I believe it to be as essential that they come at that spectre through such a preparation of gathering gloom and darkness, as it would be for them to go through some such ordeal, in reality, before they could get up a private Ghost of their own."[50] Published in mid-December, with John Tenniel, later to illustrate *Alice's Adventures in Wonderland*, doing the illustrations, *The Haunted Man*, his final Christmas book, sold over seventeen thousand copies in two weeks for a profit to him of almost eight hundred pounds. That same month, there were two marriages in the family. His brother Augustus married Harriet Lovell, whom ten years later he deserted after she became blind. Frederick, whom he dressed down strongly for marrying with debts and attempting to borrow money from him, finally married Anna Weller, from whom he later separated. Relenting, he lent—for all practical purposes gave—his brother the money for which he had asked.

Fanny's death intensified Dickens' strong autobiographical preoccupation. Now his parents' eldest living child, he clearly also was the only one of their children to have any significant intellectual or artistic gifts. In the middle of January 1849, his latest, and he hoped his last, child was born. He decided on the name Henry Fielding Dickens after rejecting Oliver Goldsmith Dickens, thus emphasizing his identification with the eighteenth-century novelist and having in mind the autobiographical novel, perhaps with *Tom Jones* as his model, that he had decided to write. His parents' eldest son had begun the process of giving birth to what he later called his favorite child, *David Copperfield*, a version of himself the creation of which would give him the further opportunity to dramatize his adult sense of his childhood traumas. At first, with Fielding in mind, he intended it to be a third-person narrative. On Forster's suggestion, and perhaps because of the autobiographical fragment, he soon decided to use the first-person. The narrator's voice would be a fictional surrogate for his own. The story could absorb, with little change, some of the autobiographical fragment, particularly his responses to the blacking-factory experience, to parental neglect, and to mistakes of the heart.

At the start of the second week of January 1849, he set off by train on a midwinter working vacation to Norwich and Yarmouth, in Suffolk, with John Leech and Mark Lemon, his intrepid walking companions. The new novel was much on his mind. April was the likely date of publication of the first monthly number. Crucial decisions had to be made, among them "a local habitation and a name." His awareness of his strong personal identification with Kent may have alerted him to the desirability of finding an alternative setting to provide some distance to the autobiographical elements. The journey was tedious and cold, "only improved by the Sparkler's conversational powers" and afterward by the pleasure of good company on long walks. Norwich, where he bought Catherine a shawl, proved a disappointment. "The success of the trip," though, was the seacoast fishing village of Yarmouth, "the strangest place in the wide world: one hundred and forty-six miles of hill-less marsh between it and London." The Suffolk marshes may have reminded him of the Medway estuary. Soon after returning, he decided definitely to "try my hand" at the Suffolk setting. South of Yarmouth, he had seen a sign for the village of Blundeston, a name that appealed to his ear. He was soon in eager search of names, particularly for his main character and for the title. "Walking perpetually," with scenes and character possibilities dancing in his mind, he felt the anxiety of finding the right name, without which he could not settle on other things, let alone begin. Getting it right was crucial. The night before his eldest son's twelfth birthday party, he awakened, frightened that he had forgotten how to dance the polka, which he had recently learned from his daughters. He insisted on practicing it before going back to bed. " 'Remember that for my Biography,' " he told Forster.[51]

A brief family vacation in Brighton with the Leeches during the third week in February alleviated the tension. Sea scenes and colorful promenades delighted him, calmed him, with resonances of Paul Dombey's death and of the water imagery of the novel he was contemplating. "The people, in carriages, on horseback, and afoot, jingling up and down the esplanade under the windows like gay little toys; and the great hoarse ocean roaring unheeded beyond them, and now and then breaking with a deep boom upon the beach, as if it said sullenly, 'Won't anybody listen?' But nobody does; and away they all go, jingling up and down again, until the sun sets, and then go home to dinner." He was listening, though, and beginning to speak in his own voice. One tone was comic, his call to Lemon to join them at Brighton:

> Oh my Lemon round and fat
> Oh my bright, my right, my tight 'un,
> Think a little what you're at—
> Don't stay at home, but come to Brighton!—

Another was serious, his "mind running, like a high sea, on names," though still not satisfied.

During the last week in February, "in the first agonies of a new book," he transformed "Mag's Diversions, Being the personal history of MR. THOMAS MAG THE YOUNGER, of Blunderstone House," through various stages into six alternatives, all of which involved the name Copperfield or David Copperfield. On March 21, with the announcement of the first number for May 1, he told Bradbury and Evans to "let it stand. And may Heaven speed us!" The full title, "The Personal History, Adventures, Experience, and Observation of David Copperfield the Younger, of Blunderstone Rookery, which he never meant to be published on any account," he soon shortened to *The Personal History of David Copperfield*. When Forster pointed out that his main character's initials were the author's reversed, he was at first startled. But he immediately granted that such a coincidence was not remarkable at all. "Why else should I so obstinately have kept to that name when once it turned up?"[52]

Other suggestions and autobiographical elements were turning up with magical timeliness. On the journey to Norwich he met some acquaintances, one of them Alfred Mellon, the musical director of the Adelphi Theatre. Mellon had done the music for the recent dramatization of *The Haunted Man*, a semiauthorized adaptation that Dickens had helped with. The name and the association with music stuck in his mind for the creation of the flute-playing Mr. Mell. In Brighton, the raving mad daughter of one of the hotel guests, and then "her father . . . too, for company," became even much more mad, putting in mind the dramatic possibilities of madness that soon contributed to the portrait of Mr. Dick. On his return from Yarmouth, he had received a letter from a committee that had been set up to present a testimonial to his old schoolmaster William Giles, which reminded him that he had lost the advantage of being his pupil "when I was very young indeed," a subject he had already written about in the autobiographical fragment and that he had in mind to dramatize in *David Copperfield*.

In late January, his father had been ill, "low and weak," though not as "*exceedingly* unwell" as his mother had indicated. He had visited again, and described his sickbed with an economical tenderness that suggested how much he had on his mind and in his feelings the alternate versions of his father that had afflicted him since childhood: the lovable Mr. Micawber and the hateful Mr. Murdstone. Fanny's son had died at the end of January, and he comforted the religious Burnett with the good but unexceptional news that "he has rejoined his mother, and for ever cast away his early sorrows and infirmities." Early in March, the Leeches' twenty-month-old daughter, the baby who had been born in the Victoria Hotel on the way back from Manchester, died, "spared from greater uneasiness and pain."[53] The autobiographical impetus, the self-identification, was strong. The boy who had believed himself to have been the victim of "boyslaughter" but who had lived to be especially sensitive to the deaths of children was preparing himself and being prepared to create his favorite child, whose early life would dramatize the neglect, the loss, the desolation, and the death threats of his own.

Finishing the first number late in March 1849, he was pleased with what he had done. Moving ahead with the second, he completed it by early May, though he soon lost the head start. By the summer, he was writing each number immediately prior to its month of publication. Though he made outlines or memoranda ("Mems," as he called them), a practice he had started with *Dombey*, he found that the pain he felt depicting David's childhood resulted in his writing in fits and starts at the beginning. In mid-April, struggling with the creation of the Murdstones and his idealized mother's destruction, "the long Copperfieldian perspective look[ed] snowy and thick." Anxious about whether the book would be successful, he took an obtuse position with his publisher about pricing policy simply out of nervousness. On the twelfth of May, the Dickenses gave a dinner and then a music party, attended by Thackeray, Forster, Jerrold, Browne, Rogers, the Carlyles, and others, a moment of social and communal affirmation. Fortunately, the sales of the first number, and those that followed, were favorable, though not as good as *Dombey*'s, as Forster had anticipated. But they were sufficiently strong so that Dickens felt reassured, sensible enough to realize that *Copperfield*, as a departure from his previous work, would need to build its own audience. He now raised for serious consideration his long-simmering commitment to edit a new periodical for Bradbury and Evans. He wanted to be liberated from such strong dependency on the sales of his novels.

By June 21, he had finished the third number, containing the death and burial of David's mother. "Quite confident in the story," he planned the special features of the next three. The fourth was particularly challenging since it incorporated a large portion of the autobiographical fragment, which had been the core of the original conception. "Fourteen miles to-day in the country," he told Forster, "revolving number four!" By mid-July, after a brief working holiday in Broadstairs, in response to

feeling bruised and ill from "an awkward fall . . . on my weak
side . . the left, where there is an inflamed kidney sometimes,"
he finished it. "I really think I have done it ingeniously, and
with a very complicated interweaving of truth and fiction." The
pain of the childhood kidney weakness went away after he had
completed the most painful part of the novel. The bruises
healed. "I am getting on like a house afire in point of health."54

But as he brought David through the trauma of childhood,
his own health and healing powers were on his mind, prompted
by two aspects of his summer holiday. With Leech, he went for
three days in mid-July to the Isle of Wight to find a summer
house particularly encouraged by a new friend, James White,
a nonpracticing clergyman who lived and owned property
there. A successful minor playwright who had inherited a substantial estate from his wife's father, White had written a series
of historical dramas that had brought him into the Dickens
circle through Macready, who had produced one of them in the
spring of 1846. A vain, moody, but good-hearted man, he and his
wife, whom Dickens liked ("He is excellent, but she is better"),
were eager to have the Dickenses for summer neighbors. Both
Leech and Dickens thought Wight and the Whites wonderful.
Making up his mind almost immediately, Dickens took "a most
delightful and beautiful house," called Winterbourne Villa, "belonging to White, at Bonchurch—cool, airy, private bathing,
everything delicious—I think it is the prettiest place I ever saw
in my life, at home or abroad." Leech took a smaller house close
by that also belonged to their friend.55 Thackeray, his wife in a
mental institution, his domesticity and passions unsatisfied, saw
the Dickens entourage arriving on the pier at Ryde, "the great
Dickens with his wife his children his Miss Hogarth all looking
abominably coarse vulgar and happy."

It was *not* a completely happy summer, though it started
well, with picnics, long walks, excursions throughout the island,
whose "views . . . are only to be equalled on the Genoese shore
of the Mediterranean. . . . No such scenery in England, certainly." Leech agreed. "This is such a place—perfect freedom—
do as you like, beauty everywhere, and in everything." They
were entertained at tea by Lady Jane Swinburne on the ram-
bling gardens and lawns of the house where the "golden-haired
son of the Swinburnes," home from his first term at Eton,

played with his children, who found the island a sporting paradise. At White's home, they had games, dinners, amusements,
including "a mighty conjuring performance" by Dickens "for
all the children in Bonchurch." They played "great games at
rounders every afternoon, with all Bonchurch looking on."
With Leech and Georgina, Dickens "attended an examination of
the childrens and Infant School." To Leech's "horror" a child
brought him "(in the presence of all the rank and beauty of
Bonchurch) a sum in arithmetic of the most terrific nature to
look over, and see if it was correct. I looked at it for some time,
went through pantomime expressions of decided approval—and
passed it on to Dickens who immediately (to my confusion)
found no end of blunders. . . . Miss Hogarth I have found out
sent this fiend in childish shape to me." On the first of August
they watched the queen sail past from her summer home in
Osborne on her way to Ireland. Talfourd visited late in August,
glowing with the happiness of his elevation to the bench. The
three friends celebrated with "a most cheerful dinner," and
what seemed to the ebullient Talfourd a wonderful walk to
Ventnor and back "by a mountain course, over the bare
downs—all the way talking as authors talk."[56]

Late in the summer Leech had a serious accident. While
bathing, he "was knocked over by a bad blow from a great wave
on the forehead." He was alternately unconscious and unable to
sleep, having suffered a severe concussion, which Dickens described as "congestion of the brain." Despite "twenty of his
namesakes on his temples" as well as ice packs, bleeding, and
other medical attention, he became worse. "His restlessness had
become most distressing, and it was quite impossible for him to
maintain any one position for five minutes." Deeply worried,
Dickens spent hours at his bedside. With medical powers of his
own, he finally persuaded the distressed Annie Leech, who had
called for him at 2:30 A.M., to allow him to try to mesmerize her
husband. "It was more than half an hour before I could so far
tranquillize him . . . by the magnetism . . . as to keep him
composed. . . . Then, that effect began, and he said he felt comfortable and happy . . . and in a few minutes fell fast asleep."
Later in the morning, the doctor pronounced him greatly better.
Dickens slept at the Leeches' the next night, "to be called if he
were restless," and the next day mesmerized him again.[57] He had

not practiced his mesmeric powers since leaving Italy. They were undoubtedly still there, still available to him.

One of the initial attractions of Bonchurch had been Dickens' belief that it had a healthy climate. For some time he had been drinking each morning and evening a pint of water, convinced that it was good for his health and that he had been free from illness because of the practice. He had also been taking a cold shower each morning, partly to brace himself for the day, mostly because he believed that the body responded favorably to the invigoration of the nervous system. Indoor showers had to be created with cisterns and gravity pipes. In Broadstairs, he delighted in his favorite shower. At Winterbourne Villa he felt semiecstasy at a 150-foot-high waterfall (in a passion of enthusiastic boasting it gained 350 feet) that he had a carpenter transform into a partly enclosed "perpetual shower bath" under which he stood every morning "to the unbounded astonishment of the aboriginal inhabitants."

By mid-August, though, he was worried by "a monstrous cold, which has now resolved itself . . . into a cough," an ailment he seems to have had since his arrival. He went to see a doctor, who used a stethoscope, Elliotson's recent importation from France. Probably he feared consumption, concerned that Fanny's illness was an indication of a general family propensity toward tuberculosis. Though he finished number four in July and wrote five and six in August and September, he felt a general lassitude and depression that worried him. It seemed perfectly reasonable to him to blame his physical and mental state on the peculiar climate of the Isle of Wight. Maintaining the privacy of his mornings for writing, whatever the social alternatives, he was deeply absorbed in mediating between and combining his life and his fiction. That he was writing a series of episodes in which his fictional alter-ego experiences variants of the most painful episodes of his own childhood may have had something to do with how he felt. But that did not occur to him. "I am perfectly convinced, that, for people suffering under a wasting disease," the Isle of Wight "is madness altogether." The doctors who prescribed the climate were mad or stupid. "The whole influence of the place . . . is to reduce and overpower vitality. . . . Naples is hot and dirty, New York feverish. Washington bilious, Geneva exciting, Paris rainy—but Bonchurch, smashing. I am quite convinced that I should die here, in a year. It's not hot, it's not close, I don't know what it is, but the prostration of it is *awful.*" As soon as he could, with his family and the ongoing manuscript of *David Copperfield,* he fled to Broadstairs, where the air was "brisk and bracing."[58]

CHAPTER EIGHT

No Need for Rest
(1849-1853)

❧ I ❧

WHEN COMPLETING *DAVID COPPERFIELD*, DICKENS EXPERIENCED A
powerful aftereffect that left him confused about "whether to
laugh or to cry . . . strangely divided . . . between sorrow and
joy." He felt that he had been turned inside out, his inner life
now visible, in partly disguised forms, in the shadowy world of
ordinary daylight. The story he had written was so deeply personal that "no one can believe [it] in the reading, more than I
have believed it in the writing." Having transformed his private
memories and his emotional life into a public myth about himself, particularly his development from an abandoned child into
a great popular artist surrounded by love and success, he felt the
excitement both of exposure and catharsis. Exorcising the
wounds of childhood and young adulthood, he also dramatized
the unresolved problems of his personality and his marriage,
anticipating the turmoil that was to come. Though energized by
the process of writing, he was also exhausted by "heaps of Copperfieldian blots," by that "tremendous paroxysm of Copperfield." Toward the end, he felt "rigid with Copperfield . . . from

head to foot." When he finally put down his pen in October 1850, he took up his "idea of wandering somewhere for a day or two." Almost inevitably, he went back "to Rochester . . . where I was a small boy."[1]

In *David Copperfield* he re-created in mythic terms his relationship with his mother, his father, his siblings, particularly Fanny, and with his wife and his wife's sisters. The novel was more precious to him than his own children because the favorite child was himself. Soon after beginning, he confessed that he had stuck to that fictional name through the exploration of alternative titles because he had, even at the earliest stage, recognized that he was writing about himself. His passion for names also expressed his need to pattern and control. After the birth of Katie in 1839, he assumed the right to name all his children (Catherine had "little or nothing to say" about that). The elaborate christening of Alfred D'Orsay Tennyson Dickens provides the representative example of the novelist imposing his literary constructs on other people's lives as well as his own.[2] When it came to his family, he did not admit of any distinction. When it came to his novels, the distinction between self and other was subordinated to the dramatization of the many varieties of the single self. Changing Charles Dickens into David Copperfield had the force both of unconscious reversal and of minimal autobiographical distancing. At the heart of the novel was a partly mediated version of himself that represented his effort to claim that he had come through, that all was well with him as he approached the age of forty.

There was much, though, that was troublesome. He had fatherhood with a vengeance, particularly difficult for someone who both embraced and rebelled against patriarchy. He had a superficially successful marriage that provided him with neither romance nor companionship. He had ostensibly left behind a childhood whose experiences and memories still galled him in the present. He had a future whose patterns promised to be similar to those he already knew, his opportunities for adventure limited by his personal and professional obligations, by the restraints of success, and by the pressure to keep earning at a high level. No longer a young man, he assumed, becoming an honored public figure of prominence and distinction, a Victorianism that he was not fully ready for and that the artist within him was uncomfortable with, perhaps even rebelled against. There were the first visible signs of middle age. The mobility of his face had now the counterpoint of some permanent lines. His luxuriant hair began to show a receding silky thinness. Having been forced from an early age to look after himself, he now had to look after others as well as to anticipate the trials of middle age, though he had hardly had the pleasures of a real childhood. Time and nature were re-creating him along their own lines, and the social world that he had built as a secure pleasure house contained more restraint than he had anticipated. In fact, he had anticipated very little.

From his adult perspective, he combined fiction and autobiography into an expression of the truth about his emotional life at the end of the 1840s. Telling his own story, the artist-writer, like the adult David Copperfield, imagines his own birth, beginning with a prelapsarian fantasy of perfect harmony with his mother. His father has died before he is born, a convenient extermination of an ideal who is not given the opportunity to disappoint his son. John Dickens is distanced by being divided into two unsatisfactory father figures, Murdstone and Micawber neither of whom is David's real father. The boy's infantile idyl with his mother is soon shattered by her remarriage, an expression of her own infantilism, dependency, and ambivalent feeling for her son, who is shocked to discover that he alone cannot satisfy his mother's needs. Like Dombey, Murdstone represents Dickens' view of the father as an unfeeling mechanism of discipline whose life gains its shape and strength from restraining himself and others. Micawber radiates with the more subtly dangerous attractions of a father whose intentions are essentially loving but whose weaknesses undermine family stability. Micawber, though, is not David's father. David's father is safely dead. Though at great cost, his mother's second husband, Murdstone, is neutralized, and Micawber becomes the friend whom David can help, eventually off to Australia, where he is out of sight if not out of mind. A Falstaffian figure, with innumerable touches of language and outlook derived from John Dickens, Micawber is neither allowed the power to hurt David nor disallowed the warmth of his basic benevolence.

David's mother dies under the heartless regimen of her second husband, whose cruelty provides Dickens with a mechanism for making David an orphan. Just as Dickens sends Micawber to Australia, he sends David's mother to the grave. But the fictional mother that he buries, broken-hearted, is a counterimage of his feelings about his own. She is the mother that Dickens would have preferred to have had. An idealized representation of unselfish maternity, she is forced to desert her son from her first marriage, a hapless innocent caught in the web of Murdstone's sexual and social authority, without the strength to liberate herself except through the grave, to which she also takes her second son. Though he is Murdstone's progeny, David's "baby brother" is an image of his sense of loss and abandonment, the mother he hardly had, the sibling who came between them. "So I lost her. So I saw her afterwards, in my sleep at school—a silent presence near my bed—looking at me with the same intent face—holding up her baby in her arms." As an adult, he remarks that "if the funeral had been yesterday, I could not recollect it better. . . . The mother who lay in the grave, was the mother of my infancy; the little creature in her arms, was myself, as I had once been, hushed for ever on her bosom." In his childhood and into his adult life, David is sustained by a "fanciful picture of my mother in her youth, before I came into the world. It always kept me company." When remembering how Elizabeth Dickens had sat him on a railing when he was a small boy in Rochester to watch the prince regent go by, the adult Dickens parethentically, as if it were a constant emotional epithet, remarked, "my mother, may God forgive her."[3]

Using passages from the autobiographical fragment, Dickens propels David through a fictionalized version of his early school experiences and then into the infamous blacking factory in the form of a wine warehouse, to which Murdstone consigns him, supposedly to make his way in the world but really to degrade and humiliate him. Whereas Dickens *felt* like an orphan, David *is* one. David's vision of himself as a scholar and a gentleman, like Dickens', is tested by adversity. Unlike his creator, though, he becomes headboy, the culmination of a school career normal for the children of the privileged, and he looks "down on the line of boys below me, with a condescending interest in such of them as bring to my mind the boy I was myself, when I first came there." Dickens also draws with autobiographical vividness on his vocational development, associating David with the law, with stenography, with Doctors' Commons, with parliamentary reporting, with writing short fiction, and then with becoming a famous novelist. The narrator-author, though, is never deflected from his intent to write a story of inward vocation, the story of the development of a wounded child whose good heart and happy progress have been impeded by lost and false parents, social distortions, mistakes of perception, and emotional inexperience. Reality is turned into fable, loss into blessing, trouble into convenience, weakness into strength, restlessness into energy, and emotional confusion into clarity by the gift of love.

Born in Suffolk, David finds the first gift of love in Kent. Dickens provides him with a second mother, his Aunt Betsey. Her love and generosity resolve his initial familial and financial problems. Her "object in life . . . is to provide for [his] being a good, a sensible, and a happy man." Unlike Peggotty, whom she initially dislikes, Betsey Trotwood represents the social class to which David aspires, the security of the middle class that his experience with poverty has made particularly attractive. Through the instrument of her bankruptcy (in which she is faultless and which turns out to be a temporary deceit) Dickens compels David to discover Dickens' virtues. Like his creator, he has the capacity "to concentrate [himself] on one object at a time, no matter how quickly its successor should come upon its heels," to try "with all my heart to do well . . . whatever I have tried to do in life. . . . There is no substitute for thorough-going, ardent, and sincere earnestness. Never to put one hand to anything, on which I could throw my whole self; and never to affect depreciation of my work, whatever it was." David's rise to middle-class status through professional achievement, described in a distancing, nostalgic retrospect, has some of the effortlessness of an assertion of the indomitable will. His voice in the present tense of his adulthood is calm, self-satisfied, an expression of Dickens' ideal of a life without anguish, disappointment, restlessness, or incompletion. As David moves toward the age of the author, he seems increasingly a mythic version of what his creator would have liked to have become. Dickens could most readily afford to see himself with emotional honesty in the past rather than in the present. "My own dreams are usually of twenty years ago. I often blend my present position with them, but very confusedly, whereas my life of twenty years ago is very distinctly represented."4

What passionately concerns Dickens, though, is the reworking of the history of his inner life to deal with his dissatisfactions in the present. For "a man's happiness, after all, [doesn't] depend upon himself. With employment for the mind—exercise for the body—a domestic hearth—and a cheerful spirit—there may be many things wanting to complete his happiness—and he may be confoundedly miserable—as I am. . . ."5 Such misery resulted partly from the gap between his Romantic aspirations and his Victorian assumption of stolid domestic responsibility. It resulted partly from a lifelong sense that his unloving mother had left a void he could not fill, and for which he needed to find ways to compensate. And it resulted from his increasing need for a companionship that Catherine could not provide. Fantasizing about some one friend whom he had never had, union with whom would make him emotionally complete, he created in *David Copperfield* an imaginative, though fragile, antidote to his restlessness, anticipating his rejection of Catherine eight years later. In his idealized version of the history of his "undisciplined heart," he provides David with a synoptic version of his own amatory experiences, beginning with Lucy Stroughill. Then there is Little Em'ly, with touches of flirtatiousness, vague hints of Maria Beadnell, who quickly participates in his tendency to transform lovers into sisters. When she becomes a fallen sister, David helps raise her to redemption. In an early passion, he falls in love with "the eldest Miss Larkins," about whom David expresses some of the same anguish that Dickens had expressed in his letters to Maria Beadnell. The dominant early passion, though, is for Dora Spenlow, in whom he combines elements of all those women in his life who have most disappointed him. Finally, there is Agnes Wickfield, the ultimate sister, with touches of both Mary and Georgina Hogarth, who eventually fulfills his strongest erotic impulse, the sister-wife, his companion of the mind and the heart.

Like his mother, Dora is flighty, selfish, and verbally childish. Like Maria, she is spoiled, teasing, and flirtatious, her father's favorite, with a companion-confidante somewhat like Maria's friend Mary Anne Leigh. Like Catherine, or the version of her that he became obsessed with, she is clumsy, careless, and,

worst of all, an inappropriate companion of the mind and heart
for David, who falls madly in love as an expression of his own
romantic projections before he realizes that he has misjudged
himself and her. "There can be no disparity in marriage like
unsuitability of mind and purpose." Her limitations force him
to take upon himself "the toils and cares of our life, and [have]
no partner in them. . . . The old unhappy feeling pervaded my
life. It was deepened, if it were changed at all. . . . I loved my
wife dearly, and I was happy; but the happiness I had vaguely
anticipated, once, was not the happiness I enjoyed, and there
was always something wanting." The qualities of character,
developed in adversity, that help him to achieve professional
success and to realize that he has chosen unwisely are the qualities that distance him from his wife. Dickens then provides
David's "child-bride" with a fatal illness and David with the
perfect replacement, the woman he should have married in the
first place. Redeeming the mistakes that only experience can
reveal, in the death of Dora he can be relieved of an otherwise
irremovable impediment to his happiness, a woman he has married because of his "undisciplined heart," a misjudgment that
arose from the deepest sources of his immature personality.
Aware that she is dying, so much does she love David that she
attempts to arrange for his union with Agnes.

Combining the qualities of both the spiritual and the erotic
ideal, Agnes is completely suitable in mind and heart, the sister
or soul mate and the perfect wife, a romantic partner and a
paragon of feminine virtues, an intellectual companion and an
absolutely competent housewife. Like his sister Fanny, she embodies the myth of a happy childhood of companionship. She
has "found a pleasure . . . while you have been absent, in keeping
every thing as it used to be when we were children. For we were
happy then, I think." "Heaven knows we were!" David re-
sponds. A heavenly light shines from her face, by which he can
see her angelic nature "pointing upwards," like Mary's happy
face in Dickens' dreams, like the resonance of her voice that he
had heard in the roar of Niagara Falls. Like Georgina, she remains by David's side, his happy domestic supporter and companion. Within the thinly concealed autobiographical fantasy of
the novel, Dickens temporarily alleviated some of his most
pressing emotional problems. But the fantasy expressed concealed wishes, as well as a reconstituted personal history, that

fiction alone could not discharge, and the novel is prescient with the turmoil that was to come.

By late November 1849, Catherine had become pregnant again. Their ninth child, named Dora Annie after David's "child-wife," was born in August 1850. Though he would have preferred no child at all, he felt pleased that at least it was a daughter. Since the births of Mamie and Katie it had seemed to him a dull succession of sons. Shortly after her birth, "working nine hours at a stretch" for numbers of consecutive days, he was preoccupied with killing his daughter's fictional namesake. "I have still Dora to kill—I mean the Copperfieldian Dora," he wrote to his wife from Broadstairs, where he had gone with the children to escape the heat and to get on with the novel. Remaining in London for her confinement, Catherine was slow in recovering from the pregnancy. She felt exhausted, depressed, and vaguely ill. Toward the end of the month, he insisted that "Mrs. Dickens is in a noble condition," the baby fragile but stable. Soon, though, Catherine was sufficiently ill for her husband and the doctors to separate her from Dora. She had "alarming disposition of blood to the head, attended with giddiness and dimness of sight . . . confusion and nervousness." She had had these symptoms at intervals for three or four years. Fearing for the life of her frail daughter, she was exhausted after having had in fifteen years nine successful pregnancies and at least one miscarriage. Youthful plumpness had been transformed into matronly obesity. And her precarious sense of self-esteem had eroded considerably in her relationship with an energetic perfectionist who dominated the life of the household with a competence that left her little room for herself. Soon taken to Malvern, a small but increasingly popular health resort, she underwent the cold-water cure, a series of baths and wrappings acclaimed for their restorative powers, particularly for the nervous system. The children were put under the care of Georgina and the servants. Catherine was "put . . . under rigorous discipline of exercise, air, and cold water."[7]

Feeling that the practical responsibilities both of family

and of professional life were all on his shoulders, he carried on assiduously with various projects, including a new journal, which had gotten started early in 1850, raising funds for the Guild of Literature and Art through regular theatrical performances by the revived amateur company, and searching for a new house, since the lease for Devonshire Terrace was to expire soon. The absence of a romantic partner was even more noticeable during Catherine's illness, particularly since he had the additional chore of regularly traveling between London and Malvern.

Late in March 1851, he learned that his father had a serious illness. Though Wilkins Micawber could be exiled to Australia, John Dickens had remained in London with the intractability on which real life insists. Continuing to work for the *Daily News*, he presumed on his son for occasional minor debts, his pension and salary sustaining his and his wife's ordinary expenses in their Keppel Street flat. To the extent that Dickens had been able in *David Copperfield* to put to rest any of the ghosts of the past, he had done so with his father. Not even the irony, though, of his being fatally ill with an "active disease of the bladder," of the sort that he had falsely claimed was a serious disability in 1824, could make it any less painful to his son that his genial, well-intentioned and self-indulgently harmful father was dying. "He had kept his real malady so profoundly secret, that when he did disclose it his state was most alarmingly advanced. . . ." On March 25, 1851, John Dickens was subjected without chloroform to "the most horrible operation known in surgery, as the only chance of saving him. He bore it with astonishing fortitude, and I saw him directly afterwards—his room, a slaughter house of blood. He was wonderfully cheerful and strong hearted." His son's hands were shaking uncontrollably. "All this goes to my side directly," Charles complained, "and I feel as if I had been struck there by a bludgeon."[8]

The next morning Charles went to Devonshire Terrace from Keppel Street. He wanted to see the children, particularly Dora, who was "quite charmed" to see him, and there was some amateur theatrical business to take care of. It was raining incessantly, the streets "in a most miserable state. A van containing the goods of some unfortunate family, moving, has broken down outside—and the whole scene is a picture of dreariness." He may have remembered the many times in his childhood his family had moved and his coming up from Chatham to London on a wet day, packed into a damp stagecoach. The Dickens family was in search of another house. And John Dickens had "slept well last night, and is as well this morning . . . as anyone in such a state, so cut and slashed, can be." He returned to Malvern with no illusions about his sixty-five-year-old father's immediate fate. He was again in London toward the end of the month for three days of rehearsals.

On the evening of March 29, returning to town, he and the messenger sent to get him passed one another on the railway. Charles went straight from the station to Keppel Street. When he arrived close to midnight his father "did not know [him], nor anyone." John Dickens "began to sink about noon . . . and never rallied afterwards." For three sleepless nights his exhausted son watched him. He died early in the morning of March 31. Charles immediately went up to Highgate Cemetery to arrange for a grave. He told Thomas Mitton, who had known John Dickens long and well, that his "poor father's death" had added "more expence" to the "much distress" that it had caused him. "But, of that, in such a case, I say nothing."9 He had already said much.

Still unwell, Catherine remained in Malvern while the family buried its prodigal father. Since Dickens had returned to London, his exhaustion had been so great that he had been unable to rest. He was constantly out in the streets both on the business of his journal and house hunting. "I have sometimes felt, myself, as if I could have given up, and let the whole battle ride on over me. But that has not lasted long, for God knows I have plenty to cheer me in the long run." Despite such self-assurances, he was depressed. He needed time to get used to his father being dead. Warmly sympathetic to his wife's ill health, he was less so to Catherine herself. With Forster, he went to Malvern by the night express on the fifth of April and then returned on the fourteenth to fulfill an engagement to preside at the annual meeting of the General Theatrical Fund, an obligation he had tried to cancel. Going immediately to Devonshire Terrace to visit the children before going to the London Tavern, he held Dora in his arms and played with her for a few minutes. At dinner, he was greeted with acclamation. Surrounded by friends, supporters, and admirers, he made a witty, gracious speech, urging contributions to the providential fund to help poor and elderly actors. The theatre was too bright a place in his memory and in the lives of the members of the audience to allow those who provided such glitter and fantasy to suffer the difficulties of poverty and old age in an economically precarious profession. He reminded his listeners, some of whom knew of his father's recent death, that "the actor sometimes comes from scenes of affliction and misfortune—even from death itself—to play his part before us." While Dickens was speaking, a servant from Devonshire Terrace delivered to Forster, who was to speak next, the message that "Dora was suddenly dead."[10]

In anguish, Forster listened to his friend conclude. "How often is it with all of us, that in our several spheres we have to do violence to our feelings, and to hide our hearts in carrying on this fight of life, if we would bravely discharge in it our duties and responsibilities." He then proposed "prosperity to the General Theatrical Fund!" When the applause subsided, the pained Forster rose and gave a grandiloquent bravura performance, praising his friend, "mentioning that he knew he was present 'at great personal sacrifice, which few men would have ventured to make.'" The solitary cry of humbug from "someone at the end of the hall" was quickly hushed. When the meeting ended, Forster and Mark Lemon told Dickens "the sad news." Returning to Devonshire Terrace immediately, he went to look at his dead child. Forster and Lemon sat up with him by her body through the night. It was a comfort to him that she had died suddenly, painlessly. Given her frailty, "if, with a wish, I could cancel what has happened and bring the little creature back to life, I would not do it." Now it occurred to him that "it was an ill-omened name," that fiction sometimes anticipated life. Concerned about Catherine, he gently provided her, in a letter that Forster took to Malvern, with a series of ascending concerns about "little Dora who is *very* ill. . . . Remember what I have often told you, that we never can expect to be exempt . . . from the afflictions of other parents—and that if—*if*—when you come I should even have to say to you 'our little baby is dead,' you are to do your duty to the rest, and to show yourself worthy of the great trust you hold in them." He was also, though, "not without some impression that this shock may do her good"; it might be a tonic to her fragile nervous system. The dead infant remained in an upstairs bedroom until she was laid in her grave three days later. The night before, about to go upstairs to strew flowers sent by a friend "over our poor little pet . . . he suddenly gave way" and wept uncontrollably in the presence of his children.[11] The shock apparently did not help Catherine. She remained sick through the spring and summer.

❦ 3 ❦

SEEKING TO BALANCE ILLNESS AND DEATH WITH COMPASSIONATE GOOD works, he continued the effort to find acceptable candidates for Urania Cottage. The earthly salvation of prostitutes seemed to him both a practical possibility, through moral retraining and emigration, and a social necessity. Emigration itself had its special difficulties. Prostitutes sometimes confused it with the transportation of convicts; corrupt crews and passengers might seduce the rehabilitated women back to their old ways on the voyage to South Africa or Australia. "In the course of [his] nightly wanderings into strange places," he regularly spoke to prostitutes. While he was writing *David Copperfield*, their problems were especially vivid to him. He wanted to use the novel to turn the public's "thoughts a little that way" in the hope of eliciting support for his efforts. Claiming, in his portraits of Little Em'ly and Martha Endell, that the problem of prostitution was essentially that of a male-dominated society in which class divisions and sexual exploitation determined that a certain number of women would be seduced into a state that made marriage improbable, he devoted a staggering number of hours to supervising Urania Cottage, to establishing rules and enforcing them, to working out overall policy, to arranging for safe passage abroad, and to finding promising candidates who were sufficiently aware that they "were trembling on the verge of destruction" to be motivated to submit to discipline but not "too miserable and low for our purpose."[12]

For those who have been unlawfully seduced, the collapse of self-esteem, he believed, almost inevitably led to self-destructiveness. Fallen women embodied the perversion of the true, high nature of women. If they could be caught before their

natures had been brutalized and provided with a disciplined
supportive environment, their essential goodness and attraction
to purity, and the naturalness of marriage and motherhood as
well, would assert itself. Since society offered few economic
opportunities for women outside the home, those who had been
deprived, by accident, by drunkenness, by poverty, by seduc-
tion, by crime, by the immoral elements within patriarchy, of
an appropriate domestic environment inevitably turned to prostitution once their alternatives had been exhausted. He had no
desire to make women economically independent of men, and
expressed no sympathy for efforts to establish vocational schools
or working communities for women. "Perfect penitence in
these women" might express itself as "a kind of active repentance in their being faithful wives and the mothers of virtuous
children."[13] Just as his awareness of how unideal his mother had
been had led to his idealization of Mary Hogarth, his emotional
elevation of the female, seeing in her the highest form of the
moral sentiments, encouraged him to visualize the redemption
of prostitutes exclusively in domestic terms.

His collaboration with Miss Coutts continued through
most of the 1850s, focusing on Urania Cottage, but also on education, housing, and sanitary reform. The relationship was curiously personal, though apparently he knew little about his
reserved friend's private life, particularly her proposal of marriage to the Duke of Wellington, forty-five years her senior.
When the Duke died in 1852, Dickens' expression of his revulsion
at "the semi-barbarous" ostentation of the funeral procession
did not take into account that he was writing to an intimate of
the deceased.

A frequent guest at her home, he allowed, probably as a
condition of the relationship, the former Hannah Meredith
(who had married William Brown in 1844) to expand the two-
some into a ménage of pleasant badinage as well as serious
philanthropy. He also borrowed Mrs. Brown's obstinacy and
habit of making statements in question form for his portrait of
Rosa Dartle, just as he took the physical characteristics of the
dwarf Miss Mowcher from a well-known London character,
who claimed to be deeply affronted by the depiction of someone
whom readers might associate with her as a facilitator of seduc-
tions. Threatened by a lawsuit and his conscience, he repaired

"Miss Mowcher's injury—with a very bad grace, and in a very ill humour." Miss Coutts, though, was not for caricature. The partial support of Charley, who had entered Eton and whose school bills she paid, she was the sole support of Urania Cottage.

Besieged by solicitations, he mediated between her philanthropic impulses and a bewilderingly large number of requests. His recommendations were humanitarian rather than radical. His liberalism did not admit a contradiction between the Westminster Ragged School, "a maze of filth and squalor, deserted by all decency," and the diamond ring that he wore on his finger and some people at the school "took occasion to admire." Miss Coutts's sense of propriety was more deeply conservative than Dickens'. There were touchy points of potential conflict, particularly the role of religion in social reform. And she let him know that she considered his amateur theatricals, "the mournful spectacle of your friend upon the boards," unseemly for a man of his position, an objection he joked away when his attempts to persuade her otherwise failed.[14]

By early 1852, Dickens had taken up her idea of creating working-class housing by clearing a London slum. At first he consulted with a new friend, Inspector Charles F. Field, who had been the source for three articles he had written and who had made regularly available to him a police escort for his late-night visits (sometimes with friends) to high-crime areas of London. Dr. Southwood Smith, an irrepressible enthusiast who spoke with "extreme rapidity and rush of words," was consulted. A Unitarian minister and medical doctor who had served as adviser to the Poor Law Commission, Smith also wrote and agitated ceaselessly on the subject of sanitary reform. Dickens had already benefited in 1842 from Smith's having brought to his attention the report on the working conditions for children and women in coal mines. Despite his being "too voluble and dashing," he assured Miss Coutts that Smith was "a very sound man, indeed." So too was Dickens' brother-in-law Henry Austin, a civil engineer, who, in alliance with Smith and the influential Dr. Edwin Chadwick, the chairman of the Poor Law Commission, had formed the Board for Sanitary Reform. A prolific propagandist, Austin involved Dickens, who had only a limited amount of time to spare, in these activities. Dickens worried, though, that both Chadwick and Smith, in their "harping so much on the past' in their legislative efforts, would associate the board with "an unjust notion of impracticality." In contrast to his uncompromising stance on social issues in the 1830s and 1840s, he had decided that "the wise thing is to take less, and make it the best that can be."15

Emphasizing the desirability of large multifamily buildings to conserve open space and make sanitary services more practical, Dickens outlined for Miss Coutts the basis of what became the Nova Scotia Gardens and the Columbia Square apartments, which were opened in 1862. But abysmal slum conditions of the sort that he dramatized in the depiction of Tom-all-Alone's in his next novel, Bleak House, were not easily abolished. Despite his conscious optimism, he revealed his sense of the intractable misery, the overwhelming social odds such efforts were challenging, in his description to Miss Coutts of a slum that he had visited while looking for potential sites to be cleared. "It is intensely poor in some parts; and chiefly supported by river, wharf, and dock employment; and by some lead mills. . . No more road than in an American swamp—odious sheds for horses and donkeys, and vagrants, and rubbish in front of the parlor windows—wooden houses like horrible old packing cases full of fever for a countless number of years. In a broken down gallery at the back of a row of these, there was a wan child looking over at a starved old white horse who was making a meal of oyster shells. The sun was going down and flaring out like an angry fire at the child—and the child, and I, and the pale horse, stared at one another in silence for some five minutes as if we were so many figures in a dismal allegory."16

Beginning in March 1850, he had a direct vehicle for expressing his views on the child, himself, and the pale horse. The child as victim, the pale horse as the social order, and he himself as reformer became the crucial elements in his new journal, which he called Household Words. In his June 1844 contract with Bradbury and Evans he had agreed that at some time in the future, with the details to be determined then, he would edit a magazine that his publisher would add to its proud, profitable flagship. Levity and amusement would be in the service of a vision of the general improvement of the individual and society. Whereas Punch was humorous, the new journal would be serious entertainment, the journals complementing, not competing with, one another. From 1844 to 1849 this proposition had had the shadowy reality of an unrealized venture. Bitterly disappointed by his contretemps with the *Daily News* and deeply involved in his many philanthropic and writing projects, he did not press his commitment to become an editor again. In March 1849, "hard at work" finishing the first number of *David Copperfield,* he began serious negotiations about the journal. Having felt energized by the excitement of a new book, he may have felt that it was the right moment for him to get the magazine started.

He had no illusion that it could be done without immense, willful effort on his part. He had come to believe, though, that he had developed "quite a remarkable power of enduring fatigue," that the more energy he exerted the more he had. Though "my cut-out way of life obliges me to be so much upon the strain," his alternation of intense work with hectic vacations, local stimulants like his daily cold shower, and occasional languid collapses kept him ready for any amount of activity. He began to elevate his energy and restlessness into the premise that they were the "condition on which I hold my inventive powers," and he believed that any attempt to restrain them would be destructive to his creativity. Given his personality, his need for control and perfection would demand his services not only as general editor but as acquiring editor, copy editor, business agent, researcher, and writer. Added to his other responsibilities, the burden would be substantial. So too, though, would be the rewards. He was not in the least self-deceitful about his paramount desire in creating the journal that it "become a good property." No matter how much hard work it entailed, "to establish it firmly would be to gain such an immense point for the future (I mean my future) that I think nothing of that."[17]

In early August 1849, on the Isle of Wight, his mind was "occupied . . . at intervals, respecting the dim design." By September, it had become at least as clear as a shadowy "name and an idea." He had made up his mind "that the Periodical must be set agoing in the spring." Within a few weeks, he had developed his idea into the firm form of "a weekly journal, price . . . two pence, matter in part original and in part selected, and always having . . . a little good poetry. . . . The original matter to be essays, reviews, letters, theatrical criticisms, &c &c, as amusing as possible, but all distinctly and boldly going to what in one's own view ought to be the spirit of the people and the time.' Despite its omission from his original overview, short stories and novels in installments soon became part of the plan. By the end of October, he had a model number set up and he had begun to assemble a staff. In the ninth installment of *David Copperfield*, available at the end of December, the new journal was advertised as "Designed for the Entertainment and Instruction of all classes of readers, and to help in the discussion of the most important social questions of the time." On March 30, 1850, after the initial tensions of miscommunication and unsatisfactory production and proofreading, the first issue appeared. It contained "A Preliminary Word" and an article, "The Amusements of the People," by Dickens, "Valentine's Day at the Post-Office" and "A Bundle of Emigrants' Letters" co-authored by Dickens, an article by George Hogarth, the first of three installments of *Lizzie Leigh*, a novel by Elizabeth Gaskell, and a poem by Leigh Hunt.[16]

His co-author, his managing editor, and his indispensable assistant in running the journal was William Henry Wills. With a limited education, having begun his career as a woodcutter and drifted into journalism for financial reasons, he was the perfect second-in-command. He readily accepted that Dickens made all the decisions, especially after an early rebuke that commanded him not to "touch my articles without first consulting me." An unsuccessful playwright, Wills, who had been born in 1810, had made himself known to Dickens in 1837 when he submitted an article, which Dickens rejected, and a brief poetic tale. which he published, to *Bentley's Miscellany*. Temporarily blind in 1838, he received a small grant from the Royal Literary Fund. Fortunately, he was well enough to join the original staff of *Punch* and then to spend three years in Edinburgh, where he had the good luck to marry the charming, socially talented Janet Chambers, the sister of the publishers of *Chambers's Edinburgh Journal*, of which he was assistant editor, and then return to London in time to sign on with the *Daily News*. Dickens took on the experienced journalist, on Forster's recommendation, as assistant editor of *Household Words* at a salary of "Eight Pounds a week absolutely, and one eighth share" in the profits. "An extremely careful, methodical man," he seemed perfect for the job. With "not the ghost of an idea in the imaginative way," he had been chosen "for a union of qualities very necessary to the business part" of the journal. From the editorial office on Wellington Street, off the Strand and close to Covent Garden, the thin, tight-lipped, conventional, but infinitely loyal, patient, and competent Wills, who always wore "a very uncomfortable look-ing hat with a very narrow brim" when he stepped out, looked after the shop for almost twenty years.[19]

In negotiating with Bradbury and Evans, Dickens remem-bered how bitterly he had resented being a salaried employee rather than a participant in the profits of *Bentley's Miscellany*. Aware of Mark Lemon's dissatisfaction with his financial ar-rangement as editor of *Punch*, Dickens soon helped him draft a letter setting out why he should be given a share in the profits. In his own case, Dickens was determined not to let the moment of maximum influence go by. The contract that he forced on the publisher stipulated that they were to receive a one-fourth share, John Forster, as consulting and contributing editor, one eighth, Wills another one eighth, and himself, in addition to his salary, one half the profits. His annual salary of £500 and Wills's of £416 were to be "charged as expenses of publication and not deducted from their respective shares."

To contributors, he was determined to pay the best going rates, and more if necessary. Initially, he pursued authors like William and Mary Howitt, Harriet Martineau, and Elizabeth Gaskell avidly, courting them with flattery, which had some of the powerful unction of coming from a man whom his preju-diced but not completely inaccurate friend, Walter Savage Lan-dor, described as "the best known man among the living," at least in England, not excluding the Duke of Wellington. He was especially successful in seducing Mrs. Gaskell, whom he called "Scheherazade" and whose work he deeply admired as a femi-nine and domesticated version of his own. Particularly attrac-tive to his middle-class audience, she became one of his most frequent contributors. With a sure sense of the taste of his read-ers, he immediately turned to her for contributions, even offer-ing to travel to Manchester for no other purpose than to discuss the matter, allaying her anxiety about undertaking "short tales" by asserting that he was "morally certain that nothing so true and earnest as your writing, *can* go wrong under your guidance.'[20] The diffident wife of a Unitarian minister, she cooperated mainly because of her respect for the editor. Despite some tensions, they were to have a mutually advantageous professional relationship for the next eight years.

By the second weekly issue, *Household Words* was a clear success. "It is expensive, of course, and demands a large circulation." The sales, though, justified the investment. After the initial unsteady figures (some purchasers may have been disappointed at discovering that they had not bought the first installment of a new novel) it maintained an average weekly sale for the next nine years of close to forty thousand copies. The addition to Dickens' income above earnings from the novels he was to write and the royalties he received from the cheap edition or from reprintings was substantial. More reliable than his other sources, it did not depend on his own writing, and though it was also subject to the vagaries of the reading public, who could choose to buy or not, it provided an assured regular income earned under much less competitive, high-pressured, and fragile circumstances than his income from writing fiction. Under Wills, the office ran with a smoothness that took its grease from Dickens' constant oiling of contributors, his ideas for articles, his own work, and his unflagging insistence that the articles be factually accurate, the subjects interesting, the level popular, informative, and entertaining, and the writing first-rate. His own contributions ranged from the delicately personal "A Child's Dream of a Star," a fictionalized reminiscence of his sister Fanny, which he created for the second issue because he felt that there was 'a want of something tender," to his article "Home for Homeless Women," which he persuaded the reluctant Miss Coutts to allow him to publish, to the approximately 120,000-word *A Child's History of England,* which he dictated to the increasingly invaluable Georgina during the next two years and published in thirty-nine installments from January 1851 to October 1853.[21]

Reading every submission, marking up many of the proof sheets of articles and stories, impatiently disparaging bad writing, especially verbosity, Dickens was an avid, even merciless editor of other people's prose. Once he good-humoredly commented on "the dreadful spectacle I have made of the proofs—which look like an inky fishing-net." He did not hesitate to suggest tactfully to authors where they might do better, even to the much-appreciated Mrs. Gaskell, who allowed *Household Words* "always [to] make titles for me." If he could have, he also would have corrected her proclivity for falls and unhappy endings, for "I wish to Heaven her people would keep a little firmer on their legs!" Having titled one of her stories "The Heart of John Middleton," he told her he had remarked to Wills that he "wished you had not killed the wife." Since she was in town, he sent Wills out to ask her if he might change the ending. " 'Oh Mrs. Gaskell's not in town,' " he reported on returning, " 'and won't be here 'til next Thursday.' 'Very good,' said I. 'Then we will print the story as it stands, and not trouble her.' Which was accordingly done."

Flooded by submissions, many of them amateurish, he soon built up a stable of authors, supplemented by a small staff who did article assignments on their own and on his initiative, receiving a regular salary and working directly under Wills. The two most important staff members were Henry Morley and Richard Henry Horne. The former, a schoolteacher, on Dickens' urging became a journalist. Born in 1822, the only university-trained person on the staff, Morley specialized initially in issues of public health, in which Dickens was keenly interested. He soon became one of the quiet, unassuming, invaluable, Dickens-worshiping members of *Household Words*, contributing a long list of articles on a wide variety of subjects during the next fourteen years. In contrast, Horne was an ambitious, moderately talented writer who had had only small success in his efforts at writing drama, poetry, criticism, and journalism. He had written glowingly about Dickens in a book of literary criticism and gossip, *A New Spirit of the Age* (1844), whose silent co-author was Elizabeth Barrett. Their co-authorship was carried on only by letter. The previous year he had had his only popular success, the pseudoepic *Orion*, whose callow derivativeness and hollow Shelleyanism were momentarily outweighed by his advertising himself as "the farthing poet." For the first two years of the existence of *Household Words*, he was its leading investigative reporter, sometimes working out suggestions that Dickens gave him. By himself or with Dickens, beginning with the second issue, he published almost ninety items in the journal before he left for Australia in 1852. Years later, Dickens drew on one of them, "Dust; or Ugliness Redeemed," for some aspects of his last completed novel.

Dickens' journalism, of course, mainly served the causes he believed in. He never, though, took his eye off the balance sheet. There was a family to support, including, to his bedazzled moroseness, another child. Edward Bulwer Lytton Dickens was born in March 1852. Despite Catherine's poor health, he had been conceived in early summer 1851. His father could not "afford to receive [this] seventh son" and ninth living child "with perfect cordiality, as on the whole I could have dispensed with him." Six months later, he provided the first of his many variations on the "strange kings in the fairy times, who, with three thousand wives and four thousand seven hundred and fifty concubines, found it necessary to put up prayers in all the temples for a prince as beautiful as the day! I have some idea—with only one wife and nothing particular in any other direction—of interceding with the Bishop of London to have a little service in St. Pauls beseeching that I may be considered to have done enough towards my country's population."[22] Nicknamed Plorn, this latest infant became his father's delight, an amusingly wonderful prodigy of entertaining willfulness and cuteness about whose childhood achievements Dickens constantly boasted, despite his preference never to have had him at all.

Back in November 1851, a relieved Dickens had moved his pregnant wife, eight children, Georgina, and various servants into a new home, where he gratefully drank a glass of champagne to Tavistock House, "and [its] illustrious architect," his brother-in-law Henry Austin. An engineer with great practical abilities, Austin had devoted hundreds of hours to drawing up plans, acting as his liaison with the contractor, and supervising daily progress. The cost for the purchase of the lease had been reasonable. The elaborate, personalized, and closely supervised renovations, though, had necessitated Dickens anticipating from Bradbury and Evans "the accounts of the last half year by . . . five or six hundred pounds." A few weeks after moving in, awaiting the statement of the balance, the sight of a letter in Austin's "hand threw [him] into a cold perspiration." The "bill is too long to be added up, until Babbage's calculating machine shall be improved and finished . . . there is not paper enough ready made, to carry it over and bring it forward again." With his lease on Devonshire Terrace expiring in 1851, a new house had been determined on as early as 1847. It would have to be large, and consequently expensive.

Having begun to look for a new house early in 1851, in late January, with Austin's approval, he bid "with fear and trembling" for one in Highgate. To his disappointment and self-criticism, he lost it, "outbidden" by another party of whom the agent had "mysteriously" hinted. "Nothing so good will ever turn up again, I believe, for the money." After looking at a number of possibilities, he offered £2,700 for Balmoral House, overlooking Regent's Park. The offer was declined, and he did not feel he could afford to offer more. Catherine was in Malvern, the children at Devonshire Terrace, which he had arranged to keep until the end of the year. And suddenly he had to face the absorbing anguish of his father's and then Dora's death, even while he continued to house-hunt. Soon the notion of sea breezes appealed to him, apprehensive that the influx of visitors for the Great Exhibition at the Crystal Palace, with "a storm of letters of introduction rising from all quarters of the earth," would make it impossible for him to get any work done or have any privacy. By the middle of April 1851, having rented Fort House in Broadstairs, he fixed bachelor rooms for himself over the *Household Words* office for his London visits. It was a satisfactory temporary solution. On April 20, he went to look at the large well-located house that Frank Stone was soon to vacate, Tavistock House, in Tavistock Square, just north of the British Museum. Stone could not afford to keep the house, half of which he rented out. By mid-July, the prospect had matured into the "great idea of buying (for five and forty years) Stone's house. . . . It is in the dirtiest of all possible conditions. . . . It is decidedly cheap," though, "most commodious—and might be made very handsome." He agreed to pay £1,500 for the house and fixtures. "Even in the midst of dirt and desolation," when he opened the blinds he saw sunlight.[23]

Leaning on Austin like "a very staff, in the invention and execution of the proposed tremendous renovations," he had major structural changes made. Stone helped expedite the work by accepting the suggestion that he and his family stay at Devonshire Terrace for a few months to give the workmen early access. Though the costs soared, so did the satisfactions. To amuse himself, willing to pay for his enthusiasms, Dickens even went to the expense of having a carpenter create 13 fictitious book shells for whose false bindings he provided a l st of mock titles some of them silly, some comic, some satirical including a "History of a Short Chancery Suit." He paid more heavily and sensibly for what had become a daily necessity for him, a shower. No detail about it was too insignificant. "The bather would be happier and easier in mind, if the [toilet] did not demonstrate itself obtrusively. I fear that I could hardly bear the box in the corner—speaking as the taker of the Shower Bath every morning. I have not sufficient confidence in my strength of mind, to think that I could begin the business of every day, with the enforced contemplation of the outside of that box. I believe it would affect my bowels. It might relax, it might confine, but I must trust its having some influence on the happy mediocrity it is my ambition to preserve." A curtain eventually was put around the toilet. After various trials of plumbing and rooftop water tanks, he finally had "a cold shower of the best quality, always charged to an unlimited extent." Finally, "the agonies of getting into [the] new house" were over. He was "beginning to find [his] papers and to know where the pen and ink are." Grateful to him for his efforts, his daughters burst into their new, brightly decorated bedroom, in which "not a single thing in it . . . had not been expressly chosen for them, or planned by him," with a sense of how privileged they were to have such a father.[24]

Though Catherine was always getting better, she was rarely completely well. The persistent pregnancies probably baffled both of them. Perhaps she felt that they demonstrated her usefulness, her importance, her maternal capability, at least an achievement of sorts. Her awareness of her husband s attitude, though, and her ill health suggest that she may have greeted them ambivalently, perhaps unhappily. The record is silent on her response. Plorn was to be their last child, though why Dickens seemed incapable of not impregnating Catherine prior to 1851 but able to avoid doing so thereafter is unclear. Perhaps physical and nervous illnesses now interfered with conception. Perhaps husband and wife discovered or now found palatable available methods to avoid conception, though abstinence is likely to have been the most useful of these. Her proba-

ble lack of interest in having more children may have contributed to her being less available. Her husband's bemused
disgust with their fecundity, his concern about expenses, his
uneasiness about his assumption of middle age, and his growing
ambivalence about his wife—her illnesses, her obesity, her
clumsiness, her inability to fulfill his yearnings for an ideal
other—may have made periods of abstinence attractive. Immediately before Plorn's conception, Dickens made a list of his
eight children, as if adding up the ledger of his domestic woes
and his paternal self-definition. "Charley, about aged 14, at
school at Eton. Mary 13. Kate 11. Walter Landor 10 (going to India
bye and bye). Francis Jeffrey 7. Alfred Tennyson 5. Sydney
Smith 4. Henry Fielding 2." To these children, "he was a strict
master in the way of insisting upon everything being done perfectly and exactly as he desired," so his eldest daughter remembered. "But, on the other hand, [he] was most kind, just, and
considerate."[25]

After the birth of his last child, a few months past his
fortieth birthday, he described himself as having grown "more
robust—less interesting—shorter haired—a more solid-looking
personage—and not younger." Except for his susceptibility to
pain related to his kidneys, he had no more than the usual
number of attacks of flu, colds, and sore throats. He sometimes,
though, awoke in the night with the sensation that he was choking, which he recognized to be the result of "disordered nerves,"
and for which "oppressive and painful sensation" he took a
pinch of snuff. In September 1851, he was fascinated by a large
number of bloated, drowned farm animals that had washed onto
shore at Margate from a shipwreck. "In every state and stage of
decay," they were being chopped open and plundered. He had
moments of spontaneous recall of the feeling of being a child or
at least young again. In responding to a letter from Maria Beadnell's father, George, with whom he'd kept up a sporadic correspondence over the years, Dickens felt that he was exactly
nineteen as he wrote the names of Maria and her sister and asked
Beadnell to give them his love. He was still always looking,
especially when starting to write, "for something I have
not found in life, but may possibly come to a few thousand
years hence, in some other part of some other system, God
knows. . . ."[26]

❧ 4 ❧

IN APRIL 1849, LADY BLESSINGTON AND COUNT D'ORSAY'S ELEGANT house of cards had come tumbling down. With "a very doleful eye," Dickens saw the auction notice pinned up to the gate of their residence, Gore House. The last splendor of Regency ostentation was dissolving into darkness. Having come to England to escape debts (on his arrival in London he had been jailed briefly for three hundred pounds owed to his boot maker in Paris). D'Orsay now fled so hastily that he had no time to say good-bye to his friends. He eluded his English creditors, who had been held at bay by the security of Lady Blessington's putative wealth. The widow, though, had an income of two thousand pounds a year on which she maintained expenses of four thousand pounds. Her expectation that she might make up the difference by earnings as a writer (not even the *Daily News* could afford to pay her the eight hundred pounds she requested) proved emblematic of Regency self-indulgence attempting to extend itself into a world of Victorian realism. The pyramid of debts collapsed. Those who had previously only requested payment now put in executions against her property. "Bill discounters, money lenders, jewellers, lace vendors, tax collectors, gas company agents, all persons having claims to urge, pressed them . . . simultaneously." The optimistic D'Orsay could not believe that this was the end. For almost two years, he had left Gore House only after sunset or on Sundays to avoid being served legal papers. A creditor, though, in a ludicrous disguise, got into the house. Within hours, Lady Blessington had persuaded D'Orsay that he must leave. That night he was on his way to Paris. The countess followed, neither of them ever to return to England again. Dickens went "to say good by'e . . . and found you gone. I cannot tell you what a blank it was to me to look at your empty house." The extravagant contents were put up for public viewing. More than twenty thousand people came in five days. Realizing over twelve thousand pounds, the sale cleared all their debts. There were, though, various morals in the tale of "the most signal ruin of an establishment of a person of high rank . . . ever witnessed."[27]

On one of the evenings preceding the auction, Dickens

made his unhappy but curious way into the crowded house. So too did much of literary and social London, partly as mourners, partly as voyeurs, partly to congratulate themselves on their own good fortune. With his strong sense of class and manners, as well as of transience, Thackeray thought it "a dismal sight— Gore House full of Snobs looking at the furniture—foul Jews, odious bombazeen women. . . . Brutes keeping their hats on in the kind old drawing-rooms—I longed to knock some of them off: and say Sir be civil in a Lady's room. . . . Ah it was a strange sad picture of Wanaty Fair." Dickens never again saw the countess, who died in D'Orsay's arms in Paris in June 1849. Gradually the count became "much improved in spirits and looks," and set up an atelier, which Dickens visited with Maclise in June 1850, and again in February 1851. The count's unexpected death in August 1852 was less of a personal loss than a reminder to the novelist of changes in himself and others. "Poor D'Orsay! It is a tremendous consideration that friends should fall around us in such awful numbers as we attain middle life. . . . But *this* is a Dream, may be, and death will wake us. . . ."[28]

There were other trepidations in the Dickens circle. Forster's poor health, the aftermath of rheumatic fever, overweight, and gout, kept his friends worried. The hardworking bachelor, ambitious and financially anxious, still kept long night hours, writing, editing, socializing. The "Lincolnian mammoth" hosted regular dinner parties at his enlarged Lincoln's Inn Fields apartment, and kept his friends tied closely to his exuberance and his supportiveness. "Anything like [a] reprimand" from Forster, Maclise confessed, "is death to me." The early triangle of friendship still had its force, and Maclise still wanted to be "first in the list of your friendships." An intimate of Carlyle, D'Orsay, Blessington, Bulwer-Lytton, and Macready, Forster fought tiredness, overwork, ill health, and occasional depression to keep his friendships strong, to have the pleasure of feeling useful to those he loved. Without any children of his own, he found paternal delight in spending time with Macready's and Dickens' children, and especially with Bulwer-Lytton's son. Despite their occasional tiffs, Dickens invariably turned to him for help with proofs and business. At *Household Words*, Forster let Wills know that he expected to be consulted on everything, and bullied the susceptible assistant editor. In September 1851, "slowly recovering from the effects of a most severe and painful illness," he stayed with the Dickenses for a few weeks. After another series of illnesses the next year, he was not in "a very healthy condition." A demanding but welcome guest, Forster was for Dickens a long-standing habit, like a member of the family. Sublimely oblivious, he dispensed temporary headaches as if they were medicinal gifts. On one long walk, Forster "was in a tip top state of amiability, but I think I never heard him *half so loud*."[29] His friendship was deeply valued, perhaps even slightly more than his presence.

Dickens' pleasures, though, were increasingly centered around Leech, Lemon, and the new friends he had made during the theatricals of the late 1840s. Of the friends of his youth, he saw less of Mitton, who had become cranky, eccentric, and even reclusive, eventually drifting away into a rural legal practice with an irregular domestic arrangement. He continued to cherish Beard; almost a member of the family, the journalist often dined informally with them and sometimes accepted Dickens' reminder, especially on holidays, that there was always "a capital spare room" for him. Ainsworth had become almost a stranger. Cruikshank's obsession with "total abstinence," and soon with rewriting fairy tales with an eye toward that subject, gradually alienated Dickens, though he disingenuously assured Cruikshank "that I have never felt the slightest coolness towards you, or regarded you with any other than my old unvarying feeling of affectionate friendship."[30] Sensitive to the denigration of imagination, Dickens attacked Cruikshank's exploitation of traditional fairy tales in an article, "Fraud on the Fairies," published in October 1853 in *Household Words*. He felt strongly that the primacy of the imagination and its pleasures were being threatened by politics, by rational and irrational ideologies, by the dry-as-dust social scientists and utilitarians.

As an antidote to overwork, Dickens pursued holidays and friendships, often at the same time. London entertainments still had their attractions, especially the theatre. Though he increasingly thought London "a vile place" and felt despondent on returning to town, he threw down the urban-entertainment gauntlet frequently. "Maclise and I," he told Lemon, "are going to the Panorama of the Nile, today at 3. . . . After that we are going anywhere. If you are disengaged, and a Man, join us at one or other of these places!" He took advantage of Charley's being at Eton to take numbers of day excursions, with Beard and Leech, to Windsor. With hampers from Fortnum & Mason's, he treated his son and his schoolmates to picnics on the river, even in the rain. Appreciative and slightly tipsy, Charley and his companions sang, "I don't care a fig what the people may think,/ But what WILL the governor say?" Usually he went to Windsor by train, walking from the station at nearby Slough, a town and an area he got to know well. With Leech or Lemon or Egg, he still took long walks, especially on the Downs. With the Stones and the Willses (both wives, but especially Janet Wills, were favorites) he went to Richmond or Greenwich, sometimes with Catherine and Georgina also. With Maclise, Dickens went to Paris for a week in late June 1850. As usual, they visited the morgue, "where there was a body horribly mutilated with a musket ball in the head, and afterwards drowned." Maclise became so sick that he ran outside and threw up on the pavement. Despite the heat, the holiday was a success, with visits to D'Orsay, conviviality with Normanby and his mistress, appreciation of the fact "that virgins were not usually to be found in French theatres," and amusement at the bohemian Maclise's being "extremely loose as to his waistcoat, and otherwise careless in regard of buttons."[31]

Having acted Macbeth in his farewell as he "never, never before acted it," the fifty-eight-year-old Macready retired from the stage in February 1851. He soon expanded the 17 miles between Elstree and central London to the 130 between his new home in Sherborne, Dorset, and his old haunts. For the actor, it was a liberation toward which all the energies of his life had been directed. He exchanged a lifetime of distaste for his profession and hatred of the tawdriness of early-Victorian theatrical life for the life of a dignified country gentleman. It is probably also likely that the corridors of his home in Elstree had echoed mournfully with memories of his dead children. One of the private dramas of the Dickens circle was the tubercular nemesis, the "fatal dowry" of Macready's wife, Catherine Atkens, that killed five of the doting Macready's children and then, one year after his retirement, their mother. At his last performance, he wore black for the recent death of his "beloved firstborn," his daughter Nina. "God knows how my heart loves thee . . . my beloved child!"

For Dickens, Macready's final performance was a milestone in his own life. "When I was a mere boy, I was one of your faithful and devoted adherents in the pit. . . . As I improved myself . . . in mind and fortune, I only became the more earnest . . . in my study of you." From Dickens' first awareness of the theatre, Macready had been an idolized presence, a model for the imaginative transformation of himself from a private personality into a major actor on the literary and social stage.

Over six hundred people crowded into the Hall of Commerce on March 1, 1851, for Macready's farewell banquet, which Dickens and Forster had organized. More ascetic than his friends, grumbling that "Dickens gives orders and goes to Paris," the actor was annoyed that they had initially chosen the smaller London Tavern because "they get a better dinner and plenty of champagne." Dickens was back in ample time, though, to join the fervid applause for Macready's tear-provoking farewell speech. "His resonant sonorous voice rang round the place like the shrill blast of a clarion," reported one star-struck young actor, "and died away like the soft breathing of a lute. . . . Every word was clearly articulated and made its mark." The same young actor reported that Dickens, who proposed the health of the chairman, Bulwer-Lytton (a choice that Macready was not particularly keen about), "was at his best. . . . His speech was as florid as his costume. . . He wore a blue dress-coat, faced with silk and aflame with gorgeous brass buttons, a vest of black satin, with a white satin collar, and a wonderfully embroidered shirt." The young actor "made some ingenuous remark upon the subject to Thackeray, who blandly rejoined, 'Yes, the beggar is as beautiful as a butterfly, especially about the shirtfront.'" With ceaselessly beating wings the bright butterfly took the opportunity to announce to his distinguished audience that he and the chairman had just undertaken a "design . . . to smooth the rugged way of young labourers, both in literature and the fine arts, and to soften . . . the declining years of meritorious age." Macready, though, had provided for his own retirement. His last tour of the United States had been profitable though controversial. Twenty people had been killed in the Astor Place riots, provoked by Anglophobia and the American actor Edwin Forrest's jealous hatred of his British rival. Nevertheless, the tour had added enough to his years of careful saving to leave him comfortable. Within six months of the dinner, he retired to Sherborne. When Forster visited him the next year, he had turned "old and grey."³³ Unexpectedly, he was to have another twenty years of rural solitude and to outlive by three of them his butterfly friend.

When the barnstorming to raise funds for the curatorship for the Shakespeare House Museum came to an end in 1848, he had given up only briefly the pleasures of that "one sea of delighted faces," that "one hurrah of applause." In November 1849, visiting Rockingham Castle with Catherine and Georgina, "the best . . . of all the country-houses and estates I have yet seen in England," he had organized a brief amateur theatrical in which he performed with a new friend, Mary Boyle. With a reputation as a fine amateur actress, Miss Boyle, the well-connected daughter of a vice-admiral, was a distant cousin of Lavinia Watson. Two years older than Dickens, she had published two novels and a volume of poetry, none of which rivaled her charm, her good looks, her warmth, and especially her ability to delight herself and others. Later, Tennyson was to call her his "girl of girls." Immediately taken by her beauty, Dickens helped transform the immense dining room at Rockingham, with its "oak-panelled walls, decorated with innumerable shields of relations and neighbours, blazoned in proper heraldic colours," into a theatre in which "hastily-concocted scenes" from *Nicholas Nickleby* and some scenes from Sheridan's *School for Scandal* were performed. Dickens was delighted to have another lovely woman in his life with whom to exchange fantasies, especially upon the safe stage of make-believe. No sooner had the company departed from Rockingham than he indulged in a variant of his usual comic lovemaking in verse, a parody of Thomas Gray's "Elegy Written in a Country Churchyard." In the epitaph, he proclaimed that "here rests his head upon his native soil/ A Youth who lived once, in the public whim:/ His death occasioned by a mortal BOIL,/ Which settled on his brain, and settled him."³⁴

In the late summer of 1850, with *Household Words* off to a good start and *Copperfield* close to its end, he relaxed with a new series of amateur theatricals. Joining forces with the wealthy

Bulwer-Lytton, who for years had had in mind a plan to build retirement cottages for artists on his estate at Knebworth, they became partners in an effort to earn ten thousand pounds within two to five years to finance the Guild of Literature and Art. A kind of "heraldic monstrosity," the enchanted castle at Knebworth became, appropriately, the headquarters of a project that combined the medieval guild mentality with modern social welfare. Heavily bearded and partly deaf, Bulwer-Lytton was, in Dickens' opinion, "the greatest conversationalist of the age."[35] A successful novelist, playwright, and mesmerist, and a notorious dandy, he also had political and social power. And despite a distinguishing streak of eccentricity, he, like Dickens, had the energy and the idealism of a charismatic enthusiast.

By late September, the preparations were proceeding briskly, the amateur company having been called out of semiretirement to act *Every Man in His Humour* and a farce. Catherine was satisfactorily replaced after badly twisting her ankle. When Mary Boyle, "the very best actress I ever saw off the stage, and immeasureably better than a great many I have seen on it," had to withdraw after more than a month of rehearsals because of the death of a dear friend, Dickens was thoroughly disappointed. Still, costumes by Maclise, scenery by Stanfield, performances by Dickens, Forster, Jerrold, Lemon, and Georgina, realized his intention "to make the nights at Knebworth *triumphant*. Once in a thing like this—once in anything, to my thinking—it must be carried out like a mighty enterprise, heart and soul." The three performances at the end of the third week in November went "off in a whirl of triumph." So too did the slightly more private theatricals at Rockingham early in January 1851 in which Dickens, "your Ever Devoted," finally got to make stage love to Mary Boyle in a comedy called *Used Up*, which Charles Mathews had adapted from the French.[36]

He was unhappy at having to return to town after the warmth and excitement of the Rockingham theatricals, confiding to Boyle that "there may be many things wanting to complete [my] happiness." The "first shadows of a new story" hovered "in a ghostly way about [him]." With "stupendous proposals" of Switzerland and Italy in his mind, he plunged more fully into the scheme for the Guild of Literature and Art. At his urging, Bulwer-Lytton, writing with his usual rapidity, dashed off a lengthy five-act historical comedy, *Not So Bad as We Seem*. Unfortunately, having read it twice, Dickens was still not quite sure what it was about, though he was sure that it "was singularly undramatic." Editing it heavily during rehearsals, and pairing it with a slapdash farce, *Mr. Nightingale's Diary*, that he and Lemon dashed off, he managed to make it performable. In May 1851, the company began a series of performances in London and around the country before a distinguished audience that included the queen, Prince Albert, and the Duke of Wellington. The fifth Duke of Devonshire, William George Cavendish, who soon became an unofficial member of the company and a contributing angel, generously lent Devonshire House in Piccadilly for the premiere. Probably Dickens had used his acquaintance with Joseph Paxton, the duke's former estate manager, who soon showed him around the Great Exhibition at the Crystal Palace, his most brilliant creation, to meet "the best of Dukes." Joseph Turner's immensely wealthy patron, the duke still had a keen and generous eye for art and artists. Dickens took the opportunity of the duke's hospitality in September to enjoy Paxton's gardens at Chatsworth, particularly the immense conservatory, and probably the extraordinary library, painting, and coin collection. He slept "in a state bedroom of enormous dimensions, with a bedstead like a brocaded and golden temple. . . . The place is the most wonderful thing in the world . . . and . . . the principal fountain is just twice the height of the Great Horse Shoe Fall at Niagara." The two performances in May 1851 at Devonshire House were "a great success, and we begin by making a great deal of money."[37]

At the end of June, Dickens went to Bath with Lemon, making arrangements for a September performance to what turned out to be "a horribly dull audience." A new friend and acting colleague remarked that they had to speak so very distinctly because of "the great size of the room . . . that the performance took longer than usual." In November, they acted in Clifton and Bristol. Exhilarated, Dickens remarked that "we never played to a better audience. The enthusiasm was prodigious." But he was happy to leave "the smoke and filth of Bristol. My eyes are so redolent of gas, that I can hardly see. . . . As to voice, I am a Raven. And my hair has got into the state from wigs, glue, and exhaustion, that it is more like a Ratcatcher's case for his game than . . . the greatest ornament of the human form." Jerrold seemed "in extraordinary force. I don't think I ever knew him so humorous." Forster continued to be his usual assertive self. "I have always a vicious desire to electrify [him] (when he is acting) violently, in some sensitive part of his anatomy.' In December, they performed in Reading, in February 1852 in Liverpool, where they "filled the Philharmonic Hall" for two nights. In Manchester, "everything went to perfection." Clearing six hundred pounds from an audience of three thousand, Dickens "stepped forward . . . after the comedy, and made them a little speech."

Leaving Liverpool at four in the morning, he was "so blinded by excitement, gas, and waving hats and handkerchiefs, that [he] could scarcely see . . . All the sights of the earth turned pale in my eyes, before the sight of three thousand people with one heart among them . . testifying to you how they believe you to be right, and feel that they cannot do enough to cheer you on. . . . I have been so happy in all this that I could have cried on the shortest notice any time. . . ." Expecting to "bank (after payment of all the heavy expenses) a thousand pounds from that short trip alone," he wanted to act endlessly. In May, performing in Birmingham, Stratford, Kenilworth, and Shrewsbury, they were breakfasted, toasted, dined, and partied, as if they "had been at a wedding."[38]

In August 1852, he took the company to Newcastle, Sunderland, Derby, Sheffield, Manchester, and Liverpool, the last series of performances for the guild. The tour was brilliant but exhausting, and Dickens had to work especially hard to clear his desk "with a view to this confounded trip." Though tired and eager to see the guild venture concluded, the intrepid manager arranged a printed travel schedule, bedroom lists, and post-office schedules for every member of the company. In Derby, where some of the clergy puritanically denounced the acting company, they nevertheless had "a very fair audience of sinners" and made "money in spite of his saints." In Manchester, they tried two new plays, having finally realized that *Not So Bad as We Seem* had been puzzling and boring audiences, most of whom came more for the sight of the literary celebrities than for the interest of the plays. While in Manchester, Dickens, with Catherine and Georgina, called upon Elizabeth Gaskell, who subsequently attended his speech celebrating the opening of the Free Library. During the long addresses, her "only comfort [was] seeing the caricatures Thackeray was drawing which were very funny . . . till [he] . . . was called on to speak & broke down utterly, after which he drew no more caricatures." Concluding at Liverpool, where they cleared another five thousand pounds, they brought the receipts up to the goal that he and Bulwer-Lytton had set. Unfortunately, ten thousand pounds was not enough to make the guild an immediate reality.39 There were also legal complications in creating the corporation. Some of the funds were tied up. When the guild came into existence toward the end of the decade it suffered an anemic life, without popular support, until its dissolution in 1897.

One addition to the company who proved himself a competent actor was Richard Henry Horne. He remained a colleague, though, at *Household Words* for only a short time. Restless, irresolute, given to romantic fantasies, at the end of 1852 he left for Australia to make his fortune in the gold fields, with an indefinite loan of fifty pounds from Dickens. Though far from sure that Horne had taken "a wise step in emigrating," Dickens attempted to enlist Miss Coutts's help on his behalf once he was in Melbourne. Kate Horne was left dependent on her husband's expectations and on the goodwill of his friends in England. Finding her attractive, Dickens enjoyed flirting with her. Catherine, who liked her as well, invited her to parties and for summer visits over the next few years. Soon Mrs. Horne faced the bittersweet challenge of penury and independence.40 The marriage was never to be resumed. Horne was not to return to England for almost twenty years.

Dickens, though, lost a dearer friend in July 1852. While in Hamburg with his family, preparing for a holiday in Lausanne, Richard Watson "was taken suddenly ill with violent inflammation of the bowels, and died (quite easily) in four days." He was fifty-two years old. Dickens' friendship with the Watsons had strengthened recently. Two weeks earlier, "on the day before he left town . . . in unusually good spirits and full of plans for future enjoyment at Rockingham," Watson had dined at Tavistock House. Dickens and Watson were bound together by their memories of Switzerland, their plans for trips to the Continent, their enjoyment of one another's hospitality, and their mutual delight in theatricals. To Dickens, he "was as true a friend as I have ever had . . . a thoroughly good man, of a most amiable and affectionate nature, and as simple hearted as a child. . . . I really held him in my heart." The body was returned to Rockingham, where Watson was buried in "his own church." Dickens' feelings for Lavinia Watson were equally strong. She now had the agony of being a young widow with four children. She "expects to be confined" in February—"which is very sad." A heroic and idealized figure of femininity, "a woman of great courage and understanding, and of a well disciplined though very affectionate nature," Lavinia soon seemed to him "very tranquil and resigned."[41]

When the stage-shy Wills had declined in March 1851 to perform the role of the valet in *Not So Bad as We Seem*, Augustus Egg had suggested his close friend Wilkie Collins. A moderately successful painter with a comfortable private income, Egg had become a worshiping intimate. Frequently in Georgina's company, he had developed strong feelings for her, and in 1852 was to propose marriage. Dickens and the twenty-eight-year-old Collins had never met. He knew, though, of his intimacy with Egg and his friendship with a group of young painters, frequent dinner guests at Egg's apartment in Bayswater. Probably Dickens also had some sense of Collins as a writer who had recently published a travel volume and a first novel. Having known his father "very well," he told Egg that he "should be very glad to know him." A successful minor painter who specialized in landscapes and genre painting, William Collins had kept his wife and two sons abroad with him for long periods, particularly in Italy, and had taken long painting trips while they remained in London.

Briefly a law student at Lincoln's Inn, Collins hoped to become a dramatist and novelist. Without an ascetic bone in his body, he enjoyed hypochondria without being seriously frail. Badly nearsighted, he wore rimless glasses that dropped low onto his moon-shaped face. His delight in food, wine, and sensual enjoyments established a reputation that his plumpness, softness, shortness (he was a little less than five and a half feet), and twinkling wittiness supported. Living with his mother in a comfortable house on Hanover Terrace, the ambitious Collins gracefully balanced the disparate elements of his life, his friendships with various pre-Raphaelite painters, his late-night writing stints, and now his inclusion in Dickens' dramatic company. With the editors of the *Leader*, his friends Edward Pigott and Thornton Hunt, he argued about the proper distinction in a newspaper between news articles and editorial intrusion, especially on religious matters. Despite his secularism, he believed "Jesus Christ to be the son of God," and that it was "blasphemy to use his name" in a newspaper.⁴² In his novels, though, he had begun to reveal a strong sensual feeling for unusual romantic situations and relationships, for the excitement of mystery and exposure, for erotic and psychological tensions.

Immediately a dedicated member of the cast, he pleased Dickens, who breathed a sigh of relief when "everything went to perfection." On short notice, "Collins was *admirable*—got up excellently, played thoroughly well, and missed nothing." Collins' good humor, his pleasant temperament, and his adequate talents as an actor encouraged Dickens to invite him, when Jerrold deserted in February 1852, to take a larger role. As the performances went on into the spring and summer of 1852, the acting colleagues crossed the line into personal friendship.

Not prone to idealize, Collins seems to have had a good sense of Dickens' personality, his restlessness, his managerial drive, his possessiveness, his emotional ruthlessness, his instinct for power. In April, he published his first contribution to *Household Words*, the oddly macabre and partly Dickensian "A Terribly Strange Bed," probably written to please the editor. He also had a sense of Dickens' vitality, excitability, and fraternal warmth, his capacity for food, wine, song, and companionship. Collins knew how to be fun. For him, it was a heady combination. For Dickens, the young writer provided relaxing companionship. With his flexible schedule, he was frequently available for recreation. With his curiosity and bohemian sophistication, his experience with women, sensual pleasures, and travel, he had none of the dark-waistcoat conservatism of some of Dickens' other friends. Unlike Dickens, he had been a habitué of casual sex since his teenage years. Partly because of his background, he had none of Dickens' drive toward respectability. He was ambitious for fame rather than social status. General sweetness of temperament, the readiness of his company, and his easy acceptance of himself and others made him a young man whose admi-

ration Dickens could respond to. By the time the guild performances came to an end in September 1852, they were sufficiently
intimate for Collins to "go (with Egg) to stay with Dickens at
Dover," where he "received the kindest and heartiest welcome.
. . . The sea air acts on me as if it were all distilled from laudanum."³

❧ 5 ❧

AS HIS GUEST IN DOVER IN SEPTEMBER 1852, COLLINS FOLLOWED
"the example of [his] host," who was at work on the eighth
number of *Bleak House*, and actually finished his "hitherto interminable" novel *Basil*. The young writer was delighted to have
his usual irregularity stiffened by his mentor's work and exercise ethic. "Our life here is as healthy and happy as life can be.
Work in the morning—long walks—sea-bathing—early hours—
famous meals." They breakfasted "at 10 minutes past eight.
. . . Dickens goes into his study, and is not visible again till
two—when he is visible for every pleasant social purpose that
can be imagined for the rest of the day. . . . When he first came,"
the tourists "used to waylay him every morning—and have a
good long stare at the 'great man' as he went to his bath."
Dickens did not find such prying eyes amusing. Dover seemed
crowded, expensive, and inordinately public. Collins' company,
though, was pleasurable. Also, Dickens' family found him an
attractive guest. And he was an appreciative audience. "Dickens
read us the two first chapters" of "a glorious number of Bleak
house . . . as soon as he had finished them—speaking the dialogue
of each character, as dramatically as if he were acting his own
personages; and making his audience laugh and cry with equal
fervour and equal sincerity." On his host's strong urging, Collins was persuaded to stay a few days more. In early October,
they walked the fifteen miles to Canterbury together, the "Cathedral white and brilliant against the brightest of blue skies."⁴⁴
Though he returned to town with Collins, Dickens went,
with Catherine, almost immediately across the Channel to Boulogne for two weeks to write the next number of *Bleak House*.
The "very bad passage over" (he felt as if he had exchanged his
"eyes for two brass bullets") did not detract from his favorable

impression of the French seaside resort, with its winding streets, unfinished cathedral, and gracious hillsides from which the town and the sea glittered. In France, Dickens could work with less interruption from the idly curious. The anonymity was restful. Having been hard at work on *Bleak House* since December 1851, he found the novelty of the French language relaxing. The previous February, less than six months after he had completed *Copperfield,* he had felt "the first shadows of a new story hovering in a ghostly way" about him, "as they usually begin to do, when I have finished an old one." The story simmered through the spring and summer of 1851. In August, he went with Henry Austin to Gloucestershire, having in mind using it as one of the settings for the new novel. While headquartered in Broadstairs from mid-May until October 1851, he delighted in "the associations of the place in which [he] finished Copperfield. . . . Corn growing, larks singing, garden full of flowers, fresh air on the sea . . . have set me to work with great vigor."45

By September 1851, he was "in the first throes of a new book." The difficulties of getting into Tavistock House set him back, but nevertheless one of the mock titles for the library was *History of a Short Chancery Suit* in twenty volumes. In mid-October, Bradbury and Evans announced a "New Serial Work by Mr. Charles Dickens." In late November, he was writing the first number of what he had decided to call *Bleak House,* and he finished it about the tenth of December. He pushed ahead, eager to get as much of a head start as possible on future numbers. In mid-February 1852, he read the first number to friends, including Miss Coutts. The hectic theatrical touring for the guild and the demands of *Household Words* did not interfere with its publication on February 28 for March 1, and the appearance of a new number on the last day of each of the next eighteen months. While he was not quite sure that he "ever did like, or ever shall like, anything quite so well as Copperfield," the new novel had "very good things in it. . . . You may come to like Bleak House," he wrote to a literary acquaintance, "as well as its predecessors! And I shouldn't wonder! For I see a something 'looming in the future' that looks pretty." Writing a new novel was partly revivification, partly additional exhaustion. He had felt in the summer of 1852 as if he had for some time "been thinking my brain into sort of a cabbage patch."[46] By late September, having finally finished the guild performances, he could enjoy Collins' company in Dover and read the eighth number of *Bleak House* with a sense of having a fairly free calendar for the first time in two years.

Soon he was "so busy, leading up to the great turning idea of the Bleak House [No. o] that I have lived this last week or ten days in a perpetual scald and boil." He advised Collins, whose *Basil* he had just read and admired, that "writing can be done [only with] the utmost application, the greatest patience, and the steadiest energy of which the writer is capable." He had been assembling the ostensible elements of *Bleak House* for many years. His long involvement with social, political, and legal matters was central. From his preoccupation with emigration and his awareness of Caroline Chisholm's Family Colonization Loan Society (her bad housekeeping and her children's dirty faces haunted him after a visit to her home), he created Mrs. Jellyby and telescopic philanthropy.[47] From Leigh Hunt and Walter Savage Landor he created Harold Skimpole and Mr. Boythorn. From images of philanthropy and benevolence, including Richard Watson, he created Mr. Jarndyce. Rockingham was transformed into Chesney Wold. From elements of Mary and Georgina Hogarth he created Esther Summerson. Most of all, though, he projected from himself a narrator so passionately angry at injustice and exploitation that his voice combines both the retrospective memories of life in the blacking factory and his biblically resonant, prophetic denunciation of what England had become.

Exhausted as well as exhilarated, he confronted the challenge of using two first-person narrators, one a female, the other his own voice. By the end of 1852, a little more than half finished, he was "already looking forward to the completion of Bleak House in August, and to bachelor wandering afterwards into Switzerland and Italy." The winter was a difficult one. His "old horrid nervous choking" at night recurred. He went to Brighton in March 1853. It poured for his entire stay. He felt rheumatic in his back. Often, though, he was "too hard at work to be able to stir." As far as *Bleak House* and the law were concerned, "I think the giant who said Fie Fi Fo Fum must have been an impersonation of the Law. Grinding Jack's bones to make his bread. . . ." His old American friend Cornelius Felton came to visit. So too did Harriet Beecher Stowe, whom he did not like. He was distressed to learn "that they have kept from me that Frank (the cleverest of all the children) stammers so horribly as to be an afflicted spirit." Eager to be out of London, he made arrangements in mid-May to summer at Boulogne. "Hypochondriacal whisperings tell me that I am rather overworked. The spring does not seem to fly back again. . . . I really feel that my head would split like a fired shell if I remained" in London.

Suddenly, at the beginning of June, he became seriously ill. The illness began in his right side. It seemed identical to what he thought of as the old illness, the weakness in the right kidney or recurrent renal cholic. It may have been a viral infection. He desperately needed to get out of London. Otherwise, he imagined, he never would recover. He made it to Folkestone, where he thought the sea air would help him. He began to get better, slowly. "I have been ill and in great pain—six days in bed for the first time in my life. . . . I have been shaving a man every morning—a stranger to me—whose appearance was rather irksome and oppressive. I am happy to say he has at last retired from the looking-glass, and is replaced by the familiar personage whom I have lathered and scraped these twenty years."[48]

By early July, he felt fully recovered, though there had been rumors he had been near death's door and had aged terribly. It was "an old afflicted KIDNEY," he explained, "once the torment of my childhood, in which I took cold." The weather at Boulogne was wonderful. "I am getting my book done in peace, and am (thank God) very vigorous and very brown." The "Manager is himself again . . . energetic, muscular, the pride of Albion and the admiration of Gaul." The cross-Channel packet brought welcome visitors, the Leeches, Collins, Beard, Forster, and Stone. Collins thought that the latest number of *Bleak House*, which he read in manuscript, "contains . . . some of the finest passages he has ever written . . . brought out with such pathos, delicacy, and truth, as no other living writer has ever rivalled or even approached." Concentrating on finishing his book, Dickens rejoiced in the celebratory dinner in Boulogne attended by Bradbury, Evans, Forster, Lemon, Browne, and Collins, and on August 25, 1853, he read the last number to family and friends.

He now relaxed into "the first drowsy lassitude" of having finished prowling "about in the wind and rain."[49] But he was eager to prowl greater distances. With Egg and Collins as traveling companions, he had made arrangements to form an "Italian Triumvirate." They would leave in early October for three months in Italy.

CHAPTER NINE

The Sparkler of Albion
(1853-1855)

❧ I ❧

THE TRIUMVIRATE CROSSED THE CHANNEL IN OCTOBER 1853 WITH
expectations of adventure and delight. For the two bachelors,
the world lay all before them, though to different degrees and
in different ways. Collins was sophisticated, self-indulgent,
amusingly and unselfconsciously conceited. He was returning
to the country of his childhood. In Rome, nothing astonished
him "more than [his] own vivid remembrance of every street
and building in this wonderful and mournful place." He saw
"all the favourite haunts" where he and his brother "used to run
about as little boys." He lectured Egg on art, drove Dickens
"into a frenzy by humming and whistling whole overtures—
with not one movement remembered correctly," and gave his
companions "a full account of his first love adventure" in which
"he came out quite a pagan Jupiter." Egg and Dickens calculated
"that at this precocious passage in his history, he was twelve
years and some odd months old."

The dark-haired, slender, idealistic, and intensely moralistic Egg had never been south of the Alps. An increasing favor-

ite of Dickens', he had had the good sense the previous year to propose marriage to Georgina, and the misfortune to be turned down. Neither the proposal nor the rejection endeared him the less to the novelist, who saw where his own self-interest lay. "It would have been a good thing for her, as he is an excellent fellow, and is well off." But "he is very far her inferior intellectually," though "five men would be out of six . . . not to mention her being one of the most amiable and affectionate of girls. Whether it is, or is not a pity that she is all she is to me and mine instead of brightening up a good little man's house where she would still have the artist kind of life she is used to, about her, is a knotty point I never can settle to my satisfaction." As they traveled, Egg readily shared the "general sentiment expressed this morning, that Georgina ought to be married." Perhaps, Dickens wryly told his wife, "you'll mention it to her!"

With his family safely in place in London, he welcomed the opportunity to be off on his own for three months with his bachelor friends, though he alternated between missing his family and delighting in his freedom. He had never had such freedom before. From Venice, Collins proclaimed that "we lead the most luxurious, dandy-dilettante sort of life here." Except for writing two brief articles for *Household Words*, Dickens also did just that. But, used to sitting up in carriages and trains in England, and having scratched among the fleas at provincial inns, eaten shabbily and on the run, and journeyed day and night to get to desired destinations during his previous visit to Italy, he wanted to travel fast and far. His companions did not, and objected. Though he had planned a whirlwind schedule that would allow him to visit Sicily for the first time, the more stately pace determined that Naples, a city he detested, would be their southern terminus. Primarily Dickens had undertaken the trip because he felt stale, restless, and burdened by having finished a long novel. Its completion had left him both exhausted and explosively energetic. The decision to go to Italy was also an attempt to return to aspects of the past, to relive youthful experiences, to see friends as well as places associated with a time when his burdens seemed less heavy. He had never been to Spain, Greece, Russia, Scandinavia, Central Europe. Yet Italy was his destination again, as if he meant to prowl inwardly. "It is so strange and like a dream to me, to hear the delicate Italian once again. . . . So beautiful to see the delightful sky again, and all the picturesque wonders of the country." Travel, though, neither provided him the opportunity for rest that it did his friends nor exhausted his compulsion to keep moving. "I am so restless to be doing—and always shall be, I think, so long as I have any portion in Time—that if I were to stay more than a week in any one city here, I believe I should be half desperate to begin some new story!!!"[2] But the new story, ultimately to be *Little Dorrit*, was the old story again, deepened and intensified, the story he carried with him into Italy and needed to exert himself not to write. In one sense, he needed rest from the most emotionally demanding activity of his life. In another, the only rest was in the activity that his restlessness promoted.

Paris in the middle of October was "extraordinarily gay, and wonderfully improving." It was, though, "literally overflowing with English travellers." The quays had been paved, the new boulevards were being constructed, "the broadest and the grandest in the world." After dining with Miss Coutts there, the triumvirate journeyed to Strasbourg "by the best railway" they had ever traveled on. They spent one morning "getting through the 'sights.'" Collins was delighted with the "fantastic puppet show . . . every time 12 o'clock strikes." At Basel, they transferred to a horse-drawn carriage. Soon they "began to get into the real Swiss country. Immense masses of hills . . . with the most vivid autumn red, yellow, and purple." Traveling together forced on them a keener awareness of one another, and mostly good-humored accommodation, of which Collins and Dickens had a great deal. Despite constant tutoring, Egg, "with a bitter bad memory," was unable to learn Italian quickly, his slowness soon declining from an irritation into an amusement. "I cannot remember what Egg called a bird yesterday . . . something compounded of English and French with an Italian termination—something like Birdoisella." They traveled "in a state of mad good spirits," Collins remarked, "and never flag in our jollity." Dickens made the arrangements and handled the funds. Collins, the most easygoing of the three, "eats and drinks everything. Gets on very well everywhere. . . ." On the road, Egg sometimes wanted "trifles of accommodation . . . which could hardly be got in Paris, and Collins sometimes want[ed] to give people too little for their trouble. But a word [put] it all right in a moment." Occasionally, to Dickens' amusement, his companions would "burst out into economy—always on some wretched little point, and always on a point they had previously settled the other way.";

Their first destination was Lausanne. Soon "miles on miles of soaring mountains . . . burst into view." The eccentric, wealthy Reverend Chauncey Hare Townshend, an expert on mesmerism, jewelry, and ghost stories, insisted on their staying in his delightful country house on the lake. There was a large dinner and an elegant evening party. The reason, though, for the Lausanne visit was to see old friends, to revive old feelings. With the exception of Lavinia Watson, who was in England, and Richard Watson, who was dead, the rest of his 1846 coterie was still in place. Dickens' heart warmed to find Haldimand "roaring with laughter, disputing, discussing, and contradicting, in exactly the old way." His vivaciousness, though, had become a regular part of a cycle of a few weeks' alternation, the other extreme of which was "a black humour," silence, and seclusion. De Cerjat was delightful company again, though he had become thin and grey. Mrs. de Cerjat was "just the same as ever, but very deaf." His Lausanne friends "crowded down on a fearful, bad morning" to see them off.4

Ascending to Chamonix and the Mer de Glace, " through pretty deep snow . . . and the climbing very difficult," he exalted in his physical strength, the headiness of a man of slight, wiry build, with legs taut from years of walking, willfully pushing himself to his limits. The Inimitable steamed "with perspiration from head to foot." Impressed, the guides "pronounced [him] 'a strong intrepid'" who "ought to ascend Mont Blanc next summer." Halfway up, the two younger men transferred from a carriage to what looked to Collins "exactly like a rotten sedan chair on wheels," which they stayed in throughout the entire climb. "Imagine almost a thousand feet of perpendicular precipice." In the brilliant sunshine, they "looked down into one of the crevices—an awful place, two or three feet wide, and *three hundred* feet deep, with the ice-walls shining blinding green all the way down." At the top, they "warmed [themselves] at a wood fire on the ice." Though the day had begun with a 4 A.M. departure from Geneva, they continued on mule to Martigny and then over the Simplon pass into Italy. The next day they drove "in the warmest brightest sunshine along the lovely shores of Lago Maggiore." An "old blind fiddler . . . sang Italian national songs" as they crossed on the ferry. Deeply moved, Collins felt like "bursting out crying." For Dickens, Italy now was like a dream revived or a dream that had somehow never ended. Even the exotic forms of transportation were fantasylike. "We have been in the most extraordinary vehicles—like swings, like boats, like Noah's arks, like barges and enormous bedsteads." In Milan, they went to the opera. Egg and Collins did the tourist sights. Two days later they were in Genoa, the second of his three personal destinations. On a wet afternoon, he took his friends to look over the Peschiere and its memories. "The garden is sorely neglected now, and the rooms are all full of boarding school beds, and most of the fireplaces are closed up; but the old beauty and grandeur of the place were in it still."[5]

Genoa itself struck him as having grown immensely, the somnolent, semimedieval town of 1846 having expanded into the bustling materialism of the nineteenth century. Dickens was both pleased and disappointed. On the one hand, growth meant progress. On the other, such change deprived him of touchstones from his past and reminded him of personal loss. One of his Genoa friends greeted him with puzzlement. " 'I expected to find a ruin, we heard you had been so ill. And I find you younger and better looking than ever. But it's so strange to see you without a bright waistcoat. Why haven't you got a bright waistcoat on?' " He "apologized for [his] black one." Her eyesight, though, was askew. There had been both subtle and gross changes. The youthful Dickens of 1846 had become, to most observers, noticeably older, his complexion ruddy and wrinkled, his hair thinner, his large, brilliant hazel-gray eyes restlessly set in middle-aged sockets and skin. In pouring rain, he visited the de la Rues and the Thompsons. The first reunion was a warm one. Emile and Dickens had corresponded regularly. Nursing "her foolish sick mother who wears out everybody near her body and soul," Augusta still suffered an attenuated version of her convulsive attacks. Though he said little about it in his letters to Catherine and Georgina, the experience with the de la Rues in 1844–45 was much on his mind, the excitement of being her beneficent doctor, the mesmeric ménage of husband, wife, and healer, the histrionics of Catherine's jealousy. The few days in Genoa strengthened his sense of having been injured by his wife's limitations. At a "ruinous Albaro-like Palace," he visited Christiana and James Thompson, who had two daughters. The talented Christiana, who now added painting to her piano playing, he thought "greatly flushed and agitated" to see him. She was as beautiful but also as unstable as ever, "her excitability and restlessness . . . a positive disease."[6]

After three days of hospitality from his Genoese friends, they boarded a crowded steamer for Naples. From a flock of small boats, obstructing their effort to leave the harbor, came vigorous "shrill choruses from Verdi's operas," accompanied by shirtless fiddlers and "coffee-coloured women with guitars." The officers of the *Valetta*, which was an English ship, shouted, "Hullo! you are in the way! I say, signora, sheer off—On, damn it: Mademoiselle *will* you sheer off!" With Genoa glittering behind them, they steamed into the bright Mediterranean on a smooth sea. As a distinguished Englishman, Dickens ' became the brother of all the officers in half an hour." His influence was soon an advantage. The ship was ludicrously overbooked, with twice as many passengers, all of whom had paid for first-class accommodations, as available beds. The agreeable passage of the first day gave way to confusion and irritation that night. 'Berths in the saloon (on the seats) had been kept for [them], but the atmosphere . . . was so stifling that [they] . . . determined to rough it with wrappers and sofa pillows on deck. . . . Just as [they] were comfortably asleep," it began to rain "like a waterfall." The stairs and cabin were crowded with people and noxious smells. The triumvirate went on deck again, and tried to sleep in the rain. A "conversational miscreant," who became known as the most prominent of the three ship bores, kept them up for hours. The next day, the captain, prompted by Dickens' constant teasing about the misconduct of the steamship line in "allowing double the number of people to take passage," took pity on the distinguished novelist and his friends. Dickens was soon superbly lodged in the steward's cabin. Egg and Collins slept in the ship's storeroom on stiff but at least private shelves, amidst flour, bread, apples, cheeses, bushes of grapes, and the clean smell of a grocery store. When they awoke, the boat was docked in Civitavecchia, "a wretched, dead place—infested by beggars and French soldiers."7

The next morning they steamed into the Bay of Naples, "wreaths of white smoke . . . curling up quietly . . . from the Crater of Vesuvius" in the distance. From his "charming apartment opposite the sea," Dickens saw that Naples had hardly changed. It seemed as overwhelmingly poor and as degraded as ever. The weather was impossibly hot. Mosquitoes soon left their "highly ornamental marks" on his skin. "The same men, with the same instruments, were singing the same songs, to the same tunes" as nine years before. With a reversal in the usual relationship between geology and culture, Vesuvius, in contrast, had completely changed since his last visit. There had been a major eruption in 1850. Now there was a great deal of smoke, but no fire. Soon after landing, they went to a public bath, where an old man, who soaped him, "kept . . . ejaculating under his breath 'O Heaven how clean this Englishman is!' " Before dinner, Collins suddenly heard the voice of the ship bore close at his ear, a man "created as a sort of moral *hairshirt* for unpenitential Protestants who won't 'mortify' the flesh with any rougher discipline than a cold bath and a rub with a turkish towel." On shipboard, they had enjoyed the company of an old acquaintance, Sir James Emerson Tennent, who, with his family, joined them on most of their excursions. Probably they had met through Forster, who had been Tennent's classmate in legal studies. A writer, traveler, and Liberal politican who supported the Reform Bill in 1832, he had lived in Greece, which he had written about, and then in Ceylon, where he had been colonial secretary.

Later, on their ascent of Vesuvius, they were also joined by the "very merry and agreeable" Austen Henry Layard, the thirty-six-year-old archaeologist, author, and diplomat, recently famous for his discovery of the ruins of Nineveh and whose parliamentary career was about to explode into a radical assault on governmental inefficiency. In the sunlight, they climbed to the cone on horseback. Making "a practice of increasing his speed when ascending a hill," Dickens, accompanied by Layard, surged ahead. Whenever they felt fatigued, Egg and Collins "discreetly rested. . . . The mountain was very quiet," Collins noticed, "no flame, no stones, no noise—nothing but thick clouds of sulphurous smoke." From the mouth of the crater, looking out over Sorrento and Capri, there was "a blood-red setting sun gleaming through the vapour." They descended by torchlight, "with a young Italian moon skimming above us."[8]

Before the middle of November 1853 they were in Rome, where Dickens paused, overcoming "the difficulties of so unsettled a life" to write a brief story for the Christmas number of *Household Words*. Soon he was looking forward to returning to domestic comforts, "though I feel I could not have done a better thing to clear my mind and freshen it up again, than make this expedition." Business problems rumbled from the distance. Sales were not as strong as he and his co-publishers had expected. Forster and Wills had hardly written to him, and Wills complained of Forster's interference and peremptoriness, which Dickens advised him to ignore. Forster complained of Wills's "not consulting him enough."

When he went sight-seeing, Dickens managed to keep his anti-Catholicism muted in the background. Since he had last been in Italy, the clerical presence had receded. Italian nationalism had become stronger. In Naples, dining at the British Embassy, he enjoyed the story of a young Englishman who had "married . . . a bare-footed girl off the Beach, with whom he had previously fulfilled all matrimonial conditions except the ceremony The better to do this, he had first turned Catholic." Another Englishman "rowed away in the dead of night with another Capri virgin—who would have gone, with the greatest cheerfulness and without any opposition from her relations and friends, in the blaze of noon." He visited St. Peter's with Egg and Collins, to whom "the high altar sparkled with hundreds of fantastically disposed lights and the voices of the full choir, sounded faint and mystical far off." But to the more pragmatic, anticlerical Dickens, the real music was in the contrast between the romance of classical ruins and the power of modernity. "The Colosseum in its magnificent old decay is as grand as ever—and, with the Electric Telegraph darting through one of its ruined arches like a sunbeam and piercing through its cruel old heart, is even grander."[9]

From Rome, they went to Siena and then Florence, happy to have had only three days of rain. On the road, they carried their own brandy, cloves, and tea. The triumvirate had no politi-

cal differences, and they triumphed over small personal irrita-
tions, such as "Collins learnedly holding forth to Egg" about
"the Fine arts" (when the subject came up, Dickens always
pretended "to fall into a profound reverie" and he never went
into a gallery with them), and Collins occasionally expounding
"a code of morals, taken from modern French novels, which I
instantly and with becoming gravity smash." Dickens found
tolerable the egotistical obsession of both friends with the mous-
taches they were growing in imitation of "the great Original."
In Venice, late in November, "in full dress and big sleeved great
coat," he was "rather considerably ashamed" by "Collins with
incipient moustache, spectacles, slender legs, and extremely
dirty dress gloves" and Egg "in a white hat, and a straggly mean
little black beard." They were conspicuously brought to their
opera seats in the traditional ceremony in which those who have
their own gondolas are escorted by their gondoliers, who lead
the way "with an enormous lantern . . . through brilliantly
lighted passages." Dickens tried to sneak away, but could not.
Though he even shaved his own small beard in the hope that
they would follow his example, such contretemps did not really
spoil their comradery. Nor did the intensely cold weather in
Venice undermine their fun. "We live among pictures and palaces all day, and among operas, ballets, and cafes more than half
the night." To Collins, among the whirl of impressions, it
seemed "seven months instead of seven weeks" that they had
been away.[10]

   Their schedule had its pressures, though. Dickens had to be
back in England by the tenth of December for family and *Household Words* business and to redeem a promise to read *A Christmas
Carol* in Birmingham. From Venice, they went in freezing
weather to Parma and then Turin, on their way to Paris, where
he had arranged that Charley, his eldest son, coming from his
business studies in Germany, would meet them. De la Rue,
whom he relied on for travel and monetary arrangements, met
them in Turin. His presence reminded him of how hard it was
"to be so near to dear old Genoa without coming back; and, if
the railroad had been finished, I think I certainly should have
done so." Something important to him still resided there. It was
not only or so much Augusta de la Rue. It was a sense of himself
that he needed both to expand and defend. He did so in an

ostensibly loving but gratuitously aggressive letter to Catherine, his anger about an incident of nine years before sufficiently strong for it to stand as emblematic of other incidents and deeper currents. Invariably confident that he could see "the plain truth," he reminded her, from Turin, that those aspects of his personality that made him different, "sometimes for good; sometimes I dare say for evil," were the same qualities that had "made you proud and honored in your married life, and given you station better than rank, and surrounded you with many enviable things."

More than anything else, "the intense pursuit of any idea that takes complete possession of me" distinguishes "me . . . from other men." His earlier preoccupation with Augusta had been an exemplification of this monomaniacal intensity, the same intensity that had brought him from the blacking factory to Tavistock Place. Her jealousy, then, had been inappropriate, and, in fact, a slander against both de la Rues, who had behaved generously in not alluding to the slur that she had forced him to cast on their honor. In his recent visit, they had been graciously solicitous of her. "Now I am perfectly clear that your position beside these people is not a good one . . . not worthy of you at all. And . . . you have it in your power to set it right at once by writing her a note to say that you have heard from me, with interest, of her sufferings and her cheerfulness . . . and that if you should ever be thrown together again by any circumstances, you hope it will be for a friendly association without any sort of shadow upon it. . . . I do not ask you to do this, or want you to do this. I shall never ask whether you have done it or not and shall never approach the subject from this hour," for "it would be utterly valueless and contemptible if it were done through a grain of any other influence than that of your own heart."[11]

Beneath his anger was a view of himself as essentially an honorable human being, incapable of purposefully deceiving others. The possibility of self-deceit hardly crossed his mind. The energetic restlessness that was inseparable, he felt, from his creativity, was a desperate force for life, amidst all sorts of restrictions. Any attempt, whatever its motives, to regulate his expression of that energy in his relationships was an attempt to diminish his creativity. He resented being coerced into giving up friends because of Catherine's banality and insecurity. That she had reason for the latter he utterly denied. That her awareness of her inferiority to her husband might have made her insecure and self-deprecatory, motivating her to dramatize her comparative incompetence while attacking him, apparently did not occur to him. Her jealousy of his intimacy with Augusta was an unacceptable limitation on his freedom to have friends and to fulfill his basic nature. And since 1845, "the skeleton in the closet" had come partly out of the closet. He had been accused of infidelities, so he later bitterly told Emile, with so many women that he deserved "respect" as an experienced man of the world. Increasingly unattractive to him, alternating between indolence and hysteria, Catherine seemed more and more like her mother in looks, in manner, and in speech. Dickens' letter from Turin was interlined with anger about and rebellion against almost twenty years of a relationship that gave him fewer and fewer satisfactions, a marriage to an ordinary, frequently depressed, modestly intelligent woman whose limitations inevitably reminded him of the constraints that he had voluntarily assumed. In Italy, traveling with his bachelor friends, he saw the advantages of independence, and the misery of a union with an unsuitable partner, the absence of "the one friend and companion" he had "never made."[12]

❧ 2 ❧

BLEAK HOUSE, COMPLETED IMMEDIATELY BEFORE DICKENS' DEPARture for Italy, is visibly dark with overtones of both his personal dissatisfaction and his increasing pessimism about the condition of England. The reconciling dynamic of the novel is the interaction between the narrator's passionate anger at poverty, corruption, and exploitation and the temperate, harmonizing goodness of the voice of the main character. For the first time, using a female first-person narrator, he created a dual narrative in which the voice of the author alternates with the voice of a character. These personae compliment and play off against one another. Drawing on the stereotypical realities of British Victorian culture, one voice is masculine, aggressively satirical, and prophetically explosive. The other is feminine, passive, innocent, loving, and infinitely gentle. The voices maintain their independence in a marriage of harmonizing opposites. They are Dickens' version of the perfect couple. Esther Summerson even eventually marries a medical doctor, whose powers of gentle healing have that touch of the feminine that he saw in himself as mesmerist, "physician." and novelist. "Most writers of fiction,' he told a contributor to *Household Words*, "write partly from their experience, and partly from their imagination. . . . I have had recourse to both sources."[13]

His absorption of personal experience into fiction had its conscious and unconscious dimensions. The former ranged from his modeling Inspector Bucket after the Scotland Yard detective who had provided him with the opportunity to write articles based on observation of police work to his projection of Georgina Hogarth onto the depiction of the idealized Esther Summerson. In creating the first detective hero, Dickens originated the genre of detective fiction. In his impressionistic depictions of London, which had become increasingly insidious, "one of the dragons" with which he was "perpetually fighting," he expanded his preoccupation with the city in an age of dehumanization into the novel of the modern urban experience. Bringing together sound and sense, he transformed the Romantic use of landscape as an equivalent for inner states of consciousness into the psychological and the symbolic novel, and to the Romantic emphasis on weather and place he pointedly added institutions, like the Chancery Court, as symbolic representations of the inner lives of individuals and the society. The biographical structure of *Bleak House*, though, rests on the emotional substructure of his preoccupation with living and dead parents, with abandonment and poverty, with the conflict between innate goodness and social degradation, and with the triumph of prophetic artistry over a chaotic world. Through fictional correlatives, he dramatizes many of the emotional conditions of his life. Like his own father, Esther's fails to make his way out of poverty. Like his mother, Esther's sacrifices her child to her own self-interest. As in his childhood he felt himself deserted, Esther is abandoned to the woeful ministrations of an evangelically demeaning false mother. Her motherlessness reflects his sense of his own, just as Lady Dedlock's feelings of loss, guilt, and unnaturalness, which compel her to endanger her status and security, reflect his desire to bring mother and child together again after a lifetime of separation. By 1852, he had found some effective strategies for distancing himself from his parents, partly through the numerous rewritings of the story of his childhood. After his father's death in 1851, he had inherited complete financial responsibility for his sixty-four-year-old mother, who had "a strong objection to being considered in the least old," and regularly appeared at Tavistock House "on Christmas Day in a juvenile cap which takes an immense time in the putting on."[14] Ever in his eyes the irresponsible parent, the bad fairy of indifference and rejection had not changed.

Within fiction, though, reconciliations were possible. With his deep attachment to his own two daughters, Dickens had little difficulty in creating for Esther in John Jarndyce a surrogate father, a man of rectitude, benevolence, and wisdom. Some of the warmth of the relationship between this "father" and his "ward" expresses his love for Mamie and Katie, but also his feelings about Georgina, who had come into his household a child and grown to womanhood there. For Dickens, emotionally and unconsciously, the line between daughter-sister and daughter-sister-wife was sufficiently blurred for there to be significant overlap. John Jarndyce proposes marriage to Esther. A surrogate father can become a real husband. Esther is everything that Catherine Dickens was not, the guiding good spirit and genius of whatever household she invests with her presence. She is an angel of competence, the good fairy of self-sacrifice, the combined figure of daughter-sister-wife into which, partly to distance himself from Catherine, he had transformed Georgina. In a notebook that he soon began to keep as a source and reminder for ideas, he sketched a partly fictionalized version of his sister-in-law in her role as surrogate: "she sacrificed to children, and [was] sufficiently rewarded. From a child herself, always 'the children' (of somebody else) to engross her. And so it comes to pass that she never has a child herself—is never married—is always devoted 'to the children' . . . and dies quite happily."[15]

The personal themes of *Bleak House* are inseparable from the social and philosophical. Esther's abandonment is as much the product of false social values as it is of maternal unnaturalness. Her redemption derives partly from the existence of benevolent forces in a generally corrupt social structure, mostly from her innate goodness, the strength and depth of her moral sentiments. Like her creator, she has the inner resources to triumph over adversity. She also has help. Standing as counterpoint to Dickens' successful struggle with abandonment and impoverishment, Jo the crossing sweep embodies his childhood fear of orphanhood and lifelong anxiety about money. Those feelings, though, are correlatives in the novel for Dickens' analysis of the sharklike materialism of nineteenth-century capitalistic England, whose wealth was, he believed, based partly on the exploitation and brutalization of surplus labor. It was a culture that needed orphans. The unprotected were malleable raw material to be purchased cheaply, for the mills, mines, and factories, for the knee-deep-mud-and-feces street crossings of London. Convinced that England was divided into the rich and the poor, without a middle class to speak of, he found the apathy, ignorance, and unwarranted power of the upper classes increasingly threatening to the social equilibrium that he believed a healthy and humane class structure promoted. Somewhere, somehow, things had gone disastrously wrong with the body politic. The symptoms were class conflict and social disease: poverty, ignorance, crime, dislocation, typhoid, cholera. Their fictional and psychological representations are shameful secrets of parenthood and plot, intricate and twisted chains of misery.

In *Bleak House* he untwists the chains and unravels the plots sufficiently to promote possibilities of personal if not societal redemption. No matter how gloomy the contemporary reality, he maintained a residual hope for social reform. As the decade advanced, he did become more selective about which causes he would actively support. His energy and his privacy became even more precious to him. He also, though, began to fear that unless some of the blatant problems were addressed, bloody revolution in the French manner would be the English fate. Though the legal system that he satirizes, remembering his costly Chancery effort to stop piracies of his novels, was in the process of being reformed while he wrote *Bleak House,* he found it convenient to use as a symbol of the society as a whole. The middle class was small, fragmented, subservient, the lower class mentally as well as physically enslaved, taught to kiss the hand of its master. And the master could not readily see that it was in his self-interest to be humane. For the characters of *Bleak House* who are not destroyed by the system or their own weaknesses, salvation resides in personal strength, in encouraging the innate moral sentiments, in rejecting materialism in favor of love and charity, and in accepting the responsibilities of constructive work. For the angry voice of the author-narrator, moving restlessly though the novel like a prophetic spirit, there seems to be no rest, no salvation, except, perhaps, in that most restless of all activities, writing novels.

Returning from Italy in December 1853, Dickens soon succumbed to pressure to write a new novel for weekly serial publication in *Household Words*. In Birmingham, he read *A Christmas Carol* twice, first to an audience of 1,700 people who came despite a heavy snow storm, then to 2,000 working people, for the benefit of the Birmingham and Midland Institute. Between those two performances, he read *The Cricket on the Hearth*. With his special interest in working-class education, he felt pleased that it would be "impossible to imagine . . . a more delicately observant audience. . . . They lost nothing, misinterpreted nothing, followed everything closely, laughed and cried with most delightful earnestness." He felt as if he were talking to a group of friends around his fireside. It had the effect of both an emotional and an intellectual high, animating him "to that extent that I felt as if we were all bodily going up into the clouds together." The sales of *Household Words* also needed to be raised. Though he had had no intention of beginning a new novel until the next autumn, "there is such a fixed idea on the part of my printers and co-partners . . . that a story by me, continued from week to week, would make some unheard-of effect . . . that I am going to write one."[16]

It did not take much persuasion. The security of a valuable property was sufficient explicit motivation. As an editor, he diffused himself "with infinite pains through Household Words," leaving "very few papers, indeed, untouched."[17] But the expectation of the readers that a magazine conducted by their most famous living novelist would excel in the publication of fiction was hard to fulfill. Constantly flattering contributors like Elizabeth Gaskell, and extensively editing manuscripts for the *Household Words* format, he knew how difficult it was for writers to tailor their novels to the requirements of weekly serial publication. All too often, he found himself having to decide

From an unsigned miniature, said to be the earliest portrait. *Courtesy of the Dickens House Museum.*

John Dickens, from an oil painting by John Jackson

John Dickens, c. 1845

Elizabeth (Mrs. John) Dickens, c. 1845. *Courtesy of the Dickens House Museum.*

Mrs. John Dickens, engraved by Edwin Roffe

Top left, no. 18, St. Mary's Place, Chatham, Dickens family residence, 1821–1823. From a photograph by Catherine Ward. *Top right*, Wellington House Academy, Hampstead Road, Dickens' school, 1821–1823. From a photograph by Catherine Ward.

Private Theatricals, *Clari*, etc., April 27, 1833

Maria Beadnell, c. 1835

PRIVATE THEATRICALS.

Stage Manager, Mr. CHARLES DICKENS.

On SATURDAY Evening, APRIL 27, 1833,

At Seven o'Clock precisely.

THE PERFORMANCES WILL COMMENCE WITH

AN INTRODUCTORY PROLOGUE;

THE PRINCIPAL CHARACTERS BY

MR. EDWARD BARROW ; MR. MILTON ; MR. CHARLES DICKENS ; MISS AUSTIN ; AND MISS DICKENS.

Immediately after which will be presented the Opera of

CLARI.

The Duke Vivaldi	..	..	..	MR. BRAMWELL.
Rolamo, .. Farmer, (Father to Clari)	..	MR. C. DICKENS.
Jocoso, ("alet to the Duke)	..	..	MR. H. AUSTIN.
Nicolo	..	..	..	..	MR. MILTON.
Geronio	..	..	..	..	MR. E. BARROW.
Nieapolo	..	..	..	MR. R. AUSTIN.
Pages to the Duke	..	..	MASTERS F. DICKENS and A. DICKENS.
Clari	..	..	..	..	MISS DICKENS.
Fidalma, (her Mother)	..	MISS L. DICKENS.
Vespina	..	..	..	MISS AUSTIN.
Ninetta	..	..	..	MISS URQUHART.

CHARACTERS IN THE EPISODE.

The Nobleman	..	..	..	MR. HENRY KOLLE.
Pelegrino, a Farmer	..	..	MR. JOHN DICKENS.
Wife of Pelegrino	..	..	MISS URQUHART
Leeda	..	..	..	MISS L. DICKENS

After which the favourite Interlude of

The Married Bachelor.

Sir Charles Courtall	..	..	MR. C. DICKENS.
Sharp	..	..	..	MR. JOHN URQUHART.
Lady Courtall	..	..	MISS L. DICKENS.
Grace	..	..	..	MISS DICKENS.

To conclude with the Farce of

AMATEURS AND ACTORS.

David Dulcet, Esq. (a Musical Dramatic Amateur, who employs Mr. O. P. Bustle, and attached to Theatricals and Miss Mary Hardacre)	..	MR. H. AUSTIN.	Elderberry, (a retired Manufacturer, simple in wit and manners, and utterly unacquainted with Theatricals)	..	MR. J. DICKENS
Mr. O. P. Bustle, (a Provincial Manager, but engaged to superintend some Private Theatricals)	..	MR. BRAMWELL	Tinkican, (Elderberry's Bartotum)	..	MR. R. AUSTIN.
Geoffry Muffincap, (immediarly Charity Boy, let out as a Servant at Bustle's lodging)	..	MR. E. BARROW
Wing, (a poor Country Actor)	..	MR. C. DICKENS	Miss Mary Hardacre, (a fugitive Ward of Elderberry's)	..	MISS DICKENS
Berry, (an Actor for the Heavy Business	..	MR. BOSTON.	Mrs. Mary Gossmall, (a Strolling Tragedy Actress, & a serious evil to her Husband)	MISS L. DICKENS

The Scenery by Messrs. H. Austin, Milton, H. Kolle, and Assistants. The Band will be numerous and complete, under the direction of Mr. E. Barrow.

J. & G. Nichols, Printers, Earl's Court, Cranbourn Street, Soho.

Charles Dickens, 1835. From a miniature by Rose Emma Drummond.

Catherine Hogarth (Mrs. Charles Dickens), shortly before her marriage, c. 1835. From a photograph by T. W. Tyrrell.

Charles Dickens, 1838. From a drawing by Samuel Lawrence.

Right to left: Dickens, Catherine, and Mary Hogarth, c. 1835. From a sketch by Daniel Maclise. *Courtesy of the Victoria and Albert Museum.*

Dickens, Thackeray, Maclise, and Mahony, 1836. From a sketch by William Makepeace Thackeray

48 Doughty Street, Dickens residence, 1837–1839. From a photograph by Catherine Ward.

Arrival of the *Great Western* steamer at New York, April 23, 1836, with Mr. Pickwick and other characters from *Pickwick Papers*

Charles Dickens, 1839. From a
painting by Daniel Maclise.

George Cruikshank, c. 1840

William Makepeace Thackeray. From a
sketch by Daniel Maclise.

Richard Bentley, c. 1850. From an etching by T. Brown.

William Harrison Ainsworth. From a drawing by Daniel Maclise.

John Forster, 1830. From a portrait by Thomas Warrington and Daniel Maclise. *Courtesy of the Victoria and Albert Museum.*

John Forster reading, May 22, 1840. From a drawing by Daniel Maclise. *Courtesy of the Victoria and Albert Museum.*

Daniel Maclise. From an engraving by J. Smith.

William Charles Macready, c. 1835. From a painting by Briggs.

T. N. Talfourd, c. 1845

Clarkson Stanfield, c. 1835

Catherine Dickens, 1842. From
a painting by Daniel Maclise.

The Dickens children, 1842. The painting the Dickenses took with them on their American trip. From a painting by Daniel Maclise.

Charles Dickens, 1844. From a drawing by Charles Martin.

Hablot Knight Browne (Phiz). c. 1845

No. 1 Devonshire Terrace, Dickens' residence, 1839–1851. From a photograph by C.W.B. Ward.

Edward Chapman

Frederic Chapman

Dickens' publishers

William Bradbury

F. M. Evans

Dickens and his friends in Cornwall, 1842. From left to right: Maclise, Stanfield, Dickens, and Forster. From a sketch by William Makepeace Thackeray. *Courtesy of the Victoria and Albert Museum.*

Dickens reading *The Chimes,* December 2, 1844. Seated from left: John Forster, Douglas Jerrold, Samuel Blanchard; rear: Thomas Carlyle, Charles Dickens, William Fox; seated from right: Daniel Harness, William Dyce, Clarkson Stanfield, Daniel Maclise, Frederick Dickens. From a sketch by Daniel Maclise.

Every Man in His Humour playbill, 1845, with drawings of Dickens and John Forster. Sketches by Daniel Maclise.

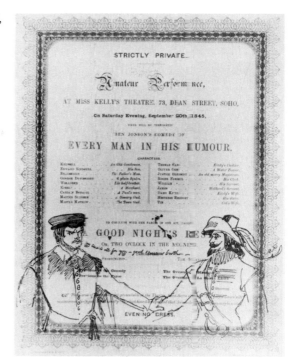

Below, Dickens in *Every Man in His Humour,* 1845. From a portrait by C. R. Leslie.

Above, Forster acting, c. 1845. From a sketch by Clarkson Stanfield.

Right, Mrs. Charles Dickens, 1846. From a painting by Daniel Maclise.

Charles Dickens, 1848. From a drawing by Count D'Orsay.

Georgina Hogarth, c. 1856.

Left, Georgina Hogarth as Lady Grace in *The Lighthouse*, 1855. From a painting by Charles Collins. *Right*, Angela Burdett Coutts, c. 1850

"The Great Social Evil," *Punch*, 1857. "Time: Midnight. Bella: 'Ah! Fanny. How *long* have you been *Gay*.'" Cartoon by John Leech.

"The Great Moral Lesson," *Punch*, 1849. The cartoon depicts the Mannings execution. By John Leech.

John Leech, c. 1850. From a drawing by John Everett Millais.

Left, Sir Edward Bulwer-Lytton, the Earl of Lytton. From a sketch by Daniel Maclise.

Sir Edward Bulwer-Lytton, c. 1840. From an engraving.

Daniel Maclise, 1851. From a contemporary sketch.

Tavistock House, Dickens' residence,
1851–1860

William Makepeace Thackeray, c. 1850

Mr. and Mrs. Richard Watson, c. 1846–1848

Above, William Charles Macready as King Lear, c. 1845. From an engraving. *Inset*, William Charles Macready, 1854. *Right*, Leigh Hunt, c. 1845. From a drawing by Daniel Maclise.

Mark Lemon, c. 1850. *Right*, as Falstaff, c. 1850
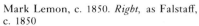

W. H. Wills, c. 1850

Augustus Egg, c. 1850. From a sketch by W. P. Frith.

Wilkie Collins, c. 1850. From a painting by Charles Collins.

Not So Bad as We Seem playbill, for the performance before the queen, May 16, 1851

Charles Dickens, Jr., c. 1851. From a sketch.

Charles Dickens, 1852. From a daguerreotype by Henri Claudel.

Sydney Dickens, c. 1860, as a midshipman

Walter Landor Dickens, c. 1855, as a military cadet

The Dickens Dramatic Company, 1854. The bottom row, from left: Charles Dickens, Jr., Katie Dickens, Charles Dickens, Georgina Hogarth, Mamie Dickens, Wilkie Collins (leaning on hand), and Helen Hogarth

Left, Dickens as Richard Wardour. From a sketch, January 17, 1857.
Below, The Frozen Deep playbill, 1857.

IN REMEMBRANCE OF THE LATE MR. DOUGLAS JERROLD.
LAST REPRESENTATION.

GALLERY OF ILLUSTRATION,
REGENT STREET.

UNDER THE MANAGEMENT OF MR. CHARLES DICKENS

On Saturday evening, August 8th, 1857, at 8 O'CLOCK EXACTLY, will be presented

FOR THE LAST TIME,
AN ENTIRELY NEW
ROMANTIC DRAMA, IN THREE ACTS, BY MR. WILKIE COLLINS,
CALLED

THE FROZEN DEEP.

PERFORMED BY THE AMATEUR COMPANY OF LADIES AND GENTLEMEN WHO
ORIGINALLY REPRESENTED IT, IN PRIVATE.

THE OVERTURE COMPOSED EXPRESSLY FOR THIS PIECE BY MR. FRANCESCO BERGER.

The Dresses by Messrs. NATHAN, of Tichborne Street, Haymarket, and Miss WILSON, of Carburton Street, Fitzroy Square
Perruquier, Mr. WILSON, of the Strand.

CAPTAIN EBSWORTH, *of The Sea Mew*	. . . .	Mr. EDWARD PIGOTT.
CAPTAIN HELDING, *of The Wanderer*	. . . .	Mr. ALFRED DICKENS.
LIEUTENANT CRAYFORD	. . . .	Mr. MARK LEMON.
FRANK ALDERSLEY	. . . .	Mr. WILKIE COLLINS.
RICHARD WARDOUR	. . . .	Mr. CHARLES DICKENS.
LIEUTENANT STEVENTON	. . . .	Mr. YOUNG CHARLES.
JOHN WANT, *Ships Cook*	. . . .	Mr. AUGUSTUS EGG.
BATESON } *Two of The Sea Mew's People*	. . . .	Mr. SHIRLEY BROOKS.
DARKER }	. . . .	Mr. FREDERICK EVANS.
(OFFICERS AND CREWS OF THE SEA MEW AND WANDERER.)		
MRS. STEVENTON	. . . .	Miss HELEN.
ROSE EBSWORTH	. . . .	Miss KATE.
LUCY CRAYFORD	. . . .	Miss HOGARTH.
CLARA BURNHAM	. . . .	Miss MARY.
NURSE ESTHER	. . . .	Mrs. FRANCIS.
MAID	. . . .	Miss MARLEY.

THE SCENERY AND SCENIC EFFECTS OF THE FIRST ACT, BY MR. TELBIN.
THE SCENERY AND SCENIC EFFECTS OF THE SECOND AND THIRD ACTS, BY MR. STANFIELD, R.A.
ASSISTED BY MR. DANSON.
THE ACT-DROP, ALSO BY MR. STANFIELD, R.A.

To Conclude with the Farce, in Two Acts,

UNCLE JOHN.

NEPHEW HAWK	. . . .	Mr. WILKIE COLLINS.
EDWARD EASEL	. . . .	Mr. FREDERICK EVANS.
UNCLE JOHN	. . . .	Mr. CHARLES DICKENS.
FRIEND THOMAS	. . . .	Mr. MARK LEMON.
ANDREW	. . . .	Mr. TOPID CHARLES.
NICE HAWK	. . . .	Miss HOGARTH.
ELIZA	. . . .	Miss KATE.
MRS. COMFORT	. . . .	Miss MARY.

TERMINATING WITH A DANCE BY THE CHARACTERS.

Musical Composer and Conductor of the Orchestra, Mr. FRANCESCO BERGER,
WHO WILL PRESIDE AT THE PIANO

The Audience are respectfully desired to be in their places by Ten minutes to 8 o'clock.

STALLS, ONE GUINEA. AREA, TWO SHILLINGS AND SIXPENCE. AMPHITHEATRE, FIVE SHILLINGS.
Tickets for Stalls, Area, and Amphitheatre, to be had at the Committee's Office, Gallery of Illustration, Regent Street every day from 2 to 4

REFRESHMENTS—The Audience are respectfully informed that the Committee have made arrangements with Mr. RICHARDSON to supply, during the evening, Tea, Coffee, Cream and Water Ices Lemonade, Soda Water, &c., &c., at the cost Price: at those charged at his Establishment in Morrimotts Street.
The Overture to THE FROZEN DEEP, composed by Mr. Francesco Berger, is published by Messrs. Drew & Co., and can be had in the room.

Hans Christian Andersen, c. 1857

Ellen Ternan. c. 1857. *Courtesy of the Victoria and Albert Museum.*

Catherine Dickens, c. 1857. *Courtesy of the Huntington Library.*

The Ternan sisters, c. 1860. From left: Maria, Ellen (standing), Fanny. *Courtesy of the Victoria and Albert Museum.*

Ellen Ternan, c. 1870. *Courtesy of the Dickens House Museum.*

Edmunc Yates, c. 1858

Right, William Makepeace Thackeray, c. 1859

Charles Dickens, 1859. From a photograph
by Mason

Dickens giving a reading, 1859. From a
photograph by H. Watkins.

Dickens, 1859. From a painting by William Frith.

Elizabeth Dickens, 1860

Dickens, c. 1861. From a photograph by C. Watkins.

Dickens, 1861. From a caricature by Andre Gill.

Gad's Hill Place

Dickens reading to Katie and Mamie at
Gad's Hill Place, c. 1860

Katie Collins, 1865. From a painting by
Marcus Stone.

Francis Dickens and Henry Fielding
Dickens, c. 1862

Alfred D'Orsay Tennyson Dickens,
c. 1862

Edward Bulwer Lytton (Plorn)
Dickens, c. 1868

Dickens and friends on porch at Gad's Hill, 1865. From
left, standing: Henry Chorley, Katie Dickens, Mamie
Dickens, Charles Dickens. Seated: Georgina Hogarth,
Charles Collins. From a photograph by Mason.

Dickens getting over a fence at Gad's
Hill, c. 1845

Dickens at the Staplehurst accident, June 1845. From a
contemporary engraving.

Dickens and Charles Fechter, c. 1868. From a
drawing by Alfred Bryan.

Wilkie Collins, c. 1870. From a photograph
by H. Watkins.

John Forster, c. 1870. From a photograph by
Elliott and Fry. *Courtesy of the Victoria and
Albert Museum.*

Marcus Stone, c. 1860

James T. Fields, c. 1860

Mrs. James T. Fields, c. 1860

The British Lion in America, 1857. From a caricature in the *New York Daily Joker*.

George Dolby, 1868. From a photograph by J. Gurney.

Dickens and Dolby, 1868. From an American caricature.

Dickens, 1867. From an American caricature: "The great novelist appears in various characters, all, however, showing the same prolific 'head.'"

Above, Dickens reading in his garden at Gad's Hill, c. 1866. *Left,* Dickens, 1867. From a photograph by J. Gurney.

"For God's sake! Bill

FAGIN

Dickens reading from *Oliver Twist.* From two contemporary sketches.

Dickens c. 1869. From an anonymous
crayon-and-pencil sketch

The Swiss chalet at Gad's Hill. From a
photograph by Catherine Ward.

Mrs Charles Dickens, 1870

Dickens, c. 1870. Drawing by "Spy."

Dickens dreaming about his characters, c. 1870. From a painting, *Dickens's Dream*, by Robert William Buss.

between rejecting a manuscript or undertaking the time-consuming, thankless work of heavily editing it for publication. It
was inevitable, then, that he would himself have to write fiction
for *Household Words*. At some point, the readers would demand
it. Since his inner imperative demanded that he write novels, he
found it sensible to combine a practical advantage with one of
the necessary expressions of his restlessness. Once he returned
to London, writing a new novel became only a matter of sooner
rather than slightly later. By late January 1854, its first page
stared at him "from under [the] sheet of note paper" on which
he was writing a letter to Miss Coutts. The main idea of the new
story, which was to be one fourth as long as his novels in twenty
monthly parts and to appear over five months in *Household
Words*, was one "[of] which you and I and Mrs Brown have often
spoken."

Its two central concerns had been with him for some time.
In 1842, in his letter to the *Morning Chronicle* on the "Mines and
Collieries Bill," he had attacked industrial working conditions
and exploitative owners. Influential proponents of industrial
and social laissez-faire continued their effective advocacy of a
free-market economy and a social system in which the laws of
supply and demand could not be managed for social and humanitarian purposes. The working poor had to survive without any
help or protection from government. In 1853, in "Fraud on the
Fairies," he had criticized utilitarian efforts to rationalize fairy
tales and to use them for propaganda. "Kaye-Shuttleworthian"
social and educational reformers, associated with Jeremy Ben-
tham, James Mill, and John Stuart Mill, had been reforming the
educational system to take the "fairy" out of "tale," the fanciful
out of literature and life. In the presence of "the supernatural
dreariness" of such people, he felt as if he "had just come out of
the Great Desert of Sahara where my camel died a fortnight
ago." The imagination was treated as a poor second cousin of
reason logic, and science.

At some point, he had shared with Miss Coutts his thought
of writing a novel connecting "dry-as-dust" political economists
for whom unfeeling and abstract rationality was more important than human happiness with educational rationalists who
were choking the imagination to death. Many of the utilitarian
political economists and educational reformers focused on the

working class. In a climate of economic and class tension that became increasingly raw in the early 1850s, it occurred to him that he could provide fictional focus for his attack on utilitarianism and strike a blow against dehumanization and the "wicked masters" of the Midlands factories by dramatizing the destructive economic, social, and class conflicts of an archetypal industrial city, "Coketown." In November, he had read in an Italian newspaper about "disturbances in Lancashire, arising out of the unhappy strikes" and about industrial actions that threatened violence in Preston. In the middle of January 1854, "the sad affair of the Preston strike remains unsettled; and I hear, on strong authority, that if that were settled, the Manchester people are prepared to strike next." In his judgment, the English were "the hardest-working people on whom the sun shines. . . . They are born at the oar, and they live and die at it. Good God, what would we have of them!" The provocation for a strike, which had then resulted in a lockout, had to be extreme. A few days later, he sent Forster a list of possible titles, among which "there are three very good ones."[18] They soon agreed on the sixth, *Hard Times*.

On the spur of the moment, at the end of January 1854, Dickens went north to see for himself what Preston was like. He had been led to think it a model town. Instead, it was "a nasty place" that seemed especially frigid with the absence of smoke from the chimneys, the unnatural silence and emptiness. The workers huddled in their houses. The streets were peaceful. The next day, he saw the dull drama, insidious in its meagerness, of the distribution to the locked-out strikers of small amounts of money raised by subscription from workers in other towns. The Bull Hotel, described in the Italian newspaper as "the Palazzo Bull," was an "old, grubby, mean, intensely formal red brick house with a narrow gateway and a dingy yard." The imagination could not survive, let alone flourish, in such physical and aesthetic poverty. The strike, which was to fail by April, hardly spoke to the real problems. The range of social issues, which included low wages, poor sanitation, and dangerous working conditions, also included social and educational brainwashing through the creation of schools that served as extensions of the factory assembly line.

On the issues of industrial safety and the efficacy of striking, he quickly spoke out in *Household Words*. Though his initial impulse was to support the right to strike, he increasingly saw himself as a mediating voice supporting neither the workers nor the masters but common sense. The enemy was an abstract political economy that broke human beings on the wheel of iron theory, the dogma that government interference in a free economy was destructive tampering with the sacred laws of nature and god. Statistics seemed weapons manipulated to undermine humane considerations. Both the strike and the lockout were "a deplorable calamity. In its waste of time, in its waste of a great people's energy, in its waste of wages, in its waste of wealth that seeks to be employed . . . in the gulf of separation it hourly deepens between those whose interests must be understood to be identical or must be destroyed, it is a great national affliction."[19] Refusing to believe that the interests of workers and masters significantly diverged, he saw stupidity and stubbornness as the source of the strike. With the advantage of education and training, with the responsibility for enlightened leadership, the masters were more to blame than the men. Unions existed only because incompetent masters had made ignorant workmen vulnerable to the manipulations of venal union leaders.

Early in February 1854, he took two brief holidays, a day excursion to Gravesend to celebrate his birthday with a "walk to Rochester, and return through Cobham woods," and a week in Paris. There were "motes of new stories floating" before his eyes, possibilities for *Hard Times* and perhaps some of the motifs for what was to become *Little Dorrit*. By the middle of the month, the plural had become a singular. He was now preoccupied with "*my* story." With the main plan for the novel clear to him, he asked Mark Lemon to send him any "slang terms among the tumblers and circus people, that you can call to mind." To his surprise, he found the limited elbow room of weekly serial publication chokingly restrictive, "absolutely CRUSHING." He had written both *Oliver Twist* and *Barnaby Rudge* that way. But it had been long ago, he had paid less attention to structural problems, and he had been a less self-consciously purposeful artist. "Nobody can have an idea of it who has not had an experience of patient fiction-writing with some elbow-room always, and open places in perspective." The first installment, contrasting, on the one hand, the imagination and circus life represented by Sissy Jupe with, on the other, utilitarian rationalism represented by M'Choakumchild, Gradgrind, Bitzer, and Bounderby, appeared on the first of April. He complained that he was "in a dreary state, planning and planning the story . . . out of material for I don't know how long a story, and consequently writing little."

Sensitive to claims that he had gotten the idea for *Hard Times* from the Preston strike, he exaggerated just how long before visiting Preston he had had the story in mind. Sensitive to the concern that he would support the strike, he assured Elizabeth Gaskell, also writing a novel about industrial relations, that he was "not going to strike. So don't be afraid of me." He was interested in compromise, not confrontation. "I often say to Mr. Gradgrind that there is reason and good intention in much that he does—in fact, in all that he does—but that he over-does it. Perhaps by dint of his going his way and my going mine, we shall meet at last at some halfway house where there are flowers on the carpets, and a little standing-room for Queen Mab's chariot among the steam engines." By late spring, he was in Boulogne, having the end of the novel in sight. "Bobbing up, corkwise, from a sea of Hard Times," he felt "three parts mad, and the fourth delirious, with perpetual rushing" at it.[20] By the middle of July, he had finished the novel, and on August 12 the final installment appeared.

The one-volume edition that appeared in August 1854 was dedicated to Carlyle. "It contains nothing in which you do not think with me, for no man knows your books better than I." *Hard Times,* though, has less of the radical Carlyle in it than Dickens liked to imagine. Democratic in principle, elitist in practice, he always sought pluralistic compromise. He was unambivalently against revolution. He did not have, as did Carlyle, the anger of the prophetic anarchist, for whom conditions are so intolerable that even total destruction sometimes seems better than the perpetuation of the current situation. What to him seemed a human muddle was for Carlyle a cosmic disease. He recognized that Carlyle's anger took him to places his own could not approach. "You know that it is impossible for anyone to admire him as a great original genius . . . more than I do," Dickens told Forster in May. "The extraordinary peculiarity of his mind," though, "always is a respect for power when it is exercised by a determined man. Some years ago when I was not familiarly acquainted with his writing, I said to you, after meeting him one night in your rooms with Emerson, that it was an anomaly I could not get out of mind, to hear him immensely lauding even the present Emperor of Russia. . . . A Tyrant is always a detestable creature, publicly, however virtuous privately. . . . Spare him two hundred years after he is dead, and you don't know what you do towards the birth of his successor next year."[21] On social matters, Carlyle thought Dickens well intentioned but superficial, an exemplification of the Whig delusion that nineteenth-century secular culture could be redeemed by liberal good works. It was a skepticism that Dickens was to share more fully in the next decade.

Even in *Hard Times* though, Dickens is as much concerned about individual salvation and human relations as he is about social problems. Key elements of the story draw on his personal preoccupation with father-daughter and father-son relationships and on the seemingly intractable problem of his marriage. Thomas Gradgrind educates his children into an insensibility of the heart that their hearts rebel against. Intent on being a good father, he denies his children their human patrimony. Eventually, father and daughter are reconciled; father and son are not. Louisa contains within herself an inherent goodness that her father's system does not destroy, though she is badly damaged. Young Thomas Gradgrind is destroyed by a combination of his father's utilitarian world and his own insufficiencies. With an affinity for daughters rather than sons, Dickens locates the crucial drama of the novel in the relationship between Louisa, Sissy Jupe, whose father has deserted her out of misplaced love, and Thomas Gradgrind. Eventually, patriarchy is redeemed by sisterhood, by daughters and sisters. In the portraits of the young women, including Rachael, there are resonances of Georgina, Mamie, and Katie, and memories of Mary Hogarth. The shadowy emotional outline of John Dickens appears in the transformation of Thomas Gradgrind into a redeemed father. The unredeemed father who put him to work in the blacking factory appears in aspects of Mr. Bounderby, the mother who insisted on his remaining there in the portrait of Mrs. Sparsit. With a sharp twist of the knife of his imagination, his view of Catherine's incompetence, clumsiness, withdrawal from responsibility, and

unsuitability as his wife appears in his depiction of Stephen
Blackpool's alcoholic wife, from whom he is separated. The rigid
divorce laws prevent him from marrying Rachael. Trapped in an
inappropriate marriage, frequently depressed, and morally self-
conscious, Stephen can do nothing but shoulder his burdens and
carry on manfully. Dickens was soon to write in his notebook the
idea for a story of "a misplaced and mismarried man. Always, as
it were, playing hide and seek with the world and never finding
what Fortune seems to have hidden when he was born."[22]

On a bright summer day in 1854 a kite rose into "half a gale
of wind," climbing briskly into the cloudless sky over the Villa
du Camp de Droite in Boulogne. The two kite makers, like
Daedalus, were proud of their achievement. "Jointly produced
by the labour and ingenuity of Dickens and your humble servant," Wilkie Collins boasted, it is "capable of taking up more
string than ever can be brought to accommodate it." For Dickens, midsummer brought the exhaustion of having finished *Hard
Times*. He tried to knock himself into relaxation by "a blaze of
dissipation" in London: the opera, dinner engagements, sitting
for his portrait. His tiredness distressed him. It seemed un-
characteristic, unacceptable. Back in Boulogne, with his friend's
summer-long company, he felt a luxuriant indolence, a stupor
out of which he could hardly stir himself to write letters. For
a few weeks he delighted in refreshing breezes, "reading books
and going to sleep on the grass," curling into a comfortable
haystack to take the sun and dream in "a state of Elysian laziness." *Household Words* business, though, infringed, dealings
with authors like Gaskell, whose *North and South*, the size of
which alarmed him, he was about to begin publishing. As August began, he tried to balance relaxation and restlessness. But
he was aware that the kite could take more string, that there
could never be enough to accommodate it. The image of ascension attracted him. If not a kite, then a balloon, on which he
would rise. By October, he "had dreadful thoughts of getting
away somewhere" altogether by himself, a "floating idea of
going up above the snow-line in Switzerland. . . . *Restlessness*

. . . is always driving me, and I cannot help it. I have rested nine or ten weeks, and sometimes feel as if it had been a year—though I had the strangest nervous miseries before I stopped. If I couldn't walk fast and far, I should just explode and perish."[23]

Summer in Boulogne, though, had its delights. This was the second of three that he was to spend there with his family. Close to London, with an excellent hotel, a lively seafaring industry, a fertile countryside, and about twenty-five thousand residents, it seemed relatively unspoiled. Its attractions in 1853 having encouraged him to come again, his landlord, Ferdinand Beaucourt, provided him with an even better house in 1854, high on the hill overlooking the town, with luxuriant roses and a long field for early-evening impromptu cricket matches. With the addition of a few friends Dickens had enough sons to comprise a team. "A trap, bat, and ball on the premises, and a fine field to play in. Post every night, parcel communication every day, electric telegraph every minute." Beaucourt hardly needed to add the pride he felt at being the landlord of a distinguished novelist to his own childlike appreciation of his property. Thinking it "the finest situation" he had ever lived in with the exception of Genoa, Dickens sent laudatory and beseeching letters to friends about this "AMAZING!!" place. "Range of view and air, most free and delightful; hill-side garden, delicious, field stupendous." And the costs were modest. The house was five guineas a week. He drank the best inexpensive wine he had ever tasted. The villa, "bright, clean, and lively," was "a regular triumph of French domestic architecture . . . all doors and windows. Every window blows every door open, and all the lighter articles . . . fly to all points of the compass." Unlike the hot oven of London, where there was a record heat that summer, "the cool sea-breeze blows over us by day and by night." When he returned in 1856, writing his way "through the summer in rosy gardens and sea airs," he was again in the Villa du Camp de Droite, which Beaucourt had improved even more, a paradise of roses and geraniums.[24] Boulogne also had a year-round attraction, an English-run school that Dickens thought well of and in which he enrolled two of his sons. They could be visited on his way to Paris. They could be left there at the end of the summer holidays.

In addition to the kite, a bright Union Jack and a Tricolor, "hoisted . . . on a haystack" in honor of the English-French alliance, flapped in the breeze at the Villa du Camp de Droite in 1854. In Boulogne, loud drums and bugles resounded in every street. Concerned that they might be disturbed, he was pleased that not a sound penetrated his privacy. "We never see or hear of it, unless we choose." The pageantry was stirring. At the end of August, he and Collins attended "military mass" at the nearby camp in honor of Napoleon's birthday. "When the Host was raised, the artillery fired their great guns and the ten thousand men presented arms—the bayonets and swords all flashing up together into the sun." Up close, the British and French soldiers looked like filthy rascals, and the camp was threateningly unsanitary. In early September, the royal yacht, "decked out with streamers," with Prince Albert "in a blazing uniform, left alone on the deck for everybody to see," sailed into the harbor. A blaze of salutes punctuated the silence. Making his own contribution to the celebratory spectacle, he illuminated the villa English-fashion. "The French illuminate outside their houses, with oil lamps . . . with which the wind interferes. . . . *We,*" Collins boasted, "shut all the front windows in the English way, and put candles in them. . . . We had 114 candles burning, stuck on 114 nails, driven into the window sashes. When we were ready to light up, every soul in the house . . . was stationed at a window. Dickens rang a bell—and at that signal we lit up the whole 114 candles in less than a minute. The effect from a distance was as if the whole house, was one steady blaze of light. It was seen for miles and miles round. The landlord went into hysterical French ecstasies—the populace left their illuminations in the town . . . to stare in amazement." Dickens, who rushed to a distance to look at it, was thrilled.25

Ardently patriotic, he felt deeply concerned about the war and allied leadership. Detesting Louis Napoleon, who seemed not only a corrupt tyrant but a dangerous incompetent who had risen to a new level of threat when he left his exile in the drawing rooms of England for the throne of France, he thought the French-British alliance a weak basis on which to confront the Russians. In the middle of September, returning with Georgina from a country walk, he suddenly found himself "face to face with Albert and Napoleon." He took off his hat, "whereupon the Emperor pulled off his cocked-hat; and Albert (seeing,

I suppose, that it was an Englishman) pulled off his. Then we went our several ways." The emperor had changed for the worse since "the old times when we used to see him so often at Gore House." In early October, Dickens attended the review at which a telegram erroneously reporting the fall of Sebastopol brought flushes to the checks of the empress, whose beauty he admired, and cheers to the lips of the vast assembly. This was theatre of a high order, though with more than the usual amount of ambivalence and heartache. With "mixed feeling about the war—admiration of our valiant men, burning desires to cut the Emperor of Russia's throat," Dickens felt "something like despair to see how the old cannon-smoke and blood-mists obscure the wrongs and sufferings of the people at home."[26] Also, those who were actually directing the war seemed dangerously incompetent. Reports from the Crimea made it clear that stupidity, elitism, and sclerotic bureaucracy were damaging the war effort severely. Many "valiant men" were being needlessly killed on the battlefield. They were also, though, being killed in their camps and hospitals. Convinced that the war was a just one, Dickens felt that the country was being betrayed by its leadership and its rigid structure. When the suffering took its toll and when the cost became clearer (an income tax had been instituted), he feared that the public would tire of the war much before Russia, feudally autocratic and a major threat to British power, was soundly defeated. The main obstacle, though, to a strong Britain abroad was a weak Britain at home. The same forces that were responsible for domestic misery would be responsible for foreign tragedy. Still, Dickens' full anguish about the war was months away. Pageantry had the upper hand for the moment. And Boulogne was a wonderful vantage point, a place where he could work and play as comfortably as his restlessness would permit.

Enthusiastic invitations brought visitors during these summers in Boulogne, some for long stays, others for brief appearances en route to other places or as short breaks from work in London. Always ready to provide a bed, "two to a space, at a pinch three," or a booking at the best hotel in town, Dickens usually met friends at the dockside customs house, where a card in hand introducing the visitor as his guest produced expeditious service.[27] Whisked through the door into the tumult of bargainers and beggars, the new arrival was soon embraced by the friendly arms of "the Inimitable." In moments of good humor, such ritual self-flourishes were an essential part of his persona. So too was hospitality. Frank Stone brought his family to spend the summers of 1853 and 1854. Usually pinched, his recent election as an associate of the Royal Academy of Art had helped make the summer holidays possible. Particularly fond of Marcus Stone, the younger of Stone's two sons, Dickens put Georgina to work to find them a house. Almost a part of the family, Collins stayed with them for much of the first two summers, working at his own fiction, which his mentor praised highly, and on writing projects for *Household Words* and for the stage.

An otherwise likely visitor unexpectedly died in March 1854. Talfourd had been among the friends of the first years of Dickens' success, an ardent supporter whose association with *Pickwick Papers* contained both the comic allusion to his role in the Norton-Melbourne trial and the serious development of his strong support for international copyright. A warm, vain, generous man, with a strident wife, he had been an early companion from the older, successful generation that included Macready and Procter. Talfourd's hope that he himself would be the great writer of the new age had been disappointed. That, though, had not undermined his worshiping admiration of Dickens. In 1849, on the Isle of Wight, he had shared with him his happiness at being appointed a judge of the Court of Common Pleas. In January 1854, he had sent him a copy of his new book, the preface to which was "an example to all of us," Dickens told him, "of modesty and of that genial disposition to be pleased which is one of the finest qualities to be found in the heart of man. . . . It has cleared away the fog of the morning and lightened the day." Under no illusion about the limitations of Talfourd's talent, Dickens always searched for grounds on which to praise him. Recently, the friends had made "two engagements," one to visit a farm Talfourd had recently purchased, the other to visit Talfourd's burial plot in Norwood cemetery, which he "was very fond of," having "accustomed himself to associate it with a day of rest." In the middle of March 1854, while "walking in Covent Garden," Dickens met Mark Lemon, who had just seen an evening newspaper with the news of Talfourd's death. While summarizing an appeal on behalf of the accused, Talfourd had "faltered, his thoughts seemed to wander for a second or two and then he fell senseless," apparently the victim of a stroke. "Three doctors instantly pronounced that he was dead." Dickens immediately went to Talfourd's London home, where the family knew from a telegram only that he had been suddenly taken ill. He soon fulfilled one of his two engagements with Talfourd, prematurely. Soon after the funeral, Forster, also deeply affected, told Leigh Hunt that "we turn to old friends at such a time as this—when the past seems all that really belongs to us."[28]

The aging Hunt probably did not attend Talfourd's funeral. Recent tensions in his relationship with Dickens may have affected his feelings about members of his circle. In the 1840s, Hunt and Dickens had become friends of sorts. He had received from the younger writer some of the formal veneration due a senior citizen of the literary community who had become a convenient symbol around which to rally the profession to raise funds and to criticize the government for neglecting the arts. When, after his pension had been granted, Hunt tactlessly returned to his friends for additional help, Dickens felt put upon. Well known for his financial carelessness, Hunt soon became the model for Harold Skimpole in *Bleak House*, the irresponsible artist whose sponging self-indulgence is immoral. That he made the identification of Hunt as the source for Skimpole unavoidable, even to the extent of using Hunt's house as the model for Skimpole's, angered Hunt's friends.[29]

But Skimpole's hypocrisy, immorality, and oily rhetoric were Dickens' invention, not Hunt's characteristics. Used to transforming life into fiction, Dickens forced an equation between Hunt and Skimpole when consciously he meant the resemblance only as the loosest starting point. Slow in making redress, he felt resentful in being called to account. For a time he managed to keep out of Hunt's way, though Hunt went out of his to demonstrate that he had no hard feelings. More interested in smooth relations than in confrontation, he wanted some public expression from Dickens that they were friends. Dickens was slow to comply, though, suggesting both that he resented being held to account for Skimpole's origin and that he had had a good deal less respect for Hunt than he had ever admitted outside the pages of *Bleak House*. In the spring of 1855, he begrudgingly made amends with a favorable notice in *Household Words*, "the best means," he told Hunt, "that could possibly present themselves of enabling me to express myself publicly about you as you would desire." After many postponements, he accepted one of Hunt's invitations to tea. "But I hope you will not now think it necessary to renew that painful subject with me. . . . In that better and unmistakeable association with you by name, let all end." The episode was not over, though. At Hunt's death in 1859, the obituaries mentioned the identification with Skimpole. Again, trying both to make amends and to exculpate himself, Dickens admitted in an article in *Household Words* that he had "privately referred the proof sheets of the first number" of *Bleak House* "to two intimate friends of Leigh Hunt . . . and altered the whole of that part of the text on their discovering too strong a resemblance to his 'way.' " He had not "thought," though, "that the admired original would ever be charged with the imaginary vices of the fictitious creature."[30]

With Forster, relations were always intense. During the Crimean War, they often found themselves not seeing eye to eye politically, though Forster's blustering insistence on taking rhetorical responsibility for the whole conduct of the war left Dickens more amused than bored. Forster's ill health sometimes kept them apart. His rheumatoid arthritis, his gout, his overweight, and probably angina, made him partly an invalid, though he continued his economically necessary editorship of *The Examiner*, his book writing, and his occasional lecturing. One night in 1854, when he was bedridden, Dickens read to him "something out of Goldsmith," their mutual favorite. "I fell upon She Stoops to Conquer, and we enjoyed it with that wonderful intensity, that I believe he began to get better in the first scene, and was all right again in the fifth act." Though Forster made occasional visits to Boulogne, Dickens saw more of him on his own monthly visits to London. The shocked author enjoyed with hysterical hilarity the secret news in March 1856 that Forster was engaged to marry Eliza Colburn, the wealthy widow of the publisher Henry Colburn. It is "the most prodigious, overwhelming, crushing, astounding, blinding, deafening, pulverizing, scarifying secret of which Forster is the hero, imaginable by the united efforts of the whole British population. It is a thing of that kind, that after I knew it (from himself) this morning, I lay down flat, as if an Engine and Tender had fallen upon me." His friends could not resist teasing him and amusing themselves. Maclise gave Dickens "the most wonderful account of Mrs. Colburn. . . . 'By God Sir the depreciation that has taken place in that woman is fearful! She has no blood Sir in her body—no color—no voice—is all scrunched and squeezed together—and seems to me in deep affliction—while Forster Sir is rampant and raging, and presenting a contrast beneath which you sink into the dust. She *may* come round again—*may* get fat—*may* get cheerful—*may* get a voice to articulate with, but by the Blessed Star of Morning Sir she is now a sight to behold!' " When Forster told Stanfield that he had a grave secret to tell him, the overjoyed painter thought he was going to tell him that he "was about to turn Catholic!"[31]

Stanfield's Catholicism did not dampen his ardor for the theatre. Nor did his health. Though "he seems to be subject to some little disorder, which is half internal and half nervous," he frequently came down from Hampstead to Tavistock Place, set on a half-price theatrical evening with Dickens and any other friend who could be enlisted. Despite his age and the recent death of a chronically ill son, he was capable of bursts of saltwater enthusiasm. Soon he was willingly drafted by Dickens into painting marine backdrops to two amateur theatricals. But visits to Boulogne, in fact traveling at all, did not especially appeal to him.

Macready's rare visits to London seemed to Dickens like the return of his old friend from a premature grave. It filled him "with pity to think of [Macready] away in the lonely Sherborne Place." John Elliotson, "everybody's friend," who, with his network of mesmeric and medical associates, traveled frequently, did come to Boulogne for a short stay. The impish Marcus Stone noticed during his 1853 visit that Elliotson's "only flaw was his habit of dying his hair a quite improbable colour." During the next summer, Thackeray stayed in Boulogne, his large, burly, but gentle presence noticeably out of scale in the small streets of the old town. Working hard at his new novel, aware of illness behind and illness to come, he enjoyed Dickens' company. One evening in July he dined with the family of "9 children 7 boys." They played parlor games afterward. The next day, returning to London briefly, Dickens played the role of Thackeray's postman, carrying letters across the Channel.[32]

Among the welcome guests was Thomas Beard, for whom

his affection, going back to his days as a journalist, never diminished. Beard's journalistic duties, though, allowed him only brief vacations. Invitations to come to Boulogne notwithstanding, Thomas Mitton had grown increasingly peripheral. Like Beard, he knew intimate family details—Dickens had known him from his early years—and Mitton kept for safekeeping in a locked box in his office a cache of letters between Dickens and his family that told the unhappy story of constant requests for money.

Among the necessary, and welcome, guests at Boulogne was William Henry Wills, who had become invaluable at *Household Words* and whose qualities as a human being Dickens strongly admired. He had managed to combine self-interest with Wills's interests by stipulating that the assistant editor would be a partial owner. When Wills's mother died, when his health became acutely troublesome, Dickens immediately offered additional financial as well as emotional support. When Miss Coutts decided to employ an executive secretary on an annual retainer to help her with correspondence of a sort that Dickens could not continue to add to his heavy responsibilities, he was successful in persuading her to employ Wills. The shy, competent assistant editor, ferociously loyal, was delighted to hold the fort at Wellington Street, to exchange an endless number of letters with "the Sparkler" and with contributors, to travel across the Channel with articles and page proofs in his briefcase, and to become partly absorbed, especially through the talents of his wife, into the Dickens amateur theatricals.

Though Dickens was able to free himself from a tight umbilical cord to London, John Leech and Mark Lemon were not. Making considerably less money than he did, both lived more modestly, Leech with his small family on Kensington High Street, Lemon with his many children as close as possible to his favorite child, *Punch,* just a short distance from Tavistock Square. Leech constantly needed to negotiate wood blocks for illustrations with engravers, publishers, and authors. The highly nervous, unsmiling artist anguished about meeting his weekly obligation to provide *Punch* with a cartoon. To Marcus Stone, he was "not really melancholy, his somewhat rare smile was exquisite, like the dawn of a summer day." Always working under pressure, though, "there were no long holidays for him.' When he spent a few weeks in lodgings in Boulogne in 1854, 'the French sunlight dazzlingly bright on white houses," there were no indications of the heart disease that he was soon to develop. Lemon had to be at the office regularly, but when he, "so irresistibly funny and amiable with children," came across for numbers of visits in 1853 and 1854, Dickens and his family delighted in "Uncle Mark's" boisterously amiable company.³³ He took up an immense amount of space graciously and well. Companionable with the children and Georgina, he also got along easily with Catherine, for whom, as part of his own domestic commitment and good spirits, he felt warm affection. An editor, writer, and expert amateur actor, he was for some years the perfect companion. Neither competitive nor possessive, he would gladly share in the fun but also unselfishly accept that others were having fun without him. He responded to Dickens' gift for making all his friends feel special. And when he visited Boulogne, he happily joined Collins and Dickens on their excursions.

When, at the beginning of January 1854, Dickens returned from reading *A Christmas Carol* in Birmingham, he "found the children getting up a dull charade" for Twelfth Night and Charley's birthday. In 1852, they had put on *Guy Fawkes*, a burletta by Albert Smith, a well-known popular lecturer, dramatist, and impresario whom Dickens liked, an eccentric, "always badly dressed" man in his late thirties, "with large head, large body, short legs; long hair, long reddish-brown beard and moustache." In 1853, it had been a popular extravaganza, *William Tell.* Now they put on a version, created by their father of Fielding's *Tom Thumb,* with little Henry Fielding Dickens playing the role with minuscule cuteness. The family theatricals, performed before private audiences, had become a tradition that the children continued even when Dickens seemed too busy to dominate the arrangements. He always, though, had enough time to ensure that they were up to standard. They "derived considerable notions of punctuality and attention from the parental drilling." Unwilling to allow a performance to go on without a role for himself, he played "the Ghost, and Mr Lemon (as great a child as himself) the Queen of the Giants." In early January 1855, Dickens was "in the agonies of getting up a gorgeous fairy play for the children," his own adaptation of James Planché's *For-*

tunio and His Seven Gifted Servants, with "Mr. Wilkini Collini" as
Gobbler and Mark Lemon as Mudperiod the Dragon.34 Though
the theatricals were always partly for the children, they were
also important to him, an excitement and an anodyne, an emotional connection between the boy in Chatham who had stood
on the table to perform for *his* father's friends and the famous
novelist for whom stage performance had become a necessary
part of life.

Aware that he had more than enough commitments without becoming a paid public performer, Dickens was assisted in
resisting that temptation by sharing to some degree the Victorian position that gentlemen do not appear on the stage, except
privately. When the Dickens theatrical company performed in
the 1840s and then in 1851, the proceeds were entirely for charity. Like Macready, Dickens believed it was the rare actor who
could overcome society's prejudice against the profession. Yet
it was also clear to him that he could risk a limited number of
unpaid public performances without endangering his social status. The subject was occasionally on his mind in the early 1850s.
Public lectures by literary people had become increasingly popular. In the 1830s and 1840s, Carlyle had lectured successfully on
historical subjects. Emerson had lectured unsuccessfully,
mostly unheard because of his droning monotone and the rustle
of newspapers. Thackeray lectured humorously on his version
of eighteenth-century history and literature, and Forster, somewhat uneasy about propriety, had lectured on the civil war.
Dickens disagreed with Forster's long-standing uneasiness
about "paid public lecturing" undermining the dignity of literature. "On the contrary, if the lecturing have any motive
power at all (like my poor father this, in the sound!) I believe
it would tend the other way." He was not ready, though, to
put his principle into practice. The plays at home were private
performances. Also, he had nothing to lecture on in the intellectual way.

But reading his own works was another matter. After the
successful readings in Birmingham at Christmas 1853, he was
deluged with requests, particularly to read for nonprofit institutions, some of which offered to pay him well, and to speak at
dinners. He curtly turned down one of the requests, explaining
that he did "not read for money or as a commercial specula-

tion."[35] In late December 1854, however, he read *A Christmas Carol* as a favor to Talfourd, at the Literary and Mechanics' Institute in Reading, as a favor to Macready at the Literary Institution in Sherborne, and then for the Educational Temperance Institute at the huge hall in Bradford, where they sat 3,700 people.

The next Christmas, in bitter cold weather, he returned from Paris briefly to fulfill promises to read *A Christmas Carol* in Birmingham, Sheffield, and Peterborough, where "they took the line 'and to Tiny Tim who did NOT die,' with a most prodigious shout and roll of thunder." The effect was hypnotically exhilarating for both reader and audience. They shared a text. They shared cultural values. They shared an unforgettable experience. So strongly did he sense the possibilities that he tried to expand his repertoire "to get out of the restriction" of the two Christmas books, particularly for his favorite audiences in Birmingham. Early in 1855, in a retrospective mood, he pored "over Copperfield (which is my favourite), with the idea of getting a reading out of it . . . by some such name as 'Young Housekeeping and Little Em'ly.'" The aesthetic and emotional challenge defeated him. For two months, he reverted to it constantly. When, by the end of February, he had "not advanced an inch," he gave it up for the time being. But he soon elevated amateur theatricals to a new level of commitment. This project was to be "a *grown-up* Play" performed in the middle of June 1855 in "the children's theatre" in the schoolroom at Tavistock House. It had been expanded to create a larger stage at the expense of fewer seats, about sixty. Since "the real Theatre is so bad . . . I have always a delight in setting up a sham one—besides deriving a pleasure from feigning to be somebody else—with the addition of the odd novelty that this sort of invention is executed in company." It was his first independent production, associated neither with a birthday nor with a charity. "Mr. Collins has written an odd MeloDrama" called *The Lighthouse.* "He shewed it to me for our advice, and some suggestions." Stanfield, almost as if young again, "full of nautical and theatrical ardor, has taken possession of the Schoolroom, and will really paint and make out an illusion of a very fine kind."[36]

With himself in the starring role, with the talented regulars in place, with a clamorous demand for seats, Dickens' expectation of a brilliant success was high. He asked the police to put a man on at his expense each of the three nights "to direct the setting down and taking up of carriages, and to prevent the intrusion of any stragglers into the enclosure before the house." Performed in "THE SMALLEST THEATRE IN THE WORLD, LESSEE AND MANAGER MR. CRUMMLES," the play was "perfectly wonderful." A professional actress, Elizabeth Yates, archly complimented him: "O Mr Dickens what a pity it is you can do anything else!" His energy and restlessness intensified by the excitement, he and the company, after the final performance, "turned to Scotch reels . . . and danced in the maddest way until five" in the morning. The next day, exhausted though still exhilarated, he expected "the postmen . . . to sink under the fatigue of delivering letters of enthusiasm from three audiences. They come showering in every hour."[37]

❧ 4 ❧

ON HIS FORTY-THIRD BIRTHDAY, WITH WALLS OF SNOW "FROM THREE to six feet high on either side," Dickens saw Gad's Hill Place again. After a festive banquet in Gravesend, he sauntered, with Beard, Lemon, and Collins, through the country of his childhood. The square stone tower of Rochester Cathedral was visible in the distance through the leafless trees. Rooks flew overhead. The Medway valley was warm in its white silence. Having returned frequently to Kent for day trips and holidays, the walk on the Gravesend Road on February 7, 1855, past the Falstaff Inn and over Gad's Hill, brought him through the most familiar landscape of his life. This time, though, something was significantly different. Gad's Hill Place was for sale, "the spot and the very house . . . literally 'a dream of my childhood,' " inhabited by the ghosts of Shakespeare and of John Dickens.[38] Aware of his patrimony, he imagined that he could be comfortable there. He had never owned property before; his houses had been leased. Like Shakespeare, he could return to his childhood home as a country gentleman. He could fulfill the dream that his father had not been able to achieve. Before leaving Kent, he got the particulars from the business agent. They were formidable but not insurmountable. Until he was ready to live in it himself he could treat it as an investment. The rental income could help pay the purchase cost.

The powerful memories that Gad's Hill evoked made him receptive to another highly charged talisman from the past. Unexpectedly, he relived an important episode of his youth as intensely as he had when writing *David Copperfield*. In January, when attempting to create a reading from that novel for his Christmas performance at Birmingham, he had tried to fashion it from material that dealt with Dora and first love, the conflict between romantic passion and the need for an appropriate person to be passionate about. Two evenings following his birthday visit to Gad's Hill, he paused, while reading at his fireside, to look at the envelopes of "a handful of notes" that were laid down on his table. Since none of them had any personal meaning to him, he returned to his reading. His mind, though, kept "wandering away through so many years. . . . At last it came into [his] head that it must have been suggested by something in the look of one of those letters." Suddenly he recognized Maria Beadnell's familiar handwriting. "Three or four and twenty years vanished like a dream, and I opened [her letter] with the touch of my young friend David Copperfield when he was in love."[39] He was not exaggerating. The effect was overpoweringly dislocating.

The Beadnells had not been altogether out of sight since Maria had rejected him in May 1833. Possibly he, Catherine, and Georgina had been her guests for dinner soon after her marriage to Henry Winter, a businessman, in February 1845. Georgina made that claim years later.[40] If it is true, it is a measure of the changes that had occurred in him. In 1845, on the drive back from that putative dinner, he had apparently laughed at his former feelings. In February 1855 he felt overwhelmed by the strong emotions her reappearance provoked. He had not, though, been out of touch with the Beadnell family. As sore a wound as Maria's rejection had left, he had sufficient warmth for the family to maintain a correspondence with her father, who had apparently found the young Dickens as likable as he had found him inappropriate as a suitor. The circumspect exchange of greetings over the years carried guarded but pleasant regards to George Beadnell's children. Also, just as occasionally Dickens must have heard something about them in conversations with

Letitia and Henry Austin, who remained friendly with the Beadnells, he must certainly have been an occasional topic of conversation, and perhaps regret, among the Beadnells. For whatever the reason, Maria, thirty-five years old at her wedding to a man who had no special distinction of position or wealth, was noticeably late in marrying. In the years of her spinster-hood, Dickens had become famous and rich. The balance of power between them had shifted. It was now she who was writing to him.

His initial response was to an image, a handwriting, a text like *David Copperfield*, what Maria represented in his feelings rather than what she had been or had become. She was an autobiographical moment, a reconstituted personal fiction come alive at a time when his feelings were desperately in search of a new self-definition in which the past had to play a formative role. If her letter had not unexpectedly come, he would have found another form in which to send himself the message that he needed to have. His restlessness, his dissatisfactions, were rooted in the past. At least part of the explanation for his sensi-bility in the present focused on some powerful moment of coa-lescence in his experience as a rejected suitor, including his resolve never to be rejected again, never to be unsuccessful at whatever he did. The deadness that he felt in his cold relation-ship with his mother had its necessary antidote in the quicken-ing of feeling that he felt in romantic attachments. Those passions in which he could entirely immerse himself were al-ways based on the remembrance that he had never felt more vitally alive than he had in his affair with Maria. To the degree that he associated her rejection of him with his mother's, he had located an unhealthy aspect of himself, which he was to drama-tize in Pip's relationship with Estella in *Great Expectations*. To the extent, though, that his heart beat faster when he saw that handwriting, he yearned again for some romantic fulfillment that he felt he had never had. Now, with Maria, he had little to fear. His passion was for himself, not for her.

The next morning, answering her letter, he told her how much he had been moved by hearing from her. "There was something so busy and so pleasant in your letter—so true and cheerful and frank and affectionate." She could not "more ten-derly remember our old days and old friends" than he did. Most of all, though, he told her, her letter "is more touching to me from its good and gentle association with the state of Spring in which I was either more wise or more foolish than I am now. . . . You so belong to the days when the qualities that have done me most good since, were growing in my boyish heart. . . ." That she now had two daughters seemed "a prodigious phenomenon. . . . What strange stuff all our little stories are made of," and not necessarily all happy and desirable stuff both in the details of personal history and in the passage of time. Less than a week later, from Paris, where he remembered that Maria Beadnell, "the Angel of my soul . . . had been sent . . . to finish her education," he wrote to her again at length. He had arranged for her letter to be forwarded to him. When she took him up on his offer that he choose some trinkets for her and her daughters while he was in Paris, he was delighted. His response to the rediscovery of Maria was partly romantic flirtation. He had been practicing with Mary Boyle, who had visited him in Boulogne, and he had had the opportunity to practice again the previous winter with Frances Colden, who had been visiting in London, though he had been initially inattentive because of business pressures. His response, though, was mostly a reinforcing of the personal myths by which he lived, for "whatever of fancy, romance, energy, passion, aspiration and determination belong to me," he wrote to Maria, "I never have separated and never shall separate from the hard-hearted little woman—you—whom it is nothing to say I would have died for, with the greatest alacrity. . . . It is a matter of perfect certainty to me that I began to fight my way out of poverty and obscurity, with one perpetual idea of you. . . . I have never been so good a man since, as I was when you made me wretchedly happy. I shall never be half so good a fellow any more."[41]

As revealing as all this was, he apparently had little intention, from the first moment he saw that handwriting, of attempting to re-create the old relationship. On the one hand, his tone was confessionally revelatory. On the other, it was reserved, almost secretive, the expression of a man who had the ability to tell without revealing, to create self-protective stories in which the emotional truths and the real messages had to be read between the lines. His passion was all for the past, for what had not been The satisfactions were redemptive. The wound could be staunched by rewriting the past, or at least filling in what the past had omitted. On his return from Paris, he was followed by a letter in which she claimed that she had indeed loved him all those years ago. She had rejected him only because of parental pressure. It was a message that he was eager to hear. "Though it is so late to read in the old hand what I never read before, I have read it with great emotion, and with the old tenderness softened to a more sorrowful remembrance than I could easily tell you." If he had known that then, he would have overcome all obstacles. That he knew it now allowed him to take up the challenge of her desire that they become confidants "in perfect innocence and good faith." For whom, he asked, "can you ever trust if it be not your old lover?"

Still, he did not want "to begin afresh." He could accept the offer of friendship that she proposed, and their correspondence could be private. But their meetings would have to be public and mediated. "I am a dangerous man to be seen with, for so many people know me." His comic impulse supported his desire that this was not to be that kind of affair. "At St. Paul's the Dean and the whole chapter know me. In Paternoster Row of all places, the very tiles and chimney pots know me." The best procedure would be for Catherine to call on her, and for Maria to return the visit at a time when she knew Catherine would not be at home. They could then have their first meeting privately. Thereafter they would meet as friends among family and friends. "Remember," he concluded, "I accept all with my whole soul, and reciprocate all.—Ever your affectionate friend."[42]

Catherine was persuaded to make the call. Maria soon came to Tavistock House. He probably saw her privately, and then certainly a number of times in company in the next month or so. She had warned him that she was " 'toothless, fat, old and ugly.' " That was a purposeful exaggeration. She was certainly, though, substantially less good-looking. She showed her age, and she was noticeably overweight, looking more like the Catherine of the present than the Maria of the past. Undoubtedly her appearance in the flesh made her less useful to him as a catalyst for remembering and invoking his youth than her appearance in the letter and the spirit. He was not interested in her in the present other than as a momentary sounding board for unresolved needs that she could no more respond to now than she had been able to twenty years before. Though he may not have been frank with himself about that until after he had seen her, his letters, even before their first meeting, are not about her or them but about himself. not about a present relationship but about one that was over long ago. Though he switched momentarily from "My Dear Mrs. Winter" to "My Dear Maria," the change indicated distance rather than endearment. Under the disguise of a gentle rhetoric he made clear his ultimate message. She was the Maria of his memory. The Maria of the present had only a limited, brief usefulness. By April, he had politely discarded her. She was to make her most vital appearance in parodic form as Flora Finching in the new novel that he had begun to think about and that he started writing in the spring of 1855.

CHAPTER TEN

Superfluous Fierceness (1855-1857)

❧ I ❧

IN PARIS AGAIN IN THE WINTER OF 1856, DICKENS SAT AT HIS DESK
on New Year's Day in a large apartment of many small rooms,
with a wonderful view of the "whole panorama" beneath his
front windows on the Champs-Élysées. The snow fell heavily
around him. The streets were clogged with slush and mud. On
Christmas Day, he had had "seven sons in the banquet-hall of
this apartment—which would not make a very large warm
bath." After dinner, everyone played a game of forfeits, and he
brewed "a famous glass of Punch" for his family and friends.
His sense of humor helped him both to dislocate and to relocate
himself. Restless, he had moved to Paris in October 1855, to stay
until the next summer. Housing was scarce, rentals expensive.
He had "the wildest and most absurd adventures trying to get
us established under a roof," including a sleepless night in
which the dirtiness of the apartment seemed almost threateningly alive. "Sallow, unbrushed, unshorn, awful, stalk[ed] the
Inimitable through" 49 Champs-Élysées until it was
"thoroughly purified. . . . The cleaning that was necessary to

make" the rooms "habitable, will take its place in the mind of posterity, among the wildest fictions known to mankind."[1]

In his New Year's retrospective, he looked back on a difficult period. Having at the beginning of 1855 felt again the anguish of his youthful affair with Maria Beadnell, he found that dissatisfactions that had been repressed or partly exorcised suddenly became vividly revitalized. Forster tried to calm him, pointing out disproportions and exaggerations. But the power of the episode had not diminished. His friend's cautionary deflations seemed not only irrelevant but incomprehensible. "I don't quite apprehend," he told him that December, "what you mean by my over-rating the strength of my feeling of five-and-twenty years ago. . . . Only think what the desperate intensity of my nature is. . . . You are wrong, because nothing can exaggerate that." He could not help "going wandering away over the ashes of all that youth and hope in the wildest manner." The ashes of the past, though, were being stoked by the fires of the present. He had little to no interest in Maria or the past except insofar as he was being driven by a "desperate intensity" now. Aspects of his life angered and depressed him, particularly what he felt was his lovelessly perfunctory relationship with Catherine. When the painter John Everett Millais married that year—Collins had just introduced Dickens to him—Wilkie could not resist jesting about the wedding night, remarking that "it is such a dreadfully serious thing afterwards that one wants to joke about it as long as one can."[2] Dickens, though, was beyond any kind of joke about his.

He was also disturbed throughout 1855 by the corrupt, inefficient administration of the Crimean War. The conflict seemed justifiable; its aims sensible. "Russia must be stopped." The "future peace of the world" depended upon that.[3] But if his past and his domestic life galled him into bitter complaint and frequent restlessness, the public world of British politics infuriated him. After fury came depression. Government and politics had none of the tidiness of his desk and mind. Accounts of mismanagement on the home front and abroad deeply offended him. Reports of insufficient clothing and supplies, of medical neglect and stupidity, of inflexible narrow-mindedness on the field and in the camp prompted unsuccessful, self-justifying efforts by the administration to ameliorate and to obfuscate. Routine and patronage had atrophied the vital organs of government. Though an increasingly reluctant, often pessimistic, reformer, Dickens' lifelong instinct to be a strong voice for change asserted itself. He wrote editorials for *Household Words*, increasingly anathematizing administrative and policy failures in the conduct of the war, particularly on the home front. A new novel began to germinate, one of whose trumpet themes would be exposure of the bureaucracy, a satirical slash at the Britain that had become a country specializing in "how not to get it done." For the half year or so of its useful life he vigorously supported his friend Austen Henry Layard's Administrative Reform Association.

An impressive, charismatic man, Layard invested much of his energy in a bold effort to rally public opinion at a time of national crisis to pressure Parliament into substantial governmental reform, particularly of the army. Despite early training in the law and a diplomatic career, he had essentially the temperament of an adventurer, an explorer, a traveler. In his desert years in the Middle East, as anthropologist and archaeologist, he had relied on instinct, courage, force of personality, and dramatic self-presentation. His strong point was dominance, not persuasion. After his triumph at Nineveh, he turned to politics, attacking the encrustations of governmental atrophy with the same willfulness with which he had uncovered Babylonian antiquities. His political career was brief, stormy, and unsuccessful. From 1855 to 1857 he served as the Liberal member for Aylesbury, then from 1860 to 1869 for Southwark, during five years of which he was undersecretary for foreign affairs. Dickens supported him throughout, and valued his friendship. He liked and admired Layard. They had climbed Mount Vesuvius together in 1853.

In April 1855, after seeing him at Miss Coutts's, Dickens volunteered to put all his and his friends' resources behind the Administrative Reform Association. It seemed a duty, a national crusade in which the media resources at his command could be invaluable. The people needed to be roused. Without reform, revolution was inevitable. To the accusation that he and Layard were creating class conflict, Dickens responded that the classes were already in opposition. The aristocratic class was responsible for the division. He assured the frightened Miss Coutts, who

thought him impetuous, that he was a reformer because he
wanted "to interpose something between . . the people . . . and
their wrath. For this reason solely, I am a Reformer heart and
soul I have nothing to gain—everything to lose (for public quiet
is my bread)—but I am in desperate earnest, because I know it
is a desperate case." For all that, though he was a cautious
national reformer, eager to persuade rather than coerce. He did
not want to alienate the middle class, without whose support he
thought reform impossible. And he had learned to temper his
private anger with due attention to public decorum and the
realities that determined success in public matters. His profession and his personal history had made him more communal,
more socialized, and more pragmatic than Layard. He had had
long training in the advantages of strategy and flattery. When,
in May 1855, the brusque Layard, speaking with his heart, made
a serious tactical mistake in an important speech, he defended
him. "For Heaven's sake, be careful . . . The most useful man
in the house" might undermine his own usefulness.4

In late June, Dickens spoke to a large meeting of the Administrative Reform Association at Drury Lane Theatre in support of Layard's motion in Parliament that "this House views
with deep and increasing concern the state of the nation, and
. . . that . . . merit and efficiency have been sacrificed in public
appointments, to party and family influences, and to a blind
adherence to routine." He did not think, he assured Miss Coutts,
he would "do anybody any harm—but I feel a little vicious
against Lord Palmerston." The association did not set "class
against class. . . . No, it finds class set against class, and seeks to
reconcile them." The speech was a stirring, witty, bravura performance. At a dinner party at Lord John Russell's, Dickens
"gave them a little bit of truth" about the oppressive govern-
ment-supported Sunday legislation, restricting public entertainment and closing public places on Sunday, "that was like
bringing a Sebastopol battery among the polite company."5

Heavy cannon, though, could be ineffective. Layard's thundering speeches had little practical result. His parliamentary
resolution was overwhelmingly defeated. For Dickens, with a
novelist's concern for origins and realities frustrated in his
political efforts and in the early stages of conceiving a new
novel, the question of who was at fault took on increased impor-

tance. It occurred to him that perhaps because it was every-body's fault it was also ironically nobody's fault.

Dickens took on another reform challenge in the spring of 1855. Unable to resist, his anger stirred by inefficiency and stupidity, he urged the Royal Literary Fund to reject its own constitution and obtain a new charter that would allow it more flexibility. The constitution invested all authority in a general committee dominated by nonliterary dignitaries primarily interested in social privilege. Badly constructed, "utterly defective and rotten," the constitution permitted neither the committee nor the membership to amend it. To Dickens the fund seemed a perverse bureaucratic nightmare expensively administered by conservative incompetents (none of whom were his personal friends) whose Tory deference to rank and privilege he detested. Their disinclination to adapt its charitable activities to contemporary conditions seemed emblematic of what was wrong with Britain as a whole. For years he had been advocating the "dignity of literature." That the most prominent organization in his profession was unprofessional and unwittingly self-demeaning infuriated him. In 1854, in protest, he resigned from the general committee. Entering into an alliance with Forster and Charles Dilke, the elderly editor of the *Athenaeum* who had been his father's colleague in the navy pay office and who had probably seen him at the blacking factory, he planned to speak, to lobby, and to pressure the committee to make changes.

In March 1855, he began the first of four annual efforts at the general meetings of the fund to defeat the reactionaries. Appointed chair of a special committee to make recommendations to the membership, he proposed that the fund expand its activities. It should be no longer only a charitable fund for indigent authors but also a literary society with a library, lectures, and distinguished writers from all countries as associate members. Fighting on his own turf, with resources of influence and prestige, he thought that he would succeed. Once the stupidity and absurdity of the whole arrangement were exposed the rotten structure would fall like a flimsy house of cards. Rather than admit that they had been wrong, he imagined that the conservative members of the committee would resign. They could not survive, he thought, his withering satire and their public exposure. "I wish you could have seen [me]," he boasted to Collins, "beleaguer the Literary Fund. They got so bothered and bewildered that I expected to see them fade away under the table; and the outsiders laughed so irreverently whenever I poked up the chairman that it was quite a facetious business. Virtually, I consider the thing done. . . . I am not about to let go, and the effect has far and far exceeded my expectations already."[6]

His optimism was more than premature. It was unwarranted, a combination of naïveté and arrogance. Dilke, who was thoroughly disliked, had made some of the same proposals years before. That there were so many recommendations from the special committee offended the conservative majority, who were averse on principle to any change at all. At a special general meeting in June, the recommendations, even those to provide loans and pensions, were defeated soundly. The widespread opinion was that Dickens and his friends were "the mouthpiece of a sort of conspiracy . . . and the arguments of the malcontents, though possessing some truth . . . have proved nevertheless injurious to the cause, from the captious spirit in which they have been brought forward." By the next general meeting it was clear that the thing would never be done. Dickens' forceful, witty speech did not help. Conservative gentlemen found his and Forster's styles distasteful. Class values were more important than substantive issues in determining the outcome. Not even a resolution to examine the administration of disbursements, which all agreed could be improved, succeeded, primarily because its advocacy had become contaminated by general hostility to the reformers, who were insufficiently deferential to God, Queen (in this case, Prince Albert), and country. Their next effort, in March 1857, was rewarded with charges of "bad taste." With unwarranted bravado, Dickens boasted that he was "resolved to reform it or ruin it—one or the other."

In March 1858, with a final flourish of opposition, the reformers attempted to rally public opinion by publishing *The Case of the Reformers in the Literary Club*, a pamphlet most of which he wrote. It did no good. The fund rejected even the motion that a subcommittee be created to inquire into the administration of the budget. His old enemy Richard Bentley, the "Burlington Street Brigand" of the early 1840s, with whom he had recently become cordial again, took great pleasure in sup-

porting conservative principle. "Ah! You should see the virtuous grey hairs of Bentley . . . voting on their conservative side,
and going direct to Heaven in their company. It's like the apotheosis of an Evangelical (and drunken) butler." The next year,
the fund rejected Forster's offer of his manuscripts, books, and
an endowment of ten thousand pounds if it would agree to some
minor changes in the constitution. It seemed too much like a
bribe. Despite his vow of ceaseless dissent from within, Dickens
never publicly addressed a Literary Fund meeting again.[7]

❧ 2 ❧

THE MOVE TO PARIS IN OCTOBER 1855 TOOK SOME OF ITS IMPETUS
from the good time that he had had there with Collins the
previous February. Unlike London, and despite the freezing-
cold weather, Paris amused "itself as gaily as ever, and only talks
occasionally on the miserable subject of the war in the East."
With "motes of new books in the dirty air, miseries of older
growth threatening to close in upon [him]," Dickens felt in
February 1855 that Paris was the perfect holiday city, Collins the
perfect companion. Maria Beadnell had been much on his mind,
and the cluster of feelings associated with domestic dissatisfaction, starting a new novel, reactionary forces in London, and the
grimness of the war created a combination of tiredness and
restlessness, a desire for amusement and escape. In a "gor-
geously-furnished" apartment in the elegant Hotel Meurice,
miraculously warm despite the "snow and ice," he and Collins
had lived comfortably like a compatible odd couple. Dickens felt
"like an elderly gentleman . . . in a negative state of virtue and
respectability." Temporarily invalided, Collins remained "perfectly cheerful under the stoppage of his wine and other afflictions." Each day Dickens wrote until two, then walked all over
Paris. Every evening they dined in a different restaurant and
went "sometimes to two theatres, sometimes to three." At midnight, he drank lemonade with rum before a bright fire.[8]

The previous month Dickens had begun to jot down ideas
for stories and character sketches and lists of titles and names
for characters in a small notebook, titled "Memoranda." It became a constant companion, with spare but pregnant entries,

the twenty-five pages of notes, about half of which were made between January and May 1855, providing the basis for most of the novels and stories he was to write thereafter. He had never before kept a working notebook. He had never been so imaginatively fertile in such a brief time. Despite, or perhaps helped by, the inner turmoil, the disappointments, and his sense of impending change, his orderly pattern of anticipating one novel at a time gave way to explosive fragments of alternate possibility, which might or might not be connected, which might or might not become literary realities. Under pressure, the departure manifested his recognition both of the necessity, on the one hand, to conserve his creative energy and plan for the future, and, on the other, to allow himself the spontaneity of comparatively unstructured creativity, the free flow of an imaginative idea whose initial nondevelopment made the next idea possible. With him in Paris, or on his desk at home, or in his pocket while walking and reading outdoors, the notebook unified his restlessness and his creativity.

After returning from his February 1855 holiday, he had begun "writing and planning and making notes [for his new novel] over an immense number of little bits of paper." *Household Words* continued to prosper, with the help of Wills and Morley, though not without his constant attention. Mrs. Gaskell finally stipulated that her proofs were not to be altered "even by Mr. Dickens," after he had gone over them "with great pains" and "taken out the stiflings—hard-plungings, and other convulsions . . . her weakenings and damagings of her own effects." As an editor, he had a sure hand, and he always felt that he knew better. But he could be tactful. "I do not like to use my pen upon a paper," he told Morley, encouraging him to revise his essay, "that is so feelingly done from the heart." Through the spring and summer he continued his activities at Urania Cottage. And he helped Miss Coutts, who had supported Charley in Germany and assisted him to employment at Baring Brothers, with her private charities. One case particularly interested him, that of Frederick Maynard and his sister Caroline Thompson, who had become a prostitute in order to support her child. Fascinated by the loving closeness between the respectable brother and his prostitute sister, he interviewed both of them numbers of times. "Rather small, and young-looking . . . pretty, and gentle," she elicited from him the feeling that "there can never have been much evil in her, apart from the early circumstances that directed her steps the wrong way. . . . I cannot get the picture of her out of my head." To his novelistic imagination, Maynard's "undiminished admiration" and love for his sister "is a romance at once so astonishing and yet so intelligible as I never had the boldness to think of."9 In late March, he read *A Christmas Carol* in Ashford.

Soon he was in a "wandering-unsettled-restless uncontrollable state of being about to begin a new book. . . . I sit down to work, do nothing, get up and walk a dozen miles, come back and sit down again next day, again do nothing and get up, go down a Railroad, find a place where I resolve to stay for a month, come home next morning, go strolling about for hours and hours, reject all engagements to have my time to myself, get tired of myself and yet can't come out of myself to be pleasant to anybody else, and go on turning upon the same wheel round and round and over and over again until it may begin to roll me towards my end." In early May 1855, he felt "restlessness worse and worse. Don't at all know what to do with myself. Wish I had a Balloon." He did have, though, what he thought a good title for his novel. It would be called, with an ironic ring, "Nobody's Fault." By late May he had begun writing "the first chapter of a new long twenty number Green book" to begin publication in November. That did not prevent him from "walking about the country by day—prowling about in the strangest places in London by night," and tearing out his hair, which, he joked seriously, he could not "afford to do." Beginning was always the most difficult part. "I say to myself sometimes when I am a little impatient, 'how can you be such an erratic, wayward, unsettled, capricious, incomprehensible Beast? I am ashamed of you!"

He was not really ashamed, though. And he had three balloons, the performances of *The Lighthouse* in June, the early stages of negotiations for purchasing Gad's Hill Place, and the summer in Folkestone. Moving to 3 Albion Villas, on the cliff, near the church, with Collins as a companion, he expended "his superfluous vitality . . . in taking prodigious walks and climbing inaccessible places," constantly smoking cigars and cigarettes. Thackeray, who came to dinner, seemed to Collins "pleasanter and quieter than . . . ever . . . before." By late August, Dickens was hard at work, rising and falling "by turns into enthusiasm and depression." The new story was "everywhere—heaving in the sea, flying with the clouds, blowing in the wind." By the middle of October, when he arrived in Paris, eager to have as much head start as possible, he had finished the first three numbers. Early in November, he changed the title to "one which has a pleasanter sound in my ears, and is equally applicable to the same story, *Little Dorrit.* "[10] Probably he did not want his readers to assume that the novel would be unrelievedly or even primarily satirical.

He visited London unexpectedly for ten days, in "the vilest and most intolerable weather," to help with the funeral of William Brown, Hannah's husband, who had died in Montpellier while on holiday with his wife and Miss Coutts. With characteristic generosity, Dickens made all the arrangements. While there was a self-serving element, and he did not particularly like Hannah Brown, who "has many excellent qualities" but "would do anything conceivable or inconceivable, to make herself interesting to Miss Coutts." he felt deeply and sincerely for the spinster philanthropist. In mid-December 1855, in freezing weather, he traveled from London to Manchester, Sheffield, and Peterborough to read for charity. It was "a grinding and snorting . . . perpetually on rail roads" week. On a brief, sad visit to Rockingham, where he felt "a chill and blank" at the reminder of the loss of Watson, he brought with him in his pocket the second number of his new novel, "the great start of my Little Dorrit herself." Mary Boyle was there. He did not want to leave. The parting made him feel desolate. When he and Lavinia came in from looking at her husband's grave, she asked him, he reported, "to go up in the gallery, which I had last seen in the days of our merry play. . . . She looked out of one window and I looked out of another, and for the life of me I could not decide in my own heart whether I should console or distress her by going and taking her hand, and saying something. . . . So I said nothing. . . ." On the journey down to London, it began to snow. "At Peterboro' . . . the lady in the refreshment-room was very hard upon me. . . . She gave me a cup of tea, as if I were a hyena and she my cruel keeper with a strong dislike to me. I mingled my tears with it, and had a petrified bun of enormous antiquity in miserable meekness. . . ."[11]

The image of imprisonment appealed to him strongly these days. He felt trapped in a cell whose bars were made by personality and history. He struggled with his sense of being imprisoned in himself. The image resonated in his letters. While writing a brief autobiographical account, he felt "like a wild beast in a caravan describing himself in the keeper's absence." The image was inseparable from shifting and uncertain self-portraiture. He did not always know what kind of beast he was. He often did not recognize himself in the mirror that hung in the prison. In responding to another formal request to furnish biographical information, he was candidly evasive. The first reason why he would not is "that I do not desire to identify myself with such memoirs during my lifetime; the second is, that I may probably leave my own record of my life for the satisfaction of my children."

He had a difficult time, though, describing himself. He had "aged somewhat," adding a moustache and scanty medium-length beard. The outer appearance was unmistakably solid, a slim well-anchored man of five feet nine, with a complexion to which weather had added deep wrinkles, with long thinning brown hair and a receding hairline, who gave the impression of being frequently in motion with sparks of energy and cheerfulness. Instinctively, he believed that a moving target was hard to hit. People noticed that he appeared always to be about to be someplace else. To many admirers, like Marcus Stone, even his physical appearance was inspirational, "his body light and spare, his hands somewhat large but fine in form. . . . His eyes, dark green grey hazel, were of unforgettable beauty. A splendid frankness and honesty shone out of them, such a keen perception and observation and such rare powers of unconscious expression. . . . His nose well formed with the nostrils . . . sensitive and mobile. A well cut mouth . . . his face . . . strongly lined" and weather-beaten. The external image also had the moral glow that the world sometimes invests in genius and success. "Take from his writings," a reverential foreign visitor remarked, "the absolutely perfect, the warm feelings, indeed, everything that is good and noble; make from it a man, and you will have the true picture of Charles Dickens."[12]

His awareness of his own lack of self-recognition was heightened when he agreed to have his portrait painted by a well-known Parisian artist, Ary Scheffer, who began to "peg away" at him in November 1855. He rushed every day from his desk to Scheffer's studio "with the monotonous regularity of a pendulum swing," fulfilling his promise with suppressed but increasing irritation. By the time each sitting was over, there was no daylight left. He missed his afternoon walks, and "to have to sit, sit, sit, with Little Dorrit on [his] mind," and the new Christmas story also, was sheer torture. Worst of all, though, he did "not discern the slightest resemblance" to himself in the painting. By late January 1856, "the nightmare portrait" was almost finished. With "a good eye for pictures," Collins thought it well done about the eyes particularly, "a wonderful portrait." Dickens politely granted that it had great merit. But if the portrait were shown to him without his knowing who it intended to represent he doubted that he would recognize himself to be the original. Of course, it "is always possible that I may know other people's faces pretty well, without knowing my own." He was startled that others thought it an excellent likeness, "and yet I don't see myself. So I come to the conclusion that I never *do* see myself."13

Later, when it was shown in London, he took belated satisfaction in the opinion of his artist friends "that it wants something . . . that it has something disappointing in it." Apparently, he did not ask himself whether the blandness of Scheffer's portrait reflected the artist's unwillingness to see and to paint his subject's inner turmoil or whether it effectively embodied his own unwillingness to let Scheffer see who and what he really was. Both artist and subject ostensibly believed such clear vision possible. Dickens was, of course, different things to different people. In the portraits and photographs of him that had begun to circulate widely by the late 1840s, he preferred, as did his public, a simplified version of the view of himself that a superficial reading of his novels suggested. By the mid-1850s, he was ready for something more, of the sort that his novels increasingly implied, both in his portraits and in his life. But that something more contained tensions and shifting perspectives of feeling and self-definition that traditional portraiture could rarely represent. He did not see himself in Scheffer's portrait because the self that he was increasingly feeling was not there. Quoting his "friend the Boots" in his recent Christmas story, he commented sadly about himself to Mary Boyle, that "when you come to think what a game you've been up to ever since you was in your cradle, and what a poor sort of chap you are, and how it's always yesterday with you or else to-morrow, and never today, that's where it is."14

WHEN THE FIRST NUMBER OF *LITTLE DORRIT* WAS PUBLISHED ON December 1, 1855, Dickens had three or four in reserve, mostly written through the late summer and autumn. When the last was published on June 1, 1857, he had been for some time writing to the moment. By late spring 1856, he was only one to two numbers ahead, though the pressure to keep ahead—he was busier than ever with *Household Words* and soon with new theatricals—did not obscure his enjoyment of the challenge or undermine his self-confidence. In Paris, in early January 1856, he read the second number to an appreciative audience of personal guests. Praise poured in from friends. The reviews, though, were mixed, with strong opposition from those who felt that he should stick to comedy and domestic drama. He felt no such thing, confident for the moment that his political satire would have some practical effect. "There is a dash in No: 3 that will flutter the doors in the House of Commons lobby, I flatter myself!" The public appreciation, though, tended to be less for the satire than for the sentiment. From the beginning, it was "an immense success" commercially, with thirty-five thousand copies of the second number sold on New Year's Day, the first soon rising to forty thousand, and then every number hovering at that level thereafter. By May, with number six being snatched from the bookstands, *Little Dorrit* had so far "beaten all its predecessors, in circulation."15

The strain of sitting tediously for Scheffer while still in the early stages, with crucial narrative decisions to be made, caused him to feel desperate. His pace through *Little Dorrit* revealed his usual writing rhythms, periods of uncertainty, depression, and intense restlessness, for which he applied his usual remedies: complaints, long walks, then a return to his desk, "prowling about the rooms, sitting down, getting up, stirring the fire, looking out of window, tearing my hair, sitting down to write, writing nothing, writing something and tearing it up, going out, coming in, a Monster to my family, a dread Phaenomenon to myself." Fortunately, he had companions with whom to find relief in Paris entertainments when he felt his head stinging "with the visions of the book." He found an apartment for Collins on the same street. Macready, Lemon, and James White visited. The "strange places" of Paris nightlife attracted his voyeuristic compulsions. He needed to observe people of all classes, of all types, at play and at work. Late one night he paid three francs to go into a dance hall, where dance partners and prostitutes were for hire. "Some pretty faces, but all of two classes—wicked and coldly calculating, or haggard and wretched in their worn beauty." He was attracted to "a woman of thirty or so, in an Indian shawl . . . handsome, regardless, brooding, and yet with some nobler qualities in her forehead. I mean to walk about tonight and look for her. I didn't speak to her there, but I have a fancy that I should like to know more about her." By day, the weather alternated between torrents of rain and snow, muddy thaw, and sharp, clear coldness, "as bright as Italy . . . these Elysian Fields crowded with carriages, riders, and foot passengers. All the fountains were playing, all the Heavens shining." Paris "went at quick march down the avenue, in a sort of hilarious dance."[16]

During the short winter days, he looked ahead to the summer in Boulogne and "the long summer mornings" in which to write, though Paris social life had its attractions and diversions. They included meeting "the illustrious" George Sand, "chubby, matronly, swarthy, black-eyed," with "nothing of the bluestocking about her," though assertively self-confident in all her opinions. When Collins came in February 1856, he found Dickens waiting for him at the flat that he had acquired for him, "like a cottage in a ballet." Dickens was "all kindness and cordiality, with a supper for me at his house." As always, Collins' company was a tonic, energizing Dickens to think that they might do a series together for *Household Words* on the most interesting sites of Paris. Dickens spent hours encouraging him with suggestions when, at the beginning of April, Collins read to him an outline of the plot of his new novel, *The Diary of Anne Rodway*. Between them they conceived "a mighty original notion," which was

Dickens' "in the beginning," for another play that they might write together and then put on at Tavistock House in January 1857.

Lemon came with two of his daughters, playmates for the Dickens children. The two girls stayed on for a short time after their father's visit. Dickens wrung a promise from a reluctant acquaintance to accompany them later to London on the grounds that "they will cause . . . no trouble, as they are too young to require any gallantry." When Macready came in April, he stayed with the Dickenses, who had added some additional rooms from a vacant apartment next door. With Macready, Dickens probably visited the Brownings, Macready's friends rather than his. They were a prominent part of the English colony in Paris, some members of which he entertained at dinner parties.[17] As a guest, he was in heavy demand. The demands, though, were not nearly as insistent or as undeniable as they would have been in London.

As *Little Dorrit* progressed, Dickens felt that he was "writing [his] head off—or rather, round and round like a Harlequin's." He was "so busy . . . that my head simmers—occasionally approaches boiling point." Sometimes, while writing letters late in the day, he joked seriously that he was not sure that he could see the paper in front of him. Some of this perceptual dislocation was the result of physical exhaustion. Probably it was also emotional fragmentation, different parts of himself at war with one another, the dizziness of both the outer and the inner whirl. When he discussed *Little Dorrit* with friends, he focused on its satirical dramatization of administrative incompetence embodied in the "Circumlocution Office," the England of "how not to do it." The energy of the novel, though, was intensely personal, the expandable dark emanations of his personal life, the "game you've been up to ever since you was in your cradle. . . ."

There is intense deflected self-portraiture in *Little Dorrit.* For the first time since *Pickwick Papers,* he returned to a debtors' prison for his setting. Though no longer functioning as a prison, it had retained its hold on his imagination. For years he had taken detours to avoid the site. In the depiction of William Dorrit, the Father of the Marshalsea, John Dickens is a living presence. The image of Dickens' recently deceased father rose in the author's imagination as if his memory were stronger than the reality of his death. The nightmare father, though. had been absorbed into the harmlessness of Mr. Micawber. Despite William Dorrit's pride and blindness, his daughter's love is unshakable. In her devotion to her father and her motherlessness, the main character embodies one of Dickens' earliest fantasies. In Amy Dorrit, he combines his various favorite female archetypes, the daughter who loves her father beyond any possibility of betrayal, the "little" woman whose moral sentiments are intuitive, and the sister to some chosen man to whom she will also become a wife. Mary and Georgina are his touchstones. In Amy Dorrit, he provides the fictional model for the "one friend and companion I have never made."[18] Inverting the realities of his childhood, wealth becomes a prison, the Marshalsea becomes a place where freedom, gained only through self-discovery, is possible, and the world of experience provides the context in which honesty, moral rectitude, and hard work determine self-worth.

In Arthur Clennam, Dickens presents an autobiographical hero who is badly mothered with a vengeance, for whom a childhood of motherlessness would have been a blessing. Exiled as a child to China with his businessman father, somber and joyless in his early middle age, Clennam returns to England to confront his mother, his vague sense of a family history of wrongs, even misdeeds, compounded by a dour Calvinism, and his displaced and damaged sense of self. For Clennam. England is a grim, gray place. London is a joyless city, where the natural moral sentiments have been distorted and repressed by social pressures. Except for Little Dorrit and Daniel Doyce, the engineer who becomes his friend and paternal model, England luxuriates in materialism, hypocrisy, and incompetence. False patriarchs abound. Like Dickens, he has had the misfortune of a mother who powerfully determines much of his unhappy emotional life. Sending him to China at an early age, part of her revenge on her adulterous husband, she provides him with not even the illusion of nurturing.

In the portrait of Mrs Clennam, Dickens created the most abysmal and frightening variation on the bad mothers of his fiction. By the mid-1850s, his own mother, Elizabeth Dickens, had been exiled almost beyond the pale. He continued to support her modestly. She remained in London apparently, perhaps at Keppel Street, throughout the decade, until her death in 1863. He did see her occasionally. There is some distant fluttering of the family wings that brings her to Letitia, that has her other children aware of her. As far as his letters are concerned, though, she seems not to exist. She continues until her death to make grim fictional appearances, particularly in *Great Expectations*. In the brutal device of Mrs. Clennam's vengeance and viciousness, "Do Not Forget," there is an inverted representation of Dickens' own inability to forget what he felt his mother had done to him. No doubt Elizabeth Dickens had long ago forgotten, or more likely had never known. In the end, Mrs. Clennam turns out not to be Arthur Clennam's mother at all. That in the unraveling of the plot she eventually feels remorse for her crimes and dies in the collapse of a house that embodies her inner corrosion aptly represents the complicated anger toward his mother that Dickens never relinquished. Apparently it was a fertile wound that still sustained him.

It was a wound that also intensified his marital problems, and in the depiction of the various women of *Little Dorrit* he wrote very close to the bone of his present situation with some anticipation of what was to come. With humorous harshness, he exaggerated Maria Beadnell into Flora Finching, the portrait "extraordinarily droll" to the writer but undoubtedly painful to the subject. Like some of his literary victims, she may have chosen not to see herself in her fictional counterpart. To Dickens, such exaggerations were imaginative reworkings essential to his creativity. He chose not to see them as damaging to the real-life models. If Maria had confronted him with the identification, he would have felt surprised, misunderstood, and defensively apologetic, as with Leigh Hunt. That the obese, incompetent, garrulous, persistently tedious Flora also suggests his view of his wife probably escaped his conscious attention. "We have all had our Floras (mine is living, and extremely fat)," he told a friend. But he was also unhappily, even bitterly, preoccupied with the realization that he was stuck with his Flora forevermore.[19]

The contrast between the Flora/Catherines, the comic side of the mothers who devour by neglect, and the Mary/Georginas, the loyal, loving, slim sister-wives, was being sharpened by depression, anger, and rebellion, much of it turned against himself. He had, he felt, neither a satisfactory mother nor a satisfactory wife. He began to believe that his decade-long restlessness, certainly since the mid-1840s, took its impetus from the interaction between his art and his motherlessness. He had no place to rest, certainly no place within himself. While he accepted such distresses as the destiny of his characters, he was not content to accept them as *his*, and he focused his discontent on the only target he could readily identify—his marriage. Catherine was the obvious victim. In Paris, in early spring 1856, he had the courage of his despair. "I have always felt," he told Forster, "that I must, please God, die in harness. . . . However strange it is to be never at rest, and ever trying after something that is never reached, and to be always laden with plot and plan and care and worry, how clear it is that it must be, and that one is driven by an irresistible might until the journey is worked out. . . . As to repose—for some men there's no such thing in this life." There had been a time, though, when things were different, when there had been an emotional harmony in which his restlessness had been balanced by marital and familial pleasures, some past in which neither his mother nor his wife put him into the bleak mood he now felt, the time when the children were young, when Catherine was still his "little mouse," when he was preoccupied with the struggle for success, fame, and friendship. "The old days—the old days! Shall I ever, I wonder, get the frame of mind back as it used to be then? Something of it perhaps—but never quite as it used to be. I find that the skeleton in my domestic closet is becoming a pretty big one."[20]

The startling news in 1856 that Forster was going to be married provided both intense, almost breathtaking amusement and an ironic counterpoint to his feeling of alienation from Catherine. With Collins, Stone, Stanfield, Macready, and Maclise, who joined him in London in May of that year, he joked almost endlessly about the bluff, hefty, domineering, lifelong bachelor of forty-four marrying a petite widow of thirty-six "with as many thousand pounds as she is years of age." That Forster would give up editing *The Examiner* was to be regretted, since "he is one of the most responsible and careful of literary men associated with newspapers. . . . That he *does* hustle an unoffending company, sometimes," was a minor fault. He could always be counted on to do more than justice to his friends. When they argued, he would be forthcoming in the reconciliation. Such arguments were an essential part of the relationship, the result of the differences between them that had made the friendship productive. As Dickens coped with his own frustrations in the next two years with what seemed to Forster unwise, compulsive decisions, he sometimes found his friend's conservatism unbearable. Often he seemed insufficiently empathetic. When Forster opposed his giving readings for profit, Dickens unkindly concluded that Forster seemed "extraordinarily irrational about it. . . . His money must have got into his head."

In his sympathy with Dickens' unhappiness, about which he knew more than anyone else, Forster urged patience, tolerance, optimism, reminding him of the problems "that might and must often occur to the married condition when it is entered into very young." Forster had been an intimate of the household for so long that his association with Catherine and the Dickens marriage had a degree of loyalty and respect that Dickens himself hardly felt at this point. Since the late 1830s, Forster had held in his hand the third glass of champagne at birthday parties and anniversary celebrations. He had been Catherine's guest and friend for over two decades. She had welcomed him into a share of the Dickens domesticity, which had meant much to him. Though not a man to indulge in idealizations, he was completely sincere in telling her thankfully in May 1856 "that I associate you so much with the change that is about to befall me—and that I have never felt so strongly as within the last few months how much of the happiness of past years I owe to you." There was tactful indirectness in signing the affectionate letter "with increasing wishes and prayers for your continued happiness."[21]

In his Paris apartment, which Dickens made a temporary home and a workplace, Catherine was an institutional reality rather than an emotional necessity. Georgina took care of many of the practical daily details. Charley worked at Baring Brothers in London, living at Tavistock House with the Hogarths, who were house-sitting. Walter, Frank, and Alfred were at school in Boulogne. Henry might soon join them. Sydney had lessons at home. The two-year-old "Little Plorn" continued to be his father's delight. Mamie and Katie, like younger sisters to "Auntie," took lessons in languages and in the arts of domesticity.

Each night at dinner, Dickens, surrounded by "my women," schooled them all, especially the impressionable children, in the complications of his personality. His dissatisfaction was frequently visible, though usually debited against the account of genius working at a new novel. Like an uneasy patriarch, he kept himself and his family on edge. He felt no urgency to return to London, which he expected to do in the autumn. And there was at least the prospect of the new theatricals, which he began to anticipate.

What most excited, and for a while frustrated, him, though, was the purchase of Gad's Hill Place. The negotiation proved more complicated and time-consuming than he had anticipated. When he first saw the for-sale sign in February 1855, he imagined that it would soon be his. When he finally paid the purchase money in March 1856, he "turned around to give it to Wills, and said 'Now isn't it an extraordinary thing—Friday! I have been nearly drawing it half-a-dozen times, when the lawyers have not been ready, and here it easily comes round upon a Friday, as a matter of course.' " He never doubted that he wanted to buy it. When he saw it in the February snow, he immediately recognized that it was "a dream of my childhood," connected to his own mythology about his origins as a writer. "I used to look at it as a wonderful mansion (which God knows it is not) when I was a very odd little child with the first shadows of all my books in my head."[22] He associated it with the Shakespearean model for authorship, with the nurturing memories of Rochester and the stable cathedral, with the need to become the success that his father was not. From the summit of the hill "a noble prospect" glowed across all the landscape of the happiest portion of his childhood, the valley of the Medway, the river and Rochester in one direction, the distant Thames and Gravesend in the other, Cobham woods close by.

The delay in purchasing the house resulted partly from the slowness of the legal procedures, partly from his haggling about the price, though with his increased income he could readily afford it. At moments, the negotiations seemed "to be a sort of amateur Chancery suit which will never be settled." He did not want to overpay, as a matter both of principle and of patrimony. He felt that he needed to keep in mind that his savings were small, that he had a large family for which to provide, and that

his earnings depended on his maintaining his reputation, popularity, and health. Previously he had only leased. This was to be
a freehold purchase. Wills, who had accidentally discovered,
soon after Dickens learned that Gad's Hill Place was for sale,
that it belonged to the writer Lynn Linton, whom he had met
at a dinner party and who seemed to him charming, acted as his
negotiator-messenger.

In July 1855, the invaluable Henry Austin, his engineer
brother-in-law who had supervised the renovations at Tavistock
house, offered to evaluate its condition and appraise the prospective purchase. Dickens was grateful for being put "in such complete possession of the facts" about the roofing, water supply,
plumbing, foundation, and so on. His commitment unqualified
by anything but the price, he immediately began to explore
renovations, such as raising the roof to transform the garret into
full-size rooms. The owners were asking over £2,000. Though he
would give up to £1,750 or £1,800, he empowered Wills to begin
with an offer of £1,500. He doubted that they would take even
the larger sum. He felt, though, that he could not "afford to buy
the place" for his "own occupation, or it might be worth more
to me. I can only regard it as an investment, and test it by the
return it would give to me in money, for so much money laid
out."[23] By November, with the negotiations still unresolved, he
became momentarily adamant about his offer, partly because
Austin had advised that "£1,800 would be too much." He agreed,
if Austin would concur, to offer £1,700, then £1,750. "If he does
not," he told Wills, "let it go, since they won't take our money."

But wanting the house too much to take the chance of
losing it, a few days later he offered the higher sum, which was
soon accepted. Rather than use savings, he sensibly borrowed
the money from the compliant Bradbury and Evans, to be repaid from future earnings. He took advice from Wills and
Forster, but he had a well-known solicitor, Frederic Ouvry,
draw up the contracts. He hoped to complete the purchase by
the end of January 1856. His plan was to renovate modestly,
complete the furnishing, and rent it as an investment, at least
for the time being. He would occupy it himself only if he could
not find a tenant to replace the "old Tory" Reverend Joseph
Hindle, who had lived there for twenty-six years and whose
wish to stay until the lease expired at the end of March 1857 he

readily agreed to. As the negotiations drew to a conclusion, he decided that he would occupy the house himself for the summer of 1857 to have the pleasure of living in it and improving it before he let it out. With potential tenants in mind, he queried Miss Coutts and then Frank Stone, and wanted the word spread that he would soon have a fine property available for a suitable tenant. When he went down with Wills in mid-February, "the country, against every disadvantage of season," seemed beautiful. ' The house is so old fashioned, cheerful, and comfortable, that it is really pleasant to look at." On March 14, 1856, the purchase was finally completed. He gasped at the amount of money paid. But he was excited. Next March "we will dash in with our improvements and furnish the place . . . occupying it for that summer."24 The house became of inestimable value to him, and his last home. He never rented it to anyone.

When his Paris stay was over in May 1856, he returned briefly to Tavistock House, still occupied by the Hogarths and Charley, where the dust lay an inch thick on the first floor. He was irritated by the presence of his in-laws and by the dirty condition of the house, transferring his anger at Catherine to her parents, though he had always previously felt affection for George Hogarth. "Getting books and papers put away," he wallowed in the dust for four hours, describing plans for his and Collins' new play to Stanfield, who hung "out of the centre back-window of the schoolroom, inventing wonderful effects." Soon he had "purified every room from the roof to the hall," as if the house had been defiled, and celebrated with his friends over a bowl of punch (Catherine was in Paris, soon to go with Georgina, the children, and the servants to Boulogne). "Headache!" he said the night after, "there is no such thing in my punch." In late May, as the country celebrated the end of the Crimean War, he stood with some friends at the top of St. Paul's and remarked, "what a wonderful sight Illuminated and Fireworked London was."25 He then joined his family in Boulogne, the last summer he was to spend at any resort town. There was a great deal of *Household Words* business to manage, a great deal of *Little Dorrit* still to be written. At the Villa des Moulineaux again, surrounded by roses and geraniums, with "sweet peas nearly seven feet high," whose "blossoms rustle in the sun, like Peacocks' tails," he was absorbed in work. His spirits were high with anticipation. "We have honey-suckle that would be the finest in the world if that were not at Gad's Hill."

Invitations brought brief visits from Stanfield, Benjamin Webster, Collins' good friend Edward Pigott, Shirley Brooks, a young writer and literary journalist, Lady Blessington's two nieces, and Mary Boyle. The Reverend Chauncey Hare Townshend stayed close by. Despite the latter's jewelry collection and expertise, when Mary bought "an emerald ring for a *franc and a half*" he was completely taken in and "admired the mock emerald as something quite priceless."²⁶ A warm invitation to Hans Christian Andersen, whom Dickens had met in London nine years before, made another visit likely, perhaps the next summer. The Danish writer idolized Dickens, who responded gallantly to his "dear and worthy Hans" with an affection that far exceeded any actual friendship between them. At the moment, it was a relationship of idealization and expectation. They had spent only a few hours together. The premier visitor, though, constantly expected and finally appearing in mid-August, was Wilkie Collins. The entire family, and particularly Mamie and Katie, wanted the new play, *The Frozen Deep*, written immediately. Though the initial idea had been Dickens', the first draft was to be Collins'. Ideas had already been exchanged, the outline was clear, new effects were being improvised, difficult turns of plot and character resolved. The two girls were to have starring roles. Georgina and Janet Wills had committed themselves to parts. Mark Lemon was to have an important one. The chief supporting role was Collins', and Dickens was to be the star. There were no plans for Catherine to participate.

By the end of August, the play, which Collins had been working on since April, was mostly completed. For a few weeks the leaves had been "tinged with yellow, and the berries . . . turning red." They had "already begun to talk sometimes" of their "return home early in October." Suddenly, precipitately, at the beginning of the fourth week of August, a month before his lease was up, Dickens rushed his sons, with Catherine, back to London. He had had an urgent warning from a friend in Paris, Dr. Joseph Olliffe, the medical consultant to the British Embassy, about a typhoid epidemic in Boulogne. It had broken out in June. The townspeople, though, had suppressed the news "for the sake of their own interests." Its initial symptom was "malignant sore throat," followed by brain fever. In June, twenty children had died. "Being far out of town," they had "only heard vaguely about the disease." When Katie developed a cough and lost her appetite, she and Mamie were sent home. Fortunately, it turned out to be only the whooping cough. Though Mr. Gibson, his sons' headmaster, determined that there was "no reason for postponing the opening of the school," Dickens decided to keep his children in London until he felt absolutely certain. Death, though at a slight remove, suddenly made Boulogne seem desolate and wretched. The popular dramatist and companionable member of the *Punch* staff Gilbert à Beckett had become ill at his boardinghouse. The visiting Douglas Jerrold, a good friend of Beckett's, brought Dickens daily reports. They walked about the garden together, "talking about these sudden strikings down of the men we loved in the midst of us.' While Beckett raved, his son died in the next room. His friends hoped that Beckett would rally, "but he sank and died, and never even knew that the child had gone before him." On September 3, Dickens was in "all the confusion and bewilderment of moving" to England, to be followed the next day by Georgina and the servants.[27]

❧ 4 ❧

COVENT GARDEN THEATRE HAD BURNED TO THE GROUND IN EARLY March 1856. From Paris, Dickens lamented that "such a Fire should have come off in my absence," a little less than a week before he was due in London with number five of *Little Dorrit*. He had mixed feelings, both for having missed such a fiery spectacle and for what the theatre had embodied. A century of history and decades of personal memory smoldered in its ruins, the theatre in which Macready had acted triumphantly, in which the novelist had for over two decades seen Shakespeare performed, opera sung, melodrama declaimed. The moment he reached London, four days after the fire, he went to see the ashes. Though the "audience part and the stage were so tremendously burnt out" and nothing remained "but bricks and smelted iron lying on a great black desert, the theatre still looked so wonderfully like its old self grown gigantic that I never saw so strange a sight." The magic of imagination and transformation still hovered in the smoking shards. The roof had come down bodily. The fragments were "like an old Babylonic pavement, bright rays tessellating the black ground, sometimes in pieces so large that I could make out the clothes in the Travatore."[28]

He had, though, his own living theatre at Tavistock House. The impetus for the play that he and Collins conceived that same month came from Dickens, who, covering all the costs of its production, saw nothing incompatible in producing, directing, and acting while writing a novel and editing *Household Words.* With theatre and a theatre community, the solitary hours at his desk could be balanced by company and communal creation. Personal frustration could be forgotten or even discharged. He was to have the unique opportunity of producing and directing the premier performance of a play that he himself had helped to write. As co-author, he would have control over the script. The words as well as the manner in which the actors recited would embody his vision. The roles would be created with the casting already in mind. The setting and lighting would be created while the script was being written. All aspects of the production would be enhanced by a cohesiveness of a sort that he had never had the chance to experience before. This was to be an act of creation in which text and performance would be a unified expression of his view of human nature.

The vision was lifelong; the catalyst was recent. He had heard of Sir John Franklin and his expedition to discover a northwest passage through the Arctic before the publication, in October 1854, of Dr. John Rae's report on the fate of Franklin's latest effort. An experienced officer who had fought at Trafalgar, Franklin's determination to find the passage had culminated in a major expedition that had left England in May 1845 and was last heard of in July. The searches that had begun in 1848 were unsuccessful. The reward of ten thousand pounds offered by the government remained unclaimed until Rae, an officer in the Hudson Bay Company, reported that he had sufficient testimony from Eskimo witnesses and from physical remains of the party to prove that Franklin and his men were not only dead but that they had prolonged their lives by cannibalism. The image of Thyestes' feast shocked the Victorians. It had strong resonances for Dickens. Dismemberment and cannibalism had been powerful images in his life from childhood on and had been direct and indirect motifs in his fiction, the self feeding on itself, the world broken into animistic fragments, the society engorging the individual.

Though fascinated by Rae's report, Dickens' immediate response was denial. The report was "hasty . . . in the statement that they had eaten the dead bodies of their companions." That seemed inconceivable. Those who had been the beneficiaries of European values could not do such a thing even under duress, and their cultural inhibitions were an expression of the positive virtues that derive not from external codes but from the very nature of human nature itself. Human beings were born with instinctive moral sentiments inseparable from their ability to feel. The notion that the Arctic wastes had been so cold as to freeze the capability of someone like Franklin to feel and express his moral sentiments was unacceptable. Attracted in his fiction to embodiments of evil, to destroyers and engorgers, Dickens often located the sources of such depravity in social pressures and deformation. Other times he admitted the insufficiency of such an explanation. He preferred, though, to explain human nature in the terms of eighteenth-century moral philosophy: Human beings are innately good; their goodness resides in their natural moral sentiments. We are at our best when we allow those sentiments spontaneous and full expression through intense feeling, through "sacred tears."[29]

Channeling his denial into semirational response, he examined "a wilderness of books" to show "that the probabilities are all against poor Franklin's people having dreamed of eating the bodies of their companions." The evidence, he claimed, did not support the charge. Eskimo witnesses were inherently unreliable, both because they were "savages" and because they shared the universal tendency among witnesses to tell investigators what they wanted to hear. If Franklin had endured trial by ice on previous expeditions, would it not be inconsistent with his demonstrated heroism for him to succumb in this instance? In two articles that Dickens wrote on "The Lost Arctic Voyagers" (published in *Household Words* in December 1854), he argued that no British gentleman could do what Franklin was now accused of doing. His arguments were "calculated to soothe the minds" of Franklin's friends, particularly the mind of his wife, with whom he began an acquaintance, as well as his own. When he read a memoir written by one of Franklin's intimates, he saw a mirror image of his own most highly valued relationships. The "manly friendship, and love of Franklin" that it expressed seemed to him "one of the noblest things I ever knew in my life. It makes one's heart beat high, with a sort of sacred joy."[30] When he conceived a "mighty original notion" for a new play in the spring of 1856 it was the Franklin expedition on which it was to be loosely based, an expression of his commitment to the values expressed in the articles he had written in 1854.

There was also another level of interest for him in the new play. It would allow him to tackle directly some of the challenges of defining art and expressiveness that had been disturbing him in recent years. It could embody a response to the criticism that the main male characters of his novels were simplistically one-dimensional, that they were not "real" flesh-and-blood men with a complexity of moral and material life, especially in comparison to the protagonists of European novels by Balzac and George Sand. The tendency on the Continent to create realistic literary characterizations had been resisted in England with the tenacity of both a moderately Puritan culture and of a community of artists who still emphasized the idealistic element in art. Dickens was among the resisters, though he was sometimes ambivalent. When John Everett Millais depicted an ordinary boy in a commonplace carpenter's shop as Jesus, he felt sufficiently offended to denounce the conception as indecent, even blasphemous.[31] Some things, he felt, should not be subject to art's increasing assimilation of the ideal into the ordinary. Despite his public denunciation, though, Dickens' notion of the ideal was nontheological, and he shared with Millais, whom he personally liked, Carlyle's notion of natural supernaturalism, of finding the sacred in everyday life. He needed to distinguish between a realism that enhanced the ideal and a realism that devalued hope, beauty, art, and human nature.

With Collins as a working partner, Dickens had an additional reminder of the complications of literary realism. Even Collins, with his penchant for direct statements about daily life, took into account Victorian conventions about what could be said and depicted in literature and what could not. Both detested hypocrisy of the sort exemplified by Martin Chuzzlewit's Pecksniff, who was based on the editor and journalist Samuel Carter Hall. When Dickens read, in July 1856, an account of a speech that Hall had given, he denounced "the snivelling insolence of it, the concentrated essence of snobbery in it, the dirty Pecksniffianity that pervaded it, and the Philoprogullododgetiveness wherein it was steeped." Pecksniff soon was to be expanded into Podsnap, an embodiment of self-serving British hypocrisy on moral and sexual matters, the narrow-minded closing down of avenues of experience and life. But both writers had their eyes fixed firmly on just how far they could push the British public without damaging their sales.

Generally the more artistically daring of the two, Dickens was radically conservative in his combination of realistic psychological portraiture and moral idealism. To the realists, though, even his sharp psychological portraiture lacked a fullness of dimension that would make the depiction true to life. Clennam was an instance at hand, as *Little Dorrit* progressed. Despite his complications of history and character, Clennam embodies conventional decency, and never struggles with the anger, violence, vengefulness, sexual fulfillment, even self-serving irrationality of the sort that such a man might naturally be expected to feel. Having gone as far as he thought it sound to go, Dickens felt the frustration of his situation as a Victorian writer. If "the hero of an English book is always uninteresting— too good—not natural, etc. . . . . what a shining imposter you," the English critic, "must think yourself and what an ass you must think me, when you suppose that by putting a brazen face upon it you can blot out of my knowledge the fact that this same unnatural young gentleman (if to be decent is to be necessarily unnatural) . . . *must be* presented to you in that unnatural aspect by reason of your morality, and is not to have, I will not say any of the indecencies you like, but not even any of the experiences, trials, perplexities, and confusions inseparable from the making and unmaking of all men!"[32] The hero of the new play was to be both the kind of character he had heretofore not been able to depict and a partial self-portrait.

By mid-September 1856, they had a draft of *The Frozen Deep*. Loosely based on, though actually only alluding to, the Franklin expedition, it contained no references to cannibalism. The moral issues were to be dramatized without the unpleasantness of dealing with the charge directly. In April, after Janet Wills had agreed to play the part, they had decided that the first act, which would take place in Devonshire, would have as its major effect the clairvoyant "second sight" of an old Scotch nurse (Mrs. Wills) who would tell Clara Burnham, Frank Aldersley's fiancée, that she saw in a vision disasters occurring to an Arctic expedition, one of whose members was Frank. Clara, played by Mamie, and her friend Lucy Crayford, played by Georgina, accompanied by Nurse Esther, set out toward Newfoundland to learn what they can. The second act, set in the Arctic, and the third, set in Newfoundland, were refined in September and October, the dramatic excitement inhering in the conflict between Richard Wardour, Clara's rejected suitor and also a member of the expedition, and Frank, who is ignorant of Wardour's love for his fiancée.

The *"admirable idea"* that became the crux of the drama was that Wardour, mad partly with jealousy, partly with despair, and partly with unextinguished hope, should struggle against his desire to murder Frank. For much of the third act his fellow crew members and the audience suspect that that is precisely what he has done. Wardour was Dickens' role. Collins played Frank. Mark Lemon played his genial alter ego, Lieutenant Crayford, Lucy's brother. At the climax, Wardour produces a completely safe and unharmed Frank Aldersley, whom he has valiantly rescued, carrying him across "the frozen deep" at the cost of his own life. In his final moments, he embraces Frank and has his last look at Clara. "My sister, Clara!—Kiss me, sister, kiss me before I die!"[33] Overcoming his initial ambivalence, Wardour demonstrates his inherent moral sentiments, his nobility of character, and his heroic virtue.

Tentative rehearsals began in September. The casting was completed, with Charley, Katie, Alfred Dickens, Edward Pigott, Augustus Egg, Helen and Edward Hogarth (Georgina's younger sister and brother), and Frederick Evans, Dickens' publisher, in minor roles. At the beginning of October, both authors agreed to small changes, Dickens tactfully acknowledging Collins' priority. Soon, in solemn council with Lemon, Dickens "abandoned the idea of doing a new farce." As a companion piece, they would do one of their old standbys, *Animal Magnet-*

ism, since *The Frozen Deep* "is so difficult and will give us all so
much to do." In mid-October, they "read the new play" to the
full cast for the first time. In the schoolroom, "the clink of
hammers [gave] awful note of preparation." Acting as his own
architect, he had redesigned it. The stage, now thirty feet long,
was constructed opposite to where it had been previously, and
the bay window at that end had become the entrance and exit
to a small extension that would deepen the stage, allow for more
sophisticated effects, and also permit room for a larger audience.
"The sounds in the house are like Chatham Dockyard—or the
building of Noah's Ark."[34]

Under Stanfield's supervision, the renovation proceeded.
Soon "in ecstacies at its proportions," he and William Telbin,
also a well-known stage designer, were good-humoredly competing. Stanfield did the scenery and stage effects for acts two
and three, Telbin for act one. Neither would allow the other to
know his plans. Concerned about "Stanny's" delicate health,
fearing that this would be his last hurrah, Dickens encouraged
him not to resist the most dramatic effects and settings possible.
The work was rejuvenating. "If you were to see my young man
perpetually painting here for the Christmas play, in the midst
of 70 paint pots and a cauldron of boiling rise, you would never
forget the spectacle." As the rehearsals became intense, Dickens'
commitment to his role and to the experience of the play became
passionate. The "Sparkler" was now "the manager" also. The
cast was drilled intensely. "All the elder children are wildly
punctual and businesslike to attract managerial commenda-
tion." He boasted that they "go through fearful drill under their
rugged parent," justifying such discipline not only as necessary
for the success of the play but as moral training, "a lesson in
patience, order, punctuality, and perseverance . . . a bond of
union among all concerned . . . the best training in Art and
respect for Art, that my young people could receive." In December, he had some moments of calm, capable even amidst the
heavy workload of humorously telling Macready that "your
aged friend glides away on the Dorrit stream, forgetting the
uproar for a stretch of hours, refreshing himself with a ten or
twelve miles' walk, pitches headmost into foaming rehearsals,
placidly emerges for editorial purposes," and then "again calmly
floats upon the Dorrit waters."[35]

For Dickens, the play was a unique event. Nothing like it would "ever be seen again." For the actors, he had one sacred rule: "WHEN THEY APPLAUD, INVARIABLY STOP, UNTIL THE APPLAUSE IS OVER." For the audience, he had one expectation—that they be sympathetic. For the performance itself, he had one standard—that it be as perfect as possible. Tickets were at a premium, to be obtained only through friendship and influence. Friends and acquaintances from literature, the arts, the bar, government, and wherever received letters of invitation, some of which Catherine wrote, accompanied by "a beautiful play bill in black and red ink," and any ticket declined had to be returned for allocation to the name highest on the waiting list. To the final rehearsal, he invited the servants and local tradespeople. At the last moment, he wrote a prologue, to be recited by Forster, who was more in character as a declaimer than as an actor. On New Year's Day, Dickens remembered that there were still "all those icicles to be made," and urged Stanny to come over quickly. The rewards of ten weeks of hard work were about to be realized. It had been "like writing a book in company; a satisfaction of a most singular kind, which has no exact parallel in my life." He had the opportunity to blow off his "superfluous fierceness" in the actual presence of his readers "instead of in my own solitary room, and to feel its effect coming freshly back upon me from the reader."[36] For the first time in his amateur career as a producer, director, and actor, he invited reviewers from the major newspapers, as if the restraints that he had felt previously no longer applied and probably also because of the importance he attached to the message of the play.

At the premiere, the audience responded rapturously, the critics enthusiastically. The performance on January 6, 1857, touched a nerve of response. The setting and lighting effects seemed spectacular, including "a Sunset," Dickens boasted, "far better than has ever been done at the Diorama or any such place." The stage illusions were astoundingly realistic. Reviewers commented with almost awestruck praise on Dickens' innovative naturalistic performance, in which he acted with an emotive restraint that made the character's feelings especially expressive. Macready, in the audience, may have recognized that his own efforts at stage realism were being carried beyond anything he had done. And the audience sensed the identification between Dickens and his role, though only some were consciously aware of it. After each performance, he felt exhausted, brooding, unapproachable, as Richard Wardour's "ghost sat by the kitchen fire in its rags." After one performance, he fainted.⁷ For the immediate audience, the identification was between the novelist and the literary nature of his conception of Wardour, between the themes of his novels and the themes of the play. For the critics, Dickens was publicly dramatizing his ability both to conceive and to perform a complex character who inwardly struggles with the contradictions of his personality. For himself, he was acting out one of the personal myths that energized him, the restless hero whose wounds and afflictions provoke the creative energy for noble acts. For the larger audience of Victorian culture, he was affirming what the middle- and upper-class public had established as self-defining: that human nature was basically good, that the English gentleman could triumph over any adversity, that the morbid voices of degradation could be dismissed.

After the premiere, Dickens hosted a champagne supper. There were to be three more performances. "How they fly!" he told Collins. With the closing performance approaching, "by an absurd coincidence" attended by "three fourths of the Judges I know," Dickens exalted in the "delightfully strong . . . impression that the play has made. . . . I actually have never seen audiences so affected." He felt overwhelmingly affected himself. Two days later he was "in the depressed agonies of smashing the Theatre." The realism of the production, including the costumes that might have allowed the cast to "have gone straight to the North Pole itself, completely furnished for the winter," did not disguise for long that the stage was an illusion, the schoolroom now 'a mere chaos of scaffoldings, ladders, beams, canvases, paint-pots, sawdust, artificial snow, gas-pipes, and ghastliness." As always, when a project was finished, the imaginative excitement over, he felt "shipwrecked—as if I had never been without a play on my hands before."

Having seen the snakes being fed at the zoo, he now kept imagining that the legs of all the tables and chairs at Tavistock House were serpents that were eating "all possible and impossible small creatures." The image would not go away. Recognizing that he was "generally in a collision state," he absorbed himself in *Little Dorrit*, "transcendentally busy, drawing up the arteries." He also had some of the usual family anguish to torment him, particularly Frederick's request for a small loan. He resolutely declined, accusing his brother of "bad faith" in an agreement he had entered into with Wills and Austin as guarantors. Apparently, like John Dickens at his worst, Frederick had defaulted. Charles reminded his brother that a loan would be throwing good money after bad since it would not free him from his creditors. Having suffered through a decade of debts, adulteries, and now a collapsing marriage, Frederick responded bitterly. "The World fancy that you are the most tolerant of men. Let them come under your lash." If he were to be judged by how he treated his "own flesh and blood, God help them." And he provided Charles with the opportunity to focus again on his own restless imperfections with the accusation that the danger of having "had the world at your feet . . . for a quarter of a century" is that "of placing yourself upon a Pinnacle, upon the assumption that your nature is perfection." Charles dismissed the accusation, though, ironically distancing himself with the response that "a touch of simple manly gratitude, fresh from the honest and overcharged heart, is so delightful in this world."38

Fortunately, he also had Gad's Hill to preoccupy him. Anticipating spending the summer there, he began the improvements that gave him so much pleasure. First he attended to the furnishings, sending his servant to the London markets to bargain for pieces he had already picked out in order to get them at a lower price. "If you should see such a thing as a mahogany dining table or two marble washing-stands, in a donkey cart anywhere, or in a cat's meat cart or any conveyance of that kind, you may be sure the property is mine." He hired a contractor to paint and wallpaper. The two most pressing renovations were raising the roof six feet so that the garret floor would have full-size rooms and redoing the garden early enough in the spring so that he might have neat flower beds with bright geraniums that summer. He urged Frank Stone to consider using it as "a light place to paint in during the winter months . . . for what you can afford to pay." The late winter was made bearable by *Little Dorrit* and by his anticipation of his "extensive freehold, where cigars and lemons grow on all the trees." In early March, he took a long weekend with Collins in Brighton "for a breezy walk on the downs." It improved his spirits to be away from Tavistock House, and Lavinia Watson was there. He had strongly regretted that she had not been able to attend a performance of *The Frozen Deep*. His admiration for her had increased. She seemed younger and more beautiful than ever. He briefly delayed calling on her when, on a walk on the Downs in which he was "rained upon, hailed upon, snowed upon, and blown," his hat became an unwearable "solid cake of ice, half an inch thick." He could not borrow Collins', since his "head being triangular with a knob in the middle, and small besides, his hat is of no use to anybody but himself."

In April, he stayed at a hotel in Gravesend, to be closer to the work at Gad's Hill, which, he crowed, "is full of the ingenious devices of the inimitable writer. . . . If you don't like it," he joked to Miss Coutts, "I shall set it on fire—particularly as it is insured." Invitations soon went out to friends to come to visit him just "an hour and half from town" at his "good little old fashioned breezy, shady, sunny, leafy place." On May 11, 1857, he finished *Little Dorrit*. A week later, triumphantly, always at his best at a party, he took a "small and noble army" of friends and relations down with him for a cold-meat dinner to inaugurate Gad's Hill Place.39 It was the first piece of property that any member of the Dickens family, past or present, had ever owned.

❧ 5 ❧

THOUGH THE SUMMER OF 1857 BEGAN WITH QUIET DAYS, IT SOON WAS transformed into a whirl of activity and a decisive crisis. The crisis had come for which Dickens had unconsciously spent years preparing. The contentment existed only on the surface, the glow from the green landscape that he surveyed from his Kentish hilltop. Beneath it were bitter memories and the vague hope of radical change. In early May, before going to Gad's Hill, he went to the Borough to see if he could find "any ruins of the Marshalsea." The visit had nothing to do with *Little Dorrit*, which he was within a few days of finishing. "Found a great part of the original building. . . . Found the rooms that have been in my mind's eye in the story. Found . . . a very small boy, who

. . . told me how it all used to be. . . . He was right enough.
. . . There is a room there—still standing, to my amazement—
that I think of taking!" It was the room in which he had watched
his father and the other prisoners signing a petition. But "the
spikes are gone, and the wall is lowered, and anybody can go out
now who likes to go, and is not bedridden."[40] It was a wish for
repossession and transformation. That room in the Marshalsea
now represented freedom, a place into which he could come and
from which he could go at will.

At the end of May, he attended a testimonial dinner at
Greenwich for a new friend, W. H. Russell, the foreign correspondent for the *Times,* whose dispatches exposing the malad-
ministration of the Crimean War he had admired. With Russell
and Jerrold, he took advantage of the lovely day to go down by
steamboat, particularly to have a good view of the *Great Eastern,*
which was under construction. When they met at Leicester
Square, Jerrold seemed slightly ill, having been sick the previous
three days, attributing it to "the inhaling of white paint from his
study window." Suddenly he "fell into a white, hot, sick perspiration, and had to lean against the railings." He felt much better,
though, on the boat trip. In Greenwich, they took a ride in an
open carriage. Though he was very quiet at dinner, Jerrold had
recovered some of his good spirits, sipping some medicinal
water and wine. Before they said good-bye—Dickens got a ride
up to London with Leech—he invited him to visit Gad's Hill,
and Jerrold assured him that he was all right now. Dickens,
though, thought that he still looked sick. The next morning
Jerrold was so ill that he could not get out of bed. He rallied
slightly, but had a relapse and died two days later, " 'at peace
with all the world' . . . and asking to be remembered to friends."
If he had offended anyone with his sharp tongue, he asked to be
forgiven.

Dickens at this point knew only that Jerrold had been ill
and was better. But he dreamed on the night of his friend's death
that Jerrold came and showed him something that he had written, eager that he should read it. He "could not make out a word
of it," and "woke in great perplexity, with its strange character
quite fresh in my sight." The next day, coming up by railroad
from Gad's Hill to London, he heard a passenger, unfolding his
newspaper, say to another, " 'Douglas Jerrold is dead.' "[41]

Dickens' relationship with the *Punch* wit had not been a particularly intimate one. The tiny, semicrippled Jerrold, from a pinched, lower-middle-class background, was a waspish, sensitive man, with a sharp, sometimes cruel tongue. He was also generous, loyal, and often quite tender. He had flourished as a *Punch* raconteur, as an editor, and as a comic writer of a considerable but minor talent, best known for his successful popular play *Black-eyed Susan*. He and Dickens had argued impersonally but sharply in 1849 about capital punishment, which Jerrold opposed under any circumstances, whereas Dickens had been willing to settle for the banning of executions in public. After months of estrangement, they found themselves dining separately but in the same room at a club. Jerrold "openly wheeled his chair around, stretched out both his hands in a most engaging manner, and said aloud, with a bright and loving face . . . 'For God's sake, let us be friends again! Life's not long enough for this!' "[42]

Even before the funeral, Dickens began organizing a series of memorial benefits for the widow and children. Far from destitute, the family was not in want, though it had not been left in the comfort that Jerrold's prominent career initially led his friends to expect. He had been "in the course of making a good provision for them, and would have succeeded in doing so, if his life had been spared a little longer." Later, "young Jerrold," whom Dickens thought "just contemptible," objected to what he felt was a slur on his father's and his family's honor by an exaggeration of the family's condition. Such ingratitude made Dickens "sick at heart on the subject," though he was determined "to let the whole matter rest until the Resurrection Day." His insistent generosity was most probably partly an expression of his need to disrupt his summer, to be active if not frenetic again, to find an outlet for his "superfluous fierceness," of which there was none more appropriate for him than the stage and fraternal charity.[43] Pressing into service Jerrold's friends in the theatre, Dickens had the satisfaction of seeing them undertake a benefit performance of *Black-eyed Susan*. He committed himself to two readings and at least two performances of *The Frozen Deep*. He was not yet ready to forsake Richard Wardour.

Dickens was also, perhaps, looking for an excuse to neglect his long-awaited guest, Hans Christian Andersen, "tall, gaunt, and rather ungainly," who had arrived at Gad's Hill on June 11, 1857. He had come to England expressly to see Dickens, with the promise that "you will have me with you a week or a fortnight, and . . . I shall not inconvenience you too much." Nothing could have been more of an understatement. Andersen idolized Dickens; but, in return, he needed lavish praise, attention, and the assurance that his work was admired and he loved. For Andersen, there could never be "enough sugar in the tea." Dickens was too busy, too self-centered, too superficially committed to supply these reassurances, though probably no amount of attention would have been sufficient. To the increasing irritation of everyone in the family, except the frequently absent paterfamilias, Andersen's visit became twice the length that had been intended. In the continental fashion, he needed to be shaved each morning. When the boys refused to do it, he had to be driven into and back from Rochester. Probably he thought walking socially demeaning. His poor English was both held against him and used as a justification for neglect. With the children, his malapropisms, gaucheness, and egoism prompted occasional bad manners. He found the boys pleasant companions sometimes, but mostly insolent. Georgina was "piquante, lively and gifted, but not kind," Catherine beautiful, though plump and "rather indolent." Mary, who resembled her mother, and Kate, who has "quite Dickens's face," seemed to him the centerpieces of "a harmonious household." One evening, "Mary and Miss Hogarth played from Lucia," the next day they played "the whole of Don Juan."[44]

Dickens did little for his guest except to be companionable at dinner, to chat with him some evenings as they walked about Gad's Hill, watching the sun glitter "upon the windows in Rochester," and to console him when his new novel was harshly reviewed. Catherine apparently found him pleasant, even soothing, company, responding warmly to his affection. Blinded by his self-centeredness and ignorance of English patterns, Andersen could hardly see, let alone have a clue to, the tensions of the household. He admired Catherine, praising "a certain soft womanly repose and reserve about her"; but when he occasionally saw her crying and once saw her "come out of a room together with her mother with her eyes full of tears," he made no suppositions about the marriage until later events forced interpretation on what he had seen. When he left, Dickens cruelly wrote on the mirror over the dressing table in the guest room that "Hans Andersen slept in this room for five weeks—which seemed to the family AGES!" Actually, he had stayed part of the time with other friends, particularly in St. John's Wood with Bentley, who was his publisher, part of the time at Tavistock House. He visited the Crystal Palace, "like a fairy city,' and attended the theatre. He disliked, though, the "horrid dust, heat, smoke, and noise" of London. Gad's Hill, especially with Dickens there, was a place where "dew-spangled gossamers lay spread like veils over meadows and ditches." And the visit had been extended when Dickens begged him "most charmingly not to go before I had seen the performance they were giving for Jerrold's widow . . . that he, his wife and daughters were so glad to have me with them." Before he left in early August, Andersen acknowledged that this "highlight of my life" could not have been easy for the family, and he humbly asked his friend to "forget in friendship the dark side which proximity may have shown you in me."[45]

In his glory again as Richard Wardour, Dickens performed his own dark role brilliantly. Andersen was astounded. Dickens "showed himself to be a quite remarkable actor, so free from all those mannerisms one finds in England and France in tragic parts. It was so true, so natural . . . the death-scene so moving that I burst into tears at it." The farce went as well as the tragedy. In the worshiping Andersen's eyes, Dickens was "so rich in humor and fun that it was a fresh revelation." This particular performance, on July 4, 1857, was a private one before the queen and her guests, including the king of Belgium, Prince Albert, and the prince of Prussia, for whom "the entrance and stairs were beautifully decked with flowers." The queen had agreed to attend at the Gallery of Illustration when Dickens respectfully declined to put the play on at Windsor. Her appearance was a compromise between her desire to see the play, after he had called her attention to it, without surrendering her principle of never formally supporting private charities through public appearances, and his reluctance to put it on at the court, mainly because he felt it inappropriate for his daughters to act where they had not been officially introduced. To the delighted queen's invitation to come to her box to accept her thanks, he replied that he could not, since he was in his "farce dress." He did not see himself, as a matter of self-definition as well as an assertion of the dignity of literature, appearing in makeup off-stage. When she tried a second time, he "again hoped her Majesty would have the kindness to excuse my presenting myself in a costume and appearance that were not my own."46

Apparently she did, and so did the audiences in London on July 11, July 25, and August 8. Those who managed to get tickets to see the performances, which were wildly praised in the press and by word of mouth, had the excitement of seeing well-known literary figures performing what had become a national ritual in which glamour, art, and charity were united. After the royal performance, the company had an exultant champagne supper at the *Household Words* office. After the first public performance, they reveled at Albert Smith's large suburban house at Walham Green, everyone in evening dress feasting in a tent on the green lawn in the afternoon, then drinking iced claret on an "Italian warm" evening. At St. Martin's Hall, on the 24th, before two thousand people whose "enthusiasm was something awful," Dickens read *A Christmas Carol*. Before the middle of July, he received an invitation to follow up another such reading on July 31 in Manchester with one or two performances of *The Frozen Deep*. He had not himself thought of doing it there. He would, though, "if a sum of any importance could be gained" that would move him closer in a quantum leap to his goal of raising two thousand pounds.47

But there were significant obstacles. He particularly feared the Free Trade Hall was so large that, in such "a wilderness of space," the stage effects would be obscured and his amateur actresses would not have the power of voice to make themselves heard. "We are committed to nothing," he assured Miss Coutts, who had been sour on his theatricals for decades. He was under pressure, though, to make a decision, and his inclination, despite his exhaustion—"it is rather hard work, after a long book"—was for action and engagement. He decided on July 25 that he "would today discuss our engaging actresses." There was precedent for doing so. In Montreal, in 1842, for the sake of propriety, he had replaced Catherine and the other amateur ladies with professionals. The moral climate in regard to acting as a profession had changed somewhat. His own feelings had changed considerably. Now it was not a question of propriety but of practicality. During the intermission in his reading in Manchester on the thirty-first he made the decision. "Some of the foremost people" urged him to do *The Frozen Deep* "in their city." They "were absolutely certain of the success of two consecutive nights in the Free Trade Hall. . . . If careful calculations should prove the likelihood of a good result," he would do it. "We went into them immediately after the readings—worked them out—and got the advertisement into the next day's paper, before going to bed." As he had already determined, the "Free Trade Hall is too large and difficult, and altogether too public for my girls. So we shall take down actresses in their stead."48

❧ 6 ❧

AT GAD'S HILL, EARLY IN AUGUST 1857, HE ATTENDED TO TWO problems related to the Manchester performances. He did not want to have to perform in the farce immediately after the "agitation and exertion" of playing Wardour. Would Frank Stone relieve him of the burden? Dickens, embarrassed, had to resume the obligation when the Manchester people and Arthur Smith, Albert's brother, whom he had begun to rely on for business advice, urged upon him "in the strongest manner that they were afraid of the change. . . . There was a danger of it being considered disrespectful." On August 2, Dickens asked Emmeline Compton, a professional actress in semiretirement who had acted in his amateur theatricals, to play the role of Lucy Crayford, "Compton and babies permitting." They did not. He then consulted theatre friends, including the manager of the Haymarket, John Baldwin Buckstone, who was also the author of *Uncle John*, the farce accompanying *The Frozen Deep*. He needed three competent professionals on short notice. Perhaps on Buckstone's recommendation, probably on the advice of Alfred Wigan, who managed the Olympic Theatre, he immediately hired Frances Ternan and two of her three daughters, Maria and Ellen.49

After reminding Wills to have "the ladies parts in the 1st and 3rd acts . . . immediately copied," in the next two weeks he rehearsed them for hours and hours.50 To his delight, they were not only thorough professionals, part of an acting family whose commitment to the stage had begun in the latter part of the previous century, but charming people. Frances Ternan's father had worked as a prompter at the Theatre Royal in York. His wife, a minor actress, had a moderately successful career whose descent she alleviated by devoting herself to the rise of her infant prodigy, Frances, who, as Fanny Jarman, had a series of starring provincial roles in the 1820s and 1830s. In 1834, Frances married the handsome Irish actor Thomas Ternan, whom Macready worked with and disliked. Ternan's career did not go well. Under the strain of a failing career and a growing family of young daughters whom their mother began to train for the stage, Ternan went from disappointment to depression to despair. He last performed in 1844. When he attempted suicide, he was placed in a mental home, where in 1846 the impoverished actor died. Macready insisted on helping the family financially, and he also offered work. Supporting her three daughters and herself, Frances Ternan now acted in supporting roles to Macready. Most likely, Dickens saw her in Shakespeare or in *Virginius.*

Frances Ternan's daughters could not escape the family fate. The eldest, Fanny, born in 1835, the year before Dickens' marriage, became a minor child star. With an attractive singing voice, she soon aspired to opera, which she pursued until she gave that up for writing fiction. She had a sharp mind, varied talents, and a distaste for the ordinary stage. Born in 1837, Maria joined Fanny in their joint debut as professional actresses in March 1840, and in 1842 the third daughter, three-year-old Ellen, made her debut. Unlike her two sisters, Maria, whom Dickens remembered seeing perform when she was a little child, would remain on the stage into the 1860s. By the mid-1850s, Frances, wanting a stable life in London for herself and her daughters, had given up touring. Fanny had recently begun to sing professionally. Further training would be necessary. Maria was successful in small comedy roles with Charles Kean at the Olympic. The least theatrical and stage-assertive member of the family, Ellen made her adult debut at the age of eighteen in April 1857. In skimpy male attire, she played Hippomenes in an extravaganza called *Atalanta,* by Frank Talfourd, Thomas Noon Talfourd's son. Having known and liked Frank since his infancy,

Dickens may have been at the performance at the Haymarket, and his friend Buckstone may have introduced him to the young actress, who is reputed to have been in tears, embarrassed by her costume.[51]

Whatever Dickens knew about the Ternans, they knew more about him, though it was all information of the sort available about celebrities. Clearly, they would not damage their careers by participating in such a high-level amateur production, and an association with Dickens and his friends might prove useful. Probably they felt some titillation in coming so close to an international celebrity whose photograph appeared prominently all over England. Maria had already seen him act, having attended one of the performances of *The Frozen Deep* at the Gallery of Illustration. Frances was to appear as Nurse Esther, Maria as Clara Burnham, and Ellen as Lucy Crayford, formerly Georgina's role. In the farce, Dickens was to play Uncle John to Ellen's Eliza Comfort, a complacent young girl whom he rejects in favor of her mother when he discovers that she prefers her young drawing master. At an early rehearsal, Maria confessed, perhaps archly, that she might not be able to bear the pain of the death scene in *The Frozen Deep*, for "it affected me so much when I saw it, that . . . I am afraid of myself." Dickens was deeply impressed, even astounded, at her infusion of personal feeling into her acting performance.

The company went up on August 20, accompanied by Catherine and the now retired amateur actresses. Dickens was slightly ill with facial neuralgia. In Manchester, on the twenty-first and twenty-second, the audiences applauded ecstatically. As he lay dying on the stage in the role of Richard Wardour, "excited by the crying of two thousand people," he imagined "with surprising force and brilliancy . . . new ideas for a story" of noble self-sacrifice, the germ of *A Tale of Two Cities*. Maria leaned over him. "Tears streamed out of her eyes into his mouth, down his beard, all over his rags—down his arms as he held her by the hair." Ellen and her mother stood to the side. Maria "sobbed as if she were breaking her heart, and was quite convulsed with grief." He whispered to her not to be so distressed. There was nothing really the matter. "She could only sob out 'O! It's so sad, O it's so sad.' . . . By the time the curtain fell, we were all crying together."[52]

At Gad's Hill a few days later, he could not find distraction enough to keep him from anger, depression, and restlessness. With the theatricals over, he felt "shipwrecked" again. Prompted by another visit to the zoo to see the snakes fed with live animals, he clung to the image of "two small serpents, one beginning on the tail of a white mouse, and one on the head, and each pulling his own way, and the mouse very much alive all the time, with the middle of him madly writhing." He may have remembered the white mice that ran the machines the boys made at Wellington House Academy. The image of being trapped and devoured pursued him. He had been feeling dispirited in July. The water problem at Gad's Hill, which had already cost him a great deal of money, had been feverishly comic. The well had become blocked, "forlornly, overblown with black and choked . . . garden chaotically dragged up by the roots—everybody tearing their own hair and mine too—what *could* I do! Hahaha! Yah-ho-ho! Manically." Not even finally breaking through to a deep spring of water that would permit a steady flow was more than a temporary relief. At the end of August, it was blocked again, and the frustration "of looking at the dry bath, morning after morning—is gradually changing the undersigned honey-pot into a mad bull."[53]

Nothing seemed to help. He felt "as if the scaling of all the mountains in Switzerland, or the doing of any wild thing until I dropped, would be but a slight relief." Though he explained his feelings to Miss Coutts as the necessary penalty of "an imaginative life and constitution," he expressed himself more personally about the sources of his unhappiness to Collins. "I want to escape from myself. For when *I* do start up and stare myself seedily in the face, as happens to be my case at present, my blankness is inconceivable—indescribable—my misery amazing." What stared back at him in the mirror of self-scrutiny was the numbness that resulted from feeling that life with Catherine was insufferable, not because of her essence but because of his needs. He did not want to live without love, romance, idealization. The thinning hair, the graying beard, made him even the more emotionally keen for life.

He was also experiencing with great discomfort very strong feelings about Ellen Ternan. He could not get her out of his mind. He soon proposed to Collins a diversion, a trip that would both distract him and provide an opportunity for a jointly written "gossipy description" for *Household Words* "of all that we see and all that we don't see." At Gad's Hill, at the beginning of September, the rain was falling, "very sadly—very steadily." If he was not going off shortly, he would "slink into a corner and cry." Having decided on "a foray into the bleak fells of Cumberland," he felt, with the day of departure approaching, that he had "come out of the dark corner into the sun again." After Cumberland, they were to go to Doncaster, ostensibly for the races. As a sport, racing hardly interested him. But Charles Keans's company from the Princess's Theatre, including Maria and Ellen, was to inaugurate on September 14 the opening of the Theatre Royal. Before leaving London, he made the hotel arrangements, reserving the apartment for the entire week, stipulating that he would pay for the full time even if he left sooner in order to make certain that they would have accommodations at such a busy season.54

Before leaving, he raised with Forster his thought that there might be some way to put an end to his marital misery. His friend was not encouraging. Dickens' justification of his restlessness and willfulness as an inherent part of his life as an artist seemed, to Forster, a description, not a justification. He reminded Dickens that he had less reason to complain about his marriage than was often the case when the parties had married very young. Dickens was beyond argument, though, and had not raised the subject for the purpose of amelioration. "The years have not made it easier to bear for either of us; and, for her sake as well as mine, the wish will force itself upon me that something might be done. I know too well it is impossible. There is the fact, and that is all one can say." He went on, though. "Nor are you to suppose that I disguise from myself what might be urged on the other side. I claim no immunity from blame. There is plenty of fault on my side . . . in the way of a thousand uncertainties, caprices, and difficulties of disposition; but only one thing will alter that, and that is, the end which alters everything."55 But his assumption of his share of the blame at this time and in this context may have been part of his preparation for some change short of death. He was used to challenging the impossible.

Only with Forster could he confess such feelings. The subject exceeded the limits of his other friendships, intimate as numbers of them were. Also, despite his general impulsiveness, he was shy about personal matters, and there was an aspect of him that was more than private in the ordinary sense, that was indeed secretive, perhaps going back to the need to suppress some of the facts of early family life and his experience at the blacking factory. Since Forster knew so much, Dickens felt comfortable with his knowing even more, though such knowledge at times strained their relationship and made it more difficult for him to relax with Forster than with some other friends. Once he began confiding his thoughts about his marriage, however, he could hardly stop. It was a great relief to him, "and I can get this from you, because I can speak of it to no one else." Catherine and he simply were "not made for each other. . . . She is . . . amiable and complying; but we are strangely ill-assorted for the bond there is between us." They had done nothing but make one another unhappy, and each would have been much better off with someone else. The incompatibility was insurmountable. "Her temperament will not go with mine." And something had changed. "It mattered not so much when we had only ourselves to consider, but reasons have been growing since which make it all but hopeless that we should ever try to struggle on." Perhaps he was alluding to his feelings for Ellen. He now read the past as an inevitable pattern that had been in progress since Mary Hogarth's death, though he preferred to make the explicit reference to her namesake's birth. "What has now befallen me I have seen steadily coming, ever since the days you remember when Mary was born; and I know too well that you cannot, and no one can, help me."

Perhaps, though, Forster could help with something else. Immediately before leaving for Cumberland, as if future alternatives were very much on his mind, Dickens raised the idea of paying for Gad's Hill "by reviving that old idea of some Readings from my books. I am very strongly tempted. Think of it. . . ." Gad's Hill Place, though, had already been paid for. His accounts with Bradbury and Evans were superlative: £2,317 of *Little Dorrit* proceeds to be paid shortly, his regular income from *Household Words,* and the plan to work his copyrights more effectively by creating a deluxe edition of his complete works "for the better class of readers," which "would keep me well before the public without wasting me."[56] The advance he had gotten against future royalties could be retired easily and comfortably from his ongoing income. In raising the prospect of readings at this time, Dickens may have had in mind the likelihood that an alteration in his marital arrangement would add expense to his existing obligations.

With Collins, in misty, rainy Cumberland, he felt energetic, temporarily relieved of the emotional drain of family and wife. Whatever plans were on his mind, he found relief in action. "Too late," he told Forster the next month, "to say, put the curb on, and don't rush at hills—the wrong man to say it to. I have now no relief but in action. I am becoming incapable of rest. I am quite confident I should rust, break, and die, if I spared myself. Much better to die, doing." In Cumberland, there were literal hills to rush at. In a heavy rain, they climbed Carrick Fell. They went up in the afternoon. It became dark more quickly than they had expected, "rain terrific, black mists, darkness of night." Their guide turned out to be incompetent. Dickens triumphantly pulled a compass out of his pocket as they began the descent. In a short while, the compass broke. "Darker and darker," they went "round and round the mountain." When they came to a roaring stream, they followed it, on his suggestion, down toward the river. "Leaps, splashes, and tumbles, for two hours. C. lost. C.D. whoops. Cries for assistance from behind. C.D. returns. C. with horribly sprained ankle, lying in a rivulet. . . . C.D. carrying C. melodramatically (Wardour to the life!) everywhere." In Wigton, in Lancaster, and then in Doncaster, Collins could hardly walk. He "never goes with me on any expedition," Dickens sighed, "without receiving some damage or other." The two traveling celebrities were constantly recognized and helped. Collins soon got around "with two thick sticks like an admiral in a farce." In the hotel suite they shared, where they began writing "The Lazy Tour of Two Idle Apprentices," which appeared in *Household Words* in five installments in October, Dickens was "perpetually tidying the rooms . . . and carrying all sorts of untidy things which belong to [Collins] into his bedroom, which is a picture of disorder."[57]

In his self-portrait as Francis Goodchild in "The Lazy Tour," Dickens provided himself with the titillation and the relief of admitting to the public what the public would not take as literally true, that he was experiencing the pangs of having fallen in love. He probably unselfconsciously rehearsed his anger at and rejection of Catherine in the painful, harsh story, inserted in "The Lazy Tour," of a man who hates his wife so much that he is literally successful in willing her death. In Doncaster primarily to see Ellen, he felt a combination of secretiveness, playfulness, and pleasure. He teasingly confided to Wills that he wished he "was as good a boy in all things" as he was in not replying to "young Jerrold." But "Lord bless you, the strongest parts of your present correspondent's heart are made up of weaknesses. And he just come to be here at all (if he knew it) along of his Richard Wardour! Guess that riddle, Mr. Wills."

At the Theatre Royal, he saw Maria and Ellen perform in one of Mark Lemon's comedies. Both writers, instantly recognized when they entered the theatre, "at once became objects of the most marked attention and conversation." Dickens "had been behaving excessively ill in the way of gasping and rubbing [his] head wearily . . . without the slightest idea that anybody knew" him when, "at the fall of the curtain . . . the pit suddenly got up without the slightest warning, and cried out 'Three cheers for Charles Dickens Esquire!' Thereupon all the house took it up" and "the actors came back and joined in the demonstration." With Frances Ternan and her eldest daughter also in Doncaster, the Ternan presence was larger, though not more prominent, than his. The attention he attracted must have given him increased warning of how public a man he was, though private meetings with the Ternans and even a public outing to the race course could not have been damaging. To Wills, he riddled again, "so let the riddle and the riddler go their own wild way, and no harm come of it."[58]

At Tavistock House, harm did come of it. Catherine's anger, depression, and self-disparagement exploded into one of her periodic outbursts of jealousy. Whether or not she had any specific target in mind in addition to her husband is unclear. He told Emile de la Rue, from whom he expected knowledgeable sympathy, that she "has obtained positive proof of my being on the most confidential terms with, at least fifteen thousand women of various conditions in life . . . since we left Genoa. Please to respect me for this vast experience. . . . We put the skeleton away in the cupboard, and very few people, comparatively, know of its existence." The image of the skeleton and the closet was not entirely accidental, and was unintentionally ironic. In his feelings, the weighty Catherine had become reduced to flesh without bones, a person without inner substance, someone to be locked away. With casual hostility, he disparaged her as mother, wife, and human being, and praised Georgina. Just before the middle of October, he ordered two separate rooms to be created out of what had been before one bedroom, a bathroom, and a large dressing room. "The sooner it is done, the better."[59] As far as he was concerned, the marriage was over.

CHAPTER ELEVEN

My Own Wild Way
(1857-1859)

❧ I ❧

"A MISPLACED AND MISMARRIED MAN," DICKENS WROTE ABOUT himself in his notebook. "Always, as it were, playing hide and seek with the world and never finding what Fortune seems to have hidden when he was born." The prison of his childhood had closed more tightly around him now, and he had difficulty in distinguishing between formative feelings that derived from those early days and the adult realities of his present life. In being fettered to Catherine, he was still being victimized by his mother. "Only last night, in my sleep," he would tell Macready in late winter 1858, "I was bent upon getting over a perspective of barriers, with my hands and feet bound. Pretty much what we are all about, waking, I think?" He believed that he faced a life-and-death struggle for survival, that his sanity and creativity depended on his becoming happy again. He defined happiness as both the absence of someone whose very presence depressed him and as the opportunity to express his ability to recapture from hostile forces "the Princess whom I adore—you have no idea how intensely I love her! . . . Nothing would suit me half so well . . . as climbing after her sword in hand, and either winning her or being killed."[1]

That the princess was Ellen Ternan mattered less than that he needed a princess. The prospect of being killed in those fantasy terms had a romantic fascination. The struggle would be revitalizing, the threat of literally dying hardly serious. The threat of madness or extinction seemed greater in remaining with his marital obligations than in making the long-anticipated, deeply feared change. Better to die feeling alive in the struggle than to continue an unsatisfactory half-life half-death, without love, romance, or idealization. Forty-five years old in 1857, he had no reason to believe that he would live to a contented old age. Having been discontented all his life, he accepted that now as his natural state. But much more of life was behind him than ahead, even without taking into account the dismal family figures on longevity. Only Elizabeth Dickens seemed to be defying them, and, given the Hogarths' demonstrated longevity, he had the frightening prospect of a premature old age with an undesired wife who would probably outlive him. The primary issue was not Ellen Ternan but his own future. Only his will could save him from an intolerable marriage.

His willfulness, though, flared and faded, and then flared again. He needed reasons to be angry enough to act. In October 1857 it was far from clear what more he could do other than what he had just done. Probably it had taken an exacerbating incident for him no longer to share a bedroom with Catherine. Perhaps she had become aware, through a jeweler's error, of a bracelet he may have sent to Ellen. The story, and its date, have a fragile source. Certainly Catherine knew about his preoccupation with the actress, probably because he told her, attempting to disguise his romantic feelings as paternal concern. She felt bewildered, tearful, and angry at his moodiness, his flirtations, his impatience, repeatedly accusing him of adultery. Ellen seemed only the latest in a long history of unfaithfulness. Dickens' elaborations on his mismarriage became obsessive. He thought Catherine insensitive, even in public, to his achievements. Just her presence had become an unconscious reminder of irresponsible mothering and obese insensitivity. Toward the middle of the month, after one turbulent argument, he performed his "celebrated feat of getting out of bed at 2 in the morning and walk-

ing" to Gad's Hill "from Tavistock House—over 30 miles—
through the dead night. I had been very much put-out; and I
thought, 'After all, it would be better to be up and doing something, than lying here.' So I got up and did that."[2] It may have
been after this desperate hike or after another of the bitter
arguments that the family had been used to for years that he
wrote from Gad's Hill to change their sleeping arrangement.
Because her accusations of infidelity were not literally true, they
had an additional power to infuriate him. They provoked and
intensified his defensiveness, his sense of moral grievance, his
self-righteousness. Their emotional accuracy increased his guilt
and strengthened his will to free himself from such painful
truth telling.

There were ineffective efforts at mediation. Georgina tried.
The differences, though, were beyond her powers of amelioration, let alone reconciliation. Her own temperament and loyalty
were more inclined to Dickens, who had made himself the center of her life, than to Catherine, who could not effectively
compete with him for children, family, or friends, even for the
loyalty of her own sister. Some of her lassitude over the years
may have been an effort to make a passive virtue out of unavoidable defeat. He was perfectly capable of insisting on managing
everything himself, and then blaming Catherine for being dependent on him. Aware of the estrangement, the Hogarths tried
to reconcile their daughter and son-in-law. Dickens' resentment
of his in-laws had increased in tandem with his anger at Catherine. They seemed another family burden, an exploitation, a
cannibalizing of his substance, even the more painful because he
had at times encouraged their dependency. He did not want to
hear the family's Scottish accent ever again. Probably the reti-
cent George Hogarth did little more than keep his fingers
crossed. Dickens had never liked the elder Georgina Hogarth.
Her efforts to rally her daughter both doubled Catherine's tearful, irritating presence and strengthened his detestation of both
of them. The Hogarths were in no position to help their daughter. When, in February 1858, Catherine wrote to Miss Coutts for
help in finding a job for her brother Edward, whose unemploy-
ment was "a serious and anxious thing," Dickens' anger flared.
He was being used again. "I hope you will forgive her," he told
Miss Coutts, "more freely and readily than I do."[3]

In November 1857, he sent Collins the little he had done of the new Christmas story on which they were collaborating. "Hope you are all right at last?" He himself was dismal, alternating between fantasies of escape and episodes of depression. Not even hard work was sufficient relief. The Christmas number, "The Perils of Certain English Prisoners," which he had "planned with great care" and of which he had written two of the three chapters, was an effort to celebrate "some of the best qualities of the English character that have been shewn in India." His depiction of the natives, displaced from India to the South Pacific, was bitterly racist, as were his many private comments on British enemies in the Orient in these years of the India Mutiny and the Chinese wars. The heart of the story, though, was a personal fantasy that dramatized variants of himself as St. George rescuing from a devouring dragon a slim, blond English beauty, who, as Mary Hogarth had, lives with her sister and brother-in-law. The narrator, much beneath Lady Maryon's station, devotes his life to protecting the woman he loves. He is contented that she be happy in another man's deserving arms as long as he may continue to serve her. One of the ways in which Dickens could serve Ellen was through the power of his influence, his friendships. In October, he had expressed his appreciation to Buckstone for employing her at the Haymarket Theatre. "I need hardly tell you that my interest in the young lady does not cease with the effecting of this arrangement, and that I shall always regard your taking of her and remembering her, as an act of personal friendship to me. On the termination of her present engagement, I hope you will tell me, before you tell her, what you see for her, 'coming in the future.' "4

Whatever he could envision of his own future, apparently he imagined Ellen playing an important role in it. Whatever the combination of daughter, sister, lover, and wife his romantic fantasies and his lifelong female archetypes created, his emotional commitment probably was strengthened by his sense of the obstacles that had to be overcome. "I don't like the Realities except when they are unattainable—*then*, I like them of all things." At this point, he could hardly put the obstacles in concrete terms. At times he found it easier to express himself as if he were being a father to a fatherless child, a protector and friend of the family. In March 1858, he responded to a request from Richard Bentley that he had no influence with theatre managers. If he had "any really serviceable influence in such wise," Dickens told Bentley, "there are claims upon it which would go before all others and exclude all others."5 Dickens' attempts to advance Ellen's and her sisters' careers had some of the urgency of his efforts for his own children. But he was not a man who needed or wanted more children. Using his influence for Ellen's advantage could not have been misunderstood by his friends. His own confusions were understandable.

Through the fall and winter of 1857–58, he struggled to get his work done. He found it difficult to sleep. When awake, he could not keep to any one task. He did keep up with his *Household Words* chores, but there he had Wills, Morley, and Collins to rely on. He fulfilled his usual pattern of long walks and private dinners, and managed to maintain an air of business and social normalcy. Occasionally, though, domestic desperation and romantic obsession burst through, especially when writing at length to old friends. A few of them, and certainly his family, knew of his distress. His association with Ellen was not hidden, only disguised. He missed Bryan Procter's birthday party in November for the first time in years, for "a special, made, engagement—not to be broken." Worst of all, he found it difficult to write. Much of the energy for writing "Perils" came from the imposition of immediate fantasy onto his restlessness. Also, the *Household Words* deadline imposed an unavoidable discipline that not even he could escape. After it was done, he felt in the Richard Wardour mood again. At the end of January 1858, he discussed with Forster his "growing inclinations of a fitful and undefined sort . . . to fall to work on a new book." If he could start now and work on through the summer, "the anxious toil . . . would have its neck well broken before beginning to publish, next October or November." He had a possible title, "One of These Days." But he was ambivalent, indecisive. "I had better not worry my worried mind for a while. . . . I think it would be of no use if I did, for I couldn't settle to one occupation."6

The first weeks of 1858 passed with an absence that those in his immediate circle could not avoid noticing. For the first time in years, he had neither the desire nor the energy to organize Twelfth Night theatricals in honor of Charley's birthday. He

made improvements at Gad's Hill, yet he did them almost me-
chanically. "I have no interest in the place," he told Forster on
New Year's Day. Against his better judgment, he had made
commitments long before to read *A Christmas Carol* for charity,
unable to resist the flattery and the challenge. He read three
times in January 1858, in Rochester, Coventry, and Bristol,
where an observer noticed that "his hair had been thinned upon
his head, and the lines have been deepened upon his face. . . ."
He had also committed himself to read in Edinburgh in April.
In December 1857, though, he had told his old friend Arthur
Ryland, a wealthy Birmingham businessman, that he could not
read in Birmingham "this Christmas. . . . I have nothing to
read." He did not want to repeat *A Christmas Carol.* "My work
in the summer for the Jerrold Fund—and very hard work indeed, it was—completely deprived me of the opportunity I had
expected to have, of getting some new reading together. . . . I
have not a chance of getting to the work of considering any of
my larger books; and when I look at your letter again, I drift
away, bodily, out to sea. You know I don't want the will. But
what am I to do without the power?"7

His explanation to Ryland was mostly candid. He had for
some time desired to create readings from his novels, particularly from *David Copperfield,* and he had not done so. He already
had more commitments than he wanted. In addition, the idea of
doing readings on a more extensive scale for his own profit still
simmered. It would be foolish to take on more charity readings
(though he could not tell that to Ryland) at a time when that idea
was becoming increasingly attractive. And he was tired, certainly depressed. The dark winter months were unusually difficult. He did find the energy in February to fulfill his promise
to preside at a dinner to raise funds for the new Hospital for Sick
Children on Great Ormond Street. He gave a lengthy, moving
speech, invoking a neglected infant he had seen in an egg box
in Edinburgh years ago, asking "why, in the name of a gracious
God, such things should be!" With unconscious resonances of
his own childhood neglect always available to him, he could
summon energy on that topic no matter what his resources
otherwise. In March, all his misery seemed focused on one
source. "The domestic unhappiness remains so strong upon me
that I can't write, and (waking) can't rest, one minute. I have

never known a moment's peace or content since the last night of *The Frozen Deep*. I do suppose that there never was a man so seized and rended by one spirit. In this condition though nothing can alter it."[8]

What was the "one spirit"? Was it hatred of his life with Catherine? Was it love of Ellen Ternan? Was it seemingly irresolvable conflict and confusion, for which he had always had so little tolerance? Though the answer is not forthcoming, the condition was intensely felt. He responded to it characteristically. Better to consume himself in outward action than in immobilizing introspection. He had a stage at hand. He had been preparing himself to give public readings for his own profit for many years. Ample precedent existed for public lectures by distinguished literary people, like Carlyle and Thackeray, who had been well paid for reading from their own writings. Previously he had acceded to Forster's objections to his idea that he do a reading series for profit. His own desires and reservations, though, had been expressed in comic form, a sure sign of his seriousness. Anyway, his preference was for acting rather than for reading, and it remained that. But professional acting seemed incompatible with his career as a writer and troublesome to his hard-earned status as a gentleman. Public readings from his own works were less dangerous.

In September 1857, before going to Cumberland, he had again raised the idea. Forster remained opposed, primarily on the grounds of the dignity of literature. Going onstage seemed too much like going to the public with hat in hand. Probably Forster also had in mind that the energy expended on the stage would be lost to literature. With the success of *Household Words* and royalty income from copyrights, the financial justification seemed hardly compelling. Conditioned by a lifetime of insecurity, Dickens had put it as a monetary proposition, connecting it to the high cost of purchasing Gad's Hill. Forster's opposition was based partly on his own long-standing ill health having made him cautious about wasteful expenditures of energy, partly on the scars he still felt from many bitter years of ambivalent social standing. Also, his profitable marriage had made him less sensitive to Dickens' financial anxiety.

If Dickens had any self-protective conservatism, it was only about the status of the literary profession. In March 1858, he argued persistently against his friend's strongly stated objections. Forster worried that readings would put an additional strain on his marriage. Dickens, though, urged him to consider it as a totally separate subject that could have no effect on what was essentially a dead relationship. He wanted advice "apart from all personal likings and dislikings and solely with a view to its effect on that particular relation (personally affectionate and like no other man's) . . between me and the public." In spite of Dickens' urgent request for guidance, it is likely that he was well on his way toward making up his mind. As a favor to the author, he had just spent a stultifying evening, exerting himself not to fall asleep, listening to a minor playwright, Westland Marston, read "a very bad play." Afterward, at Tavistock House, over cigars with Wilkie Collins, Dickens "fell into a chair with such a sudden relief from the oppressive bottling of a cask of absurdity through three long hours" that he laughed himself "into hysterics."[9] What Marston did so badly, he could do superlatively well.

After a brilliantly successful reading in Edinburgh in late March (he never tired of emphasizing how successful his readings were) Dickens had made up his mind to go ahead. For months, in a state of "energetic restlessness," he had been "devising all sorts of things." As much as he desired to, he could not be Richard Wardour again upon the acting stage, with the "transitory satisfaction of sending my very heart out of my body. . . . It was a good thing to have a couple of thousand people all rigid and frozen together, in the palm of one's hand." It was not, then, mainly a question of money. "The mere physical effort and change of the Readings," he told Collins, "would be good, as another means of bearing" his marital situation. He seemed unable to do anything else that was productive. After consulting Miss Coutts, whom he reported not at all dismayed by the idea, though she had always opposed his theatrical activity, on March 15 he raised it as a business proposition to Evans. How would such readings influence the sales of his next book? "If it had any . . . at all, would it be likely to be of a weakening or a strengthening kind?" He put it to him as if he had already made up his mind. After his last benefit reading on April 15, 1858, he would give in May and June a course of four or six readings at St. Martin's Hall in London and then "in August, September and

October, in the Eastern Counties, the West of England, Lancashire, Yorkshire, and Scotland. I should read from 35 to 40 times," and afterward return to those places where it had been successful. "By March or April *a very large sum of money* would be cleared and Ireland would be still untouched; not to speak of America where I believe I could make (if I could resolve to go there) ten thousand pounds."[10] Probably Evans did not demur. It could only increase the sale of books. If he had, it would have made no difference.

To Forster's objections, Dickens granted that the question was "a balance of doubts." No one felt more deeply the honor of the literary calling. "But . . . do you consider that the public exhibition of oneself takes place equally, whosoever may get the money? And have you any idea that at this moment . . . half the public at least supposes me to be paid . . . ? Out of the twenty or five-and-twenty letters a week that I get about Readings, twenty will ask at what price?" When he returned from Edinburgh, where he had been given a lovely cup to the applause of two thousand people, he confessed that all the rational arguments were unavailing. "My determination is all but taken." Of course he would not do it unless there was the opportunity for immense profit—he was a professional man, with large expenses. With a collapsing marriage and the possible expense of separate homes, perhaps even new dependents, of course he would need every penny he could earn. But he had to make some change anyway. The emotional pattern of his life was unbearable. "I must do *something,* or I shall wear my heart away. I can see no better thing to do that is half so hopeful in itself, or half so well suited to my restless state."[11]

Throughout April 1858 "a crowd of cares" pursued him. He kept as best he could to his usual activities and away from Catherine, eliminating her from invitations he accepted with the excuse that she hardly ever dined out. On April 29, he walked "rather stiffly, right shoulder well forward," with a geranium in his buttonhole and his gloves in his hand, to the front of the platform of a crowded St. Martin's Hall. There was "a roar of cheering that might have been heard at Charing Cross." The most popular author of his generation, whose words and face were a household vision in the English-speaking world, found himself basking alone in the spotlight of a curiosity and adulation so strong that it was as if audience and author had been preparing a lifetime for such a mutual apotheosis.

There were some preliminaries to dispatch. These were his friends, his supporters, his lifeblood, if not intimate at least precious companions. He had an intuitive sense of what was the right thing in their relationship. He owed them an explanation. At an expense of time and money, he told them, he had for years been giving readings for charity. Under the pressure of more requests than he could fulfill, he had either to give up reading altogether or to make it a regular part of his professional life. He had satisfied himself that "it can involve no possible compromise of the credit and independence of literature," that "whatever brings a public man and his public face to face, on terms of mutual confidence and respect is a good thing," and that he already knew from experience how helpful such readings were in "strengthening those relations—I may almost say of personal friendship—which it is my great privilege and pride, as it is my great responsibility, to hold with a multitude of persons who will never hear my voice or see my face. . . . I proceed to read this little book, quite as composedly as I might proceed to write it, or to publish it any other way."[12] He opened *The Cricket on the Hearth,* and began to read.

❦ 2 ❦

ON THE MORNING OF MAY 10, 1858, HE TOLD HIS ELDEST SON THAT HE and Catherine had decided to live separately. The stunned young man, taken entirely by surprise, was the only one of the children to be faced with a choice, perhaps because he was the eldest, perhaps because he was a male, perhaps because his father feared criticism if Catherine had none of her children living with her. He could either maintain his residence with his father or live with his mother. The rest of the children would stay with their father at Tavistock House and Gad's Hill Place, since to allow Catherine to have more than one child would undermine his claim that the separation was justified partly because of her incompetence. To others, he implied that Charley was the only one of the children willing to live with her. Clearly, though, it was his son's decision. Later, Dickens persuaded himself and repeatedly claimed that he had generously determined that their eldest son would live with his mother, as an expression of his own fairness, generosity, and concern. That afternoon, Charley told him "that I am afraid I did not completely make myself clearly understood to you. . . . Don't suppose that in making my choice, I was actuated by any feeling of preference for my mother to you. God knows I love you dearly, and it will be a hard day for me when I have to part from you and the girls."[13]

In early May Dickens had begun action to "put a wider space" between himself and Catherine "than can be found in one house." Whether any specific event precipitated what was to be an unshakable resolution is unclear. Perhaps the misdelivered-necklace incident occurred now. Perhaps he had attempted to force her to pay a social call on Ellen, as his daughter years later claimed. Perhaps Mrs. Hogarth put heavy pressure on him to redress her daughter's grievances, with the threat of publicity or even legal action. Perhaps the immediate success of the readings raised his spirits and determination to free himself from what seemed interminable conflict. Perhaps Catherine again expressed her preference for being discarded rather than humiliated. Her aunt claimed that "the affair was brought to a compromise, to avoid a public court, that she should agree to a separate maintenance, after various absurd proposals he made, of her going abroad to live alone, or keeping her to her own apartment in his house in daily life, at the same time to appear at his parties, still as mistress of the house . . . and to visit their friends in turns with him, and at another time proposing that when he and his family lived in the town house, she should occupy with a servant the country house or vice versa." Everyone's nerves may have been stretched so far that any resolution seemed better than perpetuating the anxiety. Over a month before, Dickens had told Forster that "nothing can put" this marriage "right, until we are dead and buried and risen. It is not, with me, a matter of will, or trial, or sufferance, or good humour, or making the best of it, or making the worst of it, any longer. It is all despairingly over. Have no lingering hope of, or for, me in this association. A dismal failure has to be borne, and there an end."[14]

When it came, the termination was a heavier burden than Dickens had anticipated. Practical arrangements had to be made, emotional scores settled, other people's as well as his own anger dealt with. The thought of divorce was instantly dismissed. He could not afford it. Despite recent simplification of the law, divorce threatened irretrievable damage to any public man who needed broad support, whether for office or art. He held a unique position that demanded the constant approbation, expressed in sales, of his constituency, for whom he represented a value system, a way of life. Divorce seemed too great a risk. The dangers of a separation were fewer. Of course there would be private talk. There would be broader rumors. He had high hopes, though, that the damage could be readily controlled. To negotiate the practical terms, he turned to Forster. With weary loyalty, he took on the charge. They readily agreed to Catherine's request that Mark Lemon, the genial, domestic Uncle Porpoise, represent her. It was to be a family affair.

By the middle of May 1858, the negotiations were in progress. Now that he had made up his mind to do it, having it done quickly seemed of desperate urgency. The legal niceties would be attended to by lawyers. The terms, though, would be negotiated between husband and wife through their appointed emissaries. Evans was proposed as a trustee. Suspicious that he was hostile, Dickens and Forster vetoed that. Legally, Dickens' property and other resources were neither the family's nor the marriage's. They belonged to him alone. With all the cards in his hands, he dealt them in a way he thought reasonable, even generous. He would "do anything for her Comfort, and spend anything upon her." He would maintain her at the same level of support, as if the marriage still existed, except that she would live in a new residence of her choice. The initial draft of the deed of separation provided her with "£400 a year and a brougham." Charley would live with his mother, in a place in London to be determined later. At a meeting on May 21, everything was "as good as settled." The next day Lemon wrote to Forster that "Mrs. Dickens thankfully accepts the proposal."[15]

While the negotiations proceeded, Dickens took some pains to justify his decision. The effort was entirely private, and done with the low-keyed urgency of minimally threatened self-interest. Catherine's mother and youngest sister, Helen, fumed in the background. Dickens told Miss Coutts, who he believed was "not quite unprepared for what I am going to say," that his marriage had been for a long time "as miserable a one as ever was made." They were incompatible on every level. She was the only person he had ever known with whom he could "not get on somehow or other." There was no "interest, sympathy, confidence, sentiment, tender union of any kind between them." Probably all this *was* news to Miss Coutts, who had seen them over the years provide a reasonable facsimile of getting on. It was shocking news to be told that Catherine was estranged from all her children, that she was an incompetent, unnatural mother, that her children "harden into stone" in her presence. Georgina, "the best, the most unselfish, and most devoted of human Creatures," knew this. Within months of their marriage, the long-dead Mary Hogarth had recognized it. "It is her misery to live in some fatal atmosphere which slays every one to whom she should be dearest. It is my misery that no one can ever understand the truth in its full force, or know what a blighted and wasted life my married life has been." He asked her not to "think the worst" of Catherine, who could not help being the way she was. "If she had married another sort of man she might however have done better. I think she always felt herself to be at a disadvantage of groping blindly about me, and never touching me, and has so fallen into the most miserable weaknesses and jealousies. Her mind has, at times, been certainly confused besides."[16]

At best, it was an ungenerous letter, presenting a position that he had repeated frequently enough over many years to attest to his having persuaded himself of its truth. It is unlikely that he persuaded Miss Coutts, who made an effort ten days later to reconcile the couple. "But nothing on earth—no, not even you—no consideration," he told her, "human or Divine, can move me from the resolution I have taken." To his American friend Cornelius Felton, he wrote more coolly. "I have been much distressed for some weeks past, by domestic matters. Although they are not yet finally arranged, they were last night . . . as good as settled; the end being, that Mrs. Dickens and I have agreed to live apart henceforth. . . . It is all for the best. We have tried all other things, and they have all broken down under us." Life would not be substantially different. Everything would remain the same, except for Catherine's absence.

His distress, though, was far from over. Rumblings of trouble had surfaced in the previous week. Naïve and overconfident, he was hardly prepared for them. Inevitably, there would be talk about his relationship with Ellen Ternan. That he had some sort of involvement was the obvious conclusion friends and acquaintances reached. Dickens wanted the relationship described in nondamaging terms. Even his immediate community, though, was not likely to cooperate. By mid-May there was comment that the separation had occurred because he had fallen in love with another woman. Some of the remarks identified her as an actress. Some specifically mentioned Ellen. Suddenly he was additionally distressed to learn that the charges might be coming from the Hogarth family, particularly Mrs. Hogarth, Helen, and Catherine. Certain that his wife, both by personality and principle, would not attempt to do him public damage, he began in the middle of May to believe that "her wicked mother" and sister had no such scruples. Apparently Mrs. Hogarth and Helen had gone with Catherine to see Miss Coutts. His sweeping rejection of her effort to mediate was strengthened by his anger at what seemed a cabal, with overtones of blackmail. "I can not enter—no, not even with you," he told Miss Coutts, "upon any question that was discussed in that woman's presence."

"That woman," though, had raised a more shocking consideration, either as inference or as accusation. Word now reached him that people were saying the marriage was breaking up because he and his sister-in-law had been having an incestuous affair. That he believed the rumor to have originated with Georgina's own family added bitterness to outrage. The allegation had more fascination for curious minds than any consideration of mere adultery with an actress. Reverberating with the horrors of a sacred taboo, it transferred with a vengeance from literature to life his fascination with the female who combines the qualities of both sister and wife. The charge had its basis in the awkward situation that forced Georgina to decide to stay with her idolized brother-in-law in the only home she had known since her youth. Her sole other alternative would be to move into some shadowy, undefined Hogarthian world in which the main consolation would be an affirmation of solidarity with her sister and family. The affirmation would have struck her as meaningless. She had little in common with Catherine. Her parents had relieved themselves of responsibility for her years before. In her brother-in-law's home, she had a role, a future, a rationale for being. She had the love and respect of nieces and nephews. She had the love and respect of her brother-in-law. She had the congenial atmosphere of literary life, the companionship of artistic people. Whatever the awkwardness, she seems not to have hesitated long, if at all. She chose to stay with Dickens. To the Hogarths, it seemed like a blood betrayal.

To her brother-in-law, her decision could not have been surprising. It had been inherent already in the early 1850s in her rejection of Augustus Egg's marriage proposal. Perhaps she had also turned down a proposal from John Forster. As it became apparent that she would remain unmarried, her alternatives had narrowed. Her future seemed irretrievably cast with Dickens' world. That she was Catherine's sister became increasingly secondary. Her efforts to smooth things over, to keep the marriage together, had been at least partly motivated by her awareness that the end of the marriage would force her to make such a choice. The decision would be no less inevitable than the awkwardness. Probably he had no doubt about what her decision would be and counted, in fact, on her remaining with him. That may have been understood between them, silently or not, in the months before the separation. He had not anticipated, though, that they both would have to pay the price of such a decision—the charge that she had been and was his mistress, that the marriage was being ended to facilitate their incestuous relationship.

By the end of the third week in May the allegation had become a public sotto voce of scandalous proportions, soon to become the property of strangers throughout England and the innuendo of newspaper gossip. The threat to his career and livelihood frightened him. The assault on an aspect of his character and honor that he had believed beyond reproach shocked him. Thackeray, aware that "all sorts of horrible stories" were "buzzing about," was told "that D is separated from his wife on account of an intrigue with his sister in law. No says I no such thing—its with an actress." He would "have said nothing about it but that I heard the other much worse story whereupon I told mine to counteract it." He soon heard from an unhappy Dickens authorizing him "to contradict the rumour on his own solemn word and his wife's authority." Though he would have liked to kill two birds with one stone, Dickens must have been hard put to determine whether he should focus on denying incest with Georgina, adultery with Ellen, or both. Despite an immediate campaign of damage control, composed mainly of vigorous denials of both allegations, the rumor concerning Georgina spread rapidly, pregnant with subrumors. Even by October it still had force, coming back to him in the allegation that "he was the outcry of London," and that his "sister in law had three children by him."[18]

There had already been tensions in the negotiations. That was inevitable. They had partly to do with the role of the wicked mother, an archetype that always had his emotions on edge, in pushing for what she believed were her daughter's interests and probably included the mention of Ellen. Some aspect of the negotiation troubled Lemon sufficiently for him to limit his role as intermediary on the twentieth. "I shall never refuse to see Mrs. Dickens but whatever she may do for the future must be done without my interference." On May 25, Dickens composed a long statement, which he gave to Arthur Smith, instructing him to show it where he thought appropriate. It gave an account of the reasons for the separation, strongly praising Georgina in order to emphasize Catherine's incompetence, claiming that family support of Dickens' position was unanimous, and complaining that "two wicked persons who should have spoken very differently of me, in consideration of earned respect and gratitude, have (as I am told, and indeed to my personal knowledge) coupled with this separation the name of a young lady for whom I have a great attachment and regard. I will not repeat her name—I honor it too much. Upon my soul and honor, there is not on this earth a more virtuous and spotless creature than that young lady. I know her to be innocent and pure, and as good as my own dear daughters. Further, I am quite sure that Mrs. Dickens, having received this assurance from me, must now believe it."[19] The two wicked people were Mrs. Hogarth and her daughter Helen, the spotless creature probably Ellen. That Catherine accepted her husband's assurances was a dubious, self-serving claim. Also on the twenty-fifth, Dickens told Collins that soon he would give him the details of this "rather long story—over, I hope now."

Late that same day or early the next, Dickens withdrew the proposal that Catherine had "thankfully accepted" on the twenty-first. He now felt certain that the rumors about Georgina and himself had originated with the Hogarths. Counterattacking, he declined to provide any financial support unless he received their unstinting cooperation in counteracting an allegation more damaging than any that had been made before. Through his lawyer, he insisted that they deny the rumors. Realizing how harmful they were even to his own client's interests, Catherine's lawyer urged compliance. Genial, amiable George Hogarth immediately wrote a memorandum denying the charge of an affair between Dickens and Georgina. Believing this insufficient, Dickens and his lawyer, Frederic Ouvry, demanded that the two alleged perpetrators, the originators of the accusation, sign a statement exculpating him. Reluctantly, under pressure, aware of the interests at stake, on May 29 Mrs. Hogarth and Helen stated in writing that since, "in reference to the differences which have resulted in the separation of Mr. and Mrs. Charles Dickens, certain statements have been circulated that such differences are occasioned by circumstances deeply affecting the moral character of Mr. Dickens and compromising the reputation and good name of others, we solemnly declare that we now disbelieve such statements. We know that they are not believed by Mrs. Dickens, and we pledge ourselves on all occasions to contradict them, as entirely destitute of foundation."[20]

Aware that the statement might be interpreted as having been elicited by economic pressure, Dickens had Ouvry delay drawing up the final deed of separation. The disclaimer was immediately attached to the statement that he had written on the twenty-fifth and put in Smith's hands. Together they dealt with the allegations about both Ellen and Georgina. No written statement, though, had the power to deal effectively with damaging rumors. The initial intent had been that it be shown only privately to interested, even friendly, people, whose denial of the rumors could then be ever the more persuasive because based on authentic statements by the interested parties. Later, when the statements did become public, they turned out to be more damaging than helpful. Those who valued him tended to disbelieve or to think irrelevant the first of the charges. The second was immediately dismissed. To antagonists, both provided amusement or self-righteous but titillating shock. The general public, despite the publicity, had sufficient skepticism about such things to suspend judgment. to forget reasonably quickly, and to continue to value him highly for the same reasons that they had previously.

In late May 1858, Dickens continued to defend himself, counterattacking in letters to friends and acquaintances. The letter campaign drew some snickers from the neutral and the hostile. To Maria Beadnell, an odd, unpromising choice. he had Georgina write, though probably he dictated the letter, that for reasons of incompatibility, "by *mutual consent* and for the reasons I have told you, *and no other,*" he and Catherine had come to this arrangement. The point of the letter, though, was practical. "To a few of our *real* friends Charles wishes the *truth* to be stated, and they cannot show their friendship better than by quietly silencing with the real solemn truth any foolish or wicked person who may repeat such lies and slanders." Many were to supporters. "The change had become indispensable and unavoidable," he told Macready, "and . . . we must all be the happier for it." With his extraordinary capacity for being willful once a decision had been made, he did not have "the faintest lingering doubt upon the subject . . . and I steadily desire to dismiss it."

To Mary Boyle, who had "seen something of the great misfortune of my life" and who knew "the truth," he responded, probably about Ellen, that "my only surprise in the matter of your note, is, that you have heard nothing worse!!! I have been the hero of such bewildering and astonishing lies during the last week, that this merely infernal one seems quite a favor. It is the penalty I pay for my conspicuous position. It is a very heavy one; but it is what I owe to the knaves and fools, and I must take their receipt for it." There was nothing to be done "but to circulate the truth. And if you will do that . . . you will gratify your own earnest and generous nature in serving the friend who loves you." To another sympathizer, he confessed that he had "heard such bewildering and thronging multitudes of wonderful and inexplicable lies about myself during the last week, that it almost bewilders me to find you in possession of the truth." At some length he rehearsed his version of the facts of the separation, for "it would be a poor example to be driven mad myself or to drive Mrs. Dickens mad; and one or both of the two results must have happened, if we had gone on living together." It was a consolation to him to claim that "there is no anger or ill-will between us . . . that it is calmly and moderately done; that whatever doubt or passion there has ever been on either side, has already died out; that I am sure we only want to forgive and forget, and live at peace."[21]

There was no peace, though. The rumors did not desist. The private-letter strategy did not work, or was not working quickly enough. Speculation about his separation rippled outward from semiprivate discussions into public newspapers. He felt frantic with being attacked by forces that he could not control, as if he were under siege or being held hostage to ignorance and maliciousness. The circle of rumor widened from England to the Continent and to America. Some of the private response was contemplative and compassionate, if not for Dickens then for Catherine. "I'd give £100 if it weren't true," Thackeray said. "To think of the poor matron after 22 years of marriage going away out of the house!" From Paris, Elizabeth Barrett Browning bewailed "this sad story about Dickens and his wife. Incompatibility of temper after twenty-three years of married life!—What a plea!—brook then irregularity of the passions, it seems to me . . . taking the mother from one child and the father from another, and the sense of family love and union from them all. . . . Poor woman!—She must suffer bitterly."[22] Much of the impersonal public comment, though, delighted in a thoughtless nastiness, some of it gossip for its own sake. Some of it, however, expressed the puzzlement, even bewilderment, of those attempting to reconcile their view of him derived from reading his novels and the view of him implicit in this scandal. To this latter group he decided to address himself publicly.

At the beginning of June 1858, Forster recommended that, as an extension of the personal-letter campaign, Dickens write to some well-known American who, with the facts before him, would help counteract the rumors there. Consulting with Ouvry, Dickens decided that the "American idea is altogether untenable. Surely on your knowledge of human nature (to say nothing of the peculiarity of the American character . . .), you cannot think it possible that I should write to any distinguished man in America, asking him to do for me *what I have not done for myself here*! It is absurd. And it is just because no public step can possibly be taken for my good, anywhere, until I have taken one here, that I feel I *must* move—somehow." Having made this determination, he composed a statement for publication, which he sent to Catherine. "I will not write a word as to any *causes* that have made it necessary for me to publish the enclosed in Household Words. Whoever there may be among the living, who I will never forgive alive or dead, I earnestly hope that all unkindness is over between you and me. But as you are referred to in the article, I think you ought to see it. You have only to say to Wills . . . that you do not object to the allusion."[23] He also intended to have it published in all the journals and newspapers, and to encourage its republication abroad. Apparently she did not object or her objections were dismissed. On the day on which he solicited her consent to his referring to her in the statement, she signed, in Brighton where she was resting, the final version of the separation deed. It provided two hundred pounds per annum more than had the earlier draft.

The next day Forster talked for an hour and a half with John Delane, the editor of the *Times*, about the wisdom of publishing the statement. Having been forced by Forster's doubts to reconsider, Dickens soon triumphantly reported to Macready, who "will see that some printed words of mine were laid on the breakfast-table this morning in the Times," that "Delane on the whole decided *in favor of the publication*. This turned the balance—as we had settled that it should, either way." On June 8 Dickens' statement appeared in the *Manchester Guardian*, and he expected its publication in other newspapers and journals. He had arranged for its front-page appearance in the next issue of *Household Words*, on June 12, under the heading PERSONAL. To Macready, he was specific and named names. "The question was not I myself; but others. Foremost among them—of all people in the world—Georgina! Mrs. Dickens's weakness, and her mother's and her youngest sister's wickedness, drifted to that, without seeing what they would strike against—though I warned them in the strongest manner."

Naturally, the published statement was bland, much like the letter he had written on May 25 and entrusted to Smith. "Some domestic troubles of mine, of long-standing" have "lately been brought to an arrangement" with "no anger or ill-will. . . . By some means," though, "arising out of wickedness, or out of folly, or out of inconceivable wild chance, or out of all three, this trouble has been made the occasion of misrepresentations, most grossly false, most monstrous, and most cruel—involving not only me, but innocent persons dear to my heart."[24] Whatever there was of truth in the statement, it was sufficiently awkward to convince no one not already convinced. The rhetoric seemed hollow at best, cowardly at worst, an excess of protestation, both an unnecessary falsehood and an inappropriate truth. It brought to the attention of otherwise uninformed people that their favorite writer was the center of a domestic scandal.

IN THE WEEKS FOLLOWING THE PUBLICATION OF HIS PERSONAL STATEment, Dickens found himself even more on the defensive. Depression and exhaustion came to his rescue. He made no more public statements. He tried to free himself from his need to be defensive, at least to do whatever he could to force it out of his mind. At first, he was only partly successful. He felt the pain of being a victim, reliving an adult variation of the feelings he had had as a child. "If you could know how much I have felt within this last month, and what a sense of wrong has been upon me, and what a strain and struggle I have lived under, you would see that my heart is so jagged and rent out of shape, that it does not leave me hand enough to shape these words." By the middle of June 1858, he was claiming normalcy, particularly to Edward Tagart, the Unitarian minister whose church he had attended and with whom he maintained a friendly acquaintance. "Though I have unquestionably suffered deeply from being lied about with a wonderful recklessness, I am not so weak or wrongheaded as to be in the least changed by it. I know the world to have just as much good in it as it had before" and "I hope to regain my composure in a steady manner." He had Wills, though, raise with Ouvry the possibility of suing the *Court Circular* and *Reynold's Weekly Newspaper* for libels against him.[25] His lawyer sensibly advised against additional self-inflicted wounds, though probably the argument that worked was that libel judgments were difficult to obtain.

At moments he affected philosophical composure. "I will not complain. . . I can never hope," though, "that any one out of my house can ever comprehend my domestic story . . . I have been heavily wounded, but I have covered that wound up, and left it to heal. Some of my children or some of my friends will do me right if I ever need it in the time to come." He appealed to the judgment of posterity, and to the sifting of literature from the vagaries of life. "I hope that my books will speak for themselves and me, when I and my faults and virtues, my fortunes and misfortunes are all forgotten." He was tempted, though, into an access of self-justifying gratitude when he received, through Fanny, from a cousin of the Ternans' in America, a strong affirmation of his innocence. Rehearsing for the role of Podsnap, a character in a novel he was to write six years later, he thanked his supporter "most heartily for the comfort and strength I have derived from the contemplation of your character . . . my admiration of the noble instinct with which the upright know the upright, all the broad world over." There was not "a man more blamelessly and openly" a friend of Fanny and her mother and sisters than he. While "wild misrepresentation and amazing falsehoods" are "a dark place in the social life of many countries and especially of America, I know well . . . the chivalry and integrity of the general American character and I trust myself to it with implicit confidence."[26]

With those who did not see things his way he ranged from being short-tempered to being irrationally vindictive. He saw no place for neutrality, only for taking sides. Only one acceptable side existed. Desiring personal testimonials from friends, either in letters or in oral exchanges he put them to what became an absolute loyalty test. The dividing line was not Catherine but the Hogarths. Forster, Collins, Wills, and others were allowed to maintain their cordiality with her as long as it was clear that it did not mean giving any credence to the charges against him. As far as Dickens was concerned, Catherine was innocent of those. She had cooperated with the separation on the grounds of general incompatibility. Though he wanted to have nothing more to do with her, he had no objection to friends of his who had known her for decades remaining in social contact with her.

Of course she was to have free access to the children, where the children resided or at her home. But when he thought Leech had told someone that Charley lived with his mother because he sided with her, he lectured his old friend harshly, strengthening the myth that he had determined Charley would reside with her.[27]

In the middle of July, Charley fulfilled the awkward obligation of clarifying for his mother a confusion that had arisen in regard to access to her children. It resulted from Dickens' insistence that those who had cast aspersions on his personal integrity were anathema to him. On the grounds that they were a slight upon her, Dickens had had removed from the separation deed "the usual formal clauses" about her visiting rights. She was welcome at Tavistock House or anywhere, with an important proviso. Since he would never forgive his children's maternal grandmother and her youngest daughter, just as he as a child had vowed never to forgive his mother, the Hogarth women were neither to be seen nor spoken of. Anyone whom he had any control over was not to come into their company. The children were even forbidden to go to any home at which the Hogarths were received. If they were to find themselves by accident or by someone's design in their company, they were to leave immediately. "I positively forbid the children ever to utter one word to their grandmother or to Helen Hogarth. If they are ever brought into the presence of either of these two, I charge them immediately to leave."

Charley painfully enunciated to his mother that "he has, as their father, an absolute right to prevent their going into any society which may be distasteful to him, as long as they remain under age." Charley's own bed of torture was made more painful by two further prohibitions. "In regard to Mr. Lemon, I positively forbid the children ever to see him or to speak to him, and for the same reason I absolutely prohibit their ever being taken to Mr. Evans's house."[28] For reasons that must have seemed tenuous, incredible, and even vindictive, he had decided that Lemon, having performed honorably as Catherine's intermediary, had betrayed him. So too had Evans. As editor and publisher, they had declined to publish his personal statement in *Punch* on the grounds that it was incompatible with the humorous tone of the magazine.

Neither intended the declination as taking sides in the dispute. Though Evans had expressed criticism of Dickens, Lemon had not. The former believed Catherine to be "absolutely free from the offences charged against her. . . . Mr. Dickens's temper was so ferocious to her that his nearest friends could not bear to go to the house." Sympathetic to Catherine, Evans helped her to find a house near his own. Dickens felt that he had been betrayed, and used the *Punch* declination to condemn both publisher and editor. Lemon felt hurt, bewildered. Evans was angry. Though he had been a general friend of the family, his children were close friends of Dickens', particularly Mamie, Katie, and Charley. Actually, Charley and Bessie Evans were in love. Charley's position was miserable. "I have had stern occasion to impress upon my children," Dickens wrote to Evans, "that their father's name is their best possession, and that it would be trifled with and wasted by him if either through himself or through them he held any terms with those who had been false to it in the greatest need and under the greatest wrong it has ever known. You know very well why (with hard distress of mind and bitter disappointment) I have been forced to include you in this class. I have no more to say." Three years later, in November 1861, Charley married Bessie Evans. Dickens, who would not separate his grudging consent from tacit disapproval, refused to attend the ceremony or the reception. "My father was like a madman when my mother left home," Katie said afterward. "This affair brought out all that was worst—all that was weakest in him. He did not care a damn what happened to any of us. Nothing could surpass the misery and unhappiness of our home."[29]

Dickens had an effective way to punish Bradbury and Evans. If they would not support him, he would not support them. When his statement did not appear in the June 17, 1858, issue of *Punch*, he immediately decided to change publishers. The next day the incredulous Bradbury and Evans learned of his intention. Probably his determination had been hardened by a critical remark of Evans' having been repeated to him. Just finishing his first London readings and preparing for a provincial tour, he decided to postpone taking action, especially since his business sense told him that he would do well to initiate the change at the half-yearly audit meeting in November. Bradbury and Evans had been his publisher since he had left Chapman and Hall in 1844 (some of his copyrights were still partially in his former publisher's hands). His arrangement, though, did not allow them any residual rights in his novels. They were partners only in the publication of *Household Words,* of which the publisher owned 25 percent; Wills and Dickens owned the remainder. "No proprietor was permitted to sell or transfer his share without first offering it to his partners."[30] Either they would sell him theirs or they would purchase his, leaving him free to start a new journal. Otherwise he would refuse to produce *Household Words,* which would then make the publisher's investment worthless. Its primary asset was its editor.

Though Bradbury and Evans resisted, their efforts were futile. The incorporation agreement did not provide a procedure for ending the agreement if the partners disagreed. Since each of the owners had a single vote, the result was easy to predict. In accordance with Dickens' decision to have nothing to do with them ever again, he refused to participate in the negotiations. On November 9 he informed them in writing that he wished to end their partnership agreement. On November 15, Forster appeared at the half-yearly meeting with Dickens' power of attorney, which Bradbury and Evans refused to recognize. Acting as secretary, Wills took the minutes. While the publisher insisted that Forster could not act for Dickens, Forster insisted that he could. He proceeded to do so, proposing "that the present partnership in Household Words be dissolved by the cessation and discontinuance of that publication on the Completion of the Nineteenth Volume" at the end of May 1859. Wills seconded the motion. Then "Mr. Forster and Mr. Wills voted in favour of the resolution,—but Messrs. Bradbury and Evans" declined to vote. The resolution seemed to them "contrary to the deed of partnership and therefore illegal."

When, in December 1858, they declined his offer of one thousand pounds for their share plus an additional sum for the stock, Dickens proceeded with his plan. If they would not accede, he would advertise the end of his association with *Household Words* and his initiation of a new journal. By late January 1859, he had a title, "really an admirable one," *All the Year Round,* " 'The story of our lives from year to year,'—Shakespeare. . . . A weekly journal conducted by Charles Dickens."[31] Forster had had to dissuade him from his initial preference for the title "Household Harmony." In March, on legal advice, Dickens advertised his intention in a separate handbill. The publisher took him to court. Later that month, the infamous Chancery, basically ruling in his favor, declared that the property was to be put up for sale. The ruling stipulated, as Bradbury and Evans desired, that it be sold as "a going concern." But that made no practical difference.

Though a war of words followed, the result was predictable. At the auction on May 16, Dickens bought the entire ownership and all the stock for £3,550. With the assistance of friends and confederates, including Frederic Chapman, the new young power at Chapman and Hall who had eagerly agreed to become his publisher again, he successfully conspired, "to the great terror and confusion of all the room," to mislead those bidding on behalf of Bradbury and Evans. That evening he celebrated a prearranged victory dinner at Verey's on Regent Street, his favorite gourmet restaurant. There was much to celebrate. Most of the purchase was purely on paper. Of course he did not have to pay anything to himself. Wills's payment took the form of a slightly increased share of the ownership of the new journal. He immediately sold the stock, valued at £1,600, for £2,500 to his new-old publisher, who was not allowed any ownership interest in *All the Year Round.* Whether or not he shared any of the £900 difference with Wills, Dickens had made a handsome profit there since he had to pay Bradbury and Evans only their one-fourth share of the purchase price, excluding the value of the stock, or about £500. It was a small amount for such a heavy loss and half of the £1,000 that he had originally offered. He told Emile de la Rue only part of the story. "The simple truth is, that I am not pleased with Messieurs Bradbury and Evans . . . that I am resolved to have no more of them—and that I have made up my mind to work what I do with my own capital, and to have no publisher at all except as a paid agent and instrument."[32]

At the same time, he fought another battle on another front, a more complicated, tenuous, and less forthright struggle. For decades he had had an amicable relationship with Thackeray, originating in the young artist-journalist's interest in illustrating *Pickwick Papers,* his publishing in *Bentley's Miscellany,* and his gradual emergence during the 1840s as a successful member of the London social-literary establishment. His two daughters became close friends of Mamie's and Katie's when they were neighbors in Paris for part of 1855-56. With the success of *Vanity Fair* in 1847-48, Thackeray had become, in some people's minds, Dickens' rival. Members of some of the same clubs and circles, both writers made nothing of it publicly and little of it privately. They genuinely admired one another's works, Thackeray lavish throughout the 1850s in his praise of Dickens' novels, particularly *David Copperfield.* There were some moments of tension, even antagonism, but they were quickly diffused. Thackeray bore gracefully his occasional jealousy of Dickens' success and his feeling that he was not loved as a writer with the unreserved passion with which Dickens was. Until the summer of 1858 their relationship had remained amiable, with touches of intimacy or at least generous good feeling.

On March 29, Dickens introduced Thackeray, who was chairing the dinner of the Royal General Theatrical Fund, with lavish praise as a writer and as a man of "truth and wisdom." On the first of May, following Dickens at the annual Royal Academy of Art banquet, Thackeray good-humoredly recalled walking up to his chambers "with two or three drawings in my hand" all those years ago. Later in the month, Dickens asked his assistance in putting a stop to the rumors about himself and Ellen Ternan, probably because he had heard about Thackeray's less than satisfactory response to rumors about Dickens and Georgina ("no such thing—its with an actress"). Dickens "fancies that I am going about abusing him! We shall never be allowed to be friends that's clear."[33] Among the most private of men, with two skeletons of his own in the closet, his institutionalized wife and his love for Mrs. Jane Brookfield, Thackeray's impulsive comment had been meant as a defense.

On the same June day that Dickens' "PERSONAL" statement appeared in *Household Words,* a young friend, Edmund Yates, published a brief article about Thackeray in a gossipy weekly called *Town Talk.* Bitterly furious to read that "his success is on the wane; his writings never were understood or appreciated even by the middle classes," and his lectures in America done purely for the money, Thackeray was especially pained to have the world told that "his bearing is cold and uninviting . . . his wit biting, his pride easily touched," and "there is a want of heart in all he writes. . . ." An inveterate sentimentalist, Thackeray's heart was his best feature.

Soon to become Dickens' protégé, Yates had warmed himself in Dickens' estimation by strongly supporting him in the previous weeks. An ambitious, hardworking journalist, earning his living with a post-office position, he was additionally dear to Dickens for his mother's sake. Elizabeth Yates, a successful minor actress known for her wit and social grace, had been on the stage with her actor husband, Frederick Yates, when Dickens had come to young manhood. Having performed in adaptations of his novels, the Yateses were associated with the warmth of his early struggles. Aware of the connection, Thackeray immediately speculated that Dickens had had something to do with the younger Yates's article. It is unlikely that he did. Yates later claimed that it had been a last-minute, midnight composition, written in the office with the printer at his elbow. Except for having met him once at Tavistock House, Thackeray had never seen him anyplace other than at the Garrick Club. Yates had been a member now for ten years. His father had been a founding member. Thackeray had made the Garrick his second home for over twenty years. Convinced that Yates's misknowledge of his personality had been derived from conversations overheard there, Thackeray made it a Garrick Club matter. By definition, all conversation within the club was private, not to be repeated outside and certainly never in print. Publishing such comments threatened the tenability of the club itself, for who would feel comfortable with the thought that anything one said there might appear the next day in the newspapers? Furious, Thackeray wrote to Yates emphatically, demanding an apology and an assurance that "you will refrain from printing remarks or opinions respecting my private conversation; that you will forego public discussion, however blundering, of my pecuniary affairs; and that you will henceforth please to consider the question of my truth and sincerity as quite out of the province of your criticism."[34]

Yates immediately consulted his mentor, for whom it was a simple matter. Thackeray had not supported him in his hour of crisis. Yates had. "I needn't tell you," Dickens told him on the same day, "that you may in all things count upon—Yours ever."

His young friend was being falsely attacked, his honor as a gentleman questioned, just as his own had been by those who spread or did not deny the rumors about himself and Ellen. Yates quickly replied to Thackeray, his words written in consultation and collaboration with Dickens, that he would not respond to such insulting demands. Throwing Thackeray's words back at him, he rejected the "slanderous and untrue" interpretation of his article. His pride wounded, Yates could not retreat. His honor unsatisfied, Thackeray could not give up. On June 26, 1858, at a special meeting of the Garrick Club committee, it responded to Thackeray's request that it adjudicate and Yates's claim that it was not a club matter by declaring that "it is competent to the Committee to enter into Mr. Thackeray's complaints . . . that Mr. Thackeray's complaints against Mr. Yates are well founded." The committee concluded that "Mr. Yates is bound to make an ample apology to Mr. Thackeray, or to retire from the Club; and if Mr. Yates declines to apologise or retire, the Committee will consider it their duty to call a General Meeting of the Club to consider this subject."[35] Naturally, Yates refused to apologize or resign.

"The Garrick is in convulsions," Dickens told W. H. Russell. "The attack is consequent on Thackeray having complained to the Committee (with an amazing want of discretion, as I think)" about Yates's article, which "is in bad taste, no doubt, and would have been infinitely better left alone. But I conceive that the Committee have nothing earthly, celestial, or infernal to do with it. Committee thinks otherwise. . . ." In the meantime, the latest installment of Thackeray's novel-in-progress, *The Virginians,* had appeared, with a hostile depiction of Yates as "young Grubstreet." Yates "can't apologise (Thackeray having written him a letter which renders it impossible) and won't retire. Committee thereupon call a General Meeting, yet pending. . . ." With Dickens' support and counsel, Yates hoped that at the general meeting on July 9 he would be vindicated. Neither Yates nor Thackeray attended. Dickens and Collins spoke on Yates's behalf. By a vote of seventy to thirty-six, the membership voted to support the committee. Yates refused to allow, when the decision went against him, that the general meeting had authority in the dispute. He decided to sue. To do so he had to force his physical ejection from the premises. That was not easy to arrange. To sue, he also had to find a legally responsible defendant. That was almost impossible. After a depressing half year of effort, he gave up the unlikely possibility of a satisfaction that could be pursued only at great cost in time and money.

Though his assistance had not been useful, Dickens tried again in November in a more conciliatory way. Perhaps he could mediate the conflict, he wrote to Thackeray, after talking to him briefly, "with the hope and purpose of some quiet accommodation of this deplorable matter." When Thackeray had first written to Yates, he "brought your letter to me. He had recently done me a manly service I can never forget, in some private distress of mine (generally within your knowledge) and he naturally thought of me as a friend in an emergency. I told him that his article was not to be defended; but I confirmed him in his opinion it was not reasonably possible for him to set right what was amiss, on the receipt of a letter couched in the very strong terms you had employed. . . . I was very sorry to find myself opposed to you; but that I was clear that the Committee had nothing on earth to do with it. . . . If this mediation that I have suggested can take place, I shall be heartily glad to do my best in it—and God knows in no hostile spirit towards any one, least of all to you."[36]

"Grieve[d] to gather," actually to have confirmed, "that you were Mr. Yates's adviser in the dispute between me and him," Thackeray immediately declined his offer. "Ever since I submitted my case to the Club, I have had, and can have, no part in the dispute." Dickens felt rebuffed. Forster expanded his anger into fury. To the Dickens circle, it seemed that Thackeray was being vindictive. To Yates, it seemed as if he were being persecuted in "one of the wickedest, cruellest, & most damnable acts of tyranny, ever perpetrated." At Forster's for dinner early in December 1858, Thackeray thought his host "admirably grotesque and absurd. I was glad to get out of the house without touching on the Dickens affair." The Thackeray-Yates "affair still roars on bravely. Three articles this week. Two against me and accusing me of persecuting Yates."

When, in February, Yates abandoned his intent to take Thackeray and the club to court, the imbroglio was in effect over. It left the Thackeray-Dickens relationship badly bruised.

Thackeray felt convinced, probably rightly, that Dickens had dictated Yates's letters to him, that it was he "who made him submit to the Committee, then call a general meeting, & then go to law." Dickens' own affair died much more slowly, if at all. Thackeray, visiting Catherine in late February 1859, probably sensed that Dickens' actions in the Yates affair were an echo of and a response to his marital problems. He now reversed his earlier position, perhaps on the basis of something she told him, perhaps more comfortable with the conclusion that Dickens was neither incestuous nor adulterous. "The row appears to be [about] not the actress, but the sister in law—nothing against Miss H—except that she is the cleverer & better woman of the two, has got the affections of the children & the father—thank God for having a home where there is nothing but sunshine." In December 1858, though generally temperate and courtly, Thackeray had allowed himself to pass on in private correspondence someone else's not singular opinion that "CD is a miscreant. He is ½ mad about his domestic affairs, and the other ½ mad with arrogance and vanity."[37]

Dickens' inclination to use his pen to justify himself had come home to haunt him in September 1858. The publicity resulting from the publication of the personal statement in June had seemed finally to be dying out at the end of the summer. Perhaps it had done some good in counteracting salacious rumors. Now, when he thought the worst over, his private problems suddenly blazed again into public fireworks. His readings in August had been brilliantly successful. From the west of England he had gone to Ireland for the first time, then to Gad's Hill, before continuing on to Edinburgh and Glasgow, eighty-eight readings in a little more than ninety days. While resting for a short time in Kent in early September, he was stunned to learn that the document he had composed in late May, "written as a private and personal communication" and given to Arthur Smith to use selectively, had "found its way into some of the London papers, extracted from an American paper." It had first appeared in *The New York Tribune* on August 16. Though "painfully necessary at the time when it was forced from me, as a private repudiation of monstrous scandals . . . it was never meant to appear in print." He wanted Catherine's lawyer to know that he was "no consenting party to this publication; that it cannot possibly be more offensive to any one in the world than it is to me; and that it has shocked and distressed me very much."

Though he carried on with the readings, he was depressed. "Sometimes I *cannot* leave it. I had one of those fits yesterday, and was utterly desolate and lost. But it is gone, thank God, and the sky has brightened before me once more." Still, "to know that any man who wants to sell anything in print, has but to anatomize my finest nerves, and he is sure to do it—It is no comfort to me to know . . . that when I spoke in my own person it was not for myself but for the innocent and good, on whom I had unwittingly brought the foulest lies."38 Though he bitterly referred to the document as the "violated letter," it is not at all clear who had violated it. He did not blame his friend and partner in his public reading career. More likely than not, Smith had had numbers of copies made. Concerned with his reputation in America, Dickens would not have objected to Smith's showing the letter there. He had stipulated only that Smith use it as he saw fit. Railing at unspecified violators, he preferred to deal with anonymous enemies rather than with his own responsibility for what had occurred.

Unfortunately, its republication throughout England in the autumn of 1858 gave new life to the scandal and to his misery. Even by as late as the following March, the normally cordial Elizabeth Gaskell reported to a friend that "Mr Dickens happens to be extremely unpopular just now,—owing to the well-grounded feeling of dislike to the publicity he has given to his domestic affairs," as if he were his own worst enemy, embarrassing even his friends.39 The audiences at his readings, though, hardly noticed. Or if they did, they did not care. Despite pain and exhaustion, he went on, through the autumn, from one reading success to another. He meant to his Victorian audiences more than the sum of his parts, and he had a hold on their hearts that transcended scandal.

❧ 4 ❧

FROM EARLY IN THEIR RELATIONSHIP, DICKENS ACTED AS ELLEN's and her family's protector, the powerful friend of four women living in London without a man in the house. After their appearance in Doncaster in September 1857, they returned to town. Maria acted at the Lyceum. Fanny, who had been touring successfully in the provinces, resumed her effort to replace her acting with an operatic career. Throughout 1857–58, Ellen performed in minor roles at the Haymarket, supported more by Dickens' influence with Buckstone than by her native ability or her enthusiasm for the theater. During the summer of 1858, she acted in Manchester, where the company had a two-month engagement. His readings in August took him close enough to visit her there. Though the loyal Wills and Smith would have facilitated any private meetings or communications, perhaps his sense of danger overcame his usual impulsiveness. Also, his schedule was mercilessly businesslike.

In late September 1858, the Ternans moved from Park Cottage, Northampton Park, Canonbury, to 31 Berners Street, near Oxford Street, close to the theatre district. Probably Dickens had strongly urged Mrs. Ternan to move from the lodgings in Canonbury, which he thought "unwholesome." Apparently he had visited them there. Aware that she needed additional professional training, Fanny decided to go to Florence, and Mrs. Ternan escorted her eldest daughter there, with Dickens' financial support and his letters of introduction. "You are to understand," he confided to Wills, "between you and me, that I have sent the eldest sister to Italy, to complete a musical education." Two of the people with whom his name might be of use were Frances Trollope, whose career as a writer he knew well and whose book on America he had read, and her eldest son, Thomas Adolphus, both influential members of the Florentine English community. Soon Thomas was to be a regular contributor to *All the Year Round*, from whom "it will give me real pleasure . . . to hear . . . at all times and seasons." Dickens introduced Fanny to Mrs. Trollope as "a professional lady of great accomplishments and the highest character, who purposes establishing herself in some very respectable family in Florence, probably for a year, that she may complete her musical education. . . . Let me beg you to shew her any aid or attention in your power: assuring you that if you bestowed it on one of my daughters, it could not be more welcome to me. . . . In this young lady and in her family, I have the warmest interest."[40]

He could not depend on those to whom he wrote letters on

Fanny's behalf not being reached by rumors of his relationship with Ellen. If his financial sponsorship were to become known, his denial of a sexual relationship would lose some credibility. At best, why was he being so imprudent? More likely than not, he felt protected by technical innocence. Still, many of those who saw Ellen perform in September and October would have known that this was the young lady with whom he had strenuously denied having an affair. Dickens' interest rose, momentarily, from concern to outrage when in late October 1858 Ellen and Maria reported to him that they were being pestered by a policeman who he thought had been bribed by a man sexually interested in either or both of them. He instructed Wills to visit the young ladies, "both of whom you know," to "get the particulars from them." Then he was to go to a friend in Scotland Yard to ask him to inquire into this "extraordinary, and . . . dangerous and unwarrantable conduct in a Policeman," who "should be dismissed." There should be no question of the ladies' respectability—they live "in the family lodgings," with their own furniture, not "in furnished lodgings."[41]

When Mrs. Ternan returned, Maria was performing in the enormously successful *The Maid and the Magpie,* which Dickens saw in mid-December 1858. Two years later he adapted the name of one of the characters, Pippo, for the name of the main character of *Great Expectations.* Ellen was still at the Haymarket, her career descending into very minor roles until she made her last appearance on the stage in July 1859. She was never again during his lifetime to be employed. Mrs. Ternan had no ostensible income. On March 24, 1859, Frances Eleanor Ternan and Maria Susannah Ternan, spinsters, of 31 Berners Street, purchased the substantial remainder of the ninety-nine-year lease of 2 Houghton Place, Ampthill Square, a sizable four-story house in residential Somers Town into which they soon moved. When Ellen reached the age of twenty-one, on March 3, 1860, her sisters sold it to her, probably transferring ownership for a token payment. She was to remain owner of the leasehold for much of her life and to receive income from it as rental property for many years after Dickens' death. "Since my said purchase I have had quiet enjoyment of the said premises and have received the rents and profits thereof." Since there is no hint of a legacy or of substantial savings or of sufficient income to purchase the leasehold, it seems likely that it was a gift from Dickens in which, with their mother's knowledge, her sisters served as proxy owners until she came of age.⁴²

In the eyes of Dickens' bewildered children the separation that occurred in May 1858 was not only painful but partially blinding. They may have heard rumors of their father being involved with an actress, even of "Auntie" being somehow to blame. Only the three oldest were formally told in the sense of having the situation described and partly explained to them. The six others learned of it as a fact of their daily lives. Their mother no longer lived with them. Even the older children had only a partial view of the crisis, protected by Victorian decorum, by the elaborate soundproofing of servants and domestic distances. They were observant enough, though, particularly Katie, Mamie, and Charley. Much after the deaths of her parents, Katie, close to her own, contributed a foreword to a selection of her father's letters to her mother in which she remarked that, though "the cause of the parting of my father and mother, is not unknown to me . . . I do not enter upon any details respecting it, for I consider it a subject with which the public has no concern." Her words resonate with the ironies of cultural change. Dickens always maintained that his rejection of his marriage preceded his relationship with Ellen Ternan. If anything, she was the catalyst, not the cause.

No conclusive evidence has surfaced to determine whether or not their relationship was sexual. If it was, there is no indication of precisely when it became so. It became an intimate one, probably by late 1857 or 1858. By Victorian private and modern public standards sexual relations would have been likely. Like many of his contemporaries, Dickens did have the opportunity (assuming Ellen was willing) to have both a marriage and a mistress. Catherine rejected that alternative. Anyway, his talent was for romantic passion. He preferred a single intimate relationship. His masks were all romantic. He did not find it in the least dishonorable to be secretive. But he could not tolerate being consciously hypocritical. After 1858, with the exception of his sister-in-law and his daughters, he had a close relationship with no other women besides Ellen. That he seems almost to have ceased his characteristic flirtations suggests that his friendship with her was emotionally satisfying in ways that his life with Catherine had not been.

Though intent on idealization, neither he nor his "Princess" were courtly lovers pledged to abstinence and/or death. Before meeting her, he had had a lifetime of training in expressing himself romantically and sexually. Even when the romance went out of his marriage, the sex remained, at least until the mid-1850s. Having had sexual relations for much of his adult life, he was not likely to renounce them voluntarily when he found himself deeply in love with an attractive young woman. He had no ascetic impulse. He detested prudishness. His concerns were of this world, and his long-held values and personality affirmed the naturalness of sexual union between lovers. That these lovers were not married, that they could not marry even if they had desired to, would have been cause for regret and concealment. It would not have been, though, sufficient reason for him to deny himself the fulfillment of being Ellen Ternan's lover.

Only she could have denied him that. Though she may have been star-struck initially, there is no reason to doubt that she loved him and committed herself to their relationship. That she was intelligent, willful, witty, playful, and certainly bold in small ways makes it even more likely that she would have behaved, with proper precautions, in an unconventional manner.[43] Her mother, her older sisters, and certainly Dickens had a sophisticated awareness of how such situations were managed. That her feelings would have struck some compromise with conventional moral values seems likely. In having such a relationship, she gained as well as forfeited much. Given the intimacy and duration of the attachment, though, and given the necessary secrecy, since the world would make assumptions whatever the private reality, she had ultimately to deal mainly with her own feelings. No matter what the facts, she would have to pay the penalty of secrecy. There is no reason to believe that either was sufficiently rigid or perverse not to behave normally in their private world.

By December 1858, Dickens was dividing his public energy between his readings and his editorial work, with the possibility of a new novel also in mind. His private energy went into controlling his anger and restoring emotional balance to his life. "Vengeance and hatred have never had a place in my breast." The only way, though, to keep them out was to insulate himself as much as possible from provocations. Just as he declined to read reviews of his work, he tried now to avoid reading gossip, including private letters to him about what other people had heard. Even without such provocations, he confessed to Mary Boyle, "I am a man full of passion and energy, and my own wild way that I must go is often—at the best—wild enough."44 That wild way had gotten him out of his marriage. It was the only way available to him. Whatever mistakes he had made, whatever pain he had caused, he accepted as the determinatives of his nature and the source of his creativity. That same energy had created his relationship with Ellen. By 1860, particularly after the Ternans moved to Ampthill Square, it became one of the two domestic poles of his life, combining relaxed privacy with romance and passion. He was a regular visitor, for musical evenings of songs and piano playing, for games of charades, for dinners, for the start of day excursions. And though Mrs. Ternan had her place and her role, by the spring of 1860 Ellen was of age and the house hers. It was a suitable time for his passion and energy to assert themselves.

This period in Dickens' life was one of revitalization. The readings sometimes tired him. But they were always contained within a condensed schedule, so that the weariness had its clear limits. In addition to the pleasure of being widely praised, the gains were so large that it made the occasional exhaustion worthwhile. Not even the cost of children, wife, friends, and retinue could deplete the two-hundred-pound average profit per reading, with the possibility of even more astounding sums from America and Australia. His father had never made more than twice that amount in an entire year, and there had been no significant inflation between 1820 and 1860. The turmoil of his marital separation had made things worse before they got better. But they were certainly better by early 1859. Though there were irregular reminders of heartache, he did manage to sustain periods of comparative tranquillity. In appearance, he had aged rapidly. In experience, he had always felt romantically young and imaginatively wise, and the threat of becoming imaginatively dead and morally cynical provoked a resistance so strong that it probably was a driving force in his rejection of his marriage. His rediscovery of his young, romantic self in a context in which he could perform his devotions without draining conflicts contributed significantly to his creativity in the next few years. Secrecy did not seem too high a price to pay for romantic revitalization.

In 1859, "for a private reason, rendering a long absence particularly painful," he rejected a tempting offer to read in America. He did not wish to leave Ellen. In January, an American entrepreneur, Thomas C. Evans, visited him at Tavistock House with a proposal for a reading tour that autumn. Since he would "never go, unless a small fortune be first paid down in money this side of the Atlantic," he proposed the figure of ten thousand pounds for eighty readings, expecting that to put an end to it. Ouvry argued against it. Wary, Dickens advised George Henry Lewes, when Evans approached George Eliot, to be careful with this "unaccredited agent, who, if he could make any bargain here, would take it to New York and sell it to any buyer who would pay enough. . . . Dollars (as you say) are good things. But a dollar in Wandsworth is worth fifty in New York." He assured Evans that he did not intend his stipulation "as a bargaining challenge to you to make another offer." In June, he told the Boston publisher James Fields that "several strong reasons would make the journey difficult to me, and—even were they overcome—I would never make it unless I had . . . reason to believe that the American people really wanted to hear me." He confessed to Forster that he "should be one of the most unhappy of men if [I] were to go, and yet I cannot help being much stirred and influenced by the golden prospect held before me." He queried Fields about possible schedules and alternatives. With a sure eye for one aspect of Dickens' personality, Collins told his mother in mid-July that nothing is "settled yet about Dickens's trip to America, except that he will lose a fortune if he does not go. So his departure sooner or later seems inevitable." By early August, though, he had decided that he would *"not go now."*45 At the moment, personal considerations outweighed financial ones.

After the completion of his provincial tour in November 1858, Dickens had returned to his desk. For the first time in almost two years (he had finished *Little Dorrit* in May 1857), he was approaching the state of controlled imaginative excitement that he needed to write a new novel. First he had to dispose of the Christmas number. Collaborating with Collins again, he wrote two of the eight chapters of *The Haunted House*, combining self-conscious gothic horror with his perennial skepticism about ghosts and fashionable spirit-rapping. Georgina appears as the main character's "maiden sister . . . very handsome, sensible, and engaging," Frederic Ouvry as "Mr. Undery, my friend and solicitor." The ghost of John Dickens, "my father, who has long been dead," appears in the mirror while the narrator is shaving. A long suppressed memory of gloom in the Dickens household, when they moved from Chatham to London in 1822, rose to consciousness in the narrator's evocation of his youth. "I was taken home, and there was Debt at home as well as Death, and we had a sale there." His "own little bed" was sold. "Then I was sent to a great, cold, bare, school of boys . . . where the boys knew all about the sale . . . and asked me what I had fetched, and who had bought me, and hooted at me, 'Going, going, gone.' " The financial anxiety that made the American prospect so tempting still haunted him.

In January 1859, he prolonged his stay at Gad's Hill, turning the new story over in his mind. It had been in back of his mind since he had played the part of Richard Wardour in Manchester in August 1857. The "vague fancy" of noble self-sacrifice had come to him, as he "lay on the ground, with surprising force and brilliance." He had jotted down some notes for it in his *Book of Memoranda*. He had used a version of it in "The Perils of Certain English Prisoners." During the personal turmoil that followed, he had not been able to do anything more with the idea, except to incorporate into it his love for Ellen Ternan. She had been on the stage when he had conceived it. Now she was central to the conception of his new novel. In late February, he struggled with the beginning. "I cannot please myself with the opening . . . and cannot in the least settle at it or take to it." By the middle of March, with the first few chapters under way, he was hard at work on *A Tale of Two Cities*.

Beginning with the phrase "It was the best of times, it was the worst of times," he had high hopes of "a magnificent start." His plan was to inaugurate his new journal, *All the Year Round*, on April 30 with the first of thirty-one weekly installments. The new novel would keep readers of *Household Words* from drifting away. It would emphasize continuity. It would inextricably identify the journal and its success with him as a writer. With the loan of books from the London Library and from Carlyle, whose inspiration he was to warmly acknowledge in his preface to the novel, and from the London Library through Carlyle, Dickens worked up the French Revolution background, hoping "to add something to the popular and picturesque means of understanding that terrible time, though no one can hope to add anything to the philosophy of Mr. CARLYLE'S wonderful book."[46] Carlyle, though, continued to decline invitations to visit. His own interests and introvertedness kept him away from Dickens' "cheerfulness," which he admired more than his novels, though he strongly extolled *A Tale of Two Cities,* to the author's delight. The public read and praised it avidly. By early July, *All the Year Round* was selling even more strongly than *Household Words* ever had, and back numbers with portions of the novel were in heavy demand.

Drawing upon decades of English fascination with and anxiety about the French Revolution, Dickens combined historical drama, social awareness, and nonsectarian Christian archetypes of compassion, forgiveness, and sacrifice. With stringent structural economy forced on him by his decision to write it for publication as a weekly serial, "nothing but the interest of the subject, and the pleasure of striving with the difficulty of the forms of treatment, nothing in the mere way of money . . . could also repay the time and trouble of the incessant condensation." As he struggled through the summer, he had a sense of both the challenge and his achievement. "The best story I have written," it "has greatly moved and excited me in the doing, and Heaven knows I have done my best and believed in it." The public was dazzled by the sureness of style, the firmness of tone, the combination of literary qualities and noble feelings whose ultimate referent was the model of Christ. With the appearance of the final installment at the end of November 1859, he felt firm in his conviction that he had created a novel in which dialogue and action represented tragic patterns in life and divine forces in the universe. There was a consonance between art and providence in both the preparation and the revelation of the plot. "These are the ways of Providence, of which ways all art is but a little imitation." From the beginning, he had designed the novel so that the development of "the contrasts and dialectic" would represent "an act of divine justice," which seemed to him "to be in the fitness of things."[47]

The providence at work, though, was a personal and autobiographical one. A novel about the eruption of long buried people and things, about putting right or at least finding ways to resolve the mistakes of the past, even at the cost of turmoil and death, *A Tale of Two Cities* dramatizes the confluence of

Dickens' past and his recent present. In the depiction of Lucie Manette, he portrayed aspects of Ellen Ternan and his vision of her: "a short, slight, pretty figure, a quantity of golden hair, a pair of blue eyes . . . with an inquiring look, and a forehead with a singular capacity (remembering how young and smooth it was) of lifting and knitting itself into an expression that was not quite one of perplexity, or wonder, or alarm, or merely of a bright fixed attention, though it included all the four expressions."[48] Lucie, though, must undergo a trial by suffering, the threat of the loss of her husband and child, before her bright eyes can shine happily. The two patriarchal figures of the novel, Dr. Manette, Lucie's father, and Jarvis Lorry, provide a ballast of competence, authority, and paternal responsibility, some of the bittersweet sense of what his own father lacked. Put to the test, they both pass. In the figure of Miss Pross, Dickens provides the counterbalance to Madame Defarge. The two matriarchal figures of the novel are literally childless, but through love and loyalty Miss Pross becomes a mother to Lucie. In the final battle to the death between the matriarch of revolution and blood and the matriarch of love and loyalty, it is Miss Pross who is triumphant.

The novel's most intense autobiographical energy focuses on the relationship between Sydney Carton and Charles Darnay, the former Marquess St. Evrémonde. They are aspects of Dickens' internal dialectic. Evrémonde has renounced his family's past, his inheritance, in order to begin anew, to be reborn as Charles Darnay, who, like David Copperfield, has the author's initials. History and human nature, though, reject that renunciation. The Revolution still considers him Evrémonde. His conscience reminding him of his responsibility, even if only indirectly, for what others are suffering, Darnay, unlike Dickens, leaves the wife he loves to return to France to set things right. He can return only through the assistance of Sydney Carton. In the depiction of the semidamned, Faust-like Carton, who has wasted his life with the anguish of writing someone else's scripts and with willful suicidal dissolution, Dickens created an alternate version of himself. This version of himself continued to haunt him when, a few years later in Paris, he saw a performance of Charles Gounod's *Faust* that caused him such anguish he could hardly bear to sit through it.

Like Dickens, Sydney Carton feels himself redeemed by his love for his princess. Like Darnay, he falls in love with Lucie. Unlike Darnay, he cannot have her in life. But through the transcendent and Christ-like self-sacrifice of love he can have her as long as she lives and remembers him. Like St. George rescuing his princess, Carton saves Lucie's husband and her daughter, though at the cost of his own life. The ploy is based upon a strong physical resemblance between Darnay and Carton. They become one figure, two parts of Dickens' personality that are united in art, though it is Carton whose energy and imagination most resemble his. Between the two characters, he creates an antiphonal self-portrait that, while it emphasizes the heavy hand of the past and the potential for self-destruction, unites opposites into an idealized version of love. Self-sacrifice and imaginative initiative triumph. Though Carton dies, he lives in Lucie, Darnay, and their daughter. At the end, Darnay is an idealized version of Carton transformed and Dickens fulfilled. While playing the role of Richard Wardour, he had imagined Sydney Carton. While creating him, he imagined himself as himself and as playing Carton's role. "I have a faint idea sometimes, that if I had acted him" onstage, "I could have done something with his life and death."[49] He already had.

CHAPTER TWELVE

A Splendid Excess
(1860-1864)

❧ I ❧

WEDDING BELLS REVERBERATED THROUGH THE SUMMER-GREEN
Kentish countryside. At St. Mary's Church in Higham, at a
height from which the nearby weather vane of Gad's Hill was
visible, a radiant Katie Dickens married Charles Collins,
Wilkie's brother. The church was resplendent with flowers.
Crowds of working-class neighbors created floral arches and
fired celebratory guns the night before and throughout the
morning of July 17, 1860. A special train brought guests down
from London. Dickens' oldest intimate friend, Thomas Beard,
was in the poignant but anomalous position of being the only
person at the wedding who had also been at the wedding of the
bride's father. Dickens ironically compared it to "a similar ceremony performed in a metropolitan edifice some four and twenty
years ago." Catherine, though, was not there. She had not been
invited. To family and friends, hers must have been an awkward, expressive absence. Elizabeth Dickens also was not there,
though only her son and her sister may have noticed. The crowd
of guests came back to Gad's Hill for a sumptuous wedding

breakfast, "a gorgeous affair. . . . Everything on the table in the way of decoration was white, none but white flowers."[1]

At twenty years of age, Katie was high-spirited, restless, and troubled. She looked more like her father than any of her brothers. The thirty-two-year-old groom was an introspective, self-doubting painter of minor achievement who had turned to writing brief articles and travel essays. Like Wilkie, he had a small patrimony that needed to be supplemented and a vigorous, protective mother, Harriet Collins, who had more personal energy than either of her sons, "a woman of great wit and humour—but a devil," her daughter-in-law later remarked. Possessing a fragile constitution, Charles Collins had had a necessary nurse in his mother, with whom he lived until his marriage When the brothers visited Gad's Hill together in July 1859, Wilkie told his mother that Charlie "is still trying hard to talk himself into believing that he ought to be married." On this festive summer morning, the celebrants shed the usual tears, drank the expected toasts, and did their best to forget the inevitable anxieties. Intensely loyal to his brother, Wilkie may have seen the marriage as a tightening of his bond with Dickens. Charley's "darling" and his "dearest," his mother, disguised her feelings with good cheer and flirtation.

The ceremony meant many things to many people. To the bridegroom, it seemed "like a dream." To the bride, the wedding was an escape from the tension of her relationship with her father. The man she had always relied on for stability and strength had become noticeably unstable. To Georgina, it had to be evident that she was the only member of the Hogarth family present. To Dickens, no amount of hopeful thinking could overcome his troubled thoughts. He had evicted his wife from his home. Soon afterward his daughter was leaving, voluntarily to marry a man whom her father suspected she did not love. At the beginning of June, Dickens had been ill with "rheumatism . . . which remains hovering about my left side."[2] The day before the wedding he had learned that his brother Alfred was seriously ill.

The wedding breakfast took only an hour. The host had promised everyone that there would be no speeches. The bride and groom "sat down at the table for a moment, then disappeared while the guests played games on the lawn." When they reappeared for the going away, Katie was dressed in black. She "cried bitterly on her father's shoulder, Mamie dissolved in tears, Charlie [Collins] as white as snow. No end of God bless yous. . . . King John Forster," who had been a witness, added "in his d——d stentorian voice, 'Take care of her, Charlie, you have got a most precious treasure.'" Mamie's tears may have expressed something of a survivor's relief, though her father expected, despite her not having "started any conveyance on the road to matrimony," that it was likely enough that she would get married, "as she is very agreeable and intelligent." He had little confidence that Charley Collins could take care of anyone, even himself, nervously confiding to a friend soon after the wedding that "the whole was a great success—SO FAR." Though he disapproved of Collins giving up painting, in which he was "attaining considerable distinction," and falling back "upon that worse of cushions, a small independence," he had not opposed the marriage. But he had no doubt that Katie "might have done much better." The ascetic groom, who had had periods of religious obsession some years before, probably had little to no sexual experience, and faced an unknown trial and its consequences. He had *his* doubts about Dickens. In late June, just before going to Gad's Hill for a short visit, he confided to his close friend the painter William Holman Hunt that of all the remarkable men he had known, he never knew "one who was not injured by success." Wilkie, though, put Dickens' success in a different light when he proposed to Hunt that they consult with him on a reasonable price to ask for Hunt's most recent painting, *The Finding of the Saviour in the Temple*.[3]

The thirty or so guests crowded onto the gravel pathway to shake hands, to throw old shoes, and to wave good-bye to the newlyweds, who were planning to live indefinitely on the Continent. In London, "we are paupers—abroad we are rich." Katie's sister and her brothers (except Charley, who had gone to Hong Kong on a business venture) tearfully relived the departure of their mother from the household. "They soon recovered. Mary in particular," her father noted, "commanded herself extremely well." The guests relaxed with an excursion to Rochester Castle and to Chatham to hear a military band. They played croquet on the Gad's Hill lawn early in the evening. Then they had dinner and danced until they had to dash to the Higham station for the special 11 P.M. London train that their host had arranged. "After the last of the guests not staying in the house had departed, Mamie went up to her sister's bedroom. Opening the door, she beheld her father upon his knees with his head buried in Katie's wedding-gown, sobbing. . . . When at last he got up and saw her, he said in a broken voice: 'But for me, Katey would not have left home.' " A year later, he declined an invitation to the wedding of a friend's daughter by confessing that "I should really have a misgiving that I was a sort of a shadow on a young marriage."4

Ten days later the death of Dickens' thirty-eight-year-old brother provided a ritual counterpoint to the wedding festivities. In his feelings, though, the events had a similarity. Dressed in black, Katie had embraced what was to be a childless, perhaps sexless, marriage. During the next five years, as Charles Collins' weak health became more specifically life-threatening, Dickens increasingly saw in his son-in-law an emblem of death and a reminder of his daughter's unhappy situation. Rather sour on marriages in general, he did have special reasons to be sour about this one. Alfred's unexpected death soon after the wedding increased his guilt about Katie and also brought to mind the unhappy and threatening fact that two of his siblings had died in childhood. Fanny, like Alfred, had been thirty-eight at her death. Of his two remaining younger brothers, one was to die in his late forties, the other just past his fortieth birthday. The eldest son, he was to outlive all his brothers.

When Charles had seen Alfred early in the summer, he had been "greatly shocked and impressed by his shattered condition." The illness had come suddenly, the same pleurisy or tuberculosis that had killed his sister, and that in 1849 he had worried he was showing signs of. "It is a dreadful thing," Charles Collins wrote to his mother, "so strong and apparently healthy as he was." After receiving a telegram on July 27, Dickens left immediately for Manchester. He arrived three hours too late. "The poor young widow," Helen, and "five little witnesses,' the eldest thirteen, were in the first shock of mourning. An expert at funeral arrangements, Dickens took on the responsibility of seeing the body into its grave next to his father's in Highgate cemetery and providing temporary help for the widow and children. All this was at his expense. Alfred had died in debt and financial confusion, though not of a substantial sort. A few hundred pounds easily cleared it all. He had left, though, absolutely nothing for his family. It helped that Dickens liked the widow, "a good, true, striving wife" whom he could "trust with all [his] heart." The "black figures" were lodged temporarily at a farmhouse near Gad's Hill. Then he found a house for them near Hampstead Heath. "Day after day I have been scheming and contriving for them . . . and I have schemed myself into broken rest and low spirits."5

Beginning in the late 1840s, there had been increasing estrangement among the brothers. Alfred had been his favorite, the only one whom he respected, primarily because he had honorably pursued a career and had been financially independent. Though he had had only moderate success as an engineer, it had not been for lack of effort. That only slightly mitigated Dickens' fear that his father's ghost lived in all his brothers. Unlike Hamlet's father, this ghost always asked for money.

By 1850, Frederick's indebtedness had become chronic. Dickens tried to move him from the treasury department into a life insurance office, offering security for six hundred pounds of debts. Though "he has been heedless enough . . . there is not the least harm in him." By the late 1850s, Frederick's marriage to Anna Weller had collapsed, partly because of financial strain, in an atmosphere of adultery and recrimination. Occasionally Frederick made unexpected appearances, once when Charles was reading in Ireland, another time in Brighton, peremptorily demanding small favors, as if they were to be the price for his disappearing again. Charles's youngest brother, Augustus, with less dramatic flair but also aggressively, played out the same ghostly debtor's scenario and his own variant of marital turmoil. Having married Harriet Lovell, with whom he had a son, in the late 1850s he deserted them when she became blind, leaving his eldest brother to support both wife and child. From America, to which he fled in 1859, Augustus pressured him to advance money and favors. "He has always been, in a certain insupportable arrogance and presumption of character, so wrong, that, even when he had some prospects before him, I despaired of his ever being right. . . . I have no hope of him."6

Dickens also began to fear that the family ghost embodied in his father's inability to stay out of debt might be rising again in the third generation, in his own sons. Their pattern of vocational indecisiveness made him anxious. Charley wanted a business career but didn't seem to make much progress. Walter and Frank were mediocre students for whom, after some diversions, the army seemed a likely possibility. Frank unsuccessfully competed for a foreign-office position. Walter and Frank handled money badly. Sydney had his mind set on the navy, and soon went off, with his father's assistance, as a teenage midshipman. Alfred went into business, without notable success, and was to go to Australia. Henry and Plorn were still at home, beginning the divergent paths that were to lead Henry to a successful legal career, Plorn to Australia and a withdrawn life as an unprosperous sheep farmer "whose besetting sin was his love of gambling."7 At the time of their parents' separation, Plorn was six, Henry nine. What terrified Dickens was the thought that some of them had inherited both their mother's laziness and his own father's tendency toward chronic indebtedness, as if the blood of the family had been poisoned. No one of them had genius. They also, though, had no extraordinary scars or special debilities, except for Frank's stutter. The patterns of his children's lives were hardly the cause for more than the ordinary parental disappointments. For Dickens, though, small signs seemed grave warnings. He felt himself potentially the indefinite financial guarantor of a family of unpromising sons, whose insufficiencies rose up before him with some of the pain of his anger at his wife's incompetence and some of the fear that he would suffer again through them the anguish he had suffered because of his father.

In the spring of 1862, Elizabeth Dickens asserted herself briefly. She had become senile, probably incontinent, and in need of constant attention. Charles continued to take responsibility for her care and support. How to do so sometimes exasperated him. He could count for help only on Letitia though she was not in a position to contribute financially. In late March, the lady with whom Elizabeth lived became "terrified by the responsibility of her charge and utterly relinquishe[d] it." Charles had "the difficult task of finding good hands" for her "and getting her into them without alarming her." Within a few weeks, he had found another place for her to live, hopeful "that all will go well, and that [she] will become no worse, but will go on very gently." Alfred's death in August was beyond her comprehension. Her son humorously but bitterly dramatized his own grim Shakespearean scene. "My mother, who was also left to me when my father died (I never had anything left to me but relations), is in the strangest state of mind from senile decay; and the impossibility of getting her to understand what is the matter, combined with her desire to be got up in sables like a female Hamlet, illumines the dreary scene with a ghastly absurdity that is the chief relief I can find in it." In her last years, she became increasingly like her son's caricature of her as Nicholas Nickleby's mother. The young boy who had so keenly felt the want of mothering was forced to become his mother's keeper. It was costly, both financially and emotionally. In late November, she felt a little better than usual. "Helen and Letitia were poulticing her poor head, and, the instant she saw me, she plucked up a spirit and asked me for 'a pound.' "[8]

His own health had its unpleasant turns. In June 1859, he had contracted "a small malady," which "my bachelor state has engendered," and put himself under treatment to Dr. Frank Beard, Thomas Beard's youngest brother. It probably was a stomach and bowel problem, with a persistent secondary skin infection. By late July, he was "very little better, really very little." In early August, he hoped that he had "thrown the enemy." By the end of the month he was still not well. He felt depressed. "I am a wretched sort of creature in my way, but it is a way that gets on somehow. And all ways have the same finger-post at the head of them, and at every turning in them." A holiday at the seashore and then finishing *A Tale of Two Cities* helped. The next spring, the month before Katie's wedding, he had a severe attack of what he called rheumatism. He could hardly stand. At the end of the year, working at his new autobiographical novel, *Great Expectations*, he was ill again, and "being doctored," with the same "disagreeables," accompanied by a painful, intractable "local irritation" that had possessed him the previous summer. By late January 1861 he seems to have recovered. In May, his facial neuralgia appeared. He associated it with the tension of writing. His faced ached "all the time." There were no other symptoms.

Though by September the distressing pain had subsided, it was to recur intermittently for many years, especially in stressful circumstances. "As my poor father (who was asthmatic too, and the jolliest of men) used philosophically to say, 'one must have something wrong, I suppose, and I like to know what it is.' " In the early 186os, the pain in his side associated with the renal cholic of his childhood returned, and frequent sleepless nights kept him emotionally and physically on edge, though he had great confidence in his powers of recuperation.9

In August 1860, anxious to liberate himself from the expense of two homes, he sold for two thousand guineas the remaining thirty-six years on the lease of Tavistock House to J. P. Davis, whom he identified to Mitton as a "Jew Money-Lender." Suspicious, expecting him to attempt to bargain and manipulate, he was relieved to have his anti-Semitic stereotypes disappointed. Without hesitation and without apparent sense of loss, he disposed of what had been the family home for ten years. "The bargain was made in five minutes . . . and the money paid within as many days." With five small rooms over the office of *All the Year Round*, he had no need for any other permanent residence in London. Romantic domesticity was available whenever he desired it at Ampthill Square. Gad's Hill would serve as the family home. If Mamie and Georgina wanted to be in town during the social season, he would take a house for a few months. Three or four days a week in London, three or four in the country, though for longer periods during the summer, seemed attractive and practical. With the success of the readings, he had no doubt that there would be long periods when he would be on the road. But it was a matter of temperament as well as practicality. He joked seriously to Miss Coutts that if he came to visit he would "want no bed," for he had "an adventurous satisfaction in exploring hotels, and am quite as likely as not to leave in the middle of the night for the coast of Cornwall."10 One of the advantages of change and travel was that other people could not readily perceive where his restlessness found rest at any particular moment.

He absolutely declined to travel backward toward reconciliation with Catherine or to mitigate his anger at her parents. To Miss Coutts, who in April 1860, probably having consulted with Catherine, again suggested that he reconsider the separation, he granted that he did "not suppose himself blameless, but in this thing as in all others know . . . how much I stand in need of the highest of all charity and mercy." The exculpating fact, though, was clear. "When I was very young, I made a miserable mistake. . . . The wretched consequences which might naturally have been expected from it, have resulted from it. That is all." As to simply meeting with her in some neutral place, "in the last two years, I have been stabbed too often and too deep. . . . It is simply impossible. . . . That figure is out of my life forevermore (except to darken it) and my desire is, Never to see it again." He assured his friend that he was the same "hopeful, cheerful, and active" man he had always been, that he had not changed, that he had not soured, and that he still desired through his art "to sweeten the lives and fancies" of others. He could not, of course, hold Miss Coutts's efforts against her. "Many reasons, old and new, unnerve me," but "I think you know how I love you." In September he and Miss Coutts saw one another, and he felt that "we renewed our old friendship and affection—or rather, perceived when we saw one another that no renewal was needed."

To Albert Smith, who tried to persuade him to attend a social event at his home, he was more peremptory. He could "not be a guest at any house where Mrs. Hogarth's youngest daughter is received in the same capacity. There are some considerations in life that are superior to one's ease and pleasure. The lowest self respect on my own behalf, and on that of the girls, and Georgina's, imposes this rule upon me." He found Smith's response objectionable, but had the satisfaction of repaying an account. At the time of the separation from Catherine, Smith had written him "a very manly letter indeed, the remembrance of which has never since been disturbed. It is my turn now. I set that against this, and am always Faithfully Yours."[11]

What the many "old and new" reasons were for being unnerved can only be guessed at. Probably one of them was his mother's condition. Perhaps another was his relationship with Ellen. Approaching fifty years of age, a grizzled-looking veteran of family and profession, he had the challenge of finding common ground and practical accommodation with a young woman barely twenty years old. If they were lovers, the range of challenges must have been delicate and unnerving. If they were not, his expectations must have kept him on edge. In addition to the delicacy of his relationship with her, he had to make the adjustment to being a bachelor and a single parent. He attributed his malady in 1860–61 to his "bachelor state." Whether that meant sexual activity as well as irregular meals and frequent travel is not clear, though probably only the latter. Despite his voyeuristic restlessness, his interest in night life and prostitutes, and his occasional excursions with the casually libertine Wilkie Collins, Dickens would have found it difficult to have casual sex. Morally self-righteous, physically fastidious, he was also widely known and would have feared recognition, even in Paris. Strongly self-censoring, his powerful imagination created fantasies that frequently ran up against the boundaries of expression in ways that must have been unnerving.

As a single parent, he worried about his children, particularly his sons. Concern was inseparable from exasperation. Like his father, he boasted on those few occasions when they gave him the opportunity, though his candid evaluations of their abilities usually had an edge of disparagement. Having been born to neither wealth nor title, his sons, Dickens assumed, should go out, as he had, into the world, and make their fortunes.[12] Since opportunities at home were limited, there were seas to sail and continents to conquer. Frustration at home could be overcome by imperial challenges abroad. Whatever the mixture of motives, after 1858 he promoted their early departure, even when it pained him to see them leave. His need, though, to force on them the model of his own success, to distance himself from their likely failures, and to decrease his daily responsibilities as a parent probably contributed to the pattern. As soon as the ghostly specter of what they would do with their lives rose, he felt sufficiently ill at ease with them to want to see them gone. His daughters, though, were a different matter. In his eyes and in society's, their natural position was dependency, and they were emotionally congenial to him in a way that his sons were not. By embracing them, he could distance himself even further from his mother and his wife. Katie's departure pained him. For Mamie, one or two echoes of matrimonial possibility surfaced. Hardly heard, they soon faded away. She began to settle into her role as the ostensible matron of her father's house. Compared to Georgina, though, she was neither particularly competent nor reliable.

During the first half of the 1860s, both daughters found

ways to express their dissatisfaction. In the second half, both
found ways to express outright unhappiness. Indirectly struggling with a possessive father who dominated their lives, they
had an almost impossible time establishing separate identities.
Katie, more energetic than "Mild Gloucester," initially made
the more dramatic attempt. Both, though, paid the heavy cost of
accepting that the price of their father's love was their rejection
of their mother. They were not forbidden to visit her. But the
message was clear. After the separation, they hardly saw her,
and the Hogarth family was beyond the pale. During the second
half of the decade, Mamie particularly showed the strain of her
spinsterhood and the oddity of her domestic position. She was
never to marry. And by the late 1860s, as her husband's health
declined, Katie's marriage collapsed.

For the next ten years, Georgina was the woman in Dickens' life on whom he most relied. Unlike Ellen, she could live
openly with him, and she had the self-protective good sense to
accept her brother-in-law's mistress as a friend. During the
1860s, in discreet ways and at convenient times, Ellen visited at
Gad's Hill, becoming companionable with Mamie and Georgina. When she and her husband returned from the Continent,
Katie kept her distance. Georgina's reverence for her brother-
in-law, though, was sufficiently powerful to accept that he was
to be spared the judgments of ordinary convention and morality. The practical situation was also clear. He could not divorce,
he could not remarry. Having chosen sides at the time of the
separation, she could not very well reconsider when one of its
natural consequences became clear. She and both daughters, of
course, were among the intimate circle of fifteen or so who knew
about the relationship. Certainly numbers more knew that
Dickens loved "deeply, passionately, madly," without necessarily knowing Ellen or having any sense of what arrangements
had been made. Georgina, who "think[s] of everything," was
necessary for his domestic comfort. She "would make the best
wife in the world, but the children are so dependent upon her
that I doubt if she will ever marry. (I don't know whether to be
glad of it or sorry for it)." He found the subject "perplexing—
not being a judge of marriages." But, on the whole, he was glad
of it.[13] Georgina served his domestic needs. Ellen served his
romantic needs. Together, they made the perfect wife.

❧ 2 ❧

THE PAST WAS MUCH ON HIS MIND. AS ALWAYS, THE CRUCIAL STORY
of his life, the sustaining myth of his childhood, needed to be
seen and reformulated in response to his vision of himself in the
present. All crisis was a spur to creativity, all fiction a mirror
of imaginative distortion in which the model of his own life
became a portrait of his culture and his world. A half year after
the separation, he had begun writing *A Tale of Two Cities*, whose
hero redeems himself by his death. Dickens was in the process
of demonstrating that his own creativity had not been diminished, that the separation had been the necessary prelude to its
resurgence, that Sydney Carton had died so that Dickens might
live.

With the book's completion in October 1859, he anticipated
only a short rest from writing fiction. Tempted to pursue *A Tale
of Two Cities* onto the stage, at least to the extent of supervising
a Paris production, in his imagination he had cast himself for the
role. In January 1860, unable to prevent Tom Taylor's adaptation of the novel being staged at the Lyceum, he "devoted" two
weeks to "trying to infuse into the conventionalities of the
Theatre, something not usual there in the way of Life and
Truth." He even wrote a slightly altered ending to "make a
better exit" where the actor playing Carton "justly felt the want
of something."[14] In his next novel, Carton was to be transformed
into a character who lives rather than dies, who survives various
internal and external threats, rising to an act of self-sacrifice
through which he achieves moral transformation and a meaningful life.

In November 1859, he had it in mind that in two years or
so he would write another serial novel of about the same length
as *A Tale of Two Cities*. *All the Year Round* was too valuable a
property for him not to strengthen its successful inception with
another story of his own as soon as he could draw sufficient
breath. Meanwhile, he had Wilkie Collins' *The Woman in White*,
which would last about eight months. To fill the period between
it and his own new story, he pursued George Eliot through his
longtime acquaintance with George Henry Lewes, building on
a brief congratulatory correspondence he had had with her in

1858. When *Scenes of Clerical Life* had appeared, he had immediately intuited that the pseudonymous author was a woman. When in July 1859 he had read *Adam Bede,* he was overwhelmed by its brilliance. Though he had in mind the possibility of her contributing to *All the Year Round,* his extensive praise was sincere. "Every high quality that was in the former book, is in [*Adam Bede*], with a World of Power added thereunto."¹⁵ Reading it closely, he was deeply moved, particularly by the "extraordinarily subtle and true" depiction of Hetty Sorrel's character. Encouraged by Lewes, he began to negotiate through him with the author, tactfully referring to her as Mrs. Lewes. Dickens was aware, of course, that she and Lewes were not actually married. Lewes' marriage had collapsed in 1849; soon, by mutual arrangement, his wife began to live with Leigh Hunt's son, with whom she had had numbers of children. In the process of becoming George Eliot, Mary Ann Evans went to Germany with Lewes in 1854. After returning, they lived together in Chelsea, in that shadow-land of social ambivalence created by Victorian private and public attitudes. They made no secret of their relationship. Unlike Dickens, though, neither was a great popular novelist whose livelihood depended on the goodwill of a vast middle-class audience.

Dickens met with Lewes, and perhaps George Eliot, early in November 1859. "The question is, whether it would be consistent with her perfect peace of mind and comfort . . . to enter into terms for such a story." Money was no barrier. She would be paid at the highest possible rate. Aware of hesitation, he urged her, through Lewes, to take it on. "An immense new public would probably be opened to her, and I am quite sure that our association would be full of interest and pleasure to me." He would say little about "the extent to which I have it at heart as an artist, to have such an artist working with me." George Eliot's ambivalent response puzzled him. He still thought, though, that the answer was essentially yes, that her hesitancy had to do with the schedule. To give her more time, he proposed another novel, probably by Mrs. Gaskell, between Collins' and hers. When, after further procrastination, Lewes wrote to him in February 1860 that she had decided on an indefinite postponement, he was disappointed and even angry. He went immediately to visit them to see if the matter was still open. But it did no good. She "is terrified by the novel difficulties of serial writing; cannot turn in the space; evidently will not be up to [it]."

When Mrs. Gaskell, not wanting to chop her novels into weekly segments, turned him down, Dickens still needed someone to follow Collins. And then someone to follow whoever followed Collins. For the latter position, he queried Bulwer-Lytton. Charles Reade was another possibility. For the immediate need, he turned to Charles Lever, a prolific minor novelist living on the Continent. Lever was thrilled at the opportunity to publish in *All the Year Round,* partly because the payment was so high, partly because he hoped that what he felt was Chapman and Hall's neglect would be remedied by this additional association with them. The terms were generous. Lever's name would be published with his story. Dickens would push Lever's novels with Frederic Chapman. that "Monstrous Humbug," who seems "to be making holiday one half of his life, and making mistakes the other half, and making money . . . in spite of himself, always." When it became clear in February that George Eliot would not be a contributor, Dickens asked Lever to begin in July, and not to be "afraid to trust the audience with anything that is good." Despite his praise, though, of the "life, vivacity, originality, and humour" of the opening of *A Day's Ride,* the readers of *All the Year Round* soon expressed their opinion in a striking falloff in sales. Lever's story was "a dead-weight."[16]

At first concerned, then alarmed, then desperate enough to take action, he determined in early October 1860, after "a council of war at the office," that the "new big book" that he had been meditating since August, and which by the middle of September he was "on the restless eve of beginning," would be transformed from the projected twenty monthly pamphlet numbers into a weekly serial. It would begin on December 1, 1860, and run concurrently with the remainder of Lever's novel. "If the publication were to go steadily down, too long, it would be very, very, very difficult to raise again." There were Lever's feelings to be assuaged. There was no way of disguising that *A Day's Ride* had failed to hold its readers, but "some of the best books ever written would not bear the mode of publication. . . . This might have happened with any writer. . . . I hate to write—dread to write—can't write—this letter." All he could do was assure the deeply disappointed author that "my original opinion of your serial remains quite unchanged." Though he tried to help publish it in book form and to get Chapman and Hall to back Lever with more publicity, it was clear to both men that he would not have a second chance with *All the Year Round.*

Preoccupied with his own new novel, Dickens had little thought to spare for Lever. The title, he told Forster at the beginning of October 1860, is "GREAT EXPECTATIONS." In the previous month, while working on a short piece, he had suddenly conceived "a very fine, new, and grotesque idea" that so excited him that he decided to cancel the short paper and "reserve the notion for a new book. . . . It so opens out before *me* that I can see the whole of a serial revolving on it, in a most singular and comic manner." The novel idea was the dramatic encounter on the Thames marshes between a young orphan and a convict escaped from the prison hulks on the river. "The grotesque tragic-comic conception that first encouraged" him was that the boy would assume, for some superficial, self-serving reasons, that the benefactor to whom he owes his "great expectations" is a bitterly disappointed, domineering, well-to-do local woman when it is actually the convict whom he has befriended. What opened out so immediately and fully before him was the ultimate reworking of the story of his own life into a fiction that would capture the emotional truths by which he had lived. Initially, the "hero [was] to be a boy-child, like David. Then he will be an apprentice." From the start, he had no doubt that it would be autobiographical, and he soon reread *David Copperfield* in order to avoid unintentional repetition, "affected by it to a degree you would hardly believe."[17]

Beginning sustained writing at the end of September, he soon had the equivalent of three weekly installments to show Forster. Through the first two weeks of October he wrote obsessively. As usual, he gave up writing all but the most essential letters, explaining to Macready that "when I have done my day's work, I rush into the air and take fierce exercise: the pen once laid down, is leaden—and not feathery—to take up again that day." By late October, he had "four weekly numbers ground off the wheel." In early November, he made a five-day visit to Cornwall with Collins, for a setting for the Christmas story, "A Message from the Sea," on which they had agreed to collaborate.

Preoccupied with that obligation, he did not resume work on *Great Expectations* until early December, soon after the first installment appeared. Also, he had been feeling ill. The "disagreeables" returned. He prepared for a month's hard work at Gad's Hill, "in actual bondage." He was soon cheered by the great success of the new novel. The sales of *All the Year Round* had immediately recovered.

At the beginning of the new year, he feared for a brief moment that his health would force him to miss an installment. He managed, though, to keep working, and soon felt better. The challenge of brevity and condensation was matched in its pain with the pleasure of success. He gave a short series of readings in London in March and April 1861. But he was happy to be out of them quickly and to be able to concentrate on his story. Hoping to be finished by mid-June, he went to Dover in late May to have the benefit of the sea air. The neuralgia in his face ached painfully. There, he worked "like a steam engine." He was feeling "the worse for wear, and the work has been pretty close. But I hope that the book is a good book, and I have no doubt of very soon throwing off the little damage it has done me."[18] He thought he had finished on June 11, 1861. Later in the month, though, he was persuaded by Bulwer-Lytton to cancel and then rewrite the ending.

The story gripped him with the passion of self-exploration, self-reconstruction. The landscape of the novel, Rochester, Kent, and London, was to be that of his childhood and young manhood. It was also the landscape of the present of his life. It contained the weather and the places to which he had returned in these recent years, both literally and emotionally: the Cooling churchyard, the flat marshes between Gravesend and the Medway, the streets of Rochester, the London law offices and courts in which he had served his apprenticeship, the essential mediation between his memory of the voice of his childhood and the voice of his adult experience. Like *David Copperfield*, it was to be narrated in the first person. Writing in the house that he had purchased as an affirmation that he was both his father's son and more, Dickens created transmutations of the important people and relationships in his life, some of it in fantasy terms, much of it, for the first time, both realistic and personally liberating, an adult fairy tale close enough to the reality to allow him to align his inner needs with his personal myths. His emotionally powerful adult misrepresentations of his childhood became the source of a subtle, resonant work of fiction about birth, class, guilt, self-deceit, betrayal, moral values, and personal redemption. Like all his orphans, the main character, Pip, is a projection of his childhood feelings of isolation and parental betrayal. He is a survivor, though, whose punishment for outliving his infant siblings and parents is a strong sense of guilt and confusion. The penalty for such independence is complete dependence on his one living sibling, his older sister, who provides him with harsh nurture, bringing "him up by hand," constantly reminding him that he is unworthy to have survived and that he has been born to failure and a bad end. Not even an orphan, then, can escape having a bad mother.

In the form of his sister's husband, Joe, this orphan is provided with an amiable, loving, but ineffectual father who cannot protect him from his wife. Like John Dickens, Joe has a good heart. Apprenticed to him at the blacksmith's forge, Pip has ahead of him the prospect of a working-class life, with a hearth potentially as glowing, fulfilling, and stable as that found in middle-class or upper-class households. Without any special talents, he possesses neither intellectual ambition nor artistic ability. Unlike his previous orphan-heros, from Nicholas Nickleby to David Copperfield, Pip is utterly unheroic, unromanticized, his sensibility and moral core free of the complications of talent and of authorial self-glorification. He is as close to the self stripped bare as Dickens could ever get.

Brought to Satis House in "Rochester" for the entertainment of Miss Havisham, an eccentric, semimad spinster who stopped her clocks and her life when jilted on her wedding day, Pip falls in love with her ward, Estella. Years later he is to discover that Estella is the daughter of Magwitch, the convict whom he had fed in the churchyard cemetery, and that her mother has been saved from the gallows by Mr. Jaggers, Miss Havisham's lawyer. Worst of all, he discovers that his wishful hope, which he had elevated into a stubborn belief, that Miss Havisham is his benefactor and intends Estella to be his wife is completely false. Miss Havisham has raised her to be his and all men's tormentor. The games the young Pip plays with her at Satis House are sadomasochistic enactments of the mutual pleasure of victim and victimizer, of the interaction of guilt, self-deprecation, and romantic hope, and a seemingly hopeless confusion of hostility, shame, vengeance, casual brutality, and class torment.

Unexpectedly told in his early adolescence by Mr. Jaggers that he now has "great expectations," that prospect becomes inseparable from his hope of fulfilling his love for Estella. He believes Miss Havisham has intended them for one another. With extraordinary acuity, Dickens reduces romantic emotion to its class basis, dramatizing the shabby contortions through which Pip feels himself compelled to wriggle up to respectability. Arrogant, snobbish, and insecure, he values becoming a gentleman more than he values Joe's good heart and his love. Memories of the blacking factory and dirty fingernails rise to the surface of the text. " 'Have you seen anything of London, yet?' " Pip asks Joe. " 'Why, yes, sir . . . me and Wopsle went off straight to look at the Blacking Ware'us. But we didn't find that it come up to the likeness in the red bills at the shop doors.' " Estella has ridiculed Pip's coarse hands, his working-class world. The daughter of a criminal and a prostitute wears the clothes of a lady. The orphan of the working class aspires to rise to her level. Actually, his expectations are being paid for by Estella's ex-convict father's labor as a sheep farmer in Australia. Magwitch mistakenly believes that he is fulfilling an honorable role by helping the little boy who fed him in the cemetery to become a gentleman.

Yet Magwitch's mistake is a mistake of the caring heart, and Pip's misplaced love for an unloving, badly damaged woman is as much an expression of his innate ability to love as is his eventual compassion for Magwitch. The ultimate model for the good heart is Joe (one of Dickens' self-christenings in his correspondence with Mary Boyle), who unites with Magwitch in the New Testament patriarchy of the novel to become the ultimate good father, the combination of Jesus and Jehovah, of love and power, and of power redeemed by love. Though Pip betrays Joe, his betrayal can be redeemed through repentance. Though Pip, when his false class pride is shaken by the revelation of his true benefactor, initially detests Magwitch, he redeems himself by learning to love the man who has loved him so much. In the end, Magwitch dies so that Pip may be reborn into a truer, more realistic sense of human values and class structures, into self-reliance and self-respect.

In his portrait of Estella, Dickens dramatized the tension that he had felt throughout his life between the romanticized female as both an idealized star of love and a tormentor who has been conditioned by society to remain out of reach. Through much of the novel she is an extreme version of Maria Beadnell, the woman for whom he had longed desperately but of whom he had been deprived by social conditioning and external circumstances. Though this deprivation partly derived from his own self-deceit, it also expresses his failure to find an appropriate person to love. In Biddy, Dickens presents Pip with an attractive example of the good sister, like Georgina, who has all the feminine virtues except erotic attractiveness. Pip cannot love her romantically. He is irresistibly drawn to a woman whose rejection of him is part of his erotic attachment to her, whose romantic unattainability marks her as the effective fulfillment of his emotional needs. Pip's pursuit of Estella, though, takes an extraordinary turn. In his devotion to Magwitch, realizing and rejecting the falseness of his earlier values, it becomes less erotic and considerably more domestic, realistic, and moral. When she is revealed to be the daughter of the man who has become a father to Pip, incest becomes sufficiently distanced to be legitimized and domesticated, the relationship a metaphor for the union of erotic and sibling love.

Conveniently, the main female characters ultimately contribute to and support Pip's salvation, his moral and emotional triumph. His unnurturing, punishing sister, the only mother he initially feels he deserves, is reduced to harmless ineffectualness. Brutally beaten by Orlick, she becomes a mute cripple whose death soon liberates her husband and "son." The powerfully grotesque Miss Havisham, who has manipulated him into maintaining the illusion that she is his benefactor, loses her power over him when he discovers that he owes nothing to her. Her portrait benefits from some touches of the senile Elizabeth Dickens, who was to outlive this last of her fictional variants by only a short time. In this final depiction of perverse, indifferent matriarchy, Dickens found the energy to transform even Miss Havisham into a repentant witch, regretting what she has done to Estella and Pip, rejecting, moments before her death, her years of bitterness, her self-destructive morbidity, and her efforts to pervert Estella's innate moral sentiments. Estella's ability, though, to learn from experience, to recover her capacity to love and to feel compassion, has not been irretrievably damaged. Her moral sentiments have not been destroyed. They cannot be. Years pass. Pip constructs a moral, self-reliant, realistic life for himself. After a marriage in which she is brutally mistreated, Estella remarries. Driving in a carriage in London, she sees and speaks to Pip, who "was very glad afterwards to have had the interview; for, in her face and in her voice, and in her touch, she gave me the assurance that suffering had been stronger than Miss Havisham's teaching, and had given her a heart to understand what my heart used to be."

With that final sentence, the last section of the novel went to galley proofs. He sent a copy to Bulwer-Lytton about the middle of June 1861. Undoubtedly, Ellen read them or had them read to her, probably by the author. Having recently read to her the proofs of *A Strange Story*, Bulwer-Lytton's new novel for *All the Year Round*, Dickens told him that he "implicitly trust[ed]" her judgment in which he "frequently observed (in the case of my own proofs) an intuitive sense and discretion that I set great store by." Bulwer-Lytton immediately argued that the ending that sent the lovers on their separate ways again was false to the direction of the story overall, that the regeneration of Pip and Estella demanded some symbolic representation in the plot, at least the suggestion, at the minimum a shadowy expectation, that they would not part again, either in the spirit or in the flesh. Probably Ellen agreed. To the extent that she and Dickens may have seen some aspect of herself in the portrait of Estella, a hint of her occasional teasing imperiousness, a touch of her beauty, some distant suggestion of the challenges and obstacles they both had faced in making their love a reality, Bulwer-Lytton's argument may have had a personal force. He "stated his reasons so well," Dickens told Collins on the twenty-third, "that I have resumed the wheel and taken another turn at it."

Once he began unraveling, he had to exert himself not to unravel too much. Having canceled the previous final passage, he wrote an ending in which Estella and Pip, reborn to love and compassion, join hands, leave the ruined garden of Satis House, and begin the difficult, fragile possibility of a life together. "And in all the broad expanse of tranquil light" the subdued but optimistic Pip "saw no shadow of another parting from her." Dickens soon made up his mind definitively. Yes, "upon the whole, I think it is for the better."19 Like Pip, he had come through one of the most painful, destructive periods of his life with subdued optimism. Personal anguish had been transformed into artistic triumph.

EACH CHRISTMAS GAVE NEW LIFE TO DICKENS' OLD CHRISTMAS works, partly because of their enduring popularity, partly because each Christmas issue of *All the Year Round* contained a new Christmas story, some or all of which he wrote. That was a sacred financial obligation. The fatuous "A Message from the Sea" of 1860, done with Collins, was followed in 1861 by "Tom Tiddler's Ground," of which he wrote two of the seven chapters. Mainly a moral fable preaching against "unnatural solitude" embodied in a perverse hermit, the final sermon has a personal resonance. "You cannot do better," the hermit is told, "than imitate the child, and come out too—from that very demoralizing hutch of yours." Busy with an intensive reading tour, he could not devote as much time to "Tom Tiddler's Ground" as he could to his next three Christmas stories. "Somebody's Luggage" (1862) was a potpourri of self-satire, partly narrated by a waiter, with *All the Year Round* as one of the genial targets. By Christmas Eve, it had "sold the rather extraordinary number of one hundred and ninety one thousand and odd hundred copies." By late summer 1863, he had in mind a new novel in twenty monthly parts.

Despite his need to "clear the Christmas stone out of the road" and to rid himself of a short paper under the rubric of the "Uncommercial Traveller," a persona he had created in 1860 to unify his disparate articles for *All the Year Round*, he found himself entranced with his new Christmas story, "Mrs. Lirriper's Lodgings." Its success prompted him to write a sequel, "Mrs. Lirriper's Legacy" (1864). "I had a very strong belief in her when I wrote about her, finding that she made a great effect upon me; but she certainly has gone beyond my hopes." Early in 1864, he boasted that "the Christmas number has been the greatest success of all; has shot ahead of last year; has sold about two hundred and twenty thousand; and has made the name of Mrs. Lirriper so swiftly and domestically famous as never was."[20] With some of the features that had made a success of Mrs. Gamp, the widowed Mrs. Lirriper seemed to him "indeed a most brilliant old lady," a rough-spoken, sentimental, good-hearted lodging-house keeper, who narrates a redemptive tale of betrayal, suffering, rebirth, and new life, of a deserted orphan adopted by a fairy godmother and godfather who proves himself to be a wise, talented son.

Through myth and storytelling, the young hero celebrates love, self-worth, and well-deserved worldly success.[21] The emotional power of his goodness rewrites the story of his parents' lives, affirming that "unchanging Love and Truth will carry us through all!" Frederick Dickens makes a cameo appearance as Joshua Lirriper, the irresponsible younger brother of Mrs. Lirriper's deceased husband. The dismal forty pounds for which John Dickens was imprisoned in the Marshalsea echoes in the dispossession that Miss Wozenham's indebtedness produces—"after all it was just forty pound, and—There!" Like Aunt Betsey in *David Copperfield*, Mrs. Lirriper glows with a maternal warmth, love, and commitment that makes the timing of her creation particularly ironic. On August 5, 1863, Mrs. George Hogarth died. Dickens gave Catherine a letter of authorization to the manager of Kensal Green cemetery to open the grave in which Mary had been buried and to which he had given his mother-in-law "the right in perpetuity." On September 12, 1863, Elizabeth Dickens died. The previous September her rapid recovery had seemed "quite amazing." She had been, though, "in a terrible state of decay." With another funeral to look after, he postponed a visit from the de la Rues, but only until the day after the burial. There was to be no period of mourning. For her gravestone, he wrote the cold words HERE ALSO LIE THE REMAINS OF ELIZABETH DICKENS WHO DIED SEPTEMBER 12TH 1863 AGED 73 YEARS. Two days after her death, he wrote to Wills, highlighting that Mrs. Lirriper had just been born. He added, as an afterthought, that "my poor mother died quite suddenly at last. Her condition was frightful."[22]

With a genius for transforming personal loss into aesthetic

wealth, he was hardly surprised by, though he exalted in, the success of the two Mrs. Lirriper stories. Ironically, the perverse maternal legacy was commercially golden. Beginning with the resuscitative success of *Great Expectations, All the Year Round* never seriously faltered again, though his contributions thereafter were to be confined to articles and Christmas stories. When *Great Expectations* appeared in book form in July 1861, the bookstores could not stock enough copies. He excoriated the inefficiency of the publisher and the printer, who "caused it to be out of print for a fortnight! Imagine that, with a second edition all sold to the trade, a third edition already being ordered away, and not a copy of either producible until next Saturday!"[23] By the end of August, the fourth edition was going to the press.

Having in mind the importance of not allowing readers to drift away from *All the Year Round,* he arranged to have the first installment of Collins' *The Woman in White* appear in the same week as the last of *A Tale of Two Cities,* with "a few words . . . between the end of mine and the beginning of his—to the effect that" he would always reserve "that first place for a continuous story" and that he hoped "this series will take its place in English literature." The hardworking, ambitious Collins, "shut up at [his] desk" in Broadstairs, had been cooperating through the summer and autumn of 1859, "every day . . . slowly and painfully launching [his] new serial novel. The story is the longest and the most complicated I have ever tried yet—and the difficulties at the beginning of it are all but insuperable." By July 1860, he had "wound [it] up in a very new and pretty manner," and felt the relief of having "written at the bottom of the four hundred and ninetieth page of my manuscript the two noblest words in the English language—*The End.*" He went out to "walk off the work and the excitement of winning the battle against the infernal periodical system, *at last.*" Throughout its serial publication, despite a mixed reception from the critics, it sustained and increased the already high weekly sales of *All the Year Round.* Dickens congratulated him on having "triumphantly finished your best book." Within a week of its volume publication in August, it had sold 1,350 copies. By September, Collins crowed, "Cock-a doodle-doo! The critics may go to the devil!" With 1,400 pounds in his pocket, "with the copyright in [his] possession . . . all sorts of good news" kept coming. From

Paris, Katie soon wrote to Harriet Collins, "How is my illustrious brother-in-law? (Private and satirical.) We have heard of his riches and his growing magnificence and plumpness. . . ."[24]

With a genius for subtle but symmetrical complications of plot in a mystery structure that exceeded his mentor's. Collins had created the first of his two extraordinary detective narratives. He had learned a great deal from the older writer, and certain aspects of Dickens' skills continued to be sharpened by his appreciation of Collins' major strength. Lacking, though, a whole arsenal of talents that Dickens possessed, Collins' spare, effective prose had none of his poetic resonances. Without the social compassion, psychological insight, or linguistic resources at the master's command, he excelled as an entertaining writer of one-dimensional fictions whose brilliance with suspenseful plot brought him great popular success throughout the 1860s. Amidst his unstinting praise, Dickens occasionally, but tactfully, offered advice. Collins objected in general to "the nonsense talked in certain quarters about [his] incapability of character-painting," which he discussed in his preface to *The Woman in White*. Dickens affirmed that the novel was "a great advance on all your former writing, and most especially in respect of tenderness . . . in character it is excellent. . . . No one else could have done it half so well. I have stopped in every chapter to notice some instance of ingenuity, or some happy turn of writing." He did, though, "always contest your disposition to give an audience credit for nothing, which necessarily involves the forcing of points on their attention."

Collins' major objection to Dickens' fiction, explicit in his suggestions about *A Tale of Two Cities*, was that he did not tell his audience enough. For Collins, the art of fiction demanded a series of self-conscious signposts directing the reader toward an unraveling of a well-constructed plot. For Dickens, plot revelation needed to rise organically from the interaction of characters in a narrative pattern in which suggestion and symbol appealed to the reader's intuition. The differences were oddly complementary, and Dickens even believed that Collins' procedure was one he could effect, if he chose to. "One of these days" they might "do a story together" that would combine their strengths. When, in October 1862, Collins feared that a bad episode of a recurrent illness might prevent him from continuing a serial novel, his friend offered to take up the artistic challenge and the fraternal obligation. "Say you are unequal to your work, and want me, and I will come to London straight and do your work. I am quite confident that, with your notes and a few words of explanation, I could take it up at any time and do it. Absurdly unnecessary to say that it would be a makeshift! But I could do it at a pinch, so like you that no one should find out the difference. . . . The trouble would be nothing to me, and the triumph of overcoming a difficulty great."25 Collins recovered in time to do the installment himself.

By April 1861, the commercial success of *The Woman in White* had made it clear that his moment had come to be rewarded financially far beyond what it was sensible for *All the Year Round* to provide. Lever had proved a failure. Bulwer-Lytton's *A Strange Story* had successfully followed *Great Expectations*. In March 1862, Collins fulfilled the last of his obligations to the journal with the beginning of the serial publication of *No Name*. Having been "slowly—very slowly—building up the scaffolding of the new book," in July 1861 he had *"tried* the outline" on Dickens, who "was immensely struck by it, and . . . gave such an account of it to Wills . . . that the said Wills's eyes rolled in his head with astonishment when he and I next met at the office. If I can only write up to my design. . . ." Manuscript in hand, Dickens thought it "extremely clever and careful . . . quite up to the mark of the Woman in White—but the creaking of the wheels is so very loud, that" he sent Collins "a little advice on that head." From the sale of the copyright and the serial rights, he earned £4,600. "Not so bad, for story-telling," Collins boasted to his mother. Dickens wrote glowingly to Collins that from the time of his first novel he "was certain . . . that you were the Writer who would come ahead of all the Field—being the only one who combined invention and power, both humourous and pathetic, with that invincible determination to work, and that profound conviction that nothing of worth is to be done without work."26 He felt pride and pleasure in his friend's accomplishment, and concern about his deteriorating health, a combination of gout and rheumatism so debilitating that he soon began to go regularly to spas on the Continent.

With the completion of the publication of *No Name*, Dickens was sorry "that we part company (though only in a literary sense}. . . ." Even if Collins' health had allowed him to remain on the staff of *All the Year Round,* money and ambition would have prevented it. With "Dickens's full approval," he signed a contract in April 1861 with Smith and Elder for their exclusive rights to his next novel, "to be published either as a *separate serial,* or in the Cornhill Magazine, as they please," for five thousand pounds. "No living author (except Dickens) has had such an offer as this for *one* book. If I only live to earn the money, I have a chance at last of putting something by against a rainy day." That it was likely to be published in *Cornhill,* a rival of *All the Year Round* that Thackeray edited and in which a satirical depiction he did of Forster had appeared, did not give Dickens a moment's hesitation in encouraging him to accept. In effect, "Smith & Elder have *bought* me away from All the Year Round and in circumstances which *in Dickens's opinion* amply justify me in leaving." Such an offer reflected well on Dickens' longtime confidence in Collins. His own pioneering success as a professional author and *All the Year Round*'s generous treatment of its contributors had helped make the offer possible. He hardly had to extend himself to sympathize with Collins' exalting that "if I live and keep my brains in good working order, I shall have got to the top of the tree, after all, before forty."[27]

Dickens continued to supplement his royalty income and his earnings from the journal by public readings. After the first reading tour in 1859, he had no doubt that through carefully planned tours he could guarantee his and his family's financial security as well as have the satisfaction of constant applause. In the spring of 1858 he had stepped onto the platform with some hesitation. The success of the provincial tour in the autumn and Smith's sure grip on the business details had increased his confidence. Having resisted the temptation to read in America in the fall of 1859, he found it a small matter to read in the provinces in October, with only the final chapters of *A Tale of Two Cities* still to be written, and to "have a Christmas series in town." Stepping into the *All the Year Round* breech with *Great Expectations,* struggling with the "terribles," he did not read again until March 1861, when he gave six performances in London. "After paying a large staff of men and all other charges," including Smith's 10 percent, he still had over five hundred pounds profit. Suffering painful facial neuralgia, finding it a strain both to read and to continue writing, he felt glad when the series ended, though the demand for tickets was so great that he could have extended it indefinitely.

The readings at St. James's Hall were wildly successful, partly because of Arthur Smith's business expertise, mostly because of Dickens' increasing professionalism in creating a stage atmosphere and projecting a distinctive image. He had a special reading desk constructed. Dressing identically for each performance, he kept his formal hat and gloves in a special place on the desk, the elbow of the hand in which he held his book resting against the lectern. The stage lighting was manipulated by dark curtains and gas illumination that he provided, employing his own "gasman" even when he traveled, in order to throw completely even light on his face and figure. Purposefully, he made no attempt to perform from memory. These were to be readings by a great author from his own works. Usually beginning in a flat, somewhat nasal voice, he wanted the audience to be aware, no matter how empathetic and dramatic the eventual presentation, that these were characters in a book and that he was their creator.

In the summer of 1861 he concentrated on preparing new readings, having committed himself to an extensive series in the fall. Each morning he labored for at least three hours at Gad's Hill, condensing the narratives and perfecting his delivery. By August, he had "the Copperfield reading ready . . . and am now going to blaze away at Nickleby, which I don't like half as well." Finally, after great effort, he had "made a continuous narrative out of Copperfield," something that had been on his mind for years, "that I think will reward the exertion it is likely to cost me." It became his favorite reading selection. Though he made constant efforts to add to the repertoire, particularly from Christmas stories such as "Going into Society" and "Doctor Marigold," the core of his readings were the selections from *Copperfield* and *Nickleby*, the death of Paul Dombey, the trial scene from *Pickwick*, the selections from *Oliver*, including Sikes's murder of Nancy, created in 1863 but not performed until 1868, and the reliable *A Christmas Carol* and *The Cricket on the Hearth*. [28] Though he later experimented with a reading from *Bleak House*, on the whole he seems to have found the novels after *Copperfield* not as amenable to condensation for reading performance.

In late October 1861 he was to begin a series of forty-six readings throughout England and Scotland. For good measure he had agreed to read his six-chapter version of *David Copperfield* in mid-January 1862 in "the place with which my childhood is inseparably associated," for the benefit of the Rochester Mechanics' Institute. To his distress, the one man he credited with the business success of the readings became ill during the summer. Dickens shared with Arthur Smith a fellowship of common-sense labor and mutual protectiveness. They were business partners in a successful venture in which each respected the other's strengths and weaknesses. Smith kept Dickens' nervous world calm. Used to carrying the business burden of life mainly himself, Dickens felt secure in Smith's competence, free to devote himself to other things. When he first heard a "bad account" of his health in early September, he was shaken. He urged him to come to Gad's Hill, where they "would take the most careful charge" of him. He seemed to be making himself worse with his worry that he would not be able to supervise the fall reading tour. On October 1, he died, "a friend whom I can never replace—who always went with me . . . and without whom, I fear," the readings "will be dreary and weary to me." For his tombstone, Dickens wrote a loving epitaph: HERE ALSO LIE THE REMAINS OF MR. ARTHUR SMITH, IN THE GRAVE OF HIS BROTHER AND FATHER, HE DIED IST OCTOBER 1861 AGED 36 YEARS. FOR HIS ZEAL, INTEGRITY, AND FIDELITY, HE WAS WIDELY BELOVED AND HONOURED. AND IT IS BELIEVED BY THOSE WHO KNEW HIM BEST, THAT HE HAD THE CLEAREST HEAD IN AFFAIRS OF LIFE, THAT WERE EVER UNITED TO THE SIMPLE TASTES, THE SWEET TEMPER AND GENTLENESS, OF AN AFFECTIONATE CHILD.[29]

On the day of Smith's burial, Henry Austin died. Weak in the chest and throat, he expired of "inflammation of the windpipe." Dickens had visited earlier in the day. One funeral followed another. His macabre sense of humor allowed him to comment that "the manner in which every body sat against the wall was wonderful. And there was the usual ghoul-like indispensability of cake and wine." Austin had been one of his earliest friends, a companion in amateur theatricals when they had been young bachelors together, a mature collaborator in sanitary reform in the 1840s. Always self-reliant, Austin had been a welcome addition to the family, a loving husband, whose unexpected death at the age of forty-nine left Letitia in shock. With his fear of emotional scenes, her brother initially "had a dread of going near her. . . . God forgive me." Given the circumstances, though, "she certainly came out better today than I had expected." Since Austin had left little besides an insurance policy and the value of the lease of their house, Dickens immediately offered "ready money" and practical advice. As executor, he supervised the payment of outstanding bills.

Worried about Letitia's health, he was keen "to know how you are, and that you are finding some rest and support under your heavy trial." When she began to suffer choking spasms, he recommended an "intensely bitter" medicine that John Elliotson had prescribed fourteen or fifteen years before, when he had had "a nervous seizure in the throat." He soon began a tactful campaign to have her awarded a government pension in recognition of her husband's contributions as an engineer and sanitary reformer. The day after his fiftieth birthday he reminisced with her about how twenty-eight years before Henry had celebrated with him his twenty-first birthday at Furnival's Inn, "and stayed there all night. . . . All wounds want time—wounds of the heart and mind, most of all." When, after correspondence with Shaftesbury and Palmerston, the pension of sixty pounds a year was finally granted in June 1864, he was "so delighted that I can hardly write to congratulate you."[30]

After Arthur Smith's funeral, reading was difficult. Dickens had to force himself "to open one of the books, and screw the text out of [him]self, in a flat dull way." It was as if his right hand were gone. The opening performance in Norwich seemed to go badly, his ghostly presence an absence that pained him. He was not at all himself. The next day he went for a brisk walk in the bright air, exhorting himself to get command of himself. "The readings must be fought out, like all the rest of life." Though he missed "poor Arthur dreadfully," and "the sense I used to have of compactness and neatness about me while I was reading is gone," he felt the loss not because of anything to do with the readings "but because I loved him and he deserved it well." His new manager, Thomas Headland, seemed noticeably undeserving, "a very honest fellow, but what we shipmates call a dull sailor." He was "the best man I could lay my hand on when I lost the man who is never to be replaced." Soon Head-

land appeared incompetent, "the worthy man with the genius
for mistakes," whom Dickens would tolerate only as long as
necessary. For the time being, though he was "damned aggravat-
ing," he would not "blow him up." Whatever his abilities, he of
course could not compete with the memory of Arthur. 'Headland and all the rest of them are always somewhere, and he was
always everywhere."[31] The second night in Norwich went better. The following afternoons and nights through the next three
months in Bury Saint Edmunds, Colchester, Hastings, Brighton, Canterbury, Dover, Newcastle, Berwick, Glasgow and Edinburgh, went from satisfactorily to brilliantly.

The new readings, particularly *Copperfield*, were, in Dickens' self-laudatory rhetoric, "a wonderful success." In Canterbury, the audience seemed "positively perfect . . . an intelligent
and delightful response in them, like the touch of a beautiful
instrument." Everywhere he "found that peculiar personal relation between my audience and myself on which I counted most
when I entered on this enterprise." In Scotland, in late November and early December 1861, Headland broke down totally.
Dickens, though, had already risen to exhilaration and remained
there temporarily. In Newcastle, he prevented likely injuries
when the threat of fire from a fallen gas batten caused a momentary panic in a huge audience. "A lady in the front row of stalls
screamed, and ran out wildly towards me, and for one instant
there was a terrible wave in the crowd. I addressed that lady
laughing . . . and called out as if it happened every night,
'There's nothing the matter, I assure you; don't be alarmed; pray
sit down'; and she sat down directly, and there was a thunder
of applause." In Glasgow and Edinburgh the large crowds,
when tickets were oversold, were accommodated on the stage,
"like some impossible tableau or gigantic picnic; one pretty girl
in full dress lying on her side all night, holding on to one of the
legs of my table."

In Liverpool, in the middle of December, when he learned
of Prince Albert's unexpected death, remembering that "the
Queen has always been very considerate and gracious to me,"
Dickens postponed the performances as a sign of respect,
though he later thought the queen's protracted mourning unhealthy. The prince himself "was neither a phenomenon, nor
the saviour of England; and England will do exactly without

him as it did with him. He was a good example of the best sort
of perfectly commonplace man." At Gad's Hill for Christmas,
Dickens took advantage of readings in Plymouth, Leamington,
and Birmingham early in the new year to visit Macready, "decidedly much older and infirm."[32] When he read *Copperfield,* he
was amazed and deeply touched to see tears running down the
retired actor's face. After the Plymouth readings, he went back
to Liverpool to do those he had postponed earlier. He had already committed himself to another spring series in London, as
if once he had gotten started he could not stop.

From March to June 1862, having exchanged Gad's Hill for
"the nastiest little house in London," near Hyde Park, he gave
eleven readings at St. James's. By the beginning of May, he felt
exhausted, "the readings . . . becoming very trying; the continuous effort and exertion, in so large a place, being quite wearing
on a hot night." He went to France with Ellen for a week before
the last performance, which "ended with a most tremendous
crowd and great enthusiasm." Then he took a long holiday. He
entreated Forster, who wanted the rest to be an indefinite one,
"to go back to what you know of my childish days, and to ask
yourself whether it is natural that something of the character
formed in me then, and lost under happier circumstances,
should have reappeared in the last five years . . . in the never to
be forgotten misery of this later time." To Georgina, he remarked that he "never could have borne the marriage" even for
as long as he did if he "had not been reading." He had partly
replaced his marriage with a more dramatic version of the most
sustained relationship of his life. "Success attends me everywhere, thank God, and the great crowds I see every night all
seem to regard me with affection as a personal friend."

During the summer and autumn, he flirted again with the
temptation to read abroad, this time in Australia. The offer was
for ten thousand pounds for eight months' work. "If it were not
for the hope of a gain that would make me more independent
of the worst, I could not look the travel and absence and exertion
in the face. I know perfectly well before-hand how unspeakably
wretched I should be. But these renewed and larger offers tempt
me. I can force myself to go aboard a ship, and I can force myself
to do at that reading-desk what I have done a hundred times."
If he went, he would travel as an independent entrepreneur,

with his own staff, the Australians acting as paid agents. With the prospect, he now imagined, of at least twelve thousand pounds in six months, he "should come back rich." Though he would have to postpone the novel in twenty monthly parts that he had in mind to start soon, the experience probably would enrich his writing. If he put off the trip for a few years he might then "not be so well fitted for the excessive wear and tear."33

The indecision went on for months. He consulted with Bulwer-Lytton, who "was all for going." The whole population would attend. He would get ideas for a new book. Both the readings and the book would make a fortune "over there as well as here." Such unlimited confidence seemed even to Dickens almost absurd. Richard Henry Horne wrote from Melbourne, as usual asking for a favor but also urging him to come to Australia. Dickens could not determine "altogether to abandon the idea, and yet it is immensely difficult to pursue it." Vacationing in Paris, he spent much of November 1862 trying to make a decision. "There are so many reasons for and against, and I am so very unwilling to go, that it causes me great uneasiness of mind in trying to do right and decide for the best " The prospect of leaving family and friends for such a long period depressed him, and he could not take Ellen with him.

There was a new pressing anxiety. In the summer, Georgina had become ill with "degeneration of the heart." Weak and short of breath, she had palpitations and "excruciating pain in the left breast." In June, he took her to Dover "in the hope of doing her service through a little change." He was "so anxious and distressed about her " though, that he felt "altogether dazed' for weeks. "Our best and dearest friend," Georgina was "the most unselfish, zealous, and devoted creature that ever lived on earth. . . . No one can ever know what she has been to us, and how she has supplied an empty place . . . since the girls were mere dolls." She was soon "certainly better than she was." But she was also depressed, perhaps frightened by her physical condition, perhaps also experiencing some traumatic long-delayed nervous response to the separation and its tensions. "All that alacrity and cheer of spirit' that used to distinguish her, are gone. . . . And she is very low about herself, almost as soon as one has ceased to speak to her after brightening her up." Though she was noticeably improved by late fall, there was still "cause for great anxiety about her."[34] By the end of the year she seemed considerably better. To Dickens' great relief the threat disappeared almost as suddenly as it had come.

If he went to Australia, Dickens hoped that Thomas Beard, who was in need of employment, would go with him to help keep him in good spirits and to take care of personal details, "seconding the Inimitable in the ring, delivering him at the scratch in fine condition, keeping off the crowd, polishing him up when at all punished, and checking the local accounts." Beard's profit would be substantial. Would he do it? "There are not six men in the world I would go with—and I don't know the other five." Beard said no. By early December 1862, Dickens had decided nothing. The balance, though, was slightly turning in his mind "against Australia." The week before Christmas he was not absolutely sure that he would *"not* go." By Christmas Day he had decided against it. Beard's declination "unquestionably . . . brought down the scale on the home side."[35] Feeling immensely relieved, he solaced himself and his restlessness with the prospect of a few weeks more in Paris at the beginning of January 1863 and perhaps a trip to Genoa.

⁂ 4 ⁂

FRIENDS BEGAN TO DIE. THE ELDERLY PROCTER, FRIGHTENED, FEELING his decrepitude, moaned to Forster that "everybody seems to die and leave us." When the once lovely Frances Yates died, it seemed as if "a beautiful part of [his] own youth" were gone, "and the dream that we are all dreaming seems to darken." Some of the casualties were Dickens' contemporaries in age as well as in spirit. Dinner with family and friends in October 1864 was interrupted by a telegram. He kept his eyes on the paper and quietly read aloud its condensed, definitive message, LEECH DEAD. A sudden "silence fell upon us," Marcus Stone remembered. "No one said a word. What was there to say? We had been laughing a moment before. We now all remained with bowed heads until Dickens rose from the table saying, 'I must go up early tomorrow morning to see his poor little wife. I may be of some use.' "

Five years younger than Dickens, Leech had struggled for

the last year with angina. In late 1863, Thackeray had felt frightened at the state of Leech's health. Frank Stone had dined with him at the Garrick the week before his death. They had "talked much of the beloved Dickens." Depressed, looking "weary and ill," Leech said that he had had a horrible attack the other day. "I thought I was going to die, and managed to get off my horse and lean against a gate." He forced himself out of bed a few days later to participate in a children's party at home, in order to create the appearance of normalcy. Annie Leech was in tears. His pain relieved by an opiate, he returned to bed. The party went on downstairs. Alarmed, Frederick Evans and Shirley Brooks came from the *Punch* office. John Everett Millais, one of his closest friends, who had that day returned from the Continent and found his dinner appointment with Leech postponed, received a message to go to his home immediately. As Millais entered, racing up the stairs, Leech died in his bedroom. Downstairs, the noise of the children's party still tinkled through the house.[36]

Weary, deeply saddened, having helped Millais make the funeral arrangements, Dickens returned to Gad's Hill the next day. The widely liked Leech brought together at Kensal Green cemetery a lifetime of friends and associates in art and literature. Dickens took his place, following the coffin on "a bitterly cold" November afternoon, next to Lemon, Evans, W. H. Russell, Edmund Yates, Hablot Knight Browne, Cruikshank, Edwin Landseer, William Frith, Millais, Tom Taylor, and Marcus Stone. The reading of the funeral service seemed "pathetically" bad. "Shocked and distressed," Wilkie Collins felt too fragile to attend the burial of a man with whom he had had "many nervous troubles in common." Constantly ill with "pain in face and head," Katie's husband wrote to his mother from Geneva, where they had stopped on their way back to England, "poor fellow how he suffered, and people thought it fancy."

At Gad's Hill again, Dickens felt dessicated, unable to work. "He could do nothing; seemed for the time to have quite lost the power." With someone wanting to write "a Biographical account" of himself, he would not cooperate, "as I may think it time to pursue the subject when my life is over."[37] Apparently he still had it in mind to do a memoir or autobiography. When the man who had read the funeral service so badly solicited information for a biography of Leech, Dickens responded that "it is a pity to write that kind of Biography at all. It seems to me that such a man's life is always best told in his works." And what would he say of Leech in that hypothetical memoir? He might say that, despite his gloomy shyness, his nervous temperament, and his disappointment in his inability to paint in oils, he had become the premier illustrator of Victorian domestic life, a generous satirist who loved the world he satirized. Deeply devoted to his wife and two daughters, he took his recreation as a gentleman hunter.

But in his private memory, Dickens would recall that, always pressed for money, Leech had too generously supported an exploitative father, who outlived him, and numbers of unmarried sisters, and he would note the similarity between John Leech, Sr., whom he employed briefly on the *Daily News* in 1848, and John Dickens. He would most remember their warm companionship during the 1840s and early 1850s: his contributions to the Christmas books; his participation in their amateur theatricals; "all our near intercourse of many years in the confidence of autumn holidays by the sea . . . all the little jokes we humoured and exaggerated"; their long walks and excursions of exorcism and revival; Leech's wife's giving birth to a daughter in the railroad hotel at Euston Station in 1847, a baby who died soon afterward, an anticipation of the heartache he was to feel at his own infant daughter's death; the mesmeric healing of Leech in Bonchurch in 1849; and his special relationship with little Sydney Dickens. Whenever Sydney was home from a cruise, Leech would take him to the Garrick for dinner and to the theatre. "On the first of these occasions the officer came out so frightfully small, that Leech told us afterwards he was filled with horror when he saw him cutting his dinner . . . with a large knife. On the other hand he felt that to suggest a small knife to an officer and a gentleman would be an unpardonable affront. So after meditating for some time, he felt that his course was, to object to the club-knives as enormous and gigantic—to remonstrate with the servant on their huge proportions—and with a grim dissatisfaction to demand small ones. After which, he and the officer messed with great satisfaction, and agreed that things in general were running too large in England."[38] Also, Dickens would remember that they had never quarreled, except for the one instance in which he had rebuked Leech for accepting, without checking with him, the claim that Charley was to live with his mother on his own volition rather than on his father's wish. Though Leech may have known that Dickens was wrong even in his claim of what the truth was, he had been, and continued to be, for twenty years a loyal friend.

At the funeral, he would have been reminded of a fellow artist with whom he had been less intimate. Leech's gravesite was next to Thackeray's, one of Leech's oldest, closest friends, with whom Dickens had never been completely reconciled after the hostility of the Yates–Thackeray–Garrick Club affair.39 There had been no coldness, though, between Katie Dickens and Thackeray and his daughters. Since the mid-1850s, they had been warm friends. Only abroad intermittently now, since expenses on the Continent were "fast becoming dearer than England," Katie had seen the Thackerays regularly in London, where she and her husband had an apartment. Aware that Thackeray, sometimes depressed, brooded about his estrangement from her father, she had encouraged him to take a reconciling initiative. " 'Oh, you mean I should apologise,' " he said. " 'No, I don't mean that exactly,' " she said, "hesitating . . . 'You know he is more in the wrong than I am,' said he. . . . 'Even if that were so . . . he is more shy of speaking than you are, and perhaps he mightn't know that you would be nice to him. He cannot apologise, I fear.' 'In that case there will be no reconciliation,' " Thackeray said decisively. After a long pause, he added, " 'And how do I know he would be nice to me?' . . . 'Oh,' " Katie said, " 'I can answer for him.' " Soon, at the Athenaeum, he had broken away from a conversation to confront Dickens at the head of the stairs. "It is time this foolish estrangement should cease" and "we should be to each other what we used to be. Come; shake hands." Dickens responded amiably. Afterward, Thackeray had told Katie, " 'Oh . . . your father knew he was wrong and was full of apologies . . . and we are friends again, thank God!' "

They had never been close friends, though. The reconciliation, mostly perfunctory, satisfied Dickens' conscience and his sense of decorum without touching his feelings. Dickens knew that Thackeray "had long been alarmingly ill." Katie had a note on Christmas Eve 1863 asking her to come to nearby Palace

Green to celebrate the holiday with the Thackerays. Feeling depressed, she declined. In the morning, his daughters found him "lying as though peacefully asleep," dead from a cerebral stroke at the age of fifty-two. At his funeral a few days later, "Dickens clasped the hand of his old friend Mark Lemon, when, as each looked into the moist eyes of the other, bygone became bygones." Whatever the degree of truth in his daughter's accounts of these incidents, he did not become intimate with Lemon again. They still went their separate ways. Dickens was not the forgiving sort, except in principle and when the cost was minimal. When an intermediary had tried in October 1863 to promote a meeting with Catherine, neither the five years that had passed nor their children in common could make the slightest dent in his defenses. "My wife has gone her way and I have gone mine and when we took our separate courses I took mine for ever." When Miss Coutts tried once again to promote an informal meeting between them at a time of mutual mourning, he claimed that "a page in my life which once had writing on it, has become absolutely blank, and . . . it is not in my power to pretend that it has a solitary word upon it."40 Though he could manage formal reconciliations with Thackeray and Lemon, the scars still remained.

In bitter December weather, Thackeray's coffin was watched into its grave by the tearful eyes of family and friends. Though he had never been intimate with Thackeray but "always met on friendly and pleasant terms," Wilkie Collins eulogized later that "he has left a great name, most worthily won." Dickens obsessively stared at one of the black crepe funereal decorations of the kind whose lachrymose ostentation he had always deplored as an insult to honest feelings and to the simplicity of death. Supposedly, he looked at the grave for some time after almost everyone else had left and had such difficulty talking with people that he walked away by himself. Pressured by Thackeray's friends, he agreed the next month to write a eulogy, published in February 1864. "The injudicious and absurd writing of some of his—miscalled—friends had made it a very difficult thing to do, with his children looking on."

The difficulty had to do partly with ambivalent feelings about Thackeray, partly with the closeness of so many deaths. The list had become long. In November 1859, his neighbor Frank

Stone, fifty-nine years old, had suddenly died of an aneurism, a "spasm of the heart," two days after they had walked together in Tavistock Square. Dickens went to Highgate cemetery "and bought the spot of ground . . . appointed the funeral," counseled the family, gave Arthur Stone, Stone's eldest son, shorthand lessons, and Marcus Stone letters of recommendation. Having been in Stone's confidence about his intentions, Dickens supported the surviving daughter and her brothers in fulfilling Stone's wish that the children and their mother live separately after his death.

The news in March 1862 that the sculptor Angus Fletcher had died touched his memory and his feelings, more a reminiscence than a trauma. The "affectionate and gentle creature" had lived to a respectable old age. The next month, Cornelius Felton, fifty-five years old, his oyster-eating companion on the streets of New York, died three thousand miles away. With "a shock of surprise," he regretted that their "ways had [not] crossed a little oftener." Closer to home, the recent death rate in the White family, all of whom Dickens and his older children knew intimately, had been high. The mordant sixty-two-year-old James White, his friend and landlord in Bonchurch, had by the spring of 1861 become chronically ill. White began indulging in morbid, humorously grotesque predictions. "Whenever they go away from home, he minutely calculates how long it will take him to return by a particular day, *to be buried*. And he cheers them of an evening by calculating in how many months there will be none of them left but the little dog. . . ." In April 1862, he "was seized with such excruciating pain that it was very difficult indeed to get him to bed. For the last two or three hours he seemed to have no pain . . . but passed very quietly away."[41]

One year later another April had brought an even sharper blow. The slim, gentle, loyal Augustus Egg, who had long ago proposed to Georgina, died while traveling in Algiers. Dr. Frank Beard, who thought him sickly, probably had recommended the North African trip. On his way there he had briefly visited Dickens and the recuperating Georgina in Paris, and Dickens was forebodingly "struck by his extreme nervousness." Four years younger, he had been both friend and protégé, and had almost become a variant of a brother-in-law. With a talent for friendship, he had been the warm host and unostentatious

center of an artistic circle of talented young men with whom
Wilkie and Charles Collins were also intimate, and he had
helped provide Dickens with a link to the new generation of
painters. Holman Hunt brought "the dreadfully shocked and
distressed" Wilkie Collins the news. "Nothing can replace the
loss," Collins moaned, "he was a man in ten thousand. It is a
calamity, in every sense of the word, for everyone who knew
him." Dickens was deeply pained. He would not cooperate with
Hunt in making public "private companionship and confidence.
. . . His words and ways, in that half-gypsy life of our theatricals," were now "sanctified by his death." He had "always been
sweet-tempered, humourous, conscientious, thoroughly good,
and thoroughly beloved. . . . There is not a single grain of alloy,
thank God, in my remembrance of our intimate personal association."

Memories of all their happy days together rose with persistent vividness—Egg vainly trying to learn Italian when the
triumvirate went to Italy, Egg sitting in their hotel room in
Venice "eternally posting up" long entries in his mysterious
travel diary, "that wonderful necromantic volume which we
never shall see opened," Egg falling out of a hammock during
rehearsals of *The Frozen Deep*. That brought to mind how many
of the actors in the play had already succumbed to "the Great
Frozen Deep" that "lay under those boards we acted on!" He
attempted to turn away from his melancholy. "This won't do.
We must close up the ranks and march on." Dickens' willful,
self-exhortatory affirmation of positive thinking had a hollow
sadness to it. He intoned the gloomy necrology. Of the participants in that play, Alfred Dickens, Arthur Smith, Albert Smith,
Frank Stone, Henry Austin, and now Augustus Egg were
dead.42 With barely suppressed anguish, he realized "what a
great cemetery one walks through after forty!"

On New Year's Eve 1863 he had been eerily disturbed by a
symbol and a premonition. Playing charades with the children,
he made, out of black cloth hung on a stick, "something to carry,
as the Goddess of Discord. . . . It came into my head as it stood
against the wall while I was dressing, that it was like the dismal
things that are carried at Funerals." He cut away some of the
black calico in order "to remove this likeness." While using it
in the charades he "noticed that its *shadow* on the wall still had

that resemblance, though the thing itself had not." When he went to bed, he brought it into his bedroom. It still looked exactly like the object at which he had obsessively stared a few days before at Thackeray's funeral. Disturbed by the insistence of that resemblance, he "took it to pieces" before he went to sleep. At five-fifteen the next afternoon, his second son, Walter Landor Dickens, died at the age of twenty-two in Calcutta. Exhausted and ill, he had been hospitalized to regain his strength for the journey back to England. His army career had been a gradual, then precipitous, failure, mainly because of chronic indebtedness. Charley had visited him in 1860, paying, "as he supposed, Everything. Yet before he got back to England, there was more to pay "

When Walter expressed his desire to put his name down for home service, his father rebuked him for his folly, including the loss of overseas supplement, and turned down his request for additional money. "He must now, as a matter of common reason and justice to his other brothers, live upon his own means." Vowing to Georgina that they would not hear from him until he was out of debt, Walter did not keep the resolution. In early December he wrote to Mamie to say that he was "so weak that he could hardly crawl." A few days before Christmas, not having seen his son for six years, Dickens sent Frank "out to Calcutta," also to make a career in the army. On the afternoon of New Year's Day Walter "was talking to the other patients about his arrangements for coming home." He "became excited, coughed violently, had a great gush of blood from the mouth, and fell dead . . . in a few seconds." He had an "extensive and perfectly incurable aneurism of the Aorta, which had burst." His father had "reason to believe (but I do not tell them so, on Georgina's account) that if he had lived, as I could have wished he had, to see home again, he might probably have . . . died at the door." When Frank arrived in India, he found that his brother had already been dead for a month. The attending doctor wrote from Calcutta on January 4. The letter arrived on February 7, 1864, Dickens' fifty-second birthday. Six months later he received a request from the colonel of Walter's regiment asking him to pay the last of his son's outstanding debts.[43]

CHAPTER THIRTEEN

The Sons of Toil
(1864-1868)

❦ I ❦

THE EXPRESS TRAIN FROM DOVER TO LONDON, ITS BRAKES SCREECH-
ing its speed down to twenty-five miles an hour, hurtled off the
tracks on a sun-bright afternoon in June 1865. On the morning
of the accident, Dickens was returning from a ten-day holiday
in France. At Folkestone, he boarded the train. Its hours varied
each day with the tide, whose advantage the cross-Channel fer-
ries needed to enter the harbor. Forty miles southeast of London, the foreman of the work crew replacing worn timbers at
the small Staplehurst viaduct from which two sections of rails
at the eastern end had been removed had misread his schedule.
He expected the express two hours later. Ordinary safety rules
"had been consistently disregarded. . . ." The engineer saw a red
flag, then the gap in the rails. The rudimentary brake system
was partly in control of guards who did not see the danger. The
work crew was helpless.

Leaping the forty-two-foot gap, the engine smashed
through the side of the viaduct. Within seconds all but one
first-class carriage tumbled into a muddy ravine. In the carriage

caught by the bridge, the "beating and the dragging" threw the passengers against whatever resistance chance provided. On Dickens' left, Ellen Ternan screamed. Opposite him, Mrs. Ternan cried, "My God." He "caught hold of them both." Quieting their panic, he asked them not to " 'cry out. We can't help ourselves. Let us be quiet and composed.' " " 'Rely upon me,' " Mrs. Ternan replied, " 'upon my soul, I won't call out or stir.' " Huddled "in a corner of the carriage," unaware of how they had gotten there, they stayed "perfectly still" for a short while. " 'Will you remain here without stirring, while I get out of the window?' " "They both answered quite collectedly. 'Yes.' " Carefully, reassuringly, he crawled out of the carriage, which hung "inexplicably in the air over the side of the broken bridge." Looking down, he saw that that side of the viaduct was gone. Below was a sheer ten-foot drop, at the bottom a scene of bloody, mangled bodies and traumatized grief. The first quiet crying and moaning for help had begun. Dickens "could not have imagined so appalling a scene."[1]

Above him, the two women remained in the suspended carriage. People in "other compartments were madly trying to plunge out the window," with "no idea that there was an open swampy field . . . below them, and nothing else!" Two distracted guards, one with a bleeding face, were running about quite wildly. Dickens called out sharply, " 'Look at me. Do you know me?' 'We know you very well, Mr. Dickens.' 'Then . . . for God's sake give me your key, and send one of those labourers here, and I'll empty this carriage.' " Tilting the planks into a ramp, he helped Ellen and Mrs. Ternan down. Going back into the carriage, he got a half bottle of brandy from his luggage tied it around his neck, and climbed down to the wreck He filled his hat with water. Carrying it in his hands, he gave himself up to almost three exhausting hours of trying to help the survivors. Many were partly crushed under "the extraordinary weights . . . twisted up among iron and wood, and mud and water." One man was so "wedged under a carriage, with another over it, that they could only manage to convey some brandy to him but could by no possibility get him out. He sighed there calling for help for more than 2 hours and then . . . gave up the ghost, suffocated, crushed to death."

A man with a frightful cut in his skull staggered against

Dickens. After giving him brandy and laying him down on the grass, he watched him die. Stumbling over a woman "on her back against a little pollard-tree, with the blood streaming over her face," he asked if she could swallow. When she nodded, he "gave her some [brandy] and left her." The next time he passed, "she was dead." Soon the tree-shaded ground, where Ellen and the other "unhurt ladies" were gathered, "had as many dead in it as living." One dazed man, whom he helped pull "out of a most extraordinary heap of dark ruins in which he was jammed upside down," unaware that he was bleeding from the "eyes, ears, nose, and mouth," searched vainly for his wife. A few seconds before the crash he had changed places with a Frenchman who disliked having the window down. The Frenchman was dead. So too was the man's wife.[2]

Twice Dickens returned to the carriage, once to get the remaining full bottle of brandy, the other when he "clambered back" to retrieve the manuscript of a number of his novel-in-progress, *Our Mutual Friend.* It was "soiled, but otherwise unhurt." Writing the end of that book four months later, he remembered the accident, remarking that he could "never be much nearer parting company with [his] readers for ever" than he was "on Friday the Ninth of June in the present year ... until there shall be written against my life, the two words with which I have this day closed this book." Ten people had died, seven of them women. Forty were seriously injured. Though he had saved his manuscript, he noted the extraordinary phenomenon that at the moment of impact people's pockets had emptied, as if they were being relieved of material things in preparation for death. Soon the railroad accident became a "horrible ... terrible" reminder of mortality. While Mrs. Ternan seemed unharmed, Ellen had aches, bruises, and whiplash and Dickens became stiff in the limbs. His hands shook. Two days later, at Gad's Hill, he still looked "something the worse for wear." Attempting to reassure family and friends, he wrote, or dictated when he trembled too much to write, note after note, repeating how horrible it had been and how shaken he was from "getting out the dead and dying." He even answered a query of concern from Catherine. Sedatives helped. His pulse, though, was feeble. Noise distressed him. He felt "very nervous [and] faint." For years afterward, when traveling even short distances, he would sometimes "suddenly fall into a paroxysm of fear, tremble all over, clutch the arms of the railway carriage, large beads of perspiration standing on his face, and suffer agonies of terror. . . . Sometimes the agony was so great, he had to get out at the nearest station and walk home." He tried to talk himself into feeling better. He was, though, "curiously weak . . . as if [he] were recovering from a long illness."[3]

Worried about Ellen, the poor "patient," who seemed to be taking a long time to recuperate, he did not flag in his attention to all the Ternans. He continued helping Maria's acting career. "I have a high opinion of the young lady and take a strong interest in her self and her family." He urged her employment "not because I have a great friendship for her and know her to be one of the best and bravest of little spirits . . . but because I . . . believe her to have more aptitude in a minute than all the other people of her standing on the stage in a month." Fanny soon gave up her operatic aspirations for a writing career. Having met when Fanny went to Italy in 1858, she and Thomas Trollope, Anthony's brother, were married in 1866. He was an established writer who had already been published in *All the Year Round,* and in the early 1860s he became a welcome visitor to Gad's Hill. Dickens was always eager to see him and took pleasure in reminding him that since he had paid for Fanny's trip and effected the introduction to the Trollopes, he had unwittingly played Cupid. "Bear me in your mind then as the unconscious instrument of your having given your best affection to a worthy object." He was "heartily glad, both for her sake and for yours, that she is with you."[4] Dickens had published a poem by Trollope's first wife and Fanny soon became a contributor as well.

In the early 1860s, Dickens' intimacy with Ellen became one of the open secrets of the Dickens circle and the Ternan family, though what any individual knew and when is difficult to determine. Occasionally rumors surfaced. They were denied or ignored. Private conversations in the London literary and social world sometimes contained parenthetical references to the relationship as one of the acknowledged givens of the great man's life. Sometimes the echoes were supportive, other times disparaging. Occasionally, despite attempts to be prudent, they were noticed in one another's company, at the theatre, in the country, while traveling. A shrewd, experienced woman, Mrs. Ternan either accepted or encouraged the relationship, perhaps both, equally concerned about her daughter's reputation and her material well-being. Her role as a sometime chaperone did not liberate Dickens from the need to be discreet.

The many letters that he wrote immediately after the Staplehurst accident either omit all reference to his traveling companions or refer to them anonymously. More than his own reputation mandated secrecy. What other people knew existed independent of Ellen's awareness of their knowledge. She desired to maintain the illusion that the relationship was secret, her privacy unpierced. One of his friends, defending him, discovered that no defense was possible. Dickens confided that Ellen's " 'magic circle' " consisted of but one member. Not even with her sister Fanny, whom Dickens distrusted and who "is infinitely sharper than the serpent's tooth," could the subject be discussed. Ellen "would not believe" that anyone "could see her with my eyes, or know her with my mind. . . . It would distress her for the rest of her life." . . . If she knew that others knew of her relationship with him, "she could not have the pride and self reliance which . . . has borne her, alone, through so much." When Dickens had attended the performance of Gounod's *Faust* in 1862, he had been deeply moved by Marguerite's situation, the "mournful shadows overhang[ing] her chamber window, which was innocently bright and gay at first"; "Mephistopheles surrounded by an infernal red atmosphere of his own." The scene probably reminded him of Ellen's position and the price she paid for their relationship.5

France and Ellen became his two main safety valves. Beginning with the summer of 1862, he was "perpetually oscillating between Paris and London." The former had the attraction of otherness. Its very differentness was resuscitating. In October 1862, he moved there, with Mamie and Georgina, for the fall season, intending to stay until Christmas. He partly hoped that the change would revive Georgina's low spirits and help her recover from her frightening cardiac episode. From "a most elegant little apartment" on the Rue du Faubourg-St.-Honoré, with "the lively street in front, and a splendid courtyard of great private hotels behind, between us and the Champs Elysee," everything seemed "pretty, airy, and light." To the visiting Mrs. Lirriper, Paris is "town and county both in one," where "everybody seemed to be playing at everything in the world. . . . And as to the sparkling lights . . . after dark, glittering high up and low down and on before and on behind and all round, and the crowd of theatres and the crowd of people and the crowd of all sorts, it's pure enchantment."

Though Paris was "as wicked and extravagant as in the days of the Regency," it also seemed "more amazing than ever." The familiar city had been changing so rapidly under Louis Napoleon's reconstruction that Dickens had to use a map to find his way to the post office, to which he had been "at least 50 times before." Change seemed everywhere. Change, though, was expensive, both in literal and in human terms. "The Genius of the Lamp is always building palaces in the night.—But he charges for them in a manner altogether Parisian and not Arabian." When Dickens had last lived in Paris, he had gone to the theatre with Eugène Scribe. "The last time but one Victor Hugo had the most fantastic apartments . . . a little fine-featured fiery-eyed gallant fellow. Now, Scribe is in Pere la Chaise, and the fantastic apartment is in the Channel Islands and Victor Hugo is an old photograph in the shops with a quenched eye and a stubbly beard. and no likeness to any one I ever saw."[6]

From Paris, he managed to exchange with Wills by mail "an astonishing quantity of proofs" and his 1862 Christmas story, "Somebody's Luggage." He went to the theatre regularly. He encouraged Wilkie Collins, for whom the "only one true friend to the afflicted in body . . . is Brandy and Water," to visit him in Wilkie's "city of dissipation." He walked at all hours the entertaining streets, often by himself, sometimes with Georgina and Mamie, whose little Pomeranian, Mrs. Bouncer, "muzzled by the Parisian police," was "a wonderful spectacle to behold . . . restrained like a raging lion." Self-imposed restraints, though, provided text and subtext to his life. In November 1862, he learned of the death of Maria Beadnell's father. "For all the old Past comes out of its grave when I think of him, and the Ghosts of a good many years stand about his memory." Continually living "over again, the years that lie behind us," he was startled in early December by a telegram claiming that the aging John Elliotson was fading into senility. Returning briefly to

London, he had "a weary time . . . with an old friend's miseries," though Dickens felt he had "quite enough of his own . . . to keep me going (or not going) when such affairs fail me." Fortunately, the claim was exaggerated, though he soon concluded that Elliotson could no longer be relied on to function effectively as a doctor. In Paris again, he learned that Stanfield, for whom "there cannot be in this world a heart more affectionately and faithfully yours than this that beats in me," had been painfully "ill three mortal months."[7]

Though at first he thought he would not "entertain the idea," partly because of the prospect of reading in Australia, partly because he had in mind late-winter readings in London, Dickens soon agreed to read for charity at the British Embassy. Spending Christmas at Gad's Hill, he had seven of his children at home. He tried to "contemplate their levity as a Sage should" and not be driven wild by "fourteen pairs of creaking boots." During the first two weeks of January, he saw Ellen regularly in London. Soon he returned to Paris for six weeks. He had thoughts of going on to Genoa. He dreamed "of getting back to Italy; but I am always waking, and never knowing when I shall look on its beloved face again. . . . Visions of going back and living there, beset me at odd times and make me restless."

In Paris, he gave three readings from his usual repertoire in the elegant mirrored throne room of the embassy, in which Queen Victoria had held court on her visit in 1856. Wildly responsive "in a most astonishing and rapturous manner," the audience expressed its enthusiasm after the final reading on the last day of January 1863 by applauding him out of the embassy and down onto the Rue du Faubourg-St.-Honoré. Afterward, he could not sleep for the excitement. "If I had carried out my original intention and had Readings of my own in Paris, I don't know where they would have stopped." People "who don't understand English, positively understand the Readings!" But, though he "could have made a great deal of money, the dignified course was to stop." He already had arranged London readings for March through June. Before returning to England in February, he claimed that he took "a ten day's tour" outside Paris, visiting Robespierre's birthplace at Arras, remembering Carlyle's descriptions of the "amiable Sea-Green." He was there on his fifty-first birthday. He wrote to Forster that he was 'as little out of heart as you would have me be."[8]

Dickens' relationship with Ellen provided much of the heart that he had. Still living with her mother at 2 Houghton Place, she entertained him regularly. During his visits to France between 1862 and 1865, he and Ellen usually coordinated their movements. Some of his trips were public, others were not, the latter barely acknowledged, even in letters to friends. Often they were concealed by lies of omission or commission. Occasionally, on his way to Paris, he would "vanish into space for a day or two" or become noticeably vague about his destination and his routes. His usually full correspondence became distinctly porous, often for periods of ten days to two weeks, and the tracer remains of his visits to France in his letters leave shadowy dark holes to indicate the other, more secret visits. "Few men are more restless than I am, and . . . few sleep in more strange beds and dine at more new cooks' shops." Sometimes, while in England, he stayed neither at Gad's Hill nor at his office apartment in London. He was simply "out of town all day," or for a few days, though apparently close by. By the summer of 1862 his main holiday destination had become a villa owned by the discreet, affable Ferdinand Beaucourt, his summer landlord from 1853 to 1856, near the Norman castle of Hardelot, in the village of Condette, about five miles south of Boulogne.[9]

Convenient to London and Paris, Condette also offered privacy. The only public part of the trip was the Channel crossing, which Dickens made so frequently that, despite his tendency to seasickness, he joked that when "I retire from a literary life I think of setting up as a Channel pilot." Flamboyant, though seemingly intent on secrecy, he was recognized on one of the ferry trips by a hostile observer. "Traveling with him was a lady not his wife, nor his sister-in-law, yet he strutted about the deck with the air of a man bristling with self-importance, every line of his face and every gesture of his limbs seemed haughtily to say—'Look at me; make the most of your chance. I am the great, the *only* Charles Dickens; whatever I may choose to do is justified by that fact.' " At Condette, he had the nonjudgmental hospitality of villagers, whose occasional awareness that they had a great man among them was not complicated by

British moralism. He stayed frequently at "La Maison Dickens," a substantial, handsome, single-story bungalow nestled against a grove of trees, with an attractive courtyard.

In late June 1862, he was "in France, and in London, and in other parts of Kent, and everywhere but [Gad's Hill] for weeks and weeks." To a more confidential correspondent, he acknowledged that he had spent a week "wandering in the strangest towns in France, and I will go back again for another adventure again next week." He called the visit in July "going to Paris." Probably his destination was Condette. Sometimes, crossing the Channel with Ellen, he went on to Paris while she stayed in Condette. She may have been there during part of his stay in Paris in the fall of 1862. After spending time together in London at the beginning of the new year, they probably crossed the Channel together. After his return to Paris in mid-January 1863, he left for several days for some destination in France. When he wrote to Forster on his birthday from Arras, on his "perfectly quiet tour for ten days, touching the sea at Boulogne," undoubtedly he was on a day excursion from Condette. The tour had no datemarks other than from Arras and nearby Amiens.[10]

Some "anxious business" took him across the Channel for five days in March 1863. He claimed to be happy to say that "it is not my own." He disappeared again on another mysterious absence in April, then in August. In mid-November, and then the next summer, he had another "Mysterious Disappearance" in the direction of France, with the false trail of "a ten days' or twelve days' visit to Belgium" mentioned to a less intimate correspondent. In November 1864, he again went to France, and he was away during the first two weeks in May 1865. On at least some of these trips, he had with him the latest number-in-progress of his new novel, portions of which were written in Condette. In late May, for the second time that month, he went to France for ten days with Ellen and her mother. He had felt near a breakdown, partly from the accumulated fatigue of work.[11] Financial insecurity (despite the facts of his balance sheet), his editorial duties, and the gap between his public position and the secrecy of his private life contributed to a constant low level of anxiety. They returned on the morning of the ninth of June to their unhappy encounter with the forty-two feet of steel at Staplehurst viaduct.

❧ 2 ❧

THE CHARACTERS WHO IN THEIR "MANUSCRIPT DRESS" HE HAD RES-
cued from the railroad carriage were some of the principals in
a novel in twenty monthly parts that he had begun writing in
late 1863. He had partially conceived the germ of *Our Mutual
Friend* in 1855, when he had entered into his newly begun notebook, "Found Drowned. The descriptive bill upon the wall, by
the waterside," and "A 'long shore' man—woman—child . . .
connect the Found Drowned Bill with this?" In 1850, he had
encouraged Horne to write for *Household Words* an article called
"Dust; or Ugliness Redeemed," which dramatizes the rescue of
a seemingly "drownded man," describes London dust heaps or
refuse mounds in detail, includes a character with one wooden
leg, and makes use of the device of a document buried in a dust
heap that determines a legacy. In 1853, he touched on some of the
same subjects in his own article "Down with the Tide." In 1862,
when he conceived the "LEADING INCIDENT FOR A
STORY. A man—young and eccentric?—feigns to be dead, and
is dead to all intents and purposes, and . . . for years retains that
singular view of life and character," he brought closer to realization elements for a novel about the heavy hand of the past,
materialistic corruption, and death and resurrection that had
been in his mind for over ten years.[12]

After the completion of *Great Expectations* in 1861, he had
devoted much of two years to profitable public readings. With
Wills's tireless help, he kept *All the Year Round* flourishing. His
own hand guided its editorial revisions and decisions. In
March 1862, he was "trying to plan out a new book, but have
not got beyond trying." By April, his frustration on being unable to hit upon anything for a story, though he had "again
and again . . . tried," led him to blame the "odious little
house," 16 Hyde Park Gate, that he had exchanged for Gad's
Hill Place for the spring season. His London reading series at
the Hanover Square Rooms, which became more enervating as
the weather became warmer, may have had as much to do with
his difficulty in coalescing his notebook materials into a defi-
nite plan for a novel as the uncomfortable house. On a hot
night, the readings "in so large a place" were "quite wasting."

Georgina's heart condition worried him terribly. In April and May 1863, he read twice in each week, and then once, and put together a reading from *Oliver Twist* that seemed to him so frightening that he was "afraid to try it in public."[13] In June, he went to France. Between the need for change of scene, concern for Georgina, relaxation in Paris and Condette, readings at the embassy, Australian possibilities, work on *All the Year Round,* and his spring 1863 readings, he had sufficient "ordinary occupations and botherations."

By late summer, spent mostly in France with Ellen, he was "full of notions" for "the new twenty numbers." Returning to the form of publication with which he had begun his career as a novelist was a formidable challenge. His initial hesitation, his inability to draw immediately on his usual concentration and discipline, may have had as much to do, though, with feelings associated with his youthful beginnings and his sense of the changes that had occurred as with any possible decline in creativity. His last novel in monthly numbers, *Little Dorrit,* had been written almost ten years before. In August, he felt that as soon as he could "clear the Christmas stone out of the road," he could "dash into it on the grander journey." In early September, he got down to business with Chapman and Hall "in reference to a new monthly work in 20 monthly No.s as of old." Having reviewed the balance sheets of his previous monthly serials, he proposed that they pay him "£6000 for the half copyright throughout and outright," assuring them that "I do not press you to give the sum . . . and that you will not in the least inconvenience or offend me by preferring to leave me to make other arrangements. If you should have any misgivings on this head, let my assurance that you need have none set it at rest."[14] They did not prefer. They had no misgivings.

In September, he wrote "Mrs. Lirriper's Lodgings," clearing that "stone out of the road." He wanted both to "get into the field before next spring is out" and to be "well on before the first No. is published." Shirking his usual day at the office, he arranged five consecutive days at his writing desk at Gad's Hill in early October, "exceedingly anxious to begin. . . . I am bent upon getting to work on it . . . but I am determined not to begin to publish with less than five numbers done. I see my opening perfectly, with the one main line on which the story is to turn; and if I don't strike while the iron (meaning myself) is hot, I shall drift off again, and have to go through all this uneasiness once more." By late October, his writing discipline had reasserted itself. He allowed no one to disturb him, "shutting [himself] up from breakfast to lunch." Sorting out his ideas, making number plans, he had his beginning under way sometime in November 1863. Despite a full house for the Christmas holidays, he knew by mid-December that he would keep his May 1864 engagement with his reading public. By the end of January, he had completed the first two numbers and was well into the third. "It is a combination of drollery with romance which requires a great deal of pains and a perfect throwing away of points that might be amplified; but I hope it is *very good.*"15

Soon "various distractions" slowed him down, one the painful news of his son Walter's death. He grimly joked to Macready that the delay "was quite superfluous, for I was bad enough before," though he kept working "in a rather dull slow way for the moment." In mid-February 1864, he moved to 57 Gloucester Place, Hyde Park Gardens, which he had rented until June "to be in town when my book is preparing and begins to come out."16 He had the printer set the first two numbers in type, and then met with his new illustrator to "take counsel together" about "what little indication of the story" to have in the illustration on the cover of the first number. He had decided to end his collaboration with Browne, which had begun in 1837. It had become less personal as the years went by, partly because of Browne's move away from central London, partly because Browne became increasingly unsocial, partly because there were few grounds of attraction between them other than their common enterprise. Busy with the time-consuming work of making his living as an illustrator, Browne took on as many commissions as he could manage. During the six years since *Little Dorrit,* working only on serial novels for weekly publication, Dickens had had no need for an illustrator of monthly parts. Browne's professional virtues now no longer seemed sufficient. With changes in the aesthetics and technology of book illustration, he was out of fashion. He was also out of Dickens' mind. With his usual loyalty to friends, Dickens turned to Frank Stone's son, the deeply admiring, modestly talented Marcus, who was at the beginning of a career that could benefit from a Dickensian boost.

Though he gave Stone specific guidance for the cover of the

first number and had his say occasionally thereafter, Dickens was less insistent than he had ever been in controlling the choice of subjects for illustrations. Often he allowed Stone to choose what he liked. One afternoon, in search of "some eccentric calling" for a character, Stone introduced him to "an articulator of skeletons, a stuffer of birds, and dealer in bottled monsters . . . 'It is the very thing I want. . . . It couldn't be better." Having "grown hard to satisfy," he wrote very slowly. "I have so much not fiction—that *will* be thought of when I don't want to think of it—, that I am forced to take more care than I once took." While working on the "golden dustman," he took long walks in the dusty street, in the "utterly abominable and unwholesome" March weather when London seemed at its worst. "Such a black shrill city, combining the qualities of a smoky house and a scolding wife; such a gritty city; such a hopeless city, with no rent in the leaden canopy of its sky." By early April 1864, he had the satisfaction of having in hand the five numbers that allowed him to breathe more easily on May 1, the date of publication, and soon to take pleasure and profit in the success of *"Our Friend*, now in his thirtieth thousand, and orders flowing in fast."17

The advantage of being in town while his novel was being prepared for publication had been partly offset by social demands, "the most severe dinner-eating I have ever known in London. Every week" he swore "to go out no more, and every week I have perjured myself several times." Vowing to "stick to [his] book and dine no more until next year," he repossessed Gad's Hill. To desert it for anyplace but France would make him vulnerable again to the temptation of self-perjury. Before Dickens departed for Condette in late June, Stone had chosen the scenes to illustrate for number six, and number seven was in proof. Though he worked hard at the manuscript in July, he felt his imagination flagging. The new Christmas story, which had to be written in the next three months, began to seem a burden. For the first time since 1856, he was working on both that and a novel. Desperate not to lose any of his five-number head start, he felt his advantage slipping away. By the end of July he had fallen behind almost one full number. In poor health, Wills had become sufficiently ill to force him "to do all the office needful." Dickens himself felt quite unwell with some unspecified ailment. At Gad's Hill, in "this beautiful but painfully hot" rainless summer, he struggled on with the novel, soon losing part of another number of his head start.[18] The cleaned-up proofs of eight were ready for Stone in September 1864. In early October, though, he had to break off before completing number nine to take up his part in the Christmas number. Soon back in form, he was happy with eight and "pleasing [him]self *very much* with Mrs. Lirriper" again. Working hard, "though No. 10 is unborn," he had the benefit of a holiday with Wilkie Collins and Georgina. In Dover, which was very quiet, even Collins had restful nights like those he remembered having when he was a boy.

Soon, though, Dickens was staggered by Leech's death, put "out woefully." He could not write in the first week of November. In the next he was "only by slow degrees getting back into the track." He did finish number ten in time to leave a little after the middle of November for two weeks in France. Probably he had the beginning of number eleven in hand. In December, January, and February he was in writing form again, with "the proofs of No. XIII back to the printer" at the middle of February 1865. But he was invalided by a painfully "wounded foot," whose lameness he attributed to frostbite from "walking continually in the snow, and getting wet in the feet daily." Forcing his boot onto his swollen foot and going out as usual, he "fell lame on the walk, and had to limp home dead lame, through the snow, for the last three miles." He was mostly confined to a sofa at Gad's Hill and at his office apartment, and then at 16 Somers Place, Hyde Park West, which he had rented for the spring. By late March 1865, he still suffered tortures, the "confounded foot as bad as ever again." In April, though he could again walk his ten miles a day without inconvenience, he worked "like a dragon." At the end of the month he went to France. At the end of June he went again, and he and the manuscript of number sixteen barely survived the return journey. Late in July, the number, delayed by the frightening accident and his shakiness afterward, went to the printer. When he received the proofs, he was distressed to learn that he had "under-written . . . by two and a half pages—a thing" that had not happened since *Pickwick*. The miscalibration of nerves, invention, and judgment indirectly brought to mind the trauma of Mary Hogarth's death. With the end in sight, he had proofs of number seventeen by the end of the third week in August.[19] On the second of September, he was finished, and wrote the postscript "with devout thankfulness" that he had lived to complete it and address his readers once more.

Indirectly speaking to his Jewish readers, Dickens attempted to provide redress for what he saw as their misunderstanding of his motives in depicting Fagin in *Oliver Twist*. Critical of overt anti-Semitism, he was less sensitive to his own more covert prejudices. His liberal imagination detested illiberality; yet the common idiom of anti-Semitism occasionally surfaced, even while writing *Our Mutual Friend*. He was sufficiently unselfconscious about it to feel defensive when it was brought to his attention by Jews as ostensibly English and acceptable as Eliza Davis, the wife of the businessman to whom he had sold the lease of Tavistock House. In July 1863, he had had a letter from her, raising the "great wrong" he had done to the "Jewish people" in the depiction of Fagin, which he answered at length. Typically, his defense was an attack. For "if there be any general feeling on the part of the intelligent Jewish people that I have done them what you describe as 'a great wrong,' they are a far less sensible, a far less just, and a far less good-tempered people than I have always supposed them to be." Fagin, he claimed, was historically accurate, a representative of a race not a religion, a Jew "because he is one of the Jewish people, and because it conveys that kind of idea of him which I should give my readers of a Chinaman by calling him Chinese. . . . I have no feelings towards the Jewish people but a friendly one. I always speak well of them, whether in public or in private."

He was enough affected by the accusation, though, to transform his defensiveness into the powerful Jewish-Christian motif of redemption in *Our Mutual Friend*. Reversing the historical stereotype, he depicts Christianity as responsible for the fiction of the materialistic perversion of the Jew in Christian culture. Under economic pressure, oppressed by racial and cultural stereotypes, Riah, the good Jew, is forced to become the front man for the Christian moneylender and slum landlord Fascination Fledgeby. Without a sense of otherness, Dickens conceives of the Jew in stereotypical Christian terms and the Christian in stereotypical Jewish terms. As fiction, it is brilliant. As racial apologetics, it is limited. Later, accepting the gift of a Hebrew-

English Bible from Mrs. Davis, he stressed that he would not "willfully" have done such an injustice to the Jewish people "for any worldly consideration."[20] But he could not get beyond the cultural evasion inherent in the word "willfully" nor escape subtly associating material terms with those to whom he was supposedly apologizing.

His new novel replicates powerfully the themes that he had developed throughout his career. Set partly in London, partly in the countryside, it follows the flow of the waters of the Thames from the city to the country, from ignorance to education, from separateness to union, from death to life, refracting across a wide range of interlinked characters and plots the novelist's fascination with rebirth and with human nature. In this world, society shapes the individual into unnatural contortions. This society that unnatural people create embodies their preoccupation with money, power, exclusion, exploitation and cannibalism. Symbolized by the dust heaps of Harmon's Bower, the obsession with wealth provides the tension between innate feelings, such as love, generosity, and communal responsibility, and the socially produced deformation of human nature into material ambition.

In Lizzie Hexam's relationship with her father and her brother, he sharply delineates the potential and the limitations of the working-class family. In Bella Wilfer's dissatisfaction with her shrewish, pretentious mother and her lovable but inadequate father, he depicts the misplaced values of a family whose internal dynamic dramatizes the stultification of the lower-middle-class household. In his depiction of the Veneering-Podsnapian world of high bourgeois pretension, he dramatizes the failure of the familial hearth to be anything but a surface fire. Having internalized the values of a rigid social system, the family is captive to the limitations of its own class identification. Since survival depends on the minimal protection that such identification provides, social exploitation is a given. Efforts to alter the family structure have only the limited potential to effect change in personal relationships, mainly through the efforts of those rare people from whatever social level who have some capacity to change themselves. Attempts to alter the larger social world directly are fated to be dissipated or smashed. The structure is a triumph of inertia and self-interest.

Lizzie Hexam and Noddy Boffin, "the golden dustman," have an innate goodness so concentrated that familial and social pressures cannot damage their ability to love generously and compassionately. Pretending to have drowned in order to explore his possibilities for life undamaged by other people's material considerations, John Harmon shows himself a man of inner and outer moral resolution. Why and how these characters can escape normative social conditioning the novel does not make clear, though Dickens implies that they are special people whose innate moral sentiments are so strong that they are invulnerable to deformation. But others can escape the structural vise only at the cost of painfully reconstructing themselves to become emotionally and morally independent of the external structures that they cannot change. Bella Wilfer and Eugene Wrayburn are the dynamic characters of the novel for whom deprivation and deformation have taken the form of a frenetic verbal materialism and emotional paralysis. Under the elaborate tutelage of Boffin, who pretends to be a miser, Bella's essential moral sanity asserts itself. She prefers love to money, compassion to exploitation. Despite the resistance of his upper-class values, Eugene's love for Lizzie motivates him to change. His deathly passivity gives way to emotional vibrancy. The threat of physical and emotional death makes his resurrection an act of self-assertion so powerful that it transforms him into a compassionate, energetic human being.

Redemption, though, in *Our Mutual Friend* is a Christian affair in a frighteningly un-Christian culture. Material and psychological disintegration are constant threats—death by exploitation, death by brutalization, death by dehumanization, death by spiritual atrophy, death by one's body being inhabited by the materialism that the society promotes. In this world, the possibilities for individual and social rebirth have been diminished, in some instances to nonexistence. Without the paradigm of rebirth in life, after the final death-in-life there may come no life-in-death. The necessary intimations of immortality that life's experiences and values should provide have almost disappeared. In Silas Wegg, Rogue Riderhood, and Mr. Veneering, Dickens portrays the spiritual vacuity of human beings damaged beyond the possibility of regeneration. In Bradley Headstone, perhaps his most powerful negative self-portrait, he depicts the psychologically tortured lower-middle-class aspirant toward self-fulfillment who has so completely internalized middle-class repression as a tool for ascendancy that his uncontrollable passion for Lizzie Hexam destroys him.

The most psychologically dynamic character in the novel, he is torn apart by a passion that his conventional qualities of prudence, outward deference, and total self-control cannot deal with, except at the cost of violence and death. Here Dickens perhaps dramatizes the dark side of his own passion, willfulness, and creativity, the self-destructiveness of which he had powerful glimpses in his anguish and hysteria during the late 1850s. The depiction of Bradley resonates with his own experience in applied madness. Having failed in his attempt to murder Eugene, his rival for Lizzie, Bradley meets his soul mate of retribution in his vicious lower-class counterpart, Rogue Riderhood. When Riderhood attempts to blackmail him, Headstone succeeds in drowning his nemesis, his primitive alter ego. In a vicious struggle, they are both dragged down into the waters of the Thames. Locked in one another's arms, they finally rise to the surface, an ironic representation of their inability both to rise in life and to rise to heaven.

Fragments of the author's sense of identity rise to the surface of the novel. In John Harmon and Eugene Wrayburn there is the Dickens who had transformed his separation from Catherine into a personal rebirth. Throughout, Harmon has the appropriate Dickensian characteristics of resolution, energy, and creativity. He too is a novelist of sorts, at least the creator of a plot and a story, the maker of a self and other-testing fiction by which he gains a world, including Bella Wilfer, that he thought he had lost or might not want. Initially aimless, lazy, and irresolute, Eugene Wrayburn embodies the Dickensian myth of regeneration through the redemptive power of love. The interaction between Lizzie and Eugene, older, more worldly, and socially superior, suggests some of the distance between Ellen and himself that Dickens needed to overcome.

In her purity of moral sentiment, in her absolute incorruptibility, Lizzie is the culmination of a series of idealized heroines who are both sister and lover and whose psychic origins are in his childhood relationship with his sister Fanny, in his feeling that his mother had deserted him, and in the reinforcement of

his feeling of being deserted that the early death of Mary Hogarth provided. In the portrait of Bella, he combines some of
Ellen's traits, particularly her occasional teasing, with some of
Katie's. For where there is a sister and lover, usually there is also
a father and daughter. The playful teasing between Bella and
her father evokes the favorite daughter that he had partially lost.
An idealized version of John Dickens, Mr. Wilfer is ineffectual
but loving, just as the benevolent Mr. Boffin completes the resolution of Dickens' lifelong effort to reconstruct out of the
materials of John Dickens a satisfactory father figure. In Mrs.
Wilfer, he creates a character whose similarities to the Elizabeth
Dickens of the Mrs. Nickleby days are balanced by the depiction
of Mrs. Boffin, so idealized a mother that she has only the children she chooses to adopt. Combined with Mrs. Wilfer, she
provides an acceptable image of mothering of a sort that none
of his previous novels has had in this sustained way. There are
no witches in *Our Mutual Friend,* no representation of the child-
adult's nightmare of Elizabeth Dickens as the neglectful, unloving destroyer.

✤ 3 ✤

BUT THERE WERE PUBLIC DESTROYERS AT LARGE, ESPECIALLY THOSE
who believed that parliamentary democracy was the glory of the
nation. In January 1866, attending a banquet at the Mansion
House, Dickens could hardly suppress his fury as he listened to
"the imbecility of constitutional and corporational idiots." Having begun his career as a parliamentary reporter covering the
election campaigns preceding and following the passage of the
Reform Bill of 1832, he harbored no illusions about the venality
and stupidity of that legislative body. The genial satire of his
depiction of the Eatanswill election in *Pickwick Papers* had become the bitter despair of the Circumlocution Office in *Little
Dorrit.* On many matters even his Whig-radical sympathies had
become more conservative, though not on the fundamental issues of education and the franchise.

However, the enfranchisement of the sanitized middle
class had not, he believed, significantly improved either the
intelligence or the liberalism of parliamentary legislation and

governmental administration. "Every inventor of anything designed for the public good, and offered to the English Government, becomes *ipso facto* a criminal, to have his heart broken on the circumlocution wheel. It is as certain as that the whole Crimean story will be retold, whenever this country again goes to war."[21] With politics, his anger was likely to overcome his usual class identification. He had such "a very small opinion of what the great genteel have done for us, that I am very philosophical indeed concerning what the great vulgar may do." Though fetishistic about personal cleanliness, he did not fear the contamination of the great unwashed. He saw no reason to fear the working-class enfranchisement that was inherent in the Reform Bill of 1867, partly because he did not believe any elected body in contemporary England could effectively govern the nation.

Inherent within his distress at the condition of England was his implicit admission that his novels, his stories, and his journalism had contributed little to social and political reform. Taking his lead from Carlyle, whom he self-delusively claimed he had always striven to follow, he found himself, after the failure of the Administrative Reform Bill that Austen Henry Layard had championed and the publication of *Little Dorrit*, increasingly uncomfortable with political discourse. He declined emphatically a number of new opportunities to serve in Parliament. His tendency during the 1850s to emphasize social progress as a factor of individual regeneration rather than organized political activity found its counterpart in his increased need for privacy and a sharper distinction between his public and private life after 1859. He continued to express strong opinions in *All the Year Round*, and vociferously in private conversation. The Poor Law seemed "infamously administered." Patronage was "one of the curses of the country," the inference that high birth implied superiority inseparable from government by well-connected incompetents. Between 1859 and 1866 it appeared to him that "the general mind" was as weary of debates as was his own, that there was no "strong feeling" on the subject of reform, and that the society as a whole had "taken *laissez-aller* for its motto."

On the subject of capital punishment his idealism had diminished in the face of what seemed incontrovertible evidence of the recalcitrance of the habitual criminal. He had not changed his mind about the barbarity of the separate or solitary system. There had been, though, some wear and tear around the edges of his optimism about prison reform. On occasion he would even express himself about a particular criminal barbarity with a passionate exclamation that the only protection society had from such madness was to throw away the key. Though more likely to advocate capital punishment for non-English and particularly nonwhite malefactors, sometimes his anger overlooked even that distinction. In 1849 he had expressed his opposition to capital punishment. In 1863 he still believed "*public* execution to be a savage horror . . . affording an indecent and fearful gratification to the worst of people." But he had come to believe "Capital Punishment to be necessary in extreme cases; simply because it appears impossible otherwise to rid society of certain members of whom it *must* be rid, or there is no living on this earth."[22]

Dickens' increasing outrage with society had a comic side, particularly his hysterical fury at the noise of street musicians, many of them immigrants attempting to make a poor living with an organ and a monkey. Their persistence seemed blackmail. When they played beneath his window, he fumed, partly the resentment of the writer whose privacy is being violated, partly his characteristic fury at what he believed an infringement of his dignity and rights. Wilkie Collins complained that he had lost five working days recently "through nothing but pianos at the back of the house and organs, bagpipes, bands and Punches in front." In May 1864, Dickens joined other writers, partly distinguished by their inability to sympathize with the inconvenient poor, in signing a petition, whose vivid wording has his flair and tone, urging legislative control of street musicians. At Somers Place in 1865, he was "a terror . . . to all the organs and brass bands in this quarter."

In regard to more serious crimes, his identification with what drives the criminal to criminal acts had decreased. When in 1868 two street thieves tried to rob him, he recklessly, and then with a relentless persistence, pursued them to capture and imprisonment; he pressured the police into arresting and a magistrate into convicting a young girl " 'for using bad language in the streets.' " In 1865, at Gad's Hill, his gardener "came upon a man in the garden and fired." The shot missed. "The man returned the compliment by kicking [the gardener] in the groin." Dickens "set off, with a great mastiff-bloodhound . . . in pursuit. Couldn't find the evil-doer, but had the greatest difficulty in preventing the dog from tearing two policemen down." In an 1868 article, "The Ruffian," he scathingly denounced street violence, advocating public or at least private flogging. In response to a notorious murder in 1865, he made clear that he had a graphic sense of sex and violence, and a preoccupation with both that had none of the softening disguises of his fiction. He theorized that "the father was in bed with the nurse. The child was discovered by them, sitting up in his little bed, staring, and evidently going to 'tell Ma.' The nurse leaped out of bed and instantly suffocated him in the father's presence. The father cut the child about to distract suspicion . . . and took the body out to where it was found."[23] The threat of telling "Ma" had grim overtones of his childhood and marriage. The horror stories told by his nurse were the realities of adult life, and most of the formulas for reform that he had believed in as a young man now seemed untenable as social policy.

Though he felt the need for a strong hand at home, his international perspective condemned illiberalism abroad, particularly in his two favorite European countries, France and Italy. Louis Napoleon, whom he had met in England during the emperor's exile, appalled him. A poor simulacrum of his talented uncle, he seemed an adventurer with "no chance but in the distraction of his people's minds, and in the jingle and glitter of theatrical glory." Scathing in his condemnation of British politicians who deferred to the emperor, Dickens predicted that the latter's policies would end in blood, some of which might be English. "Louis Napoleon's last great card for the temporary union and pacification of France is War with England." In Italy, Austrian oppression had for some time been shedding the blood of Italian patriotism. When Prussia competed with Austria for influence, he felt that they were equally contemptible. "If each could smash the other," he would be "perfectly satisfied." Napoleon's policy was "like his position in Europe at all times, simply disheartening and astounding," partly because a "united Italy would be of vast importance to the peace of the world, and would be a rock in Louis Napoleon's way." Dickens felt "for Italy almost as if [he] were an Italian born."

The country that was "an abiding dream with him" con-

tinued in the stupor that he had bewailed during his visits in
1844–45 and 1853. "Rome and I," he complained, "are wide asun-
der . . . morally." Detesting dogmatic Catholicism, "that abominable old priestly institution," he distinguished Italian
nationalism from Italian religion. He was sick of the spectacle
presented in England "by the indecent squabbles of priests of
most denominations" and especially of the small-minded dog-
matism of the Anglican Church, which had its "hand at its own
throat." Any increase in the power of the Roman Catholic
Church, "that tottering monster," would make a bad matter
worse. He supported Giuseppe Mazzini, Camillo Cavour, and
Giuseppe Garibaldi, whose humanity he admired, hoping that
enlightened nationalism would destroy the Church's power. To
the extent that he wanted any church at all, he wanted one "with
less arbitrary pretensions and stronger hold upon the mantle of
our Saviour." Because "man's forms of religion tend to what is
diabolically irreligion," he "would not therefore abolish all
forms of religion."[24] And he cautioned that criticism of the
papacy in England and in any country in which Catholics were
in the minority should be moderate.

The outbreak of war in America provoked Dickens' fascination and disgust. In early 1861, "the American business" was
"the greatest English sensation." He predicted "that the struggle of violence will be a very short one, and will be soon succeeded by some new compact between the Northern and
Southern States." He shared the British view that Northern
attempts to force conformity of law and social custom on the
South arose from the desire of the North to continue to exploit
the South economically. Detesting slavery, he believed that opposition to slavery had nothing to do with Northern policy. In
fact, "any reasonable creature may know, if willing, that the
North hates the Negro, and that until it was convenient to make
a pretence that sympathy with him was the cause of the war, it
hated the abolitionists. . . . For the rest there is not a pin to
choose between the two parties. They will both rant and lie and
fight until they come to a compromise; and the slave may be
thrown into the compromise or thrown out of it, just as it
happens." Sensitive to the likelihood that programs to en-
lighten, let alone liberate, distant peoples, particularly in Africa,
would be bought at the expense of efforts to help the poor and

oppressed in England, he had in *Bleak House* satirized the missionary mentality.

In the Jamaica insurrection of 1865, he strongly supported the governor, Edward Eyre, who had been charged with using excessive violence in suppressing the rebellion. "That platform-sympathy with the black—or the Native, or the Devil—afar off, and that platform indifference to our own countrymen at enormous odds in the midst of bloodshed and savagery, makes me stark wild. . . . But for the blacks in Jamaica being over-patient and before their time, the whites might have been exterminated, without a previous hint or suspicion that there was anything amiss."[25] He joined Thomas Carlyle, John Ruskin, and Alfred Tennyson on a committee of defense, though he did not take an active role in raising funds or in the public debate. The affair provoked a number of his characteristic attitudes: patriotism, chauvinism, a combination of paternalism, callousness, and moral condescension in regard to "primitive" people, distaste for the personality as well as the theology of "Exeter Hall," or missionary evangelicism, and contempt for those concerned with the ill-treatment of distant people rather than with misery at home.

Always ambivalent about America, he had developed a realism that bordered on cynicism, prompted by his visit in 1842, the aggressive pirating of his books, and the reaction to *American Notes*. Some friendly feelings notwithstanding, he shared the widespread British disparagement of the United States as an overcommercial country too slowly struggling out of the barbarism of its origins, the shortness of its history, and the mixed blood of its ethnic components, a "distracted land of troublesome vagabonds." The American "people . . . are the most extensive and meanest of scoundrels." Sharing the European notion of community based on biological identity, he had some sympathy with the view that Procter stated, "what can you expect from a people who are made up of the off-scourings of other countries?" When war erupted, he thought both sides venal. He was more provoked, though, by Northern materialistic self-righteousness than by what seemed to him Southern defense of its traditions. Uncomfortable with coercive Federalism, he argued that it was possible the Founding Fathers did not consider secession to be rebellion.

His conviction that it was to be a short war terminated by a "contemptible" compromise only gradually gave way to obvious facts. Though he accepted the claim that the North could put down the South speedily because "the South has no money and no credit," he believed that it "will neither raise the money nor the men required." In fact, "the one chance for the miserable country . . . is, that those two blatant impostors Lincoln and McClellan will fail to get the 300,000 new men they ask for." In a country, though, in which the devil is "the ruling power," anything could happen. In May 1863, Dickens still responded to the opinion "that the conscription will succeed . . . and that the war will be indefinitely prolonged," with a firm " 'No' . . . however mad and villainous the North is, the war will be finished by reason of its not supplying soldiers." No analysis of the conflict and its likely perpetuation other than his own, no matter what the evidence to the contrary, seemed worth consideration. "I can *not* believe . . . that the conscription will do otherwise than fail, and wreck the War. . . . Of course the more they brag, the more I don't believe them."26

Compromise was not forthcoming. A Southern victory soon appeared impossible. Southern social values and class stratification seemed preferable to Englishmen who valued traditional notions of gentlemanliness. The South, of course, did not threaten British commercial and manufacturing interests. Its agrarian economy supported British imperialistic industrialization. The North seemed vulgar, arrogant, and ambitious. It also had the power to interfere with British trade. British cotton manufacturing interests flexed their self-defensive muscles in favor of a steady supply of Southern cotton, raising fears of economic depression if factories closed. "The Americans northward are perfectly furious on the subject." Fearing that irresponsible British responses to American embargoes, and then a series of confrontations between American sea power and British trade, would increase tension, from the beginning Dickens felt "the North to be utterly mad, and war to be unavoidable."

Though he had no American investments, he had flirted with invitations to do a reading tour there. The war made it impossible even to consider that for the time being. When a friend sailed for the North on a business trip, Dickens suggested that they "drink confusion together to your customers for light steel and my customers for light reading." There was serious concern that Britain would intervene in the war on behalf of the South. A British-American conflict would eliminate the possibility of his giving readings in America, perhaps for the rest of his lifetime. When the danger of such a war diminished temporarily. he responded to a query from an American friend, "Think of reading in America? Lord bless you, I think of reading in the deepest depth of the lowest crater in the Moon, on my way there!" In 1865, he again feared that American "swagger and bombast" and "claims for idemnification" would "embroil us in a war."[27] Two years later he was to be storm-tossed on a Cunard steamer, once more on his way to a tumultuous and this time profitable welcome in America.

❋ 4 ❋

WHILE ON A READING TOUR IN MARCH 1867, DICKENS TOOK AN AFTERnoon holiday by the sea at Tynemouth. "There was a high north wind blowing, and a magnificent sea running." Huge waves suddenly broke over the bar, knocking him down, drenching him, filling his pockets with water. For a moment, he felt "wonderfully well, and quite fresh and strong." The sky turned golden. Beyond the waves, he saw "a quiet rainbow of transcendent beauty" arching over "one large ship, as if she were sailing direct for heaven." Stanfield, whom the scene brought to mind, died two months later. Alerted by Stanfield's son, he went up to Highgate for a last visit. When he "saw what had happened," he did not have "the courage to ring. . . . No one of your father's friends can ever have loved him more dearly than I." He had a keen sense of ships sailing directly to heaven, of the changing of the tide that age and time determined. He clung to old friendships as best he could. With the death of his parents, his sister Fanny, and his brother Alfred, his links to his childhood had diminished. His brother Augustus died in Chicago in 1866. In October 1868, Frederick died, "a wasted life, but God forbid that one should be hard upon it, or upon anything in this world that is not deliberately and coldly wrong." His memory conveniently lapsing, he could "not recollect . . . that a hard word . . . passed between us." He "was my favourite when I was a child, and . . . I was his tutor when he was a boy." With one of his oldest friends Dickens now had almost no contact; Thomas Mitton had withdrawn into eccentricity and seclusion.²⁸ But with Thomas Beard he sustained an easy, intimate affection.

Of the friends of his early manhood, Macready was the oldest in years, Maclise in intimacy. The latter's obsession with his work and his frequent depressions prevented "the old associations," though it had "not a jot abated the old regard." Always hoping to come out of his isolation, Maclise became by 1867 a little more accessible. The old relationship, though, was mostly a memory. Dickens watched Macready live almost the length of a second postprofessional life in his Cheltenham retirement. Having left the stage early in the 1850s, he remarried, fathering a second family while the tubercular remains of his first continued to fade away. "Poor Macready," Procter moaned, expressing the heartache of his friends, "are all his children to die, or to desert him?" He had remarkable flashes of liveliness, though, his "old fire" reviving whenever Dickens encouraged his "dearest old friend" to talk about drama, art, and the artist. Unquestionably, Macready "was wrong in excluding himself from . . . the world of occupation and Art." On occasional trips to London, he also traveled the additional thirty miles to Gad's Hill. At Cheltenham soon after the birth in 1862 of Macready's youngest child, Dickens found the second Mrs. Macready an excellent wife, and seized an umbrella when Macready "had the audacity to tell me he was growing old, and made at him with Macduff's defiance." The retired actor "fell into the old fierce guard, with the desperation of thirty years ago. . . . Repentantly possessed" of one of the Macreadys' bath towels, Dickens soon sent him a claret jug with their names inscribed upon it, "in token of our many years of mutual reliance and trustfulness."

Four years later, Macready had "aged exceedingly," though not enough to prevent Dickens suspecting that there was "some prospect of another addition to the family party." On his seventy-fourth birthday in March 1867, Dickens sent him his "most affectionate and long-cemented love." The next month, when he read in Cheltenham, Macready was too ill to attend. He joked that he meant "to go on reading the Trial," Macready's favorite, in Cheltenham, "at intervals, until you come to hear it. Let them therefore expect no variety from *me.*" The next year he was delighted to find his dear friend "in a tone so bright and blooming."[29] But by 1868 Macready's slow decline had brought him noticeably close to an end that did not occur until three years after Dickens' own.

In the summer of 1862, Forster had remarked with purposeful casualness about the estrangement since 1860 between himself and Macready, " 'If I was wrong . . .' " Dickens "immediately struck in, 'There is no doubt upon it in my mind. You *were* wrong.' " Forster said nothing more. A year later, he inquired about Macready's health. After Dickens replied, he said, "in a softened manner, that we were all growing older, and that it made him uneasy to think of the terms on which" he and Macready stood. He then added, " 'I should like Macready to know that I believe I was wrong, and that I am sorry for it.' " Excitable and intemperate, Forster had, since his marriage in 1856, become wealthy without becoming wise. In late 1862, he moved into a new house, the formidable bourgeois-palatial Palace Gate near Hyde Park. Pushing himself puritanically, he maintained both his writing schedule and his position as secretary to the Commission on Lunacy, which demanded frequent travel. In 1861, he became a commissioner on the same committee, often "smoking all over his head and fuming exactly like a steamboat ready to start," fulminating at people and institutions with a regularity that occasionally had him as estranged from his closest friends as from his enemies. At a dinner in 1860 at Tavistock House, he had been "a little ferocious . . . but calmed down afterwards. Lord!" Dickens had told Macready, "I wish you could have seen him in Montague Square a fortnight ago, concerning some oysters that the fishmonger had opened tardily."

Nineteen years younger than Macready, Forster had gout, rheumatism, circulatory difficulties, and bronchial problems. Frequently ill, increasingly reclusive, he seemed to Dickens to have "gotten into *an old way* which is not wholesome. He has lost interest in the larger circle of tastes and occupations that used to girdle his life, and yet has a morbid sort of dissatisfaction in having subsided into an almost private personage," a change that influenced "his health quite as much as his bodily illness." Deeply loyal, Forster still read manuscripts, corrected proofs, and assisted with personal and professional matters. His com-

mitment beyond question, his combination of bluster, stubbornness, and experience often served Dickens well. Ready to argue
with anyone, he was also ready to love, respect, and work for the
friends with whom he argued. Wills and he growled "at each
other like angry dogs" whenever they met at the office. Despite
Forster's compulsive argumentativeness, though, Dickens had
no doubt that he "has great tenderness under a tough exterior."
When they fought, the estrangement conveyed the emanations
of an inseparable friendship. After one argument, as Dickens
"conversed in the hall with all sorts and conditions of men,"
Forster "flitted about the Athenaeum . . . and pretended not to
see me—but I saw in every hair of his whisker (left hand one)
that he saw Nothing Else." As with most of their brief aliena-
tions, the sacred "Nothing Else" was their transcendent friendship. Neither of them would behave in any way that would
permanently damage it. Responding in 1864 to the publication
of Forster's life of John Eliot, Dickens had thought it "as honest,
spirited, patient, reliable, and gallant a piece of biography as
ever was written. . . . And what I particularly feel about it," he
told him, "is that the dignity of the man, and the dignity of the
book that tells about the man, always go together and fit each
other."30

During the 1860s Wilkie Collins also had serious health
problems. His professional success was undercut by the problems of gout, obesity, arthritis, digestive disorders, fainting
spells, and heart palpitations. Sometimes he felt as if "the gout
has attacked my brain. My mind is perfectly clear—but the
nervous misery I suffer is indescribable." His ill health was so
widely known that it seemed at best an ironic April Fool's joke
to learn that he had been reported dead, a Frenchman writing
"to say he has betted ten bottles of champagne that I am alive—
and to beg I will say so, if I am!" The view in the mirror was
unflattering. Frequently abroad for his health, he wrote to his
mother that "here is 'forty' come upon me—grey hairs shrinking fast . . . rheumatism and gout familiar enemies for some time
past—all the worst signs of middle age sprouting out on me."
Feeling "fat and unwieldy," his own "horrid corpulence" distressed him. Despite all this, though, "I don't *feel* old, I have no
regular habits, no respectable prejudices."

He did have an unrespectable semidomestic life. Though

he protected its privacy as much as possible, his friends were familiar with it. Middle-class women frightened him, marital restrictions repelled him. His first loyalty was to his mother, Harriet Collins. " 'The British female,' " he wrote to her, "is as full of 'snares' as Solomon's 'Strange Woman'—a mixture of perjury and prudery, cant and crinoline—from whom (when we travel in railways) may the guard deliver us!" The "danger from virtuous single ladies whose character is 'dearer to them than their lives' " was greater than from traveling thieves and murderers. He channeled his fears and susceptibility into two long-term relationships, neither of them marriages, neither of them subjects of discussion between him and his mother. In 1857, with Caroline Graves and her daughter, Harriet, he moved into 90 Gloucester Place, Portman Square. Charles Collins had made the matrimonial break from his mother's home in 1860 when he married Katie. Wilkie Collins made no such commitment to Caroline.

A "young woman of gentle birth," her liaison with him had started no later than the spring of 1860. Dickens watched with interest, eventually accepting, probably liking, Caroline. In August 1860, he reported that Wilkie had finished writing *The Woman in White* and "if he had done with his flesh-coloured one, I should mention that too."[31] The relationship continued. During the 1860s it had all of the flavor of a marriage, with few of its restrictions. Collins took parental pleasure in Caroline's daughter, the three of them spending evenings at home entertaining themselves and close friends, including Dickens, who sent his "love to the Butler," his nickname for Harriet Graves, "from her ancient partner in the card trade." He also sent his "kind regards to the Butler's Mama." When Collins was in great pain from gout, Caroline would mesmerize him "into sleeping so as to do without the opium" to which he had become addicted. They wintered in Rome in 1863–64, where she had health problems of her own, particularly "nervous-hysterical" attacks with nightlong palpitations.

In October 1868, the relationship changed radically. Caroline married Joseph Clow, Wilkie attending the wedding. His "affairs defy all prediction," Dickens commented. "For anything one knows, the whole matrimonial pretense may be a lie of that woman's, intended to make him marry her, and (contrary to her expectations) breaking down at last. . . ."[32] It may have been her response to Collins' affair with Martha Rudd, a working-class woman who soon took her place in his home and gave birth to three children within a short period. Dickens did not live to see the further developments. Caroline returned to live with Collins in the 1870s. What happened to Martha Rudd and the three children is unclear. Apparently he set up a second household, provided financially for both of them, and alternated between them. With the same first name as his mother, Harriet Graves became his secretary and emotional support in his old age.

In 1867 Dickens lured him back as a contributor to *All the Year Round*. Attracted by the money, his health somewhat better, Collins proposed that he write a new novel, *The Moonstone*, for serial publication. Dickens urged him also to collaborate, "we too alone, each taking half," on a new Christmas story. "The thought that we shall have a bout of work together again . . . fills me with pleasure and interest. . . . Wills is ready to go into the 'figures' (as he calls it), and there is no chance of any difficulty in that direction. . . . Of course it will be for you to name your own convenient times of drawing money here. All times are alike to us." The collaboration on *No Thoroughfare* gave them both great pleasure, though the actual writing became an irritating burden to Dickens as he began in the fall to move in the direction of America. Collins had long before predicted that he would eventually cross the Atlantic again. Unlike Forster, who opposed the decision, he thought it inevitable. Different as they were, and differing in their attractions to Dickens, he and Forster maintained a pleasantly distant companionship throughout the 1860s, connected by their mutual friend, who frequently had them together as his guests. There were some moments of estrangement. In 1861, though, Collins barely stretched the truth by stating that Forster "is a very intimate and valued friend of mine." Later that year, he delighted in hosting on "a capital day on the river, in a private steamer . . . the Dickenses, Forster, etc." The plural of the "Dickenses" probably included Ellen.[33]

The "etc." also meant Wills, who was a close companion during the 1860s, partly because they worked together on *All the Year Round*, partly because he had no competing loyalty, partly because he had become a combination of private secretary, confidant, and trusted friend to Dickens. Shrewdly binding him with an annual salary and a partnership interest amounting to two thousand pounds a year, Dickens made him the indispensable quiet man who knew his place, filled it well, and found it consequently one of high trust. No other two men "can have gone on more happily and smoothly, or with greater trust and confidence in one another," as if a more reliable Frederick were running the errands again. In late 1864, Wills gave him an attractive small carriage, proof, Dickens felt, of Wills's "ever generous friendship and appreciation, and a memorial of a happy intercourse and a perfect confidence that have never had a break, and that surely never can have a break now (after all these years) but one."

The gradual deterioration of Wills's health, which had long been fragile, did threaten that final break a few times during the 1860s. Severe illnesses in the late 1850s and thereafter evoked Dickens' compassion. They also forced him to carry much of Wills's load at the office, with the help of Henry Morley and sometimes Collins. Throughout much of the spring and summer of 1864, Wills was an invalid. In the fall, he had the great disappointment of being blackballed at the Garrick, albeit with the support of the resignation of Dickens, who had proposed him, and Collins, who had seconded him. The next month, seeing that his health was still precarious, Dickens urged him not to return too soon. Just as his health was a concern to Dickens, the latter's worried Wills. In the spring of 1866, when Dickens undertook a brief reading tour, Wills, "partly that he may have assurance of there being nothing amiss with me, and partly that our All the Year Round business may go on as usual," accompanied him everywhere. When he left for America in 1867, Wills put in his hands confidential instructions about his business and personal affairs. The next year, Wills, a hunting enthusiast and a fearless rider who had just moved to the country, received a concussion in a fall from his horse. It left him hearing "doors slamming" in his head for the rest of his life.34

The late 1850s and the belated, even tired, 1860s, brought the refreshment of new friends to supplement the old. Some were young, with the admiring attitude of disciples, some his contemporaries. The editor of the *Sun*, Charles Kent, became a hero-worshiping friend and a contributor to *All the Year Round*. Other journalists and writers became minor companions in work and pleasure, to some extent Augustus Henry Sala and particularly Percy Fitzgerald, twenty-two years younger than Dickens. He never completely warmed to the dashing, unstable, pleasure-loving Sala either as a friend or as a writer, but he developed a strong affection for Fitzgerald, who became a regular contributor to *All the Year Round*, a visitor at Gad's Hill, a guide during the Irish part of his 1867 reading tour, and, for a short while, a potential husband for Mamie. Fitzgerald, who met Dickens in 1858, cultivated the relationship slowly but assiduously. A handsome, self-centered, ambitious Irishman, he ultimately transformed the friendship into a self-serving industry of personal glorification. It was not an exaggeration, though, that he "was received always as a friend and an intimate." Dickens continued to take a protective, even fatherly interest in Edmund Yates, who was amused one night by Dickens' exemplifying his own theory that "no one ever liked to be thought that he or she could sleep in public." Dickens fell into a doze on the train. When he awoke, Yates said, " 'You've been asleep, sir!' [Dickens] looked guilty, and said, 'I have, sir! and I suppose you're going to tell me that *you* haven't closed an eye!' "[35]

Eccentric, passionately devoted, often at Gad's Hill, Henry Chorley became a satellite member of the family. A thin tall man with a squeaky voice that "reminded one of a guinea pig" and blond hair that had turned white, he was a well-to-do aging bachelor in search of companionship and a home. A heavy drinker, in the 1860s he would "sometimes . . . arrive at a friend's house for dinner in a very confused state, assume that he was in his own . . . and start ordering the servants about." As he grew older, he became "more feeble, more cantankerous, and more bibulous," though his friends' affection for a while generously absorbed his performances. By 1869, when Dickens visited him in his rooms, he seemed "a sad and solitary sight. . . . Poor Chorley reposed like the dregs of last season's wine." Devoted to Mamie, perhaps in love with her, he insisted on incorporating into his will a legacy for her, "an honest desire to pledge himself as strongly as possible." A prolific writer of novels, plays, and opera librettos, Chorley maintained great power in the contemporary musical world through his position as music critic for the

Athenæum. A contentious and musically narrow man, who never missed a chance of showing his "immense importance," he used his power to reinforce his prejudices. When he gave public lectures on musical topics, Dickens advised him on elocution, and then complimented him on the amazing "improvement in [his] delivery." Under pressure, Dickens published a few of his turgid articles in *All the Year Round.* [36] Chorley, though, excelled as a sumptuous host at his home on Eaton Place, obsessed by his dinner menus for weeks in advance, and as a friend whose desperate search for affection made him always loyal, sometimes sweet, and occasionally generous. He was frequently in Dickens' and his daughters' company at Gad's Hill, at Eaton Place, and at Woodlands, the Highgate home of Frederick and Nina Lehmann, Janet Wills's niece.

Born in Germany, Lehmann had come to England as a young man to initiate a successful business career, becoming a partner in the industrial firm of Naylor Vickers. In 1852 he had married Nina Chambers, a perky, dark-haired, and beautiful daughter of the successful Scottish publisher Robert Chambers, who had moved to London to be near the libraries when he launched *Chambers's Encyclopaedia* in 1859. Through Wills, affectionately known as "The Dodger," Nina Lehmann had been introduced to Collins and then to Dickens. She already knew Bulwer-Lytton, George Henry Lewes, and George Eliot. She soon knew most of Dickens' and Collins' friends. A frequent house guest, Collins probably was half in love with her, and Chorley became infatuated with her sister Amelia, "Tuckie," one of Katie's bridesmaids. Through Frederick's brother Rudolph, a minor, moderately successful painter, the Lehmanns got to know most of "the Victorian artistic establishment."

Nina's spacious Highgate home soon became an informal salon and familial visiting place for the Dickens family and Nina and Mamie intimate friends. Restless, Mamie spent long periods at Woodlands and traveled abroad with Nina. Dickens liked and respected Frederick Lehmann, whose expertise on American affairs provided the facts that gradually reduced his prejudices and misconceptions. A generous friend and a good companion, Lehmann gave gifts, favors, and his company at Woodlands, in London and Paris, and on long city and country walks. Their young son, who regularly attending Dickens' London readings,

vividly remembered how "the face and figure that I knew" as
Dickens transformed himself into Mr. Justice Stareleigh in *Pickwick Papers*. Dickens "seemed to vanish as if by magic, and there
appeared a fat, pompous, pursey little man, with a plump imbe-
cile face, from which every vestige of good temper and cheerfulness . . . had been removed." After the performance, his parents
took him to the dressing room, where, as soon as Dickens caught
sight of the boy, "he seized me up in his arms and gave me a
sound kiss."[37]

In his reading career Dickens had become a professional
stage performer. Though always amiable, he rarely was intimate
with theatre people in these years. He did become a warm admirer and close friend of the actor Charles Fechter. Of German,
probably Jewish, background, with a French mother, Fechter
came to England in 1860, where he overcame the disadvantage
of his accent to have a successful though brief career as a romantic actor and as the director of the Lyceum Theatre. He reminded Dickens, who first saw the thirty-five-year-old actor
perform in Paris in 1859, of one of the fine performers of his early
London days, Edmund Yates's father, Frederick. "He has the
brain of a man combined with that strange power of arriving,
without knowing how or why, at the truth, which one usually
finds only in a woman." Offstage, in repose, he appeared "a fat,
clumsy-looking figure with a very dark sallow face and close
black hair." When he performed, "his countenance reflected all
he heard," his face lit up, his expressions became dramatically
mobile and moving. Sharp in conversation, idealistic in his
friendships, he seemed "the greatest all-around actor" of his day,
with "a tenderness and delicacy that was absolutely inimitable."

Impressed with performances that he thought intuitively
brilliant in the creation of character, Dickens became Fechter's
confidential adviser and semiprofessional impresario in London. When, in loyalty to Wills, Dickens resigned from the Garrick, Fechter, in loyalty to him, resigned also. By the early 1860s,
the friendship was an intimate one. With an invalid French wife
and one child, a second having been accidentally killed by his
closest friend in a stage duel, Fechter became Dickens' constant
companion in amusement both onstage and off. Dickens believed in Fechter's genius, "a man of remarkable capacity . . .
with the quickest and brightest understanding." When, in 1862,

he did *Hamlet*, it "was a performance of extraordinary merit; by far the most coherent, consistent, and intelligible Hamlet" he "ever saw. . . . Foreign accent, of course, but not at all a disagreeable one. And he was so obviously safe and at ease, that you were never in pain for him as a foreigner." The combination of picturesqueness and romanticism on the one hand and "a remorseless destruction of all conventionalities" on the other deeply impressed him. Fechter's performance that same season in *Othello*, though, he thought "an utter and unspeakable failure." Always a temperamental artist, Fechter sometimes brought to the stage stubborn misconceptions. Quarrelsome, "given to fits of ungovernable temper," he needed Dickens, the one friend he never alienated, to provide mediation and advice. His management of the Lyceum was a moderate success. In 1867 his performance in the stage version of *No Thoroughfare* helped the dramatization to a long run. In 1865–66, certainly as a favor to his friend, he provided Frances Ternan with her final acting roles in two plays in which he himself acted and in the production of which Dickens assisted.[38]

For Fechter's own American tour in 1869, Dickens provided advance publicity in a laudatory article for the *Atlantic Monthly*, praising, among other things, the rapture of Fechter's "passion—that sheds a glory on its object, and raises her, before the eyes of the audience, into the light in which he sees her." Seeing in Fechter a mirror image of some of his own idealistic impulses and self-definitions, particularly his transforming energy and passion, he had found himself in the summer of 1865 sitting in a two-story summer house, a miniature chalet that the impulsive, generous Fechter had given him as a gift. Early in the year the residents at Gad's Hill Place had been astounded by the appearance on the front lawn of fifty-eight boxes containing the ninety-four parts of some mysterious whole. Having been "constructed in France in bits," it was put together in England and erected amidst the shrubbery on his small piece of land across the Gravesend Road at Gad's Hill, "with the British Thames and British ships visible from its windows." Varnished a warm blond-brown, with decorative chalet trim, it had two rooms, one on each floor, a small balcony, and the atmosphere of an expanded dollhouse or tree house for grown-up children. It was like a set for a stage, a place for performance. Fechter "completed his charming present . . . by furnishing it in a very handsome manner."39 Dickens added mirrors on all the walls of the second floor, finding in the brightness, light, and beauty of the reflections an expansion of his small space and enclosure into a brilliant world of imaginative openness.

※ 5 ※

THE INFANT PHENOM, THE BOY PRODIGY, THE PERFORMANCE PERsonality, the inimitable Boz had become the grizzled, sunbronzed squire of Gad's Hill. He delighted in his possession of the property, in "the golden beauty of an early harvest," as if his English landscape had been additionally internalized by ownership. The lower-middle-class orphan of the feelings was proud of the harvest he had brought in. The reality of Kent, though, was not all golden sunshine. There were hot, uncomfortable summer days. There were winter mornings so cold that water froze in the basins and the piercing wind made his study uninhabitable. As much as he identified with Gad's Hill, his family was scattered, his domestic arrangements unusual. His sense of dislocation and his private needs motivated him to seek alternatives both to Kent and to London. But the "stout, red-faced . . . old-fashioned family house . . . with a wide porch and a bell tower" was made as comfortable as possible.40

On the right, from the central entrance, was his study, about eighteen by fifteen feet, lined partly with false book titles brought from Tavistock House and shelved into the back of the door. Built-in bookshelves extended around the room to a fireplace decorated with twenty delft tiles. A bow window like a glass triptych faced northeast toward the Gravesend Road. To the left, the living room. Behind the study, the billiards room, one wall half-tiled to prevent cue-stick damage to the plaster. Behind the living room, the dining room. Upstairs, off the central hallway, four bedrooms and a bathroom. Tiles brightened the house, mirrors extended it. To the living room he added an extension, to the dining room he added in 1869 a conservatory with a tile floor in a traditional pattern of brown, blue, and white and large glass windows with curved window-top frames. Into opposite walls of the extended living room he had floor-length mirrors embedded that "gave the effect of an endless corridor." Between the main house and the coach house he added a servants' hall. The upper floor of the coach house became a dormitory for children and visitors. A tunnel constructed under the Gravesend Road created safe, private access to his small property opposite. In 1862, he negotiated successfully with the Sir Joseph Williamson's Free School in Rochester for the exchange of a parcel of land he owned in return for the meadow behind his house, thus rendering his "little property more compact and complete." He now had twelve acres in all. From the gardener's cottage behind the coach house the staff kept the acres well trimmed, the flower beds bright in season. Responding to his pride at glass and flowers, Katie remarked, " 'Well, really, papa, I think when you're an angel your wings will be made of looking-glass, and your crown of scarlet geraniums!' "[41]

Each morning, before going to his desk, the squire of Gad's Hill inspected his property, including his stable of dogs, most of whom accompanied him in a small pack on his hikes through the lanes. Most were presents, including Turk, a mastiff; his favorite Linda, a St. Bernard; and Sultan, a magnificent Irish bloodhound, a gift from Percy Fitzgerald. They earned their keep by providing early alarm against the tramps who in the mild weather found the Gravesend Road their natural route between Rochester and London. Fascinated by the tramps, Dickens wrote about them with a mixture of attraction and repugnance that resonated with his sense of his hard-fought elevation to middle-class status, his sympathy for the homeless poor, and his own restlessness. Disguised as the squire, he too was often on the road. Performing the squire's role, he had neighborhood working people onto his back meadow for cricket matches and foot races for which he sponsored prizes.

To his regular guests from the Higham Cricket Club he was fastidious, even priggish enough to complain that it "did not escape [his] notice that some expressions were used the other day which would have been better avoided." He dismissed them from his mind, though, "as being probably unintentional." At Christmas 1866 he had "two thousand people here. . . . The road between" Gad's Hill "and Chatham was like a Fair all day. Having distributed to the visitors a sententious printed bill stating that "Mr. Dickens puts every man upon his honour to assist in preserving order," he felt his liberal civic-mindedness redeemed when there were no arguments, no drunkenness, not a rope or a stake displaced. He was delighted when one of the workingmen raced 120 yards and jumped ten hurdles *"with a pipe in his mouth, and smoking it all the time,"* and came in second. " 'If it hadn't been for your pipe,' " Dickens said to him at the finish line, " 'you would have been first.' 'I beg your pardon, sir,' he answered, 'but if it hadn't been for my pipe I should have been nowhere.' "42

When his sons assembled during holidays, there were dramatic performances, particularly old favorites from childhood like *The Miller and His Men,* cricket on the meadow, croquet and bowls on the lawn, and continuous bouts of billiards. "Cool cups and good drinks. Good beds. Harmony, most evenings." To the stomach-tortured Charles Collins there seemed always to be "eating and drinking on an alarming scale." For some life at Gad's Hill was delightful. "You breakfasted at nine, smoked your cigar, read the papers, and pottered about the garden until luncheon at one. All the morning Dickens was at work, either in the study . . . or in the Chalet." Then came a long, quick-paced walk. With family and friends competing, the billiard and cricket matches were intense, each participant having a reputation and handicap. At cricket matches, he tended to be an umpire, in the billiard rooms an observer, in croquet an occasional participant, and in the theatricals a regular performer.

Alfred, and then Henry, edited a home newspaper, the *Gad's Hill Gazette,* published irregularly during the holidays and supported by subscriptions. It contained capsule accounts of arrivals and departures, of most major events, such as a plague of tramps with their "Runaway Rings," or a persistent hot drought, or a storm so violent that the flagpole in front of the house had been knocked down, or outrageous things done by the family pets. When it faltered because of a defective printer, Wills donated a surplus machine from the *All the Year Round* office. After 1865, it became defunct. The last editor sent the Christmas number to each of his "subscribers free of cost, as a *very* slight token of my gratitude to them for their consideration to me and my journal."43 The heavy footsteps of boys running on the stairs lightened and disappeared. With increasing departures to foreign places, the theatricals and the games declined.

His son Walter's death in 1864 was the first of many farewells that were, for all practical purposes, just as final. Feeling "undoubtedly one of the sons of TOIL . . . for having brought up the largest family ever known with the smallest disposition to do anything for themselves," he joked that he expected to be given the proverbial "pewter watch" in honor of his achievement. "I never sing their praises, because they have so often disappointed me." He did boast, though, about his midshipman son, Sydney, who in the summer of 1866 received an appointment to sail on the *Bristol* off the west coast of Africa. She had the reputation of being an unlucky ship. He was destined to be an unlucky young man, dying in 1872, at the age of twenty-five, probably of consumption. Frank's failure at the war office seemed "quite unaccountable" to his father. Seemingly useless at the *All the Year Round* office, he left for India in 1864, not to return in his father's lifetime. In May 1865, at twenty, after two years of unsatisfying work for an import-export business in London, Alfred left for Melbourne, eager to seek his fortune, his father glad "to dispose of this boy of mine in Australia." Two years later he found it convenient to believe "the very best tidings of Alfred. He is hard at work in the veritable Bush life—has never had an hour's illness of any kind—is highly interested in what he has to do—and reports himself as perfectly happy. His industry and adaptability to the strange circumstances, have put him on a pecuniary footing which enables him to be quite independent, and he leaves untouched some money that I had banked for him in case of need."44 The most difficult departure, as final as Alfred's, was Plorn's in 1868 to join his brother as a sheep farmer.

Only his eldest son, who by 1868 had made him a grandfather five times over, and the next to the youngest, Henry, remained in England. An unsuccessful businessman, Charley seems to have had even less of his father's unqualified affection after his marriage in 1861 to Bessie Evans. He only hoped that his son's marriage would "not be a disasterous one," since he believed that it had been schemed by "his foolish mother" and "he cares nothing for the girl." Their annual production of a child must have been distasteful to Dickens. Used to being disappointed, Dickens only hesitantly, and then gradually, recognized his good fortune when Henry, who seemed brighter, more purposeful, and more disciplined than his brothers, began to show talent as a scholar. At the age of sixteen, he told his father "that he did not wish to enter the Indian Civil Service" but to go to Cambridge. Among his reasons may have been his image of Walter's sudden death in Calcutta. His father resisted. "Many of us have many duties to discharge in life which we do not wish to undertake . . . we must do the best we can to earn our respective livings and make our way." He wanted the terms of his cooperation absolutely clear, for the family name "is too notorious to help him, unless he can very strongly help himself. . . . I bear as heavy a drain as can well be attached to any one working man, and . . . could by no means afford to send a son to college who went there for any other purpose than to work hard, and to gain distinctions. After consulting with his son's teacher, he thought his chances worth the risk and expense. Soon there was highly gratifying praise for Henry, and then, to his father's pleasure, a scholarship.[45]

In different ways, Mamie and Katie were also problems. "Attractive . . . decidedly pretty," Mamie had a small *"petite* figure" with "well-shaped features." Aggressively witty, "her power lay in her interesting character—its curious spirit of *independence* and haughty refusal of submission." Her independence sometimes seemed eccentricity. Her wit often took the form of badinage. Her father felt "grievously disappointed" that she could "by no means be induced to think as highly" of Fitzgerald as he did. By 1866, though, she seemed "round and matronlike," increasingly like her mother. Probably stifled by her triangle with her father and aunt, she looked for alliances elsewhere. Katie confided to a friend that Mamie was "to be pitied . . . but added mysteriously, 'she takes her happiness where she can, and a few visits to town have given her all she cares for.'" Mamie's dissatisfactions were widely noted in the Dickens circle. She "may blaze up in firework any day." Rumors circulated that both sisters were "going to the devil as fast as can be."

Katie's problems were more concrete. Family and friends generally agreed that Charles Collins "was guilty of an 'infamy' in marrying at all." Undoubtedly as aware of his daughter's sexless marriage as of her childlessness, by 1864 Dickens had come to the conclusion that she "was likely to be left a young widow." Increasingly impatient, angry, and probably guiltily self-protective about her situation, he began to make bitter remarks, sometimes in other people's presence, perhaps in the presence of his daughter and son-in-law as well. Collins' semi-invalided appearance at the breakfast table at Gad's Hill became a painful death's head At moments, apparently, Dickens wanted nothing but that Collins should die and get it over with. The situation was awkward for Wilkie, aware of the tensions and deeply loyal to his brother. Dickens, though, had moments of constructive sympathy for his children, even for "the charming, attractive, feckless Charlie [Collins]." In May 1867 he "doubled . . . Katie's marriage portion." Wilkie thought that "liberal and just" and hoped that his brother's luck was turning.46 But Charlie's fortunes remained as bad as ever. His stomach ulcers, eventually cancerous, kept him in torment until 1873.

Katie, meanwhile, made do with an unhappy father, an ill husband, and a troublesomely large amount of unexpressed life and spirit of her own. At a party at Chorley's, she and her sister behaved frenetically and impolitely. When she "smiled, something of her former pretty self appeared, only to make the pained and woebegone expression that would follow more distressing." She took up acting "on the private stage." She had, like her father, theatrical talent. She also was gifted as a painter. But she had no marketable skills, and few hopes. When an aristocratic friend put on "a series of Tableaux for the Prince of Wales," she took a small part, Charlie (Collins) noting that "our future monarch is very nearly as broad as he is long" and "getting bald very fast. . . . He talks the language of the country which he is to govern with a foreign accent, and will be in a year or two a little fat Hanoverian of the type of the three first Georges." Friendly with Thackeray's daughters, in June 1867 she attended Minny's wedding to Leslie Stephen, "a somewhat dry uninteresting personage—a Saturday Reviewer and Pall Mall Gazattier of the modern type." Trying to survive on Collins' small inheritance, sporadic earnings as a writer, and their marriage portion kept them close to their bourgeois-genteel, nonworking grindstone. "Rather delicate—about the chest and heart," through much of the 1860s she suffered from unexplained debilitating illnesses, with some serious episodes that worried her father and her friends. When she was ill in late 1866 with a "low nervous fever," he felt that "she is a bad subject for illness, having long been in an unsatisfactory and declining state." Flirting and teasing regularly, she appeared "so discontented . . . so intensely eager to find other lovers," that she was "burning away both character and health slowly but steadily."[47]

Fortunately, the sunshine at Gad's Hill shone on Ellen as well as on his daughters and friends. The *Gad's Hill Gazette*, of course, makes no mention of her comings and goings, and the carefully expunged record conceals any indication of how frequently she visited. With relatives in Rochester, she had occasion to be in the area separate from her friendship with him. Mamie, Katie, Georgina, and a few intimate friends had partial to full knowledge of the relationship, but her visits need not have revealed to those on the perimeter more than the impression that she was a friend of the family. The younger boys undoubtedly were told nothing other than that. A veteran of the 1858–59 conflict, Charley Dickens would have assumed that the relationship was an intimate one. As they grew up and then survived their father, some of his other sons learned the basic facts, including the possibility that their father and Ellen had had a child. Whether that was one source of Dickens' anxieties is unclear. Diligent detective work has not uncovered the secrets of the supreme detective, capable of throwing even himself off the trail of self-awareness. There are only shadows of possibilities, a circumstantial network of connections between one of his pseudonyms and the name of a child on a birth certificate, a few dim, half-thoughtless recollections that they had had or someone had said that they had had a son, and the less circumstantial statement by Henry Fielding Dickens in 1928 that unto them had been born, etc.[48]

Though the "patient," whose health never fully recovered after the Staplehurst accident, may have enjoyed the recuperative sunshine of Kent, she had a comfortable residence of her own at Ampthill Square. By December 1865 Ellen felt well enough to attend a dancing party, hosted by the brother of her brother-in-law-to-be, Anthony Trollope, with scarlet geraniums in her hair. In January 1866, she moved to Elizabeth Cottage in Slough, seventeen miles from London, across the river from Windsor and three miles from Eton. The proceeds from subleasing the Ampthill Square house probably helped support her and her mother. Using the pseudonym "Charles Tringham," partly borrowed from the name of his tobacconist in Covent Garden, partly from a story that Thomas Hood had published in 1839 about a scandal in the "tattling village of Tringham," Dickens paid the rent and the taxes for the comfortable cottage. A frequent visitor, he could easily see across the river the towers of the castle outside of which he and Maclise had romantically rhapsodized about the young queen. Slough provided both ready access from the *All the Year Round* office and sufficient privacy for him to move through the neighborhood with semianonymity. Undoubtedly, Georgina, his daughters, and Wills knew that he might just as well be there as in London or at Gad's Hill. Often, as far as the extended circle of friendship and business knew, he was at the other of the two acknowledged places.

The move to Elizabeth Cottage may have been prompted by a desire for greater privacy. If there had been a pregnancy in late 1865, then the move in January 1866 would have been sensible. In October 1866, Ellen did not attend the Paris wedding of her eldest sister to Thomas Trollope, though Maria and her mother did. Frequently at Slough, at least during the summer of 1866 and almost certainly from January 1866 to May 1867, Dickens did his usual lying to disguise either his whereabouts or why he was there, dating his letters from Eton or from town. With deceptive casualness he explained the Eton postmark. He was "merely walking in the Park here, but write from this place, in consequence of having omitted to do so in town." Usually, though, he was in Eton waiting for the train to London, having walked across the back fields from Slough, as the Eton station was on a line more convenient to the *All the Year Round* office. He also preferred to be noticed, if at all, at the Eton rather than the Slough station.49 In March 1867, he gave up Elizabeth Cottage and rented, using a variant of his Tringham pseudonym, a larger, more comfortable house much nearer to central London and Gad's Hill, Windsor Lodge, at Linden Grove in Peckham, not far from Herne Hill and Dulwich. Ellen moved there in May 1867. A frequent visitor, he wrote one of his most psychologically revealing autobiographical stories there, "George Silverman's Explanation." Very few nonfictional explanations were forthcoming from the increasingly secretive novelist.

His departure for America later that year involved good-byes at all his residences. Perhaps the most dramatic good-bye had already taken place in October 1866. Now huge in size, Sultan, Fitzgerald's gift, was docile and loving, though aggressively possessive. He had become his master's favorite, partly because of his affectionateness, partly because he rejected and detested everyone else. "So accursedly fierce towards other dogs" that he had to be muzzled in order to be taken out, he attacked everything moving or still, with a special "invincible repugnance to soldiers." Dashing "into the heart of a company . . . he pulled down an objectionable private." The price of such total love was the problem of how to deal with his creature's unmitigated enmity to the rest of the world. To Dickens, he was the finest dog he had ever seen. "Between him and me there was a perfect understanding." Breaking his muzzle frequently, though, he came home "covered with blood, again and again." One day he swallowed an entire blue-eyed kitten, afterward suffering "agonies of remorse (or indigestion)?" When he seized the little sister of one of the servants, Dickens flogged him. The next morning he took the dog to the meadow behind the house, accompanied by a half-dozen men with guns and a wheelbarrow. Sultan bounded out cheerfully, anticipating "the death of somebody unknown." He paused, meditatively, with his eyes on the wheelbarrow and the guns. "A stone deftly thrown across him . . . caused him to look round for an instant, and then he fell dead, shot through the heart."[50]

CHAPTER FOURTEEN

A Castle in the Other World
(1867-1870)

❧ I ❧

Glasses were raised high to honor the great novelist of the age. The arched top of each of the twenty wall panels in Freemason's Hall had had inscribed on it in great gold letters the name of one of his novels, "the post of honour over the chair being given to the Immortal Pickwick." When the doors were thrown open on the evening of November 2, 1867, Dickens and Bulwer-Lytton entered arm in arm. "A cry rang through the room, handkerchiefs were waved on the floor and in the galleries . . . and the band struck up a full march." The faces looking up at his radiated with the belief that they were attending "a high historical event." The 450 distinguished literary and social gentlemen who glowed through the crowded dinner and the 100 women sequestered in evening-gown splendor in the gallery had no doubt that the young newspaper reporter from somewhere had long ago arrived to help make them themselves. He was the author whose name Queen Victoria was soon told "will hereafter be closely associated with the Victorian era."[1]

The dinner arrangements had been made mostly by

Charles Kent, with Dickens' encouragement. The honor appealed to his vanity. It would provide an infusion of communal warmth before he sailed into a comparatively solitary adventure. It would generate publicity that would precede him to American shores. It would provide him with a forum in which to speak of his positive feelings about the former republic of his imagination. Determined that in this second coming there would be no politics, no international copyright, no divisive speeches, he wanted only amity and financial success. At a dinner hosted by Wilkie Collins a few evenings before, he responded to all eyes being drawn to "a most wonderful pin" in his cravat, "large in size, strange in form," with a substantial jewel at its center, "I hope, that there is no such pin as this in America. I have invested in it for the whole and sole purpose of pleasing my friends over the water, and I hope you all think I shall succeed." Public and private celebratory dinners filled his engagement book. There could not be enough memorializing. The enlisting of a huge honor role of stewards for the farewell banquet gave Forster the opportunity to reaffirm the platform of nonpatronage, that "vile" custom of listing aristocrats separately on the program. Among other things, the dinner was to affirm "the common fellowship of professors and lovers of literature," the lifelong effort that his career represented to make literature a respectable profession.[2]

Surrounded by the community that he had been instrumental in creating, Dickens seemed radiantly happy, his excitement unaffected by Bulwer-Lytton's garish makeup and his "ingeniously bad" speech, by the "drunken waiters . . . greasy fragments of tepid dishes . . . cold plates with the soup. . . ." The mood was laudatory, the self-praise of an idealizing culture in which tears and cheers went together. If there was a sepulchral resonance, it was regal, congratulatory, expressing a sense of the momentousness of the occasion. This was to be, as Procter told the ailing Forster, "the Dickens apotheosis." One of the speakers declaimed, "Happy is the man who makes clear his title-deeds to the royalty of genius while he yet lives to enjoy the gratitude and reverence of those whom he has subjected to his sway. . . . Seldom . . . has that kind of royalty been quietly conceded to any man of genius until his tomb becomes his throne." The title had been conceded long ago. There was no need for quiet now. When Dickens rose to speak, "the air . . . full of electricity," the entire company surged to its feet. His friends at the front tables rushed forward, forcing their way up the aisles until only a solid wall of admiring faces glowed before him. "Men leaped on chairs, tossed up napkins," spilled champagne, "waved glasses and decanters over their heads." In the galleries the women, "scarcely able to breathe for the smoke and heat," waved their handkerchiefs. Flushed with excitement, his "wonderful eyes" flaming "around like a searchlight," he waited a long while until the storm of shouts faded into silence. His voice faltered. He needed to take "a desperate hold" of himself or he "should have lost [his] sight and voice and sat down again." "Tears streamed down his face. . . . It seemed to be a sacred moment."3

In his best oratorical style, he thanked his audience of brother artists for testifying that the cause of art had been safe in his keeping, "and that they think it has never been falsely dealt with by me." His fondest hope was that he might "leave its social position in England something better than I found it." For "the public believe, that with a host of imperfections and shortcomings on my head, I have as a writer . . . tried to be as true to them as they have ever been to me." As always, he spoke not from a text but from memory and inspiration. He kept in mind the prepared image of his speech as a wheel, with spokes as its subtopics. As he turned the wheel, each spoke dropped away. He turned to the spoke of literature as free enterprise, as an open community. He had heard "a great deal about literary sets and cliques, and coteries, and barriers, about keeping this man up, and keeping that man down, and about sworn disciples, and sworn unbelievers, and mutual admiration societies" obstructing the upward path that he had begun "to tread when [he] was very young, without influence, without money, without companion, introducer, or advisor," but he had never encountered these barriers.

For the moment, the blacking factory, the struggle to find a vocation, his battles with Bentley, his sense that he could never run too fast or too far to keep ahead of rivals and detractors, his pursuit of friends of influence and a supportive community faded into the background. He then turned the wheel to the spoke of America. With the flags of the two great nations above his head, he did not hesitate to say that "the story of my going again . . . is very easily and briefly told." Since he had last been there, the best known of his books, *David Copperfield*, had been published, "a vast entirely new generation [had] arisen," and he had been beseeched to visit by many strong American voices of personal interest . . . and personal affection." He wanted to see for himself "the astonishing change and progress of a quarter of a century over there, to grasp the hands of many faithful friends whom I left upon those shores, to see the faces of a multitude of new friends upon whom I have never looked, and . . . to use my best endeavour to lay down a third cable of intercommunication and alliance between the old world and the new. . . . And so, as Tiny Tom observed, 'God bless us every one!' "4

The story, though, was more complicated, the blessing less generalized. He and his friends had no doubt in their minds and in private discussions that his main motive for going was financial gain. What an American might have frankly stated, English Victorians had to disguise. With his sensitivity to being thought mercenary, he felt compelled to idealize his intentions. With Wills, Forster, and his new business manager, George Dolby, he was unflinchingly candid. "To get that sum in a heap so soon is an immense consideration to me—my wife's income to pay—a very expensive position to hold—and my boys with the curse of limpness on them. You don't know what it is to look around the table and see reflected from every seat of it (where they sit) some horribly well remembered expression of inadaptability to anything."

For his spring 1866 reading tour he had been paid £1,500 by the theatrical management firm of Arthur and Thomas Chappell, "speculators, though of the worthiest and most honourable kind," who took care of all the arrangements that could be made from their office and by their agents. He had settled in advance with them for a guaranteed fee, the Chappells receiving all the profit beyond that and his expenses. From mid-January to May 1867, he had done a series of forty-two readings in London and the provinces, for which he had been paid £2,500. With his usual passion for getting it right, he had worked up new selections, particularly from his recent Christmas stories, "Barbox Brothers" and "The Boy at Mugby," which by January 1867 had reached "the extraordinary circulation [of] 256,000 odd hundred of copies." For the first time he learned all his readings by heart, "so as to have no mechanical drawback in looking after the words." Since the completion of *Our Mutual Friend* in November 1865, his mind had not been on fiction, except for some short pieces and the loose agenda of a new novel somewhere off in the distance. The reading experience (and "when I read I *don't* write . . . I only edit") sustained him emotionally and bolstered him financially.5

It was never *only* a matter of money. During the winter and spring of 1867, in England, Ireland, and Scotland, "constantly travelling . . . here, there, and everywhere, and (principally) nowhere," through snow sleet, rain, cold, on trains that set his nerves trembling, through insistent evenings in hot crowded reading halls, he revived at the sound of applause, his energy surged at the sight of waiting audiences. His performance personality and his financial insecurity were catalysts for one another. two sides of the same coin of his neediness. Every seat was always taken and usually "the success the most brilliant" he had ever seen. In one mood and to one kind of correspondent he found the most idealized terms for his fascination with the readings. "When I first entered on this interpretation of myself . . . I was sustained by the hope that I could drop into some hearts, some new expression of the meaning of my books, that would touch them in a new way. To this hour that purpose is so strong in me, and so real are my fictions to myself, that, after hundreds of nights, I come with a feeling of perfect freshness to that little red table, and laugh and cry with my hearers, as if I had never stood there before." Dolby had no hesitation, though, in confessing what they sometimes both felt. In the tedium of business "our travelling life had become so much a matter of system with us. that the routine of it became almost monotonous. Day after day we were doing the same things at the same time."6

No sooner had Dickens finished the spring 1867 readings than he started to succumb to the lure of the American invitations. Early in May he was so tired that he could "hardly undress for bed." On the same day he felt frustrated by "expenses . . . so enormous" that he began to feel himself "drawn toward America, as Darnay in the Tale of Two Cities was attracted to the Loadstone Rock, Paris." Darnay had had a narrow escape.

Dickens must have sensed the implication of the comparison. Through much of 1866 he had been unwell, with contradictory diagnoses about his lameness that pointed to gout or erysipelas, with undiagnosed long-standing neuralgic symptoms, with some indication of cardiac illness, which one doctor called " 'great irritability of the heart.' " Still, in February 1866 he "sold" himself "(rather in the Faust way!) for 30 readings." In September 1866, twice in one week he was "seized in a most distressing manner—apparently in the heart." Persuading himself that it was "only in the nervous system," through the winter and spring he suffered from various ailments, constantly in the diagnostic shadow-land between overexertion and the possibility of serious illness. Exhaustion and rationalization obscured organic symptoms. Illness contributed to exhaustion, which he blamed on overwork.

Until February 1867, he dismissed any relationship between his symptoms and the possibility of "degeneration of some functions of the heart." Thereafter he resisted but could not completely deny the possibility. Reading in Liverpool in January 1867, he became "so faint afterwards that they laid [him] on a sofa at the hall for half an hour." He attributed "it to [his] distressing inability to sleep at night, and to nothing worse." Two nights later it happened again. Though "heavily beaten," he consoled himself with the claim that he "was not faint . . . only exhausted." The next week, "severely shaken on an atrocious railway," he could not sleep. In February, he began to feel "a curious . . . soreness all round the body." Soon he had a recurrence of bleeding from piles, which he had not suffered from so severely since the early 1840s. He managed to make it to the end of the readings in May. On May 9, he told his sister that, "thank God, I am getting on splendidly, and resting amazingly."[7] The next day was the one on which he could hardly undress himself.

For five months he hesitated to announce that he had succumbed to the magnetic attraction. The decision was implicit in his feelings in May and an almost inevitable expression of his character. America had been long on his mind, as a concept and as a business enterprise. When he had declined to read there in 1859, he had reserved the likelihood of a more propitious time. A world of American connections needed attending to, needed to be fully reconciled with. Also, there was a market for his works and his readings. Feeling a constant grievance about the lost royalties from the American sale of his books, the proceeds of which would have made him rich, he could, by giving readings there, reclaim some of the gold that rightfully belonged to him, the unrewarded sweat of his brow during thirty years as a writer. And the emanations from America were fraternal as well as financial. He responded warmly whenever the two came together. His Boston publisher, James T. Fields, and his wife, Annie, had visited him in London and at Gad's Hill in July 1859. A petite, dark-haired, intelligent, and attractive woman, eager to transform hero worship into friendship, Annie Fields quickly become one of his platonic female favorites. Seventeen years older than his second wife, James T. Fields was a soft-spoken, generous, hospitable man whose social and professional position made him a prominent representative of New England literary culture. Dickens liked him immensely, and was especially pleased with his compact edition of *Our Mutual Friend*.[8] Editor of the *Atlantic Monthly* and the active partner in the firm of Ticknor and Fields, Fields urged him to give America another chance.

This time he would have a reliable business companion to accompany him. George Dolby, an experienced theatrical agent and the brother of the well-known singer Madame Santon Dolby, had initially been employed by the Chappells as their representative. Brawny, balding, cigar-smoking, with a wide moustache and a huge waist, the worshiping Dolby deserved his reputation for efficiency, competence, and insensitive toughness in dealing with business matters. Not even his habitual stutter, forcing "him to become suddenly stately in the middle of a homely phrase and to give a queer intonation to his voice," detracted from his effectiveness.[9] He quickly became confidant, protector, and essential companion. Nurturing and protecting his frail, often exhausted, and frequently depressed "Chief," he more than earned his 10 percent commission, which the Chappells paid. Everywhere that Dickens read in 1866–67 Dolby went also, attending to the safety of the props, providing sandwiches, protection, and security, seizing, securing, and counting the receipts each night, dealing with business problems on the spot, worrying about his health during the performances, checking from his next-door room on whether the exhausted and often ill performer was having another of his sleepless nights.

On the face of it, Dickens carefully deliberated the decision to go to America; but much of the rational process, including considerations of health, was superfluous. The balance sheet dominated his thinking. When Fields in April 1866 queried him, he responded that he would need a very substantial financial incentive to commit himself to the wear and tear when he had merely to say yes to the Chappells "to pluck fruit that grows on every bough at home." He would put no price on "fifty readings in America, because I do not know that any possible price could pay me for them. And I really cannot say to anyone disposed towards the enterprise, 'Tempt me,' because I have too strong a misgiving that he cannot in the nature of things do it. . . . The chances are a thousand to one that the answer will be no." A direct no would have ended the matter. In effect, his response challenged Fields to tempt him sufficiently. The Bostonian of course took up the challenge. One of the important unmentioned obstacles to the "very large proposal from America" was that he could not "bear the thought of the distance and the absence" from Ellen. The temptation and its difficulties were much on his mind during the summer of 1866. In mid-October, he wrote to Fields that "a faint outline of a castle in the air always dimly hovers between me and Rochester, in the great hall of which I see myself reading to American audiences. But my domestic surroundings must change before the castle takes tangible form. And perhaps *I* may change first, and establish a castle in the other world."

After working his way into exhaustion through his series of fifty readings, he was ready again in May 1867 to return to the American temptation. "On behalf of a committee of private gentlemen at Boston," Fields guaranteed ten thousand pounds to be banked in London. American speculators besieged Dolby and the Chappells. If there was a time to go, it was soon, while the fever was strong, for the Americans, he believed, "are a people whom a fancy does not hold long. . . . They are bent upon my reading there, and they believe (on no foundation whatever) that I am going to read there. If I ever go, the time would be when the Christmas number goes to press. Early in this next November." The qualification that it was "on no foundation" was partly for Forster, who strongly opposed the trip, partly momentary self-deceit. "It is *possible,*" he admitted, "that I may enter into some extensive 'Reading' engagements as the winter begins, though I cannot at present decide . . . and in the meantime the impending possibility obscures my whole prospect." In June, he told Fields that he was "trying HARD" to free himself so "as to be able to come over to read this next winter!" In the meantime, "don't contradict the rumour." That might cause confusion and affect the success of the readings. For "no light obstacles will turn me aside, now that my hand is in.'"10

Wills, and Forster particularly, opposed the venture, the former because of the potential damage to Dickens' health, the latter because he also believed the readings incompatible with the dignity of literature. Others, like Carlyle, muttered quietly about intemperate greediness. Procter felt sorry that he was "expatriating himself," though he would be "very glad if he come back safe—and brings a heavy bag full of American coin— *No* paper." Concerned friends in New York sent "letters about Danger, Anti-Dickens feeling, Anti-English feeling," and "New York rowdyism." As for 'the patient," Dickens acknowledged to Wills that his desire not to be separated from her was "the gigantic difficulty. But you know I don't like to give in before a difficulty, if it can be beaten." He proposed bringing her with him. He would read in America on his own account, without benefit of the Chappells or any intermediary. The generally agreed on estimate of ten thousand pounds' profit was conservative. He could easily make that sum even with restricting himself to the large cities of the East Coast to lessen the strain of travel. His visit would help the sales of the collected edition of his works. His "exceptional faculty of accumulating young feelings in short pauses, which obliterates a quantity of wear and tear," would protect his health. He even felt comfortable arguing from the premise that though "my worldly circumstances are very good" and "I don't want money, for all my possessions are free, and in the best order . . . still, at 55 or 56, the likelihood of making a very great addition to one's capital in half a year, is an immense consideration."11 Though he easily outargued Wills and Forster, it did not matter anyway. He had made up his mind to go.

For his own protection and expecting conclusive justification, he sent Dolby to America to provide an expert analysis of the facts and figures. Unhappily, just before his manager's departure at the beginning of August, Dickens' left foot became swollen and inflamed again. There are "so many reasons against supposing it to be gouty," he insisted, "that I do not really think it is." He could not get his boot on, let alone walk, the pain so intense that he went to see a specialist as soon as he returned from Liverpool to London. Dr. Henry Thompson diagnosed it as the result of "pressure on a bone received in much walking and engendering a tendency to inflammation." In great pain, immediately consigned to complete rest on the sofa at the office, he wrote to Dolby to assure him that "the cause of all the annoyance is the action of the boot on an unidentified part of a bone," which had developed into "erysipelas in the foot," an infection of the skin and subcutaneous tissue. (Dolby diagnosed America with equal optimism, though with sounder justification.) At home, Dickens did everything possible to stifle the rumor that he was seriously ill, though he remained lame for almost two months. He still claimed in the middle of September that he had "not the least idea whether I am going to America or not," though "everybody else seems to know all about it."¹² He would decide when his manager returned.

That was only technically true. Later in the month he lied to Kent, urging him to contradict rumors, to tell people that "I never was better in my life—doubt if anybody ever was or can be better—and have not had anything the matter with me but a squeezed boot, which was an affair of a few days." The rumors spread persistently, by word of mouth and in newspapers. "The undersigned innocent victim," he insisted, "is NOT in a *critical state of health*, and has NOT consulted *eminent surgeons* and . . . has not had so much as a head ache for twenty year." Apparently he found it humorous, when Charles Reade, the popular novelist, and Wilkie Collins visited Gad's Hill, that "the joke of the time is to feel my pulse when I appear at table." He drew up a precise statement of "the case in a nutshell" for Wills's and Forster's responses. As a business document, it was completely sound. But it did not mention his physical and emotional health. Toward the end of the month, he seemed to Collins, as they worked on the Christmas number, to be "greatly harassed about *finally* deciding on the American tour. On Mon-

day next, he must definitely decide—Yes, or No." The next day
he told Kent that the telegram would go out on the twenty-
eighth. "Solar System shall be apprized immediately afterwards." He went to Ross-on-Wye, where Dolby lived, and
where the Forsters were vacationing, for a final conference. The
main point was clear to him. "I cannot set the hope of a large
sum of money aside."₁₃ He listened to Forster's objections, and
then sent the telegram.

�֍ 2 ✖

DESPITE DICKENS' EXHILARATION AT THE BRILLIANCE OF THE BAN-
quet, he was depressed and restless for the month preceding his
departure, not "in very brilliant spirits at the prospect" before
him, the fatigue of the journey, the absence from loved ones. He
miswrote and blotted the last word of the phrase "your affectionate Father—I can't write the word"—in an explanatory letter to Henry about not being able "to neglect so promising a
prospect of being so handsomely remunerated for hard work."
He was uneasy about what awaited him. Notwithstanding his
frequent persuasions to the contrary, he did know that his
health was fragile, that the "puny, weak youngster" with "violent spasmodic attacks" had been reincarnated as a sickly elderly
man. He ordered a small medicine chest to be provisioned for
the venture with what he usually carried on tour "for neuralgic
touches, namely Laudanum—Ether—Sal Volatile," and a form
of digitalis for the heart. In the middle of October, Wills and
Collins were prowling around at Gad's Hill "with their hands
in their pockets," while he prowling around in his mind, wrote
a letter to Dolby, who had gone again to America to make the
final arrangements. Fechter stuck his head in—"Pough Bang he
dies!" He felt "in the pause as if [he] were not in England, not
in Europe; not in America, Africa, or Asia," but nowhere, between two worlds, on the edge of a kind of extinction.₁₄ The
possibility that he might not return occurred to him, though he
held it at a distance.

He still hoped to have Ellen join him. Having charged
Dolby on this second trip to consult with the Fieldses, both of
whom knew about her, and to get his and their opinion about

whether it would be safe to have her come, he was "quite prepared for your great Atlantic-cable-message being adverse.
. . . I think it so likely that Fields may see shadows of danger
which we in our hopeful encouragement of one another may
have made light of, that I think the message far more likely to
be No than Yes. I shall try to make up my mind to it, and to be
myself when we meet." He provided Forster "general and
ample Power of Attorney" and wrote detailed business memos
for Wills, who would handle most daily matters while he was
gone. Mary and Georgina were given access to his checking
account to pay Gad's Hill expenses. Ouvry was to send Catherine her money. All letters to him, whether addressed to Gad's
Hill or to the office, were to be opened only by Wills. Letters
to Ellen that he sent to Wills, whose responsibilities may also
have included paying any obligations connected with Ellen,
probably at least the quarterly taxes on Windsor Lodge, were to
be hand-delivered or forwarded discreetly.

Unfortunately, the telegram from Dolby was not determinative either way. He immediately worked out a code that
would signal, soon after his arrival in Boston, whether or not he
would risk her joining him. "Tel: all well means *you come.* Tel:
safe and well, means *you don't come.*" Wills was to forward the
message to Ellen in Florence, where she would be staying with
her sister at Villa Trollope. There was to be no mistake in his
carrying out his instructions. "If she needs any help . . . NELLY
. . . will come to you, or if she changes her address, you will
immediately let me know. . . . On the day after my arrival out
I will send you a short telegram at the office. Please copy its
exact words . . . and post them to her . . . by the very next post.
. . . And also let Gad's Hill know—what the telegram is. . . ."
And also Forster, who "knows Nelly as you do, and will do
anything for her if you want anything done."15

Tossed again by heavy Atlantic seas, Dickens made his
second crossing from Liverpool to Boston, this time on the
Cunard steamer *Cuba.* He had an officer's cabin on deck "big
enough for everything but getting up in and going to bed in."
Mamie, Katie, Wilkie, Kent, and Yates saw the voyager off. As
usual, he refused to say good-bye, and found circumlocutions to
avoid the pain and bad luck. This was *not* good-bye. It was not
even his farewell to the stage. When the ship left Liverpool in

bright calm weather on November 8, 1867, he already had arranged another reading tour. The Chappells had accepted his proposal that on his return he do a series of seventy-five "farewell readings in town and country," for which they would cover all expenses and commissions and pay him six thousand pounds. On shipboard, the popular celebrity was treated to the captain's right hand and to the adulation of the mostly American passengers. Believing that they did wonders in preventing seasickness, he began to eat baked apples frequently. Finding the dining room stuffy, he often dined in his small airy cabin, where he had a miniature writing desk, and read constantly. Halfway out a heavy gale sprang up, the ship rolling and plunging. It became impossible to pass a teacup from one pair of hands to another or to write. "My heels [are] on the paper as often as the pen. . . . My desk and I have just risen from the floor."[16] At Sunday services the tossing kept everything and everyone sliding comically. Though his foot remained sore from the episode in August, he still tried to get exercise walking on deck. Fortunately, he was not seasick at all. As the *Cuba* steamed down from Halifax against heavy winds, he sang and amused himself at a farewell party with the other passengers.

In Boston, expectations were high. There was an overnight queue, stretching for nearly half a mile, in front of Ticknor and Fields. The rapid sale of tickets shocked even Dolby. Every seat for the first four readings sold in a little over eleven hours with receipts of fourteen thousand dollars, or two thousand pounds. For the Bostonians it was simultaneously a theatrical, a social, and a cultural event. The most famous literary man in a world in which the printed word was king and the only royalty available again and at last was coming to the city that defined itself as the cultural capital of America. For Dickens, Boston was "his American home . . . all his literary friends lived there." On the eighteenth a telegram from Halifax claimed that the *Cuba* would arrive the next day, "with Mr. Dickens on board." When Dolby read it to the crowd waiting for tickets, standing on long lines in frigid weather, the first sign of what proved to be an unusually hard winter, "there was a terrific *furore*," some of which expressed the greed of speculators who were attempting to buy as many as possible to resell for profit.

Accepting an offer to meet the *Cuba* in a United States

customs steamer, Dolby sailed through a shower of welcoming
rockets and flares illumining the ship as it entered the harbor
in the moonless night. As the steamer came alongside, Dickens
called down from the deck, having anticipated that Dolby
would pick him up "from a pilot boat, or some other impossible place between Halifax and Boston." Soon he was warmly
embracing Dolby and Fields. Evading the crowds at the wharf,
they made their way into the Parker House Hotel, where "all
the notabilities of Boston" had gathered to greet him. He
seemed to Fields to be in excellent health and spirits. Finally,
he ascended to his apartment, high up in a quiet corner, with
"a hot and cold bath in his bedroom," for rest, food, "the old
brew of punch and a cigar," and some private moments with
Dolby. Annie Fields had decorated the rooms with bright
flowers. While he ate, people frequently looked in through the
doors the waiters left open, reminding him of how he had
been exhibited like an animal on his previous visit. He felt
peevish, fatigued, and suddenly "very depressed in spirits."[17]
But he had a little more than ten days to refresh himself before
the readings were to start.

The ten days proved an irritant. More than anything, he
wanted to get the readings done and return to England. It became clear to him immediately that in this inconsistently moralistic world neither his cultural image nor the available
conditions of limited privacy could withstand Ellen's arrival.
"All New England is primitive and puritanical. All about and
around it is a puddle of mixed human mud with no real quality
in it," though it was "a good sign maybe, that it all seems immensely more difficult to understand than it was when I was
here before." His pessimism had been sound, his caution the
preliminary to inevitable disappointment. Two days after arriving he telegraphed to Wills, SAFE AND WELL EXPECT GOOD LETTER
FULL OF HOPE. Soon he had a telegram back through Fields. The
next week he was "yearning already for spring and home."[18]
Characteristically impatient, he found waiting more stressful
than acting. Incapable of sitting still, his delight in his Boston
friends and his interest in the changes in American culture kept
him constantly active. The day after his arrival, Henry Wadsworth Longfellow, Ralph Waldo Emerson, Oliver Wendell
Holmes, and Louis Agassiz called on him. The next day the elite

of Boston literary society gathered at Fields's Charles Street
home for a welcoming dinner party.

There were striking absences and changes. The much-
loved Cornelius Felton was dead. So too was Nathaniel Haw-
thorne. Though the Civil War had taken its toll, Dickens seemed
to notice that much less than natural causes and ordinary time.
A brilliant scientist and professor, Agassiz was "the most natural and jovial of men." Annie Fields feared that Holmes, "so
simple and lovely," bored him by talking at him. Dickens particularly liked the young writer and scholar Charles Eliot Norton.
Having turned "perfectly white in hair and beard, but a remarkably handsome and notable-looking man," Longfellow greeted
him warmly, happy to "see [him] again after so many years, with
the same sweetness and flavor as of old, and only greater ripe-
ness." Emerson had a more reflective response, later telling
Annie Fields that "I am afraid he has too much talent for his
genius; it is a fearful locomotive to which he is bound and can
never be free from it nor set at rest. You see him quite wrong;
and would persuade me that he is a genial creature, full of
sweetness and amenities and superior to his talents, but I fear
he is harnessed to them. He is too consummate an artist to have
a thread of nature left." With Fields, Dickens took long walks
every day, one of them to Cambridge, where he dined with
Longfellow again in "his old house, where his beautiful wife
was burned to death." Dickens, who told funny stories and did
his "irresistible imitation" of Carlyle, could not get out of his
mind the vivid image of her being "in a blaze in an instant" and
rushing "into his arms with a wild cry."[19]

With all tickets sold at the highest price, he made his
American debut on December 2, reading *A Christmas Carol* and
the trial scene from *Pickwick* to an overflow audience of aggressively laudatory Bostonians, including many of his literary
friends, most of whom found themselves happily attending
every performance. To his "pleasure and amazement," he found
in his room, before leaving for the Tremont Temple, a lovely
flower for his buttonhole that Mary Boyle in England had arranged to have delivered to him, as was her practice in London.
He walked to the stage "as cool . . . as though I were reading at
Chatham." Everything was "brilliant beyond the most sanguine
hopes," the whole city "perfectly mad" with excitement. He

wired to Wills, probably for Ellen's eyes also, TREMENDOUS SUC-
CESS GREATEST ENTHUSIASM ALL WELL. They were making "a *clear
profit* of £1200 per week," and he and Dolby amused themselves
with just how much the case in a nutshell had overstated their
expenses and underestimated their profits.

The ticket speculators were a problem, though, their success threatening his credibility and his principles. The rumor
that he was in collusion with them surfaced. The notion that
anyone but he and those he designated were profiting from the
readings infuriated him, and his populist desire that the ticket
prices be low enough to allow average people to afford them was
being frustrated. They devised various schemes to thwart the
speculators, with little success. While he finished his first series
of Boston readings, Dolby in New York vainly tried to quell
riots, insurgencies, and well-organized professional entre-
preneurs on lines that dwarfed those in Boston. By two o'clock
in the afternoon of the first day, every ticket at Steinway Hall
was sold. The amount taken was over sixteen thousand dollars
(about £2,285) for the first four readings alone. Since the value of
the tickets was so great, many respectable people resold theirs.
Soon the professionals "were selling the best seats at enormous
premiums" no matter what Dolby did.[20] With up to fifty people
at work for them on each ticket line, they went about their
completely legal profiteering hardly discouraged and mostly
triumphant.

Dickens' triumphs were on the stage as well as at the box
office. Too consummate an artist to leave anything to chance, he
managed his performances punctiliously. Dolby applied equally
professional standards to the business arrangements. At every
theatre, he tested the acoustics in advance. While Dickens stood
at his table, Dolby walked to all areas of the hall as they carried
on a conversation in a low tone of voice. Neither illness nor
depression nor fatigue nor anger at the speculators would keep
him from performing. "No man had a right," he insisted, "to
break an engagement with the public, if he were able to get out
of bed." At the beginning, he was steady and steadily on his feet.
Long walks and standing during performances gradually took
their toll. The Boston success during the first week was overwhelming. In a glow of pleasure he graciously tolerated the
newspapers' familiarly referring to him as "Dickens" or even

"Charlie," and he balanced the "Bar Loungers, dram drinkers, drunkards, swaggerers," and loafers who gathered every night in the lobby of his hotel with the "delightful domestic life— simple, self-respectful, cordial, and affectionate'—that he saw in Cambridge. In New York, at the beginning of December, he found the Westminster Hotel almost faultless, with excellent food, unobtrusive service, and a quiet private apartment with its own access to the street.

"One might be living in Paris," he said about New York. The city had changed immensely. The ground at Irving Place on which his hotel now stood had been farmland in 1842. New York has "grown out of my knowledge, and is enormous. Every- thing in it looks as if the order of nature were reversed, and everything grew newer every day, instead of older." In a "very smart carriage and pair . . . furred up to the moustache . . . and with an immense white, red, and yellow striped rug for a cover- ing," looking like he was of "Hungarian or Polish nationality," he did not allow a severe cold spell to prevent him going to the theatre and sightseeing. One morning at 3 A.M., visiting the central police station, he could hardly pull his eyes away from "a horrible photograph-book of thieves' portraits." He soon ex- changed the carriage for "a red sleigh covered with furs," join- ing "ten thousand other sleighs" in the park, bells ringing, fine horses "tearing up 14 miles of snow an hour." During the snow- storm a small fire broke out in the hotel. He enjoyed the spec- tacle of people turning out into the lobby, having put "the strangest things on!" and helping with the fire hoses. It was colorful and amusing, and to his surprise "everybody talked to everybody else."[21]

At Steinway Hall, the New York audience delighted him with its sophistication. He doubted that he ever saw a better one except in Paris. Though he did not see any change for the better "in public life . . . great social improvements in respect of man- ners and forbearance have come to pass since I was here before." New York had become a cosmopolitan city, its rough edges softened. There was "improvement in every direction." *The Tribune, The New York Herald, The New York Times,* and William Cullen Bryant's *Evening Post* all now seemed to him excellent newspapers, creating "generally a much more responsible and respectable tone than prevailed formerly." Raucous yellow journalism had abated. Even the police seemed better than anyplace else. Both the city and Dickens had definitely changed, though, unlike New York, he did not have the power to reverse the order of nature. With his "success here beyond all precedent or description," expecting "to make a very handsome sum of money," he was in a superlative mood. Even the enormous cost of living, which "happily we can afford," did not distress him.

One thing that had gotten worse, though, were the railways, which seemed "truly alarming." Perhaps his sensitivity to railway travel since the Staplehurst experience influenced his response. Still, the cars were badly ventilated, the track rougher than in England, the unrenovated lines suffering from their heavy use during the war. He felt himself beaten about on the return trip to Boston on December 21, as outrageously mistreated as most of his luggage, which arrived in fragments. He had not been feeling well. During his last readings in New York he felt ill. After one performance he had been "laid upon a bed, in a very faint and shadey state," to recover from some "low action of the heart, or whatever it is." The next day he stayed in bed until the afternoon. In Boston, after a walk in the bright sunlight, he felt better. But he had caught a slight cold. Soon it was "a frightful cold." When he was back in New York on December 26, he was "exceedingly depressed and miserable." The next day he felt so unwell that he sent for a doctor, who raised the possibility that he might have "to stop reading for a while."[22]

He rejected the medical advice. Dr. Fordyce Barker, "a very agreeable fellow," had it explained to him that there were commitments that had to be met. "I must go on if it could be done." It was not to be thought of as more than "a very heavy cold indeed, an irritated condition of the uvula, and a restlessly low state of the nervous system."[23] On Christmas Day, most of which had been spent on the train from Boston to New York, his spirits had been particularly depressed. The very genius of Christmas seemed low, semiextinguished, pursuing profit rather than charity, transported like Scrooge to scenes of his former life that were alien and cold. He felt painfully homesick. As advance man, Dolby constantly kept ahead of him on the road. The Fieldses were mostly now behind him in Boston. Greeted like a star, Dickens felt the isolation of someone without friends and family to talk to at a trying time. He forced himself to pretend, particularly in letters home, that his cold was getting better, that he was in high spirits. Snow, thaw, snow again, constant travel, sleepless nights, four readings a week, the excitement of unexpectedly high profits, the anxiety of planning the schedule and trying to keep tickets out of the hands of speculators all contributed to his being noticeably off-balance, slightly feverish.

By early January 1868 the pattern had established itself unalterably. "The work is hard, the climate is hard, the life is hard; but so far the gain is enormous. My cold steadily refuses to stir an inch. It distresses me greatly at times, though it is always good enough to leave me for the needful two hours. I have tried allopathy, homoeopathy, cold things, warm things, sweet things, bitter things, stimulants, narcotics, all with the same result. Nothing will touch it." He and his "American catarrh" were well matched. Nothing would shake him from his schedule other than a balance-sheet analysis of his commitments and profits. When it became clear in December that he could make his goal without going west, he had canceled the Chicago plans. In the latter part of the month, he had read, to his amusement and with great success, in Ward Beecher's Plymouth Congregational Church in Brooklyn, the only building in the borough large enough to put a dent in the demand for tickets. Hearing him read on New Year's Eve in New York, the young Mark Twain was very disappointed. There seemed "no heart or feeling in it," all "glittering frostwork."

In the harsh winter, which dried his hair and broke his nails, he went on to Philadelphia, then back to New York, then to Philadelphia again, then to Baltimore and Washington. Looking in the mirror, he saw that he was losing his hair "with great rapidity, and what I don't lose is getting very grey." At the end of most readings, he felt exhausted and faint. He kept his eyes, though, as steadily focused on his audiences and on outward scenes as his cold would allow, and "left off referring to the hateful subject, except in emphatic sniffs . . . convulsive wheezes, and resounding sneezes."[24] In Philadelphia at the middle of the month, giving his twenty-sixth reading of a projected eighty-four, he had the satisfaction of sending to his bank ten thousand pounds "in English gold," for which he had exchanged his dollars despite the loss on rates and commissions. When he arrived in the capital on the first of February he had gotten through half his readings.

Washington also had changed for the better. Having been warned that it was widely "considered the dullest . . . most apathetic place in America," he found his audiences superb. After a newspaper announcement of his impending birthday, his room became "a blooming garden." Letters and presents poured in, his hosts observing the day as if he "were a little boy." At night his audience stood and cheered until he returned to the stage. Though "in all probability I shall never see your faces again . . . I can assure you that yours have yielded me as much pleasure as I have given you." That afternoon his cold had been so bad that, plastered with a mustard poultice and almost voiceless, he despaired of being able to read. Dolby assured a visitor that "you have no idea how he will change when he gets to the little table." Five minutes into his performance, he was not even hoarse. Some of the faces were far from anonymous. President Andrew Johnson had a "whole row for his family every night." Justices of the Supreme Court and members of the cabinet attended. Dickens had already met most of them, particularly Johnson, who insisted on entertaining him at the White House. A short, stout man "with a remarkable face," not "imaginative but very powerful in its firmness . . . indicating courage, watchfulness," his manner "suppressed, guarded, anxious," the president impressed him. "Each of us looked at the other very hard." He soon discovered some of the political reasons why Johnson, who was soon to be impeached, had "an air of chronic anxiety about him," though he seemed "a man not to be turned or trifled with. A man . . . who must be killed to be got out of the way."25

The deaths of presidents was much on his mind. At a dinner hosted by Charles Sumner, Secretary of War Edwin Stanton, "a man . . . famous for his acquaintance with the minutest details" of Dickens' books, told a remarkable story that fascinated him. Both Stanton and Sumner had attended the cabinet meeting on the afternoon of the day of Lincoln's assassination and had been "the first two public men at the dying President's bedside," remaining "with him until he breathed his last." At the cabinet meeting, "the President sat with an air of dignity . . . instead of lolling about in the most ungainly attitudes, as his invariable custom was. . . . 'Have you received any information, sir, not yet disclosed to us?' 'No . . . but I have had a dream. And I have had the same dream three times. . . .' 'Might one ask the nature of the dream sir? . . 'Well,' replied the President . . . 'I am on a great broad rolling river—and I am in a boat—and I drift—and I drift!—but this is not business—' suddenly raising his face and looking round the room. . . ."26

Unable to resist the gray area between foreshadowing and clairvoyance, particularly anticipations of death, from childhood on Dickens had been sensitized to nightmare, mystery, and the unexpected, and he had had that sensitivity reinforced by his own dreams, his own stories, and his adult experiences. Committed to the importance of the emotional current of dreams, he was convinced that the striking and unlikely coincidences that frequently occurred had psychological significance. Unexpected reversals in which people actively but unconsciously pursue their own deaths fascinated him. On the evening of Thackeray's death an ordinary household object had transformed itself in his imagination into a symbol of death. The Lincoln story became a fixation, one that he told and retold, as if he were the Ancient Mariner, who sought release and relief by retelling the primal tale of himself. He so identified with it that every retelling seems to have been a rehearsal of his anxieties about his own death.

When Dickens went to Baltimore again, he felt that "the Ghost of Slavery" still 'haunted the town." Emancipation seemed a self-serving Northern trick, pretending that the black man was free when both prejudice and inferiority enslaved him still. He believed that blacks "will die out of this country fast," for it is "absurd to suppose it possible that they can ever hold their own against a restless, shifty, striving, stronger race." His cold was as bad as ever. From Baltimore, Dickens went to New York and then to Boston, with a side trip to give a reading in Providence. The pressure from speculators became even more damaging when Dickens discovered that one of his staff had engaged in a form of profiteering. Profits still were immense, much beyond initial expectations. It seemed increasingly likely, though, that the country's preoccupation with impeachment proceedings would diminish his audiences. People talked about nothing else. Suddenly it seemed sensible to cancel some readings in the hope "that the public may be heartily tired of the

President's name by the 9th of March," when he was scheduled to resume. He himself felt tired of his "wearying life, away from all I love."[27]

In the cold February weather his health was no better. Annie Fields kept his room "always radiant with brilliant flowers." Attempting to amuse, or at least to raise his low spirits, Dolby arranged with James Osgood, Fields's junior associate, to test Dolby's superiority as an Englishman against the American in a race dubbed the "Great International Walking Match," partly in emulation of, partly a mark of respect for, Dickens' passion for walking. The walking match did amuse him. He insisted on acting as Dolby's trainer, taking him for eight-mile-long fast-paced trial runs through mud, snow, and sleet, and he composed a comic statement of the articles of agreement for the rules of the race, the prize to be "two hats a side and the glory of their respective countries." He and Fields, the "Gad's Hill Gasper" and "Massachusetts Jemmy," paced off the thirteen-mile route to Newton Centre and back on February 28. The next day, "the worst day we have ever seen," Dolby and Osgood, the "Man of Ross" and the "Boston Bantam," slogged vigorously through "half-melted snow, running water, and sheets and blocks of ice" over the mostly deserted Boston streets. The air was freezing, the wind biting. "Our hair, beards, eyelashes, eyebrows, were frozen hard and hung with icicles." Though the two were almost shoulder to shoulder until halfway through the course, Osgood astonished Dolby and Dickens by forging ahead "at a splitting pace and with extraordinary endurance, and won by half a mile." They had not believed that Osgood, or any American, had it in him. Dolby felt crushed, as if he had let down his "Chief," his team, and his country. Dickens good-humoredly consoled him and readily forgave Annie Fields, who, claiming that she would have done it for whoever was in the lead, had come onto "the ground in a carriage" and put *bread soaked in brandy* into the winning man's mouth as he steamed along." To Dickens, who hosted a "splendid" postrace dinner at his hotel for the participants and all his Boston friends, "the whole thing was a great success, and everybody was delighted."[28]

Soon he was on the road once more, this time to upstate New York, particularly Albany, Syracuse, Utica, Rochester, and Buffalo, mostly for the reading tour, partly to see Niagara Falls again. Syracuse seemed "a rather depressing feather in the eagle's wing," as if it had begun to be built yesterday. Rochester appeared dismally isolated in the snow. One could not expect much from Buffalo, he felt, since it overflowed with Irishmen, "all or most of whom are mad." As he moved away from the seacoast cities, he noted that the usual sparkle of female beauty gave way to hard, blunt faces. The sparkle of Niagara Falls, where in mid-March he spent two days with Dolby, had hardly dimmed. His memory and imagination came alive again. In 1842, he had had a visionary experience there, the glow of Mary's soul visible to him in the resonances of immortality that the magnificence of the falls evoked, as if through this sublime manifestation of nature the natural world could be momentarily transcended. Everything about the falls was still *"made of rainbow."* His response now was less vibrant, less mystical, though still very powerful. Not even "Turner's finest water-colour drawings" are "so ethereal, so imaginative, so gorgeous in colour. . . . I seem to be lifted from the earth and to be looking into Heaven." His feelings of some twenty-five years before returned, though now there was something more of a reflected than a primary glow.

His strongest glow came from the expectation and the exhortation in thinking and saying "it is nearly all 'back' now, thank God!" Unexpectedly, he had a smaller body of water to cross before the larger one. A sudden spring thaw had flooded three hundred miles of towns, valleys, and railway track between Rochester, Utica, and Albany, "drowned farms, barns adrift like Noah's arks, deserted villages, broken bridges." The railway officials, making an intense effort to get the famous visitor through, inched the train toward Albany. The workmen, coming across a large train into which cattle and sheep had been locked, freed the animals, which, "in their imprisonment," had begun "to eat each other." Their flesh was torn, their faces haggard.[29]

As the April departure date came closer, Dickens felt tired and acutely homesick. He felt "depressed all the time (except when reading)" and had lost his appetite. On reading days, at seven in the morning he had fresh cream and two tablespoons of rum, at noon a sherry cobbler and a biscuit, and at three a pint of champagne. Five minutes before his performance he had an egg beaten into a glass of sherry, during the intermission strong beef tea, and afterward soup, altogether not "more than half a pound of solid food in the whole four-and-twenty hours." Dolby hovered over him, "as tender as a woman and as watchful as a doctor." He took laudanum to help himself sleep. In Boston, for his farewell readings at the beginning of April, he looked pale and exhausted, worried that the catarrh might have done him some "lasting injury in the lungs." The Fieldses joined Norton and Longfellow "in trying to dissuade him from future Readings. . . . He does not recover his vitality after the effort . . . and his spirits are naturally somewhat depressed by the use of soporifics," which had become "a necessity."

Dickens felt further depressed by the news of the Reverend Chauncey Hare Townshend's death, and by the grim, ludicrously comic realization that soon after he returned to England he would have to write and edit a new Christmas number of *All the Year Round,* as if he "had murdered a Christmas number years ago . . . and its ghost perpetually haunted me." He was right, in the sense that he had long ago turned Christmas into a commercial imperative, and his reading tour was the logical extension of that transformation of the spirit into money. Procter remarked that Dickens must be tired of "Yankee applause," for "what is *any* applause worth, except from our friends." Actually, a large number of his English colleagues had a very firm sense of the value of Yankee applause. His determination to meet his material goals was an instance of his particular personality expressing a general sense among English writers that it would be foolish not to profit from the American market.[30]

Now that the end was near, Dickens could admit that he felt "nearly used up. Climate, distance, catarrh, travelling, and hard work, have begun . . . to tell heavily upon me. Sleeplessness besets me; and if I had engaged to go on into May, I think I must have broken down." The excuse of the impeachment proceedings at the beginning of April came just in time. Only the Boston and New York farewell readings remained. Though he feared that the political climate would "damage the farewells by about one half," they had no effect on the size of his audiences. In the usual pattern, each afternoon at four he felt as if it would be impossible to read that night. But when he walked onto the platform, his spirits rose, his energy spiraled, his voice returned. Afterward, he collapsed. Fordyce Barker prescribed a tonic that seemed to help. Dickens assured Wills that he was "very weary, but no worse." When he went onto the platform on April 8 for his final Boston reading, he found his table covered with flowers. He thanked "the great public heart" and "the private friendships that have for years upon years made Boston a memorable spot to me." The receipts for this one reading, the largest for any single reading in America, amounted to $3,456 (about £494).

After the performance he spoke briefly, tears trembling in his eyes, his voice quavering. He had "never until this moment really felt" that he was "going away. In this brief life of ours it is sad to do almost anything for the last time. . . . It is a sad consideration with me that in a very few moments from this time, this brilliant hall and all that it contains, will fade from my view—for evermore." As he wished them farewell, the audience rose, shouting, cheering, waving hats and handkerchiefs.[31] With his last flicker of energy, beginning on the thirteenth he gave his New York farewell readings. Since he found it almost impossible to walk, he had to make a major effort to get to the platform. A severe attack of erysipelas now threatened his attendance at a banquet in his honor on the eighteenth at Delmonico's. He might have to cancel his final reading on the twentieth.

Dolby, meanwhile, tussled with an ambitious federal tax commissioner, who refused to accept the ruling from his Washington superiors that Dickens' earnings were exempt from the 5 percent income tax. Since the stakes were high, Dolby played a cat-and-mouse game of bluff and appeal to higher authority. Dolby's own commission was £2,888. Ticknor and Fields received a £1,000 fee and 5 percent of the receipts of the Boston readings. The expenses in America had been $39,000 (about £5,570), the preliminary expenses £614. Dickens' profit, after all costs and commissions, was about $140,000 or £20,000. The tax commissioner threatened to prevent their leaving the country. In the past two years, Dickens had earned from his readings alone approximately £33,000—£20,000 from the American readings and £13,000 from the tours for the Chappells, the equivalent of at least £1 million or $1.5 million to $2 million today. Neither Dolby nor Dickens wanted to give up a penny of it.

The two hundred gentlemen who assembled for the banquet at Delmonico's, hosted, ironically, by the New York press, which had reviled him in 1842, became restless when the guest of honor did not appear. Finally, an hour late, Dickens arrived. Since he had found it impossible to get a boot on his swollen, heavily bandaged foot, he had had to drag himself to the restaurant. Dolby had spent half the day finding a gout bandage with which to cover it. Leaning on Horace Greeley's arm, he was conducted to the platform amid cheers while the band played "God Save the Queen." In response to Greeley's toast, which nostalgically evoked the day over thirty years before when he had published in his new magazine a story by an unknown writer known as Boz, Dickens warmly, appreciatively recalled his days as a young reporter, "always steadily proud of that ladder" by which he had risen.

In his best oratorical style, he thanked America and Americans, praised their "national generosity and magnanimity," verbally embraced his American friends, and emphasized that, despite any differences that had and that might arise, America and England were bound together by their commitment to justice. The amazing changes that he had seen were all for the better. "Nor am I, believe me, so arrogant as to suppose that in five-and-twenty years there have been no changes in me, and that I have nothing to learn, and that I had nothing to learn and no extreme impressions to correct from when I was here first." He was sincere in more than acknowledging that "I have been received with unsurpassable politeness, delicacy, sweet temper, hospitality, consideration, and . . . respect for . . . privacy. . . . This testimony . . . I shall cause to be republished, as an appendix to every copy of those two books of mine in which I have referred to America." To laughter and applause he repeated the pledge he had made that he had no intention of and absolutely would not write another book set in or about America. "The fact is exactly the reverse, or I could not have spoken," he later told an acquaintance, "without some appearance of having a purpose to serve."[32] This testimony was his final statement on the republic of his imagination.

They were almost his last public words in America. He did not think he would be able to read on the twentieth. The evening before, though, he persuaded himself that he could do it one last time. Dr. Barker composed a statement to distribute to the audience medically certifying that "Mr. Dickens is suffering from neuralgic affection of the right foot. . . . But I believe that he can read to-night without much pain or inconvenience (his mind being set on not disappointing his audience), with the aid of a slight addition to his usual arrangement," a rest stool and partial seat to relieve some of the pressure. Making a public concession to his health for the first time, he wanted his audience to be neither unprepared nor disappointed. He told the surprised Dolby, from whom he had concealed the extent of his pain, that he was so exhausted that he could experience nothing but his own exhaustion and that "if I had to read twice more, instead of once, I couldn't do it." He ended, as he had begun, with *A Christmas Carol* and the trial scene from *Pickwick*, and with a brief speech that had some of the feeling but none of the passion of his Boston farewell. He wanted nothing more than to be aboard the *Russia*, to have the ocean wind sharply in his face, to feel himself steaming homeward.

On April 23, he and Dolby nervously boarded the ship. The federal tax collector had pledged to have them removed. New York police officers, though, provided by the sympathetic chief of police, physically protected them from arrest by the tax agents who had come aboard. At the same time, the Cunard people were hosting an elaborate farewell lunch on the ship. Just before sailing, Anthony Trollope came alongside in the mail tender "to shake hands." Seeking his own American fortune, he had arrived the day before. Fellow members of the Athenaeum, they had an understood but unexpressed family connection through Fanny Ternan's marriage to Thomas Trollope. Amazed to see him, Dickens euphorically thought him "the heartiest and best of fellows . . . a perfect cordial to me, whenever and wherever I see him." All those who were going ashore soon descended to the mail ship and other small boats, except Fields, who lingered for one last moment between them. For a few seconds the friends embraced. "You will never know how I loved you both; or what you have been to me in America, and will always be to me . . . or how fervently I thank you." As the evening fell rapidly, steamboats, police tenders, and private tugs followed the "magnificent ship" for some distance down the bay, extending their final salutes by fading whistles and distant cannons.[33]

❧ 3 ❧

In early May 1868 the conquering hero stepped off the Grave-send train into the carriage that was waiting to take him to Gad's Hill Place. He drove between houses dressed with flags of welcome and on a road crowded with farmers who had come out in "their market-chaises to say, 'Welcome home, sir!'" Lavishly decorated with banners and flags, Gad's Hill had hardly a brick visible. Driving up, he was overwhelmed by the cheerful brightness and the happy open arms of his family. A few days later, on Sunday, at St. Mary's, he could not prevent the bellringers dashing out at the end of the sermon and ringing "like mad" to celebrate his return. Deeply relieved to be home, where various "birds sing all day, and the nightingales all night," from his chalet, high up among the branches of the trees, he watched "the birds and the butterflies fly in and out, and the green branches shoot in, at the open windows, and the lights and shadows of the clouds come and go. . . ."[34] Kent was in its springtime beauty. London and American shadows seemed far away.

When he had stepped off the ship at Liverpool, he had surprised those who feared that the returning millionaire would look deathly. After three days at sea, he had begun to feel revitalized. On some of the fine days he walked and sat in the sun. When a delegation of passengers had asked him to give a reading, he politely replied that sooner than do it he "would assault the captain, and be put in irons." Arriving home with a suntan that had bronzed his ruddy cheeks into a glow, he boasted that he was in his "usual brilliant condition. . . . Katie, Mary, and Georgina expected a wreck, and were, at first, much mortified." His belief in his recuperative powers took on comically grandiose proportions. "My doctor was quite broken down in spirits when he saw me, for the first time, since my return. . . . 'Good Lord!' he said, recoiling, 'seven years younger!' " His friends were heartened, and he took special pleasure in disappointing expectations, as if the great magician were an artist of self-healing as well as of literary fictions.

He returned, though, to a heavy *All the Year Round* workload, forced on him by Wills's riding accident. Morley took up some of the slack, and Wilkie Collins lent a hand. When it became clear that Wills would not be returning, Charley's request that he be given the chance to turn his "liberal education to account" as a staff member began to seem sensible. His business venture having failed, he had filed for bankruptcy, some of the costs of which his father paid. For someone who felt that he could not get his "hat on" because "of the extent to which my hair stands on end at the costs and charges of these boys," saving a salary and having his son gainfully employed was attractive. "Why was I ever a father! Why was *my* father ever a father!" In November 1868, Charley replaced Morley as a regular staff member. Dickens assured Morley that "I value your cooperation so highly and respect you so much that I would not for any consideration be misunderstood by you. I earnestly hope that you will not write the less for All the Year Round or give it a wider berth in any way, because of my making this experiment." Fortunately, after a year's trial, he had reason to conclude that "Charley is a very good man of business, and evinces considerable aptitude in sub-editing work." Disgusted by his own inability to create a new Christmas story, Dickens decided not to "reproduce the old string of old stories in the old inappropriate way, which every other publication imitates to death."35 In October he abandoned the idea of a Christmas number for 1868.

The previous month he had seen his youngest child for the last time, the son whom "of all his children he loved . . best . . . truly his Benjamin." In late September 1868, he took Plorn to Southampton for his departure to join Alfred in Australia. To Mamie, he was the "dearest and best loved of all [her] brothers." His father could not forget "the many fascinations of the last little child" he would ever have and felt the parting painfully. Though there were to be letters between him and his Australian exiles, there were also to be extended silences. When Plorn's debts came to light, he felt angry, betrayed. When Sydney's debts (he had developed "an inveterate habit of drawing bills that will ruin him") threatened to be laid at his door, he had more reason to fear that the ghost of his father lived in his sons. Charley's bankruptcy did not help. His brother Frederick's death in October added another skeleton to the closet of insolvency and failure His daughters' problems distressed him, while Charles Collins, "who will never be well on this earth," created daily his own life portrait of death and abandonment.

He did not feel well himself, despite the shipboard and summer suntan that had begun to fade by early autumn. To his surprise, the American catarrh returned, though not as strongly as before.[36]

In the late summer, in preparation for his farewell tour from October 1868 to May 1869, Dickens created a new reading, based on one he had fashioned in 1863 but had decided against using, a version of Bill Sikes's murder of Nancy in *Oliver Twist*. He wanted something fresh and extraordinary, partly an expression of the showman's search for novelty, partly of his need to find a new challenge. Practicing outdoors at Gad's Hill, he frightened those who overheard him rehearsing his most demanding, most exhausting, performance. Though worried that it might prove too upsetting, even revolting, to his audiences, he loved the experience of being absorbed in it, of acting it out, of being both murdered and murderer. Finding it difficult to distinguish between himself and his text, after each rehearsal, as he walked the streets, he had the "vague sensation of being 'wanted.'" When he began the tour, he had not yet decided whether to include it. The old formula worked well enough. The enthusiastic crowds at the inaugural reading at St. James's Hall, and in Manchester and Liverpool later in the month, "were beyond all former experience." A thousand people were turned away. In London, the demand was so great that "it seems as though we could fill St. Pauls." But the same problems he had experienced while reading in America surfaced quickly, weariness, hoarseness, sleeplessness, and frenetic, pulse-racing exhaustion after each performance.

In mid-November, he read the "Murder of Nancy" as an experiment to an audience of over one hundred invited guests. The opinion of his friends confirmed his desires. "The verdict of ninety of them was: 'It must be done.' So it is going to be done." There were warnings in the form of compliments and compliments in the form of warnings. A doctor said, "My dear Dickens, you may rely upon it that if only one woman cries out when you murder the girl, there will be a contagion of hysteria all over this place." A well-known actress replied, "Why, of course, do it. . . . Having got such an effect as that, it must be done. . . . The public have been looking for a sensation these fifty years or so, and by Heaven they have got it."[37]

Through the late fall and winter of 1868–69 in England,

Scotland, and Ireland, he went on "murdering Nancy" with a
regularity that became addictive. Worried, Dolby began to advise him to read it less often. The constant railway journeys
made Dickens' nerves tremble, his lips turn white. He looked
additionally haggard, the illusion of health with which he had
returned from America long gone. He clung, though, to the new
reading stubbornly, passionately. In mid-February 1869, his
foot, the left one this time, to his surprise, "turned lame again,"
forcing him to cancel a reading. He had known "for some days
that the inflammation was coming on; but it is impossible to
guard against it when that amount of standing in a hot place has
to be encountered for months together." A well-known Edinburgh doctor disparaged Dr. Henry Thompson's previous diagnosis, laughing away contemptuously the suspicion that it was
gout and attributing it instead to fatigue and walking in the
snow. The enforced withdrawal was even more painful than his
swollen foot, and he felt "as restless as if [he] were behind bars
in the Zoological Gardens." If "I could afford it, [I] would wear
a part of my mane away as the Lion has done by rubbing it
against the windows of my cage."

At the beginning of March, his friend Emerson Tennent,
with whom he had climbed Mount Vesuvius sixteen years before, was much on his mind. He talked about him with Dolby.
The next morning news came that Tennent had died. With
split-second timing and hardly a moment's leeway, he engi-
neered a trip from York to London that enabled him both to give
his reading in York that evening and to attend the funeral.
When he read the murder of Nancy in Cheltenham, Macready
authoritatively pronounced it to be equal to "two Macbeths!"
Soon Macready's tubercular daughter, Katie, died. Her death
brought "a rush of old remembrances and withered joys" that
struck him to the heart. To commemorate his final reading in
Liverpool, he allowed the corporation to host early in April a
farewell banquet in his honor that over 650 people attended. In
the brilliantly lit St. George's Hall, decorated with plants,
flowers, and silver, with hundreds of additional people in the
gallery, he gave an unusually long speech of thanks, reminding
his listeners of what a warm and long relationship he had had
with Liverpool audiences, concluding with a strong statement
about the dignity of literature as a profession.

Soon after the banquet, reading in Leeds, he appeared so

utterly exhausted that Edmund Yates, who had been pleasantly surprised at his appearance when he returned from America, was shocked. He lay stretched out on a couch, one of his boots off, the foot swathed in bandages. "He looked desperately aged and worn; the lines in his cheeks and round the eyes, always noticeable, were now in deep furrows; there was a weariness in his gaze, and a general air of fatigue and depression about him." A few days later Dickens told Mark Lemon, who had begun a reading tour of his own, that perhaps if he had given a timely rest to his favorite watch, which had had "palpitations" for six months after the Staplehurst accident, the watch might have recovered sooner.[38]

The lines that Yates noticed etched into Dickens' face at this point had nothing to do with a need for rest. They were physiological self-portraiture by a man who for a long time had been transforming inner images into external equivalents, images of tiredness, resentment, restlessness, insecurity, and financial anxiety, images of denial, resistance, fear of age, and fear of death. Christmas and renewal had mostly long since faded into transparency. Recognizing that he was "a difficult subject," Dickens did not like most of the efforts to capture his image, as if the inner vision that he had attempted to portray in his fiction had a reality for him that any photograph of his external appearance denied. Frequently photographed and much more frequently besieged to sit for portraits for sale and display, he did not believe that any photograph embodied his own sense of himself. He felt "intense weariness and horror" at the prospect of sitting for "a new photographic portrait . . . an unremunerative investment of time and temper." He seriously joked with one photographer that his snapshot had "a grim and wasted aspect, and perhaps might be made useful as a portrait of the Ancient Mariner."[39] When Yates saw him on his couch of exhaustion at Leeds, he did indeed have some resemblance to the Ancient Mariner. He had also just come from compulsively retelling in his readings the story of his life.

What his contemporaries saw when they looked at him varied from one perspective to another. The photographers mostly missed the realities of personality, though some did better than others in capturing aspects of his public presence. He rarely appeared in group photographs, and then only by the accident of a few impromptu snapshots at Gad's Hill. Most depict him alone, partly disguising his shortness and the premature shrinking of an inch or so from his original five feet eight, his slightness most apparent when he was not inflated by the excitement of performance, when he relaxed or collapsed into exhaustion, when the mask of his ruddy cheeks became transparent enough to reveal that the energetic look was at best skin-deep. Nearsighted, he refused to wear glasses in public or to be photographed wearing them at home. His gray-blue eyes still sparkled, sometimes with more life than his body normally supported, intensely focused when concentrating on talking to someone, otherwise seeming to gaze off into the distance. By the late 1860s his hair had thinned so much that he could hardly bear to joke anymore about his partial baldness. His longer, straggly beard gave him the impression of being off-balance. Often, partly to disguise baldness, he wore a hat, particularly a jaunty bowler. His sporty street clothes, especially checks and plaids, spoke of the country gentleman. But his wrinkles, his weariness, his thinness, and his appearance of pained concentration did not speak of country relaxation, of the balanced life, of a personality at rest.

Some of the verbal portrait painting projected his culture's expectations about what the greatest writer of the age should look like. Some of these stereotypes were internalized or at least acted out. There were various Dickenses: the meticulous editor, the sharp businessman, the responsible father, the reliable friend, the writer of genius, the good citizen of literature, the man of the theatre, the public performer, the national celebrity, the patriotic Englishman, the friend of the poor, the liberal reformer, the stylish dresser punctilious about his clothes, the narcissist constantly combing his hair, the well-traveled European sophisticate, the sporty country squire with dogs and walking stick, the London boulevardier who "always was theatrically dressed." Often his public image combined sober Victorian responsibility with a touch of Romantic theatricality. But he was a whole cast of characters himself, a performance personality with as long a list of disguised and fully dressed variants on the basic model as the list of characters in any one of his novels. He delighted in consciously and unconsciously playing many roles, partly as a relief from the burden of an otherwise singular, rigid, brittle personality. One evening in 1863, after hearing him read, Carlyle said, "Charlie, you carry a while company of actors under your own hat." To some, he seemed "about as odd a character as any he had ever drawn from his fruitful imagination."[40]

At the office, he smoked cigarettes insatiably. At home or with friends, he smoked cigars. Alcohol appealed to him in the form of wine with dinner, champagne at celebrations, and, after dinner, port, sherry, or brandy to punctuate good fellowship. Convivial in company, he seemed to many a paragon of cheerfulness, a public image that his association with Christmas, hearth, and friendship encouraged. His seeming good spirits, though, did not mean self-exposure, confidences, intimacy. In that regard, he kept a narrow company, mostly Forster and Georgina, sometimes Collins and a few others, probably Ellen. Otherwise his emotions, like his private life, were played close to the vest. Only appropriate, carefully censored feelings were allowed verbal expression other than in the disguised forms of his fiction. Deeply private in that sense, he often expressed gaiety in public as a performance in which the real Dickens usually was far out of sight, though he attempted to keep as narrow as possible the distinction between cheerfulness and happiness. An American visitor, during a visit in the summer of 1869, thought the Gad's Hill household and its master "perpetually jolly." Sometimes, though, his joviality seemed forced, overwhelming and wearying people, as if they doubted its spontaneity or felt it inhumanly exhausting in its powerfulness, almost a physical assault. Often when he seemed happy, he was moody, depressed, and angry. Annie Fields remarked that it is "wonderful, the flow of spirits C.D. has for a sad man."[41]

Generous when unchallenged, his notion of compromise was total victory. His aggressiveness, stubbornness, and inflexibility seemed tyranny to some, the power of genius to others. Yates, to whom he was a surrogate father, felt the force of both his love and his authority as a son would. "He was imperious in the sense that his life was conducted" on the principle that his will was his command. "Everything gave way before him. The society in which he mixed, the hours which he kept, the opinions which he held, his likes and dislikes, his ideas of what should or should not be, were all settled by himself, not merely

for himself, but for all those brought into connection with him.
. . . Yet he was never regarded as a tyrant; he had immense
power of will, absolute mesmeric force."

Completely loyal, Dickens expected total loyalty in return. "His nearest and dearest friends were as unwilling to
face as they were unable to deflect the passionate pride which
suffered neither counsel nor rebuke." Thackeray complained
that " 'there is nobody to tell him when anything goes wrong.
. . . Dickens is the Sultan, and Wills is his Grand Vizier.' "
Bulwer-Lytton remarked that one of the signs of his mastery
of "the practical part of Authorship beyond any writer" was
his creating "a corps of devoted parasites in the Press." When
he went to friends for advice, he expected unflinching support
once his decision had been made, as if they were cabinet members pledged to the will of the chief executive. Even his gaze
struck some people as imperial, the kind of "economy of ap-
prehension" of his "merciless *military* eye" that one would expect of a general surveying a battlefield. Often he was both
general and private, a man used to shouldering the burden of
leadership and of performance. Having set the highest standards, he regularly punished himself wherever he failed to fulfill them. To avoid certain forms of self-punishment he was
punishingly rigorous with himself. "He was so anxious to be
in time that he was invariably before time."[42] He found relaxation almost impossible.

When Dickens looked at himself, always an indirect and
deflecting activity, he had shadowy glimpses of an evasive and
evading self-portrait. "I cannot see myself," he constantly complained. Often he did not care to. He had trained himself into
willful, then habitual secretiveness. He "can even be insincere
but unconsciously so," Bulwer-Lytton remarked. In the two
most revealing activities of his life, though, he was sincere, his
public readings and his writing of fiction, both intensely autobiographical, the disguised self-revelation that he was attracted to
and with which he felt comfortable. Though constantly on his
own trail, he was determined never fully to catch the "him" that
he was following, ultimately more successful as the pursued
than the pursuer, the criminal than the detective. The readings
were an "interpretation of myself." So too were the writings.
His 1868 short story "George Silverman's Explanation" revealed

his most concentrated psychological portrait of the mono-identity of the pursuer and pursued. As he wrote it, the story seemed to him strange and unusual, exercising a powerful fascination, the source of which he could not identify.

His fascination with murdering Nancy, "continually done with great passion and fury," was also partly self-portraiture in which he played both victim and victimizer.43 Nancy resonated with his vision of the innately good women in his life. In her murder he enacted the lives and deaths, both physical and emotional, of Mary Hogarth, Little Nell, Little Em'ly, his sister Fanny, and the emotional sacrifices of Georgina Hogarth and Katie Dickens, the ideal vision of moral purity embodied in the life of a prostitute who by her very nature must love and help the deprived child. Some of his terror in presenting her murder derived from his knowledge that the murderer was not only Bill Sikes but also her author and creator. When he enacted Sikes's killing of Nancy, he created the stage illusion that he was Sikes, that his will and his heart were committed to the crime. They were. In repeatedly murdering her, he expressed himself with displaced violence against the horrible women of his life, his mother and his wife. Perhaps he also expressed some of his occasional ambivalence about what he had done to Georgina and Ellen. In murdering Nancy, he committed a crime of vengeance and self-assertion available to him only within fiction. So powerful was his identification with Sikes that not even Sikes's death could free him from the emotional grip of that identification. An unworthy criminal still prowled on the loose, within himself. After the reading, when he left the theatre, he almost expected to be arrested in the streets. He looked over his shoulder to see who was pursuing him.

❀ 4 ❀

WALKING ON THE BEACH IN BLACKPOOL IN APRIL 1869, DICKENS unhappily faced the possibility that he would have to cancel the remaining twenty-six in this farewell tour of one hundred readings. The buoyant, healthy Dickens had disappeared. Instead, there was an elderly man with lines of exhaustion so deeply etched into his face and posture that the couch of weariness

Yates had witnessed seemed preparation for the final bed. On
Saturday, April 17, in Chester, he had felt giddy, "with a tendency to go backwards, and to turn round. Afterwards, desiring
to put something on a small table, he pushed it and the table
forward, undesignedly. He had some odd feelings of insecurity
about his left leg, as if there were something unnatural about his
heel . . . some strangeness of his left hand and arm." He "missed
the spot on which he wished to lay that hand, unless he carefully
looked at it." Unable to lift his left hand readily, especially
toward his head, he could not get the brush to where he wanted
it when he tried to brush his hair. The weakness and deadness
were "all *on the left side.*" Writing to Dr. Frank Beard immediately, asking if the medicine he had prescribed could possibly be
responsible for these effects, he had gone on to Blackburn, then
Blackpool on the twenty-first. "Nothing would uphold [him]
through such work . . . but the prospect of soon *working* it out."
He still hoped to complete the tour. "Six weeks will carry me
through the Readings," he wrote to Beard, "if you can fortify
me a little bit, and then, please God, I may do as I like."44 At
the end of his "delicious walk by the sea" and his day's rest at
a charming beach-front hotel, he felt some flickers of optimism.
He had slept well. His appetite improved, his foot felt better.

Beard responded peremptorily. Immediate medical attention was necessary. "There can be no mistaking the symptoms,"
the doctor wrote, though he resorted to their favorite euphe-
mism of "overwork. . . . I wish to take you in hand without any
loss of time." While Beard hurried northward on the London-to-
Preston train, Dickens still expected to continue with the readings. His friend knew, though, what Dickens admitted to only
with evasions, qualifications, and vague references to a disorder
of the nervous system. For over three years Dickens had had
symptoms of coronary illness. Beginning in 1866, in response to
"degeneration of some functions of the heart," he had been
taking a combination of iron, quinine, and digitalis, prescribed
by Beard, "to set [the heart] a-going, and send the blood more
quickly through the system." Stethoscopic examination revealed some "fluttering" of the heart. His left vision played
tricks. Sometimes he could not read the right half of signs in the
streets. Recently, he had difficulty remembering names and
numbers, though he claimed that he had always done that, and

admitted that "sometimes [he] lost or misused a word." In fact, he did so regularly, dyslexically reversing syllables and stumbling over consonants, occasionally while reading before an audience. Now the discomfort was in the left foot. For over three years, he had been willfully deceiving himself. Echoing what must have been the judgment of many of his friends, Yates remarked that "he has pain, inflammation, every possible gouty symptom in the foot, the chosen locality for gout, but it is *not* gout. . . . As he walks along the street one day, he can read only the halves of the letters over the shop-doors that were on his right as he looked. 'He attributed it to medicine' . . . It is really almost too astonishing."

In Chester, Dickens had probably had a minor stroke. In Preston, where he was scheduled to read that night, the symptoms he had had in Chester returned. After examining him, Beard, who had arrived in the afternoon, ordered him to cancel the readings for the next few days and to return with him immediately to London for consultation with a heart expert. Though he claimed that Beard only confirmed what he had himself already fully realized—"that the readings must be *stopped*"—he now for the first time accepted that it would be physically impossible for him to go on.45

Returning to London that night, he was examined the next day by Sir Thomas Watson. The verdict was dismal. Dickens felt sure, though, that a week or two of rest would take care of the whole matter. Try as he would, he could not induce the doctor "to hear of more Readings anywhere." Still, the only practical consequence was that he could not do the London farewells in May. Yes, Watson granted defensively, "preventive measures are always invidious, for when most successful, the necessity for them is the least apparent." He had been, though, "on the brink of an attack of paralysis of his left side, and possibly of apoplexy . . . the result of extreme hurry, overwork, and excitement, incidental to his Readings." There was no mention of the likelihood that he had already suffered a stroke, that he had perhaps had a series of minor strokes during the last three years, and that there may have been permanent damage to the heart. Since he still owed the Chappells twenty-six readings, the answer to that debt was to do the London readings at a later date, probably the next winter. When he had left Preston, he had worried that if he were seen walking onto the London train, his credibility would be questioned by the press. He now had Watson and Beard sign a certificate for public distribution. "The undersigned certify that Mr. Charles Dickens has been seriously unwell, through great exhaustion and fatigue of body and mind consequent upon his public Readings and long and frequent railway journeys. In our judgment Mr. Dickens will not be able with safety to himself to resume his Readings for several months to come."

Pledging "implicit obedience" to his doctors, confident that rest would make him completely well, he refused even to imagine it possible that he would or even should never give public readings again. Unable to "bear to be hurried or flurried," feeling all right "except for a rather dazed sensation of being greatly fatigued," he declined a dinner invitation from Forster. Resting, the next day he felt that he had begun "to recover himself." Soon he announced that he was "in a quite brilliant condition already. . . . I should be almost ashamed of myself, if I didn't know the unconditional knocking off for a time, from all 'reading' wear and tear, to be a cautionary rather than a curative measure." Still essentially denying the seriousness of his condition, he returned to Kent, the place from which all his "early imaginations dated. . . . I took them away so full of innocent construction and guileless belief, and I brought them back so worn and torn, so much the wiser and so much the worse!"[46]

The notion of leaving something unfinished distressed him. At Gad's Hill, at the beginning of May, he attended to two necessary tasks, the first to convince his doctors to sanction his redeeming "in a careful and moderate way, some of the reading engagements, to which he had been pledged before those threatenings of brain-mischief in the North of England." He felt an obligation to the Chappells and to himself, partly professional, partly financial. Since he did seem to feel perfectly well, Watson gave in. The readings were scheduled for early in the new year.[47] The second was to write his will. If this too were only cautionary, it may have arisen from a new awareness that he could not afford any longer to be unprepared and unprotected. Having locked into his desk drawer at the office an "Important Memorandum," he now sent for it. On May 12, 1869, he signed and had witnessed the will that he had composed himself, with Ouvry's assistance. The initial provision gave "the sum of £1000 free of legacy duty to Miss Ellen Lawless Ternan, late of Houghton Place, Ampthill Square." That it came first suggests that he was playing his obsessive game of revealment and concealment, pursuer and pursued. The bequest's prominent position made a bold public announcement about her importance to him. But, though the amount was sufficiently large to force additional notice, it was not large enough to make the statement complete and unmistakable. More likely than not, Ellen's finances had already been provided for, including her ownership of the lease at Houghton Place, which produced an income of about three hundred pounds a year. It is inconceivable that he would have left her without reasonable financial security.

The remaining provisions were unexceptional. To his unmarried daughter he also left one thousand pounds and an annuity of three hundred pounds, separate from her share in the division of his estate. To Georgina he left eight thousand pounds, his personal effects, and his papers. To Charley he gave his library, and, a year later, in a codicil, his interest in *All the Year Round.* Also to Charley and to Henry, living in the London area and in regular touch with their mother, he left a total of sixteen thousand pounds, the income from which was to be used to support "my wife during her life," the money thereafter to revert to all his children. The remainder, and by far the bulk, of his real and personal estate, including his copyrights, were to be divided equally among his children, probably producing for each a legacy of about six to eight thousand pounds. To his "dear and trusty friend" John Forster he bequeathed his favorite watch and all the "manuscripts of my published works as may be in my possession at the time of my decease." Georgina and Forster were to be executors and guardians of the underage children. Dickens solemnly urged his "dear children to remember how much they owe to the said Georgina Hogarth, and never to be wanting in grateful and affectionate attachment to her . . . their ever-useful self-denying and devoted friend. AND I DESIRE here simply to record the fact that my wife, since our separation by consent, has been in the receipt from me of an annual income of £600, while all the great charges of a numerous and expensive family have devolved wholly upon myself. I emphatically direct that I be buried in an inexpensive, unostentatious, and strictly private manner; that no public announcement be made of the time or place of my burial; that at the utmost not more than three plain mourning coaches be employed; and that those who attend my funeral wear no scarf, cloak, black bow, long hat-band, or other such revolting absurdity."[48]

During the unusually rainy summer of 1869, he went about his tasks and his pleasures with no more self-pity or sense of imminent danger than the will expresses. His major work was to rest while also fulfilling his responsibilities to *All the Year Round.* "I am really *all right,*" he assured Wills in early May. The danger had been only topical, the railways again. He had not even really been ill to begin with. He had only "begun suddenly to be so shaken by constant Express travelling, that I might very easily have been ill. Said the Doctors: 'take warning, stop instantly.' I made the plunge, and became, please God, well." He was grateful to the doctors for their insistence, and, fortunately, "rest and a little care immediately *unshook* the railway shaking." In late May and June, the Fieldses and Annie's friend Mabel Lowell visited. Entertaining them at Gad's Hill and in London, staying at a hotel in Piccadilly, with Mamie and Georgina, in order to facilitate their day excursions and night prowling to slums and police stations, he went with Fields to visit a dockside opium den, where curls of hallucinatory smoke rose from long-stemmed pipes into his imagination for later use. One of their theatre visits had to be canceled because one of the ladies was "knocked up" and "destroyed our evening." They went to Canterbury, evoking the experiences that had been fictionalized in *David Copperfield.* Ellen came to visit at Gad's Hill, where probably she met the Fieldses. When Katie, who came soon after, heard that Ellen had participated in a game of cricket, she derisively remarked, "I am afraid she did not play the game!"[49] In early June, he stayed overnight at Lord John Russell's, an odd personalization of his cordial but distant relationship with an elderly great leader from the past.

But Dickens was more visited than visiting. Gad's Hill was comfortable, "immensely improved," with its blaze of red geraniums and neatly cut lawns. He had in mind a further improvement, a glass conservatory extension to the dining room. With the purchase of an additional small piece of land, he now owned about twenty acres. Except for his visits with Ellen and brief excursions, he thought it best to stay put. With well-intentioned imperception, he had for months been attempting to mediate a separation agreement between Frances Dickinson Elliot and her husband. The process soon became a benign version of his own. Insufficiently self-aware and conveniently forgetful, he told her that "your repudiating your marriage on the one hand, and requiring that the Dean shall live with you at such and such times to keep up appearances on the other" is a "monstrous absurdity." When the inevitable "miserable complications arose," he finally begged off, "painfully reminded of the caution given me by the Doctors to add nothing, this summer and autumn, to the pressures of my own affairs." Thomas Trollope urged him to visit Italy in the fall. No, he replied, "there is no chance of my being able to quit England this year." When Ellen's brother-in-law reminded him that a new year was coming, he responded, "Walk across the Alps? Lord Bless you, I am 'going' to take up my alpenstock and cross all the Passes, and I am 'going' to Italy; I am also 'going' up the Nile to the Second Cataract, and I am 'going' to Jerusalem, and to India, and likewise to Australia. My only dimness of perception in this wise is that I don't know when. If I did but know when, I should be so wonderfully clear about it all."[50]

During the summer he appeared to an American visitor to be "physically (as well as mentally) . . . immensely strong, having quite regained his health and strength." In June, he wrote his brief article for the *Atlantic Monthly* in praise of his favorite actor, in preparation for Fechter's American tour. In July, the news of Henry's scholarship of fifty pounds at Cambridge gave him the longed-for opportunity to boast. "The bigwigs expect him to do a good deal there." In late August, he gave a lengthy toast at the banquet for the Oxford and Harvard crews at the Crystal Palace, a celebrity having been persuaded to attend a celebrity event honoring the English-American alliance. In September, prevailed upon by his friend Arthur Ryland, he addressed the Birmingham and Midland Institute, of which he had been elected president for the next year. Though he entertained "the heretical belief" that "our own country . . . is an over-talked one," he could not resist lauding education and denying that the age was materialistic. "The one serviceable, safe, certain, remunerative, attainable quality in every study and in every pursuit is the quality of attention. My own invention or imagination, such as it is . . . would never have served me as it has, but for the habit of commonplace, humble, patient, daily, toiling, drudging attention."

Before the end of the summer, he was at work on a new novel, at least to the extent of making publication arrangements and determining on that most necessary of all preconditions, a title that he liked. After some initial hesitation, he decided not to publish it as a serial in *All the Year Round* but in twelve monthly numbers to be sold for a shilling each, the first to appear on March 31, 1870. Publishing in twelve monthly numbers would have the advantage of breathing room between each without the disadvantages of the length of twenty monthly numbers or the pressure of weekly serial publication. Chapman and Hall agreed to pay over eight thousand pounds for half the profits.[51] His painstaking creative habits of "toiling, drudging attention" were called upon once more.

Eager to get ahead before starting his London readings, he wrote the first two numbers of *The Mystery of Edwin Drood* in the late summer and early fall. Rummaging through his notebook, he found usable ideas, names, and character sketches. The notion of two young people having been separated for many years after having been pledged to be married had been jotted down as early as 1861, perhaps in 1857. By mid-October 1869, he was well into "the preliminary agonies" of working out the characters, situations, and events of the novel. The central plot had become less the problem of betrothed nonlovers than the relationship between the main character, John Jasper, the organist at a cathedral like Rochester's, his ward, Rosa Bud, and his nephew, Edwin Drood. The obsessive, addictive passions of Jasper's imagination and heart dominate the novel. It is a loving and creative heart. Also it is a grotesquely damaged, perversely destructive heart. For Dickens, writing in the detective mode, fascinated by pursued and pursuer, the plot was crucial. Jasper's nephew, the betrothed of his ward, whom Jasper loves, disappears under circumstances that suggest that his uncle may have murdered him. Whether he is actually dead or not, though, is unclear.

If John Jasper has murdered or attempted to murder

Edwin, under what circumstances has he done so? In addition to being an artist-musician, he is both a mesmerist and an opium smoker. In the first scene, the "Ancient Cathedral Town" of the novelist's Kentish childhood is invoked from the curling smoke of Jasper's hallucinating imagination as he puffs an opium pipe in a version of the den that he and Fields had visited. In its special way, *Drood* is as autobiographical as *David Copperfield,* set in a dark Kentish landscape, with shadows of death, with Dickens dramatizing aspects of himself. Taking place in sight and under the spell of the "massive grey square tower" of his childhood, the novel begins in the waning of the year, in the "drowsy city" of Cloisterham, at a time when he was young, and resonates with the autumnal tone of his premature old age. What roles would mesmerism, opium addiction, and the mysterious characters introduced early in the novel play in the development of the story? He seems to have told no one the full plot. To Charles Collins, who at his own request did the design for the overall cover, he told only what was necessary. When Collins, in ill health, was replaced by a young man, Luke Fildes, who "promises admirably" and whom Dickens liked, he told him no more than he needed to know.52

By late autumn Dickens felt ill again. The London farewells were scheduled to begin in early January 1870. In mid-December, heavy snowstorms through much of England gave an accurate foretaste of what was to be a "very long, dark, and *bitter* winter." Fortunately, he had finished the first two numbers by late November, and told the printer that he wished he *"could* set up the whole of the book before we begin! But if I get nearly half of it ready by that time, I shall be more than satisfied." To his shock, just before Christmas the printer told him that they were, "altogether, *twelve printed pages too short!!!"* He had to transpose and rewrite immediately at a time when he had turned from the book to preparing the readings.

At Christmas, he was not in good spirits. He wrote his usual end-of-the-year letters, assuring the aged Macready that "it needs not Christmas time to bring the thought of you and of our loving and close friendship round to my heart, for it is always there." He indulged both of them in the fantasy that in the summer they would sit together in the new conservatory. It was finished in January, "a brilliant success—but an expensive one!" There was now the likelihood that Henry's scholarship would become a fellowship, though his father had "learned to moderate" his "transports as to hopeful children."

Reminded by the presence of a grandchild that he was something as deleterious as a grandfather, Dickens felt it particularly inopportune that his foot had become painfully lame again. Probably he worried that the inflammation would affect his readings. One evening, because "he had been ailing very much and greatly troubled with his leg," he lay on the sofa while his guests were playing "The Memory Game." Soon he joined in. "After many turns," he "successfully [went] through the long string of words, and finished up with his own contribution, 'Warren's Blacking, 30 Strand.' "53

Having decided that it would be best to be in town to supervise *Drood*'s inauguration, he moved, at the beginning of the new year, into 5 Hyde Park Place, near Marble Arch, renting the large, comfortable house until the end of May 1870 from a well-connected acquaintance, Milner Gibson. Mary was delighted to be in London, close to Katie. The sisters plunged themselves and pulled their father, who needed some tugging, into a bustling social season. At dinner at the home of Arthur Stanley, the dean of Westminster Cathedral, he again told the story of Lincoln's anticipation of his death. In early January, he went to Birmingham to distribute the prizes at the institute before a huge audience. The next day, with one of his sons, he visited "some of the large factories. . . . As we walked through the crowded rooms, perspiring, smoke-begrimed workmen kept asking Henry, " 'Is that Charles Dickens—is that Charles Dickens?' " The effort, particularly the railway trip, tired him.

A few days later he began the series of twelve final readings to overflow audiences at St. James's Hall. Though he regretted interfering with his writing schedule, he felt that he could read once or twice a week and still continue at his desk. Later in the month, he fulfilled a commitment postponed from the previous year to give a special morning reading of the murder of Nancy for professional actors and actresses. Ellen, who was present and still referred to as "the patient," sent her regards to Wills, too much an invalid now to attend. Dickens' ordinary pulse of 72 rose to 112 at the end of the reading. It was madness, he recognized, "to do it continuously." Watching, waiting, Frank Beard had begun attending every performance. One night Dickens "found it impossible to say Pickwick, and called him Picksnick, and Picnic, and Peckwicks and all sorts of names except the right," giving "a comical glance of surprise" at his family and friends occupying their usual front seats. He treated it lightly afterward. "If he attributed it to any special cause at all, [he] referred it, as he referred the disordered vision, to the effects of medicine he was taking." Beard had workmen erect steps at the side of the platform. He told Charley that "you must be there every night, and if you see your father falter in the least, you must run up and catch him and bring him off with me, or, by Heaven, he'll die before them all."54

By late February, there were "only three more readings now!" "Charles is *quite well*, thank God!" Georgina told Annie Fields. Though eager to have the readings over, he was saddened by the notion that soon they would be over forever. "There is always something sad about—'the last'—of anything." He invariably found it difficult to say good-bye, as if it were bad luck. He told Georgina, though, that he would also "feel the absence of the *money* made by the Readings." The small world around him quietly provided comment on his past and present. George Hogarth, his once-upon-a-time friend and father-in-law, died in February. Probably Georgina visited her sister, both in mourning. Mary and Katie visited their mother, who, on one of the only two occasions in which she ever referred to her husband in Katie's presence, asked, "looking towards his photograph . . . 'Do you think he is sorry for me?' "55

With the last reading scheduled for mid-March, Dickens was looking forward to rest and quiet. With the first number of *Drood* to appear March 31, he pleasantly anticipated reestablishing his old role with his audience. On March 15, 1870, tired, sad, his left foot in pain, the exhausted Prospero made his dreaded final appearance on the platform. He read *A Christmas Carol* and the trial scene from *Pickwick*. Against expectations, finding the energy to make one last effort, he read with verve and brilliance. The applause was overwhelming, and seemed to go on and on and on. Finally, it was quiet again. In the absolutely silent hall he confessed how he closed "this episode in my life with feelings of considerable pain. For some fifteen years, in this hall and in many kindred places, I have had the honour of presenting my own cherished ideas before you for your recognition; and, in closely observing your reception of them, have enjoyed an amount of artistic delight and instruction which, perhaps, is given to few men to know. . . . In but two short weeks from this time I hope that you may enter, in your own homes, on a new series of readings, at which my assistance will be indispensable; but from these garish lights I vanish now for evermore, with a heartfelt, grateful, respectful, and affectionate farewell." He walked slowly from the platform into the wings, as if in deep mourning. Tumultuous applause and handkerchief waving brought him back one last time. Tears rolled down his cheeks. He kissed his hand to his friends, good-bye.[56]

Before leaving the public stage forever, he appeared briefly on the most sacred private stage of Victorian culture. Arthur Helps, a minor writer, upper-level civil servant, the queen's adviser, and Dickens' friend, manipulated an introduction that resulted in Victoria inviting the star performer of her age to a private audience. "They had known one another, though they had never met, for a long time." She had happily attended a private performance of *The Frozen Deep* in 1857, though she may not have fully understood his refusal to be introduced to her then. He now pressed Helps to repeat the explanation. In 1863 she had purchased for her private library Thackeray's presentation copy of *A Christmas Carol*. In February 1870, Helps encouraged Dickens to send her the Civil War photographs he had brought back with him in 1868. In return, she sent him photographs of herself. Somewhat amused and impressed by the honor, he accepted an invitation to appear at Buckingham Palace on March 9, joking that "we will have of 'Gad's Hill Place' attached to the title of Baronetcy, please—on account of the divine William and Falstaff." Apparently, though, he did not want a title or was ambivalent enough to disguise his feelings. Whether one was offered is unclear. When rumors persisted, he remarked that "I am going to be nothing but what I am." Helps prepared the queen for the visit. "His Christian name is Charles. . . . One of his best works is David Copperfield; and it is supposed that it gives a . . . narrative of the author's early life. Your Majesty might naturally say that Your Majesty's many cares and duties have prevented your reading all the works of your most eminent authors, and might, playfully, ask Mr. Dickens's advice whether David Copperfield would be the work of his which he would wish your Majesty to read next . . . and might ask him whether he would read to her at Windsor."

Instead of lasting the expected ten or fifteen minutes, the interview went on, by Helps's account, for half an hour, by Dolby's for an hour and a half. Initially, they were both shy. With Helps as facilitator and the queen standing to put him at ease, they chatted lightly about superficial things. Dickens was at his most Victorian, optimistic, conservative, social, entertaining. The queen found his voice and manner pleasant. "He talked of his latest works, of America, the strangeness of the people there, of the division of classes in England which he hoped would get better in time. He felt sure that it would come gradually." Again he told the story of Lincoln's dream before his assassination. Helps thought the interview "interesting and amusing." They exchanged gifts of books, the queen an author of sorts herself. Soon Dickens accepted an invitation that resulted in Mary and him being presented formally at court. After the interview, when he arrived late for their dinner appointment, Dolby impatiently implored him to "tell me everything." " 'Everything! my dear fellow, everything! I tell you what, it would be difficult to say what we did *not* talk about.' "[57] It was mostly, though, a tale of the butcher, the baker, and the candlestick maker. He soon declined the queen's request that he give a private reading at Windsor. He needed a larger audience, and his reading days were over.

His London obligations, though, continued into the spring, writing and reading proofs, seeing friends, and attending dinner parties. The social whirl became wearisome. He had gotten "into that complicated state of engagements that my life is positively made wretched." On many days, he felt as if he were making only slow headway with his novel. Though he felt restless, he persevered. With the publication of the first number on April 1, he felt relieved at its immediate success. In early May, Georgina remarked that "I think he never wrote more quickly. The two first numbers have had an enormous sale—and an enormous success—he has just now finished the 5th—so he keeps well in advance." When Mary gave a large party, newspaper gossip implied that he had become a worshiper of the aristocracy. At dinner at Lord Stanhope's, he chatted with Disraeli, who noticed "the charm of his conversation, his brightness, and his humour," an exception to "the general rule of authors being so much less interesting than their books." At the end of April, he blandly addressed, fulfilling an old promise, the annual dinner of the Newsvendors' Benevolent Institution. Early in May, he attended a breakfast hosted by William Gladstone. He preferred the Liberal "Tweedledum" to the Conservative "Tweedledee," as Carlyle called them, having come to admire Gladstone's policies on Ireland and other issues. Gladstone seemed more congenial to the vestiges of his own youthful radicalism, some fallen aspect of which he had superficially alluded to in his speech in Birmingham when he had remarked that his "faith in the people governing, is, on the whole, infinitesimal; my faith in The People governed, is, on the whole illimitable."58

Through much of the spring Dickens felt ill, though not enough to desist from his usual activities. He had brief attacks, which he referred to as "uneasiness and hemorrhage," coming with "a sudden violent rush," from which he recovered quickly enough to insist that they had "not the slightest effect on [his] general health." On April 28 he was shocked to read in the newspaper at a railway station that Daniel Maclise had died in his Brighton lodgings. Wrenched into memories and miseries by the death of his "dear old friend and companion," he struggled to get some command over himself, and only succeeded by "at once thinking of it and avoiding it in a strange way." Maclise had briefly surfaced from his seclusion a number of times in recent years, even attending the farewell banquet in 1867. He had sustained himself mostly, though, with memories, invoking for Forster in 1868 his unforgettable image of "you clambering up the goat path" near "King Arthur's Castle of Tintagel" when the two of them, with Dickens and Stanfield, visited Cornwall in 1842. "In my vain wish to follow I grovelled and clung to the soil like Caliban and you in the manner of a picksy spirit and stout Ariel actually danced up and down before me." Forster had recently said to Dickens that "we should one day hear that the wayward life into which he had fallen was over, and there should end our knowledge of it."

As if circumstance, that wonderful web that Dickens believed in and wove into his novels, had conspired like a masterful artist to bring all things round into a formal circle, he was scheduled the day after the news of Maclise's death to give the principal address at the annual banquet of the Royal Academy of Art at their new Burlington House home. "Since first I entered the public list, a very young man indeed, it has been my constant fortune," he told the members and guests, "to number among my nearest and dearest friends members of this Royal Academy. They have so dropped from my side one by one that I already feel like that Spanish monk . . . who had grown to believe that the only realities around him were the pictures he loved, and that all the moving life he saw, or ever had seen, was a shadow and a dream." Amid the ghostly realities of his artist friends, he invoked a golden myth of the man whose intimate companion he had been for many years.59 The speech was a supreme fiction of Victorian eulogy. But he deeply believed his own words, and he mourned Maclise as he celebrated their shared ideals and as he eulogized the days that were no more.

For a few brief moments at the beginning of May 1870 he seemed quite well. Suddenly his foot flamed up again. He took heavy doses of laudanum in order to sleep. Extremely hot poultices were applied night and day, causing severe blistering. Limping between his office and Hyde Park Place, he carried on with his work, slightly drugged and in frequent pain, but making as light of it as he could. He begged off some dinner engagements, "literally laid up by the heels," with "a neuralgic infection which usually seizes me about twice a year." He went back to the myth of its originating "in over-walking in deep snow." He did not disguise, though, from Forster that he was in "horrible pain." He had to cancel his commitment at the middle of the month to address the Royal General Theatrical Fund dinner. "I could no more walk into St. James's Hall than I could fly in the air." The pain and invalidism went on for three weeks. Without exercise, which he needed, he believed, in order to write, he felt additionally depressed. Toward the end of the month, just before finally leaving Hyde Park Place, he claimed to be "much shocked to hear" that Mark Lemon, old Uncle Porpoise, had died. He blandly assured Lemon's son that "there never was any serious estrangement between us," though his old companion's death does not seem to have touched him deeply.60

With his foot heavily bandaged, Dickens left for Gad's Hill. The conservatory had been filled with scarlet geraniums for his return amid June brilliance. He went back to town almost immediately, partly for *All the Year Round* business, partly to direct Mamie and Katie's performances at a friend's home on Wednesday, June 1, in a play called *Prima Donna*. The scenery had been designed by Millais. "Behind the scenes the whole time . . . his well-worn . . . haggard face, flitting by," he stayed overnight at the office, he and Dolby having their usual Thursday business lunch. On parting, as they shook hands across the table, Dolby noticed that he seemed in great pain and could hardly walk. But he was unwilling to ask him about it. "So without another word on either side," they parted. On Friday morning, he remained secluded, working in his office, with his door open. Finally, at 1 P.M., Charley, leaving for a weekend in the country, went into his father's office and "saw that he was writing very earnestly. After a moment I said: 'If you don't want anything more, sir, I shall be off now,' but he continued his writing with the same intensity as before, and gave no sign of being aware of my presence. Again I spoke—louder, perhaps, this time—and he rested his head and looked at me long and fixedly. But I soon found that, although his eyes were bent upon me, and he seemed to be looking at me earnestly, he did not see me, and that he was, in fact unconscious for the moment of my very existence."[61]

During the weekend, at Gad's Hill, though Dickens worked at *Drood* and wrote some letters, he clearly was not feeling well, his complexion unnaturally gray, his breath short. After a brief walk with Katie on Sunday afternoon, he felt strikingly tired. He proudly showed her the new conservatory. "It is positively," he said, "the last improvement." In the evening, at dinner with his daughters and Georgina, he seemed better. Afterward, smoking his customary cigar, he invited Katie to tell him at length about her plans, particularly her thoughts about going on the stage, which he advised against. The life would be too difficult, too crass. " 'I will make it up to you.' He went on to speak of other subjects—with regret. He wished, he said, that he had been 'a better father—a better man.' " They talked until 3 A.M. Before she left the next morning, she insisted on going to the chalet to say good-bye. "As a rule, when he was busy, he would just put up his cheek to be kissed. But this day he took her in his arms, saying 'God bless you, Katie!' " When she was halfway back to the house through the tunnel under the Gravesend Road, "something said to me, 'go back,' and I immediately ran up the steps, through the shrubbery, into the Chalet and tapped on the door. My father—who was seated with his back to it—called out, 'Come in'; turning and seeing me he held out his arms into which I ran, when he embraced me again and kissed me very affectionately."[62]

On Monday afternoon, too fatigued to take his usual walk, Dickens went for a drive with Georgina through Cobham woods. He felt strong enough to walk back. After dinner, he sat for an unusually long time, chatting with her about how much he loved Gad's Hill, watching "the effect of some Chinese lanterns he had hung in the conservatory." On Tuesday and through much of Wednesday, he seemed well and in good spirits. He intended to make his usual Thursday visit to the office. At about one o'clock on Wednesday he came back into the house from the chalet and smoked a cigar in the conservatory. Going back to the chalet, late in the afternoon he put a flourish to the end of the last chapter of the sixth number of *The Mystery of Edwin Drood*, exactly the halfway point of the novel. Returning to the house an hour before his usual time, he sat down to dinner with Georgina. They were alone in the house, except for servants. Suddenly she noticed a striking change in his color and expression. He responded to her question, was he ill, " 'yes, very ill; I have been very ill for the last hour.' " She wanted to send for a doctor immediately. But he said no. He would be all right. He would go on with dinner and he would be all right. And then he would go to London afterward. He began talking "rapidly and indistinctly—mentioning Forster." She begged him to lie down. " 'Yes, on the ground,' he answered." He got up from the table. She tried to hold him but he slid through her arms, suddenly, immediately, and totally unconscious.[63]

Calling for the servants, who lifted him onto a sofa, she tried to make him comfortable. He did not respond. In the hope that he might be moved, a bed was brought into the dining room. Doctors were sent for, telegrams dispatched. Forster, receiving his in Cornwall, turned homeward immediately. Mamie and Katie were at a dinner party in London. Before they had gone out for the evening, Katie had suddenly said, " 'Mamie, I feel something is going to happen to us.' 'Nice or nasty?' returned Mamie. 'I cannot say,' " she replied. On receiving the message, they left at once for Gad's Hill with Frank Beard. The doctor from Rochester had already arrived and cut away his coat and other clothes. When Mamie saw the look on Georgina's face, "the last faint hope" died within her. Entering the house, they could hear their "father's deep breathing." Watching him through the night, they took turns putting hot bricks at his icy cold feet. He never moved or spoke. Knowing that there was no hope, they prayed that he would not become conscious again, so that he might be "spared the agony of parting," the farewells that he hated so much. When Charley arrived in the morning, the ninth of June, with an eminent specialist who later sent a bill for twenty guineas, the doctors "found unmistakable symptoms of brain haemorrhage." At 6 P.M. his breathing declined. Ten minutes later a tear "trickled down his cheek." He gave a deep sigh, and stopped breathing altogether.

When Henry arrived from Cambridge the next morning, bright sunlight flooded the room. His father's body had been moved onto the bed. Millais soon came to do a death cast, but settled for a pencil drawing. To Georgina, the house already seemed "dreadful now, without him," the first moments of the long cold lonely years without his sunshine. "The light has gone from our lives, and they can never be the same again and our hearts are very desolate and broken."[64] Katie left to break the news to her mother. She returned with Ellen. Forster arrived, and then went immediately to London. Unable to hold back his violent sobs, Forster arranged with Dean Stanley, who agreed to the conditions stated in the will, that Dickens be buried in Westminster Abbey. Arrangements under way for burial in Rochester Cathedral were canceled. A grave had already been dug there. Bells had been tolled.

Three carriages entered the Abbey yard at 9:30 A.M. two days later. The closed coffin was waiting. During the night it had been delivered from Rochester to London, "like game," though it had not "rained hard all the way." The son of Kent was again to become part of the dust of London. At the graveside, his only surviving sister represented the family of his childhood. Georgina represented the sisters and wives of his imagination and desire. Other than his two daughters, the only other woman present was his eldest son's wife, whose wedding he had declined to attend. His disappointing namesake and the successful scholar of the family represented the survivors of his exiled tribe of unhappy and unhappy-making sons. Of the five friends who accompanied the coffin and watched it lowered into the earth it was appropriate that one was his doctor, another his lawyer, and one the son-in-law to whom he had reluctantly given his favorite daughter. The other two were his closest friends and collaborators, Forster and Collins, the men who knew best the secrets of his heart. Without applause, without an audience other than these twelve, without Ellen's presence, without an echo of his wife other than in the quiet attendance of four of her children, he was buried silently on a beautiful summer morning "in that vast space of the Abbey." Dean Stanley pronounced to believers and unbelievers alike the resonant phrases of the Anglican burial service. The Sparkler, the Inimitable, the manager, became part of the great majority. As the procession left the cathedral, the dean asked Forster "whether, as it would be a great disappointment to the public, he would allow the grave to be kept open for the remainder of the day." Forster said, " 'Yes; now my work is over, and you may do what you like.' "65

Notes

ABBREVIATIONS

The following abbreviations and short titles are used in the notes:

MANUSCRIPTS

Berg Henry W. and Albert A. Berg Collection, the New York Public Library, Astor, Lenox and Tilden Foundations
BL British Library
DHM Dickens House Museum
HH The Henry E. Huntington Library, San Marino, California
Morgan Pierpont Morgan Library, New York
NLS National Library of Scotland
PH The Free Library, Philadelphia
PR The Parrish Collection, Princeton University
TEX The Harry Ransom Humanities Research Center, University of Texas
V&A Forster Collection, Victoria and Albert Museum
Yale Beinecke Rare Book and Manuscript Library, Yale University

PEOPLE

ABC Angela Burdett Coutts
AD Alfred Dickens
AR Arthur Ryland
AS Albert Smith
ASM Arthur Smith
AT Augustus Frederick Tracey
B&E Bradbury and Evans
BP Bryan Procter
CaD Catherine Dickens

C&H Chapman and Hall
CC Charles Collins
CCF Cornelius C. Felton
CD Charles Dickens
CDJr Charles (Charley) Dickens, Jr.
CK Charles Kent
CL Charles Lever
CS Clarkson Stanfield
CW Charles Ward
DJ Douglas Jerrold
DkD Duke of Devonshire
DM Daniel Maclise
EBL Edward Bulwer-Lytton
ED Edward B. L. (Plorn) Dickens
EG Elizabeth Gaskell
EP Edward Pigott
ER Emile de la Rue
ET Edward Tagart
EY Edmund Yates
FB Fanny (Dickens) Burnett
FD Frederick Dickens
FDN Frances Dickinson
FE Frederick Evans
FL Frederick Lehmann
FO Frederic Ouvry
FS Frank Stone
GC George Cruikshank
GD George Dolby
GH Georgina Hogarth
GHL George Henry Lewes
HA Henry Austin
HB Henry Burnett
HC Harriet Collins
HCA Hans Christian Andersen
HFD Henry Fielding Dickens
HMB Hannah Meredith Brown
HWL Henry Wadsworth Longfellow
JD John Dickens
JET James Emerson Tennent
JF John Forster
JL John Leech
JM John Macrone
JTF James T. Fields
KD Kate (Katie) Dickens
LA Letitia (Dickens) Austin
LB Lady Blessington
LH Leigh Hunt
LW Lavinia Watson
MB Mary Boyle
MD Mary (Mamie) Dickens
ML Mark Lemon
MS Marcus Stone

MW Maria (Beadnell) Winter
PC Philip Collins
PF Percy Fitzgerald
RB Richard Bentley
RBL Robert Bulwer-Lytton
RHH Richard Henry Horne
TAT Thomas A. Trollope
TB Thomas Beard
TC Thomas Carlyle
TJT Thomas James Thompson
TM Thomas Mitton
TNT Thomas Noon Talfourd
WC Wilkie Collins
WCM William Charles Macready
WFC William F. de Cerjat
WHA William Harrison Ainsworth
WHH William Holman Hunt
WHR W. H. Russell
WHW William Henry Wills
WJC William J. Carlton
WMT William Makepeace Thackeray
WSL Walter Savage Landor

BOOKS

Dickens' Works

The Clarendon Dickens (Oxford, 1966–1982) has been used for *DC, DS, ED, LD, MC,* and *OT.* For all other works, including the Christmas tales and stories, *The Oxford Illustrated Dickens* has been used with occasional textual corrections from the Penguin edition, with the exception of *BkM,* which has been cited from the text (1981) published by the New York Public Library, and *PI,* which has been cited from the edition (1973) edited by David Paroissien. *Miscellaneous Papers* (1914), ed. B. W. Matz, contains many otherwise uncollected short pieces.

AN American Notes, 1842
BH Bleak House, 1852–53
BkM Charles Dickens' Book of Memoranda, 1981
BR Barnaby Rudge, 1841
DC David Copperfield, 1849–50
DS Dombey and Son, 1846–78
ED The Mystery of Edwin Drood, 1870
GE Great Expectations, 1860–61
HT Hard Times, 1854
LD Little Dorrit, 1855–57
MC Martin Chuzzlewit, 1843–44
MP Miscellaneous Papers, 1914
NN Nicholas Nickleby, 1838–39
OCS The Old Curiosity Shop, 1840–41
OMF Our Mutual Friend, 1864–65
OT Oliver Twist, 1837–38
PI Pictures from Italy, 1846
PP Pickwick Papers, 1836–37
RP Reprinted Pieces, 1850–56
SB Sketches by Boz, 1833–36

TTC *A Tale of Two Cities*, 1859
UT *The Uncommercial Traveller*, 1860, 1865, 1875

HCD *The Heart of Charles Dickens*, ed. Edgar Johnson, 1952
KJF *The Speeches of Charles Dickens*, ed. K. J. Fielding, 1960
MM *Mr. and Mrs. Charles Dickens. His Letters to Her*, ed. Walter Dexter, 1935
N The Nonesuch Edition of *The Letters of Charles Dickens*, ed. Walter Dexter, 3 vols., 1938
P The Pilgrim Edition of *The Letters of Charles Dickens*, volumes 1–5, ed. Madeline House, Graham Storey, Kathleen Tillotson, K. J. Fielding, 1965–81
Wills *Charles Dickens as Editor*, ed. R. C. Lehmann, 1912

Journals
AYR *All the Year Round*, 1859–70
D *The Dickensian*, 1905–
DSA *Dickens Studies Annual*, 1970–1987.
GHG *Gad's Hill Gazette*, 1863–65. Berg; DHM.
HW *Household Words*, 1850–59

Reminiscences, Articles, and Books
Adrian Arthur Adrian, *Georgina Hogarth and the Dickens Circle*, 1957
Allen Michael Allen, "The Dickens Family at Portsmouth, 1807–14," D (1981), 131–43; "The Dickens Family at London and Sheerness, 1815–1816," D (1982), 3–7; "The Dickens Family at Chatham, 1817–1822," D (1982), 67–88; "The Dickens Family in London, 1822–1824," D (1982), 131–51; "The Dickens Family in London 1824–1827," D (1983), 2–20
Bred *Hans Christian Andersen and Charles Dickens, A Friendship and Its Dissolution*, Anglistica 7, 1956
Christian Eleanor E. Christian, "Recollections of Charles Dickens," *Temple Bar*, 1888
CD Jr Charles Dickens, Jr., "Reminiscences of My Father," *Windsor Magazine*, 1934
Davies James A. Davies, *John Forster, A Literary Life*, 1983
DD Gladys Storey, *Dickens and Daughter*, 1939
Dolby George Dolby, *Charles Dickens as I Knew Him*, 1912
F John Forster, *The Life of Charles Dickens*, 2 vols., 1876
Fitz Percy Fitzgerald, *Memories of Charles Dickens*, 1913
Frith W. P. Frith, *My Autobiography and Reminiscences*, 1889
Gaskell A. V. Chapple and Arthur Pollard, ed., *Letters of Mrs. Gaskell*, 1966
HFD.M Henry Fielding Dickens, *Memories of My Father*, 1929
HFD.R Henry Fielding Dickens, *The Recollections of Sir Henry Dickens*, 1934
IR Philip Collins. ed., *Charles Dickens, Interviews and Recollections*, 2 vols., 1981
J Edgar Johnson, *Charles Dickens, His Tragedy and His Triumph*, 2 vols., 1952
JTF James T. Fields, *Yesterdays with Authors*, 1882
Langton Robert Langton, *The Childhood and Youth of Charles Dickens*, 1891
Lehmann John Lehmann, *Ancestors and Friends*, 1962
MD Mamie Dickens, *My Father as I Recall Him*, 1900
MS Marcus Stone, "Reminiscences," DHM
Nisbet Ada Nisbet, *Dickens & Ellen Ternan*, 1952
P&P Frederic G. Kitton, *Charles Dickens by Pen and Pencil*, 1889–90
Patten Robert Patten, *Charles Dickens and His Publishers*, 1978
Ray Gordon N. Ray, *The Letters and Private Papers of William Makepeace Thackeray*, 4 vols., 1945–46
Slater Michael Slater, *Dickens and Women*, 1983
WCM.D William Charles Macready, *The Diaries of William Charles Macready*, ed. William Toynbee, 2 vols., 1912

WCMLR William Charles Macready, *Macready's Reminiscences and Diaries*, ed.
   Frederick Pollock, 875
Wright Thomas Wright, *The Life of Charles Dickens*, 1935
Yates Edmund Yates, *Recollections and Experiences*, 1884

CHAPTER ONE
Scenes of His Boyhood
(1812–1822)

1. CD to WHW, 9/4/1860, N 3, 176–77; CD to WCM, 3/1/1865, N 3, 416; DD, 106–7.
   Though Storey states that it was Katie who tried to save some of the letters, it is
   likely to have been Mamie or Georgina; Katie was in France.
2. CD to WCM, 2/1/1865 N 3, 416.
3. Christian, 483–84; Allen ("Portsmouth"), 137; CD to ABC, 8/30/1849, P 5, 602.
4. F, I, 1, 5; CD to ABC, 1/25/1855, HCD, 289; MS. DHM.
5. "The First of May" ("A Little Talk about Spring and the Sweeps"), SB (June 1836),
   170.
6. J 2, 1160–61 provides genealogies for the Dickens and Barrow families that go back
   to 1633 and 1510 respectively. I do not believe that they are historically valid; DD, 31–33.
7. Allen ("Portsmouth"), 131–32, 137; WJC, "The Barrows of Bristol," D (1949), 33–36; DD,
   37.
8. Allen ("Portsmouth"), 38–39, 142.
9. "Dullborough Town," UT, 126; "The First of May," SB (June 1836), 169; "Travelling
   Abroad," UT, 62.
10. Allen ("Chatham"), 67–68.
11. "Travelling Abroad," UT, 67; "Chatham Dockyard," UT (AYR, 1860?), 260–62;
    "Dullborough Town," UT, 116–17; the question of the precise nature of his childhood
    and life long ailment has not been satisfactorily resolved. The most plausible guesses
    are made by W. H. Bowen in CD and His Family, 1956, 134–59.
12. KJF, 50–51; Langton, 25; F, I, 7, 10.
13. F, I, 1, 9–11.
14. MS; Arthur Heran, "Those Wonderful Eyes," D (1926), 25–29; F I, 1, 10–11.
15. *Memoirs of Grimaldi*, ed. CD, 1838, ed. Richard Findlater, 1968, 9–10; F 2, 93.
16. Jane W. Stedman, "Good Spirits: Dickens's Childhood Reading." D (1965), 150–54; F,
    I, i, 10; "Dullborough Town," UT, 120.
17. "Dullborough Town," UT, 118.
18. "Dullborough Town," UT, 118–19.
19. "Dullborough Town," UT, 119.
20. "Night Walks," UT, 131; "Nurse's Stories," UT, 156–57.
21. DD, 33–34; WJC, "More About the Dickens Ancestry," D (1961), 5–10; Allen ("Cha-
    tham"), 80, 76–77.

CHAPTER TWO
The Hero of My Own Life
(1822–1834)

1. "Dullborough Town," UT, 116.
2. See WJC, "The Deed in DC," D (1952), 101–6. William Oldie, "Mr. Micawber and the

Redefinition of Experience," D (1967), 100–110: "JD is the source for Mr. Micawber. . . . Perhaps this, more than anything, shows how profoundly Dickens *needed* to write about his father" (109). E. Davey, "The Parents of CD," *Lippincott's Monthly Magazine* (1874), 772–74, takes the untenable position that JD and Micawber and Elizabeth Dickens and Mrs. Nickleby have little in common and are not portraits of CD's parents.

3. Davey, 773; Ephesian (C. E. Bechhofer Roberts), "The Huffams, the Barrows, and the Admiralty," D (1928), 263–66; W. B. Matz, "Christopher Huffam, CD's Grandfather," D (1924), 121–24; Allen ("London," 1), 114.

4. F, I, 1, 18–19; WJC, "The Barber of Dean Street," D (1951), 8–12.

5. WJC, "Fanny Dickens, Pianist and Vocalist," D (1957), 133–43, and supplementary documents, DHM.

6. DD, 46–48; WJC, "JD, Journalist," D (1957), 5–11.

7. Allen ("London," 1), 135.

8. WJC, "In the Blacking Warehouse," D (1964), 11–16; for a discussion of the problem of dating the start of CD's employment at Warren's, see Allen ("London," 1), 138.

9. Kathleen H. Strange, "Blacking Polish," D (1979), 7–11; F, I, 1, 25–26.

10. WJC, "The Deed in *DC,*" D (1952), 101–6.

11. Angus Easson, "I, Elizabeth Dickens: Light on JD's Legacy," D (1971), 35–40; Allen ("London," 1), 149–50; JD to H. Perryman, 10/6/1825, D (1913), 148.

12. Easson, 40; copies of these Public Record Office documents are at the DHM. The originals are quoted in Allen ("London," 1), 146–47, and Allen ("London," 2), 4.

13. WJC, "Postscripts to Forster," D (1962), 88–89; F, I, 28; Allen, 145–46.

14. F, I, 1, 22–3, 36–37.

15. F, I, 1, 38.

16. See Albert D. Hutter, "Reconstructive Autobiography: The Experience at Warren's Blacking," DSA 6 (1977), 1–14; F, I, 38.

17. P&P, 128.

18. See "Our School," *UT,* 567, 573; Willoughby Matchett, "Dickens at Wellington House Academy," D (1911), 212–13, 180–81; C. M. Neale, "Did Dickens Learn Virgil?" D (1912), 89–91, 123–26; CD to O. P. Thomas, 1825–26. P 1, 1.

19. Langton, 89; "Our School," UT, 568; Walter Dexter, "One Hundred Years Ago, Dickens's School Days in London," D (1926), 45.

20. WJC, "The Deed," 104–6; the editor, "Two Early Homes of CD," D (1951), 198–200.

21. P&P, 129.

22. P&P, 130–31.

23. WJC, "The Strange Story of TM," D (1960), 141–52; P 1, 35 note.

24. CD to J. H. Kuenzel, 7/?/1838, P 1, 423; P 1, 9 note 4.

25. Gerald G. Grubb, "Dickens' First Experience as a Parliamentary Reporter," D (1940), 216; Samuel Carter Hall, *Retrospect of a Long Life,* 1883, 64; WJC, "JD, Journalist," D (1957), 5–6.

26. WJC, *CD Shorthand Writer* (1926), 46–7; CD to Kuenzel, 7/?/1838, P 1, 423; Grubb, 211–18.

27. F, I, 3, 55.

28. P 1, 2.

29. A. De Suzannet, "Maria Beadnell's Album," D (1935), 161–68.

30. "City of London Churches," *UT,* 88–89; Michael Slater, "David to Dora: A New Dickens Letter," D (1972), 162–66, and Slater, 54–57; "The Bill of Fare," HH MS.; despite his disappointment, he continued to feel affection for George Beadnell, who "was most hospital, friendly, & kind," and corresponded with him through the 1840s.

31. WJC, "A Companion of the Copperfield Days," D (1953), 7–16.

32. CD to MW, 2/22/1855, N 2, 633; "Birthday Celebrations," *UT,* 403.

33. CD to Maria Beadnell, 5/14/1833, 5/19/1833, P 1, 23, 29; CD to Henry Kolle, 5/19/1833, P 1, 29.
34. CD to JF, 12/30–31/1844, 1/1/1845, P 4, 244–45.
35. WJC, "Fanny Dickens," 135–36; P 4, 245.
36. CD provided a fictional account of an aspect of the preparation in "Mrs. Joseph Porter" (*Monthly Magazine*, 1/1834); Morgan MS.
37. Morgan MS.; Charles Haywood, "CD and Shakespeare; or, The Irish Moor of Venice, O'Thello, With Music." D (1977), 67–87.
38. CD to Kolle, 12/10/1833, P 1, 33–34; WJC, "An Echo of the Copperfield Days," D (1949), 149–52; Charles Mackay, *Forty Years' Recollections of Life Literature, and Public Affairs*, 1877, I, 78; P&P, 33–34.
39. JD to TB, 12/4/1834, DHM.

CHAPTER THREE
The First Coming
(1834–1837)

1. J. P Collier, *An Old Man's Diary*, 1872, IV, viii.
2. Collier, IV, 12–14.
3. P 1, 47, 60; KJF, 347.
4. P 1, 41 note 1; CD to CaD, 12/16/1835, P 1, 106–7; P 1, 106, note 3.
5. KJF 346–47; "Preface," SB (1850); "Preface," PP (1867).
6. KJF, 347; Charles Mackay, P&P, 134.
7. CD to George Hogarth, 1/20/1835, P 1, 54–55.
8. PP, 138.
9. DD, 49–50; W. Forbes Gray, "The Edinburgh Relatives and Friends of CD," D (1926), 218–23; Christian, 481.
10. WJC "An Early Home of Dickens in Kensington," D (1965), 20–25; CD to CaD, 7/1835, 7/9/1835, P 1, 67, 69.
11. CD to CaD, 5/1835, P 1, 61.
12. CD to CaD, 6/?/1835, P 1, 63.
13. CD to CaD, 6/1835, P 1, 63; Michael Slater, "How Dickens 'told' Catherine about his Past," D (1979), 3–6.
14. CD to CaD, 11/19/1835, P 1, 95.
15. CD to CaD, 12/18/1835, 12/?/1835, P 1, 110, 104.
16. CD to CaD, 11/30?/1835, P 1, 99; P 1, 131 note, 144 note; PP, supplement, 10; TB to F. G. Kitton, 1/12/1888, DHM.
17. See G. A. Sala, *The Life and Adventures of G. A. Sala*, 1895, I, 172–73, for the origin of this story and John Sutherland, "JM," DSA 13, 244 and 258 note; CD to JM, 10/27/1835, P 1, 81–84.
18. Samuel Ellis, *William Henry Harrison and His Friends*, 1911, I, 99, 121, 225.
19. Sala, *Gentleman's Magazine* (1878). Quoted in Michael Wynn Jones, *George Cruikshank, His Life and London*, 1978, 43; Blanchard Jerrold, *The Life of George Cruikshank*, 1898, 109, 47–73; John Wardropper, *The Caricatures of George Cruikshank*, 1978, 8; Kitton, *CD and His Illustrators*, 1899, 4; they had probably met in the summer of 1835. See WHA to Dear Sir, 8/30?/1835, HH.
20. Jerrold, 109; CD to JM, 12/26/1835, 12/17/1835, P 1, 112, 108; JTF, 230–31.
21. See Sutherland, 250, and Patten, 31–32, 40–41.
22. CD to RB, 9/17/1836, P 1, 174; P 1, 210 note; T. W. Hill, "Dickens and His 'Ugly Duckling,' " D (1950), 190–96.
23. Patten, 60–62; Arthur Waugh, *A Hundred Years of Publishing: Being the Story of C&H*, 1930, 16–17; "Preface," PP (1847).

24. Patten, 46–60; C&H to CD, 2/12/1836, P 1, 648; CD to CaD, 2/10/1836, P 1, 128–29.
25. Waugh, 20–21, 23; CD to Robert Seymour, 4/14/1836, P 1, 145–46; "Preface," PP (1868), xxiii; for an argument on behalf of Seymour's contributions to PP, see Diane Keitt, "CD and Robert Seymour: The Battle of Wills," D (1986), 2–11.
26. Patten, 65; CD to C&H, 4/27/1836, P 1, 147–48.
27. See Jane R. Cohen, CD and His Original Illustrators, 1980, 53–58.
28. Speech at the Royal Academy dinner, Ray I, 312; KJF, 265.
29. Ray, I, 312; CD to JL, 8/24/1836, P 1, 168; CD to C&H, 8/24/1836, P 1, 169–70; F, I, 1, 71–72.
30. Patten, 66–67.
31. CD to C&H, 11/1/1836, P 1, 189.
32. JD to C&H, 2/14/1837, DHM transcription from Fitzgerald Collection, Rochester.

CHAPTER FOUR
Charley Is My Darling
(1837–1841)

1. CD to JF, 6/20?/1837. P 1, 274.
2. WMT to Edward Fitzgerald, 5/1835, Ray, I, 287; Juston O'Driscoll, Memoir of Daniel Maclise, 1871, 20–22; Christian, 496.
3. Davies, 159–83; CD to JF, 1/8/1845, P 4, 246–47; JF to Mrs. JF, 7/8?/1869, HH; JF, "Diary," 8/1853, 7/15/1849, 2/24/1851, 8/29/1859, 10/12/1860, HH; Henry Rawlins to Whitwell Elwin, 12/20/1879, HH.
4. JF to Mrs. Bennett, 6/20/1827, HH; Miss Bennett to Thomas Chitty, 9/12/1877, HH; extract from playbill, HH; William Andrew Mitchell, Newcastle Mercury (5/17/1828); P 3, 273 note 1.
5. Davies, 10–13; CD to Dr. Belcombe, 2/8/1838, Morgan; JF, "Diary," 8/18/1859, HH.
6. P 1, 205 note 3, 210 note 1.
7. Samuel C. Hall, Memories of Great Men and Women of the Age 1877, 64.
8. WCM.D, 36, 72, 399.
9. P 1, 65 note; WJC, "The Death of Mary Hogarth—Before and After," D (1967), 69; Mary Scott Hogarth to Mary Scott Hogarth II, 5/15/1836, P 1, 689; Mary Scott Hogarth to Mary Scott Hogarth II, 1/26/1837, "New letters of Mary Hogarth and Her Sister Catherine," D (1967), 77.
10. Catherine Hogarth to Mary Scott Hogarth II, 5/30/1857, WJC, "New Letters," D (1967), 71–72, 80; CD to ABC, 5/9/1858, HCD, 354–55.
11. CD to George Thomson, 5/8/1837, P 1, 256; WJC, "New Letters," 80; CD to unknown correspondent, 6/8/1837, P 1, 268; CD to TB, 5/17/1837, P 1, 259.
12. Charles Klingman, "The Dream of CD," Journal of the American Psychoanalytical Association (1970), 783–89; P 1, 629; CD to Richard Johns, 5/31/1837, P 1, 263.
13. P 1, 632; CD to Johns, 5/31/1837, P 1, 263; CD to William Bradbury, 3/3/1839, P 1, 515; CD to CaD, 2/1/1838, P 1, 366.
14. CD to Henry Kolle, 12/10?/1833, P 1, 34; Kathleen Tillotson, ed., OT, 1966, xv–xvi.
15. From the inscription by CD on Mary Hogarth's tombstone, P 1, 259 note 1.
16. OT, LVIII.
17. OT, XXXIX, LIII.
18. Royal A. Gettmann, A Victorian Publisher: A Study of the Bentley Papers, 1960, 15–23, 97–102; CD to RB, 8/17/1836, P 1, 164–65; P 1, 648–49.
19. P 1, 650; CD to Thomas Tegg, 8/11/1836, P 1, 163.
20. CD to RB, 11/2/1836, P 1, 189–90; CD to John Easthope, 11/18/1836, P 1, 195–96; Samuel Ellis, William Henry Harrison and His Friends, 1911, I, 305–8.
21. P 1, 207. CD to RB, 12/5/1836, P 1, 207.

22. CD to RB, 12/5/1836, 1/24/1837, P 1, 207, 227.
23. CD to RB, 6/17?/1837, 9/16/1837, P 1, 272, 308–9.
24. CD to JF, 1/21/1839, P 1, 494; CD to RB, 1/26/1839, P 1, 495–96.
25. CD to TNT, 1/31/1839, P 1, 504.
26. Thomas Powell, "Leaves from My Life," *Frank Leslie's Sunday Magazine* (1877), 98, 105; Christian, 483; CD to CaD, 3/5/1839, P 1, 521; JD to C&H, 12/19/1837, Berg; CD to JF, 11/16/1838, P 1, 454.
27. Powell, 97; Christian, 484; CD to CaD, 3/5/1839, P 1, 517–18; CD to JF, 3/5/1839, P 1, 520.
28. John Greaves, *Dickens at Doughty Street*, 1975, 11–25; P&P, 138–39.
29. CD to James Hall, 11/19/1839, P 1, 603.
30. CD to RB, 3/28/1836, P 1, 392; CD to JF, 3/30/1838, 10/29/1839, P 1, 392, 595; CD to C&H, 2/9/1841, P 2, 206.
31. WCM.D, 1, 493–96; Charles H. Shattuck, *Bulwer and Macready*, 1958, 56–78; CD to TJT, 2/13/1848, P 2, 26–27, 27 note; B. R. Jerman, *The Young Disraeli*, 1960, 192, 280–81.
32. CD to JF ("Louisa" to "Dear Sir"), 7/27/1838, P 1, 422.
33. WCM.D, 1, 262; Hall 265–28?; William Jerdan, *The Autobiography of William Jerdan*, 1853, III, 168–206; Grantley F. Berkeley, *My Life and Recollections*, 1865, III, 185–200; JF to WHA, n.d/1841?, HH; DM to CD, n.d./1841?, HH; DM to "My dear friends and fellow sufferers," n.d./1840?, V&A.
34. CD to Richard Milnes, 2/1/1840, P 2, 16; CD to WSL, JF, TJT, and DM, 2/9–13/1840, P 2, 23–28.
35. CD to JF, 4/29/1841, P 2, 275; see Phillip Bolton, *Dickens Dramatized*, 1986.
36. See John Turpin, "Maclise as a Dickens Illustrator," D (1980), 67–77; DM to CD, 7/16/1841, HH; CD to DM, 8/16/1841. H. R. Woudhuysan, "Sales of Books and Manuscripts," *Times Literary Supplement* (8/14/1987), 888, and Sotheby's "Catalogue," 1987.
37. WCM D, 1, 426, 2, 25–26; P 2, 138 note.
38. See Fred Kaplan, *Thomas Carlyle, A Biography*, 1983, 131–32.
39. P 2, 310 note; F, I, 2, 168–74; R. Shelton Mackenzie, *Life of CD*, 1870, 130; KJF, 8–15; CD to C&H, 6/26/1841, P 2, 312; CD to JF, 6/30/1841, P 2, 315.
40. CD to JF, 7/9/1841, 7/11/1841, P 2, 324, 326–28.
41. CD to JF, 7/9/1841, 7/11/1841, P 2, 324, 326–28; CD to DM, 7/12/1841, P 2, 332.
42. CD to JF, 5?/1840, P 2, 70; see Kaplan, *Sacred Tears, Sentimentality in Victorian Literature*, 1987, 43–50.
43. CD to Edward Chapman, 11/4/1839, P 1, 601–2.
44. CD to John Landseer, 11/5/1841, P 2, 418.
45. OCS, LXXII.
46. CD to WCM, 1/6/1841, P2, 180; CD to JF, 1/8?/1841, P 2, 181–82.
47. CD to Mrs. George Hogarth, 10/24/1841, P 2, 408; CD to JF, 10/25/1841, 10/?/1841, P 2, 410–11.

CHAPTER FIVE
The Emperor of Cheerfulness
(1842–1844)

1. CD to TB, 5/1/1842, P 3, 227; CD to TM, 1/31/1842, P 3, 43; CD to DM, 1/2/1842, P 3, 8; CD to T.C. Grattan, 1/22/1842, P 3, 16; AN, 73.
2. AN, 60; CD to JF, 3/22/1842, 7/14/1839, P 3, 165, P 1, 564; CD to WCM, 8/10/1840, P 2, 113.
3. WJC, "Dickens's Insurance Policies," D (1955), 133–37; CD to C&H, 1/1/1842, P 3, 1–2; CD to Joseph Lunn, 11/15/1841, P 2, 421.

4. CD to Washington Irving, 4/21/1841, P 2, 267; CD to Lewis Gaylord Clark, 9/28/1841, 12/1841, P 2, 394, 445; Sidney P. Moss, *CD's Quarrel with America*, 1984, 82–87.

5. P 3, 49 note 5; JTF, 127–29; CD to JF, 1/29/1842, P 3, 33.

6. CD to JF, 2/17/1842, P 3, 71; CD to DM, 2/27/1842, P 3, 94; CD to TB, 5/1/1842, P 3, 225; "Diary of Levi Lincoln Newton," 2/5/1842, Newton family papers, American Antiquarian Society.

7. KJF, 21–22, 24–25.

8. CD to WCM, 8/24/1841, P 2, 368; CD to Jonathan Chapman, 2/22/1842, P 3, 76–77; CD to John S. Bartlett, 2/24/1842, P 3, 79.

9. CD to JF, 3/22–23/1842, P 3, 165.

10. Edward Wagenknecht, "Dickens in Longfellow's Letters and Journals," D (1955), 8; E. Lattimer, "A Girl's Recollection of Dickens," *Lippincott's Monthly Magazine*, VII, 1893, 338; CD to JF, 4/24/1842, P 3, 204–5.

11. Sam Ward to HWL, 2/22/1842, Wagenknecht, 10; CCF to Henry R. Cleveland, 1/24/1842, Wagenknecht, 10; CD to JF, 2/17/1842, P 3, 69.

12. KJF, 397; Lattimer, 338–39; *The Journal of Richard Henry Dana*, ed. Robert F. Lucid, 1968, I, 56–59; P 3, 31 note 2; Richard Henry Dana to William Cullen Bryant, 2/5/1842, Wagenknecht, 9.

13. CD to Bryant, 2/14/1842, P 3, 58–59; CD to WCM, 2/22/1842, P 3, 160; CD to JF, 2/28/1842, P 3, 96; P 3, 59 note 2; George Washington Putnam, "Four Months with CD . . . By his Secretary," *Atlantic Monthly*, XXVI (1870), 478, 588–89; N. C. Peyrouten, "Mr. 'Q', Dickens's American Secretary," D (1963), 156–59.

14. CD to JF, 2/17/1842, 2/28/1852, 3/17/1842, P 3, 70, 96, 138; KJF, 32, 28–29; Julia Ward Howe, *Reminiscences, 1819–1899* (1899), 27; CD to Lady Holland, 3/22/1842, P 3, 150.

15. CD to Albany Fonblanque, 3/12/1842, P 3, 119–20; CD to JF, 3/6/1842, 3/13/1842, 3/28/1842, P 3, 100, 170, 126.

16. CD to Fonblanque, 3/12/1842, P 3, 117; CD to JF, 3/15/1842, P 3, 133; TC to John Carlyle, 6/20/1839, *The Letters of Thomas and Jane Welsh Carlyle*, ed. KJF and Richard Sanders, 1985, XI, 138.

17. CD to JF, 3/15/1842, P 3, 134; CD to David Colden, 3/10/1842, P 3, 111; CD to Fonblanque, 3/12/1842, P 3, 118.

18. CD to JF, 2/21/1842, P 3, 140–41; CD to Lord Brougham, 2/22/1842, P 3, 145; CD to Charles Lanman, 2/5/1868, N 3, 616–17.

19. CD to JF, 4/15/1842, P 3, 192–94; *AN*, 302.

20. *AN*, 216.

21. CD to JF, 4/24/1842, P 3, 205, 208; *AN*, 225, 228, 231.

22. CD to JF, 5/26/1842, P 3, 245–47.

23. *AN*, 243–44; CD to JF, 4/26/1842, P 3, 210–11; CD to Charles Sumner, 5/16/1842, P 3, 239.

24. CD to Sumner, 5/16/1842, P 3, 239; *AN*, 245.

25. CD to Frederick Granville, 10/20/1842, P 3, 354; CD to Fonblanque, P 3, 120; CD to JF, 5/26/1842, P 3, 248.

26. See PC, "Dickens and the Prison Governor George Laval Chesterton," D (1961), 11–26.

27. CD to Colden, 3/10/1842, P 3, 111; PC, *Dickens and Crime*, 1962, 1968, 133–39.

28. CD to the Editor of the *Morning Chronicle*, 7/25/1842, P 3, 278–85.

29. CD to Charles Smithson, 2/9?/1841, P 2, 300; Samuel C. Hall, *Memories of Great Men and Women of the Age*, 1877, 404; Grantley F. Berkeley, *My Life and Recollections, 1865*, III, 201–31; P 1, 414 note; CD to TM, 7/22/1843, P 3, 525.

30. CD to Brougham, 9/24/1843, P 3, 570; PC, "Dickens and the Ragged Schools," D (1959), 95; CD to ABC, 9/16/1843, P 3, 564; "A Sleep to Startle Us" (HW, 3/13/1852), *MP*, 308–16.

31. CD to Charles Molloy, 12/28/1839, P 1, 624.
32. Diana Orton, *Made of Gold, A Biography of Angela Burdett Coutts*, 1980, 111–31; Edna Healy, *Lady Unknown, The Life of Angela Burdett Coutts*, 1978, 83–114; CD to JF, 9/24/1843, P 3, 573; CD to ABC, 2/23/1843, P 3, 533.
33. CD to ABC, 9/16/1843, P 3, 564; Norris Pope, *Dickens and Charity*, 1978, 152–99; CD to Macvey Napier, 9/16/1843, P 3, 565.
34. PC, *Dickens and Crime*, 16–26; CD to James Kay-Shuttleworth, 3/28/1846, P 4, 527.
35. CD to ABC, 9/24/1843, P 3, 572.
36. CD to W. H. Prescott, 7/31/1842, P 3, 295; CD Jr, 8; CD to Mrs. WCM, 7/4/1842, P 3, 255; CD to TB, 7/11/1842, P 3, 264; *Letters of Thomas Hood*, ed. Peter Morgan, 1973, 486 Quoted in P 3, 264 note 3.
37. CD to H. P. Smith, 7/14/1842, P 3, 270; CD to JF, 8/31/1842, P 3, 312; CD to CCF, 9/1/1842, P 3, 315; CD to WHA, 9/14/1842, P 3, 323; N. C. Peyrouton, "Some Boston Abolitionists on Boz, A Lost American Note," D (1964), 20–26.
38. *Journals of R. W. Emerson*, ed. W. H. Gilman and J. E. Parons, VIII, 222. Quoted in P 3, 271 note 4; Wagenknecht, 11; CD to HWL, 9/28/1842, P 3, 334.
39. HWL to JF, 5/8/1845, P 3, 335 note 4.
40. WCM.R, 509; Francis Crew, "A Dickens Dinner Party," *Bulletin of the John Rylands Library*, 36 (1953–54), 13; Fred Kaplan, "Dickens Mixed the Salad: Henry Rawlins' Memoir of JF," *Cahiers Victoriens & Edouardiens*, ed. Sylvere Monod, 1984, 97–105; S. M. Ellis, "Mrs. Touchet," D (1932), 184.
41. DM to JF, n.d./1846, V&A; CD to WCM, 6/9/1843, P 3, 505; Pietr van der Merwe, *The Spectacular Career of Clarkson Stanfield, 1793–1867*, 1979, 19; CD to TC, 10/26/1842, P 3, 357; Arthur A. Adrien, *ML, First Editor of Punch*, 1966, 110–137.
42. CD Jr, 11; Jane Carlyle, *Letters to Her Family*, ed. Leonard Huxley, 1924, 170–71; WMT to Mrs. WMT, 5/3/1843, Ray, II, 110.
43. CD to ABC, 11/12/1844, P 3, 367; CD to CCF, 9/1/1843, P 3, 550; CD to JF, 8/15/1843, P 3, 541.
44. CD to JF, 6/28/1843, P 3, 516–17.
45. CD to TM, 9/28/1843, P 3, 575–76; CD to John Wilson, 11/24/1843, P 3, 601.
46. CD to CCF, 9/1/1843, P 3, 551; CD to Prescott, 11/10/1843, P 3, 597; CD to Mrs. FL, 3/8/1855, TEX; P 3, 487; CD to Charles Smithson, 5/10/1843, P 3, 487.
47. CD to FB, 9/6/1843, CHM.
48. CD to Mrs. George Hogarth, 5/8/1843, P 3, 483; CD to HWL, 12/29/1842, P 3, 409; *MC*, 832.

CHAPTER SIX
An Angelic Nature
(1844–1846)

1. CD to D. M. Moir, 5/29/1843, P 3, 493; CD to GHL, 8/11/1847, P 5, 147; CD to JF, 8/29?/1843, P 3, 547.
2. CD to Thomas Powell, 3/2/1845, P 4, 346; P 2, 199 note; WJC, " 'Who was the Lady?' Mrs. Christian's Reminiscences of Dickens," D (1964), 68–77; Christian, 484–85, 491.
3. CD to JF, 5/12–17?/1845, P 4, 310; CD to Frances Colden, 2/14/1842, 4/29/1842, P 3, 80, 219–20; CD to David Colden, 4/4/1842, P 3, 183.
4. CD to CaD, 2/26/1844, P 4, 52; KJF, 56–7; CD to TJT, 2/28/1844, P 4, 54–56.
5. P 3, 446 note 2, note 4; CD to CaD, 2/25/1844, P 4, 51; P 4, 54 note 4.
6. CD to TJT, 2/28/1854, 3/11/1854, P 4, 55, 69; CD to FB, 3/1/1844, P 4, 56–57; CD to Powell, 3/2/1844, P 4, 61; CD to T. E. Weller, 3/1/1844, P 4, 58; P 3, 69.
7. CD to TJT, 3/11/1844, P 4, 69–70.

8. CD to TJT, 3/11/1844, P 4, 70; CD to WCM, 10/17/1845, P 4, 406.

9. WJC, " 'Old Nick' at Devonshire Terrace: Dickens Through French Eyes in 1843," D (1963), 142–43.

10. P 3, 472–73 notes 1, 3; CD to JF, 11/1/1843, P 3, 587–88.

11. Patten, 140; CD to TM, 12/4/1843, P 3, 604–5; P 4, 691; CD to B&E, 5/8/1844, P 4, 121–23.

12. P 4, 147 note 1; F, I, 360.

13. F, 1, 362; CD to Count Alfred D'Orsay, 8/7/1844, P 4, 166; see P 4, 155 note 1, and PI, 39–63; CD to JF, 7/14?/1844, P 4, 155.

14. CD to JF, 8/3/1844, P 4, 166; CD to DM, 7/22/1844, P 4, 158–60.

15. CD to D'Orsay, 8/7/1844, P 4, 169–70.

16. TC to JF, 8/10–11?/1844, P 4, 174; CD to TM, 8/12/1844, P 4, 178; P 4, 188.

17. CD to FD, 7/22/1844, P 4, 158; CD to CaD, 9/7/1844, P 4, 192; CD to JF, 9/10?/1844, 10/8/1844, P 4, 193, 199; CD to TM, 8/12/1844, P 4, 176–77.

18. CD to JF, 9/20?/1844, P 4, 196–97.

19. CD to FD, 12/30/1843, P 3, 617; CD to Charles Mackay, 12/19/1843, P 3, 610; CD to ET, 12?/1842–2/1843, P 3, 449; CD to CCF, 3/2/1843, P 3, 455–56.

20. See Fred Kaplan, Dickens and Mesmerism: The Hidden Springs of Fiction, 1975.

21. CD to JF, 10/6 or 8?/1844, 10/15?/1844, P 4, 199–201; CD to FB, 12/6?/1844, DHM; CD to LB, 11/20/1844, P 4, 224; CD to TM, 11/5/1844, P 4, 211.

22. CD to JF, 10/15/1844, 11/1 or 2?/1844, 11/3/1844, P 4, 201, 209–10; CD to TM, 11/5/1844, P 4, 211.

23. CD to JF, 11/12/1844, P 4, 216–17; CD to DJ, 11/16/1844, P 4, 219–20; PI, 131, 140; CD to CaD, 11/23/1844, P 4, 228.

24. CD to CaD, 12/2/1844, P 4, 234–35; DM to CaD, 12/8/1844. Quoted in KJF, "Two Sketches by Maclise: The Dickens Children and the Chimes Reading," Dickens Studies, II (1966), 13; CD to FB, 12/6/1844, DHM.

25. CD to JF, 12/30–31/1844, 1/1/1845, P 4, 244.

26. CD to ER, 12/26/1844, P 4, 243; CD to J. S. Le Fanu, 11/24/1869, N 3, 752–53.

27. CD to Dr. R. H. Collyer, 1/27/1842, P 3, 23.

28. CD to JF, 4/2/1842, P 3, 180; WCM.D II, 179–80.

29. CD to Le Fanu, 11/24/1869, N 3, 752–53; CD to ER, 1/25/1845, P 4, 219.

30. CD to ER, 1/27/1845, 2/10/1845, 2/23/1845, 10/23/1857, P 4, 253, 264, 273, Berg; CD to CaD, 12/5/1863, MM, 227–29.

31. CD to TM, 2/22/1845, P 4, 269–71; CD to ER, 2/23/1845, P 4, 272–73; CD to LB, 5/9/1845, P 4, 303.

32. CD to JF, 2/11/1845, 1/31?/1845, 5/12/1845, P 4, 266, 257, 309; CD to LB, 5/9/1845, P 4, 302; PI, 168–76; CD to GH, 2/4/1845, P 4, 261; CD to ABC, 3/18/1845, P 4, 280; CD to Angus Fletcher, 3/26/1845, P 4, 288.

33. CD to D'Orsay, 3/18/1845, P 4, 283–84; CD to JF, 3/9/1845, P 4, 277. See Leonee Ormond, "Dickens and Painting," D (1984), 3–25, and Richard Lettis, "Dickens and Art," DSA 14, 93–146.

34. CD to Charles Bodenham, 3/24/1845, P 4, 286; CD to Le Fanu, 11/24/1869, N 3, 752–53.

35. CD to Fletcher, 3/26/1845, P 4, 288; CD to Lord Robertson, 4/28/1845, P 4, 301; CD to CaD, 12/5/53, MM, 225–29.

36. CD to LB, 5/9/1845, P 4, 302–3; CD to TB, 5/20/1845, P 4, 311; CD to Thomas Chapman, 4/10/1845, P 4, 292.

37. CD to JF, 4/13/1845, 6/15/1845, P 4, 295, 320–22; P 4, 317–18 note 4; CD to ER, 6/29/1845, P 4, 324–25.

38. CD to D'Orsay, 7/5/1845, P 4, 325; CD to DJ, 7/9/1845, P 4, 329; CD to ER, 7/19/1845, P 4, 324; DM to JF, 4/1/1847, n.d./1845?, V&A; JF to WHA, 10?/1845?, HH; CD to ABC, 9/17/1845, P 4, 380.

39. CD to CS, 7/9/1845, P 4, 334; P&P, 105–10; CD to TJT, 7/28/1845, P 4, 342; CD to WCM,

8/7/1845, P 4, 343; Blanchard Jerrold, "JF," *Gentleman's Magazine*, NS. XVI (1876), 31–15; CD to Mrs. ER, 9/27/1845, P 4, 391, P 4, 388 note 2.

40. CD to AD, 9/8/1845 P 4, 372; CD to John Willmott, 9/10?/1845, P 4, 376; CD to WCM, 9/3/1845, P 4, 382; CD to Mrs. ER, 9/27/1845, P 4, 387–89; CD to Powell, 9/29/1845, P 4, 392.

41. CD to JF, 7/1845, P 4, 327–28.

42. CD to TM, 7/25/1845, 10/20/1845, P 4, 336, 410–11.

43. CD to TM, 10/20/1845, P 4, 411–12; WCM.D II, 307, 309.

44. CD to B&E, 11/3/1845, P 4, 423–24.

45. CD to Robertson, 1/17/1846, P 4, 474.

46. CD to TB, 11/4/1845 P 4, 424.

47. CD to JF, 11/1/1845, P 4, 423; CD to B&E, 11/3/1845, 11/6/1845, 11/7/1845, P 4, 423–24, 426–27, 431; CD to TB, 11/4/1845, P 4, 424; CD to Julian Harney, ?/4/1845, P 4, 425; CD to Macvey Napier, 11/10/1845, P 4, 433.

48. JD to TB, 12/20/1845, DHM

49. CD to J. H. Stocqueler, 12/1–4?/1845, P 4, 446; CD to Joseph Paxton, 1/16/1846, P 4, 473.

50. P&P. 142–43.

51. WMT to Mrs. BP, 7/7/1840, Ray I, 454; *Daily News*, 2/28/1846, quoted in PC, *Dickens and Crime*, 1962, 226; CD to the editors of the *Morning Chronicle*, 7/21/1840, 7/26/1840, P 2, 85, 90–91; CD to Napier, 7/28/1845, P 4, 340–41.

52. CD to WFC, 12/29/1840, P 5, 683; "Lying Awake," HW (10/30/1852), *RP*, 434.

53. P 4, 478 notes 1 and 3; WCM.D II, 321; CD to B&E, 1/30/1845, P 4, 485.

54. CD to JF, 10/26–29/1845, 4/17?/1845, P 4, 648, 537–38; CD to Stocqueler, 2/24/1846, P 4, 504; CD to Robertson, 2/27/1846, P 4, 508; CD to Mrs. ER, 4/17/1846, P 4, 534.

CHAPTER SEVEN
As My Father Would Observe
(1846–1849)

1. P 4, 532 notes 1, 2; CD to Mrs. ER, 4/17/1846, P 4, 534.

2. CD to JF, 11/30?/1846, P 4, 669; CD to LB, 5/26?/1846, P 4, 552.

3. CD to JF, 6/7?/1846, 6/13–14?/1846, 6/22/1846, P 4, 558, 560–61, 568; CD to DM, 6/14/1846, P 4, 561–62; CD to FD, 6/15/1845, P 4, 562–64; CD to DJ, 6/16/1846, P 4, 565–66.

4. CD to ABC, 6/25/1846, P 4, 569–70; CD to JF, 6/28?/1846, P 4, 573.

5. See John Butt and Kathleen Tillotson, *Dickens at Work*, 1957, 90–113; CD to JF, 1/17?/1841, 7/5/1846, P 2, 188, P 4, 579; CD to H. P. Smith, 7/9/1846, P 5, 582.

6. CD to JF, 6/25/1846, P 4, 571–72.

7. CD to JF, 8/30/1846, 6/28?/1846, 7/18/1846, 9/20/1846, P 4, 614, 573, 586, 622–23.

8. CD to JF, 9/26/1846, 11/30?/1846, P 4, 625–27, 670.

9. CD to JF, 8/30/1846, P 4, 612–13.

10. CD to JF, 9/6?/1846, 10/3/1846, 10/11/1846, 10/18/1846, 10/20?/1846, P 4, 618–19, 627, 631, 637–38; CD to TM, 9/24/1846, P 4, 624; CD to ABC, 10/5/1846, P 4, 630; CD to ER, 10/12/1846, P 4, 635.

11. CD to JF, 8/2/1846, 8/9–10/1846, P 4, 594, 601; CD to DJ, 10/24/1846, P 4, 644; CD to WCM, 10/24/1846, P 4, 646.

12. CD to ER, 8/20/1846, 10/12/1846, 3/24/1847, P 4, 608, 636, P 5, 41; CD to WCM, 10/24/1846, P 4, 647.

13. CD to Count Alfred D'Orsay, 8/5/1846, P 4, 597.

14. CD to ER, 3/24/1847, P 5, 43; extracts from Richard Watson's diary from "Sidelight on a Great Friendship," D (1950), 16–21.

15. CD to JF, 7/25–26/1846, 8/24–25/1846, 10/11/1846, P 4, 591–92, also 591, note 3, 633, 610; CD to ER, 8/17/1846, 8/20/1846, P 4, 604, 608; CD to DJ, 10/21/1846, P 4, 642.
16. D (1950), 18; CD to JF, 10/11/1846, 9/20?/1846, 10/26–29/1846, P 4, 631, 650, 622.
17. CD to WCM, 10/24/1846, P 4, 646; CD to JF, 11/13/1846, 11/15/1846, P 4, 656–57; CD to William Haldimand, 11/27/1846, P 4, 664–66; CD to Watson, 11/27/1846, P 4, 666–67.
18. CD to JF, 11/30?/1846, P 4, 668–69; CD to LA 1/2/1847, P 5, 2; CD to Haldimand, 11/27/1846, P 4, 665.
19. "Travelling Abroad," UT, 64; "Lying Awake," RP, 436; F, 1, 513.
20. CD to Edmund B. Green, 2/14/1842, P 3, 61; CD to Amedee Pichot, 4/10/1845, P 4, 293; CD to JF, 11/4/1846, P 4, 653; Alan Horsman, "Introduction," DS (1974); PC, "Dickens's Autobiographical Fragment and DC," Cahiers Victoriens & Edouardians, ed. Sylvere Monod, 1984, 87–95.
21. PC, 89.
22. CD to ABC, 1/18/1847, P 5, 9.
23. CD to JF, 12/6/1846, P 4, 675–76; CD to ER, 1/22/1847, 3/24/1847, P 5, 11, 42.
24. CD to LB, 1/27/1847, P 5, 13, 15; F, 1, 520–1; DM to JF, 1/13/1847, V&A; CD to ET, 1/28/1847, P 5, 19.
25. CD to CaD, 12/21–22/1846, 2/20/1847, P 4, 681–82, P 5, 31; CD to ER, 3/24/1847, P 5, 41.
26. CD to Mrs. FL, 3/8/1865, TEX.
27. CD to H. K. Browne, 3/15/1847, P 5, 36; CD to ER, 3/24/1847, P 5, 41.
28. CD to JF, 4/9/1847, 12/1847, P 5, 55, 218; CD to ER, 3/24/1847, P 5, 41–43; CD to FB, 3/31/1848, DHM.
29. DM to JF, ?/1846, ?/1848, ?/1849, 12/1850, V&A; CD to ER, 3/24/1847, P 5, 43; CD to FB, 5/24/1847?, DHM; CD to JF, 1/7/1848, P 5, 225.
30. DM to JF, 6/21/1849?, V&A; CD to FB, 5/24/1847?, DHM; Lynn Linton, My Literary Reminiscences of Dickens, Thackeray, George Eliot, Etc, 1899, 55–56; Mrs. Gaskell quoted in P 5, 497 note 3; WCM.D II, 376.
31. P 5, 227 note 1.
32. Ray II, 293–308; WCM.D II, 368; CD to JF, 6/9/1847, P 5, 82; WMT to Mrs. Carmichael-Smyth, 7/2/1847, Ray II, 308–9; CD to WMT, 3/30/1848, P 5, 267.
33. CD to JF, 9/2/1847, P 5, 156; CD to ML, 3/25/1849, P 5, 514; CD to CaD, 3/27/1848, P 5, 265.
34. CD to HA, 4/26/1847, P 5, 60; Linton, 59.
35. P 5, 698–99, 703–5; CD to ABC, 11/3/1847, P 5, 183.
36. CD to W. B. Hodgson, 6/4/1847, P 5, 77; Mary Cowden Clarke, Recollections of Writers, 1878, 321–22.
37. CD to Hodgson, 6/12/1847, P 5, 87–88; Davies, 14–24; P 5, 77 note 3; CD to the "Friends of LH," 6/23/1847, P 5, 98 and notes 1, 3; Kathleen Tillotson, "Dickens and a Story by John Poole," D (1956), 69–70.
38. CD to TJT, 6/19/1847, 7/10/1847, P 5, 95, 123.
39. CD to HCA, 7/30/1847, P 5, 134; CD to GHL, 8/11/1847, P 5, 148; CD to TM, 8/8/1847, P 5, 144–45; P 5, 133 note 2.
40. CD to GHL, 8/11/1847, P 5, 148; CD to TM, 8/8/1847, P 5, 145; P 5, "Appendix E," 700–702; CD to JF, 9/19/1847, P 5, 165; James Sheridan Knowles to WSL, 6/2/1847, V&A.
41. CD to Spencer Lyttleton, 12/10/1847, P 5, 207; CD to AD, 1/1/1848, P 5, 221; CD to GH, 12/30/1847, P 5, 217; CD to JF, 12/30/1847, P 5, 216.
42. See Charles Shattuck, Bulwer and Macready, 1958; KJF, 95–96.
43. CD to TB, 5/10/1848, P 5, 302; CD to FB, 5/9/1848, P 5, 302; CD to ABC, 5/24/1848, P 5, 317.
44. Clarke, 295–341; CD to FB, 5/1/1848, DHM; DM to JF, ?/1848, V&A.
45. Clarke, 305–25.

46. CD to Mrs. Cowden Clarke, 7/22/1848, P 5, 374; CD to FB, 3/31/1848, DHM.
47. CD to FB, 3/31/1848, 5/3/1848, DHM; CD to HB, 9/5/1848, 10/9/1848, DHM.
48. CD to FB, 5/3/1848, DHM; MD, 114; CD to ABC, 7/25/1848. P 5, 376; CD to TB, 7/28/1848. P 5, 379; CD to CaD, 9/1/1848, P 5, 399; "A Child's Dream of a Star," HW (April 1850), *RP*, 387–90; CD to HB, 9/5/1848, 1/31/1849, DHM, P 5, 482; CD to JL, 9/6/1848, P 5, 402.
49. CD to JF, 9/25?/1848. P 5, 414; CD to LW, 10/5/1848, P 5, 419; CD to William Bradbury, 12/1/1848, P 5, 451.
50. CD to Earl of Carlisle, 1/2/1849, P 5, 466–67.
51. CD to CaD, 1/8/1849, P 5, 470; CD to JF, 1/12/1849, P 5, 474; P 5, 473 note 1 and F, II, 6, 101.
52. CD to Samuel Rogers, 2/18/1849, P 5, 498; CD to ML, 2/?/1849, P 5, 496; CD to ABC, 2/27/1849, P 5, 502; CD to JF, 2/13/1849, 2/23/1849, 2/26/1849, 4/19?/1849, 3?/1849, P 5, 498, 500, 502, 526, 518; CD to B&E, 3/21/1849, P 5, 511.
53. CD to the Committee for Mr. Giles's Testimonial, 2/12/1849, P 5, 474; CD to HB, 1/31/1849, P 5, 482; CD to LA, 2/1/1849, P 5, 483; CD to JL, 3/9/1849, P 5, 506.
54. CD to JF, 4/19?/1849, 6/6/1849, 6/21/1849, 7/10/1849, P 5, 526, 551, 557, 569; CD to FE, 7/4/1849, P 5, 563.
55. CD to JF, 7/?/1849, P 5, 580; CD to CaD, 7/16/1849, P 5, 573.
56. CD to JF, 7/28/1849 8/?/1849, 8/4–5/1849, 9/23/1849, P 5, 583, 588 and notes 1 and 2, 599, 611; P 5, 606 note 2; CD to TB, 7/18/1849, P 5, 573–74; JL to ML, 7?/1849, DHM; P 5, 588 note 1, 2; P 5, 597 note 1.
57. CD to JF, 9/24/1849, 9/26/1849. P 5, 613, 615; CD to FE, 9/25/1849, 9/27/1849, P 5, 614, 616; CD to ML, 9/26/1849, P 5, 615–16.
58. CD to CaD, 7/16/1849 P 5, 573; CD to TB, 7/18/1849, P 5, 574; CD to William Bradbury, 7/28/1849, P 5, 583; CD to ABC, 8/15/1849, P 5, 594; CD to JF, 8/?/1849, P 5, 605; CD to JL, 10/5/1849, P 5, 620.

CHAPTER EIGHT
No Need for Rest
(1849–1853)

1. CD to JF, 10/21/1850, N 2, 240; "Preface" to *DC*, October 1850; CD to MB, 10/15/1850, Morgan; CD to WHW, 9/17/1850, N 2, 234; CD to Dr. William Brown, 9/22/1850, Morgan; CD to JF, 10/23/1850, N 2, 240.
2. DD, 24.
3. *DC*, VIII, IX, XIII; MS. DHM.
4. *DC*, XVIII; XLII; CD to Dr. Stone, 2/2/1851, N 2, 267–70.
5. CD to MB, 1/15/1851, Morgan.
6. *DC*, XLVIII, LX.
7. CD to LW, 3/9/1851, HH; CD to HA, 3/12/1851, Morgan.
8. CD to TB, 3/31/1851, N 2, 293–94, MM, 150–51.
9. CD to CaD, 3/26/1851, MM, 152–53; CD to JF, 3/31/1851, N 2, 293; CD to TM, 4/19/1851, TEX.
10. CD to CaD, 4/4/1851, MM, 153–54; KJF, 122; F, II, 6, 115.
11. F, II, 6, 115–16; KJF, 124; CD to CaD, 4/15/1851, MM, 155–56; CD to FE, 4/17/1851, Berg; CD to RHH, 4/17/1851, Yale; MD, 38.
12. CD to ABC, 2/4/1850, 4/12/1852, HCD, 165, 167–68; CD to ABC, 2/4/1850, 7/30/1850, Morgan.
13. CD to ABC, 2/4/1851, HCD, 164.
14. CD to ABC, 11/19/1852, 9/23/1852, 2/12/1850, 7/31/1850, 3/23/1851, HCD, 215, 208, 171, 182–83.

15. CD to ABC, 4/18/1852, HCD, 200; CD to HA, 2/27/1850, 1/21/1852, Morgan.

16. CD to ABC, 4/18/1852, 1/7/1853, HCD, 198–99, 219.

17. CD to ABC, 3/24/1849, P 5, 513; CD to Cornelius Matthews, 3/22/1849, P 5, 512; CD to ABC, 1/13/1852, 4/12/1850, HCD, 192–93, 167–68; CD to HA, 5/12/1850, Morgan.

18. CD to JF, 8/1849, 9/22/1849, 7/19/1849, P 5, 580, 611, 621–23; P 5, 622 note 3; Anne Lohrli, *Household Words, Table of Contents, List of Contributors, and Their Contributions*, 1973.

19. CD to WHW, 7/12/1850, 1/22/1850, N 2, 222, 200; Anne Lohrli, "Wife to Mr. Wills," D (1985), 23–25; CD to ABC, 2/2/1850, HCD, 164; CD to HA, 3/21/1850, Morgan; CD to EG, 12/17/1850, Berg.

20. Patten, 240; WSL to Elizabeth Landor, 5/1851, HH; WSL to JF, 8/3/1850, HH; CD to EG, 2/5/1850, Berg.

21. CD to James White, 7/13/1850, N 2, 223; Patten, 240–46; CD to JF, 3/14/1850, N 2, 210; HW (4/23/1853), 169–75; CD to ABC, 4/12/1852, Morgan.

22. CD to ABC, 3/17/1852, HCD, 198; CD to Mrs. Catherine Gore, 9/7/1852, Berg.

23. CD to HA, 1/30/1851, 3/12/1851, 7/14/1851, Morgan; CD to ABC, 2/10/1851, Berg; CD to Richard Owen, 5/7/1851, TEX; CD to CaD, 9/11/1851, MM, 156–58.

24. MS. DHM; CD to HA, 10/1/1851, 10/14/1851, 10/17/1851, 11/18/1851, Morgan; CD to ABC, 10/9/1851, 11/17/1851, HCD, 187, 190; MD, 39.

25. CD to L. H. Sigourney, 5/24/1851, Berg; MD, 47.

26. CD to George Putnam, 7/24/1851, N 2, 331; CD to ABC, 6/27/1852, Morgan; CD to FS, 9/8/1851, N 2, 342–43; CD to LW, 3/22/1852, HH; CD to George Beadnell, 5/4/1852, N 2, 391–92; CD to MB, 7/22/1852, N 2, 403.

27. R. R. Madden, *Correspondence of the LB*, 1855, I, 195–96, 205; CD to LB, 4/14/1849, P 5, 524–25.

28. CD to Richard Milnes, 5/7/1849, P 5, 535; CD to Jane Brookfield, 5/4/1849, Ray II, 532; CD to CaD, 8/8/1852, MM, 149–50. CD to JF, 8/8/1852, N 2, 408.

29. DM to JF, 12/1850, n.d 1851?, V&A; JF to John Chapman, 9/1/1851, Yale; CD to HMB, 11/3/1852, Morgan.

30. CD to TM, 2/6/1851, HH; CD to TB, 7/22/1852, N 2, 402; CD to GC, 4/25/1851, N 2, 301.

31. CD to EBL, 1/24/1851, 2/10/1851, N 2, 271–72; CD to ML, 2/22/1850, HH; CD to LW, 7/1/1851, N 2, 326–27; CD to CaD, 6/24/1850, MM, 148, 139–40.

32. WCM.D 2, 495–96; Alan S. Downer, *The Eminent Tragedian*, WMC, 1966, 200–201; CD to WCM, 2/27/1851, N 2, 274–75.

33. WCM.D 2, 493; KJF, 114–15, 117; quoted from John Coleman, *Fifty Years of an Actor's Life*, 1904; CD to HMB, 11/3/1852, Morgan.

34. MB, *Her Book*, 1902, 230–32; Tennyson, "To Mary Boyle"; CD to JF, 11/30/1849, P 5, 662; CD to MB, 12/3/1849, P 5, 665, 709; also 665, notes 4 and 5.

35. Lehmann, 181–82.

36. CD to DM, 9/16/1850, Yale; CD to MB, 9/24/1850, Morgan; MB, *Her Book*, 233–34; CD to EBL, 11/3/1850, N 2, 242–43; CD to LW, 11/28/1850, HH; CD to LW, 11/23/1850, N 2, 246–47; CD to MB, 12/2/1850, Morgan.

37. CD to MB, 2/21/1851, N 2, 273–74; MS. DHM; CD to HA, 9/28/1851, 5/21/1851, Morgan; CD to CaD, 10/2/1851, MM, 158–59.

38. WC to EP, 2/9?/1852, 9/?/1851, HH; CD to CaD, 11/13/1851, 9/12/1852, MM, 160–62, 165–66; CD to LW, 7/29/1851, HH; CD to EBL, 2/15/1852, N 2, 377–78; CD to HA, 11/13/1851, 9/13/1851, 2/16/1852, Morgan; CD to DkD, 2/17/1852, N 2, 378–79; WC to HC, 5/12/1852, Morgan.

39. CD to HA, 8/6/1852, Morgan; CD to ABC, 8/20/1852, Morgan; WC to HC, 8/25/1852, Morgan; EG to Marianne Gaskell, 9/2/1852, Gaskell, 197; WC to EP, 2/9?/1852, HH.

40. CD to ABC, 1/13/1853, Morgan.

41. CD to Dr. Brown, 8/1/1852, Morgan; CD to WFC, 12/20/1852, Berg; CD to LW, 5/6/1852, HH; CD to ABC, 8/5/1852, HCD, 204.
42. CD to Augustus Egg, 3/8/1851, Morgan; CD to EBL, 2/4/1852, N 2, 375–76; WC to EP, 2/3/1852, 2/12/1852, 2/12/1852, HH.
43. CD to CaD, 2/12/1852, MM, 165–66; WC to HC, 9/1/1852, 9/9/1852, Morgan.
44. WC to HC, 9/9/1852, 9/23/1852 10/1/1852, Morgan; WC to EP, 9/16/1852, Morgan.
45. CD to HA, 10/4/1852, Morgan; CD to MB, 2/21/1851, N 2, 273–74; CD to JF, 6/1/1851, N 2, 315. CD to DkD, 6/1/1851, N 2, 316.
46. CD to DkD, 9/28/1851, N 2, 346; CD to ABC, 10/9/1851, HCD, 187; CD to MB, 7/22/1852, N 2, 403; CD to ABC, 7/3/1852, Morgan.
47. CD to ABC, 11/18/1852, 3/4/1850, HCD, 166, 215; CD to WC, 12/20/1852, N 2, 435–36.
48. CD to WFC, 12/20/1852, Berg; CD to ABC, 3/5/1853, 4/12/1852, 4/29/1853, Morgan; CD to WHW, 5/30/1853, HH; CD to Lacy Eastlake, 6/11/1853, TEX.
49. CD to WC, 6/30/1853, Morgan; CD to ABC, 7/10/1853, 8/27/1853, HCD, 227, 231–32; CD to Peter Cunningham, 6/24/1853, PH; WC to HC, 7/29/1853, Morgan.

CHAPTER NINE
The Sparkler of Albion
(1853–1855)

1. CD to CaD, 11/21/1853, 10/16/1853, MM, 215–19, 184–85; WC to CC, 11/13/1853, Morgan; CD to GH, 11/25/1853, Berg; CD to ABC, 10/25/1853, HCD, 237–39.
2. WC to HC, 11/25/1853, Morgan; CD to ABC, 10/25/1853, HCD, 237–39.
3. WC to HC, 10/16/1853, Morgan; CD to GH, 11/25/1853, Berg; CD to CaD, 10/20/1853, MM, 189–93.
4. WC to HC, 10/16/1853, 10/28/1853, Morgan; CD to ABC, 10/25/1853, HCD, 237–39; CD to CaD, 10/16/1853, 10/20/1853, MM, 180–85, 186–89.
5. CD to CaD, 10/20/1853, 10/30/1853, MM, 185–93, 199–201; WC to HC, 10/28/1853, Morgan; CD to ABC, 10/25/1853, HCD, 237–39.
6. CD to CaD, 10/28/1853, 11/5/1853, MM, 194–97, 225–29; CD to GH, 11/25/1853, Berg.
7. WC to CW, 10/31/1853, Morgan; WC to EP, 11/4/1853, HH; CD to ABC, 11/13/1853, HCD, 240–43.
8. WC to EP, 11/4/1853, HH; CD to ABC, 11/13/1853, HCD, 240–43; CD to CaD, 11/14/1853, 11/4/1853, MM, 208–14, 207; MS. DHM; WC to CC, 11/13/1853, Morgan.
9. CD to CaD, 11/14/1853, 11/21/1853, MM, 208–14, 215–19; WC to CC, 11/13/1853, Morgan; CD to JET, 11/14/1853, Berg.
10. CD to CaD, 11/21/1853, 11/27/1853, MM, 215–19, 220–24; WC to HC, 11/25/1853, Morgan.
11. CD to ER, 12/4/1853, Berg; CD to CaD, 12/1853, MM, 227–29.
12. CD to ER, 10/23/1857, Berg; CD to JF, 2/1855, N 2, 621.
13. CD to J. S. Cummings, 9/7/1852, N 2, 415.
14. CD to MB, 1/28/1856, N 2, 735–37; CD to MW, 2/10/1855, N 2, 626.
15. BkM, 10.
16. CD to WFC, 1/16/1854, N 2, 535; CD to LW, 1/13/1854, N 2, 533; CD to ABC, 1/23/1854, HCD, 258.
17. CD to ER 12/4/1853, Berg.
18. CD to ABC, 1/23/1854, 4/1/1853, 11/27/1853, HCD, 258, 223–24, 244–45; CD to CaD, 11/27/1853, MM, 220–24; CD to WFC, 11/16/1854, N 2, 536–37; CD to Charles Knight, 3/17/1854, N 2, 548; CD to JF, 1/20/1954, N 2, 537.
19. CD to JF, 1/29/1854, N 2, 538–39; CD, "On Strike," HW, 2/11/1854.
20. CD to Robert Browning, 2/7/1854, N 2, 539; CD to ABC, 2/6/1854, HCD, 260–61; CD to Peter Cunningham, 3/11/1854, N 2, 546; CD to EG, 2/18/1854, 4/21/1854, N 2, 542,

554; CD to ML, 2/20/1854, N 2, 542; CD to JF, 2/18/1854, N 2, 543; CD to WHW, 4/18/1854, N 2, 551–52; EG to JF, 4/23/1854, Gaskell, 281; CD to Henry Cole, 6/17/1854, Morgan; CD to WC, 7/12/1854, N 2, 565–66; CD to JF, 7/14/1854, N 2, 567.

21. CD to JF, 5/15/1854, HH.
22. BkM, 10.
23. WC to CC, 8/31/1854, Morgan; CD to CaD, 7/19/1854, MM, 231–32; CD to EG, 7/31/1854, N 2, 573–74; WC to HC, 7/27/1854, Morgan; CD to WHW, 8/19/1854, N 2, 580–81; CD to JF, 10/1854, N 2, 596.
24. CD to HA, 8/20/1854, Morgan; CD to WHW, 6/22/1854, N 2, 564–65; CD to WC, 7/12/1854, N 2, 565–66; CD to Frances Colden, 8/4/1854, N 2, 575–77; WC to HC, 7/27/1854, Morgan; CD to DkD, 7/5/1856, N 2, 785; CD to ABC, 8/30/1856, N 2, 795.
25. CD to EG, 7/31/1854, N 2, 573–74; WC to HC, 7/27/1854, Morgan; CD to HA, 9/6/1854, Morgan; WC to CC, 8/31/1854, 9/7/1854, Morgan.
26. CD to JF, 9/1854, N 2, 586; MS. DHM; CD to LW, 11/1/1854, N 2, 602–3.
27. CD to FS, 6/23/1853; quoted in MS. DHM.
28. CD to TNT, 1/16/1854, PH; CD to ABC, 3/17/1854, Morgan; J. E. Davis to LH, 3/14/1854, BL; C. M. Wightman to ?, 3/?/1854, NLS; JF to LH, 3/23/1854, BL.
29. Catherine Horne to RHH, 4/4/1853, HH.
30. CD to LH, 6/28/1855, N 2, 675; "LH. A Remonstrance," HW, 12/24/1859, MP, 206–10.
31. CD to WFC, 1/3/1855, N 2, 619–20; CD to GH, 3/11/1856, N 2, 750–51; CD to CaD, 5/9/1856, MM, 248–50; CD to CS, 5/14/1856, Yale.
32. CD to WCM, 11/4/1864, Morgan; CD to JF, 4/1856, N 2, 765; MS. DHM; WMT to Elizabeth Strong, 7/18/1854, Ray II, 379–80.
33. MS. DHM.
34. Yates, 227; CD to ABC, 1/2/1854, 12/26/1854, HCD, 251, 281–82; CD to MB, 1/3/1855, N 2, 616–17.
35. CD to JF, 5/16/1855, N 2, 557; CD to David Laing, 4/15/1854, Yale; CD to Moor, 3/27/1855, N 2, 647.
36. CD to LW, 12/23/1855, N 2, 715; CD to AR, 1/29/1855, 2/26/1855, N 2, 619, 637; CD to Whitwell Elwin, 6/7/1855, N 2, 668; CD to ABC, 5/24/1855, HCD, 302.
37. CD to the inspector of police, 6/15/1855, PH; CD to CS, 6/20/1855, N 2, 673; CD to ABC, 6/19/1855, 6/21/1855, HCD, 305–6.
38. CD to ABC, 2/9/1855, HCD, 290; CD to WHW, 2/9/1855, N 2, 625.
39. CD to MW, 2/10/1855, N 2, 625–26.
40. Slater, 61, 394.
41. CD to MW, 2/15/1855, N 2, 638–39.
42. CD to MW, 2/22/1855, N 2, 633–35.

CHAPTER TEN
Superfluous Fierceness
(1855–1857)

1. CD to EY, 1/2/1856, N 2, 720; RBL to JF, 12/26/1855, HH; CD to CS, 10/19/1855, Yale; CD to WHW, 10/21/1855, N 2, 698–99; CD to HA, 10/28/1855, Morgan.
2. CD to JF, 12/25/1855, N 2, 716; WC to EP, n.d., 1855, HH.
3. CD to WFC, 1/3/1855, N 2, 619–20.
4. CD to ABC, 5/15/1855, 5/11/1855, HCD, 229–301, 298–99.
5. CD to ABC, 6/23/1855, Morgan; KJF, 198, 203; CD to WC, 7/8/1855, N 2, 678.
6. CD to WC, 5/19/1855, N 2, 644.
7. Literary Gazette, 6/23/1855, 395; quoted by KJF, 197; CD to WCM, 3/15/1857, Morgan; CD to Shirley Brooks, 3/11/1858, N 3, 10–11; KJF, 209–14, 225–28, 253–58.

8. WC to HC, 2/14/1855, Morgan; CD to JF, 2?/1855, N 2, 621; CD to GH, 2/16/1855, N 2, 630.
9. CD to WC, 3/4/1855, 5/27/1855, N 2, 637, 647; CD to Henry Morley, 5/19/1855, PH; CD to ABC, 12/11/1854 2/16/1855, Berg, HCD, 230–31.
10. CD to LH, 5/4/1855, N 2, 658; CD to ABC, 5/10/1855, Morgan; CD to LW, 5/21/1855, 9/10/1855, 11/10/1855, HH, N 2, 690; CD to WHW, 9/1/1855, 9/16/1855, HH, N 2, 688; WC to HC, 9/22/1855, Morgan; CD to TB, 8/23/1855, N 2, 686; WC to CW, 8/20/1855, Morgan; CD to Rackes Curtrie, 8/28/1855, N 2, 686.
11. CD to WHW, 3/2/1855, N 2, 728; CD to FS, 1/27/1856, PH; CD to LW, 11/10/1855, HH; CD to MB, 1/28/1856, N 2, 736–37.
12. CD to WC, 6/6/1856, N 2, 777–78; CD to Edward Walford, 10/4/1856, PH; HCA to H. Wulff, 6/18/1857, 3 ed, 94–97; MS. DHM; HCA to C.S.A. Bille, 7/10/1857, Bred, 103.
13. CD to Marguerite Power, 11/25/1855, PH; CD to JF, 11/?/1855, 1/20/1856, 3/?/1856, N 2, 719, 734–35, 754; CD to AEC, 2/10/1856, HCD, 311–13; WC to HC, 3/11/1856, Morgan.
14. CD to CaD, 5/5/1856, DMM. 247–48; CD to MB, 1/28/1856, N 2, 735–37.
15. RBL to JF, 12/26/1855, HH; CD to FS, 1/27/1856, PH; CD to J. T. Gordon, 5/2/1856, Berg.
16. CD to JF, 1/?/1856, N 2, 737–38; CD to AEC, 2/19/1856, HCD, 316; CD to WC, 4/22/1856, N 2, 761–63.
17. CD to JF, 1/11/1856, N 2, 728; WC to HC, 4/5/1856, Morgan; CD to WHW, 4/6/1856, N 2, 755–56; CD to Thomas Fraser, 4/10/1856, Berg; CD to Robert Browning, 4/12/1856, Berg.
18. CD to FS, 10/24/1856, PH; CD to ABC, 10/30/1856, 2/25/1857, Morgan; CD to JF, 2/1855, N 2, 62.
19. CD to JF, 4/7/1856, N 2, 756; CD to DkD, 7/5/1856, N 2, 785.
20. CD to JF, 4/1856, N 2, 765.
21. CD to ABC, 7/15/1856, Morgan; CD to WC, 3/21/1858, N 3, 14; CD to JF, 9/5/1857, N 2, 677–78; JF to CaD, 5/12/1856, P 1, xvii.
22. CD to GH, 3/15/1856, N 2, 751; CD to WHW, 2/9/1855, N 2, 625; CD to ABC, 2/9/1856, HCD, 311–15.
23. CD to WHW, 3/2/1856, N 2, 728; CD to HA, 7/21/1855, 8/12/1855, Morgan.
24. CD to WHW, 11/18/1855, N 2, 708; CD to JF, 11/25/1855, 2/13/1856, N 2, 712, 745; CD to HA, 4/17/1856, Morgan.
25. CD to ABC, 5/13/1856, Morgan; CD to GH, 5/5/1856, N 2, 770; CD to CaD, 5/9/1856, MM, 248–50; CD to Benjamin Webster, 5/9/1856, BL; CD to ABC, 6/1/1856, HCD, 319.
26. CD to ABC, 8/13/1856, HCD, 325–26; WC to HC, 8/19/1856, Morgan.
27. CD to HMB, 8/8/1856, HCD, 325; CD to CaD, 8/25/1856, 9/2/1856, MM, 250–52; CD to WHR, 6/10/1857, N 2, 55–56; CD to JF, 9/1856, N 2, 798; CD to ABC, 9/8/1856, HCD, 326–7; WC to HC, 9/8/1856, Morgan.
28. CD to WHW, 3/6/1856, 3/22/1856, N 2, 749–50, 752; CD to B&E, 3/3/1856, PH.
29. CD to LW, 11/1/1854, N 2, 602–3; See Fred Kaplan, *Sacred Tears*, 1987.
30. CD to ABC, 11/20/1854, Morgan; CD to JF, 4/1856, N 2, 767–68.
31. HW, 6/15/1850.
32. CD to WC, 7/13/1856, Morgan; CD to JF, 8/15/1856, N 2, 797.
33. *Under the Management of CD, His Production of "The Frozen Deep,"* ed. Robert Louis Brannon, 1966, 160.
34. CD to FS, 10/15/1856, PH; CD to HA, 10/15/1856, Morgan; CD to Whitwell Elwin, 10/17/1856, N 2, 807; CD to LW, 10/7/1856, N 2, 803–4; CD to WC, 10/9/1856, N2, 805.
35. CD to DM, 1/14/1856, PH; CD to LW, 10/17/1856, N 2, 803–4; CD to ET, 1/20/1857, N 2, 829; CD to WCM, 12/15/1856, N 2, 815.

36. CD to ABC, 12/9/1856, HCD, 330–31; CD to WHW, 1/2/1857, N 2, 823; WMT to Annie and Harriet Thackeray, 12/3/1856, Ray III, 642–43; CD to CS, 1/1/1857, PH; CD to JET, 1/9/1857, N 2, 825; CD to DM, 7/8/1857, N 2, 859.

37. CD to HMB, 1/2/1856, HCD, 333; CD to MB, 2/7/1857, N 2, 834.

38. CD to WC, 1/10/1856, 2/14/1857, N 2, 825–26, 835; CD to HMB, 1/14/1856, HCD, 333–34; CD to ABC, 1/14/1857, 2/14/1857, Morgan, HCD, 337–38; CD to LW, 1/16/1857, HH; CD to WFC, 1/17/1856, N 2, 827–28; CD to WCM, 2/27/1857, Morgan; CD to FD, 2/5/1857, N 2, 833; FD to CD, 2/7/1857, HH; CD to WHW, 2/7/1857, HH.

39. CD to HA, 2/15/1857, Morgan; CD to FS, 2/18/1857, 2/26/1857, PH; CD to Joseph Paxton, 3/1/1857, N 2, 837–38; CD to LW, 3/8/1857, PH; CD to ABC, 5/22/1857, 4/9/1857, Morgan, HCD, 338–40; CD to Catherine Horne, 5/29/1857, DHM; CD to WC, 5/17/1857, N 2, 847.

40. CD to George Beadnell, 6/5/1857, DHM; CD to JF, 5/7/1857, N 2, 845–46.

41. CD to JF, 6/9/1857, N 2, 854; CD to WHR, 6/10/1857, N 2, 855–56; CD to Blanchard Jerrold, 11/26/1857, N 2, 75–77, Yale.

42. CD to Jerrold, 11/26/1858, N3, 75–76, Yale.

43. CD to AD, 7/11/1857, Berg; CD to WHW, 9/17/1857, HH; CD to W. Hamstead, 10/4/1857, PH.

44. HFD. M 14; HCA to CD, 6/10/1857, Bred, 46; HCA, 7/1/1857, Bred, 76.

45. HCA, 6/28/1857, 6/19/1856, Bred, 70, 59; HCA to Henriette Scavenius, 6/11/1857, Bred, 93; HCA, "A Visit," 1860, Bred, 110; Bred, 127; DD, 22; HCA, 6/15/1857, 6/17/57, 6/21/1857, 8/1/1857, Bred, 53–54, 59–60, 117–18.

46. HCA, 7/4/1857, Bred, 78–80; CD to JF, 7/5/1857, N 2, 859.

47. HCA, 7/12/1857, Bred, 88; Wright, 252–53; CD to WCM, 7/10/1857, Morgan; CD to John Deane, 7/12/1857, N 2, 861.

48. CD to ABC, 7/25/1857, Morgan; CD to AR, 8/3/1857, PH.

49. CD to FS, 8/9/1857, 8/18/857, N 2, 868, PH; Malcolm Morley, "The Theatrical Ternans," D (1958), 161. Much of my information on the Ternan family background has been drawn from Morley's series of ten articles, 9/1958–1/1961.

50. CD to WHW, 8/3/1857, Berg; CD to FS, 8/18/1857, PH.

51. CD to ABC, 9/5/1857, HCD, 347–48; Wright, 244; Malcolm Morley, "The Theatrical Ternans," D (1958), 160–61.

52. CD to ABC, 9/5/1857, HCD, 347–48.

53. CD to JF, 8/1857, N 2, 874; CD to HA, 7/21/1857, 8/28/1857, Morgan.

54. CD to WC, 8/29/1857, N 2, 873; CD to HMB, 9/4/1857, Morgan; CD to HCA, 9/2/1857, N 2, 874–75; CD to ABC, 9/5/1857, HCD, 347–48; Morley, D (1959), 36–37; CD to Angel Hotel, 9/3/1857, DHM.

55. CD to JF, 9/5/1857, N 2, 677–78.

56. CD to JF, 9/1857, N 2, 887–88; CD to FE, 9/6/1857, PH.

57. CD to JF, 10/1857, 9/9?/1857, N 2, 888, 880; CD to ABC, 10/4/1857, HCD, 349–51; CD to GH, 9/12/1857, 9/15/1857, N 2, 882–84.

58. CD to WHW, 9/17/1857, HH; Morley, D (1959), 36; CD to ER, 10/23/1857, Berg; CD to WHW, 9/20/1857, HH.

59. CD to ER, 10/23/1857, Berg; CD to Anne Cornelius, 10/11/1857, N 2, 890.

CHAPTER ELEVEN
My Own Wild Way
(1857–1859)

1. BkM, 87, 18; CD to WCM, 3/15/1858, N 3, 11; CD to LW, 12/7/1857, HH.

2. Wright, 254–55; CD to LW, 12/7/1857, HH.

3. CaD to ABC, 2/1/1858, HCD, 352, CD to ABC, 2/2/1857, HCD, 352–53.
4. CD to WC, 11/1/1857, Morgan; CD to ABC, 11/9/1857, Morgan; CD to John Baldwin Buckstone, 10/13/1857; unpublished letter quoted by Slater, 207.
5. CD to LW, 12/7/1857, HH; CD to RB, 10/5/1857, 3/8/1858, Berg.
6. CD to BP, 11/25/1857, Yale; CD to JF, 1/27/1858, 1/30/1858, N 3, 5.
7. CD to JF, 1/1/1858, N 3, 3; KJF, 246; CD to AR, 12/2/1857, PH.
8. KJF, 251; CD to WC, 3/21/1858, N 3, 14.
9. CD to JF, 9/5/1857, 3?/30/1853, N 2, 677–78, N 3, 15; CD to WCM, 3/15/1858, Morgan.
10. CD to WCM, 3/15/1858, Morgan; CD to LW, 12/7/1857, HH; CD to WC, 3/21/1858, N 3, 14; CD to FE, 3/16/1858, N 3, 11–12.
11. CD to JF, 3/21?/1857, 3/28?/1858, N 3, 13–14.
12. CD to WHW, 4/3/1858, N 3, 15; CD to Mrs. Hogge, 4/14/1858, PH; EY, 99; KJF, 264.
13. CDJr to CD, 5/10/1858, N 3, 25.
14. DD, 96; K.J. Fielding, "CD and His Wife, Fact or Forgery?" *Etudes Anglais* 8 (1955), 212–22; WJC, "Mr. and Mrs. Dickens: The Thomson-Stark Letter," *Notes and Queries* (1960), 145–47; CD to JF, 3/30?/1858, N 3, 15.
15. CD to ABC, 5/9/1858, HCD, 354–56; KJF, 66.
16. CD to ABC, 5/9/1858, HCD, 354–56.
17. CD to CCF, 5/22/1858, DHM; CD to ABC, 5/19/1858, DHM.
18. See David Parker and Michael Slater, "The Gladys Storey Papers," D (1980), 4, 3–16; WMT to Mrs. Carmichael Smyth, 5/26?/1858, Ray IV, 86–87; WMT to James Wilson, 5/1858, Ray IV, 83–84; KJF, "CD and Colin Rae Brown," *Nineteenth-Century Fiction*, VII (1952), 103–10.
19. ML to JF, 5/20/1858, 5/21/1858, Morgan; 5/25/1858, N 3, 22–23.
20. CD to WC, 5/25/1858, 5/29/1858, Morgan, N 3, 23.
21. GH to MW, 5/31/1858, MM, 290–91; CD to WCM, 5/28/1858, Morgan; CD to MB, 5/29/1858, Morgan; CD to Mrs. Catherine Gore, 5/31/1858, Berg.
22. WMT to Smyth, 5/26–7/1858, Ray IV, 86–87; Elizabeth Barrett Browning to Miss Bayley, n.d. 1858, TEX.
23. CD to FO, 6/2/1858, HH; CD to CaD, 6/4/1858, MM, 257–58.
24. CD to WCM, 6/7/1858 Morgan; HW, 6/12/1858.
25. CD to EY, 6/8/1858, N 3, 26; CD to ET, 6/14/1858, N 3, 37; KJF, 71–72.
26. CD to WFC, 7/7/1858, Yale; CD to Richard S. Spofford, 7/15/1858, Morgan.
27. Nisbet, 78–79.
28. CDJr to CaD, 7/13/1858 HH.
29. Harriet Martineau to H. A. Bright, 4/8/1860; quoted in Kathleen Longley, *A Pardoner's Tale: CD and the Ternan Family,* unpublished MS., n.d., 138–40; CD to FE, 6/?/1858, MM, 282; DD, 94.
30. KJF, "Bradbury v. Dickens," D (1954), 75. 73–82.
31. KJF, 76; CD to JF, 1/28/1859, N 3, 91.
32. CD to GH, 5/16/1859, N 3, 103–4; CD to WC, 5/14/1859, Morgan; CD to ER, 3/13/1859, Berg.
33. KJF, 265; WMT to James Wilson, 5/1858, Ray IV, 83–84; WMT to Smyth, 5/?26–27/1858, Ray IV, 86–87.
34. Yates, 9–13; EY to Herman Merivale, 5/25/1858, Ray IV, 133–34; WMT to EY, 6/15/1858, Ray IV, 91.
35. CD to EY, 6/15/1858, N 3, 27; EY, 18–19, 22.
36. CD to WHR, 7/7/1858, N 3, 32; Yates, 24–8; CD to WMT, 11/24/1858, Ray IV, 116.
37. WMT to CD, 11/26/1858, Ray IV, 118; EY to Merivale, 5/25/1889, Ray IV, 133–34; WMT to Smyth, 2/20?/1858, Ray IV, 128–31; WMT to Anne and Harriet Thackeray, 12/4/1858, Ray IV, 121–22; see KJF, "The Recent Reviews," D (1955), 31–32.
38. CD to FO, 9/5/1858, MM, 258–59; CD to MB, 9/10/1858, Morgan.

39. EG to Charles Eliot Norton, 3/9/1858, Gaskell, 535–38.
40. CD to WHW, 10/25/1858, TEX; CD to WHW, 10/25/1858, HH; quoted from Nisbet, 48–49; CD to TAT, 5/16/1859, PH; CD to Mrs. TAT 9/20/1858, TEX.
41. CD to WHW, 10/25/1858, TEX; Nisbet, 48–51; G. S. Grubb, "Dickens and Ellen Ternan," D (1953), 121–29; Edward Wagenknecht, "Letter," D (1953), 28–34; KJF, "The Recent Reviews," D (1955), 25–30.
42. Assignment of Lease, 7/2/1901 DHM; quoted in part by Slater, 426; see Longley, *A Pardoner's Tale*, 194.
43. See Leslie C. Staples, "Ellen Ternan—Some Letters," D (1965), 30–35; Longley, "The Real Ellen Ternan," D (1985), 27–44; CD to MB, 12/9/1858, Morgan.
44. CD to MB, 12/9/1858, Morgan; see Staples, "Ellen Ternan—Some Letters," D (1965), 30–35; Longley, "The Real Ellen Ternan," D (1985), 27–44.
45. CD to ASM, 1/26/1859, Morgan; CD to WFC, 2/1/1859, PH; CD to GHL, 8/14/1859, Yale; CD to T. C. Evans, 2/3/1859, Morgan; CD to JF, 7?/1859, N 3, 112; WC to HC, 7/14/1858, Morgan; CD to JTF, 8/6/1859, N 3, 114.
46. See F II, 8, 284–85, 9, 350–51; CD to ABC, 9/5/1857, N 2, 876; BkM, 14–16, 95; "Preface," *TTC* (1859); CD to JF, 2/21/1859, N 3, 94–95; CD to BP, 3/19/1859, N 3, 96–97.
47. CD to JF, 8/25/1859, 8/?/1859, N 3, 117–19; CD to WC, 10/6/1859, N 3, 124–25; CD to F. J. Regnier, 10/15/1859, N 3, 125–26.
48. *TTC*, I, 4.
49. CD to MB, 12/8/1859, Morgan.

CHAPTER TWELVE
A Splendid Excess
(1860–1864)

1. CD to TB, 6/12/1860, N3, 163–64; Lehmann, 163.
2. DD, 214; WC to HC, 7/19/1859, Morgan; CD to HC, 7/19/1860, 7/29/1860, Morgan; CD to EBL, 6/5/1860, N3, 162–63.
3. KD to HC, 7/29/1860, Morgan; Lehmann, 163; CD to WFC, 5/3/1860, Berg; CD to FDN, 8/19/1860, N3, 172–73; CC to WHH, 6/20/1860, HH; WC to WHH, 5/19/1860?, HH.
4. CC to HC, 8/5/1860, Morgan; CD to Helen Dickens, 7/19/1860, N 3, 167–68; DD, 106; CD to Mrs. Milner Gibson, 7/8/1861, N 3, 229.
5. CC to HC, 8/5/1860, Morgan; CD to ABC, 8/3/1860, HCD, 371; CD to FDN, 8/19/1860, N 3, 172–73.
6. CD to W. B. Hodge, 10/24/1850, 10/30/1850, PH; CD to Helen Dickens, 11/13/1859, N 3, 135; Helen Thompson to Mrs. Stark, 8/30/1858, K. J. Fielding, "CD and His Wife, Fact or Forgery?" *Etudes Anglais* 8 (1955), 217.
7. DD, 175.
8. CD to WHW, 3/28/1860, N 3, 154; CD to Helen Dickens, 4/17/1866, N 3, 156; CD to FDN, 8/19/1860, N 3, 172–73; CD to GH, 11/27/1860, DHM.
9. CD to FB, 6/25/1859, 7/1/1859, 7/29/1859, 8/6/1869, DHM, N 3, 109–10, 113–14; CD to JF, 8/25/1859, N 3, 118–19; CD to MB, 12/28/1860, N 3, 196–97; CD to GH, 12/28/1860, 5/26/1861, N 3, 197, 223; CD to Lady Olliffe, 5/26/1861, N 3, 222; CD to WHW, 8/31/1861, N 3, 232–33; Jerome Meckier, "Some Household Words: Two New Accounts of Dickens's Conversation," D (1975), 5–20.
10. CD to Frederic Chapman, 8/24/1860, DHM; CD to ABC, 3/13/1860, HCD, 368–69.
11. CD to ABC, 4/4/1860, 4/8/1860, 3/13/1860, HCD, 368–70; CD to LW, 9/14/1860, HH; CD to AS, 2/14/1860, 2/15/1860, PH.
12. CD to ED, 9/26/1868, N 3, 667–68; DD, 123–24.

13. CD to GH, 10/9/1861, N 3, 244; CD to LA, 10/23/1861, Morgan.
14. CD to F. J. REgnier, 11/16/1859, N 3, 136–37; CD to ABC, 1/30/1860, HCD, 367–68; CD to X. Villiers, 1/20/1860, Yale.
15. CD to GHL, 11/14/1859, Berg; CD to George Eliot, 7/10/1859, N 3, 110–11.
16. CD to GHL, 11/12/1859, 11/20/1859, 2/13/1860, Berg, N 3, 150–51; CD to CL, 2/21/1860, 1/2/1860, 3/9/1860, N 3, 144, 151–52; CD to WFC, 2/1/1861, PH.
17. CD to Earl of Carlisle, 8/8/1860, N 3 170; CD to Alfred Wigan, 8/31/1860, TEX; CD to LW, 9/14/1860, N 3, 177–78; CD to CL, 10/6/1860, 10/15/1860, N 3, 183–84; CD to JF, 9/?/1860, 10/4/1860, 10/?/1860, N 3, 182–83, 186.
18. CD to WCM, 10/12/1860, 6/11/1860, Morgan; CD to JF, 10/24/1860, N 3, 188; CD to WHW, 5/26/1860, N 3, 223.
19. CD to WC, 6/23/1861, N 3, 224–25; CD to EBL, 5/15/1861, 6/24/1861, N 3, 220, 225.
20. CD to HMB, 10/24/1862, HCD, 373–74; CD to WCM, 12/27/1862, Morgan; CD to WHW, 12/20/1863, N 3, 374; CD to WC, 1/24/1864, N 3, 378–79.
21. CD to WHW, 12/20/1863, N 3, 374.
22. CD to WHW, 12/20/1863, 9/14/1863, N 3, 374, 362; CD to CaD, 8/6/1863, MM, 264; CD to LA, 9/7/1862, Morgan; CD to ER, 9/12/1863, Berg; DD, 109.
23. CD to JF, 7/1/1861, N 3, 226–27; CD to WCM, 7/31/1861, Morgan.
24. CD to GHL, 11/14/1859 Berg; WC to CW, 8/18/1859, Morgan; CD to WC, 7/29/1860, N 3, 169; WC to HC 7/26/1860, 8/22/1860, 9/12/1860, Morgan; KD to HC, 12/20/1860, Morgan.
25. WC to EP, 12/11/1859, HH; CD to WC 1/7/1860, 10/14/1862, N 3, 145, 310.
26. WC to HC, 5/24/1861, 7/11/1861, 8/12/1862, Morgan; CD to GH, 1/24/1862, HH [from Adrian, 83]; CD to WC 9/20/1862, N 3, 304–5.
27. CD to WC, 1/5/1862, N 3 275–76; WC to CW, 4/22/1861, Morgan; WC to HC, 7/31/1861, Morgan.
28. CD to WC, 8/16/1859, 5/28/1861, N 3, 115–16, 231–32; CD to JF, 4/22/1861, 9/?/1861, N 3, 215–16, 234; see PC, CD, *The Public Readings*, 1975, XVII–LXVI, 467–71.
29. CD to H. G. Adams, 10/21/1861, 10/26/1861, Berg, N 3, 242; CD to AS, 9/3/1861, N 3, 234–35; CD to JF, 9/28/1861, N 3, 240; CD to Mrs. AS, 10/9/1861, Berg.
30. CD to GH, 10/9/1861, 10/15/1861, N 3, 243–44, HH; CD to LA, 10/23/1861, 11/25/1861, 10/17/1861, 2/7/1862, 6/3/1864, Morgan; CD to "Sir," 6/5/1864, PH.
31. CD to JF, 10/?/1861, N 3 243; CD to GH, 10/29/1861, 11/1/1861, 1/3/1862, 1/8/1862, N 3, 245–49, HH; CD to MD, 10/10/1861, N 3, 244; CD to HMB, 11/3/1861, HCD, 371–73; CD to AT, 12/26/1861, TEX.
32. CD to MD, 11/4/1861, 11/2/1861, N 3, 250, 258–59; CD to JF, 11/8/1861, N 3, 253; CD to GH, 12/3/1861, 1/3/1862, N 3, 263–66, HH; CD to WHW, 12/15/1861, N 3, 267; CD to WFC, 3/16/1862, Berg, HH.
33. CD to TB, 4/5/1862, N 3 292; CD to LA, 5/8/1862, 7/3/1862, 1/4/1862, Morgan; CD to JF, 6/?/1862, 10/5/1862, 10/22/1862, N 3, 297 306, 312; CD to GH, 1/8/1862, HH.
34. CD to John Poole, 6/13/1862, Morgan; CD to JF, 11/5?/1862, N 3, 316–17; CD to TB, 11/15/1862, N 3, 319–20; CD to RHH, 11/22/1862, PH; CD to LA, 11/7/1862, 7/3/1862, 6/20/1862, Morgan; CD to WCM, 7/2/1862, Morgan.
35. CD to TE, 11/4/1862, 12/4/1862, N 3, 314–15, 328; CD to LA, 12/4/1862, 12/20/1862, Morgan.
36. BP to JF, n.d. [summer 1864–65?], V&A; CD to EY, 4/17/1860, N 3, 156; MS. DHM; CC to HC, 11/3/1864, Morgan; Simon Houfe, *John Leech and the Victorian Scene*, 1985, 206–7.
37. Houfe, 207. CD to Shirley Brooks, 12/24/1864, N 3, 407; WC to HC, 11/3/1864, 11/8/1864, Morgan; CD to JF, 11/?/1864, N 3, 404; CD to William Riddle, 7/29/1864, PH.
38. CD to E. S. Dallas, 11/12/1864, HH.

39. WMT to Whitwell Elwin, 5/31/1861, Ray IV, 237–38.
40. KD, "Thackeray and My Father," *Pall Mall Magazine,* n.s. XIV (1911), 216–17; CD to WC, 1/25/1864, N 3, 378–79, Morgan; DD, 109–11; Arthur A. Adrian, *Mark Lemon,* 1966, 136–37; CD to Joseph Hindle, 10/28/1863, N 3, 366; CD to ABC, 2/12/1864, HCD, 335–37.
41. WC to HC, 2/8/1864, Morgan; CD to WC, 1/25/1864, N 3, 378–79; CD to WCM, 2/10/1864, 6/11/1864, Morgan; CD to JF, 11/19/1859, 4/8/1862, N 3, 137, 292; CD to Ellen Stone, 11/19/1859, PH; CD to John Darlington, 3/23/1862, N 3, 289–90; CD to Alexander Duff Gordon, 4/4/1862, HH.
42. CD to WC, 4/22/1863, N 3, 348–49; WC to FB, n.d. 1863, PR; CD to WHH, 5/31/1863, PH.
43. CD to ABC, 2/12/1864, HCD, 335–37; CD to WCM, 2/10/1864, Morgan; CD to H. S. Adams, 2/25/1864, DHM; Colonel Priestly to CD, 7/16/1864, Adrian, 86.

CHAPTER THIRTEEN
The Sons of Toil
(1864–1868)

1. T. W. Hill, "The Staplehurst Railway Accident," D (1942), 38, 147–52; CD to TM, 7/13/1865, N 3, 425–26; CD to LA, 6/13/1865, Morgan; CD to FO, 6/10/1865, HH; CD to ABC, 6/11/1865, HCD, 379.
2. CD to TM, 7/13/1865, N 3, 425–26; CD to Mrs. Hulkes, 6/18/1865, PH; CC to HC, 6/13/1865, Morgan.
3. CD to TM, 6/13/1865, N 3, 425–26; *OMF,* "Postscript," 822; Hill, 148; CC to HC, 6/13/1865, Morgan; CD to Arnold, 6/12/1865, DHM; MD, 158; CD to JF, 6/?/1865, N 3, 429.
4. CD to Benjamin Webster, 9/8/1861, N 3, 234–35; CD to EY, 4/3/1862, N 3, 291; CD to TAT, 6/26/1863, PH; CD to TAT, 11/2/1866, TAT, *What I Remember,* 1888, 361; CD to TAT, 7/25/1866, Berg.
5. CD to FDN, 7/5/1867, N 3, 475–76; CD to WCM, 2/19/1863, N 3, 342–43.
6. CD to TAT, 6/16/1863, PH; "Mrs. Lirriper's Legacy" (HW, Christmas 1864, 422); CD to WCM, 2/19/1863, N 3, 342–43; CD to WHW, 10/24/1862, N 3, 313; CD to CL, 11/4/1862, N 3, 315.
7. CD to JF, 11/?/1862, N 3, 322; WC to HC, 11/6/1862, 11/18/1862, Morgan; CD to LA, 11/7/1862, 12/20/1862, Morgan; CD to MW, 11/17/1862, N 3, 320; CD to HMB, 10/24/1862, HCD, 373–74, Morgan; CD to WCM, 4/11/1863, Morgan; CD to CS, 12/18/1862, Yale.
8. CD to LA, 11/7/1863, 2/4/1863, Morgan; CD to WCM, 12/27/1862, Morgan; CD to MB, 12/27/1862, N 3, 328–29; CD to TAT, 6/16/1863, PH; CD to W. W. Story, 8/1/1863, Berg; CD to FL, 2/3/1863, Morgan; CD to WHW, 2/4/1863, N 3, 340–41; CD to JF, 2/7/1863, N 3, 341.
9. CD to WC, 1/1/1863, N 3, 333; CD to CL, 11/4/1862, N 3, 315; CD to EY, 4/3/1862, N 3, 291; WJC, "Dickens's Forgotten Retreat in France." D (1966), 69–86.
10. CD to WFC, 10/25/1864, N 3, 402–3; Catherine Van Dyke, "A Talk with CD's Office Boy, William Edrupt of London," *Bookman* (1921), 49–52, quoted in IR, 196; Julia Clara Byrne, *Gossip of the Century,* 1892, I, 225, quoted by Nisbet, 22, and Slater, 210; CD to Thomas Baylis, 7/2/1862, N 3, 298–99; CD to LA, 7/3/1862, 7/8/1862, Morgan; CD to Ellen Ternan? [name excised], 1/10/1863, Morgan; CD to Pitre-Chevalier, 1/18/63, TEX; CD to MD?, 1/31?/1863, N 3, 338; CD to GH, 1/12/1863, Adrian [HH], 79.
11. CD to FO, 3/17/1863, HH; CD to WC, 8/9/1863, N 3, 359–60; CD to EY, 11/15/1863, Morgan; CD to MS, 7/7/1864, Morgan; CD to WHW, 6/26/1864, N 3, 392–93; CD to Mary Nichols, 6/26/1864, N 3, 392; CD to MS, 11/17/1864, Morgan; CD to JF, 5/?/1865, N 3, 422.

12. *B&M*, 8, 19, 88, 100–101.

13. CD to WFC, 3/16/1862, N 3, 288–89; CD to LA, 5/8/1862, 6/20/1862, 4/22/1863, Morgan; CD to William Henry Brookfield, 5/24/1863, N 3, 353.

14. CD to JF, 8/30/1863, N 3, 361; CD to Mrs. Eliza David, 7/10/1863, N 3, 356–57; CD to C&H, 9/8/1863, Morgan.

15. CD to C&H, 9/8/1863, Morgan; CD to JF, 10/?/1863, N 3, 364; CD to ER, 10/28/1863, Berg; CD to Lady Cowley, 12/23/1863, PH; CD to WC, 1/24/1864, N 3, 378–79.

16. CD to WCM, 2/10/1864, Morgan; CD to ABC, 2/12/1864, HCD, 375–77.

17. CD to MS, 6/14/1864, 7/7/1864, Morgan; MS. DHM; CD to JF, 3/20/1864, V&A; *OMF*, I, xiii; CD to JF, 5/3/1864, N 3, 387.

18. CD to Mrs. Wreford Major, 6/17/1864, N 3, 392; CD to Mrs. WHW, 8/7/1864, N 3, 394–95; CD to JF, 7/29/1864, N 3, 394; GHG, 14: 8/6/1864; CD to JET, 8/26/1864, N 3, 396–97.

19. CD to CK, 10/6/1864, PH; CD to GH, 10/12/1864, HH; WC to HC, 10/19/1864, Morgan; CD to JF, 11/1864?, 3/3/1865, 7/?/1865, N 3, 404, 416, 429; CD to MS, 11/17/1864, 2/15/1865, 6/21/1865, 8/29/1865, Morgan, PH; CD to BP, 12/31/1864, N 3, 407; CD to Fanny Brown, 2/21/1865, Morgan; CD to FB, 3/21/1865, N 3, 418; CD to WCM, 4/22/1865, N 3, 419; CD to Mr. Day, 8/22/1865, N 3, 434; CD to WHW, 8/27/1865, N 3, 434.

20. CD to WCM, 6/11/1861, 2/2/1866, Morgan; CD to WHW, 4/2/1864, N 3, 385; CD to Eliza Davis, 7/10/1863, 11/16/1864, 3/1/1867, N 3, 356–57, 405, 512.

21. CD to CK, 1/18/1866, N 3, 456–57; CD to S. Perkes, 11/29/1866, N 3, 192–93; CD to WFC, 1/1/1867, N 3, 499–501.

22. CD to TC, 4/13/1863, N 3, 348; CD to Louisa Twining, 2/10/1860, Yale; CD to WFC, 2/1/1859, PH; CD to Harry Rawson, 3/26/1863, TEX; CD to Joshua Fayle, 1/21/1864, N 3, 378.

23. WC to HC, 7/26/1864, Morgan; CD *et al.*, 5/?/1864, N 3, 389–90; CD to WCM, 4/22/1865, N 3, 419; CD to WFC, 2/1/1861, 11/30/1865, N 3, 445–46, PH.

24. CD to Story, 8/1/1863, N 3, 358; CD to WC, 1/24/1864, N 3, 378–79; CD to WFC, 2/1/1859, 3/21/1861, 10/25/1864, PH, N 3, 402–3; CD to L. W. Morey, 7/12/1867, PH; CD to TAT, 7/25/1866, 9/6/1859, Berg; CD to ER, 7/6/1866, Berg.

25. CD to WFC, 2/1/1861, 3/16/1862, 11/30/1865, PH, Berg, N 3, 445–46; CD to Mrs. Kemble, 3/1/1865, N 3, 446; Fred Kaplan, *Thomas Carlyle*, 1831, 387–93.

26. CD to FL, 7/12/1862, 7/28/1862, 6/28/1863, N 3, 300, TEX; BP to JF, 3/13/1865, V&A; CD to WC, 8/6/1863, N 3, 359–60; CD to WFC, 3/16/1862, 5/21/1863, N 3, 288–89, 351–53; CD to JF, 7/1/1861, N 3, 226–27; CD to WHW, 8/31/1861, N 3, 232–33, TEX.

27. CD to WCM, 6/11/1861, Morgan; CD to GH, 12/3/1861, N 3, 263–64; CD to Lehmann, 7/28/1862, PR; CD to WFC, 11/30/1865, N 3, 445–46.

28. CD to GH, 3/6/1867, HH; CD to CS, 4/18/1867, N 3, 524–25; CD to George Stanfield, 5/19/1867, N 3, 527–28; CD to Dr. Howison, 10/23/1868, N 3, 674–75; CD to JF, 10/24/1868, N 3, 675; CD to MW, 11/17/1862, N 3, 320.

29. DM to JF, 5/17/1861, 5/28/1861, 8/20/1867, V&A; DM to CK, 10/21/1867, HH; CD to GH, 3/23/1866, 4/19/1866, HH, Yale; BP to JF, n.d./1862, V&A; CD to WCM, 2/9/1862, 9/30/1862, 3/3/1867, 3/26/1867, 10/2/1867, Morgan; CD to WCM, 4/5/1862, N 3, 292; CD to Mrs. CS, 4/9/1866, Yale; CD to CS, 4/17/1867, N 3, 524–25.

30. CD to WCM, 1/2/1860, 9/7/1863, 10/13/1863, 12/27/1868, Morgan; JF to EBL, 9/27/1862, quoted in Davies, 114; CD to Whitwell Elwin, 6/3/1859, TEX; Fitz, 40; CD to E. S. Dallas, 12/7/1862, N 3, 324–25; CD to GH, 1/28/1864, HH; CD to JF, 3/20/1864, V&A.

31. WC to [?], 9/28/1864, HH; WC to HC, 1/8/1864, 4/1/1866, 7/19/1864, Morgan; WC to Mrs. FL, n.d. [1866?], quoted in Lehmann, 178; BP to JF, 9/17/1867, V&A; CD to FDN, 8/19/1860, N 3, 172–73.

32. CD to WC, 7/12/1861, N 3, 229–30; WC to FB, 1/30/1863, PR; WC to CW, 11/4/1863,

Morgan; WC to FB, n.d., 1863, PR; WC to [?], n.d./1868, PR; CD to GH, 10/29/1868, N 3, 676.

33. CD to WC, 5/1/1867, N 3, 525–26; CD to WC, 5/4/1867, Morgan; WC to HC, 5/14/1867, 5/24/1867, Morgan.

34. Lehmann, 189–90; CD to GH, 9/30/1867, N 3, 555; CD to WHW, 2/2/1862, 11/30/1864, 4/28/1859, 10/1/1864, 10/16/1864, N 3, 101, 275, 399, 401, 405; CD to Mrs. WHW, 8/7/1864, N 3, 394–95; CD to WCM, 3/12/1866, Morgan; Fitz, 233.

35. Yates, 294; Fitz, 1.

36. Mrs. C. M. Ward, *Reminiscences*, ed. Elliot O'Donnell, 1911, 34; Lehmann, 206, 211–12; CD to Mrs. FL, n.d., 1869, quoted in Lehmann, 213; CD to MD, 1/31/1868, N 3, 612; CD to Henry Chorley, 3/1/1862, 3/9/1862, N 3, 284, PH; Fitz, 306.

37. Lehmann, 162, 164–65.

38. Yates, 108, 7; Lady Westmoreland to Julian Fane, 3/14/1862, quoted in "Recollections of Dickens," D (1923), 235; Ward, 149; CD to FO, 4/30/1865, HH; CD to WFC, 3/16/1862, Berg; CD to WCM, 1/9/1862, Morgan; Malcolm Morely, " 'No Thoroughfare' Back stage," D (1953), 39–42; Kathleen Longley, *A Pardoner's Tale: CD and the Ternan Family*, unpub MS, 236.

39. CD, *Collected Papers*, 1938, 116–17, "On Mr. Fechter's Acting," *Atlantic Monthly*, 1869. CD to HC, 6/13/1865, Morgan; GHG, 27: 8/19/1865.

40. CD to Story, 8/1/1863, Berg; Yates, 102.

41. Yates, 102; MD, "CD at Home," 43; CD to Governors of Sir Joseph Williamson's Free School, 6/30/1862, N 3, 298.

42. CD to H. Wright, 7/29/1862, N 3, 301; CD to JF, 12/25/1866, 1/1/1867, N 3, 493–94, 499; CD to WCM, 12/28/1866, Morgan.

43. CD to WHR, 5/26/1865, N 3, 422; CC to HC, 10/12/1865, Morgan; Yates, 103; GHG, 20: 1/21/1865; HFD to PF, summer 1865, Yale.

44. CD to WCM, 1/2/1866, Morgan; CD to WC, 10/4/1866, N 3, 487; CD to JET, 8/20/1866, N 3, 481–82; CD to W. F. Wilson, 11/6/1863, TEX; CD to Austen Henry Layard, 5/17/1865, N 3, 421; CD to Mrs. FL, 3/8/1865, TEX; CD to Dr. Christie, 2/20/1867, HH.

45. CD to LW, 11/5/1867, N 3, 565; CD to HMB, 11/3/1861, HCD, 371–73; CD to Mrs. FL, 3/8/1865, TEX; CD to Rev. W. Brackinbury [?], 9/18/1865, DHM; CD to Albert Canning, 10/4/1866, PH.

46. CD to EBL, 7/16/1866, N 3, 478; Fitz, 54–55; Lehmann, 210–11; WC to HC, 5/30/1867, Morgan.

47. Lehmann, 210–11; WC to HC, 7/8/1866, Morgan; CC to WHH, 6/23/1867, HH; CD to WCM, 2/2/1866, 12/28/1868, Morgan; CD to LA, 12/13/1866, Morgan.

48. See Thomas Wright, *Autobiography*, 1936; DD, 94; Nisbet, 37, 85; Felix Aylmer, *Dickens Incognito*, 1959, 34–92; L. C. Staples, "Ellen Ternan," D (1960), 28–29; David Parker and Michael Slater, "The Gladys Storey Papers," D (1980), 6–7; Kathleen Longley, "Letter," D (1980), 17–19.

49. Fanny Ternan to Bice, n.d., quoted in Longley, *Pardoner's Tale*, 236; Longley, B4–B5; CD to Arthur Chappell, 8/2/1866, N 3, 480–81; CD to GD, 8/2/1866, N 3, 480; CD to R. H. Mason, 8/3/1866, N 3, 480; Aylmer, 13–43; J. C. Reid, "Mr. Tringham of Slough," D (1968), 164–65; Longley, "Dickens Incognito," D (1981), 88–91.

50. CD to PF, 11/30/1865, 11/6/1866, N 3, 447. 489–90; CD to WFC, 1/1/1867, N 3, 499–501.

CHAPTER FOURTEEN
A Castle in the Other World
(1867–1870)

1. CK, *An Authentic Record of the Public Banquet Given to Mr. CD . . . November 2 1867 . . .* , 1867; *New York Tribune*, 11/18/1867, quoted in KJF, 369; Arthur Helps to Queen

Victoria, 3/5/1870; quoted in John R. DeBruyn, "CD Meets the Queen: A New look," D (1975), 85–90, 87.

2. Frith, 235–36; WC to HC, 10/26/1867, Morgan; JF to CK, 10/?/1867, HH.

3. KJF, 370; BP to JF, 11/4/1867, V&A; CK, *Authentic Record*, 14, 17; Moncure Conway, quoted in IR, 340–41; Jane Ellen Frith Panton, *Leaves from a Life*, 1908, 149; CD to WHW, 11/3/1867, N 3, 565; *New York Tribune*, quoted in KJF, 370.

4. CK, *Authentic Record*, 18–21.

5. CD to WHW, 6/6/1867, HH, CD to JF, 4/?/1866, 5/14/1867, N 3, 467, 527; Dolby, 43–44; CD to LA, 1/2/1867, Morgan; CD to WFC, 1/1/1867, N 3, 499–501.

6. CD to CS, 4/18/1857, N 3, 524–25; CD to Mrs. Ellicott. 4/2/1867, N 3, 521; CD to GH, 3/29/1867, HH; CD to RBL, 4/17/1867, N 3, 523; Dolby, 72.

7. CD to TAT, 1/17/1866, Berg; CD to WCM, 2/3/1866, Morgan; CD to Mrs. CS, 4/9/1866, Yale; CD to GH, 2/9/1866, 1/21/1867, 1/24/1867, 5/10/1867, N 3, 459–60, 502–4, 527; CD to JF, 9/?/1866, 1/29/1867, N 3, 483, 506; CD to MD, 2/17/1867, N 3, 509; CD to LA. 5/9/1867, Morgan.

8. CD to Ticknor and Fields, 4/16/1867, N 3, 523; CD to JTF, 4/22/1867, DHM.

9. M. A. DeWolfe Howe, *Memories of a Hostess*, 1922, 139.

10. CD to JTF, 5/2/1865, 10/16/1866, 5/20/1867, 6/3/1867, N 3, 470–71, 477–78, 528, 530; CD to GD, 8/2/1866, N 3, 480; CD to JET, 5/23/1867, Berg.

11. BP to JF, 10/2/1867, V&A; CD to WHW, 6/6/1867, 12/10/1867, HH. N 3, 530–31, 580.

12. CD to GH, 8/2/1867, N 3, 540; CD to Walter Thornbury, 8/5/1867, N 3, 540; CD to JF, 8/6/1867, N 3, 540–41; CD to GD, 8/4/1867, PH; CD to LA, 8/18/1867, 9/16/1867, Morgan.

13. CD to CK, 9/23/1867, 9/26/1867, Yale, HH; CD to F. D. Finlay, 9/3/1867, N 3, 544; CD to JTF, 9/3/1867, N 3, 544–45; WC to HC, 9/25/1867, Morgan; CD to WHW, 9/28/1867, N 3, 554; CD to GH, 9/30/1867, N 3, 555.

14. CD to JF, 10/5/1867. N 3, 557; CD to HFD, 10/7/1867, N 3, 558; Dolby, 38; CD to Thomas Hills, 10/7/1867, N 3, 559; CD to GD, 10/16/1867, PH.

15. CD to GD, 10/16/1867, PH; CD to FO, 10/20/1867, HH; CD to WHW, 10/?/1867, N 3, 563; Nisbet, 52–56.

16. CD to MD, 11/10/1867, N 3, 566; CD to JF, 11/18/1867, N 3, 568; CD to WHW, 11/21/1867, N 3, 570–71; CD to GH, 11/17/1867, 11/25/1867, N 3, 568, 572.

17. JTF, 165–66; CD to MD, 11/21/1867, N 3, 568–69; Dolby, 249–60.

18. CD to GH, 12/6/1867, HH; CD to JTF, 11/24/1867, Berg; CD to WC, 11/28/1867, N 3, 574.

19. CD to GH, 11/25/1867, N 3, 572; Howe, 141, 158; CD to MD, 11/21/1867, N 3, 568–69; HWL to JF, 11/23/1867, HH; CD to WC, 11/28/1867, N 3, 574–75.

20. CD to JF, 12/3/1867, N 3, 577; CD to WC, 12/2/1867, N 3, 577; CD to WHW, 12/4/1867, 12/6/1867 N 3, 579; CD to GH, 12/6/1867, HH; Dolby, 166–68.

21. Dolby, 171; JTF, 167; CD to JF, 12/14/1867, 12/22/1867, N 3, 581–82, 585–87; CD to WHW, 12/10/1867, 12/17/1867, N 3, 580, 584; CD to MD, 12/11/1867, N 3, 580–81; CD to GH, 12/6/1867, 12/16/1867, HH, N 3, 582–83.

22. CD to EBL, 12/16/1867. N 3, 583; CD to MD, 11/21/1867, 12/26/1867, 12/27/1867, N 3, 586–89; CD to JF, 12/22/1867, N 3, 585–87; CD to GH, 12/22/1867, N 3, 584–85; CD to WHW, 12/24/1867, N 3, 587–88.

23. CD to JTF 12/29/1867, N, 589–90.

24. CD to JF, 1/5/1867, N 3, 597–98; CD to GH, 1/12/1868, N 3, 600–601; Sidney P. Moss, *CD's Quarrel with America*, 1984, 288; CD to JTF, 1/15/1867, N 3, 604–5.

25. CD to MD, 2/10/1868, N 3, 619; CD to JF, 2/7/1868, N 3, 616; CD to GH, 2/7/1868, N 3, 617; CD to JTF, 2/9/1867, N 3, 618; KJF, 375.

26. CD to MD, 2/4/1868, N 3, 613–14; CD to JF, 2/4/1868, N 3, 615.

27. CD to JF, 1/30/1868, 2/25/1868, N 3, 611–12, 625–26; CD to MD, 2/9/1868, N 3, 619; CD to GH, 2/17/1868, N 3, 622; CD to Charles Fechter, 2/24/1868, N 3, 623.
28. CD to MD, 2/25/1868, N 3, 625; Dolby, 261; CD to GH, 2/27/1868, 3/2/1868, N 3, 626–29.
29. CD to JF, 3/13/1868, 3/16/1868, N 3, 631–33; CD to Mrs. JTF, 3/19/1868, N 3, 634–35; CD to WCM, 3/21/1868, N 3, 637–39.
30. CD to MD, 4/7/1868, N 3, 642–43; JTF, *Biographical Notes and Sketches*, ed. Mrs. JTF, 1881, quoted in IR, 320; CD to Fechter, 3/8/1868, N 3, 630–31; BP to JF, 3/3/1868, V&A.
31. CD to JF, 4/2/1868, N 3, 640–41; CD to WHW, 4/17/1868, N 3, 643; Dolby, 301; KJF, 378.
32. Dolby, 310–11; KJF, 379–82; CD to Alexander Ireland, 5/30/1868, Morgan.
33. "CD's Farewell Reading in America," D (1915), 237; CD to Thomas Chappell, 5/3/1869, N 3, 723; CD to TAT, 5/6/1869, Berg; CD to JTF, 4/26/1868, N 3, 644–45; Dolby, 327–28.
34. CD to Mrs. JTF, 5/25/1868, N 3, 650–51.
35. CD to LW, 5/11/1868, N 3, 646; CD to WCM, 6/10/1868, 7/20/1869, Morgan; CD to Mrs. JTF, 5/25/1868, N 3, 650–51; EY, 116; CD to Dolby, 9/25/1868, Berg; CD to Henry Morley, 10/22/1868, PH; CD to WHW, 8/9/1868, DHM.
36. MD to ED, 9/26/1868, 6/17/1870, Yale; CD to GD, 9/29/1868, HH; CD to WCM, 10/11?/1868, 11/19/1868, Morgan; CD to TAT, 9/13/1868, Berg.
37. CD to W. P. Frith, 11/16/1868, N 3, 678; CD to FO, 10/9/1868, PH; CD to WCM, 11/19/1868, Morgan; CD to Mrs. JTF, 12/16/1868, N 3, 686–88.
38. CD to JF, 2/15/1869, N 3, 703; CD to CK, 2/19/1869, PH; CD to GD, 2/15/1869, N 3, 705–6; CD to WCM, 4/3/1869, Morgan; EY, 116–20; CD to ML, 4/16/1869, N 3, 720.
39. CD to John Watkins, 9/28/1861, P&P, 80; CD to W. L. Thomas, 12/27/1869, N 3, 755.
40. David Alec Wilson and David Wilson MacArthur, *Thomas Carlyle*, 1923–34, 5, 505; Fred Kaplan, *Thomas Carlyle*, 1983, 430; IR, 303 (Cornelius Cole).
41. IR, 194 ("Dickens's Amanuensis" [1882]), 295 (Justin McCarthy, "Reminiscences" [1899]), 322 (Mrs. JTF); Franklin Philp to [?] [Solorums?], 7/31/1869, PH.
42. IR, 207 (EY), 212 (Linton), 217 (James Payn, "Some Literary Recollections" [1884]), 297 (Henry James, "Notes of a Son and Brother" [1914]), 330 (EBL), 334 (Arthur Helps).
43. IR, 330 (EBL); CD to TAT, 5/6/1869, Berg.
44. JT, 200; CD to GH, 4/21/1869, N 3, 721; CD to LW, 4/20/1869, HH; CD to FB, 4/21/1869, N 3, 721.
45. CD to JF, 4/22/1869, N 3, 720–21; CD to GH, 2/9/1866, Berg; Yates, 116–20; CD to MD, 4/22/1869, N 3, 722.
46. CD to LA, 4/23/1869, Morgan; CD to JF, 4/26/1869, PH; CD to TAT, 5/6/1869, Berg; CD to Joseph Nightingale, 4/28/1869, PH; "Dullborough Town," *UT*, 126.
47. JTF, 448–50; CD to C. Locock, 6/16/1869, PH.
48. N 3, 797–800.
49. CD to WHW, 5/3/1859, Wills, 392–93; CD to PF, 5/3/1869, Fitz, 63–64; JTF, *In and Out of Doors with CD*, 1876, 105–6, 138; CD to Benjamin Webster, 5/25/1869, PH; DD, 127–28.
50. CD to FO, 10/9/1868, PH; CD to FDN, 8/8/1869, 8/14/1869, N 3, 735–37; CD to TAT, 7/21/1869, 11/4/1869, PH, Berg.
51. Franklin Philp to Solurums?, 7/31/1869, PH; CD to WCM, 7/20/1869, Morgan; KJF, 403–6; CD to Frederick Chapman, 8/20/1869, DHM.
52. BkM, 16, 97; CD to WCM, 10/18/1869, N 3, 745–46; CD to Chapman, 1/4/1870, PH.
53. GH to Mrs. JTF, 2/25/1870, HH; CD to George Clowes, 11/24/1869, Yale; CD to JF, 12/22/1869, N 3, 754; CD to WCM, 12/27/1869, Morgan; CD to JTF, 1/14/1870, N 3, 759–60; HFD.M, 23–24.
54. HFD.M, 22; CD Jr, 30.
55. DD, 131; GH to Mrs. JTF, 2/25/1870, HH.
56. KJF, 412–14; HFD.M, 20–21.

57. CD to Arthur Helps, 3/3/1870, PH; CD to G. W. Rusden, 5/20/1870, N 3, 779–80; Dolby, 453–58; John R. DeBruyn, "CD Meets the Queen: A New Look," D (1975), 85–90.

58. CD to Mrs. PF, 5/9/1870, N 3, 775; CD to CK, 4/25/1870 N 3, 722; GH to Mrs. JTF, 5/4/1870, HH; Yates, 140; KJF, 407.

59. CD to JF, 3/29/1870, 4/29/1870, N 3, 769, 773; DM to JF, 10/13/1868, V&A; KJF, 421–22.

60. GH to Mrs. JTF, 5/4/1870, HH; CD to GH, 5/12/1870, PH; CD to Mrs. CW, 5/11/1870, Mrs. C. M. Ward, *Reminiscences,* ed. Elliot O'Donnell, 1911, 198, N 3, 776; CD to William Ralston, 5/16/1870, N 3, 778; CD to JF, 5/16/1870, N 3, 778; CD to J. B. Buckstone, N 3, 777; CD to Harry Lemon, 5/25/1870, PH.

61. Fitz, 81–82; Dolby, 464–65; CD Jr, 30–31.

62. DD, 132–34; MD, 18–19.

63. MD, 119–20; DD, 135–36.

64. MD, 123; DD, 123, 135–36; GH to Mrs. JTF, 7/4/1870; MD to Mrs. JTF, 9/1/1870, HH.

65. F II, 12, 513; A. A. Adrian, "CD and Dean Stanley," D (1955), 152–56. In *London for the Literary Pilgrim,* 1949, 83, William Kent has conjectured but not substantiated that Ellen Ternan attended the funeral.

Acknowledgments

DURING THE YEARS THAT I HAVE WORKED ON THIS BOOK I HAVE incurred many professional and personal obligations, all of which, in their various permutations, have contributed to its creation. The primary institutional obligations are to libraries and universities, and to two research centers, the Huntington Library and the National Humanities Center, which provided me with substantial fellowships. The National Endowment for the Humanities also gave financial assistance. My own college and university, Queens College (which generously granted me a Presidential Research Award and Faculty Research awards) and the Graduate Center of the City University of New York, kindly contributed to my having had time to work on this long but mostly happy labor.

Three libraries and their beneficent overseers head the list of my archival obligations: the Berg Collection of the New York Public Library and its curator, Lola Szladits, the Dickens House Museum in London and its curator, David Parker (who kindly read and made helpful comments on the manuscript), and the Henry E. Huntington Library in San Marino, California, and its librarian, Daniel Woodward. At the Dickens House Mu-

587

seum, I was also helped by Eileen Power, and at the Huntington Library by Mary Robertson, Susan Hodson, Alan Jutzi, and Martin Ridge. Other libraries and librarians whose resources and generosity I am thankful for are the Beinecke Rare Book and Manuscript Library, Yale University (Marjorie Wynn), the British Library, the Harry Ransom Humanities Research Center of the University of Texas (Cathy Henderson), the National Library of Scotland, the Pierpont Morgan Library, the Benoliel Collection of the Free Library of Philadelphia (Walter A. Frankel), the Parrish Collection of Princeton University Library (Jean F. Preston and Alexander D. Wainwright), the Sadleir Collection of the University of California at Los Angeles, and the Forster Collection of the Victoria and Albert Museum. These and other such obligations are further detailed in the citations of sources.

The Editors and Trustees of the Pilgrim Edition of *The Letters of Charles Dickens,* to whom Mr. Christopher Dickens has turned over the common-law copyright for Dickens' unpublished letters, have kindly permitted the use of summaries and brief quotations. I am especially indebted to Kathleen Tillotson for her support and cooperation. Graham Storey has kindly conveyed to me this permission on behalf of Christopher Dickens. I am also indebted to R. A. Denniston, the publisher of the Oxford University Press for permission to quote from the published letters.

Personal and professional debts begin to become indistinguishable, probably inseparable, at this point, though one has an institutional presence that allows me to acknowledge here how stimulating and helpful have been my years of participation in the Dickens Project of the University of California at Santa Cruz, and the support of its two directors, Murray Baumgarten and John Jordan, and of Edwin Eigner and my other colleagues there.

My friend and colleague David Kleinbard has contributed to some of the small moments of grace that the book may have by his kind, helpful reading of the manuscript. Rhoda Weyr, who has been the first audience for some of this book, has my warm appreciation for her help. My colleagues at the seminar in biography at New York University made useful suggestions, particularly in regard to the first chapter, and I'm especially indebted to Robert Halsband, Charles Molesworth, and Aileen

Ward for their comments. My colleague at the National Humanities Center, Donald Scott, provided me with a helpful Dickens document from the Newton Antiquarian Society archives. Kirk Beetz kindly shared with me some of his wide knowledge of Wilkie Collins' letters. I owe a debt of appreciation to Kathleen Longley, who allowed me to read and benefit from her unpublished writings on Ellen Ternan and the Ternan family. Jay Williams provided kind words and suggestions throughout.

Georges Borchardt in New York and Richard Simon in London are partly responsible for the excellent editing and production that the book has had under the capable and creative eye of Maria Guarnaschelli of William Morrow and the thoughtful suggestions that were made by John Curtis of Hodder & Stoughton. Amy Edelman of William Morrow has copyedited the manuscript with great competence and intelligence, and she and her colleagues Cheryl Asherman, Susan Halligan, and Dennis Combs have been invaluable. Sylvere Monod, during my stay in Paris, was kind enough, among his many kindnesses, to direct me to Olivier Cohen of Mazarin. Michelle Lepautre graciously brought us together. To Sylvere Monod I also am indebted for introducing me to Janine Watrin, who generously spent a day showing me all the Dickens sites and associations in the area of Condette and Boulogne. Dr. Kenneth Churchill, the cultural attaché at the British Embassy in Paris, put me in touch with his colleague Diana Neill, who graciously took me on a tour of the embassy to indulge my desire to examine the ballroom in which Dickens had given readings. Gloria Kaplan helpfully shared ideas and rendered assistance.

I am indebted, in alphabetical order, to the following people for acts of assistance that directly or indirectly contributed to my work: Laura Maslow Armand, Jerome Badanes, Maggie Blades, Doreen Blake, Charles Blitzer, Martin Blum, Philip Bolton, Charles Carlton, Philip Collins, Sandra Copeland, Mara Lemanis Cunningham, Enid Davey, Wally Davey, Morris Dickstein, Daniel Donno, Elizabeth Donno, Nan Dorsey, Robert Edwards, K. J. Fielding, Ernestine Friedl, Norman Fruman, Regenia Gagnier, Edward Geffner, Elliot Gilbert, Michael Goldberg, Harold Goldwhite, Maria Goldwhite, Mark Greenberg, Robert Greenberg, Vivian Greenberg, Edward Guiliano,

Jack Hall, Katie Higby, Robert Higby, Theo Hoppen, Jean Houston, Irving Howe, Lois Hughson, Howard Hughson, Al Hutter, Gerhardt Joseph, Alfred Kazin, Shirley Strum Kenny, Maureen Kleinbard, Uli Knoepflmacher, Barbara Leavy, Peter Leavy, Jean Leuchtenberg, Townshend Luddington, Carol Mackay, Harold Marcus, Steven Marcus, Annie Monod, Linda Morgan, Kent Mulliken, Robert Patten, Gordon Philo, Robert Polehumus, Wayne Pond, Norris Pope, John Reilly, Virginia Renner, James Riddell, Murray Roston, Clyde Ryals, Andrew Sanders, Hilary Schor, Pat Schrieber, Elsa Sink, Michael Slater, Doris Smedes, Harry Stone, James Thorpe, Charles Tolk, Robert Tracy, Allan Tuttle, Rebecca Vargha, Roland Voize, Alexander Welsh, the late Elizabeth Wheeler, and Carl Woodring.

Finally, a Dickensian acknowledgment of a philosophical sort, my expression of appreciation to that long list of people who have been helpful and kind to me. It has not been more than I deserve, to paraphrase and reverse Coleridge's sad comment. But it is a marvel to be savored and appreciated—how many people, despite the problems of life and time, generously help those who ask.

Index

About the Author

A distinguished biographer and literary scholar, **Fred Kaplan** is a professor of English literature at Queens College and the Graduate Center of the City University of New York. His *Thomas Carlyle, A Biography* (1983), was nominated for the 1983 National Book Critics' Circle Award and was a jury-nominated finalist for the Pulitzer Prize. His *Sacred Tears: Sentimentality in Victorian Literature* (1987), *Dickens and Mesmerism: The Hidden Springs of Fiction* (1975), and *Miracles of Rare Device: The Poet's Sense of Self in Nineteenth-Century Poetry* (1972) are significant contributions to the study of Romantic and Victorian British literature and culture. Co-editor of *Dickens Studies Annual,* he has edited Dickens' *Book of Memoranda* (1981). He has held Guggenheim and National Endowment for the Humanities fellowships, received a Queens College Presidential Award, and been a Fellow of the National Humanities Center and the Huntington Library.